여러분의 합격을 응원하는
해커스공무원의 특별 혜택

FREE 공무원 영어 특강

해커스공무원(gosi.Hackers.com) 접속 후 로그인 ▶
상단의 [무료강좌] 클릭 후 이용

출제예상 핵심 어휘리스트(PDF)

해커스공무원(gosi.Hackers.com) 접속 후 로그인 ▶
상단의 [교재·서점 → 무료학습자료] 클릭 ▶
본 교재의 [자료받기] 클릭

공무원 보카 어플 이용권

VVAHALFVOCA

구글 플레이스토어/애플 앱스토어에서 '해커스공무원 기출보카' 검색 ▶
어플 설치 후 실행 ▶ '인증코드 입력하기' 클릭 ▶ 위 인증코드 입력

* 등록 후 30일간 사용 가능
* 해당 자료는 [해커스공무원 기출 보카 4000+] 교재 내용으로 제공되는 자료로, 공무원 시험 대비에 도움이 되는 유용한 자료입니다.

공무원 매일영어 학습

해커스공무원(gosi.Hackers.com) 접속 후 로그인 ▶ 상단의 [무료강좌] 클릭 ▶
[매일영어 학습] 클릭하여 이용

해커스공무원 온라인 단과강의 20% 할인쿠폰

C674FB4626CAMAZU

해커스공무원(gosi.Hackers.com) 접속 후 로그인 ▶ 상단의 [나의 강의실] 클릭 ▶
좌측의 [쿠폰등록] 클릭 ▶ 위 쿠폰번호 입력 후 이용

* 등록 후 7일간 사용 가능(ID당 1회에 한해 등록 가능)

합격예측 온라인 모의고사 응시권 + 해설강의 수강권

644A3653CEDDB9N3

해커스공무원(gosi.Hackers.com) 접속 후 로그인 ▶ 상단의 [나의 강의실] 클릭 ▶
좌측의 [쿠폰등록] 클릭 ▶ 위 쿠폰번호 입력 후 이용

* ID당 1회에 한해 등록 가능

쿠폰 이용 관련 문의 1588-4055

단기 합격을 위한 해커스공무원 커리큘럼

입문
탄탄한 기본기와 핵심 개념 완성!
누구나 이해하기 쉬운 개념 설명과 풍부한 예시로 부담없이 쌩기초 다지기

TIP 베이스가 있다면 **기본 단계**부터!

▼

기본+심화
필수 개념 학습으로 이론 완성!
반드시 알아야 할 기본 개념과 문제풀이 전략을 학습하고
심화 개념 학습으로 고득점을 위한 응용력 다지기

▼

기출+예상 문제풀이
문제풀이로 집중 학습하고 실력 업그레이드!
기출문제의 유형과 출제 의도를 이해하고 최신 출제 경향을 반영한
예상문제를 풀어보며 본인의 취약영역을 파악 및 보완하기

▼

동형문제풀이
동형모의고사로 실전력 강화!
실제 시험과 같은 형태의 실전모의고사를 풀어보며 실전감각 극대화

▼

최종 마무리
시험 직전 실전 시뮬레이션!
각 과목별 시험에 출제되는 내용들을 최종 점검하며 실전 완성

PASS

단계별 교재 확인 및 수강신청은 여기서!

gosi.Hackers.com

* 커리큘럼 및 세부 일정은 상이할 수 있으며, 자세한 사항은 해커스공무원 사이트에서 확인하세요.

2025 최신판

해커스공무원

비비안 영어
매일 하프
모의고사

문제집

해커스공무원

해커스공무원

비비안 영어
매일 하프
모의고사

문제집

해커스공무원
gosi.Hackers.com

해커스공무원
gosi.Hackers.com

> 아침이 온다는 건,
> 또 한 번의 기회가 우리에게 주어진다는 의미입니다.

누군가는 한창 자고 있을 아침,
공무원 수험생들은 커피 한 잔으로 눈을 뜨고 무겁게 열리는 책장을 다시 펼칩니다.

그 시작이 쉽지 않다는 걸 누구보다 잘 압니다.
아무도 박수쳐 주지 않는 새벽,
스스로를 일으키는 일은 가장 조용한 용기이자 위대한 선택입니다.

이 책은 그런 수험생들의 새벽을 위해 만들어졌습니다.
매일 아침 10문제, 작아 보이지만 그 하루하루가 쌓여 '합격'으로 데려다줄 것입니다.

지금 걷는 이 길이 때로는 막막하고, 눈물겹더라도
이 페이지를 넘기는 순간만큼은 혼자가 아니라는 것을 느끼기를 바랍니다.

이 책을 다 풀었을 때,
'할 수 있을까?'라는 의문이 어느새
'나는 반드시 해낸다'라는 믿음으로 바뀌어 있을 거라 저는 믿습니다.

여러분들의 모든 뜨거운 아침을 응원합니다.
자, 그럼 이제 저와 함께 30일간의 기적을 만들러 가 볼까요?

2025년 5월
비비안 올림

목차

이 책만의 특별한 구성 6
공무원 영어 최신 출제경향 및 합격 학습 전략 8
합격을 위한 학습 플랜 10

■ 문제는 half, 실력은 double! **문제집**

DAY 01 하프모의고사 01회	14
DAY 02 하프모의고사 02회	18
DAY 03 하프모의고사 03회	22
DAY 04 하프모의고사 04회	26
DAY 05 하프모의고사 05회	30
DAY 06 하프모의고사 06회	34
DAY 07 하프모의고사 07회	38
DAY 08 하프모의고사 08회	42
DAY 09 하프모의고사 09회	46
DAY 10 하프모의고사 10회	50
DAY 11 하프모의고사 11회	54
DAY 12 하프모의고사 12회	58
DAY 13 하프모의고사 13회	62
DAY 14 하프모의고사 14회	66
DAY 15 하프모의고사 15회	70
DAY 16 하프모의고사 16회	74
DAY 17 하프모의고사 17회	78
DAY 18 하프모의고사 18회	82
DAY 19 하프모의고사 19회	86
DAY 20 하프모의고사 20회	90
DAY 21 하프모의고사 21회	94
DAY 22 하프모의고사 22회	98
DAY 23 하프모의고사 23회	102
DAY 24 하프모의고사 24회	106
DAY 25 하프모의고사 25회	110
DAY 26 하프모의고사 26회	114
DAY 27 하프모의고사 27회	118
DAY 28 하프모의고사 28회	122
DAY 29 하프모의고사 29회	126
DAY 30 하프모의고사 30회	130

해커스공무원 비비안 영어 매일 하프모의고사

■ 포인트만 쏙쏙, 실력 최종 완성! **해설집**

DAY 01 하프모의고사 01회 정답·해석·해설 2	**DAY 16** 하프모의고사 16회 정답·해석·해설 82
DAY 02 하프모의고사 02회 정답·해석·해설 7	**DAY 17** 하프모의고사 17회 정답·해석·해설 87
DAY 03 하프모의고사 03회 정답·해석·해설 12	**DAY 18** 하프모의고사 18회 정답·해석·해설 93
DAY 04 하프모의고사 04회 정답·해석·해설 18	**DAY 19** 하프모의고사 19회 정답·해석·해설 98
DAY 05 하프모의고사 05회 정답·해석·해설 23	**DAY 20** 하프모의고사 20회 정답·해석·해설 104
DAY 06 하프모의고사 06회 정답·해석·해설 28	**DAY 21** 하프모의고사 21회 정답·해석·해설 110
DAY 07 하프모의고사 07회 정답·해석·해설 34	**DAY 22** 하프모의고사 22회 정답·해석·해설 115
DAY 08 하프모의고사 08회 정답·해석·해설 39	**DAY 23** 하프모의고사 23회 정답·해석·해설 120
DAY 09 하프모의고사 09회 정답·해석·해설 44	**DAY 24** 하프모의고사 24회 정답·해석·해설 125
DAY 10 하프모의고사 10회 정답·해석·해설 50	**DAY 25** 하프모의고사 25회 정답·해석·해설 131
DAY 11 하프모의고사 11회 정답·해석·해설 55	**DAY 26** 하프모의고사 26회 정답·해석·해설 137
DAY 12 하프모의고사 12회 정답·해석·해설 60	**DAY 27** 하프모의고사 27회 정답·해석·해설 142
DAY 13 하프모의고사 13회 정답·해석·해설 65	**DAY 28** 하프모의고사 28회 정답·해석·해설 147
DAY 14 하프모의고사 14회 정답·해석·해설 71	**DAY 29** 하프모의고사 29회 정답·해석·해설 152
DAY 15 하프모의고사 15회 정답·해석·해설 76	**DAY 30** 하프모의고사 30회 정답·해석·해설 158

 무료 <출제예상 핵심 어휘리스트> PDF 제공
해커스공무원(gosi.Hackers.com) 접속 후 로그인 ▶ 사이트 상단의 [교재·서점 ▶ 무료학습자료] 클릭 ▶
본 교재 우측의 [자료받기] 클릭하여 <출제예상 핵심 어휘리스트> PDF 다운로드

이 책만의 특별한 구성

■ 매일 10분으로 공무원 영어 실력을 완성하는 하프모의고사 30회분!

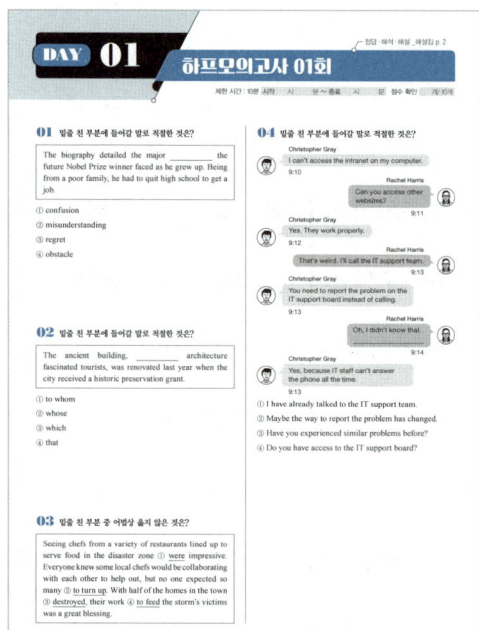

① 매일 10분 집중 학습으로 실전 감각 극대화
매일 10분, 하루 10문제씩 집중 학습을 총 30일간 꾸준히 반복하며 실전 대비와 문제 풀이 시간 관리를 동시에 할 수 있습니다.

② 공무원 출제경향 완벽 반영
실제 공무원 영어 시험과 가장 비슷한 난이도와 문제 유형으로 구성된 하프모의고사 30회분을 제공하여 탄탄한 공무원 영어 실력을 쌓을 수 있도록 하였습니다.

③ Self Check List를 통한 자기 점검
매회 하프모의고사가 끝나면 모의고사 진행 내용을 스스로 점검하여 개선점을 마련하고, 앞으로의 학습 계획을 세울 수 있도록 각 회차마다 Self Check List를 제공하였습니다.

■ 한 문제를 풀어도 진짜 실력이 되는 상세한 해설 제공!

① 취약영역 분석표
취약영역 분석표를 통해 자신의 취약영역을 스스로 확인할 수 있습니다.

② 해설 & 오답 분석
문제에 대한 정확한 해석과 상세한 해설 그리고 필수 학습 어휘를 제공하였습니다. 해설과 오답 분석을 통해 정답이 되는 이유와 오답이 되는 이유를 확실히 파악할 수 있습니다.

■ 어휘 암기까지 확실하게 책임지는 학습 구성!

① 문제집 내 QR코드를 통해 핵심 어휘 확인
매회 문제 풀이를 끝낸 직후, 해당 하프모의고사에 나온 중요 어휘와 표현을 정리한 〈출제예상 핵심 어휘리스트〉를 바로 확인할 수 있도록 각 회차마다 QR코드를 삽입하였습니다.

② Quiz를 통한 학습 내용 확인
간단한 Quiz를 통해 〈출제예상 핵심 어휘리스트〉의 어휘와 표현을 확실히 암기했는지 확인할 수 있습니다.

■ 체계적 학습 계획으로 목표 점수 달성!

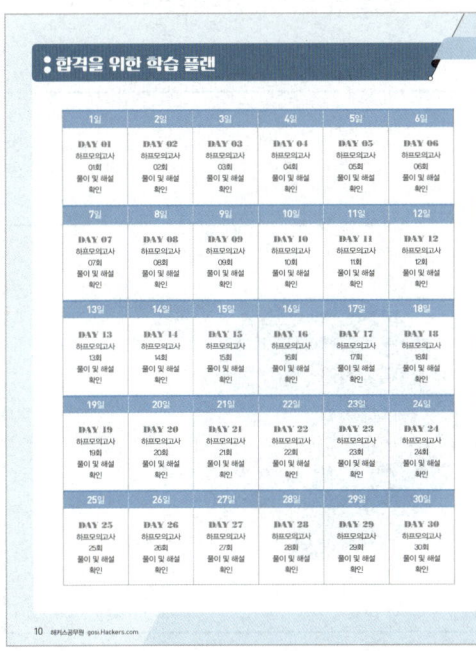

① 합격을 위한 학습 플랜 제공
총 30회분의 하프모의고사 풀이를 30일 안에 자율적으로 진행할 수 있도록 구성한 학습 플랜을 제공하였습니다.

② 학습 방법 제공
실력을 최종 점검하고 취약점을 보완해 목표 점수에 도달할 수 있도록 학습 플랜에 따라 적용할 수 있는 효과적인 학습 방법을 제공하였습니다.

공무원 영어 최신 출제경향 및 합격 학습 전략

■ 문법

문법 영역에서는 **어순과 특수 구문, 준동사구, 동사구**를 묻는 문제가 자주 출제되며, 세부 빈출 포인트로는 **병치·도치·강조 구문, 수 일치, 분사**가 있습니다. 최근에는 단문 형태의 보기에서 묻고 있는 문법 포인트에 밑줄이 적용되거나 한 문제의 모든 보기가 하나의 문법 포인트로 구성되는 등 다양한 형태의 문법 문제가 등장하고 있습니다.

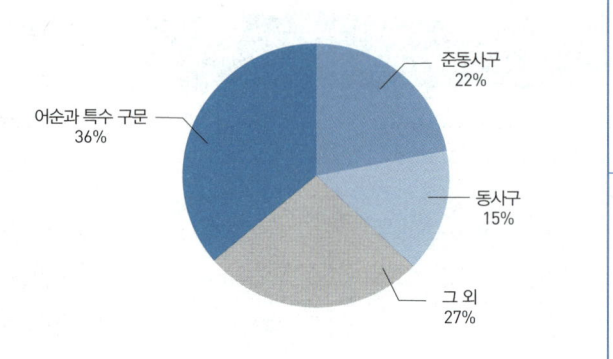

- 어순과 특수 구문 36%
- 준동사구 22%
- 동사구 15%
- 그 외 27%

■ 독해

독해 영역에서는 **주제·제목·목적·요지 파악**과 **내용 일치·불일치 파악** 유형의 출제 빈도가 증가하고 있습니다. 한편, **빈칸 완성(단어·구·절)** 유형의 경우 항상 높은 출제 비중을 꾸준히 유지해 왔으며, '문단 순서 배열'을 비롯한 논리적 추론 파악 유형도 매시험 빠지지 않고 포함되었습니다.

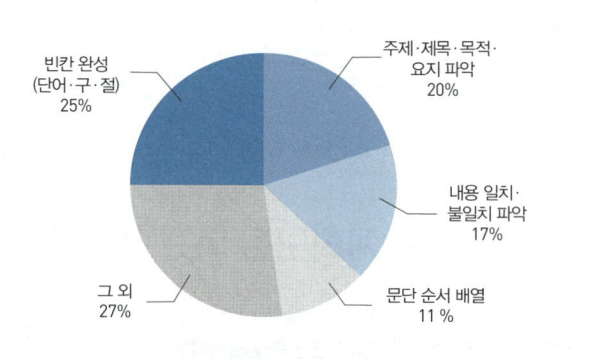

- 빈칸 완성(단어·구·절) 25%
- 주제·제목·목적·요지 파악 20%
- 내용 일치·불일치 파악 17%
- 문단 순서 배열 11%
- 그 외 27%

■ 어휘

어휘 영역에서는 **유의어 찾기** 유형의 비중이 가장 높으며, 최근에는 문맥 속에서 **빈칸에 들어갈 적절한 단어를 추론**하여 푸는 문제가 증가하고 있습니다. 생활영어 영역은 **실생활과 밀접한 주제**의 대화가 주로 출제되고, 때로는 **직무 관련 대화**도 출제됩니다.

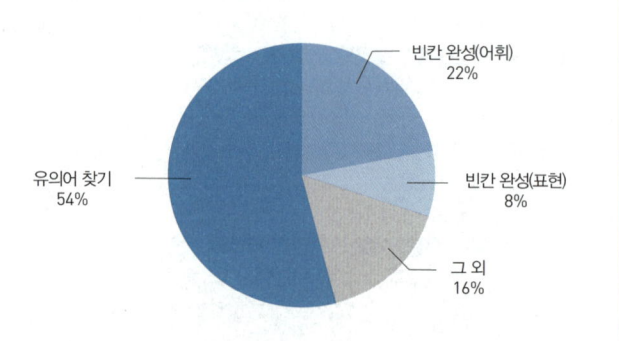

- 유의어 찾기 54%
- 빈칸 완성(어휘) 22%
- 빈칸 완성(표현) 8%
- 그 외 16%

📁 **합격 학습 전략**

실생활에서 자주 쓰이는 활용도 높은 문법 포인트 위주로 반복 학습합니다.

- 기존에 출제되던 단문형 문제의 비율이 점차 줄어드는 대신, 묻는 문법 포인트가 명확한 지문형 또는 빈칸형 문제들이 출제될 수 있습니다.
- 기본 개념을 탄탄히 한 다음 세부적인 문법 요소를 학습해 나가며 실력을 쌓는 것이 중요합니다. 문법 영역은 이론을 알고 있더라도 실전에서 혼동하기 쉬우므로, 반복적인 문제풀이를 통해 빈출 포인트들을 확실하게 확인합니다.

📁 **합격 학습 전략**

기존 문제 유형들에 대한 감을 유지하면서 다문항·실용문 등의 신유형에 대비합니다.

- 문제 유형에는 변화가 거의 없지만, 한 지문에서 두 개의 문항이 출제되는 다문항과, 이메일·안내문·웹페이지 등 새로운 형태의 지문에 익숙해질 필요가 있습니다. 유형별 문제풀이 전략을 완벽하게 숙지하고, 실제 문제풀이에 전략을 적용해 보는 연습을 하는 것이 중요합니다.
- 특히 실용문에 대비하여 공무원 직무와 관련된 어휘를 학습하고, 정부 관련 정책들에 대해서도 알아 둡니다.

📁 **합격 학습 전략**

문맥을 통해 빈칸에 적절한 어휘 또는 대화를 추론하여 정답을 찾습니다.

- 정답에 대한 단서가 문맥 속에서 명확하게 주어지며, 난이도가 높지 않으면서 활용도 높은 어휘 위주의 출제가 예상됩니다.
- 비대면 의사소통 상황을 비롯한 직무 관련 내용의 대화가 출제되는 경우에 대비하여, 관련 상황 속에서 쓰일 수 있는 빈출 표현들을 미리 정리해 둡니다.

합격을 위한 학습 플랜

1일	2일	3일	4일	5일	6일
DAY 01 하프모의고사 01회 풀이 및 해설 확인	**DAY 02** 하프모의고사 02회 풀이 및 해설 확인	**DAY 03** 하프모의고사 03회 풀이 및 해설 확인	**DAY 04** 하프모의고사 04회 풀이 및 해설 확인	**DAY 05** 하프모의고사 05회 풀이 및 해설 확인	**DAY 06** 하프모의고사 06회 풀이 및 해설 확인
7일	**8일**	**9일**	**10일**	**11일**	**12일**
DAY 07 하프모의고사 07회 풀이 및 해설 확인	**DAY 08** 하프모의고사 08회 풀이 및 해설 확인	**DAY 09** 하프모의고사 09회 풀이 및 해설 확인	**DAY 10** 하프모의고사 10회 풀이 및 해설 확인	**DAY 11** 하프모의고사 11회 풀이 및 해설 확인	**DAY 12** 하프모의고사 12회 풀이 및 해설 확인
13일	**14일**	**15일**	**16일**	**17일**	**18일**
DAY 13 하프모의고사 13회 풀이 및 해설 확인	**DAY 14** 하프모의고사 14회 풀이 및 해설 확인	**DAY 15** 하프모의고사 15회 풀이 및 해설 확인	**DAY 16** 하프모의고사 16회 풀이 및 해설 확인	**DAY 17** 하프모의고사 17회 풀이 및 해설 확인	**DAY 18** 하프모의고사 18회 풀이 및 해설 확인
19일	**20일**	**21일**	**22일**	**23일**	**24일**
DAY 19 하프모의고사 19회 풀이 및 해설 확인	**DAY 20** 하프모의고사 20회 풀이 및 해설 확인	**DAY 21** 하프모의고사 21회 풀이 및 해설 확인	**DAY 22** 하프모의고사 22회 풀이 및 해설 확인	**DAY 23** 하프모의고사 23회 풀이 및 해설 확인	**DAY 24** 하프모의고사 24회 풀이 및 해설 확인
25일	**26일**	**27일**	**28일**	**29일**	**30일**
DAY 25 하프모의고사 25회 풀이 및 해설 확인	**DAY 26** 하프모의고사 26회 풀이 및 해설 확인	**DAY 27** 하프모의고사 27회 풀이 및 해설 확인	**DAY 28** 하프모의고사 28회 풀이 및 해설 확인	**DAY 29** 하프모의고사 29회 풀이 및 해설 확인	**DAY 30** 하프모의고사 30회 풀이 및 해설 확인

하프모의고사 학습 방법

01. 각 회차 하프모의고사를 풀고 <출제예상 핵심 어휘리스트> 암기하기
(1) 실제 시험처럼 제한 시간(10분)을 지키며 하프모의고사를 풉니다.
(2) 매회 제공되는 <출제예상 핵심 어휘리스트>를 통해 부족한 어휘를 암기하고, 잘 외워지지 않는 어휘는 체크하여 반복 학습합니다.

02. 취약점 보완하기
채점 후 틀린 문제를 중심으로 해설을 꼼꼼히 확인합니다. 해설을 확인할 때에는 틀린 문제에 쓰인 포인트를 정리하면서 '포인트를 몰라서' 틀린 것인지, 아니면 '아는 것이지만 실수로' 틀린 것인지를 확실하게 파악합니다. 하프모의고사는 회차를 거듭하면서 반복되는 실수와 틀리는 문제 수를 줄여 나가며 취약점을 완벽하게 극복하는 것이 중요합니다.

03. 하프모의고사 총정리하기
(1) 틀린 문제를 다시 풀어 보고, 계속해서 틀리는 문제가 있다면 해설을 몇 차례 반복하여 읽어 모르는 부분이 없을 때까지 확실하게 학습합니다.
(2) <출제예상 핵심 어휘리스트>에서 체크해 둔 어휘가 완벽하게 암기되었는지 최종 점검합니다.

■ **하프모의고사 회독별 학습 Tip!**

1회독 [실전 문제 풀이 단계]	2회독 [영역별 심화학습 단계]	3회독 [취약점 보완 단계]
■ <학습 플랜>에 따라 매일 모의고사 1회분 집중 문제 풀이 ■ 해설 및 오답 분석을 정독하여 틀린 이유 파악 ■ Self Check List 작성 ■ <출제예상 어휘 리스트> 암기 ■ 학습 기간: 30일	■ 매일 2회분 모의고사 반복 풀이 ■ 반복해서 틀리는 문법 포인트 및 독해 유형을 파악하여, 관련 이론 및 문제풀이 전략 심화 학습 ■ 학습 기간: 15일	■ 매일 5회분씩 1~2차 회독 시 틀린 문제 위주로 점검 ■ 시험 직전 최종 점검을 위한 본인만의 오답노트 정리 ■ <출제예상 어휘 리스트>에 수록된 모든 어휘를 완벽하게 암기했는지 최종 확인 ■ 학습 기간: 6일

*3회독을 진행하며 반복해서 틀리는 문제들은 반드시 별도로 표시해 두었다가 [해커스공무원 영어 기출 불변의 패턴], [해커스공무원 실전동형모의고사 영어] 교재를 통해 추가로 학습하여 실전에 대비할 수 있도록 합니다.

공무원 영어 직렬별 시험 출제 영역

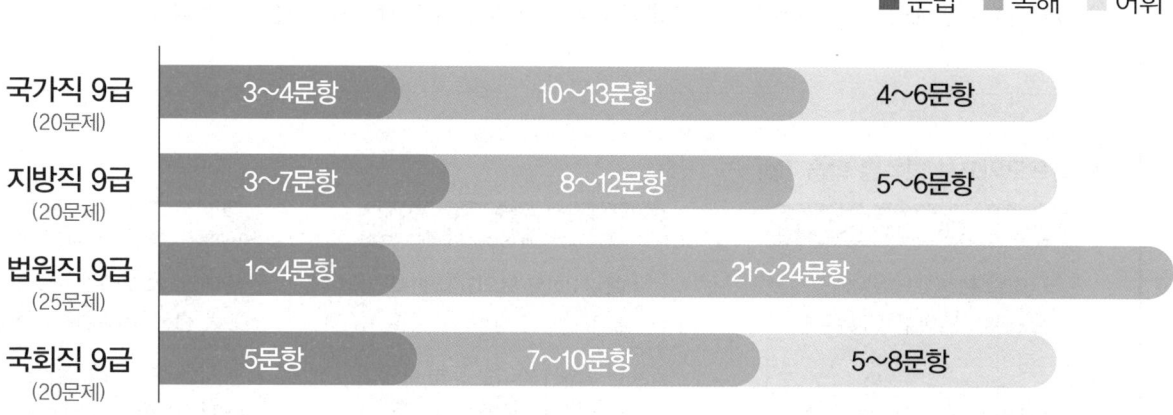

공무원 영어 시험은 직렬에 따라 20문항 또는 25문항으로 구성되며, 크게 문법/독해/어휘 3개의 영역으로 나눌 수 있습니다.

국가직 · 지방직 · 국회직 9급 영어 시험은 총 20문항이며, 독해 영역이 약 60%를 차지하고 나머지 40%는 문법과 어휘 영역으로 구성됩니다. 이때 어휘 영역의 경우 세부적으로 어휘 및 표현, 생활영어로 구분됩니다. (법원직의 경우 독해 약 80%, 문법 및 어휘 약 20%)

한편, 출제기조 전환은 2025년 국가직 · 지방직 · 지역인재 9급 공채 시험부터 적용되며, 개편 시험에 앞서 인사혁신처에서 공개한 예시문제는 문법 3문제, 독해 13문제, 어휘 4문제로 구성되어 있습니다.

공무원 영어 시험의 영역별 출제 문항 수는 변동이 적은 편이므로, 영역별 문항 수에 따라 풀이 시간을 적정하게 배분하는 연습을 할 수 있습니다.

해커스공무원 비비안 영어 매일 하프모의고사

DAY 01~30

하프모의고사 01~30회

잠깐! 하프모의고사 전 확인사항

하프모의고사도 실전처럼 문제를 푸는 연습이 필요합니다.
- ✔ 휴대전화는 전원을 꺼 주세요.
- ✔ 연필과 지우개를 준비하세요.
- ✔ 제한 시간 10분 내 최대한 많은 문제를 정확하게 풀어 보세요.

매 회 하프모의고사 전, 위 상황을 점검하고 시험에 임하세요.

01 밑줄 친 부분에 들어갈 말로 적절한 것은?

The biography detailed the major _____ the future Nobel Prize winner faced as he grew up. Being from a poor family, he had to quit high school to get a job.

① confusion
② misunderstanding
③ regret
④ obstacle

02 밑줄 친 부분에 들어갈 말로 적절한 것은?

The ancient building, _____ architecture fascinated tourists, was renovated last year when the city received a historic preservation grant.

① to whom
② whose
③ which
④ that

03 밑줄 친 부분 중 어법상 옳지 않은 것은?

Seeing chefs from a variety of restaurants lined up to serve food in the disaster zone ① were impressive. Everyone knew some local chefs would be collaborating with each other to help out, but no one expected so many ② to turn up. With half of the homes in the town ③ destroyed, their work ④ to feed the storm's victims was a great blessing.

04 밑줄 친 부분에 들어갈 말로 적절한 것은?

Christopher Gray
I can't access the intranet on my computer.
9:10

Rachel Harris
Can you access other websites?
9:11

Christopher Gray
Yes. They work properly.
9:12

Rachel Harris
That's weird. I'll call the IT support team.
9:13

Christopher Gray
You need to report the problem on the IT support board instead of calling.
9:13

Rachel Harris
Oh, I didn't know that.
_____
9:14

Christopher Gray
Yes, because IT staff can't answer the phone all the time.
9:13

① I have already talked to the IT support team.
② Maybe the way to report the problem has changed.
③ Have you experienced similar problems before?
④ Do you have access to the IT support board?

※ 다음 글을 읽고 물음에 답하시오. [05~06]

(A)

With the expansion of the city, local wildlife habitats are in danger.

The need for more land for housing is causing the rapid demolition of parts of the Red Forest. We need to protect this unique area and the animals that call it home.

The Red Forest Conservation League has taken a leading role in this fight. The group is holding an information session and fundraiser to help reach its goal. Attend to show your support and do your part for nature.

Can you imagine the area without its beautiful forests and special wildlife?

- Location: Grimley Central Park (in the event of snow: Joseph Caldwell Community Center)
- Date: Sunday, January 12
- Time: 11:00 a.m.

To volunteer to assist the group or to make a donation, please visit www.redforestleague.com or call (212) 555-9711.

05 (A)에 들어갈 윗글의 제목으로 가장 적절한 것은?

① Conserve Energy to Help Wildlife
② Make the City Great Again
③ Meet the Area's Unique Plants and Animals
④ Help Save the Red Forest

06 밑줄 친 "show"의 의미와 가장 가까운 것은?

① present   ② guide
③ depict   ④ teach

07 다음 이메일의 내용과 일치하지 않는 것은?

To: rentals@reveretheater.com
From: tinamurphey@speedmail.com
Date: April 6
Subject: Venue rental inquiry

Dear Sir,

I am writing to inquire about renting the Revere Theater for a movie premiere in October. Any evening on Friday or Saturday that month would work. The event will last four hours: one hour for arrival and appetizers, two hours for the movie, and one hour for a Q&A session with the cast and crew after the showing. We are currently expecting around 300 guests.

We plan to hire an event planning firm to handle ticketing, transportation, photography, and catering, which we hope to host in your main lobby as part of a stand-up event. To manage the actual film showing, we would like to hire a technician familiar with your venue and its equipment. Could you please recommend someone?

I look forward to your response.

Sincerely,

Tina Murphey

① 영화 시사회는 10월에 있을 예정이다.
② 행사는 4시간 동안 진행될 것이다.
③ 케이터링 서비스는 로비에서 즐길 수 있다.
④ 추천하는 기술자 명단이 첨부되어 있다.

08 다음 글의 흐름상 어색한 문장은?

Día de los Muertos, or the Day of the Dead, is a Mexican holiday celebrated on November 1 and 2. This special time honoring the dead is joyful rather than somber, as it is believed that the spirits of loved ones can come back to earth for one night. ① During the holiday, families gather together to remember those they have lost by setting up decorated tables to them. ② These are covered in offerings to welcome and refresh the spirits after their arduous journey back to the world of the living. ③ People also dress up like skeletons and celebrate with their neighbors in the streets and town squares. ④ Most Mexican towns were built around a grand plaza that acts as a meeting place and site of celebrations and official events. Today, the holiday is even observed internationally in places with large Mexican populations.

09 주어진 글 다음에 이어질 글의 순서로 적절한 것은?

Samuel Morse is famous for inventing Morse Code. However, he did not initially set out to be a telecommunications pioneer or an inventor.

(A) While there, he gained admission to the Royal Academy, where he received artistic education. Upon his return to the United States three years later, Morse took up art as a full-time career.

(B) In fact, he studied philosophy, mathematics, and the science of horses while at Yale. But none of these seemed to be his calling. After graduation, Morse traveled to England to study European art.

(C) He was so successful in his chosen profession that he was commissioned to paint the president and other aristocrats. It was not until he was in his 40s that he became interested in electrical signaling devices and devised the system for sending messages using electrical dots and dashes now known as Morse code.

① (A) – (B) – (C)
② (B) – (A) – (C)
③ (B) – (C) – (A)
④ (C) – (B) – (A)

10 밑줄 친 부분에 들어갈 말로 적절한 것은?

Fast fashion is a relatively new concept in the fashion industry in which discount retailers take high-end designer looks and recreate them at a much lower price point. The garments they produce are often simplified or made with lower-quality fabric and hardware, which allows them to be sold for a fraction of the cost of designer goods. While this may seem like a benefit for those who cannot afford to buy expensive brand-name clothing, many consider fast fashion to be bad for the less affluent considering maintenance cost. The inferior quality of the products shows that _____, as they often wear out rather quickly and must be replaced or thrown out.

① the genius of a design can't be copied
② designers are charging too much for their clothing
③ fast fashion is damaging the clothing industry
④ paying less initially doesn't always indicate saving

01 밑줄 친 부분에 들어갈 말로 적절한 것은?

Implementing the changes he proposed right now is _____ as there hasn't been nearly enough time to fully test the updates.

① current
② impractical
③ progressive
④ possible

02 밑줄 친 부분에 들어갈 말로 적절한 것은?

The detective working on the recent murder case says he has determined that the suspect _____ present at the crime scene because surveillance footage confirmed she was across town at the exact time of the incident.

① cannot be
② will not be
③ should not have been
④ could not have been

03 밑줄 친 부분에 들어갈 말로 적절한 것은?

A: You look upset. What's wrong?
B: It's my new secretary. He keeps messing up my schedule.
A: Did you miss anything important?
B: No. It's just really frustrating, though.
A: Well, give him some time. He's still learning your style.
B: You're right. Instead of grumbling about it, _____.

① I'm trying my hardest to help him.
② I should help him adjust and learn quickly.
③ a severe warning will be the only good solution.
④ an experienced secretary has agreed to join us soon.

04 다음 글의 목적으로 적절한 것은?

To: customers@TravelGurus.com
From: alerts@TravelGurus.com
Date: October 14
Subject: Holiday travel

Dear Travel Lovers,

With the holiday travel season approaching, flight prices are rising. At Travel Gurus, we know you want to save money, so we've come up with a list of ways to get the best deals on flights. Use these tips and you can save on your holiday travel:

1. Book early to avoid last-minute price increases.
2. Be flexible and consider traveling on weekdays, when prices are lower.
3. Compare offers on different airlines and routes including those with longer layovers, which tend to be cheaper.
4. Fly into an airport near your destination if possible. Even with the required ground transportation, it can sometimes cost less overall.

These tips should help you save money, but our travel experts are here to help, too. Just call Travel Gurus, and one of our agents will be glad to help you find the best flights within your budget.

Happy Travels,
Travel Gurus

① to tell customers about an increase in airfare
② to explain methods for reducing flight expenses
③ to inform travelers about optimal booking times
④ to highlight the benefits of ground transportation

※ 다음 글을 읽고 물음에 답하시오. [05~06]

Dance-A-Thon
HOME   ABOUT   DANCE-A-THON   FAQ   SEARCH
HOME > DANCE-A-THON

[A   ]

July is Childhood Cancer Awareness Month. Each year, university students hold 48-hour dance marathons during which they dance continuously without sitting or sleeping. These events not only bring attention to those who suffer from the disease but also raise funds for their treatment. By soliciting donations from sponsors, participants raise millions of dollars each year.

The student dance-a-thons began at Pennsylvania State University in 1973 but have since spread to universities across the country. Shorter versions are now also held for high school and elementary school students who wish to help out as well.

This devastating disease affects more than 15,000 young people each year. But thanks to research funded in part by the dance-a-thons, survival rates are steadily increasing.

Do your part to help childhood cancer sufferers.

How will you help?
☐ Take part in a dance-a-thon
☐ Volunteer to organize an event
☐ Sponsor a dancer for $5 per hour
☐ Direct cash donation

Dancer Sponsorship:
☐ I would like to sponsor _____ (dancer name) for _____ hours of dancing.

Direct Cash Donations:
☐ $25   ☐ $50   ☐ $75   ☐ Other: _____

05 (A)에 들어갈 윗글의 제목으로 적절한 것은?

① Development of Childhood Cancer Treatment
② Join the Fight against Childhood Cancer
③ Learn about Ways to Prevent Diseases in Children
④ Signs of Cancer in Young People

06 윗글에서 캠페인에 관한 내용과 일치하지 않는 것은?

① 이틀 내내 계속된다.
② 펜실베이니아 대학이 매년 수백만 달러를 후원한다.
③ 청소년들을 위한 별도의 행사가 준비되어 있다.
④ 기부는 두 가지 방법으로 할 수 있다.

07 밑줄 친 부분 중 어법상 옳은 것은?

Education experts are ① interesting in the effects of e-book reading on comprehension. Despite the improved quality of digital books and their low cost, many wonder ② that reading from paper might be more beneficial than reading an electronic file. One reason for this is that reading text on screens irritates the eyes and ③ makes reading uncomfortable. Another reason is that many find e-book reading ④ highly distracted due to pop-up notifications.

08 다음 글의 흐름상 어색한 문장은?

Representative money includes checks, debit cards, and credit cards, which are a type of money that represents actual currency. It has no value as a physical object but is useful when carrying large sums of money is inconvenient and enables more secure digital transactions. ① The value of representative money is that it can be used to pay for something even when one does not have cash on their person. ② Unlike cash that can be stolen or lost, these payment methods offer security features like PIN protection and fraud monitoring. ③ Digital transactions also create traceable records, providing protection against unauthorized use and enabling dispute resolution. ④ Furthermore, the advantage of paying with cash is that the transaction can proceed more quickly. As technology advances, these digital payment methods continue to evolve with additional security features like biometric authentication and instant fraud alerts, making them increasingly preferred over actual currency.

09 주어진 문장이 들어갈 위치로 적절한 것은?

Unfortunately, the sink was made of plastic and the tin set it on fire.

In a science laboratory in the 1970s, a teacher was demonstrating to his students what happens in a thermite reaction. (①) By accident, a single spark from a burner landed in a tin can of magnesium, which should have been closed but had been left open. (②) The teacher grabbed the tin and threw it in the sink, thinking to put the fire out with water. (③) The teacher then picked up a fire blanket to cover it but that too caught fire, effectively blocking the only exit in the room. (④) Everyone did manage to get out; needless to say, the rules for laboratory use were revised and flammable items were summarily replaced.

10 밑줄 친 부분에 들어갈 말로 적절한 것은?

When I think back to the teachers I had in my school days, the one who stands out for me the most is my first-grade teacher. She was a kind, soft-voiced, and perceptive woman who always did her best for everyone in her class. And of all the likeable qualities she displayed, the one that was most extraordinary for me was her _____. This became especially clear when foreign students who spoke little English joined her class, of which I was one. She was extremely patient with us when we had difficulty reading, making sure we all had the chance to practice. She treated all the students in the same way and never favored some above the others. I felt comfortable around her because she had no biases. She will always be a great role model for me.

① sense of fairness
② style of communication
③ creative instructional technique
④ empathetic listening skills

DAY 03 하프모의고사 03회

01 밑줄 친 부분에 들어갈 말로 적절한 것은?

Many civil rights activists believe that the government should _____ problems caused by social injustice to create a more equal society.

① overlook
② address
③ deny
④ build

02 밑줄 친 부분에 들어갈 말로 적절한 것은?

The controversial theory about climate change proved to _____ related policies positively despite initial skepticism.

① influence
② have influenced
③ be influenced
④ have been influenced

03 밑줄 친 부분 중 어법상 옳지 않은 것은?

Parents in Scandinavia consider *friluftsliv*, the Nordic concept of being outdoors, ① fundamental to human beings. Therefore, they will give their children, even babies, ample time outdoors ② regardless of rain, snow, and freezing temperatures. ③ It is believed that exposure to inclement weather creates resilience and immunity in young children. Also, the more children are taught to enjoy the outdoors and live spontaneously, the ④ easiest they are to manage.

04 밑줄 친 부분에 들어갈 말로 적절한 것은?

 Henry Cooper
Hi! I want to know about your catering services.
10:10

Emma Williams
Of course. How many people are you expecting?
10:11

 Henry Cooper
We're planning for about 150 attendees in our company conference center on June 15.
10:12

Emma Williams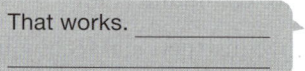
That works. _____
10:12

 Henry Cooper
I saw your three-course formal dinner in the online reviews.
10:13

Emma Williams
In that case, we offer four different meal options. I can email you the options and pricing.
10:13

 Henry Cooper
It would be great if you could send it by today.
10:14

① What is your budget range for this service?
② Did you enjoy the meal options we provided?
③ Do you have any particular menu in mind?
④ Would you like to schedule this for lunchtime?

※ 다음 글을 읽고 물음에 답하시오. [05~06]

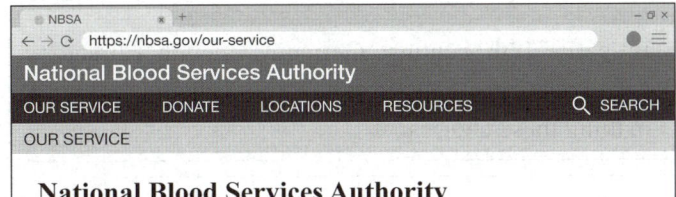

National Blood Services Authority

What We Do

We operate the largest network of blood banks in the country, collecting and testing blood before distributing it to hospitals and clinics for medical needs. We also organize nationwide blood donation drives and maintain a reserve supply of blood that medical facilities can access in the event of domestic emergencies such as natural disasters or major accidents.

Our Goals

We endeavor to eliminate blood shortages by promoting voluntary blood donation and building a reliable base of regular donors, and to continue research into blood storage technologies in order to enhance the safety and longevity of blood products.

Our Values

We uphold rigorous ethical and medical standards, ensuring every donation is handled with care and precision. We are committed to transparency, accountability, and making sure our practices adhere to global safety protocols.

05 윗글에서 National Blood Services Authority에 관한 내용과 일치하는 것은?

① It maintains a reserve supply of blood for export to other countries.
② It wants people to give blood voluntarily so there is always enough of it.
③ It has increased the budget for research into blood storage technologies.
④ It sets international safety standards for blood banks.

06 밑줄 친 regular의 의미와 가장 가까운 것은?

① generous   ② random
③ potential   ④ consistent

07 (A)에 들어갈 글의 제목으로 적절한 것은?

_____(A)_____

A day pass for Namid National Park can be purchased for $10, but those intending to spend more time at the park are encouraged to purchase the Explorer Pass for $75, which provides 12 months of access not just to Namid National Park but to more than 100 protected sites across the country. Passes can be obtained at park entrances or online and must be displayed on your vehicle dashboard.

Namid National Park is open throughout the year, but visitors wishing to use campgrounds in the winter are advised to come prepared. Please note that winter temperatures average -5°C during the day and can occasionally drop as low as -30°C at night.

Fishing is allowed in designated areas with a valid fishing license. Hunting, however, is strictly prohibited and punishable by law.

For more information, please call 1 (888) 343-9536.

① Explorer Pass Benefits across Protected Sites
② Seasonal Camping Restrictions in National Parks
③ Comprehensive Visitor Guidelines for Namid National Park
④ Temperature Fluctuations in Mountain National Parks

08 다음 글의 흐름상 어색한 문장은?

Color is easily the most obvious physical property of a mineral, but it is not useful in identifying it. This is because the real color in some minerals is hidden. ① The bare eye may see a strong blue or green, but it cannot perceive traces of other colors that affect the true color, causing it to appear different in hue. ② Mineral color can also change because of the presence of other minerals. ③ For example, quartz, a glossy mineral that is crystal in form, is colorless, but small amounts of titanium or iron can make it appear pink. ④ Quartz rocks, especially those that are dark, can be damaged by constant exposure to direct heat and sunlight.

09 주어진 문장이 들어갈 위치로 적절한 것은?

In early 19th century Germany, though, directors began to appear, and actors were no longer tasked with making these choices.

Works by Shakespeare have been staged continually since he wrote them in the 16th and 17th centuries, but how they are performed has changed immensely. (①) This is largely due to the change in direction in theaters. (②) In Shakespeare's time, theaters lacked the position of a dedicated director, relying instead on actors to direct themselves in how they delivered lines on stage. (③) This change was prompted by the increased complexity of stage productions of the time; someone was needed to oversee the larger casts of extras and more advanced stagecraft. (④) Interestingly, over the next century, directing evolved into an artistic position of its own, with people considering the director's vision to be as important as actors' performances.

10 밑줄 친 부분에 들어갈 말로 적절한 것은?

Air traffic controllers are not workers that many people think about often. However, their work is vitally important in the modern world due to the global reliance on aircraft for transporting cargo and personnel by companies and economies worldwide. These highly trained professionals monitor all of the aircraft in the sky and coordinate their movement to ensure that they remain at a safe distance from one another. Performing this task requires immense planning, as it relies on ensuring that all planes have clear flight paths in order to maintain air traffic separation rules. So essential is their work that if they were to decide to stop performing it, they could _____.
This was exactly what happened when American air traffic controllers went on strike in 1981. Without their assistance, more than 7,000 passenger and cargo flights had to be canceled, sending shockwaves through numerous sectors.

① cause the government to increase safety rules
② direct flights to less convenient locations
③ disrupt the aviation and logistics industries
④ increase the fares that passengers pay for flights

01 밑줄 친 부분에 들어갈 말로 적절한 것은?

Social media was once considered nothing more than a means of communication, but it is now understood to play a(n) _____ role in everyday life.

① secondary
② conventional
③ reasonable
④ essential

02 밑줄 친 부분에 들어갈 말로 적절한 것은?

Until the government _____ stricter environmental regulations, some companies will continue to prioritize profits over sustainability.

① will have implemented
② have implemented
③ will implement
④ implements

03 밑줄 친 부분 중 어법상 옳지 않은 것은?

Gardens have ① a timeless beauty, so growing flowers and vegetation naturally appeals to many homeowners. However, it is imperative that a gardener ② utilize the right mix of plants to promote healthy growth. Some plants have substances that repel certain bugs, and these are helpful to plants ③ that attract those insects. Additionally, some flowers and shrubs should never ④ place near each other as they compete for soil and water.

04 밑줄 친 부분에 들어갈 말로 적절한 것은?

A: Are there any electronics service centers around here? My phone isn't working properly.
B: I might be able to help. What's the problem?
A: It keeps showing an error message, and I can't send texts.
B: Oh, that's a well-known software issue.
A: So what do I need to do?
B: _____
A: That's simpler than I thought. Thanks for letting me know!

① How about getting a new phone this time?
② Maybe you should back up your data first.
③ Download the latest operating system.
④ There's nothing you can do.

※ 다음 글을 읽고 물음에 답하시오. [05~06]

(A)

The Cleveport Community Center is happy to announce that it will be offering computer literacy classes for seniors, a perfect way for older residents to improve their abilities and confidence in using technology. Don't miss this opportunity to learn and grow!

Class Schedule
- **Dates**: Monday, May 5 - Friday, May 30
- **Times**: 10 a.m. - 12 p.m.
  (Monday, Wednesday, and Friday)
- **Location**: Cleveport Community Center,
  1624 Adams Boulevard

What You'll Learn
- **Tech Basics**

Discover how to operate a computer, connect to the internet, and send email.

- _____ **Digital Skills**

Go on step further, and master the skills needed for shopping online, using online banking, and making video calls with friends and family.

- **Internet Security**

Get tips for staying safe while enjoying the services of the internet.

Classes are offered at no cost for those 60 years old and over. To sign up, call (985) 555-8472.

05 (A)에 들어갈 윗글의 제목으로 적절한 것은?

① Stay Safe While Online Shopping
② Empower Seniors through Technology Education
③ Connect with Family through Video Calls
④ Fundamental Computer Skills for Modern Living

06 윗글의 밑줄 친 부분에 들어갈 말로 적절한 것은?

① Formal
② Advanced
③ Communal
④ Unexpected

07 FactsOnly에 관한 다음 글의 내용과 일치하지 않는 것은?

A New Tool in Fighting Disinformation

FactsOnly is the government's latest tool in the battle against online misinformation. The site features a list of the top false stories currently circulating on the Internet, along with detailed fact-checks, allowing users to quickly learn the truth. There is also a search feature to look for specific stories or topics. In addition to an explanation of the issue, all articles are accompanied by a list of sources for firsthand research. The FactsOnly website is offered free of charge and contains no advertising or user data collection. Users can also download a browser extension that uses AI to scan webpages and suggest articles on FactsOnly.org related to the content.

① It is part of an effort to fight against false information on the Internet.
② Users can look for articles about particular subjects.
③ No personal information about users is collected by the site.
④ It creates new articles using artificial intelligence.

08 다음 글의 주제로 적절한 것은?

Humility may be regarded as the very root of all other virtues that lead to personal growth. Without this quality, which is an acceptance of one's shortcomings with the ultimate goal of making oneself a better person, no other virtues can develop. A humble person makes other people comfortable, whereas someone who is arrogant is unpleasant to be around because he only thinks of himself. Humility can therefore be a profitable trait to have no matter what environment a person is in. Among family and friends, it can keep relationships running smoothly, as a humble person is capable of setting their pride aside to resolve conflicts. In the workplace, it confers advantages as well, making employees receptive to change and willing to work with others. On the whole, developing the trait of humility can improve one's life and make it more peaceful.

① weaknesses that are hard to manage
② the problems associated with humility
③ advantages of being a humble person
④ ways to develop a humble character

09 주어진 문장이 들어갈 위치로 적절한 것은?

This book, like others before it, was based on the notion that there was a perfect society that once existed or had yet to be discovered.

Utopian novels can be traced back to the writings of Plato, where he described the lost continent of Atlantis. Novels and stories featuring utopias, perfect societies, have appeared occasionally throughout history ever since. (①) However, they were truly popularized by Thomas More's work *Utopia*, which introduced the word into the English language. (②) Then, Edward Bellamy's 1888 novel *Looking Backward* elaborated on the idea and speculated about a utopia in the distant future. (③) This piece of fiction was immensely popular, leading to a wealth of utopian novels describing the perfection that would be reached in the future. (④) Eventually, the genre grew outdated and was replaced by the more critical and satirical, yet equally speculative, dystopian novel.

10 밑줄 친 부분에 들어갈 말로 적절한 것은?

Adolescents undergo social and emotional changes beginning at puberty, and this can have an impact on their education in middle and high school. Even from early adolescence, their thinking is on a higher level than in childhood, which causes them to _____ _____. Psychologists say that with this new mindset, teenagers are more likely to challenge classroom norms and educational goals. Hence, teens are less receptive to attempts to control and mold them into high-achieving adults. Education can become less effective when teachers are unsympathetic to the social and emotional upheavals that adolescent students are undergoing. In addition, that students are more technologically advanced than their teachers can cause them to be less respectful toward them. Therefore, education for adolescents should take into consideration the challenges posed by students during a time when they are learning to find their way and become independent.

① prefer emotional experiences over learning
② demand more technological approaches
③ explore and search for their identity
④ resist social and emotional upheavals

DAY 05 하프모의고사 05회

01 밑줄 친 부분에 들어갈 말로 적절한 것은?

The sustainable waste management bill passed this month indicates that the legislature will _____ drastic reforms to environmental conditions in the country.

① separate
② undertake
③ abandon
④ interpret

02 밑줄 친 부분에 들어갈 말로 적절한 것은?

We packed extra supplies _____ the camping trip lasted longer than expected.

① even though
② in case
③ whereas
④ unless

03 밑줄 친 부분 중 어법상 옳지 않은 것은?

A recent study conducted by a research team in Japan ① suggests that a specific protein amino acid, called LP7, can slow down the development of dementia. Although this study has not yet reached clinical trials, it is expected ② to provide help for those at risk of the condition. Researchers will conduct further experiments to see ③ if their findings prove valid. If so, then a simple LP7 supplement ④ taking daily may be sufficient to inhibit brain cells from dying.

04 밑줄 친 부분에 들어갈 말로 적절한 것은?

Liam Anderson: I bought you a ticket for the comedy show tonight. 11:05

Camila Nelson: Thanks, but I'm not really interested in comedy. 11:06

Liam Anderson: You'll want to go, trust me. Ryan is going to be performing. 11:06

Camila Nelson: Wow! In that case, I'd love to see it too. _____ 11:07

Liam Anderson: I'll send you the online ticket. It has all the information about the performance. 11:08

Camila Nelson: I'll check it out. Thanks for getting me the ticket. 11:09

① When and where is the performance?
② Did Ryan study performing arts in university?
③ Is there a chance to meet Ryan after the performance?
④ Did you know that he's performing tonight?

※ 다음 글을 읽고 물음에 답하시오. [05~06]

A Growing Threat to Public Health

A growing concern for the National Disease Prevention Agency (NDPA) is the global public health threat posed by antibiotic resistance. Not only is antibiotic resistance responsible for at least a million deaths each year, but it also complicates what should be routine medical procedures, leading to prolonged hospital stays and increased medical costs.

Antibiotic Resistance

Antibiotic resistance occurs when disease-causing bacteria adapt to the antibiotic medications that previously killed them. Those who use antibiotics incorrectly, whether by taking them unnecessarily or failing to complete treatments as prescribed, facilitate the development of resistant strains that can spread to others.

The NDPA educates healthcare providers and the public about the proper use of antibiotics and funds research to develop new treatments. When a resistant infection is identified, the NDPA works with hospitals to <u>contain</u> its spread and provide guidance on treatment options.

05 윗글의 요지로 적절한 것은?

① The NDPA ensures that people use antibiotic medications as prescribed.
② The NDPA aims to combat bacteria's growing ability to withstand treatments.
③ The NDPA tracks deaths resulting from global public health threats.
④ The NDPA tests new treatments designed to replace antibiotics.

06 밑줄 친 contain의 의미와 가장 가까운 것은?

① prevent
② estimate
③ perform
④ document

07 National Technology in Education Conference에 관한 다음 글의 내용과 일치하는 것은?

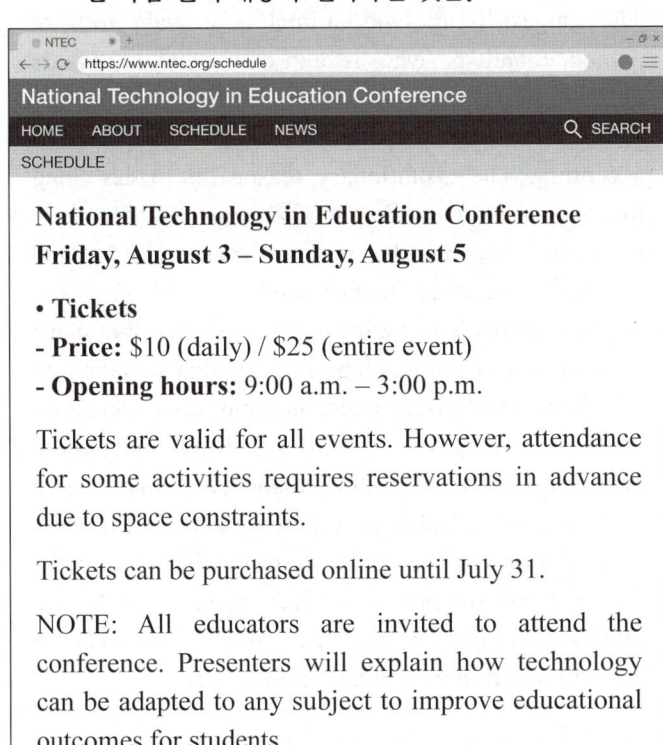

① 일일권은 할인이 적용된다.
② 일부 행사는 사전 예약이 필요하다.
③ 티켓은 7월 31일까지 현장에서 구매할 수 있다.
④ 기술 분야에 종사하는 교육자들만 초대받았다.

08 다음 글의 주제로 적절한 것은?

The longest-living land animal is a giant tortoise named Jonathan, who is approximately 192 years old. Similarly, other species of turtles such as sea turtles and the smaller box turtles can also live up to a century. The evolutionary reason for turtles' long lifespans is relatively simple. Their eggs and hatchlings frequently become the prey of snakes, birds, and raccoons. Therefore, turtles need to breed often and lay eggs throughout their long lives so that they have more chances of producing offspring that survive into adulthood. On the other hand, the biological explanation for turtles' longevity is still not fully understood. What experts are beginning to suspect is that certain turtle species are able to initiate a controlled process in the body that quickly destroys damaged cells. This mechanism prolongs life because it blocks the replication of compromised cells that could otherwise develop into tumors and later into cancer.

① reasons turtle eggs are targeted by predators
② the rationale for turtles' extended lifespans
③ advantages of a prolonged breeding period
④ the anatomy of duplicated cancer cells

09 다음 글의 흐름상 어색한 문장은?

Positive economics studies the economy by relying on objective analysis, completely free of endorsements and disapprovals. ① John Keynes was the first economist credited with developing positive economic theories based solely on fact-supported logic. ② He posited that better financial decisions can be made when the facts of the economy are prioritized over value judgements and unsubstantiated predictions. ③ Financial decisions based solely on positive economics often lead to economically inefficient outcomes. ④ Critics, however, point out that there are many factors to consider when making an economic decision apart from objective truths. They insist that a mix of positive and normative economics, the latter of which incorporates subjectivity, is needed for sound economic decision-making.

10 밑줄 친 부분에 들어갈 말로 적절한 것은?

Mindfulness practices such as meditation and breathing exercises are portrayed in popular media as ways to become aware of the emotions that cause stress in everyday life. Many people believe that by recognizing feelings instead of running away from them, an individual should be able to relieve themselves from the anxiety related to their emotions. However, actual research from cognitive psychologists suggests that a person who is merely cognizant of their emotions may suppress uncomfortable feelings, which in turn exacerbates stress levels. Therefore, experts insist that participants can derive more value from a mindfulness approach that _____ rather than just awareness of them. Doing this effectively involves identifying and acknowledging feelings without ascribing any judgment to them. With enough practice, individuals who embrace their emotions while refraining from mentally and physically reacting to them should gradually experience lower levels of anxiety.

① promotes various meditation exercises

② incorporates acceptance of emotions

③ reflects academic experiment results

④ describes the consequences of stress

01 밑줄 친 부분에 들어갈 말로 적절한 것은?

Those who forget their past accomplishments and focus on their failures tend to _____ themselves for not succeeding.

① welcome
② copy
③ blame
④ analyze

02 밑줄 친 부분 중 어법상 옳지 않은 것은?

Being the youngest in a family of four children, I would not ① be surprising if my siblings were to treat me indifferently. However, instead of dominating all conversations, my brothers and sisters have ② always considered my opinion to be as ③ important as ④ theirs.

03 밑줄 친 부분이 어법상 옳지 않은 것은?

① Her resolve to avoid relationship problems stopped her from get to know people.
② First-time skiers cannot be too careful about choosing appropriate slopes.
③ My visa had been denied by the consulate and I had to wait six months to reapply.
④ She will take the train to visit her parents however crowded it may be.

04 밑줄 친 부분에 들어갈 말로 적절한 것은?

A: How's it going with the move into your new place?
B: Well, it's going OK, but also not OK. I'm having a bit of a problem.
A: What sort of problem?
B: The former tenant left a lot of stuff. _____ _____?
A: You're within your rights to throw it out if it says so in the lease. Check the terms.
B: Oh, I didn't know that. I'd better look at what it says.

① What am I supposed to do with it
② Do you know if I can buy his stuff
③ Have you had a chance to take a look
④ How long am I allowed to keep it

※ 다음 글을 읽고 물음에 답하시오. [05~06]

Nature Conservancy

Who We Are
Composed of administrative professionals and an expert team of over 400 scientists, we are the biggest nonprofit foundation dedicated to land and water preservation. We make conservation efforts through direct projects and partnerships with local organizations in 81 countries.

What We Do
Through funding from private donations, we fight climate change by giving a voice to local leaders and lobbying for environment-first policies on both the domestic and international levels. Our main goal for the next decade is to protect 10 percent of the world's oceans through conservation programs and sustainable fishing initiatives.

How To Help
- Volunteer: Plant trees or restore a green space in your area.
- Donate: All monetary contributions directly support our mission.
- Lower your carbon footprint: Use our carbon footprint calculator to determine your footprint and _____ to reduce it.

05 윗글에서 Nature Conservancy에 관한 내용과 일치하는 것은?

① It exclusively works through collaboration with local groups.
② It receives funding from government subsidies.
③ It advocates for domestic and international environmentally friendly policies.
④ It aims to protect 10 percent of all land areas in the next 10 years.

06 윗글의 밑줄 친 부분에 들어갈 말로 적절한 것은?

① keep in touch
② hit the road
③ take action
④ run away

07 다음 글의 목적으로 적절한 것은?

To: clients@signalinvestments.com
From: no-reply@signalinvestments.com
Date: June 10
Subject: Meeting investment goals

Dear Valued Customers,

Signal Investments knows that planning for your future is about more than simply setting financial goals. You need to make smart, intentional choices to secure your life after retirement. Here are five ways that you can do that:

1. Consistently contribute to your investment account to maximize growth.
2. As your income grows, consider increasing your contributions to retirement or investment accounts to boost your long-term financial benefits.
3. Build wealth strategically through age-appropriate investments: consider aggressive portfolios in your early career, then gradually shift toward more conservative investments.
4. Diversify your investments to protect yourself from sudden changes in the market and optimize long-term returns.
5. Periodically review your investment plan to track your savings and make changes as your needs and goals shift.

For more strategies to maximize your retirement investing, please visit the Signal Retirement Planning Center on our website.

Sincerely,

Signal Investments

① to notify customers of ways to optimize their finances for retirement
② to notify customers of a new strategy to diversify investments
③ to notify customers of the importance of retirement plans
④ to notify customers of the need to review their investment plans

08 다음 글의 제목으로 적절한 것은?

The upper levels of Earth's atmosphere contain narrow bands of strong winds known as jet streams. These streams form when warm air masses converge with cold air masses. They play a strong role in influencing the weather, and are thus of great interest to meteorologists. As a general rule, greater differences in temperature cause the jet stream to flow faster, with mixtures of winter polar and subtropical air sometimes generating winds exceeding 200 miles per hour. When this occurs, these powerful jet streams dip southward, bringing sudden cold waves and triggering heavy snowfall in regions that normally experience milder conditions. As demonstrated by such effects, the jet stream's power gives it the capacity to generate powerful storms and to shape weather systems on a large scale.

① How Jet Streams Regulate Temperature
② Cold Wave Warning: Increasing Weather Volatility
③ Tracking the Formation of Tropical Storms
④ The Influence of the Jet Stream on Weather

09 주어진 글 다음에 이어질 글의 순서로 적절한 것은?

Archaeologists had long assumed that all inhabitants of Herculaneum, an ancient city located at the western base of Mount Vesuvius, consumed the same type of food. But an analysis of the remains revealed some interesting details about them.

(A) Archaeologists now know that, based on these gender differences, the men had a higher proportion of seafood in their diet compared to the women, whose main source of protein came from animal products rather than fish.
(B) However, the researchers found a significant difference between what the men ate and what the women ate upon further examination of this dietary pattern. Ratios of carbon and nitrogen isotopes of amino acids collected from the skeletons showed that women mostly took in a different source of protein.
(C) The amino acids from 17 adult skeletons indicated that the people ingested plenty of seafood. It appears that, overall, they ingested three times more fish than their modern counterparts.

*isotope: (화학) 동위 원소

① (A) – (C) – (B)
② (B) – (A) – (C)
③ (C) – (A) – (B)
④ (C) – (B) – (A)

10 주어진 문장이 들어갈 위치로 적절한 것은?

They obtain our profiles and follow what we click on online, and then provide tailored product choices based on our surfing habits.

Matthew Tobin Anderson's 2002 novel *Feed* introduced us to a culture that was strongly influenced by advertising and the use of Internet-capable brain implants called "feed." (①) Feed is designed not only to give people constant access to databases of music, movies, and other entertainment products but also to detect an individual's personal preferences and to communicate with the user through the implant. (②) This idea of directly connecting to the brains of people is comparable to the marketing landscape today. (③) Like a prediction of what we're experiencing now, Anderson's feed is a portrayal of how companies control our shopping behavior. (④) Indeed, present-day consumerism shares similarities with the strategy in *Feed*.

01 밑줄 친 부분에 들어갈 말로 적절한 것은?

After the weather report warned of an approaching hurricane, citizens rushed to gather supplies necessary to _____ the disaster.

① reveal
② ignore
③ accept
④ face

02 밑줄 친 부분에 들어갈 말로 적절한 것은?

Maslow's hierarchy of needs enables us to understand basic human needs and _____ the insights in practical settings, categorizing human motivations into different levels.

① applying
② apply
③ applied
④ is applied

03 밑줄 친 부분 중 어법상 옳지 않은 것은?

Thank you all for ① attending today's Get Out and Conquer webinar. This is your first step to freeing yourself from your office and becoming a digital nomad, allowing you ② working from anywhere in the world. Telecommunications advances have made ③ it possible to do a great number of jobs without being physically present in the office. Get Out and Conquer will teach you how ④ you can work outside the office so that you can offer your abilities to companies all over the world.

04 밑줄 친 부분에 들어갈 말로 적절한 것은?

Luna Martinez
Did you book hotel rooms for our E Corp trip?
15:03

Joseph Hughes
Yes, I reserved rooms at the Lux Hotel for the 14th to 17th.
15:04

Luna Martinez
Hmm… We may need to change the reservation.
15:04

Joseph Hughes
Why? Is there a problem with that hotel?
15:05

Luna Martinez
No, the hotel's fine. But the E Corp meeting will be postponed until the 21st.
15:06

Joseph Hughes
I see. _____
15:07

① Let's stay at the Lux Hotel in that case.
② I'll call and see if they can push back our reservation.
③ We should prepare our presentation for the client.
④ I'll check the availability of closer accommodations.

※ 다음 글을 읽고 물음에 답하시오. [05~06]

To	City Planning and Development Office
From	Arthur Mahoney
Date	September 19
Subject	Concerns Regarding an Abandoned Building

Dear Director of City Planning and Development,

This letter concerns the abandoned warehouse located off Highway 17, near the Cantu Street exit. Despite the city's assurances that this structure would be demolished, it has remained standing, which is a matter of concern for many residents.

In addition to being an eyesore, the structure appears to be unstable, with shattered windows and a partially collapsed roof. The presence of graffiti on its exterior walls suggests that people are illegally accessing the property. Given the _____ state of the structure, I feel like it is only a matter of time until someone gets hurt.

I kindly request that, for the good of the community, you honor the city's original commitment to tear down this hazardous building as soon as possible. Thank you for your attention to this pressing matter.

Respectfully yours,

Arthur Mahoney

05 윗글의 목적으로 적절한 것은?

① 근처 고속도로가 훼손된 상황을 알리려고
② 건물 외벽의 불법 낙서에 대해 신고하려고
③ 불법 건축물로 인해 부상을 입은 사실을 공유하려고
④ 시에서 약속한 폐건물의 철거에 대해 상기시키려고

06 윗글의 밑줄 친 부분에 들어갈 말로 적절한 것은?

① uneven
② firm
③ poor
④ light

07 다음 글의 요지로 적절한 것은?

Companies and public figures in the US frequently file lawsuits that they don't intend to win, solely to damage the defendant by costing them money. These suits are known as "strategic lawsuits against public participation," or SLAPP suits. Such suits are generally punitive in nature, being filed in response to some form of perceived defamation, and are aimed at discouraging others from speaking out about an issue. SLAPP suits are problematic, yet effective in leaving media outlets and individuals fearful of criticizing many public figures. While some states have legislation limiting such practices, far too many plaintiffs simply file their suits in another state.

① SLAPP suits are designed to punish defendants through excessive legal costs.
② Public figures should be careful not to insult others in their public statements.
③ Media outlets have a responsibility to defend honest news coverage.
④ Legislation preventing SLAPP suits needs to be revised.

08. Glacier Conservation Agency에 관한 다음 글의 내용과 일치하는 것은?

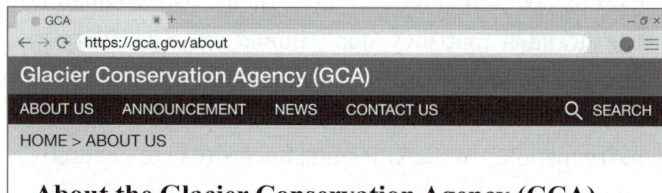

About the Glacier Conservation Agency (GCA)

The Glacier Conservation Agency (GCA) is a government agency dedicated to the preservation of the nation's glaciers. Guided by a strong commitment to science and innovation, the GCA employs advanced satellite imaging, as well as ground-based surveys, to monitor glacier size, movement, and melt rates. It shares the information it obtains with international research institutions, which it collaborates with to develop new strategies to save these vital ecosystems. In addition to research, the GCA works with other government agencies to implement legislation limiting land use in sensitive glacier areas. It has the authority to enforce this legislation through the imposition of fines, the suspension of permits, and, when necessary, legal action.

① It develops strategies to address glacier melting.

② It provides funding to international research institutions.

③ It is the only government body authorized to determine land-use policies.

④ It can impose fines to enforce related legislation.

09. 다음 글의 흐름상 어색한 문장은?

A 2009 study showed guppies can evolve in under 30 generations, making it observable to humans. A number of guppies from the Yarra River were divided into two groups. ① One of these groups was introduced to an area that had been cleared of predators, while the other was put in a section of the river that had extra predators added. ② The evolutionary changes observed in guppies were primarily caused by temperature fluctuations rather than predation levels. ③ Eight years later, within 30 generations, those in the low-predation area had evolved to have fewer babies, and become larger. ④ This evolution helped them survive the increased competition that comes from higher survival rates. Those in the high-predation area, on the other hand, had evolved to have much faster reproductive cycles with more offspring, which were generally smaller.

10 주어진 문장이 들어갈 위치로 적절한 것은?

As a result, most advertisements try to communicate how a person might feel with the marketed product in their lives.

Many advertising agencies employ psychologists in an attempt to maximize the effectiveness of their ads. The crossover between these disciplines is particularly pronounced in emotional advertisements. (①) Numerous studies have shown that customers react more strongly to emotions than reason. (②) Rather than listing a product's features, letting you imagine its application, advertising will often show the users' emotional responses, such as a sense of relief or satisfaction. (③) This invariable tactic has been used since the 1700s, when a brewery's contents were being auctioned off. (④) Advertisers said, "We are not here to sell boilers and vats, but the potential for extraordinary wealth and success."

DAY 08 하프모의고사 08회

01 밑줄 친 부분에 들어갈 말로 적절한 것은?

The couple _____ saving money rather than living luxuriously, with the goal of building up a sizable sum of money for their retirement.

① stopped
② prioritized
③ postponed
④ minded

02 밑줄 친 부분에 들어갈 말로 적절한 것은?

Furniture created by expert designers for small apartments _____ at the exhibition.

① showcased
② is showcased
③ are showcased
④ have been showcased

03 밑줄 친 부분 중 어법상 옳지 않은 것은?

The platypus has a broad, flat bill that resembles ① those of ducks and a furry body like a beaver, which surprised European biologists. ② What was later learned about the platypus made it seem like an ③ even stranger creature. It was discovered that the platypus does not give birth to live young like nearly every other mammal, but instead ④ lays eggs like a bird.

04 두 사람의 대화 중 가장 어색한 것은?

① A: Where can I find the closest convenience store?
   B: It's just two blocks ahead on your right.
② A: What do you do to relax after work?
   B: I pour myself a glass of wine.
③ A: Do you think you can come and lend me a hand?
   B: Hold on, I'll be there in a minute.
④ A: Can you recommend a dish on the menu?
   B: Yes, of course. I'll bring you the bill.

※ 다음 글을 읽고 물음에 답하시오. [05~06]

_____(A)_____

If you have a sweet tooth and a big heart, come support the bake sale for the Art for Everyone Association.

This charity organization provides children in need with opportunities to experience and participate in art. Your support helps kids discover their artistic passion!

A wide variety of baked goods will be provided by local bakeries and home cooks. All proceeds from the bake sale will be used to purchase art supplies and fund field trips to museums and other cultural centers.

Give the gift of art!

Organized by Art for Everyone

- **Location**: Sheraton Farmer's Market, Booth 121
- **Date**: Saturday, February 20
- **Time**: 8:00 a.m. to 2:00 p.m.

If you are unable to attend but would like to donate, monetary contributions can be given at www.artforeveryoneassoc.org/donationpage.

05 (A)에 들어갈 윗글의 제목으로 적절한 것은?

① Appreciation for Our Local Artists
② Fun at the Farmer's Market Art Booth
③ Homemade Desserts by Art Teachers
④ Fundraiser for Children's Art Opportunities

06 위 안내문의 내용과 일치하지 않는 것은?

① 전문 베이커리에서 만든 빵을 구매할 수 있다.
② 지역 미술관에서 행사를 주최한다.
③ 행사는 농산물 직판장에서 단 하루 동안 열린다.
④ 웹페이지를 통해 기부금을 전달할 수 있다.

07 다음 글의 요지로 적절한 것은?

If you were to estimate the length of a line in a photograph, how would you do it? Some people simply look intently at the line and provide a rough estimate. But others examine the line in relation to another object in the picture to gauge its length. Either group may think that the method used by the other seems illogical; in truth, it really depends on how you were raised. People who were raised to be more independent try to solve problems directly; hence, they focus on the line itself to measure it. Individuals who were encouraged to have a group mentality, on the other hand, consider the context, which is why they look at things other than the line. A similar difference occurs when taking a picture. The more independent person will aim at something in the frame, while the other will look at the picture in its entirety. It's like using a zoom lens versus taking a panoramic shot.

① Personal attitudes can have an impact on how one poses for a photograph.
② The perspective of an individual can depend on the way the person was reared.
③ Thinking of the group and not just the individual is more caring.
④ The choices one makes are largely determined by how one views culture.

08 다음 이메일의 내용과 일치하는 것은?

To: inquiries@vera_print.com
From: helen_strickland@FowlerRoth.com
Date: May 2
Subject: Custom T-Shirt Order Inquiry
Attachment: company_logo.pdf

Good afternoon,

Our company is planning an upcoming volunteer day and is interested in placing an order for custom T-shirts.

We need 150 navy blue cotton shirts with our company logo printed on the front left chest area and "Fowler-Roth Volunteer Day" printed on the back in white. The order should include 40 small, 50 medium, 45 large, and 15 extra-large shirts, all of which should be unisex with a standard fit. We have a strict budget of no more than $2,200 for this order.

We need the shirts delivered to us by May 25. I realize this is a tight timeline, so I would appreciate it if you could let me know if you are able to fulfill this request as soon as possible.

I hope to hear from you soon.

Best regards,

Helen Strickland, Event Organizer

① 흰색 면 셔츠 150장이 필요하다.
② 네 가지의 서로 다른 사이즈를 주문할 예정이다.
③ 각 사이즈마다 2,200달러의 예산을 편성했다.
④ 답변 기한은 5월 25일까지이다.

09 다음 글의 흐름상 어색한 문장은?

The brain is at its peak in one's early to mid-twenties and then begins to weaken, but this does not worsen thinking ability. ① Despite the physical decline, the older brain can accomplish some things better than the younger brain can. ② For example, it can process information in a superior way when it comes to making moral decisions, controlling emotions, and assessing social situations. ③ To reduce the consequences of negative changes to the brain, older people should engage in activities that keep the brain active. This is partly because older people have learned to focus better, control anxiety, and avoid distractions. ④ As a result, in tasks involving problem-solving and abstract reasoning, older adults often do better than younger people.

10 주어진 글 다음에 이어질 글의 순서로 적절한 것은?

Utilitarianism is a form of decision-making that emphasizes outcomes that produce the greatest good for the greatest number of people. Many everyday decisions are easy to rationalize through a utilitarian lens.

(A) In hypothetical scenarios, though, this reasoning becomes more difficult when the outcomes are unclear. Suppose a group of 100 and a group of five are both in imminent danger. The utilitarian would say that saving the group of 100 is clearly better.

(B) For example, a parent may buy their children ice cream to make them happy rather than save a little money and deny them a slightly unhealthy snack.

(C) However, the group of 100 is made up of adventure enthusiasts who knowingly took risks, while the five are a group of scientists about to complete a vaccine for a deadly epidemic. The utilitarian must weigh 100 immediate lives against the potential to save hundreds of thousands in the future, which is not an easy task.

① (A) – (C) – (B)
② (B) – (A) – (C)
③ (B) – (C) – (A)
④ (C) – (A) – (B)

DAY 09 하프모의고사 09회

01 밑줄 친 부분에 들어갈 말로 적절한 것은?

To others, the young child's attempts at speech were _____, but his parents were able to interpret what he was trying to say.

① extra
② junior
③ unclear
④ pure

02 밑줄 친 부분에 들어갈 말로 적절한 것은?

The ancient city _____ the birthplace of democracy by historians since the 5th century BCE.

① refers to as
② has been referred
③ was referred to as
④ has been referred to as

03 밑줄 친 부분 중 어법상 옳지 않은 것은?

Ramadan is a holy time ① when Muslims around the world reflect on their spiritual lives and focus on their faith by avoiding ② consume food and drink from sunup to sundown. The purpose of this practice is to allow those ③ fasting to escape the distractions of the material world. By concentrating solely on the spiritual world, they can dedicate themselves to ④ the healthiest practices for their moral well-being.

04 밑줄 친 부분에 들어갈 말로 적절한 것은?

 Mia Anderson
Are you planning to attend the marketing seminar next month?
14:15

 Owen Bailey
I attended a similar seminar last year, so I might skip this one.
14:16

 Mia Anderson
This year's seminar is actually quite different from last year's.
14:16

 Owen Bailey
Really? What are the differences?
14:17

 Mia Anderson
It highlights AI marketing tools and how to implement them in our campaigns.
14:17

 Owen Bailey
That sounds interesting! How can I register?
14:18

 Mia Anderson
_____
14:18

 Owen Bailey
Great, I'll do that today. Thanks for letting me know!
14:19

① The registration deadline is next Friday.
② Just let Sarah know you're interested.
③ We need your employee ID.
④ It's the pre-registration period now.

※ 다음 글을 읽고 물음에 답하시오. [05~06]

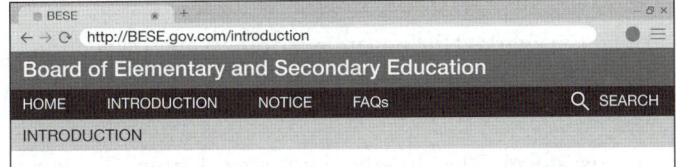

Board of Elementary and Secondary Education

Goals

We are dedicated to providing students a high-quality education that prepares them for future career success by fostering academic excellence and supporting educators. We also strive to create a more just education system and close achievement gaps.

Actions

We create educational policies and allocate resources to strengthen schools and give educators the tools they need to deliver effective instruction. This includes establishing curriculum guidelines, administering standardized testing, and providing on-going training. In addition, we collaborate with local school districts to implement programs that enhance learning and school performance.

Organizational Values

- Equity: Fairness in education is a top priority and we work to provide a high-quality education to all, regardless of background.
- Innovation: We develop new approaches to teaching and continuously seek policies and practices to improve education.

05 윗글에서 Board of Elementary and Secondary Education에 관한 내용과 일치하는 것은?

① It focuses on ensuring educators have successful careers.
② It creates rules and regulations related to education.
③ It works with local businesses to provide resources to schools.
④ It tailors education to students' individual backgrounds.

06 밑줄 친 just의 의미와 가장 가까운 것은?

① fair
② global
③ famous
④ affordable

07 다음 글의 제목으로 가장 적절한 것은?

When Europeans colonized North America, they found a massive passenger pigeon population. The birds were so numerous that it was said that large flocks could darken the sky for days. However, within a short time, the species disappeared altogether. The reason for the quick demise of a population of animals estimated at between three and five billion amazed scientists. While it seemed to be influenced by the new settlers, this didn't fully explain the extinction. Surprisingly, modern genetic research suggests that the species was in decline before the arrival of the Europeans. In fact, researchers believe that the pigeon population would have fallen to only a few hundred thousand had Europeans not arrived in North America. However, this doesn't completely free settlers from responsibility. It is likely that overhunting by the Europeans pushed the struggling species to its ultimate extinction.

① The Reality of the Passenger Pigeon's Disappearance
② The Reason North America's Pigeon Population Increased
③ Pigeon Hunting: A Source of Nourishment for European Settlers
④ Ecological Damage Caused by Colonization

08 다음 글의 요지로 가장 적절한 것은?

Safe Travels

Protecting travelers on the nation's transportation systems is the main function of the Passenger Safety Administration (PSA). Effective safety measures protect passengers, crew, and cargo across the country's vast road-, rail-, and air-travel systems.

Weapons, Explosives, and Incendiaries

Weapons, explosives, and incendiaries (WEIs) are prohibited items on passenger travel, especially air travel. These include firearms, knives, and flammable materials that pose security threats.

The PSA employs teams of inspectors working around the clock using scanners and police dogs at departure points to detect WEIs on passengers and in their luggage. When a WEI is detected, PSA staff order additional screening to positively identify the item and determine whether it is a safety threat, often ordering its confiscation and detaining the traveler if he or she is suspected of having a dangerous intent.

*incendiary: 발연성 물질

① PSA supervises the functioning of the nation's transportation systems.

② PSA aims to create detection systems that accurately identify items in luggage.

③ PSA creates lists of WEIs that are prohibited for air travelers to carry.

④ PSA's main focus is protecting travelers from transportation security threats.

09 주어진 문장이 들어갈 위치로 적절한 것은?

In fact, it sparked the enactment of the Meat Inspection Act and the Pure Food and Drug Act.

In his novel The Jungle, journalist Upton Sinclair portrayed the terrible working conditions immigrant workers experienced in the early 1900s. Sinclair documented the truth through the life of a young Lithuanian, Jurgis Rudkus, who had recently immigrated. (①) In the novel, young immigrant men faced an environment that destroyed whatever optimism they had at the start. (②) For instance, they stood for ten hours a day in dirty, poorly-ventilated meatpacking factories for five dollars a day. (③) Sinclair hoped the book would help these men; instead, the public expressed strong concerns about food hygiene. (④) Encouragingly, over a century after the book's publication, significant progress has been made in the meatpacking industry through strengthened labor regulations, technological automation, and worker rights advocacy.

10 밑줄 친 부분에 들어갈 말로 적절한 것은?

Today, robots complete 50 percent of all tasks in numerous fields including agriculture, the automotive industry, and supply chain management. As robots become even more prevalent, they will need to improve their ability to _____, which will increase their efficiency and productivity. That's why a team of researchers from MIT has devised a framework that allows robots to develop human-like social skills through an interactive model. These robots were each given a goal and programmed to recognize the aims of others. An algorithm collected data from the social interactions between them and then decided if the other machines needed help achieving their goals or not. While still early, this type of social recognition would be beneficial at an assisted living center, for example, where robots could assess how much aid an elderly person requires.

① understand and respond to social cues
② update their algorithms
③ establish task objectives independently
④ identify mechanical failures

DAY 10 하프모의고사 10회

01 밑줄 친 부분에 들어갈 말로 적절한 것은?

Freedom from _____ is essential for Consumer Protection Committee members when evaluating the circumstances of consumers with dissatisfaction.

① alarm
② bias
③ honesty
④ cooperation

02 밑줄 친 부분에 들어갈 말로 적절한 것은?

The citizens asked that the government _____ taxes on basic necessities.

① reduced
② reduces
③ to reduce
④ reduce

03 밑줄 친 부분 중 어법상 옳지 않은 것은?

In *Charlotte's Web*, Charlotte, a spider, weaves a message into her web ① in order to save Wilbur, a pig who faces death. Upon seeing the message, Wilbur's owner decides ② not to kill the animal. Two lessons emerge. One is that deep friendships can form even among very different creatures, and ③ the other is that sacrifice can have a lasting impact. Wilbur's decision to protect Charlotte's eggs after she dies lets readers ④ to see the enduring bond between the two characters.

04 밑줄 친 부분에 들어갈 말로 적절한 것은?

A: Can I get someone else to give the talk for me?
B: Why? Did something suddenly come up?
A: Not really. But I feel like I'm going to mess up the speech.
B: You will be fine. If you're too worried, _____ _____.
A: That's a good idea. Can you help me?
B: Of course. Deliver the speech to me now, and I'll give you my thoughts.

① I'd be happy to give the speech for you.
② why don't you reschedule the speech for next week?
③ you can use note cards instead of the script.
④ how about getting some feedback on it?

※ 다음 글을 읽고 물음에 답하시오. [05~06]

To	Mapleton Municipal Council
From	Jean Richards
Date	November 5
Subject	Improvement to the Town's Online Complaint System

Dear Council Members,

I trust everyone on the council is well. I am sending this letter in regard to the town's online system for filing complaints, which I believe can be improved.

The current system requires the complainant to provide their name and phone number. While I understand there are situations when the complainant must be contacted for more information, I think some complaints, like those about road or park conditions, can be made anonymously.

As we live in a small community, it's easy for rumors to spread or for personal information to be shared. By allowing anonymous complaints for certain issues, more residents would feel comfortable voicing their concerns, which in turn would lead to greater _____ in improving our town. Thank you for considering this suggestion.

With sincere regards,

Jean Richards

05 윗글의 목적으로 적절한 것은?

① to ask for road repairs near the park
② to propose a change to the town's online complaint process
③ to complain about the unauthorized sharing of private data
④ to suggest ways to improve the security of the town's website

06 윗글의 밑줄 친 부분에 들어갈 말로 적절한 것은?

① residence
② participation
③ generosity
④ indifference

07 다음 글의 내용과 일치하지 않는 것은?

The historic Loma Manor is accessible by public transportation. Visitors can take the Green Line to Freeman Station and walk north for five minutes from Exit 6 or take the 115 bus to Wolfe Avenue and walk west for three blocks. Taxis and rideshare service vehicles can enter the parking lot for free to access the pick-up and drop-off area. For those driving, parking is available for a flat fee of $20 per vehicle. Cash is no longer accepted.

General admission tickets do not cover specially ticketed programs or events. The cost of a standard adult ticket is $40. When accompanied by a ticketed adult, children under three are admitted for free. A complimentary mobile audio guide app is included with general admission.

NOTE: Although Loma Manor is open for tours daily from 9:30 a.m. – 5:00 p.m., its gardens close at 4:00 p.m. on Mondays and Tuesdays.

① Loma Manor can be accessed by foot from Freeman Station.
② The cost of on-site parking depends on duration.
③ The $40 admission does not provide all-inclusive access.
④ Loma Manor's gardens close early twice a week.

08 다음 글의 주제로 적절한 것은?

If you feel that you're stuck and can't get things moving forward, you may need to start saying "yes" more often, according to Shonda Rhimes. In her memoir, *Year of Yes*, the award-winning TV producer and show creator says that she was always an introvert who was scared to try many things. However, she decided to change when a relative told her that she never said yes to anything. Rhimes pledged to say yes to everything for one year. And the results were amazing. As Rhimes confronted new fears, she not only overcame them but also became more confident in facing other fears, so they lost their power. But it was not all about getting over things that made her uncomfortable; she also said yes to allowing herself more time for fun, which she says unlocked her creative potential. As a result, she was able to improve the level of her work and advance her career even further.

① strategies for managing reluctance effectively
② life transformation through positive responses
③ role of family support in career choices
④ TV industry challenges for female producers

09 주어진 글 다음에 이어질 글의 순서로 적절한 것은?

Some fruits and vegetables are easy to classify because they are either sweet or not sweet. This method of categorization is subjective, and can lead to different groups of people categorizing the same plant differently.

(A) For example, confusion may occur because some consider a tomato a sweet fruit, while others insist it is a non-sweet vegetable. The criterion of sweetness will make yams, carrots, and beets fruits as they all have a degree of sweetness.

(B) Instead of using taste as a classifier, botanists concur that fruits and vegetables should be viewed botanically, that is, based on which part of the plant they come from.

(C) If it emerges from the plant's flower, then it is a fruit, and this would include apples, cucumbers, and eggplants. In contrast, if it comes from any other part of the plant, such as the roots, stems, or leaves, it is a vegetable.

① (A) – (B) – (C)
② (A) – (C) – (B)
③ (C) – (A) – (B)
④ (C) – (B) – (A)

10 밑줄 친 부분에 들어갈 말로 적절한 것은?

A comprehensive outline of civil, political, economic, social, and cultural rights is the basis for the Universal Declaration of Human Rights adopted by the United Nations in 1948. The Declaration has its origins in the abuses of World War II, when governments used police and armed forces to infringe people's human rights, and was written by representatives from various cultural backgrounds. Explicit in the document is the intent to accord all human beings the right to dignity, governance participation, and remedy for rights violations given its legitimacy in all countries. Although it is considered the most significant development in the history of human rights, many see it as imperfect because _____. Should rights violations occur in any country, such as the state's use of military might against the citizenry or the denial of human rights by society, the UN does not have the legal power to act.

① the limits do not go far enough
② its principles are not binding
③ concepts of human rights change over time
④ few countries have signed on

01 밑줄 친 부분의 의미와 가장 가까운 것은?

The ambassador was recently attacked by the international community for his ignorant remarks about the ongoing refugee crisis.

① criticized
② evaluated
③ avoided
④ suspended

02 밑줄 친 부분에 들어갈 말로 적절한 것은?

Three-fourths of books _____ online are typically delivered within two business days.

① is purchased
② purchasing
③ purchased
④ are purchased

03 밑줄 친 부분 중 어법상 옳지 않은 것은?

In Western countries, social workers tend to keep parents and children together ① despite any issues that may be present in the home. Only when the risk is deemed too high ② does the social worker make a recommendation for intervention to a family court. Before that, however, social workers are willing to ③ doing everything to improve the situation of a family. If a family ④ successfully applies the advice, then there will be no need to take the step of separating children from their parents.

04 밑줄 친 부분에 들어갈 말로 적절한 것은?

① Why didn't you mention this to me earlier?
② When do you prefer to take your vacation?
③ Have you thought about what you're going to do then?
④ How many vacation days do you have left this year?

※ 다음 글을 읽고 물음에 답하시오. [05~06]

(A) _____

Pottersville invites everyone to its New Year's Eve Ball, an annual celebration of the coming of the new year that has been held for 75 years. You don't want to miss out on this fun event.

Details
- **Date**: Thursday, December 31
- **Time**: Events start at 6 p.m.
- **Location**: Doré Arena at the Pottersville Convention Center
- **Dress Code**: Formal attire required
- **Ticket Cost**: $25 per person

Highlights
- **Entertainment**
  Enjoy the talents of an assortment of musicians, dancers, and other entertainers as they put on shows throughout the evening.

- **Countdown and Fireworks**
  Count down the last moments of this year and take pleasure in the city's fireworks show at midnight in comfort from the arena's rooftop.

To request tickets, please call the city events manager at 555-2821.

05 (A)에 들어갈 윗글의 제목으로 적절한 것은?

① Visit Pottersville in the Coming Year
② See How Pottersville Changed over the Years
③ Experience a Magical Night in Pottersville
④ Be Inspired by Pottersville Creative Passion

06 New Year's Eve Ball에 관한 윗글의 내용과 일치하지 않는 것은?

① 75년 동안 진행되어 왔다.
② 별도의 복장 규정이 있다.
③ 연예인들의 무대를 볼 수 있다.
④ 티켓은 현장에서 구매 가능하다.

07 다음 글의 요지로 적절한 것은?

One of the principal theories for the interactions of people and societies is that of structural functionalism. This idea looks to explain how societies and personal relationships develop over time. The theory posits that societies evolve much in the same way that biological organisms do, with different components each serving a specific purpose, much in the same way that organs do with organisms. Sectors of a society could include education, religion, philosophy, economics, and countless other arenas. Each sector has the goal of reaching its own equilibrium, or state of stability. This, in turn, brings stability to the entirety of the organism. This theory has come under tremendous scrutiny for flaws such as taking too much of a macroscopic view of society and ignoring human nature and genetics, yet it remains influential even today.

① Social sectors operate independently for overall stability.
② Evolutionary biology determines societal structural development exclusively.
③ Structural functionalism compares society to biological organisms.
④ Human nature primarily contradicts structural functionalism principles.

08 다음 글의 흐름상 어색한 문장은?

Meet ISabelle, the Immigration Service's New Virtual Assistant.

The ISabelle chatbot is a new service offering information from the Immigration Service. ISabelle can assist users with commonly asked questions about the immigration process, including explaining visa categories, giving directions for filling out applications, and checking one's case status, all using the latest information to provide accurate and timely help. ① As part of the Immigration Service's efforts to improve customer service, the chatbot will be available around the clock. ② The Immigration Service warns users that ISabelle frequently provides outdated visa information from 2010. ③ For questions that cannot be answered, ISabelle offers users access to live operators who can provide more in-depth assistance. ④ Currently available in English, Spanish, and Chinese, the service will add additional languages in future updates, including Korean, Portuguese, and Arabic.

09 주어진 문장이 들어갈 위치로 적절한 것은?

But the truth is that discipline—forcing oneself to sit at the desk to write first without motivation— leads to inspiration.

Many wannabe fiction authors with dreams of producing best-selling novels struggle to write. (①) This doesn't mean that they don't have the talent to produce coherent or even artful prose. (②) Rather, their writing difficulties emerge from their inability to make themselves physically sit with an open notebook or a word processor and get to work. (③) For many aspiring authors, this problem seems to stem from the misconception that they must wait for inspiration to strike before they can start writing. (④) Famed writer William Somerset Maugham, among other established authors, seemed to agree with this regimen when he said, "I write only when inspiration strikes, which fortunately strikes every morning at nine o'clock sharp."

10 밑줄 친 부분에 들어갈 말로 적절한 것은?

With the enormous geographical and meteorological changes occurring on Earth, it has become more important than ever to collect information related to natural disasters. The use of modern monitoring and imaging technology has allowed scientists to understand, forecast, and respond to volcanic eruptions, earthquakes, and landslides. In addition, being able to observe and predict glacier and ice-sheet melt and the resulting sea-level change can provide governments with data for disaster response support and mitigation. In short, _____ is critical for protecting life on the planet.

① the precise monitoring of changes on and inside Earth
② international collaboration among governments
③ studies on natural disasters that occurred previously
④ sustainable infrastructure in vulnerable regions

01 밑줄 친 부분에 들어갈 말로 적절한 것은?

It is usually harder for _____ people to remember information presented at meetings than it is for those who are attentive.

① friendly
② dedicated
③ independent
④ distracted

02 밑줄 친 부분에 들어갈 말로 적절한 것은?

_____ people attending the international food festival was remarkable, which reflected the event's popularity.

① The number of
② A number of
③ A variety of
④ A little of

03 밑줄 친 부분 중 어법상 옳지 않은 것은?

The first "challenge" activity on social media to catch on ① was the Ice Bucket Challenge in which people poured large buckets of icy water on ② themselves to ③ rise treatment research funds for Lou Gehrig's disease. Unfortunately, a lot of challenges are now simply meant to create funny viral videos, lacking ④ such a worthwhile goal.

04 밑줄 친 부분에 들어갈 말로 적절한 것은?

A: Have you planned anything for next week's mini-vacation?
B: The usual, I guess. I'll get some rest and watch TV.
A: Don't you usually go somewhere?
B: No, I hardly ever do anything special.
A: You should think about using this time to treat yourself. How about finding a nice restaurant to enjoy a meal?
B: _____ I'd like to do that.

① I'm trying to save money on food.
② That's actually a good suggestion.
③ I'd rather not waste my time.
④ Restaurants will be crowded.

※ 다음 글을 읽고 물음에 답하시오. [05~06]

Office of Global Justice and Security

About

We are committed to creating a safer world through coordination with law enforcement authorities in over 180 countries. Together, we collect and share evidence to assist investigators and facilitate the secure transfer of prisoners across international borders for prosecution within the proper geographic jurisdictions.

CLOUD Act

In response to the new era of digitization, the Clarifying Lawful Overseas Use of Data (CLOUD) Act was passed in 2018 to accelerate the process of approving and sharing digital and electronic evidence among the department's <u>network</u> of international partners.

Points of Emphasis
- Balancing the protection of public safety with the individual's right to privacy
- Fighting corruption at the global level by identifying high-ranking officials guilty of bribery and similar crimes

05 윗글에서 Office of Global Justice and Security에 관한 내용과 일치하는 것은?

① It oversees law enforcement agencies around the world.
② It dispatches investigators to prosecute prisoners.
③ It applies a law to enable the quick sharing of digital evidence.
④ It prioritizes public safety over individuals' right to privacy.

06 밑줄 친 network의 의미와 가장 가까운 것은?

① authority
② community
③ access
④ agreement

07 다음 글의 주제로 적절한 것은?

Culture shock is a well-known phenomenon; still, returning home after years of living abroad can subject one to an even bigger episode—that of reverse culture shock. People have good memories of their homeland, but once the initial euphoria of being back home wears off, they may start feeling like a foreigner in their own country, especially if the withdrawal from their previous life was too swift. Having adjusted to the culture of a Western nation in surroundings very different from their motherland, native traditions can seem unfamiliar, and before long, they begin to feel foreign. The language, the sights, smells and sounds, and even the conversation can become overwhelming. Moreover, the feeling of being socially distant from people one is close to can be distressing. Like culture shock, it takes time and the empathy of loved ones to help persons readjust when they return home.

① a comparison of culture shock and reverse culture shock
② a surprising reaction to returning to one's homeland
③ the difficulties of learning new customs and traditions
④ the benefits of living in a foreign land

08. National Transportation Safety Convention에 관한 다음 글의 내용과 일치하지 않는 것은?

National Transportation Safety Convention (NTSC)

Tuesday, January 12 – Friday, January 15
Tickets:
- **Price**: $25.00
- **Hours**: Tuesday: Noon – 5:00 p.m.
   Wednesday-Friday: 10:00 a.m. – 5:00 p.m.

Tickets will be available online or at the convention center box office beginning December 1.

Sponsors and exhibitors can receive free tickets for their employees. Ticket allocation will be determined by sponsorship level or display booth size.

Tickets ensure entrance to the exhibit hall, all lectures, and most additional events. Special passes are required for VIP activities.

① 화요일 회의는 오후 12시에 열린다.
② 입장권은 12월 1일부터 판매된다.
③ 무료 입장권 제공 수량은 업체마다 다를 수 있다.
④ 입장권 소지자는 VIP 행사에 참여할 수 있다.

09. 주어진 글 다음에 이어질 글의 순서로 적절한 것은?

Door-to-door selling in the US began in the mid-1800s when David McConnell went house to house to sell books. But he struggled to find buyers, and women only opened their doors because they liked his free samples of perfume.

(A) On top of that, he wasn't the best salesperson when it came to talking to women about perfumes. So, he hired a sales force of women who loved talking about perfumes, and that is how his perfume company became successful.

(B) Looking reality in the face, McConnell realized that he should focus on selling the more popular product. He began selling fragrances with hopes they would appeal to the women who made up the majority of his customers. He experienced a degree of success, but there were still barriers.

(C) The largest obstacle was that there was only one of him. Walking for the whole day was tiring, and the profits he earned alone were less than he had anticipated.

① (A) – (C) – (B)
② (B) – (A) – (C)
③ (B) – (C) – (A)
④ (C) – (A) – (B)

10 밑줄 친 부분에 들어갈 말로 적절한 것은?

Called the big cities of the sea, coral reefs have plenty of natural competition, from organisms that feed on them to jellyfish that invade their territory. But nothing has been more destructive to reefs than ocean acidification due to rising carbon dioxide levels, and by 2011, only half of the reefs that previously existed remained. A year later, scientists thought of transplanting healthy coral that could withstand warming water onto damaged reefs. Subsequently, the method was challenged because it was slow and expensive. _____, sturdier, slow-growing coral species began being used to bolster weak ones by embedding baby coral onto damaged reefs, which is less costly and shows greater promise. In addition, by designating areas where coral reefs grow as "protected," fish that consume organisms that prey on coral can thrive, thus reducing the pest population and giving corals added protection.

① Theoretically
② Ultimately
③ Obviously
④ Honestly

01 밑줄 친 부분에 들어갈 말로 적절한 것은?

Conservationists refused to _____ their opposition to cutting the budget allocated for protecting endangered animals.

① admit
② withdraw
③ complete
④ pursue

02 밑줄 친 부분에 들어갈 말로 적절한 것은?

During our home renovation project, I decided to have all the windows _____, which dramatically improved the insulation in our century-old house.

① replace
② replaced
③ replacing
④ to be replaced

03 밑줄 친 부분 중 어법상 옳지 않은 것은?

As the fictional character Sherlock Holmes grew ever more beloved, his creator Arthur Conan Doyle began ① to resent him. The success of the Holmes detective series left Doyle's other literary works ② overshadowed. The author's seven historical novels were his real passion, but ③ they attracted little attention among his readers because they ④ were obsessing with the enigmatic Holmes.

04 밑줄 친 부분에 들어갈 말로 적절한 것은?

Emily Lewis
How may I help you today?
11:00

Ryan Murphy
I'd like to renew our current delivery service contract.
11:01

Emily Lewis
We appreciate your continued business. How long would you like to extend the contract?
11:02

Ryan Murphy
One year. The services we need would be the same as before. What about the cost?
11:03

Emily Lewis
The cost might change depending on the delivery volume.
11:03

Ryan Murphy
_____
11:04

Emily Lewis
Our pricing policy has changed. A fixed rate applies up to a certain number of deliveries, with extra charges for more.
11:05

① Do you offer any discounts for regular customers?
② We typically use delivery services twice a week.
③ I'm not certain about our exact delivery needs for next year.
④ Wasn't it a fixed rate regardless of changes in volume?

※ 다음 글을 읽고 물음에 답하시오. [05~06]

Appeal Review
Appeals Courts (AC) look at legal decisions to make sure they follow the law correctly. These courts are an important part of our justice system. They fix mistakes that could lead to people being treated unfairly under the law.

Legal Precedent
Legal precedent (LP) means decisions made by courts in the past that set rules for future cases. When courts follow LP, similar cases get similar outcomes. This makes our legal system fairer and more consistent. If judges don't follow these precedents, people might be confused about what the law really means.

AC judges check cases where legal precedent may have been used incorrectly. They study past court decisions carefully. Then they write opinions that explain legal standards clearly. This helps make sure the law works the same way for everyone across the whole court system. By doing this important work, AC judges protect everyone's right _____.

05 윗글의 요지로 적절한 것은?

① AC's top concern is looking for problems in the judicial system.
② AC is charged with establishing precedent in legal cases.
③ AC aims to be sure that laws are clear and fairly applied.
④ AC trains judges to look for inconsistencies in LP.

06 윗글의 빈칸에 들어갈 말로 적절한 것은?

① to supervise lower court decisions
② to receive fair treatment under the law
③ to evaluate court procedure compliance
④ to reinforce existing legal standards

07 다음 글의 목적으로 적절한 것은?

To: Residents@LesterCity.com
From: Info@LesterCity.com
Date: April 11
Subject: Household waste

Dear Residents,

The City of Lester is committed to reducing pollution caused by household waste. But we can't do it alone. Here are five ways residents can minimize waste:

1. Reduce the number of single-use items used by opting for reusable bags, bottles, and containers.
2. Compost food scraps and yard waste instead of throwing them out.
3. Follow recycling guidelines and sort all recyclables rather than putting them in household trash.
4. Donate or repurpose unwanted clothing, furniture, or other household items that are still in good condition to help others.
5. When shopping, be mindful to avoid purchasing products with unnecessary packaging.

Following these steps can help keep our community clean and sustainable. For more tips and resources, visit the Sanitation Department's website. Remember, small changes can have a big impact!

Sincerely,

City of Lester

① to tell residents how to separate trash properly
② to tell residents how to use food scraps to produce compost
③ to tell residents how to save money while shopping
④ to tell residents how to reduce the amount of waste they produce

08 다음 글의 제목으로 적절한 것은?

Asperger syndrome is a relatively common condition, affecting roughly 37 million people worldwide. It is classified as a form of autism, but sufferers do not exhibit the same symptoms shown by those with other forms of autism. Most notably, people with Asperger syndrome do not seem to have any form of cognitive impairment. Instead, they tend to have a decreased level of displayed emotional responses, and they may not be as perceptive as those without the condition in noticing the emotional responses of others. Additionally, they display odd peculiarities in their speech, often engaging in wordy monologues about topics they are knowledgeable about. The condition was misunderstood for a long period of time, and the public carried tremendous negative perceptions about those who had it. But as public awareness has increased, these stigmas have begun to change.

① Recent Increases in the Number of Asperger Patients
② Asperger Syndrome: The Most Common Form of Autism
③ Treatment Strategies for Asperger Syndrome
④ Common Symptoms of Those with Asperger Syndrome

09 주어진 문장이 들어갈 위치로 적절한 것은?

However, these claims expose a fundamental misunderstanding of this constitutional provision.

Over the last decade, the spread of information has become increasingly democratized as more and more people have turned to social media platforms or user-created content. (①) This has in turn led to negative reactions when one of these sites requires fact-checking, or blocks inaccurate or harmful information. (②) Certain users declare that such actions infringe upon their right to free speech guaranteed by the First Amendment of the United States Constitution. (③) The first right protected by the First Amendment is free speech, but this only limits the interference of the government. (④) Companies and other private entities are free to place whatever restrictions they want on the actions or speech of their users and members. Moreover, laws may require that these organizations limit or edit content if there is a risk associated with not doing so.

*First Amendment: (미국 헌법) 수정 제1조

10 다음 글의 흐름상 어색한 문장은?

The disposition effect refers to a change in humans' outlook due to the perceived potential for loss or gain. This was first identified in a 1985 paper written by Hersh Shefrin and Meir Statman. In the paper, they discuss investing, where they found that people are far more likely to sell stocks that increase in value, and to hold on to stocks that have lost value over time. ① Based on this research, the two researchers concluded that humans have a stronger emotional connection to negative outcomes than they do to perceived gains. ② By holding on to falling stocks, people retain hope that their fortunes may turn around. ③ The main purpose of implementing stock market regulations was to protect investors from the risks of the disposition effect. ④ Along with this, more importantly, they avoid acknowledging or finalizing a situation that would cause regret. As a result, they often end up losing additional money.

01 밑줄 친 부분에 들어갈 말로 적절한 것은?

It is unnecessary to _____ the existing system, seeing that it works well as it is and the people are accustomed to the system.

① comprehend
② establish
③ conceal
④ reform

02 밑줄 친 부분에 들어갈 말로 적절한 것은?

Were the policy implemented without proper consideration of economic factors, it _____ numerous problems.

① created
② will create
③ would create
④ would have created

03 밑줄 친 부분 중 어법상 옳지 않은 것은?

Competitive skating today is marked by a higher level of physical ability, ① compared to the figure skating of the twentieth century. While the jumps have become complex, the circular patterns, ② which gave "figure skating" its name, are seen less frequently. This means that skaters who performed with grace in the past can no longer compete in events where athletic jumps ③ performed by young and powerful skaters. Points for elegance are lower than ④ those for fantastic jumps.

04 밑줄 친 부분에 들어갈 말로 적절한 것은?

A: We had to stop the presentation midway today.
B: Your team spent weeks preparing everything. Why weren't you able to finish?
A: Because we kept getting interrupted by the audience asking for more details.
B: _____
A: You're right. I think we scheduled the presentation too tightly.
B: And it would be better to have the Q&A session after finishing the presentation.

① Setting priorities can save us time.
② Add more visuals to your presentation.
③ You should have planned time for questions.
④ We typically get fewer attendees than we hope for.

※ 다음 글을 읽고 물음에 답하시오. [05~06]

To	Consumer Protection Office
From	Ron Banks
Date	April 24
Subject	Hidden Online Fees

To whom it may concern,

I hope that you are well. I'm writing today about a problem I have encountered when shopping online, specifically hidden fees that are being charged when making purchases.

Like most people, I enjoy the convenience and selection of shopping online. However, many online retailers are now tacking on hidden fees for making purchases. Prices of items initially seem low, but at payment, the price is inflated by processing fees, unincluded basic options, or high shipping costs. So, I don't know the true cost until the last minute. This feels like false advertising.

I would like your agency to investigate this problematic practice and determine what can be done. I hope you can make advertised online prices clearer.

Respectfully,

Ron Banks

05 윗글의 목적으로 적절한 것은?

① To request help finding a product in an online store
② To complain about the selection of items offered online
③ To ask that a common tactic of online stores be stopped
④ To inquire about the fees charged by online retailers

06 밑줄 친 problematic의 의미와 가장 가까운 것은?

① troublesome
② difficult
③ messy
④ famous

07 Ministry of Digital Advancement에 관한 다음 글의 내용과 일치하는 것은?

Introduction of the Ministry of Digital Advancement (MDA)

The MDA is at the forefront of the country's push to modernize public services. The MDA focuses on developing and implementing digital versions of many government services, including permit applications, identification cards and passports, and tax payments. The MDA also offers online literacy programs to help citizens uncomfortable with technology adapt to the use of the new system. We see the MDA's actions as a step toward both improving government engagement with citizens and a mechanism for increased transparency. The MDA envisions a future in which nearly all government services will be available to citizens using their computer or other Internet-connected device.

① It does not provide passport-related services.
② It supports programs to teach people to use its new system.
③ It wants people to engage with each other online more.
④ Its plan is to distribute Internet-connected devices to all citizens.

08 다음 글의 제목으로 적절한 것은?

It's quite common for moms and dads to look over and correct their kids' homework during the early years of their education. Sometimes, this continues on into high school and even to college. If this is your habit, you as a parent are not contributing to your child's education and self-esteem. The message conveyed through such behavior is doubt regarding your child's abilities. While answering a few questions children may have is perfectly fine, going through their reports and papers meticulously is unnecessary. Reviewing and then fixing errors only reinforces the notion that you believe they are not skilled enough to do the work on their own. Instead, they should be left to find their own way with gentle guidance, not with excessive interference. The mistakes they are allowed to make will ultimately benefit them.

① The Benefits of Parental Oversight
② Ways to Motivate Lazy Students
③ Proper Role for Parents in Children's Schoolwork
④ The Connection between Education and Self-Esteem

09 다음 글의 주제로 적절한 것은?

With its brutal winters and short summers, Siberia has long been known as one of the coldest places on Earth. However, it began to experience unusually high temperatures in the first half of 2020, even reaching an unprecedented 38 degrees Celsius in June, which led to wildfires and the appearance of insects and animals that never existed in the area previously. Today, climate change continues, and the rise in Siberia's temperature remains a persistent issue. Though scientists have identified large-scale wind patterns as the primary cause for the fastest warming recorded anywhere in the world, another factor was decreased snow cover. This lack of cover reduced ground moisture and exposed the ground to solar radiation, triggering the melting of the area's permafrost.

*permafrost: 영구 동토층 (지층의 온도가 연중 0°C 이하인 땅)

① increased wildfire rates in the northern hemisphere
② extreme changes to the climate of Siberia
③ ways that animal species are affected by global warming
④ benefits of snow cover on temperature regulation

10 밑줄 친 부분에 들어갈 말로 적절한 것은?

Long recognized for their curiosity and superior intelligence, dolphins also seem to have other important abilities that make them special. One of these is the capability _____, which they use for determining where they are and where they are going. Surprisingly, unlike in other animals that are thought to have this capacity, it has been proven in dolphins. In studies, researchers presented the marine mammals with two identical objects, one with a magnetic charge and the other without. In almost all cases, the dolphins approached the magnetized object more quickly, proving that they could detect its charge and were attracted to it. From this, researchers concluded that dolphins could most likely sense Earth's magnetism and use it in their navigation.

① to remember previous journeys
② to recognize identical items
③ to sense magnetic fields
④ to use objects around them as tools

DAY 15 하프모의고사 15회

01 밑줄 친 부분의 의미와 가장 가까운 것은?

Agricultural workers are hesitant to abandon pesticides because doing so would leave their crops <u>vulnerable</u> to insect attacks.

① superior
② similar
③ helpless
④ immune

02 밑줄 친 부분에 들어갈 말로 적절한 것은?

The pilot program, advertised as a breakthrough in online education, turned out to _____ for teachers with limited classroom experience, raising questions about its true intent.

① have been designed
② have designed
③ being designed
④ be designed

03 밑줄 친 부분 중 어법상 옳지 않은 것은?

In 2021, Sotheby's hosted its first "Natively Digital" event, and ① <u>has continued</u> to showcase digital arts in the form of non-fungible tokens (NFTs) since that time. NFTs are digital files based on the same blockchain technology as Bitcoin and Ethereum. ② <u>Being published</u> as an NFT allows these digital art pieces to be owned and traded in a secure, verifiable manner. ③ <u>What</u> Sotheby's would keep ④ <u>boosting</u> the new form of art remains to be seen because blockchain asset could fluctuate anytime.

04 밑줄 친 부분에 들어갈 말로 적절한 것은?

 Mason Parker
Are you going to apply for the new customer service task force?
14:40

Chloe Wright
I'm not sure.
14:41

 Mason Parker
Why not? It's a great opportunity to learn how to deal with customer complaints and common issues effectively.
14:42

Chloe Wright
That's true. I've been wanting to develop those kinds of practical skills.
14:42

 Mason Parker
Then why are you hesitating?
14:43

Chloe Wright
I'm worried that I might be away from my current job for too long.
_____
14:44

 Mason Parker
I think it will last at least a quarter.
14:44

① How many people are allowed to join the task force?
② Where will the task force be working primarily?
③ How long is the task force expected to operate?
④ Are you interested in other training seminars?

※ 다음 글을 읽고 물음에 답하시오. [05~06]

_____(A)_____

As a Hawaiian resident, you need to know what you can do to save the state bird.

Although their numbers have slightly improved, the nene is still not safe from extinction. So, let's all do what we can to protect the native goose that serves as Hawaii's state bird.

The Nene Conservation Team is working on a plan to help the bird's population grow. They will hold an information session for the public next week. Attend and you can learn more about their efforts and what you can do too.

Can you imagine the state without its most iconic native bird?

- **Location**: Diamondhead Outdoor Pavilion
  (event will be held in the Assembly Hall in case of bad weather.)
- **Date**: Wednesday, April 10
- **Time**: 6:30 p.m.

To donate to the group, please visit www.savethenene.com or call (808) 555-6363.

05 (A)에 들어갈 윗글의 제목으로 적절한 것은?

① Join the Hawaiian Bird Watching Network
② Hawaii's Ecosystem Needs Your Attention
③ Hawaii's State Bird is in Danger
④ Volunteer to Save Hawaiian Traditions

06 위 안내문의 내용과 일치하지 않는 것은?

① 하와이의 상징적인 새를 보존하려는 단체가 있다.
② 하와이 주조의 개체 수는 현재 감소하고 있다.
③ 행사는 야외 공간에서 개최될 예정이다.
④ 기부는 웹사이트를 통해 할 수 있다.

07 다음 글의 흐름상 어색한 문장은?

Timing plays an important role in how events are presented to the world, and poor timing can cause important events to be overlooked. One example of this occurred with the early aviation pioneer Harriet Quimby. On April 16, 1912, the American pilot set off from Dover, England, and landed on a beach near Calais, France. ① The 40-kilometer flight may not seem particularly impressive today, but it marked a great feat in aviation at the time since Quimby had become the first female pilot to fly across the English Channel. ② Unfortunately, her accomplishment went largely unnoticed. ③ That's because most of the world was focused on the sinking of the *Titanic*, which had happened the previous day. ④ The *Titanic*'s tragic sinking is still a source of fascination to many people today. In fact, in *The New York Times*, the only mention of Quimby's accomplishment came in a short article on page 15.

08 다음 글의 요지로 적절한 것은?

After working for years in a children's psychiatric clinic, British psychiatrist John Bowlby formulated his theory of attachment in 1958. His attachment theory considered the significance of the relationship between mothers and babies in regard to their cognitive, social, and emotional development. Without this link, Bowlby argued, young children would not receive sufficient care and support and thus would be more likely to develop attachment issues and disorders. Subsequent studies in the 1960s were conducted to understand how healthy attachments form. Interestingly, researchers found that babies established stronger relationships not with those who satisfied their physical needs—those who fed them or spent the most time with them—but with those who were attuned to their emotional state. This sensitive responsiveness is the key to forming deep attachments, and it can be fostered through play and appropriate and timely communication.

① Attachment theory explains the importance and formation of relationships.
② Children will be poorly adjusted without sufficient care.
③ Emotional states are more important to well-being than physical states.
④ Fundamental attachment is determined in childhood and does not change.

09 주어진 글 다음에 이어질 글의 순서로 적절한 것은?

Can people who are blind be trained to use bat-like echolocation to move through their environment? According to neurobiologist Lutz Wiegrebe, it is possible.

(A) Depending on the sound that is returned, they can perceive how objects are arranged and even detect their composition. Knowing what is near them and exactly where it is located allows them to move around unaided much more easily.

(B) Wiegrebe has found a small number of blind people who have developed a rudimentary form of echolocation that helps them navigate their surroundings with ease. By making clicking sounds with their mouths and then listening for the echo, they form a mental image of the objects around them.

(C) In fact, some blind people have become so adept at this skill that they can even ride a bicycle. Such impressive mastery of echolocation is perhaps the most compelling evidence that Wiegrebe's research will continue to open new possibilities for the visually impaired.

*echolocation: 음파 탐지, 반향 위치 결정법

① (A) – (B) – (C)
② (A) – (C) – (B)
③ (B) – (A) – (C)
④ (B) – (C) – (A)

10 밑줄 친 부분에 들어갈 말로 적절한 것은?

In Thailand, people are often called by a nickname rather than their legal name. In fact, the practice is so prevalent that people can be friends for years without knowing each other's official names. While many outsiders believe that these terms of endearment are simply easier versions of the person's longer name, there is actually another reason for them. According to a traditional Thai belief, evil spirits lurk around children and try to interfere with their lives. However, it is thought that their malicious attempts can be prevented _____
_____. Therefore, Thai parents assign their children nicknames at birth and use these to refer to them instead of their actual names. Interestingly, these often take the form of names that may seem insulting, like "fatty" or "frog," as these are thought to be less likely to cause jealousy in the spirits than nicer nicknames.

① if they do not know the child's actual name
② if special charms are worn to repel evil spirits
③ if spiritual protection ceremonies are regularly performed
④ if parents maintain secrecy about their child's existence

01 밑줄 친 부분에 들어갈 말로 적절한 것은?

At the start of the year, people plan to _____ self-limiting habits in order to remove barriers to their progress.

① adopt
② strengthen
③ break
④ revive

02 밑줄 친 부분에 들어갈 말로 적절한 것은?

As long as students _____ their assignments on time, they will receive full credit, which will be reflected in their final grades.

① submit
② will submit
③ were submitting
④ will have submitted

03 밑줄 친 부분 중 어법상 옳지 않은 것은?

The mechanical double clocks in competitive chess ① keep track of time as one player or ② the other makes a move. In international tournaments, a player is permitted forty moves in two hours. If the player does not make the number of moves ③ require during the game, he loses the game—except when the opponent lacks ④ enough pieces to win the match.

04 밑줄 친 부분에 들어갈 말로 적절한 것은?

A: Don't forget to bring an umbrella for our trip today.
B: The forecast said the sky would be clear.
A: I know, but it's the rainy season and the weather on the island is unpredictable.
B: Well, in that case, should I bring a waterproof jacket too?
A: That's not a bad idea. _____
B: You're right. I wouldn't want to get soaked.

① Let's go indoors if it starts raining.
② You can never be too careful.
③ The rainy season is almost over anyway.
④ I've checked multiple weather sources.

※ 다음 글을 읽고 물음에 답하시오. [05~06]

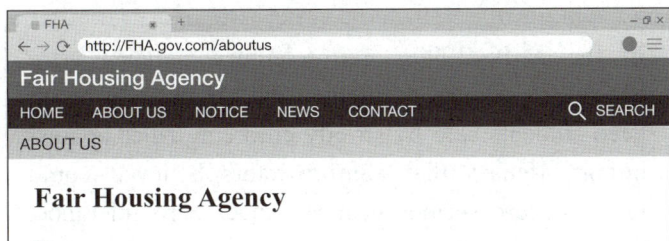

Fair Housing Agency

Purpose

Our agency was founded to advance equal access to housing regardless of race, social class, and other demographic characteristics. Our programs are meant to make sure that safe, affordable housing is available to everyone in the country and free from unlawful barriers.

Activities

We investigate complaints received from the public to ensure fair housing practices are upheld and hold violators accountable for their actions. In addition, we provide resources and training to help individuals understand their rights and give housing providers the tools necessary to foster <u>diverse</u> communities. We also partner with outside organizations to help those facing housing discrimination.

Guiding Principles
- Equity & Accessibility: We promote equal opportunity and the removal of systemic barriers to housing.
- Accountability & Transparency: We champion ethical standards and maintain openness in all our actions.

05 윗글에서 Fair Housing Agency에 관한 내용과 일치하는 것은?

① It was founded to build more affordable housing units.
② It has no power to punish violators of housing laws.
③ It offers educational tools to people supplying housing.
④ It pays outside organizations to provide housing for individuals.

06 밑줄 친 diverse의 의미와 가장 가까운 것은?

① busy
② varied
③ local
④ strong

07 다음 글의 흐름상 어색한 문장은?

Some personality traits may predict the likelihood of success in life. Studies led by psychologists point to diligence as one such trait. It reflects a tendency to work hard, set goals, take responsibility, obey rules, and be organized. People who have this trait regulate themselves and control their impulses. ① For instance, while most people choose enjoyment at the moment, industrious individuals will go home and study for a big exam or make sure they're in bed early so they can be at work on time. ② They are also the ones who avoid driving over the speed limit even when there are no other cars around. ③ Studies show that diligence is directly linked to decreased creativity since rule-following limits innovative thinking. ④ The trait is especially significant in critical areas such as relationships, financial security, and health. They are aware of the consequences of certain actions and are thus apt to be more careful than others.

08 다음 글의 내용과 일치하지 않는 것은?

To: Reservations@TimesSquareHosp.com
From: VicHadid@SimpsportCity.com
Date: July 5
Subject: Banquet Facilities

Dear Sir or Madam,

I would like to get more information about possibly reserving the facilities at your hotel.

We will be hosting an event for a delegation visiting from China on September 10. We need to book a facility that can provide a space where we can have a show by a local theater troupe. Before the performance, we need to have a catered cocktail party. After, we will have a sit-down dinner. We expect approximately 100 guests at the event, but would like preparations for at least 20 additional people to be safe.

Could you please let me know if your hotel can accommodate our needs? If so, please send me a sample menu and the price for such an event.

I hope to hear from you soon.

Kind regards,
Vic Hadid
Simpsport City Event Planner

① Visitors from another country will attend the event.
② An area for a performance is necessary.
③ Food needs to be prepared for 100 people.
④ A menu and cost estimate should be provided.

09 다음 글의 주제로 적절한 것은?

In the early 1990s, zero-tolerance policies were enacted in schools throughout the US in an effort to keep students safe by strictly enforcing rules against minor offenses that administrators believed could lead to more serious crimes. Under zero tolerance, those in violation of school rules were automatically punished, no matter the circumstances or rationale behind the violation. In theory, the threat of a strict penalty for even minor offenses would deter students from misbehaving. In practice, however, the results were less successful. Increased suspension rates didn't improve school discipline but rather caused students to fall behind in their studies, which led to discouragement and eventually more poor conduct. To make matters worse, there were even cases where victims and attackers were punished equally. For example, a student defending him- or herself against a bully would receive the same penalty as the initiator because they were both technically involved in a fight.

① Origins of zero-tolerance policies in American education
② Negative impacts of strict disciplinary approaches in education
③ The historical development of school punishment systems
④ Educational reforms aimed at reducing student misconduct

10 주어진 글 다음에 이어질 글의 순서로 적절한 것은?

The political decision to commit injustice for the sake of the citizenry is a philosophical dilemma. In Ursula Le Guin's short story which takes place in the fictional city of Omelas, this choice is aptly described.

(A) Every day in the real world, immigrants and refugees often appear at the borders of countries and are subjected to detention, deprivation, and trauma. Everyone in the country sees it but, just like in Le Guin's tale, they accept the norms they find immoral.

(B) One resident after another visits the child and feels sickened by the conditions he lives in, but no one ever tries to free him. They know that the happiness of Omelas will vanish if anyone dares to bring the child out.

(C) It is the name of a peaceful place that radiates happiness, but the contentment is dependent upon the suffering of one child. Everyone knows that he is kept in a filthy basement.

① (A) − (C) − (B)
② (B) − (A) − (C)
③ (C) − (A) − (B)
④ (C) − (B) − (A)

DAY 17 하프모의고사 17회

01 밑줄 친 부분에 들어갈 말로 적절한 것은?

The man decided to pursue a career as a lawyer, hoping to effectively _____ his combative nature by arguing court cases.

① forgive
② doubt
③ overcome
④ utilize

02 밑줄 친 부분 중 어법상 옳지 않은 것은?

Nothing made me ① more uneasy than the sense that I had no control over my life. Over the years, I found my family and supervisors taking over every significant decision in my life. I realized it was time to stop ② feeling so helpless. I told ③ to them that I wanted my choices to be respected, and after they started to allow me ④ to make my own decisions, I began feeling that I was capable of taking responsibility for myself.

03 밑줄 친 부분이 어법상 옳은 것은?

① I have to leave for work an hour early lest I ran into rush-hour traffic.
② She turned down her music because she heard someone knocked on the door.
③ By far the most influential scientist of all time was Sir Isaac Newton.
④ One fifth of our clients has been using our services for at least 10 years.

04 밑줄 친 부분에 들어갈 말로 적절한 것은?

Elizabeth Clark: You must be enjoying working the day shift now. 11:15

Logan Phillips: Not really. I'm thinking of switching back to the late shift. 11:16

Elizabeth Clark: I didn't expect that. What seems to be the problem? 11:16

Logan Phillips: _____ 11:17

Elizabeth Clark: Oh, I see. It must be difficult for you to get up so early. 11:18

Logan Phillips: Yes. And I still go to sleep late, so I'm running late every morning. 11:18

① I try to sleep eight hours every night.
② There isn't a lot to do in the morning.
③ The night shift pays better than the day shift.
④ Well, I'm more of a night person.

※ 다음 글을 읽고 물음에 답하시오. [05~06]

To	Subscribers@OrangeSecurity.com
From	Support@OrangeSecurity.com
Date	January 18
Subject	Security Notice

Dear Orange Security Subscribers,

The security of your data is now more important than ever. With a major computer virus spreading, Orange Computer Security wants to help. Here are four steps you can take to stay protected:

1. Ensure your operating system, antivirus software, and applications are up-to-date.
2. Do not open suspicious emails, attachments, or links from unknown sources.
3. Use firewalls, strong antivirus software, and two-factor authentication on your accounts to add an extra layer of security to your devices and information. Please note that these advanced security services may require additional fees.
4. Back up your important files in the cloud or on a separate external drive to prevent data loss in case you are affected by a virus.

Remaining proactive is the key to keeping your devices and information safe. To learn more about security threats and ways to protect yourself, visit the Safety & Security tab on our website.

Respectfully,

Orange Computer Security

05 윗글의 목적으로 적절한 것은?

① to alert subscribers about the threat of a computer virus
② to notify subscribers about what they can do to protect their data
③ to advise subscribers on how to update their computer's software
④ to instruct subscribers to use a cloud-based service for backing up information

06 위 이메일의 내용과 일치하지 않는 것은?

① 주요 컴퓨터 바이러스가 확산 중이다.
② 운영 체제를 최신 상태로 유지할 것을 권장한다.
③ 이중 인증 기능은 유료로 제공된다.
④ 데이터를 외장 드라이브로 유출해서는 안 된다.

07 다음 글의 주제로 적절한 것은?

Since it was published in the early 17th century, the inns that the main character in Miguel de Cervantes's *Don Quixote* stops at along his journey have been analyzed in great detail. On the surface, these can be seen for what they are literally, places of rest and refuge for tired travelers. However, if viewed more metaphorically, they can be seen in an entirely different way. The guest houses that Don Quixote and his travel partner Sancho Panza stop in are filled with a variety of characters from different social classes, from servants to nobles. In these, Panza finds comfort and a connection to others. However, Quixote is uncomfortable and would prefer to spend his nights in the wilderness under the stars. And even when he is convinced to lodge at an inn, Quixote remains disconnected from the events that occur there, much as he is with reality and society.

① Don Quixote's friendship with Sancho Panza
② The importance of buildings in Cervantes's works
③ Cervantes's use of symbolism to represent society
④ A comparison of nature and civilization in *Don Quixote*

08 다음 글의 요지로 적절한 것은?

Federal Marshal Service
As the country's oldest law enforcement department, the Federal Marshal Service (FMS) is committed to protecting its citizens. In addition to enforcing federal law, the FMS oversees special initiatives aimed at improving the well-being of those impacted by crime.

Security and Benefit Programs
The FMS manages the Witness Security Program, which provides 24-hour protection for individuals and their families who testify against dangerous criminals. Since its foundation in 1971, over 19,000 witnesses have entered the program's guardianship, and no participant has been harmed.

The FMS also has the authority to seize illegally obtained assets. Once a suspect is found guilty, these assets, including real estate, vehicles, art, and jewelry, are sold at auction, with a portion—about $500 million per year—of the total proceeds used to compensate victims of crimes.

① FMS maintains financial stability through the seizure and sale of assets.
② FMS is specially qualified to recommend changes to federal law.
③ FMS ensures that suspects appear for federal court trials.
④ FMS operates programs to aid crime victims and witnesses.

09 주어진 문장이 들어갈 위치로 적절한 것은?

Over the three-month experiment, the mice in the former group were revealed to have much better long-term memories.

Though intermittent fasting (IF) is being advocated as a means of losing weight and increasing longevity, it may have another, less publicized benefit—improving memory retention. Researchers from King's College London conducted an experiment on three groups of lab mice. (①) While one group was subjected to IF, the two others had normal and calorie restricted (CR) diets. (②) The mice on the CR diet exhibited an improvement too, but the results were not as impressive. (③) Scans of the brains of the IF mice also showed that they had undergone greater neurogenesis—the creation of new neurons, the process of which supports the speed and recovery of cognitive abilities. (④) Based on their results, the researchers hypothesized that IF could be an effective means of improving long-term memory and brain function in humans.

10 밑줄 친 부분에 들어갈 말로 적절한 것은?

In 2011, a study introduced a cognitive bias called the "IKEA effect," named after the Swedish company that produces and sells furniture that sometimes requires assembly by the purchaser. In the study, participants who had folded their own origami figures considered their amateur work to be of equal quality and more _____ than origami made by experts. Researchers concluded that individuals would place excessive worth on a product that they helped to create through their own labor. But this phenomenon only occurred when the labor resulted in success. In other words, origami structures that fell apart did not receive the same perceived boost in worth.

*origami: 종이접기

① skilled
② distinct
③ valuable
④ functional

01 밑줄 친 부분에 들어갈 말로 적절한 것은?

Tasks are repeated hour after hour for days, with little variation or rest, leaving assembly line workers at the factory feeling _____.

① patient
② jealous
③ ashamed
④ bored

02 다음 (A), (B) 중, 어법상 옳은 것끼리 고른 것은?

A recent survey revealed (A) (what / that) most consumers prefer using environmentally friendly products to (B) (choose / choosing) cheaper alternatives with higher environmental costs.

(A)	(B)
① what	choose
② what	choosing
③ that	choose
④ that	choosing

03 밑줄 친 부분 중 어법상 옳지 않은 것은?

The Isle of Man ① is enjoying the benefits of Internet connectedness as it continues to see infrastructure development advance year by year. ② For several years, the number of people using the Internet to obtain official documents has been ③ raising. Government officials are now looking for ways ④ to offer more services online.

04 밑줄 친 부분에 들어갈 말로 적절한 것은?

A: It looks like there's a tear in the suit you just bought.
B: Then I'll have to take it back and exchange it for one in good condition.
A: The store has a really rigid exchange policy.
B: _____
A: They don't allow exchanges for simply changing your mind, and the packaging can't be damaged.
B: I see. I'd better check their policy before going.

① Do I need to present my receipt for the exchange?
② Have you ever exchanged anything at that store?
③ What if the suit was damaged before I purchased it?
④ In what way is their exchange policy strict?

※ 다음 글을 읽고 물음에 답하시오. [05~06]

National Security Service

The National Security Service (NSS) is dedicated to ensuring secure and effective foreign diplomacy by protecting the nation's assets worldwide. To fulfill this mission, the NSS is one of the largest security agencies in the government, with over 100 locations across the country.

Protecting People and Property

NSS agents provide 24/7 protection for the minister during their travels and official visits. They also collaborate with personal protection teams to safeguard visiting important foreign officials, including heads of state, members of royal families, and foreign ministers.

Present at over 100 government buildings throughout the country, NSS personnel are responsible for maintaining security. Selected locations <u>feature</u> trained police dogs that patrol government buildings and other sites of national importance. On the digital front, NSS engineers design and manage advanced security systems that protect these facilities from unauthorized access and cyberattacks.

05 윗글의 요지로 적절한 것은?

① NSS emphasizes a technology-based approach to security.
② NSS is committed to deploying police dogs.
③ NSS promotes diplomacy by providing comprehensive security.
④ NSS strives to become the most widespread security organization in the government sector.

06 밑줄 친 feature의 의미와 가장 가까운 것은?

① exclude
② leave
③ pick
④ contain

07 National Institute of Origin에 관한 다음 글의 내용과 일치하지 않는 것은?

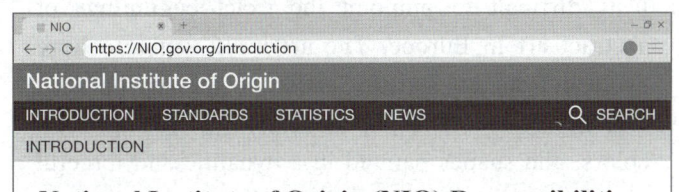

National Institute of Origin (NIO) Responsibilities

The NIO is a French regulatory body charged with ensuring wine, dairy products, and other agricultural goods are produced in specific regions using traditional methods. Only products that receive NIO approval can use regional names and designations of authenticity. This protects local farmers and artisans, as well as product reputations, from imitations produced elsewhere. It also protects consumers, as soil in other regions or different production methods can negatively affect the flavors of the finished products they buy. The institute files notices with appropriate authorities and may offer support for legal enforcement of regulations when products are marketed using region-specific names without certification.

① 전통적인 생산 방법이 사용될 것을 보장한다.
② 제품에 지역 이름이 쓰일 수 있는지를 결정한다.
③ 소비자들로부터 지역 농부와 장인들을 보호한다.
④ 관련 규정의 집행에 관여할 수 있다.

08 다음 글의 주제로 적절한 것은?

It is difficult to pinpoint the exact beginnings of abstract art in Europe. The art itself seems to have evolved from an artistic landscape that encouraged free expression. Thus, spectators began seeing lines, colors, and shapes painted in a dynamic and forceful manner rather than the familiar well-arranged pictorial subject, attributes that abstract art became well known for. It is also recognized for the great variety of styles utilized, which is the reason no single style can be associated with the movement. Notably, regardless of style, the early artworks had the characteristics of what we now call abstract expressionism—art that does not represent anything that is real.

① Dynamic expression through lines and colors in European landscapes
② Public reception of abstract art exhibitions across European museums
③ The historical context and features of abstract art
④ Exhibition strategies for abstract art in European galleries

09 주어진 글 다음에 이어질 글의 순서로 적절한 것은?

There was once a busy couple who worked hard so that they could prepare for their son's future. Their only child was a curious boy who kept asking his parents about everything in life.

(A) He hardly talked to them, however, and it was then that the parents regretted not giving their son time when he wanted to talk.

(B) He grew indifferent to his parents, preferring to study or relax alone, or spend time with his friends. But his parents were aging, and they longed to know more about what their son was doing and what his thoughts were.

(C) Despite his flourishing curiosity, his mother and father were so tired in the evenings and weekends that they just wanted to rest or do some activity with minimal conversation. As he got older, he began seeking his own identity.

① (B) – (A) – (C)
② (B) – (C) – (A)
③ (C) – (A) – (B)
④ (C) – (B) – (A)

10 밑줄 친 부분에 들어갈 말로 적절한 것은?

Studies show that people's cognitive decline after turning 20 is greater than the growth that occurs prior to that point. Intellectual growth during a person's developmental years is often swifter, more positive, and more dramatic than growth that takes place during adulthood. Other studies confirm that tasks that require the recall of information become more complex in adulthood, particularly when people's names and contextual details are involved. In addition, the slowing down of information processing due to deteriorating vision and hearing is evident in later adulthood. While such intense handicaps may seem overwhelming, people develop other methods of approaching problems and numerous coping mechanisms throughout adulthood to _____.

① accelerate cognitive development
② make up for these deficits
③ restore previous physical capacities
④ complicate memory recall processing

DAY 19 하프모의고사 19회

01 밑줄 친 부분에 들어갈 말로 적절한 것은?

If someone _____ an action or event, it could be impressive in style, often to the point of seeming pretentious.

① observes
② approves
③ resolves
④ exaggerates

02 밑줄 친 부분에 들어갈 말로 적절한 것은?

The students took detailed notes _____ to the professor's lecture on ancient history.

① listen
② listened
③ while listening
④ with listened

03 밑줄 친 부분 중 어법상 옳지 않은 것은?

Responsibility for a crime usually requires not only a guilty mind, ① but also a guilty act. ② To be considered a guilty act, the act needs to take place voluntarily. Unintentional actions would not qualify as guilty acts. Situations ③ in which the actor is unaware of his behavior are also deemed involuntary. On the other hand, the voluntary aspect of a guilty act includes deliberate inaction. Crimes or injuries that ④ are resulted from intentional inaction can constitute guilty conduct.

04 밑줄 친 부분에 들어갈 말로 적절한 것은?

Harper White
I think it's time to buy printer paper and toner.
10:18

Morgan Russell
Yes, I agree. How many should we order?
10:19

Harper White
2 toners and 5 packs of printer paper would be fine. We have to order them this week.
10:19

Morgan Russell
I see. I will place an order this afternoon. _____
10:20

Harper White
I noticed that we're running out of paper cups. Maybe we should order those too.
10:21

Morgan Russell
We won't be buying paper cups anymore because they create a lot of waste.
10:22

① Could you check when our last order was placed?
② Do we need to order any additional supplies?
③ Should we order from the supplier we used before?
④ Do you know how much of our budget is left?

※ 다음 글을 읽고 물음에 답하시오. [05~06]

To	Highway Safety Bureau
From	Sadie Bates
Date	November 12
Subject	Road conditions

Dear Sir or Madam,

Today, I am writing to you about a growing problem that I have noticed on public highways over the last year. I am referring to the increase in the number and size of potholes, which have become a driving hazard.

Since I work in sales, I must often commute to meet clients in other cities using the highway system. Recently, these trips have been affected by the condition of the roadways. As drivers have to slow down to avoid the potholes, traffic jams form. In addition, I have seen many cars sustain damage or get into accidents after hitting a broken part of the road.

The conditions of the roadways are dangerous and _____. I implore you to repair the roadways so that everyone can travel safely once again.

Respectfully,

Sadie Bates

05 윗글의 목적으로 적절한 것은?

① 도로 위 움푹 패인 곳의 잦은 발생 원인을 문의하려고
② 출퇴근 시간에 혼잡한 고속도로 상황을 공유하려고
③ 안전하지 않은 공공 시설물에 대한 복구를 요청하려고
④ 고속도로에 교통량이 증가한 이유를 설명하려고

06 윗글의 밑줄 친 부분에 들어갈 말로 적절한 것은?

① unacceptable
② narrow
③ sensitive
④ empty

07 Future City Engineering Competition에 관한 다음 글의 내용과 일치하는 것은?

Future City Engineering Competition (FCEC)

Team Registration Deadline: August 30

- **Registration Fee**: $25.00 (per team)
- **Competition Date**: 11:00 a.m., November 15

Teams must consist of at least three students of middle school age. There is no maximum limit on team size.

Final projects, which include an essay, a model of the future city, and a presentation, will be judged by a panel of engineers.

Please note: Registration must be completed by a team coach on the competition portal. Spots are limited, so we recommend registering as soon as possible.

① Each student must pay $25 to register.
② Teams can have no more than three members.
③ The competition will be evaluated by engineering experts.
④ A representative student must complete the registration online.

08 주어진 글 다음에 이어질 글의 순서로 적절한 것은?

Although the Vietnamese soup pho is a laborious dish to prepare, it is so pleasing that you may not mind the burden of making it.

(A) Once all the items are prepared, put the soup together. The meat should be thinly sliced and arranged in bowls with the vegetables and noodles. Pour the hot stock over it, and garnish the dish with bean sprouts, lime wedges, and cilantro.

(B) The secret to a great pho is the stock. Start with high-quality beef bones and rinse them repeatedly to reduce the oil. The bones must then be cooked slowly for at least three hours.

(C) When the stock is cooked, it should be strained to remove fat and bits of bone, after which it can be flavored with fish sauce, salt, and sugar. Next, prepare the other ingredients. This includes boiling and cooling the noodles and slightly burning the onions and ginger.

① (A) − (C) − (B)
② (B) − (A) − (C)
③ (B) − (C) − (A)
④ (C) − (A) − (B)

09 주어진 문장이 들어갈 위치로 적절한 것은?

In pursuit of these goals, minimalists dispose of items or habits that do not provide value.

Voluntary simplicity, otherwise more commonly known as minimalism, has been linked to higher rates of happiness. (①) One reason for this is that partakers in a minimalist lifestyle, which is centered on limiting consumption and ownership, tend to take better care of their psychological needs. (②) Instead of focusing on acquiring material objects, they pay more attention to maintaining individual autonomy, overall awareness, and positive emotions. (③) As a result, they also get rid of many sources of stress in their lives, leaving them with excess energy to support their psychological well-being. (④) The immense mental and emotional benefits that come from removing unnecessary items and simplifying one's lifestyle make voluntary simplicity a powerful tool in the search for happiness.

10 밑줄 친 (A), (B)에 들어갈 말로 적절한 것은?

Even if humans were to stop using fossil fuels this very moment, the carbon dioxide already in the atmosphere would remain. This lingering carbon dioxide would cause temperatures to rise for centuries. ___(A)___, scientists are looking for solutions to remove this gas from the atmosphere. Of course, plants and trees do this naturally. Unfortunately, while trees reliably absorb carbon dioxide and convert it to oxygen, they do so too slowly. As a result, a large number of trees would be needed to influence climate change in a meaningful way. Planting more trees requires lots of land, which may be unavailable or better used for growing crop-producing plants. A unique solution already being implemented is the planting of hyper-efficient fake trees. ___(B)___, the leaves of these artificial trees can soak up one thousand times more carbon dioxide compared to real leaves that use photosynthesis. This increased efficiency would help rid the Earth of carbon dioxide emissions and keep more land available for other purposes.

	(A)	(B)
①	Thus	In contrast
②	For example	Recently
③	Consequently	In fact
④	In the same way	However

DAY 20 하프모의고사 20회

01 밑줄 친 (A), (B)에 들어갈 말로 적절한 것은?

Journalists with know-how and experience are ___(A)___ to newspapers because practical skills ___(B)___ in the field enable them to quickly produce compelling stories under tight deadlines.

	(A)	(B)
①	challenging	admired
②	vital	accumulated
③	challenging	combined
④	vital	distorted

02 밑줄 친 부분에 들어갈 말로 적절한 것은?

The damaged vehicles are required _____ before insurance claims can proceed.

① to inspect
② to be inspected
③ inspecting
④ being inspected

03 밑줄 친 부분 중 어법상 옳지 않은 것은?

From unexpected places ① comes the best ideas. That's why the city government is accepting proposals ② to improve the quality of urban life from all citizens. ③ Whoever submits a proposal will present their ideas before a committee that will review them in order to select the best ones, lest too many projects ④ overwhelm the limited funding.

04 밑줄 친 부분에 들어갈 말로 적절한 것은?

A: What is the quickest way to get to the shopping district from here?
B: That would definitely be the subway.
A: Thanks. Isn't there a bus that goes there?
B: Sure. But it will take more than an hour.
A: It takes longer than expected. _____
B: It makes many stops along the way.

① Is this area always so congested with traffic?
② How long would it take by subway?
③ Doesn't it go straight to the area?
④ Has the road construction been completed?

※ 다음 글을 읽고 물음에 답하시오. [05~06]

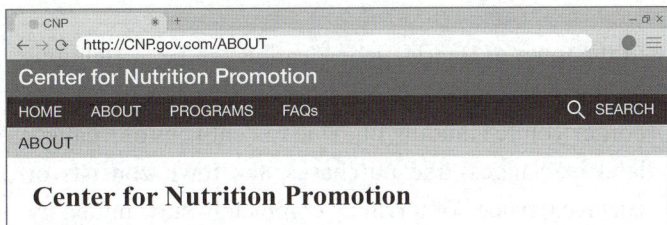

Center for Nutrition Promotion

Our Purpose
We provide science-based guidance and resources to help people make informed nutrition choices. By creating and implementing policies, we promote healthier eating and natural well-being to prevent diseases and conditions often related to diet, such as obesity, hypertension, and diabetes.

What We Do
We create nutrition guidelines that highlight eating a balanced diet rich in natural foods, fruits, and vegetables. This enables people to understand the importance of their dietary choices. In addition, we support policymakers, educators, and health professionals in providing the public with practical, accurate nutrition information.

Our Commitment
- Scientific Integrity: We conduct research experiments and studies to base recommendations on fact-based research.
- Impactful Cooperation: We partner with public health experts and organizations to encourage healthy eating habits.

05 윗글에서 Center for Nutrition Promotion에 관한 내용과 일치하는 것은?

① It provides resources to help people lose weight.
② It offers medical treatment to people with hypertension and diabetes.
③ It encourages people to eat more natural foods.
④ It gives classes to the public about practical nutrition.

06 밑줄 친 partner의 의미와 가장 가까운 것은?

① pair
② assist
③ interact
④ collaborate

07 다음 글의 주제로 적절한 것은?

Readers around the world have read the popular decades-old mystery books by an author named Carolyn Keene. As it turns out, this was a pen name for all the writers who penned the actual Nancy Drew stories, which were produced by the Stratemeyer Syndicate. These writers, whose names never appeared on the book covers, did ghostwriting, a job that involves writing something and then never claiming authorship of the material. Ghostwriting has had a long history, with the practice being used in earlier times by prominent and high-ranking persons who needed others to write for them. In later times, it was kept a secret by publishers, but perceptive readers recognized that many famous individuals did not have the time to write their memoirs. Today, however, ghostwriting is considered a profession, with as much as 25 percent of bestselling books having been written by surrogate writers in the US and Europe.

① history of pen names in literary publishing
② significance of authorship in mystery book series
③ famous celebrities hiring writers for memoirs
④ modern acceptance of ghostwriting as a profession

08 다음 글의 요지로 적절한 것은?

Volcanic eruptions can range from relatively harmless to extremely calamitous. Whether the explosion is a harmless slow flow or a devastating outpouring depends on the makeup of the molten rock, known as magma, which resides beneath the earth's surface. Magma contains dissolved gases that expand in response to shifts in pressure in the surrounding rock. Those gases then seek to escape their confinement and pull the magma up to the surface with them, causing an eruption. The severity of this eruption depends on how sticky, or resistant to flow, the magma is. The stickier the magma is, the more difficulty the gases have escaping and the more intense the eruption is. When the magma is more fluid, the gases meet less resistance and create a gentler flow. Of course, the amount of gas suspended in the magma is another factor. High concentrations of gas bubbles provoke violent eruptions; lower concentrations have less disastrous outcomes.

① Magma collides with volcanic gases to produce eruptions.
② Sticky magma is present in all types of volcanic eruptions.
③ Different kinds of magma have various concentrations of gas.
④ Magma composition determines the intensity of a volcanic eruption.

09 주어진 글 다음에 이어질 글의 순서로 적절한 것은?

In the town of Baarle, your location can be in Belgium or the Netherlands depending on which side of the border you're standing on. Due to centuries of treaties, land exchanges, and purchases, the town consists of enclaves, pieces of territory completely surrounded by the other country.

(A) All the sections of Belgian land in Baarle are enclosed by their Dutch neighbors, while these Belgian exclaves also contain areas of land belonging to the Netherlands.
(B) As a more interesting example, in the past, the Dutch food establishments in this particular town shut down earlier than their Belgian counterparts, so patrons would simply move to the Belgian side of the restaurant at closing time to continue eating.
(C) In other words, there are Dutch exclaves inside these Belgian ones. In fact, citizens of Baarle can enjoy a meal in their Belgian dining room, play in their backyard situated in the Netherlands, and then travel back to Belgium when it's time to sleep in the bedroom.

① (A) – (B) – (C)
② (A) – (C) – (B)
③ (B) – (A) – (C)
④ (B) – (C) – (A)

10 밑줄 친 부분에 들어갈 말로 적절한 것은?

To	patients@VirtuHealthNet.org
From	patientcare@VirtuHealthNet.org
Date	August 7
Subject	Virtual Visits

Dear Valued Patients,

Virtual doctor visits are a convenient way to access quality healthcare from the comfort of your home. If you've booked an online checkup, here are five simple steps to help you get ready for it:

1. Ensure your device is fully charged and has a working camera, microphone, and internet connection. Test these features in advance.
2. Find a quiet space where you won't be interrupted and you are comfortable talking about your medical concerns.
3. Have a list of your current medications, allergies, and any recent symptoms.
4. Write down questions you wish to address with the physician so you don't forget anything important.
5. Log in to the VirtuHealthNet platform five to ten minutes before your scheduled appointment time using the link sent to your email.

By following these steps, you'll be well-prepared for _____. If you need technical assistance or wish to cancel or modify an appointment time, support is available 24/7 at www.VirtuHealthNet.org/support.

Best regards,

VirtuHealthNet Patient Care Team

① finding a quiet space for telehealth interactions
② having a productive consultation with your doctor
③ keeping your digital privacy safe
④ navigating the telehealth platform

DAY 21 하프모의고사 21회

01 밑줄 친 부분에 들어갈 말로 적절한 것은?

Because the student consistently misbehaved, the principal decided to _____ her according to school regulations.

① motivate
② discipline
③ dislike
④ praise

02 밑줄 친 부분에 들어갈 말로 적절한 것은?

The judge let the defendant _____ by a public defender because he could not afford a private attorney.

① represented
② be represented
③ to represent
④ to be represented

03 밑줄 친 부분 중 어법상 옳지 않은 것은?

It is reported that a substantial portion of all bankruptcies in America ① are due to medical bills. The medical costs are clearly burdensome even for ② those with insurance, and such costs can keep people without coverage ③ seeking necessary treatment. The government is working to expand coverage, including programs like Medicaid, which is a health insurance program for low-income individuals and people with disabilities, ④ operated by both the federal and state governments.

04 밑줄 친 부분에 들어갈 말로 적절한 것은?

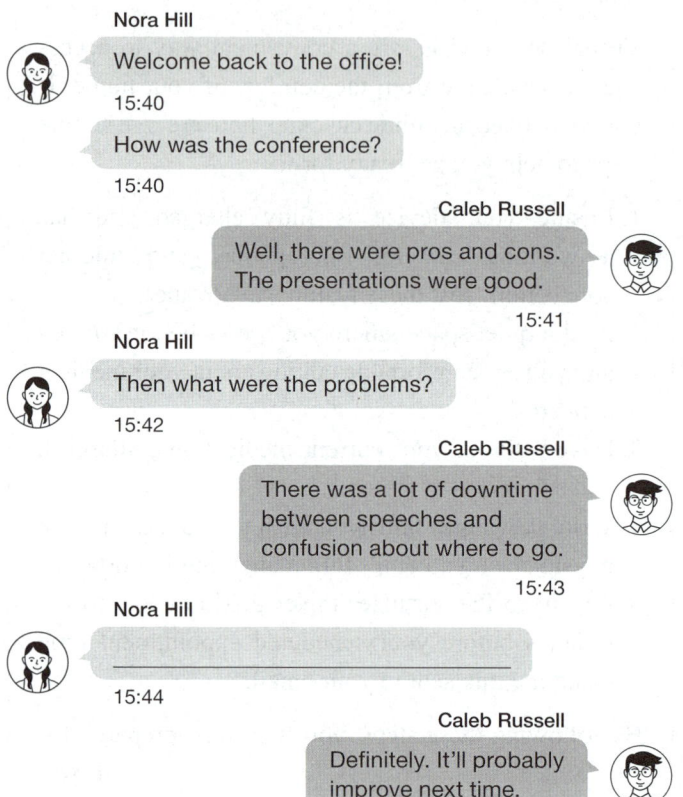

① I'm glad it was a productive experience.
② At least you were constantly stimulated.
③ You probably didn't stay for the whole event.
④ The host organization is probably inexperienced.

※ 다음 글을 읽고 물음에 답하시오. [05~06]

(A)

Everyone has the power to make a difference in the lives of animals in need.

At the shelter, we try our best to make the animals comfortable, but there are many that require more individualized care and special attention. By fostering, you can provide a safe and caring space for these animals before they are adopted.

We invite you to attend an information seminar to learn more about the fostering process. You will also get a chance to meet some of the furry friends you might be able to help.

Come see if fostering is right for you.

- **Location**: Coopersville Animal Shelter
- **Date**: Saturday, April 12
- **Time**: 10:00 a.m. (Animal meet-and-greet starts at 10:30 a.m.)

For more information or to browse photos of animals available for fostering, please visit our website at www.coopersvilleanimalshelter.com/fosterprogram.

05 (A)에 들어갈 윗글의 제목으로 적절한 것은?

① Meet Other Pet Owners
② Respect for Shelter Volunteers
③ Open Your Homes to Pets
④ Gratitude for Animal Adoption

06 위 안내문의 내용과 일치하지 않는 것은?

① 일부 동물들은 위탁 양육 가정에서 특별한 돌봄이 필요하다.
② 세미나에서 참석자들은 일부 보호소 동물들을 볼 수 있다.
③ 세미나는 토요일 아침에 열릴 것이다.
④ 웹사이트에 위탁 양육 중인 동물들의 사진이 있다.

07 다음 글의 주제로 적절한 것은?

Asthma is a chronic condition resulting in more than 400,000 deaths yearly, and there has been a marked increase in diagnoses since the 1960s. The disease has been recognized since the empires of ancient Egypt. Life for sufferers involves constant management of the condition, as there is no cure. Asthma is characterized by inflammation of the airways in the lungs, causing attacks of shortness of breath, wheezing, coughing, and general difficulty breathing. Those afflicted with the condition may be more susceptible to or suffer more severe reactions to infections of the lungs, like pneumonia. The condition ordinarily begins in childhood, and while symptoms may become less severe, with asthma attacks occurring less frequently, they persist for life. Given the increasing prevalence of the condition, it is well worth investing in its research.

*asthma: 천식
*pneumonia: 폐렴

① Ancient treatments for chronic conditions
② Various symptoms of lung diseases today
③ Lung infections complicating existing health problems
④ The need for more asthma research due to rising case numbers

08. 다음 글의 흐름상 어색한 문장은?

Smart lights for improved traffic flow

The Ministry of Public Works plans to replace traditional traffic signals at all major intersections in the city with a smart traffic light control system. ① Unlike standard signals, smart traffic lights use sensors to detect real-time traffic conditions, automatically adjusting traffic light timing based on the volume of traffic they detect. ② The implementation of the new system is expected to reduce unnecessary wait times during off-peak hours by as much as 25 percent. ③ It is also expected to improve response times for emergency vehicles, as the system can identify them and activate green lights to prioritize their movement through intersections. ④ Unfortunately, citizens' concerns about surveillance technology have resulted in the indefinite postponement of the smart traffic light system. The installation will begin in March and conclude in September.

09. 주어진 글 다음에 이어질 글의 순서로 적절한 것은?

Prisons in America are often said to have a "revolving door," as exiting the system often leads to re-entry for ex-prisoners. New research indicates that this may be directly related to punishments imposed during release.

(A) It was found that, on average, people who were sent to prison had a 20 percent higher chance of returning later than those who had only been sentenced to probation. These findings reinforce countless other studies in the field.

(B) In a 2017 study from the University of Michigan, the post-release progress of individuals in the Michigan state corrections system was tracked.

(C) These studies seem to point to the conditional release system as the main cause of these alarming statistics. Former prisoners were much more likely to be sent back to prison for violating one of the many restrictions placed on conditionally released individuals, despite the fact that such violations were not actually crimes.

*probation: 집행 유예

① (A) – (B) – (C)
② (B) – (A) – (C)
③ (B) – (C) – (A)
④ (C) – (A) – (B)

10 밑줄 친 부분에 들어갈 말로 적절한 것은?

The normalcy bias is an inescapable aspect of human nature, greatly affecting the public's reaction to everything from natural disasters to financial market collapses. This cognitive bias causes people to disregard warnings of impending threats. As a result, they often fail to act, believing the disaster won't happen or won't result in negative consequences for them. Studies have indicated that 70 percent of people display this characteristic when faced with serious threats. Some researchers believe that our inaction is a result of our being inherently _____ and considering any vagueness we detect in the warnings or threats as a sign that they won't be as serious as thought.

① realistic
② romantic
③ energetic
④ optimistic

DAY 22 하프모의고사 22회

01 밑줄 친 부분에 들어갈 말로 적절한 것은?

Some victims had such _____ injuries that they required more urgent transport to the hospital than others.

① accidental
② intentional
③ severe
④ external

02 밑줄 친 부분에 들어갈 말로 적절한 것은?

Isabella's friend asked _____ a mistake during the team project.

① when would I admit to make
② when would I admit making
③ when I would admit to make
④ when I would admit making

03 밑줄 친 부분 중 어법상 옳지 않은 것은?

Solar geoengineering is ① different from other methods of lowering atmospheric temperatures in ② a number of ways. It may have negative repercussions caused by the use of technologies that ③ are untested. Reducing temperatures can be done by ④ emit sulfur into the upper atmosphere or altering cloud cover over the ocean, both of which carry risks.

04 밑줄 친 부분에 들어갈 말로 적절한 것은?

A: I just got word from Mr. Bell that he's not going to make it on time.
B: Oh, no! Everyone's expecting him to give the first talk.
A: I know, so I asked the other speaker to take his slot.
B: That's probably the best option under the circumstances. But what about Mr. Bell?
A: He'll have to take the time slot vacated by the other speaker.
B: Well, that's a relief. _____

① Mr. Bell has never been late before.
② We should push back the first talk time.
③ The audience will complain about the change.
④ Late participation is better than no participation.

※ 다음 글을 읽고 물음에 답하시오. [05~06]

To	Federal Communications Board
From	Richard Collins
Date	April 10
Subject	Television Content

Dear FCB Representatives,

As a concerned viewer and media consumer, I feel compelled to address the increasing amount of inappropriate content in television shows and movies, specifically how much violence is being shown.

I appreciate the variety of programs aired by the networks. However, the rising levels of graphic violence being depicted are troubling, especially given their impact on young people. Repeated exposure to violent and distressing scenes can desensitize and negatively influence young minds.

I ask that the FCB review the content and issue stronger guidelines to take care of the problem and ensure content aligns with the audience's expectations and family values.

I thank you for your time and hope steps are taken to promote responsible media content.

Respectfully,
Richard Collins

05 윗글의 목적으로 적절한 것은?

① 다양한 프로그램을 방송하는 방송사에 감사를 표현하려고
② 개별 콘텐츠에 대한 심의를 강화할 것을 부탁하려고
③ 최근 방영된 TV 프로그램의 아쉬운 점을 전달하려고
④ 가족적 가치를 반영하는 새로운 콘텐츠를 제안하려고

06 밑줄 친 aligns with의 의미와 가장 가까운 것은?

① adapts to
② conforms to
③ interferes with
④ copes with

07 다음 글의 내용과 일치하지 않는 것은?

Tickets for the Yung Tower Observation Deck can be purchased in the first-floor lobby of the visitor center located at the base of Mount Slev. Admission is $15 for adults and $10 for senior citizens and children 13 years old and younger. Please note that tickets are valid only on the day of purchase from the time of purchase until the observation deck closes for the day.

Visitors must take the Mount Slev Cable Car from the visitor center up to the Yung Tower entrance, where there are elevators to the Observation Deck. During peak hours, visitors can expect to wait in line for the cable car, which has a capacity of approximately 40 people.

- If you have a reservation for Flame, the fine-dining restaurant at the highest point of the tower, please confirm your reservation at the visitor center before taking the cable car.

Please call 1 (800) 926-6543 for more information.

① The cost of admission is lower for senior citizens and children.
② Tickets for the observation deck can be purchased days in advance.
③ About 40 people can be transported from the visitor center to the tower at a time.
④ Visitors must take a cable car to get to Flame.

08 주어진 글 다음에 이어질 글의 순서로 적절한 것은?

Deep-sea mining is the extraction of valuable metals and minerals by cutting away wide areas of ocean floor with robotic equipment. While it provides a source of metals used in electronics, it is now at issue because of its projected environmental impacts.

(A) Once the foundations needed for survival are damaged, deep-sea organisms will die off. The same can be said of ocean floor corals, where many creatures live.

(B) One is the destruction of landforms through the use of techniques similar to surface mining for coal. The process involves the pressing of the sea floor, which releases masses of sediment that make the water dirty and toxic. Another disruption is the hindering of natural water flows.

(C) These two ways will alter the basic geological elements necessary for life in the deepest parts of the ocean. Resources that support biodiversity will be destroyed, and the natural transport of nutrients will be halted.

① (A) – (B) – (C)
② (B) – (A) – (C)
③ (B) – (C) – (A)
④ (C) – (A) – (B)

09 주어진 문장이 들어갈 위치로 적절한 것은?

The idea that general people could belong to a superior social class stimulated luxury goods consumption.

People are natural consumers, but before the 1900s, they mostly bought the necessities of life, such as food, clothing, and shelter. (①) Overconsumption became a lifestyle when industrialization made it possible for everyday people to purchase goods freely. (②) It was especially evident after the end of World War II, a period when marketers promoted greater spending by making it seem necessary for ordinary people to climb socially. (③) Families thought they could attain this status if they owned items that were considered luxurious back then—cars, cigarettes, and electric iceboxes. (④) It became crucial to have these possessions in order to meet the standard.

10 밑줄 친 부분에 들어갈 말로 적절한 것은?

Just decades ago, people who got tattoos were part of a cultural subgroup and had to make a special effort to find a tattoo shop. Today, pigmenting the skin is so popular that parlors can be easily found in downtown areas. About 30 percent of people in the US and in Britain have had markings etched onto their skin. Now that it is more widely accepted, more careful thought and planning is put into getting a tattoo. People who got one while in their early 20s now realize they were too young and the motif on their skin no longer suits them. This has increased the demand for skin clinics that offer laser tattoo removal. Since it can be costly and painful, professional tattoo artists encourage clients to _____ just in case they may come to dislike their body art in the future.

① consider tattoo design trends that are currently popular
② mull over the desired design before getting tattooed
③ be aware of the physical side effects of tattoos
④ choose tattoo artists with proper medical certification

Self Check List

이번 테스트는 어땠나요?
다음 체크리스트로 자신의 테스트 진행 내용을 점검해 볼까요?

01 나는 10분 동안 완전히 테스트에 집중하였다.
 ☐ YES   ☐ NO

02 나는 주어진 10분 동안 10문제를 모두 풀었다.
 ☐ YES   ☐ NO

03 유난히 어렵게 느껴지는 지문이 있었다.
 ☐ YES   ☐ NO

04 유난히 어렵게 느껴지는 문제가 있었다.
 ☐ YES   ☐ NO

05 모르는 어휘가 있었다.
 ☐ YES   ☐ NO

06 개선해야 할 점과 이를 위한 구체적인 학습 계획

_____
_____

정답·해석·해설 p. 115

하프모의고사 22회
출제예상 핵심 어휘리스트
바로 다운받기 (gosi.Hackers.com)

QR 코드를 이용해 핵심 어휘리스트를 다운받아, 언제 어디서든 공무원 출제예상 어휘를 암기하세요!

DAY 23 하프모의고사 23회

01 밑줄 친 부분에 들어갈 말로 적절한 것은?

The newly opened restaurant is receiving negative reviews from customers, as many _____ that the staff are unprofessional and make frequent mistakes during service.

① question
② complain
③ promise
④ reject

02 밑줄 친 부분에 들어갈 말로 적절한 것은?

Standing at the edge of the flooded road as rain continued to pour heavily, the driver knew it was no use attempting to cross the dangerous waters or _____ for the storm to subside.

① wait
② waited
③ waiting
④ had waited

03 밑줄 친 부분 중 어법상 옳지 않은 것은?

When applying for jobs, there are several things that can be done ① to enable one to stand out. First, tailor your résumé to the industry. For instance, in creative fields, it is advisable ② for applicants to take a more artistic approach, such as formatting their résumés in a more flexible manner. In addition, include key words from the job listings so that it can help the hiring manager ③ finding your résumé ④ when they search through job sites.

04 밑줄 친 부분에 들어갈 말로 적절한 것은?

 Riley Scott
How's the preparation for the annual performance review coming along?
11:25

Ethan Davis
All the data and reports are ready. I'm planning to ask you to review them this afternoon.
11:26

 Riley Scott
Then I'll give you feedback tomorrow morning.
11:27

Ethan Davis
Also, I've reserved meeting room A for the annual performance review on Friday.
11:28

 Riley Scott
Good. What time is the meeting?
11:28

Ethan Davis
It's 2 p.m. _____
_____
11:29

 Riley Scott
Of course. It's a very important meeting, so make sure to take enough time to prepare.
11:30

① What is the time limit for the presentation?
② Can I do a practice run for the meeting that morning?
③ How long does the meeting usually last?
④ Should I book an earlier reservation time?

※ 다음 글을 읽고 물음에 답하시오. [05~06]

Bank Failures

Guaranteeing the deposits of accountholders during bank failures is the main function of the Federal Banking Insurance Agency (FBIA). Ensuring the safety of money held by the country's banks gives consumers more confidence in their financial institutions and protects their assets.

Deposit Insurance

Deposit insurance is a _____ with the backing of the federal government that ensures the money accountholders deposit is safe, up to a predetermined limit, even in cases in which a bank goes out of business.

In the event of a bank failure and closure, the FBIA acts as a receiver for the business. It dispatches teams of professionals to take over the bank, sell off its assets, and attempt to find other banks to purchase the business. This allows it to reimburse depositors in a timely fashion, usually within the course of one business day, and minimizes disruptions for consumers.

05 윗글의 요지로 적절한 것은?

① FBIA aims to assist consumers in increasing their assets.
② FBIA focuses on ensuring banks do not fail.
③ FBIA's main purpose is to protect funds held by banks.
④ FBIA tries to sell banks that are in financial trouble before they fail.

06 윗글의 밑줄 친 부분에 들어갈 말로 적절한 것은?

① safeguard
② barrier
③ hardship
④ permit

07 The National Archive에 관한 다음 글의 내용과 일치하는 것은?

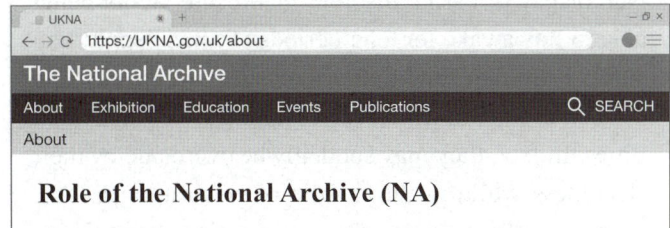

Role of the National Archive (NA)

The NA is responsible for preserving and managing important records related to the country's history and governance. In keeping with this mission, it advises government agencies on how to properly manage records to follow all legal requirements. It also facilitates online public access to these documents in order to ensure transparency. Because of the digitization efforts of the NA, ordinary citizens and researchers can easily access records dating back hundreds of years at no cost. Materials in the archive can even be printed or bound for a modest fee.

① It allows citizens to store important documents and items.
② It encourages people to visit the archive and access documents.
③ It makes centuries-old documents available to the public.
④ It will print out any record at no cost to users.

08 다음 글의 주제로 적절한 것은?

Narcolepsy is a sleep disorder that results in not being able to stay awake for long periods of time. People who suffer from this condition often have extreme daytime drowsiness and find themselves falling asleep at random times. In fact, they may suddenly be overcome by their sleepiness while in the middle of performing a task, or even in the middle of a conversation. Sometimes, this causes them to slur their words or even collapse. Unfortunately, there is no cure for narcolepsy at this time. Instead, sleep specialists offer medications that can help reduce the disorder's impact on sufferers' lives and guide them in changing their behavior to manage their symptoms. Most often, this encompasses devising sleep schedules that prevent drowsiness at inopportune times. These not only have strict nighttime sleep rules, but can also include scheduled naps so the patient can stay awake at other times.

① causes of extreme daytime sleepiness disorders
② the impact of sleep disorders on social life
③ managing narcolepsy through medication and schedules
④ novel surgical procedures for narcolepsy patients

09 다음 글의 흐름상 어색한 문장은?

After a series of studies, researchers have determined that the traditional practice of preventing foreign-language learners from using bilingual dictionaries while reading may not be wise. ① To test the effect of using a dictionary while reading, the researchers split students into two groups—one with access to electronic dictionaries and one without them—and had them read a passage in the second language. ② They then gave the students a vocabulary test to see how well they understood the new words that they had encountered. ③ It was found that the average modern English dictionary includes more than 175,000 distinct words. ④ When the results were analyzed, they showed that the students who were able to look up words understood and retained them much better than those who guessed their meaning from the context.

10 주어진 문장이 들어갈 위치로 적절한 것은?

In addition to inferior care, they argue it results in a great cost for the government.

Critics of nationalized health care contend that it has many disadvantages over a system in which care is provided on a for-profit basis. (①) They claim that a government-run system is inefficient and reduces the quality and the range of treatment options available. (②) In the United States, for example, estimates indicate that implementing a universal health care program would require an outlay of more than 15 trillion dollars over the first ten years. (③) Opponents also point to relatively longer wait times for diagnostic tests like MRIs in countries with publicly-run systems. (④) They commonly cite the Canadian system as the perfect example of this, as being sent to a specialist there can take nearly six months in some provinces.

01 밑줄 친 부분에 들어갈 말로 적절한 것은?

Readers can often _____ the meaning of unknown words thanks to context clues.

① set about
② figure out
③ carry on
④ hold onto

02 밑줄 친 부분에 들어갈 말로 적절한 것은?

The new stadium is _____ the previous one, accommodating many more spectators.

① three times as large as
② three times as largely as
③ three times as larger than
④ three times as large than

03 밑줄 친 부분 중 어법상 옳지 않은 것은?

One of the ① oldest forms of the English novel ② are the Robinsonade. It takes its name from modern English novels, *Robinson Crusoe*. The original novel is about a man ③ who was shipwrecked on an island and had to survive before escaping. Books in this genre share themes with the genre's origin, ④ centering around stories of isolation, survival, and rebuilding both the self and society.

04 밑줄 친 부분에 들어갈 말로 적절한 것은?

A: Any interest in visiting my hometown with me?
B: I'd love to. When are you going?
A: I'm going this weekend.
B: I'll be in the office all weekend. _____ _____?
A: Unfortunately, I need to go soon, and this is my only free weekend for a while.
B: I see. That's too bad. I want to join you next time, though.

① Are we still able to get tickets
② Is there any way we can reschedule
③ What time does the flight leave
④ How long will you be out of town

※ 다음 글을 읽고 물음에 답하시오. [05~06]

_____(A)_____

Don't be a couch potato—join us for the Ridgemont Potato Festival, the province's longest-running festival. Bring the entire family for a weekend of fun that celebrates our city's most important crop!

Details
- **Date and Time**: Saturday, April 8 – Sunday, April 9; 11:00 a.m. – 7:00 p.m.
- **Admission**: Entry is free; food vendors and certain activities require cash.
- **Location**: Ridgemont Fairgrounds

Attractions
- **Global Potato Feast**
  Enjoy potato-based dishes from around the world, including potato pancakes, soups, and salads. For a classic treat, don't miss out on complimentary French fries!
- **Potato Contests**
  Take part in the fun with potato peeling races and "hot" potato toss competitions, open to both children and adults.

For the safety of all guests, pets are not allowed on the fairgrounds. Additional information about the festival's schedule can be found at ridgemontpotatofestival.com.

05 (A)에 들어갈 윗글의 제목으로 적절한 것은?

① Learn Delicious Potato Recipes
② Have Fun with a Cool Crop
③ Teach Children How to Use Potatoes
④ Expand Tourism in Our Province

06 Ridgemont Potato Festival에 관한 윗글의 내용과 일치하지 않는 것은?

① 이틀 모두 같은 시간에 끝난다.
② 축제 입장료가 없다.
③ 모든 연령대의 사람들이 대회에 참가할 수 있다.
④ 축제는 반려동물 친화적인 행사이다.

07 밑줄 친 부분에 들어갈 말로 적절한 것은?

To: equipment@UrbanEvents.com
From: CarlaLandis@Tidewater.gov
Date: August 26
Subject: Equipment Rental

Dear Rental Manager,

I am writing to inquire about renting some audio equipment for the city's annual employee appreciation picnic.

We will be holding the picnic at Triton Park Pavillion the first Sunday of November. For the four-hour picnic, we will need to rent microphones and speakers to be used during speeches and various events. We will also need a projector so that we can present a slide show of the city's achievements over the last year. Keep in mind that everything will be done in the park, so all of the equipment needs to be able to be used outdoors.

Please send me a list of equipment options that _____. In addition, please note that someone will need to drop off and pick up the equipment on the day of the event.

I thank you for your time.

Respectfully,

Carla Landis, City Clerk

① would include weatherproof items
② would meet our needs for the event
③ would fall within our city's budget range
④ would support presentations throughout the entire day

08 다음 글의 요지로 적절한 것은?

Of the more than 3,000 spoken languages that exist worldwide, indigenous peoples speak about 90 percent of them. This is why indigenous communities are considered the main source of language diversity in the world. Yet, it is these languages that are the most likely to disappear. As indigenous languages vanish when young people stop speaking them and elders pass away, communities lose their political standing as recognized tribes. This loss of recognition frequently leads to governments denying these peoples their fundamental right to self-governance and tribal autonomy. This makes it crucial to preserve these languages. There are many ways to save a language, some of which are encouraging its use in the home and offering language classes to the young. In addition, social media sites may be used to communicate in the language.

① All tribal languages hold sufficient educational value.
② Tribal communities should avoid political recognition systems.
③ Language preservation ensures tribal political rights.
④ Social media threatens indigenous language prevalence.

09 주어진 글 다음에 이어질 글의 순서로 적절한 것은?

Detecting when someone is lying is easier when the person is speaking a foreign language, according to the existing theory. This hypothesis states that lying and speaking a foreign language, respectively, are cognitively more demanding than telling the truth and using a native language.

(A) A new theory based on this knowledge asserts that it is actually simpler to discern when native speakers lie because the differences in response time between telling the truth and a falsehood are much more pronounced.

(B) However, recent findings show non-native speakers take a while to respond regardless of whether they are telling the truth or lying.

(C) Owing to this increased cognitive burden, telling a lie in a foreign language would have a suspiciously long and easily detectable response time.

① (A) – (C) – (B)
② (B) – (A) – (C)
③ (C) – (A) – (B)
④ (C) – (B) – (A)

10 밑줄 친 (A), (B)에 들어갈 말로 적절한 것은?

Scientists have long assumed that Jupiter's Great Red Spot has endured for centuries because of its very depth. Researchers from the National Aeronautics and Space Administration initially presumed that it was a shallow storm because of its flat appearance. ____(A)____, it turned out that the storm was much deeper than they believed. Scientists used Juno, a space probe with cutting-edge technology, to analyze the storm's top cloud layers. Microwaves measured the clouds down to 200 kilometers but could go no farther. A Juno scientist subsequently used deviations in Juno's flight path to examine more deeply and was able to report that the Great Red Spot is about 500 kilometers deep. ____(B)____, the storm's extent cannot compare with the brown and white stripes that go around the planet, which are about three thousand kilometers in depth.

*Great Red Spot: (목성) 대적점

(A)	(B)
① However	Nonetheless
② Therefore	In addition
③ For instance	Consequently
④ Moreover	Hence

01 밑줄 친 부분에 들어갈 말로 적절한 것은?

It's important to stand your ground and refuse to _____ on issues that matter to you. Otherwise, you may lose credibility with both yourself and others.

① concentrate
② compromise
③ continue
④ decide

02 밑줄 친 부분에 들어갈 말로 적절한 것은?

The doctor _____ regular exercise could significantly improve his condition.

① explained that the patient
② explained to the patient that
③ explained to the patient what
④ explained the patient that

03 밑줄 친 부분에 들어갈 말로 적절한 것은?

Samuel: Hello. I'm interested in volunteer opportunities at municipal animal shelters. 15:30

Municipal Shelter: Thank you! Volunteer positions are always open. _____ 15:30

Samuel: Nothing specific, but I'm a dog groomer, so I could help with grooming work. 15:31

Municipal Shelter: The Best Friends shelter needs groomers. Would you be interested in volunteering there? 15:32

Samuel: Yes, that sounds perfect! How do I apply? 15:32

Municipal Shelter: You can apply online through the Best Friends shelter website. 15:33

Samuel: I'll do that today. 15:34

Municipal Shelter: Excellent! The shelter animals will benefit from your grooming service. 15:34

① Which days work best for you?
② Do you have a preference for a particular position?
③ Are you comfortable cleaning cages and walking dogs?
④ Do you know about the age requirements for volunteering?

※ 다음 글을 읽고 물음에 답하시오. [04~05]

Citizen Services

A lost or stolen passport is a serious matter as it could lead to identity theft or illegal use. It must therefore be reported immediately to Citizen Services through our website or 24-hour helpline so that it can be canceled.

If you wish to apply for a replacement passport, you must visit a passport office or consulate in person with valid government-issued identification, two recent passport-sized photographs, a completed replacement form, and the replacement fee. If you have to travel urgently and would like an emergency passport, you will be required to submit proof of an upcoming flight.

In the event that you are abroad when your passport is lost or stolen, visit your nearest embassy for assistance obtaining an emergency travel document. Your identity will have to be <u>verified</u> through additional documentation, such as an image of your lost passport.

04 밑줄 친 verified의 의미와 가장 가까운 것은?

① recorded
② protected
③ confirmed
④ shared

05 윗글의 목적으로 적절한 것은?

① to provide information about passport processing times
② to explain what to do after losing a passport
③ to announce new passport security features
④ to offer safety tips to international travelers

06 다음 글의 내용과 일치하지 않는 것은?

SUMMER SCIENCE SEMINARS

Explore, experiment, and learn at the Northshore Children's Museum during the Summer Science Seminars. Each seminar will feature hands-on exhibits, live demonstrations, and fun experiments to make science come alive.

ABOUT
Science educators and researchers from NCM and local universities will give weekly presentations examining a different scientific topic ranging from local ecosystems to space exploration. Participants will get first-hand experience with scientific topics and have their questions answered by experts.

RECOMMENDED AGES
Participants ages 6-18 are welcome.
All activities are split into three age groups, with materials and experiments tailored to the needs and knowledge of each.

SCIENCE FAIR
The summer series will end with a science fair in which participants can create a presentation about a topic they learned about during the seminars.

WHEN
Every Wednesday from June 1 to August 31
Seminars run from 10 a.m. to 3 p.m.

COST
$10 per seminar or $100 for the 13-week program when paid in advance

① A variety of scientific topics will be explored during the seminars.
② Students from local universities are invited to attend.
③ Participants will be grouped according to age for all exercises.
④ A discount is offered when paying for the full 13-week program.

07 밑줄 친 부분 중 어법상 옳지 않은 것은?

Smoking bans have become ① so commonplace that it's easy ② to forget that there was a time recently ③ in which cigarettes could be smoked in the majority of restaurants. In the United States, ④ although the initial worry that such a move would be incredibly detrimental to businesses that catered to smokers, bans followed California's successful prohibition of smoking in public restaurants in 1995.

08 다음 글의 주제로 적절한 것은?

While humans have no muscles that control the movement of the spine in the same way that hands and fingers can be manipulated with precision, it is arguably a far more important collection of bones than any other in the body. The spinal column is made up of a series of vertebrae separated by intervertebral discs, and it houses the nerves that connect the brain and heart to a person's four limbs. This structure is so integral to the functioning of the entire body. The slightest damage to any one of the spine's discs can cause severe pain and even impair movement in certain areas. Even though surgery and other forms of treatment can successfully alleviate these problems, the complexity of the spine is such that cures are often not so simple and take a long time to work.

*spinal column: 등골뼈
*vertebrae: 척추뼈
*intervertebral disc: 척추 사이 원반

① Precision control systems in human anatomy
② Similarities between hands and spine mobility
③ Medical treatments for spinal cord problems
④ Complex structure and vital role of the spine

09 주어진 문장 다음에 이어질 글의 순서로 적절한 것은?

When most people hear that someone is depressed, they immediately think that the person is simply sad, but clinical depression is a mental illness that causes not only depressed feelings, but also numerous physical effects.

(A) In fact, clinically depressed patients often suffer from rapid unexpected weight loss or gain, exhaustion, and trouble with their psychomotor abilities.

(B) Luckily, for most patients, depression and its effects can be controlled through a combination of psychotherapy and medications that balance hormone levels.

(C) As a result of these symptoms, the patients can begin to suffer even greater feelings of hopelessness, as their bodies seem to be failing them.

① (A) - (B) - (C)
② (A) - (C) - (B)
③ (C) - (A) - (B)
④ (C) - (B) - (A)

10 밑줄 친 부분에 들어갈 말로 적절한 것은?

One of the greatest challenges facing entrepreneurs today is effective marketing for their business. This is a critical aspect of developing new businesses of all sizes. Even after securing investors for their business, establishing the business and developing its operational and logistical capabilities can consume the majority of a new company's start-up capital, leaving little room in the budget to tell potential customers about their business. The most cost-effective way to do this is to focus initially on branding: reach out to those in your demographic and establish your business as a legitimate and trusted member of the community. This can mean participation in local events, doing charity work, and otherwise serving the interests of your future customers. This is often harder work than marketing a product directly. But, it ensures that customers trust you when you begin to market your products, guaranteeing that _____.

① you learn what products every age group would respond best to

② you get the most value possible for your marketing budget

③ you understand your customers' needs in future ad campaigns

④ you build efficient delivery processes for your upcoming products

Self Check List

이번 테스트는 어땠나요?
다음 체크리스트로 자신의 테스트 진행 내용을 점검해 볼까요?

01 나는 10분 동안 완전히 테스트에 집중하였다.
    □ YES   □ NO

02 나는 주어진 10분 동안 10문제를 모두 풀었다.
    □ YES   □ NO

03 유난히 어렵게 느껴지는 지문이 있었다.
    □ YES   □ NO

04 유난히 어렵게 느껴지는 문제가 있었다.
    □ YES   □ NO

05 모르는 어휘가 있었다.
    □ YES   □ NO

06 개선해야 할 점과 이를 위한 구체적인 학습 계획

    _____
    _____

정답·해석·해설 p. 131

하프모의고사 25회
출제예상 핵심 어휘리스트
바로 다운받기 (gosi.Hackers.com)

QR 코드를 이용해 핵심 어휘리스트를 다운받아, 언제 어디서든 공무원 출제예상 어휘를 암기하세요!

DAY 26 하프모의고사 26회

01 밑줄 친 부분에 들어갈 말로 적절한 것은?

The leaders at the summit vowed to _____ the commitments they made to reduce global warming, which marked significant progress.

① execute
② mention
③ identify
④ relax

02 밑줄 친 부분에 들어갈 말로 적절한 것은?

The instructions for assembling the bookshelf were _____ without any additional help, allowing even furniture assembly beginners to complete the task quickly.

① enough clear to follow
② enough clear to following
③ clear enough to follow
④ clear enough to following

03 밑줄 친 부분 중 어법상 옳지 않은 것은?

The school administration is requesting that parents ① pack an extra set of clothing for their children and make sure they wear rubber boots to school. On rain-soaked streets ② comes inconveniences like puddles, which can cause students' clothes and shoes wet, making them uncomfortable in class. In addition, a concerted effort ③ to protect against sickness during the wet months ④ is required to ensure the students' well-being.

04 밑줄 친 부분에 들어갈 말로 적절한 것은?

A: I won't be able to meet with the client next week.
B: Why not? What's going on?
A: He and I disagree rather strongly about the marketing plan. I'm not sure I'm the best fit for his vision, so I'd like you to take over the project.
B: That makes sense. _____
A: Thanks for being understanding.
B: No problem. We're all on the same team.

① How could you let this happen?
② It does seem like the best approach.
③ You need to adjust to the client's needs.
④ People should finish anything they start.

※ 다음 글을 읽고 물음에 답하시오. [05~06]

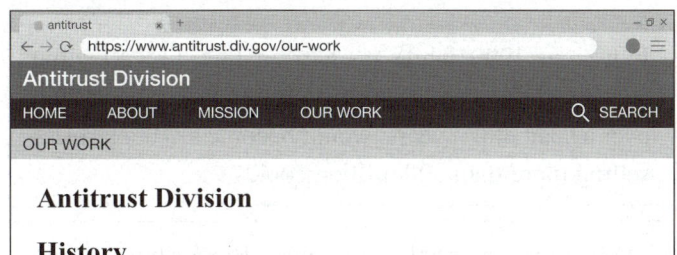

Antitrust Division

History

The Antitrust Division was established in 1919 to regulate competition among companies and protect consumers from unfair pricing. Since its foundation, it has passed three landmark laws that work to ensure competition in the marketplace so that consumers receive lower prices, more choices, and higher-quality goods.

Enforcing Regulations

When violations of antitrust laws occur, we pursue legal action against the offending company. If found guilty of monopolistic practices, companies may be issued significant fines, and key individuals involved may be sentenced to prison.

Competition Advocacy

We advocate for policies and laws that promote competition in nationally regulated industries like communications, transportation, and energy. We also review local legislation and provide legal recommendations to spur competition in areas such as real estate and professional licensing.

05 윗글에서 Antitrust Division에 관한 내용과 일치하는 것은?

① Protecting companies from unfair laws is its primary objective.
② Violations of laws will result in companies being issued warnings.
③ Energy sector regulations are beyond its advocacy scope.
④ It reviews local legislation to promote competition.

06 밑줄 친 landmark의 의미와 가장 가까운 것은?

① strict
② notable
③ costly
④ domestic

07 다음 글의 제목으로 적절한 것은?

In cities where closed-circuit television (CCTV) cameras are a common sight, people generally believe them to be helpful in providing added security. The cameras give a heightened sense of protection from criminal activity and the benefit of records that can be checked to verify facts when an incident occurs. Some feel uncomfortable, however, and for good reason, for CCTV cameras can breach privacy in both public and nonpublic areas. That a person's every move can be monitored even when he or she is not carrying out lawless activity can be cause for discomfort and offense. In fact, some people have abused the technology to catch citizens engaged in immoral rather than illegal acts or to target certain persons for the purpose of threatening them, turning the system into a means by which crimes can be committed.

① Reasons Authorities Install CCTV Cameras in Public Areas
② Types of Illegal Activities Caught by Public Monitoring Devices
③ The Unethical Use of a Surveillance System
④ Why the Public Agrees to the Use of CCTV Cameras

08 National Wildlife Conservation Conference에 관한 다음 글의 내용과 일치하지 않는 것은?

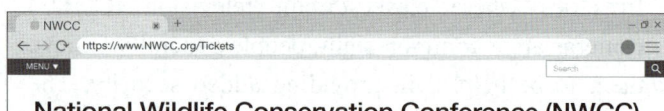

National Wildlife Conservation Conference (NWCC)

Thursday, October 10
9 a.m. – 5 p.m.

Tickets
- **Price**: $50.00 (general); $75.00 (VIP)

All tickets are valid for admission to all events. VIP tickets include reserved seating in the designated VIP section.

Tickets are available online or through the venue box office. A $10 discount is offered for tickets purchased before September 1.

NOTE: NWCC invites attendees from government agencies, businesses, and members of the general public.

① 10월 중 단 하루 개최된다.
② VIP 티켓 구매자는 예약석을 이용할 수 있다.
③ 티켓 판매는 9월 1일까지 진행된다.
④ 일반인들도 회의에 참석할 수 있다.

09 주어진 글 다음에 이어질 글의 순서로 적절한 것은?

It was in 1990 while on a train that J.K. Rowling conceived the idea for the first Harry Potter book that, over a span of ten years, would become a 7-book series selling more than 500 million copies.

(A) In time, the publishing house Bloomsbury would see some merit in her manuscript. They asked only that she change her name so that boys would be encouraged to read the book. Hence, the entire best-selling series was published under the name J.K. Rowling instead of Joanne Rowling.

(B) Rowling kept all these letters, most of which stated that her novel was too old-fashioned, too long, and too ordinary. She did not allow these refusals to make her despair but instead kept pushing forward with her book.

(C) Yet, the first book was rejected by twelve different publishers after it was completed in 1995. One publisher even sent her a rudely worded letter turning down her novel.

① (B) – (A) – (C)
② (B) – (C) – (A)
③ (C) – (A) – (B)
④ (C) – (B) – (A)

10 밑줄 친 부분에 들어갈 말로 적절한 것은?

When teaching classrooms full of young learners, we have to be prepared to support the _____ of talent and abilities we are likely to encounter. Some students learn more efficiently through physical activity, while others thrive when allowed to express themselves artistically. Similarly, certain children thrive in groups, whereas other kids work best on their own. Before we can cater to each student's unique learning style and level, however, we have to recognize them. To do this, offer choices to the children. Allow them—within reason—to dictate how they learn most effectively, so they can showcase their talent. This requires that we offer a range of learning materials, such as books about various topics, and games and puzzles with tiered difficulty levels that can provide an appropriate challenge to students with different gifts.

① balance
② addition
③ variety
④ development

DAY 27 하프모의고사 27회

01 밑줄 친 부분에 들어갈 말로 적절한 것은?

He finds it _____ to eat with his colleagues because they always bring up troublesome work-related issues during regular lunch times.

① ordinary
② inspiring
③ refreshing
④ uncomfortable

02 밑줄 친 부분에 들어갈 말로 적절한 것은?

The company implemented a six-month trial period _____ new policies were tested and refined.

① what
② where
③ during which
④ of which

03 밑줄 친 부분 중 어법상 옳지 않은 것은?

Investors ① provide startup companies the initial financial backing in the hopes of reaping ② growth profit, but an excessive concentration on these types of investments can make the whole investment ③ riskily, so they typically take up ④ no more than 10 percent of an investor's portfolio.

04 밑줄 친 부분에 들어갈 말로 적절한 것은?

Jackson Evans 11:32
Have you read over the website copy?

Amelia Jones 11:33
Yes. The text requires lots of edits.

Jackson Evans 11:34
I thought so too. There are some unsupported claims in the promotional content.

Amelia Jones 11:34
Exactly. It puts us at risk of being penalized for false advertising.

Jackson Evans 11:35
The formatting and wording seem a little inconsistent too. _____

Amelia Jones 11:36
Correcting the exaggerated parts is the most urgent.

Jackson Evans 11:36
I agree. Can you get started with it right away?

① When is the deadline for content revisions?
② Where should we begin our corrections?
③ Is there a problem with the content guidelines?
④ Didn't we proofread the entire copy?

※ 다음 글을 읽고 물음에 답하시오. [05~06]

_____(A)_____

The Pritchard Municipal Transportation Department is excited to invite you to its upcoming Summer Bike Safety and Repair Clinics, a series of free events designed to promote safe and responsible cycling for everyone in the community.

Details
- **Dates**: Every Saturday, from the beginning of June through the end of August
- **Time**: 10:00 a.m. – 1:00 p.m.
- **Location**: Southside Mall Parking Lot, 300 Novak Avenue

What to Expect
- **Free Bike Tune-Ups**
  Experienced mechanics will be on site to offer free bike tune-ups.
- **Safety Lessons**
  Instructors will provide hands-on lessons on how to navigate city streets, signal turns, and wear appropriate safety gear.
- **Giveaways**
  To encourage safe riding, we will distribute free bike lights to children (while supplies last).

For more information, visit www.pritchardbikeclinics.org or contact the Municipal Transportation Department at (208) 987-6543.

05 (A)에 들어갈 윗글의 제목으로 적절한 것은?

① Ride Safely This Summer
② Upgrade Your Bike
③ Explore New Bike Paths
④ Get Fit Through Cycling

06 Summer Bike Safety and Repair Clinics에 관한 윗글의 내용과 일치하지 않는 것은?

① 매주 개최될 것이다.
② 전문가들에게 자전거를 점검받을 기회가 있다.
③ 안전 장비에 대한 수업을 들을 수 있다.
④ 모든 참가자들은 자전거 지시등을 받을 수 있다.

07 주어진 문장이 들어갈 위치로 적절한 것은?

This process is only required once at the very beginning, so you won't need to take photos multiple times.

IDforMe is a government-approved, digital identification app that can serve as a valid proof of ID. It can be used for various purposes, including picking up mail at the post office, accessing bank accounts online, buying age-restricted items, and signing up for government services. The app securely stores your personal information using advanced encryption, ensuring that your details are only accessible by you. (①) To get started, download the app for free and create an account. (②) You'll be prompted to take a selfie and scan a piece of government-issued ID, like a driver's license or passport to verify your identify. (③) With IDforMe, your proof of identity is always available as long as you have your phone. (④)

08 다음 글의 요지로 적절한 것은?

Astronomers have gathered much information about the rings of Saturn in the 400 years since Galileo Galilei first spotted them. When viewed through telescopes on Earth, Saturn appears to have seven large rings that orbit it at different speeds depending on their distance from the planet. But through satellite imaging, these main rings have been determined to actually be a series of up to one thousand smaller ringlets that are grouped together. The rings consist of pieces of ice and shattered chunks of rock from comets, asteroids, and moons that were broken into pieces under the immense force of Saturn's gravity. Three other planets in the solar system have rings too, but they are darker, fainter, and do not fill the viewer with the same sense of awe as Saturn's. This is because of the ring system's sheer size, with a diameter of 270,000 kilometers, or more than half the distance between the Earth and the Moon.

① Astronomers disagree about Saturn's ring composition.

② Rings maintain consistent speeds around planets.

③ Moons remain intact despite Saturn's gravity.

④ Multiple tiny ringlets compose Saturn's rings.

09 다음 글의 흐름상 어색한 문장은?

A "cliff-hanger" is a storytelling tool that works to build suspense by placing the lead character in a dangerous situation or tricky dilemma at the end of a work of fiction. If executed correctly, a cliff-hanger will encourage the audience to tune back in for the next installment of the story. ① The technique itself has been in use for centuries in oral storytelling. ② However, the term only came into being in the 1930s, when British author Thomas Hardy published a serialized version of his novel *A Pair of Blue Eyes*. ③ Bookstores typically display cliff-hanger novels in prominent locations to maximize impulse purchases. ④ His work appeared in *Tinsley's Magazine* for more than six months, with each installment strategically ending in suspense. One memorable section ended with the main character literally left hanging on the edge of a cliff. Eager to learn the fate of this hero, readers purchased the following magazine issue enthusiastically.

10 밑줄 친 부분에 들어갈 말로 적절한 것은?

In 1952, the poet Dylan Thomas penned the now-famous refrain "Do not go gentle into that good night… Rage, … rage against the dying of the light." At the time, the lines expressed Thomas's grief for the impending death of his ailing father as well as his belief that a person should never simply be resigned to death. Since then, the poem has been used in popular culture to not only reflect on the end of life but also to evoke the notion that surrendering is unacceptable under any circumstances as long as there is still time and opportunity. In other words, the fundamental message of the poem is that, in the face of an inevitable and undesirable outcome, _____.

① life will go on no matter what
② one should fight until the end
③ acceptance will bring peace
④ nothing can be done about the past

DAY 28 하프모의고사 28회

제한 시간 : 10분 시작   시   분 ~ 종료   시   분 점수 확인   개/ 10개

01 밑줄 친 부분에 들어갈 말로 적절한 것은?

After three days of trial, the plaintiff won the case as his opponent lacked _____ evidence.

① flexible
② concrete
③ fake
④ complex

02 밑줄 친 부분에 들어갈 말로 적절한 것은?

The private investigator watched the subject who had been under surveillance _____ the abandoned building.

① to enter
② enter
③ entered
④ being entered

03 밑줄 친 부분 중 어법상 옳지 않은 것은?

US schools are ① similar to European schools in a number of ways. Class size is limited, which allows a teacher ② to give each student adequate attention. Both systems are co-educational, offer the same basic subjects, and ③ require nine or ten years to complete. Yet, the rate of students who go on to university in the United States is about 10-20 percent higher than ④ those of Europe.

04 밑줄 친 부분에 들어갈 말로 적절한 것은?

A: Before we go to my sister's place, can we stop by the bank?
B: Can you do that tomorrow? We have a long drive ahead of us.
A: But I'm going to see my sister's kids for the first time.
B: I know, but why do you need to drop by the bank?
A: _____
B: Oh, I didn't think of that. Let's go to the bank, then.

① I need to deposit some money quickly.
② I'm going to open an account.
③ I have to check my balance.
④ I want to give them small bills as a gift.

※ 다음 글을 읽고 물음에 답하시오. [05~06]

Maritime Safety
Maintaining the safety and security of the nation's coastal waters is the core mission of the Coast Guard. The agency actively patrols to enforce law and provide protection in order to safeguard the country and its citizens and industries.

Search and Rescue Operations
Search and Rescue (SAR) operations, in which the Coast Guard looks for and assists people in distress at sea, such as lost boaters, those experiencing medical emergencies, and passengers on damaged or capsized vessels, are a critical aspect of the service's activities.

The Coast Guard's highly trained personnel are on duty 24 hours a day. They actively respond to distress signals and coordinate rapid responses to dangerous situations. When a distress call is received, SAR teams immediately mobilize and dispatch the necessary resources to conduct a timely rescue.

05 윗글의 요지로 적절한 것은?

① The Coast Guard takes care of maintaining water quality.
② The Coast Guard is meant to protect people in the waters around the country.
③ The Coast Guard attempts to prevent boats from being damaged or capsizing.
④ The Coast Guard conducts SAR exercises to improve its operations.

06 밑줄 친 dispatch의 의미와 가장 가까운 것은?

① deploy
② secure
③ retrieve
④ command

07 Hillary-Sanders 저택에 관한 다음 글의 내용과 일치하지 않는 것은?

The Hillary-Sanders House is open to the public on weekdays from 11 a.m. to 7 p.m. and from 8 a.m. to 8 p.m. on Saturdays and national holidays. Tickets may be reserved up to one month in advance using the online ticket booking agency. Online purchasers will receive a QR code that can be scanned by the kiosks at the entrance of the museum.

- **Online tickets**: Tickets.HSandersHouse.com

The Hillary-Sanders House (part of the city's Historical District) charges $15 for full-priced adult admission. Children ages 6-18 and senior citizens can enter for $10. There is no charge for those under 5 years old. Guided tours can be arranged for an additional cost of $10 per ticket, regardless of age.

- **CLOSED**: Sundays, New Year's Day, and Christmas week (December 25-31)

There is no charge for school groups visiting the Hillary-Sanders House as part of an official field trip.

For additional information, call 1 (800) 555-2814.

① 토요일에 더 늦게까지 개방한다.
② QR 스캔용 키오스크를 비치하고 있다.
③ 티켓 구매 시 무료 가이드 투어를 제공한다.
④ 현장 학습 학생들은 별도의 입장료가 없다.

08 다음 글의 제목으로 적절한 것은?

In the days of old, sailors composed sayings about their situation when they were sailing the oceans. For example, "down in the doldrums" means that one is unable to make progress. For sailors, "the doldrums" meant that the ship could not move. Ships sailing between Europe and Africa relied on trade winds— steady breezes found north and south of the equator. These natural wind patterns essentially served as highways for ocean navigation. Specifically, Earth's rotation causes air to slope toward the equator in a counterclockwise direction in the southern hemisphere and in a clockwise direction in the northern hemisphere, known as the Coriolis effect. This effect, along with a high-pressure area, pushes the trade winds from east to west. However, the intense solar heat near the equator calms these winds, causing them to cease. This area is known as the doldrums, where ships stood still as there was no wind in their sails.

① The Science behind an Old Sailing Expression
② How Ships in the Past Navigated the Seas
③ Formation of Winds near Earth's Equator
④ The Effect of Wind on Trade in the Old Days

09 주어진 문장이 들어갈 위치로 적절한 곳은?

By that time, Benin had become a prosperous city, and it attracted the Europeans who were about to divide and conquer Africa.

In 800 AD, the people of Benin, a city located in what is now southern Nigeria, began building a defensive fortification. (①) Completed around 1460 AD, its earthen walls were 20 meters high in most parts and included defensive water channels. (②) When the Portuguese visited in 1472 AD, they described the earthwork as a structure so great that it was second only to China's Great Wall. (③) Because of its wealth, Benin was especially attractive to British traders who were attempting to convince the government to make the city a protected territory. (④) Aware of their motives, the rulers of Benin attacked first, causing the British army to invade the city in 1897 and completely destroy it.

10 주어진 글 다음에 이어질 글의 순서로 적절한 것은?

Global agricultural systems strive to meet the dietary demands of growing populations, but this has impacted the environment negatively. The process begins with the planting of crops.

(A) Aside from this impact on water, nitrogen accumulation is a threat to land and air. It affects the health of native plant species, which reduces the biodiversity of the ecosystem. Fertilizers also contribute one-fifth of total greenhouse gas emissions in the atmosphere.

(B) To ensure food security, farmers use chemical fertilizers that double the rate of food produced but also increase nitrogen and phosphorus levels in the environment. These pollutants find their way into water bodies.

(C) One especially pronounced effect is the death of lakes. Washed-away fertilizers in these lakes result in algae blooms, which deplete oxygen in the waters and create dead zones where no living thing can thrive.

① (A) – (C) – (B)
② (B) – (A) – (C)
③ (B) – (C) – (A)
④ (C) – (B) – (A)

01 밑줄 친 부분에 들어갈 말로 적절한 것은?

She felt there was no reason to trust her former neighbor, who had _____ her so many times before.

① convinced
② respected
③ deceived
④ invited

02 밑줄 친 부분에 들어갈 말로 적절한 것은?

_____ the negotiation fail again, the government will have no choice but to implement stricter economic measures.

① If
② Should
③ That
④ Were

03 밑줄 친 부분 중 어법상 옳지 않은 것은?

Humans are naturally inclined ① to seek patterns and habits. Breaking habits requires that the stimulus that results in the response ② be removed. We can also try an alternate strategy to replace the habit with another beneficial one. In this way, the catalyst that motivates detrimental behaviors instead inspires positive ③ one. ④ Such a systematic strategy can be an effective way to use our own tendencies toward patterned behavior to effect a change that we want to see in our lives.

04 밑줄 친 부분에 들어갈 말로 적절한 것은?

 Isabella Wilson
I'm reaching out because we'd like to conduct a final interview with you.
11:20

 Jack Foster
I appreciate the opportunity. When will the interview be scheduled?
11:20

 Isabella Wilson
It will be conducted online during the third week of this month.
11:21

 Jack Foster
Could you let me know the exact date and time?
11:21

 Isabella Wilson
You can choose the time slot that works best for you through the 'Recruit' section of our website.
11:22

 Jack Foster
I'll probably choose Wednesday or Thursday. How will I be notified of the confirmed interview schedule?
11:23

 Isabella Wilson
_____
11:24

① You can reschedule the interview if something urgent comes up.
② Time slots are available on a first-come, first-served basis.
③ After you reserve a time, we'll email you within three days.
④ The final candidates will be announced next Monday.

※ 다음 글을 읽고 물음에 답하시오. [05~06]

National Healthcare Funding Board

Our Primary Challenge

Life expectancy has risen thanks to advances in medicine, nutrition, and sanitation, but many individuals still spend their later years managing multiple health conditions, which not only reduces their quality of life but places a strain on the already overburdened healthcare system. The National Healthcare Funding Board was established to fund research into initiatives that predict, prevent, and reduce the impact of chronic diseases.

What We Fund

We invest in projects that promote early intervention. Through grants to academic institutions and medical research centers, we also help support studies that explore emerging diagnostic tools, technologies that monitor health conditions remotely, and interventions that delay cognitive decline in aging populations.

Our Core Values
- We consider it beneficial _____.
- All our funding decisions are based on rigorous, ethically sound research.

05 윗글의 내용과 일치하는 것은?

① Life expectancy increases have contributed to the strain on healthcare systems.
② Chronic disease treatments can receive Board funding for clinical trials.
③ The Board supports research conducted at schools and research centers.
④ Remote technologies are only funded when focused on aging populations.

06 윗글의 밑줄 친 부분에 들어갈 말로 적절한 것은?

① to shift the focus from treatment to prevention
② to expand medical insurance coverage
③ to unify the national healthcare system
④ to introduce market competition principles

07 다음 글의 목적으로 적절한 것은?

To: customers@globalsecuretravel.com
From: support@globalsecuretravel.com
Date: April 18
Subject: Travel Tips

Dear Customers,

Increased reliance on digital devices when in unfamiliar surroundings can make it easier for cybercriminals to steal your sensitive data. To help you stay safe while traveling, we've put together some essential tips to keep in mind:

1. Free Wi-Fi in public spaces can be a hotspot for cybercriminals. Use a VPN whenever possible.
2. Secure your accounts with unique passwords, and add an extra layer of protection by enabling two-factor authentication.
3. Make sure to turn off Bluetooth in public places when you don't need it. This protects your device from being detected by other nearby devices.
4. Use your own charger, and plug it into a power outlet instead of using public USB charging ports.
5. Check your bank and credit card statements frequently to catch any suspicious transactions early.

Travel with greater peace of mind by taking these precautions. For more travel and safety tips, visit our Traveler Safety Center.

Sincerely,

The Global Secure Travel Team

① to provide customers with instructions on how to find free Wi-Fi in public spaces
② to provide customers with information on how to set up a VPN before traveling
③ to provide customers with advice on how to protect their personal data during travel
④ to provide customers with details on how to turn on Bluetooth in public places

08 다음 글의 흐름상 어색한 문장은?

Some languages use a flexible order, with fluctuating word orders or meanings, depending on a variety of factors, while others employ a set order. ① Languages with fixed word orders require specific sequences for subjects, objects, and verbs, and deviating from these constructions will either change the meaning or be ungrammatical. ② Many languages have additional parts of speech that get inserted into a sentence, such as prepositions, articles, adjectives, and adverbs. ③ The most common word order to find is SOV, or subject-object-verb, accounting for around nearly 44 percent of languages. ④ Languages with a free order are substantially less common, only making up around 2 percent of languages. In these languages, words can be put in any order with little to no impact on the meaning.

09 주어진 문장이 들어갈 위치로 적절한 곳은?

It also provides invaluable consumer data, allowing businesses to continuously refine their approaches.

Social media has fundamentally transformed how businesses interact with their audience through digital engagement strategies. Companies now require established digital presences across multiple platforms—from TikTok and Instagram to emerging metaverse spaces. (①) These digital platforms emphasize visual content and necessitate constant monitoring to maintain brand consistency. (②) Brand identities are increasingly shaped through personalized content and targeted demographic approaches. (③) Additionally, customer support has evolved to multi-channel solutions, with automated chatbots handling routine inquiries. (④) This automation resolves simple repetitive problems, conserving time and energy for human representatives who address complex issues publicly, creating transparent accountability.

10 밑줄 친 부분에 들어갈 말로 적절한 것은?

The rule of law is a principle of governance whereby government and all individuals and entities are accountable to the laws of the land. This presumes that the law is consistent with international human rights standards. People in positions of authority should treat law as something higher than politics and personal advantage. Similarly, citizens should obey the law even if aspects of it are inconvenient. If rule of law goes unrecognized, it becomes impossible to achieve peace and security and to attain economic, developmental, and social progress. Under the rule of law, the state acts within a legal framework that includes the obligation to protect human rights. In this context, when operating within legal systems aligned with international standards, states may take appropriate measures to protect their populations from serious human rights violations or crimes against humanity. This is the opposite of a government that controls its citizens in a random manner through laws that have no basis in _____.

① reality
② agreement
③ safety
④ universality

01 밑줄 친 부분에 들어갈 말로 적절한 것은?

Finding no work in the city during the economic crisis put rural migrants in a(n) _____ position. They even sold the land in the countryside that had been passed down through generations.

① desperate
② temporary
③ stable
④ individual

02 밑줄 친 부분에 들어갈 말로 적절한 것은?

No sooner _____ than property development corporations sought exceptions to avoid the requirements.

① the new housing bill passed
② the new housing bill will pass
③ had the new housing bill passed
④ have the new housing bill passed

03 밑줄 친 부분 중 어법상 옳지 않은 것은?

With the world ① embraced digitalization, customers have come to rely on the convenient access to products that e-commerce provides. Nevertheless, they remain largely unaware of the enormous challenges ② involved in facilitating it. First, e-commerce businesses must ③ either hire a shipping company or have their own system of delivering goods. Furthermore, since ④ information that is sensitive is necessary in all online purchases, e-commerce firms are obligated to take special care when it comes to cyber security.

04 밑줄 친 부분에 들어갈 말로 적절한 것은?

A: What's wrong? You don't look well.
B: I know. I might have eaten something bad.
A: Do you want to see a doctor?
B: I don't think it's that serious.
A: _____
B: I can't. I have work that needs to be finished today.
A: We can probably adjust the schedule. Take care of yourself before your condition gets worse.

① How many days of sick leave can you take?
② Why don't you leave work early and get some rest?
③ Did you get the company's regular check-up?
④ Could you work from home until you're better?

※ 다음 글을 읽고 물음에 답하시오. [05~06]

To	Traffic Fines Processing Office
From	Aliyah Woods
Date	March 18
Subject	Issue with Online Traffic Fine Payment System

Dear Sir or Madam,

Please be advised of the challenges I've encountered when trying to pay a traffic fine through the official website.

Whenever I enter my citation number into the system, I receive an error message.

I have tried to submit my payment multiple times, using various devices and credit cards, and my repeated lack of success makes me feel that this problem is not unique to me but, rather, a problem with your website. My citation is due in a few days, and it would be very inconvenient for me to have to visit your office to pay it in person.

If this issue has not already been <u>reported</u> by other users, I ask that you address it promptly. In the meantime, is there an alternative remote payment option available?

Regards,
Aliyah Woods

05 윗글의 목적으로 적절한 것은?

① 잘못 부과된 교통 범칙금에 대해 항의하려고
② 범칙금 납부와 관련된 기술적인 문제를 보고하려고
③ 웹사이트의 취약한 보안에 대한 조치를 요청하려고
④ 범칙금을 온라인으로 납부하는 방법을 제안하려고

06 밑줄 친 reported의 의미와 가장 가까운 것은?

① weakened
② corrected
③ raised
④ achieved

07 ClearSky 앱에 관한 다음 글의 내용과 일치하지 않는 것은?

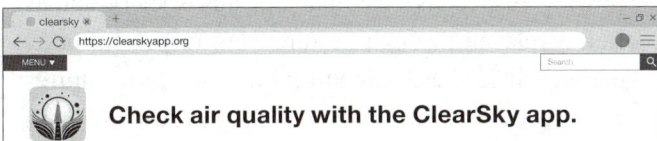

Check air quality with the ClearSky app.

The new ClearSky app helps residents stay informed about local air quality. ClearSky gives real-time readings of the air quality index, which provides information about various pollutants in the air. As part of the government's Environmental Health Awareness (EHA) initiative, the app allows users to make informed decisions about their outdoor activities. When pollution reaches dangerous levels, ClearSky provides an emergency alert warning. In the future, it will also offer seven-day forecasts for air quality. To use the app, simply download it from your mobile device's application store and turn on live location. ClearSky data can also be accessed via computer on the EHA website.

① It gives information about the quality of the air.
② Warnings are sent out when pollution becomes dangerously high.
③ Expected pollution levels are now available to users a week in advance.
④ Its information can be accessed using a computer.

08 다음 글의 주제로 적절한 것은?

Showing respect is customary in any society and is often displayed through gestures, but respectful body language differs according to culture. Western cultures demonstrate respect with the handshake, although there are variations when signifying deference, such as not putting the other hand in the pocket while shaking hands in Germany and not pumping the hand too hard in France. In other cultures, physical touch may even be considered disrespectful. For example, Eastern countries recognize someone's superiority by allowing them to remain higher in position and bestowing them more space, which is why those in a subordinate position bow about 15 degrees or bend their head and keep their limbs closer to their body. Other cultures have different ways to show respect without contact, such as the Zimbabwean clapping of the hands and the Tibetan extending of the tongue, and in certain Eastern cultures, individuals may fold their hands together or place their right hand above their heart.

① common expressions of respect across cultures
② physical space requirements for social interactions
③ global variations in respect through gestures
④ East-West perspectives on handshake practices

09 다음 글의 제목으로 적절한 것은?

Studies indicate that there are numerous health benefits that come with getting a pet, particularly if that pet is a dog. These benefits are especially notable for older individuals, as they face unique health challenges that pets can address. Pets can help combat feelings of loneliness and isolation, which is a significant factor in health decline for senior citizens. There are cognitive benefits as well, as studies show that cognitive deterioration in these individuals slows due to the presence of a pet in their lives. Furthermore, for those with dogs, the exercise boost from daily walks with the dog can translate into keeping people healthy and active as they age.

① Addressing Loneliness in Elderly Members of Society
② Ways to Keep Pets Healthy as a Person Ages
③ Effective Exercise Regimens for Senior Citizens
④ Seniors Remaining Healthier Longer by Keeping Pets

10 주어진 글 다음에 이어질 글의 순서로 적절한 것은?

You make a to-do list. You're resolved to finish everything on your list. That's because it's your objective to be productive so that you can achieve your goals.

(A) In such cases, delaying is not an act of laziness. Laziness is an unwillingness to do anything, but delaying tasks is an active process of avoiding something important because it's difficult or unpleasant. Like any other bad habit, it takes hard work and discipline to overcome the habit of delaying tasks.

(B) Begin by recognizing the fact that you are delaying. Then, you need to adopt a strategy that is encouraging, such as changing your internal dialogue from "I have to do this," to "I choose to do this," after which you can reward yourself each time you complete a difficult task.

(C) Unfortunately, the same pattern has happened again: The most important task on your list was put off for another day not because you were busy but because you focused on the less essential things.

① (A) – (B) – (C)
② (B) – (A) – (C)
③ (C) – (A) – (B)
④ (C) – (B) – (A)

MEMO

해커스공무원 gosi.Hackers.com

공무원 학원 · 공무원 인강 · 공무원 영어 무료 특강 · 공무원 보카 어플 ·
출제예상 핵심 어휘리스트 · 합격예측 온라인 모의고사 · 공무원 매일영어 학습 한국사능력검정시험 1위* 해커스!

해커스 한국사능력검정시험 교재 시리즈

* 주간동아 선정 2022 올해의 교육 브랜드 파워 온·오프라인 한국사능력검정시험 부문 1위

빈출 개념과 **기출 분석**으로
기초부터 **문제 해결력**까지
꽉 잡는 기본서

해커스 한국사능력검정시험
한권합격 　심화 [1·2·3급]

스토리와 **마인드맵**으로 **개념잡고!**
기출문제로 **점수잡고!**

해커스 한국사능력검정시험
2주 합격　심화 [1·2·3급]　기본 [4·5·6급]

시대별/회차별 기출문제로
한 번에 합격 달성!

해커스 한국사능력검정시험
시대별/회차별 기출문제집　심화 [1·2·3급]

개념 정리부터 **실전**까지!
한권완성 기출문제집

해커스 한국사능력검정시험
한권완성 기출 500제　기본 [4·5·6급]

빈출 개념과 **기출 선택지**로
빠르게 합격 달성!

해커스 한국사능력검정시험
초단기 5일 합격　심화 [1·2·3급]
기선제압 막판 3일 합격　심화 [1·2·3급]

해커스공무원 단기 합격생이 말하는
공무원 합격의 비밀!

해커스공무원과 함께라면
다음 합격의 주인공은 바로 여러분입니다.

대학교 재학 중,
7개월 만에 국가직 합격!

김*석 합격생

영어 단어 암기를 하프모의고사로!

하프모의고사의 도움을 많이 얻었습니다. 모의고사의 5일 치 단어를 일주일에 한 번씩 외웠고, 영어 단어 100개씩은 하루에 외우려고 노력했습니다.

가산점 없이
6개월 만에 지방직 합격!

김*영 합격생

국어 고득점 비법은 기출과 오답노트!

이론 강의를 두 달간 들으면서 **이론을 제대로 잡고 바로 기출문제로 들어갔습니다.** 문제를 풀어보고 기출강의를 들으며 **틀렸던 부분을 필기하며 머리에 새겼습니다.**

직렬 관련학과 전공,
6개월 만에 서울시 합격!

최*숙 합격생

한국사 공부법은 기출문제 통한 복습!

한국사는 휘발성이 큰 과목이기 때문에 **반복 복습이 중요하다고 생각**했습니다. 선생님의 강의를 듣고 나서 바로 **내용에 해당되는 기출문제를 풀면서 복습**했습니다.

해커스공무원 gosi.Hackers.com

더 많은 합격수기가 궁금하다면? ▶

해커스공무원

비비안 영어
매일 하프
모의고사

DAY 01 하프모의고사 01회

정답
p. 14

01	④	어휘	06	①	독해
02	②	문법	07	④	독해
03	①	문법	08	④	독해
04	②	생활영어	09	②	독해
05	④	독해	10	④	독해

취약영역 분석표

영역	맞힌 답의 개수
어휘	/1
생활영어	/1
문법	/2
독해	/6
TOTAL	/10

01 어휘 obstacle 난이도 중 ●●○

밑줄 친 부분에 들어갈 말로 적절한 것은?

The biography detailed the major _____ the future Nobel Prize winner faced as he grew up. Being from a poor family, he had to quit high school to get a job.

① confusion
② misunderstanding
③ regret
④ obstacle

[해석]
전기는 그 장래의 노벨상 수상자가 성장하면서 직면한 주된 장애물을 상술했다. 빈곤 가정 출신이기 때문에, 그는 일자리를 얻기 위해 고등학교를 그만두어야 했다.

① 혼란
② 오해
③ 후회
④ 장애물

정답 ④

[어휘]
biography 전기   detail 상술하다, 열거하다; 세부 항목   quit 그만두다
confusion 혼란   misunderstanding 오해   regret 후회; 후회하다
obstacle 장애(물)

02 문법 관계절 난이도 중 ●●○

밑줄 친 부분에 들어갈 말로 적절한 것은?

The ancient building, _____ architecture fascinated tourists, was renovated last year when the city received a historic preservation grant.

① to whom
② whose
③ which
④ that

[해석]
건축 양식이 관광객들을 매료시키는 그 고대 건물은 작년에 시가 역사 보존 보조금을 받았을 때 재단장되었다.

[해설]
② 관계대명사   빈칸은 The ancient building을 수식하는 것의 자리이다. 선행사(The ancient building)가 사물이고 관계절 내에서 architecture가 무엇의 건축 양식인지를 나타내므로, 소유격 관계대명사 ② whose가 정답이다.

정답 ②

[어휘]
ancient 고대의   architecture 건축 (양식)   fascinate 매료시키다
renovate 재단장하다, 개조하다   preservation 보존   grant 보조금

03 문법 수 일치 | 동사의 종류 | 분사 | to 부정사 난이도 중 ●●○

밑줄 친 부분 중 어법상 옳지 않은 것은?

Seeing chefs from a variety of restaurants lined up to serve food in the disaster zone ① were impressive. Everyone knew some local chefs would be collaborating with each other to help out, but no one expected so many ② to turn up. With half of the homes in the town ③ destroyed, their work ④ to feed the storm's victims was a great blessing.

[해석]
재해 지역에서 음식을 제공하기 위해 일렬로 선, 다양한 식당들에서 온 요리사들을 보는 것은 인상적이었다. 모든 사람이 몇몇 현지 요리사들이 도움을 주기 위해 서로 협력하고 있을 것임을 알았지만, 아무도 그렇게 많은 요리사들이 나타나리라고는 예상하지 못했다. 그 마을의 주택 중 절반이 소실되었기 때문에, 폭풍우의 피해자들에게 먹을 것을 제공하려는 그들의 노력은 엄청나게 고마운 것이었다.

[해설]
① 주어와 동사의 수 일치   주어 자리에 단수 취급하는 동명사구(Seeing ~ zone)가 왔으므로 복수 동사 were를 단수 동사 was로 고쳐야 한다.

[오답 분석]
② to 부정사를 취하는 동사 동사 expect는 to 부정사를 목적격 보어로 취하므로 to 부정사 to turn up이 올바르게 쓰였다.
③ 분사구문의 역할 이유를 나타낼 때 'with + 명사 + 분사'의 형태로 나타낼 수 있는데, 명사 half of the homes와 분사가 '주택 중 절반이 소실되다'라는 의미의 수동 관계이므로 과거분사 destroyed가 올바르게 쓰였다.
④ to 부정사의 역할 문맥상 '먹을 것을 제공하려는 그들의 노력'이라는 의미가 되어야 자연스러우므로 명사 their work 뒤에 명사를 수식하는 형용사 역할을 하는 to 부정사 to feed가 올바르게 쓰였다.

정답 ①

어휘

disaster 재해, 참사   impressive 인상적인
collaborate with ~와 협력하다   turn up 나타나다, 생기다
destroy 소실시키다, 파괴하다   victim 피해자, 희생자
blessing 고마운 것, 축복

---

04 생활영어 Maybe the way to report the problem has changed.
난이도 하 ●○○

밑줄 친 부분에 들어갈 말로 적절한 것은?

 Christopher Gray
I can't access the intranet on my computer.
9:10

Rachel Harris
Can you access other websites?
9:11

 Christopher Gray
Yes. They work properly.
9:12

Rachel Harris
That's weird. I'll call the IT support team.
9:13

 Christopher Gray
You need to report the problem on the IT support board instead of calling.
9:13

Rachel Harris
Oh, I didn't know that. _____
9:14

 Christopher Gray
Yes, because IT staff can't answer the phone all the time.
9:13

① I have already talked to the IT support team.
② Maybe the way to report the problem has changed.
③ Have you experienced similar problems before?
④ Do you have access to the IT support board?

해석

Christopher Gray: 제 컴퓨터에서 내부 전산망에 접속할 수가 없네요.
Rachel Harris: 다른 웹사이트에는 접속할 수 있나요?
Christopher Gray: 네. 제대로 작동해요.
Rachel Harris: 이상하네요. 제가 기술지원팀에 전화해 볼게요.
Christopher Gray: 당신은 전화 대신 기술지원팀 게시판에 문제를 보고해야 해요.
Rachel Harris: 오, 몰랐어요. 아마 보고하는 방법이 바뀌었나 보네요.
Christopher Gray: 네, 기술지원팀 직원들이 언제나 전화를 받을 수 있는 건 아니라서요.

① 저는 기술지원팀과 이미 얘기한걸요.
② 아마 보고하는 방법이 바뀌었나 보네요.
③ 전에도 비슷한 문제를 겪은 적이 있나요?
④ 기술지원팀 게시판에 대한 접근권이 있나요?

해설

내부 전산망에 접속할 수 없는 문제로 기술지원팀에 전화해 보겠다는 Rachel에게 Christopher가 전화 대신 게시판으로 문제를 보고해야 함을 알려 주고, 빈칸 뒤에서 다시 Christopher가 Yes, because IT staff can't answer the phone all the time(네, 기술지원팀 직원들이 언제나 전화를 받을 수 있는 건 아니라서요)이라고 말하고 있으므로, '아마 보고하는 방법이 바뀌었나 보네요'라는 의미의 ② 'Maybe the way to solve the problem has changed'가 정답이다.

정답 ②

어휘

intranet 내부 전산망   properly 제대로, 적절하게   weird 이상한, 기이한

05~06 다음 글을 읽고 물음에 답하시오.

(A)

With the expansion of the city, local wildlife habitats are in danger.

The need for more land for housing is causing the rapid demolition of parts of the Red Forest. We need to protect this unique area and the animals that call it home.

DAY 01 하프모의고사 01회

The Red Forest Conservation League has taken a leading role in this fight. The group is holding an information session and fundraiser to help reach its goal. Attend to show your support and do your part for nature.

Can you imagine the area without its beautiful forests and special wildlife?

- Location: Grimley Central Park (in the event of snow: Joseph Caldwell Community Center)
- Date: Sunday, January 12
- Time: 11:00 a.m.

To volunteer to assist the group or to make a donation, please visit www.redforestleague.com or call (212) 555-9711.

해석

(A) Red 숲을 살리도록 도와주세요

도시 확장으로 인해, 현지 야생 동물 서식지가 위험에 처해 있습니다. 주택을 위한 더 많은 토지에 대한 필요성이 Red 숲 일부의 급격한 파괴를 야기하고 있습니다. 우리는 이 고유한 지역과 이곳을 보금자리로 삼는 동물들을 보호해야 합니다.

Red 숲 보존 협회는 이 싸움에서 주도적인 역할을 맡아 왔습니다. 단체는 목표를 달성하도록 돕기 위해 설명회와 모금 행사를 개최할 것입니다. 참석하셔서 여러분의 지지를 보여 주세요, 그리고 자연을 위해 여러분의 본분을 다해 주세요.

아름다운 숲과 특별한 야생 동물이 없는 그 지역을 상상할 수 있으신가요?

- 장소: Grimley 중앙 공원 (눈이 올 경우 Joseph Caldwell 시민 문화 회관)
- 날짜: 1월 12일 일요일
- 시간: 오전 11시

단체를 돕기 위해 자원봉사를 하시거나 기부를 하시려면, www.redforestleague.com으로 방문 또는 (212) 555-9711로 전화 주세요.

어휘

expansion 확장, 팽창 wildlife 야생 동물 habitat 서식지
demolition 파괴, 철거 conservation 보존, 보전
take a leading role 주도적인 역할을 맡다 information session 설명회
fundraiser 모금 행사 do one's part 자신의 본분을 다하다
in the event of ~의 경우에 donation 기부, 기증

05 독해 제목 파악   난이도 중 ●●○

(A)에 들어갈 윗글의 제목으로 가장 적절한 것은?

① Conserve Energy to Help Wildlife
② Make the City Great Again
③ Meet the Area's Unique Plants and Animals
④ Help Save the Red Forest

해석
① 야생 동물을 돕기 위해 에너지를 절약하세요
② 도시를 다시 위대하게 만드세요
③ 그 지역의 고유한 식물과 동물들을 만나 보세요
④ Red 숲을 살리도록 도와주세요

해설
지문 앞부분에서 주택 토지 개발이 Red 숲 일부의 파괴를 야기하고 있으므로, 이 고유한 지역과 이곳에 사는 동식물들을 보호하기 위해 지지를 보여 달라고 요청하고 있다. 따라서 ④ 'Red 숲을 살리도록 도와주세요'가 이 글의 제목이다.

정답 ④

어휘
conserve 절약하다, 보존하다

06 독해 유의어 파악   난이도 중 ●●○

밑줄 친 "show"의 의미와 가장 가까운 것은?

① present
② guide
③ depict
④ teach

해석
① 드러내다
② 안내하다
③ 묘사하다
④ 가르치다

해설
밑줄 친 부분이 포함된 문장에서 show는 문맥상 지지를 '보여 주다'라는 의미로 쓰였으므로, '드러내다'라는 의미의 ① present가 정답이다.

정답 ①

어휘
present 드러내다, 증정하다; 존재하는; 선물 depict 묘사하다

07 독해 내용 불일치 파악   난이도 하 ●○○

다음 이메일의 내용과 일치하지 않는 것은?

To	rentals@reveretheater.com
From	tinamurphey@speedmail.com
Date	April 6
Subject	Venue rental inquiry

Dear Sir,

I am writing to inquire about renting the Revere Theater for a movie premiere in October. Any evening on Friday or Saturday that month would work. The event will last four hours: one hour for arrival and appetizers, two hours for the movie, and one hour for a Q&A session with the cast and crew after the showing. We are currently expecting around 300 guests.

We plan to hire an event planning firm to handle ticketing, transportation, photography, and catering, which we hope to host in your main lobby as part of a stand-up event. To manage the actual film showing, we would like to hire a technician familiar with your venue and its equipment. Could you please recommend someone?

I look forward to your response.

Sincerely,

Tina Murphey

① 영화 시사회는 10월에 있을 예정이다.
② 행사는 4시간 동안 진행될 것이다.
③ 케이터링 서비스는 로비에서 즐길 수 있다.
④ 추천하는 기술자 명단이 첨부되어 있다.

해석

수신: rentals@reveretheater.com
발신: tinamurphey@speedmail.com
날짜: 4월 6일
제목: 장소 대여 문의

친애하는 귀하,

10월의 영화 시사회를 위해 Revere 극장을 대관하는 것에 대해 문의하고자 연락드립니다. 해당 월의 금요일 또는 토요일의 어느 저녁 시간이든 가능합니다. 행사는 4시간 동안 진행될 예정인데, 입장과 전채 요리를 위한 한 시간, 영화에 두 시간, 그리고 영화 상영 후 출연진 및 제작진과의 질의응답을 위한 한 시간을 포함합니다. 저희는 현재 약 300명의 손님을 예상하고 있습니다.

저희는 입장권, 교통편, 사진 촬영, 그리고 서서 하는 행사의 일부로써 메인 로비에서 진행하기를 희망하는, 케이터링 관련 업무를 처리할 행사 기획 업체를 고용할 계획입니다. 실제 영화 상영을 관리하기 위해, 귀하의 극장과 장비에 익숙한 기술자를 고용하고 싶습니다. 누군가를 추천해 주실 수 있을까요?

귀하의 답변을 기다리겠습니다.

진심을 담아,

Tina Murphey

해설

④번의 키워드인 '기술자'를 그대로 언급한 지문의 technician 주변의 내용에서 Revere 극장과 장비에 익숙한 기술자를 추천해 달라고 요청하고 있으므로, ④ '추천하는 기술자 명단이 첨부되어 있다'는 지문의 내용과 다르다.

정답 ④

어휘

venue (행사 등의) 장소 inquiry 문의하다 premiere 시사회
appetizer 전채 요리 cast 출연진 crew 제작진 firm 업체
transportation 교통(편), 운송 host 진행하다, 주최하다; 주최(측)
technician 기술자

---

08 독해 무관한 문장 삭제   난이도 중 ●●○

다음 글의 흐름상 어색한 문장은?

Día de los Muertos, or the Day of the Dead, is a Mexican holiday celebrated on November 1 and 2. This special time honoring the dead is joyful rather than somber, as it is believed that the spirits of loved ones can come back to earth for one night. ① During the holiday, families gather together to remember those they have lost by setting up decorated tables to them. ② These are covered in offerings to welcome and refresh the spirits after their arduous journey back to the world of the living. ③ People also dress up like skeletons and celebrate with their neighbors in the streets and town squares. ④ Most Mexican towns were built around a grand plaza that acts as a meeting place and site of celebrations and official events. Today, the holiday is even observed internationally in places with large Mexican populations.

해석

'Día de los Muertos' 또는 죽은 자들의 날은 11월 1일과 2일에 기념되는 멕시코의 축제이다. 죽은 사람들을 기리는 이 특별한 기간은 침울하기보다는 유쾌한데, 이는 사랑하는 사람들의 영혼이 하룻밤 동안 이승으로 돌아올 수 있다고 여겨지기 때문이다. ① 축제 동안, 가족들은 함께 모여 그들이 잃은 사람들을 위한 장식 탁자를 설치함으로써 그들을 기억한다. ② 이것들은 산 자들의 세계로 돌아오는 영혼들의 고된 여행 후에 그들을 환영하고 생기를 되찾게 하는 제물로 뒤덮인다. ③ 사람들은 또한 해골처럼 변장하고 길거리와 마을 광장에서 이웃들과 기념한다. ④ 대부분의 멕시코 마을들은 모임 장소와 기념 및 공식 행사의 장소 역할을 하는 대광장 주변에 지어졌다. 오늘날, 그 축제는 심지어 많은 멕시코 사람들이 모인 장소들에서 국제적으로 관찰된다.

해설

지문 앞부분에서 사랑하는 사람들의 영혼이 이승으로 돌아올 수 있다고 여겨지는 멕시코의 축제 '죽은 자들의 날'을 소개하고, ①, ②, ③번에서 이 축제를 기념하기 위해 사람들이 행하는 의식들을 설명하고 있다. 그러나 ④번은 '주로 대광장 주변에 지어지는 멕시코 마을들'에 대한 내용으로, 지문 앞부분의 내용과 관련이 없다.

정답 ④

어휘

celebrate 기념하다, 축하하다 honor 기리다, 존경하다 somber 침울한
offering 제물, 제공된 것 arduous 고된, 몹시 힘든
dress up 변장하다, 옷을 갖춰 입다 skeleton 해골 square 광장, 정사각형
act as ~의 역할을 하다

---

09 독해 문단 순서 배열   난이도 중 ●●○

주어진 글 다음에 이어질 글의 순서로 적절한 것은?

Samuel Morse is famous for inventing Morse Code. However, he did not initially set out to be a telecommunications pioneer or an inventor.

DAY 01 하프모의고사 01회

(A) While there, he gained admission to the Royal Academy, where he received artistic education. Upon his return to the United States three years later, Morse took up art as a full-time career.

(B) In fact, he studied philosophy, mathematics, and the science of horses while at Yale. But none of these seemed to be his calling. After graduation, Morse traveled to England to study European art.

(C) He was so successful in his chosen profession that he was commissioned to paint the president and other aristocrats. It was not until he was in his 40s that he became interested in electrical signaling devices and devised the system for sending messages using electrical dots and dashes now known as Morse code.

① (A) – (B) – (C)
② (B) – (A) – (C)
③ (B) – (C) – (A)
④ (C) – (B) – (A)

해석

새뮤얼 모스는 모스 부호를 발명한 것으로 유명하다. 하지만, 그가 처음에 통신의 개척자 또는 발명가가 되기 위해 시도한 것은 아니었다.

(A) 그곳에 있으면서, 그는 영국 왕립 미술원에 입학 허가를 받았고, 이곳에서 그는 미술 교육을 받았다. 3년 뒤 미국으로 돌아오자마자, 모스는 정규직 직업으로 미술을 시작했다.

(B) 사실, 그는 예일 대학에 있는 동안 철학, 수학 그리고 말에 대한 학문을 공부했다. 그러나 이것들 중 아무것도 그의 천직처럼 보이지 않았다. 졸업 후, 모스는 유럽 미술을 공부하기 위해 영국으로 여행을 갔다.

(C) 그는 자신이 선택한 직업에 있어 매우 성공해서 대통령과 다른 귀족들을 그려 달라고 의뢰받았다. 그는 40대가 되고 나서야 전기 신호 장치에 관심이 생겼고 오늘날 모스 부호라고 알려진, 전기를 이용하는 점과 대시를 사용한 메시지 전송을 위한 체계를 고안했다.

해설

주어진 문장에서 모스 부호로 유명한 새뮤얼 모스는 처음에 통신 관련 발명가가 되기 위해 시도하지는 않았다고 언급한 뒤, (B)에서 사실(In fact) 그는 대학에서 철학, 수학, 말에 대한 학문을 공부한 후 유럽 미술을 공부하기 위해 영국으로 갔다고 설명하고 있다. 이어서 (A)에서 그곳(there)에서 교육을 받은 뒤 미국에 돌아와서 정규 직업으로 미술을 시작했다고 하고, (C)에서 자신이 선택한 직업(his chosen profession)에서 성공한 그는 40대가 되어서야 모스 부호를 고안했다고 알려 주고 있다. 따라서 ② (B) – (A) – (C)가 정답이다.

정답 ②

어휘

initially 처음에 **set out** ~을 시도하다, 착수하다
telecommunication 통신 **pioneer** 개척자, 선구자
gain admission 입학 허가를 받다 **take up** ~을 시작하다
calling 천직, 소명 **graduation** 졸업 **profession** 직업
commission 의뢰하다; 위원회, 수수료 **aristocrat** 귀족
electrical 전기의, 전기를 이용하는 **devise** 고안하다

---

10 독해 빈칸 완성 – 절   난이도 중 ●●○

밑줄 친 부분에 들어갈 말로 적절한 것은?

Fast fashion is a relatively new concept in the fashion industry in which discount retailers take high-end designer looks and recreate them at a much lower price point. The garments they produce are often simplified or made with lower-quality fabric and hardware, which allows them to be sold for a fraction of the cost of designer goods. While this may seem like a benefit for those who cannot afford to buy expensive brand-name clothing, many consider fast fashion to be bad for the less affluent considering maintenance cost. The inferior quality of the products shows that _____ _____, as they often wear out rather quickly and must be replaced or thrown out.

① the genius of a design can't be copied
② designers are charging too much for their clothing
③ fast fashion is damaging the clothing industry
④ paying less initially doesn't always indicate saving

해석

패스트 패션은 할인 소매업체들이 고급 디자이너의 디자인을 가져와 그것들을 훨씬 더 저렴한 가격대로 재현하는, 패션 산업에서 비교적 새로운 개념이다. 그들이 생산하는 옷은 보통 간소화되고, 더 낮은 질의 직물과 쇠붙이류로 만들어지는데, 이는 그것들이 디자이너 상품 가격의 몇 분의 일로 판매되도록 해 준다. 이것이 값비싼 유명 상표가 붙은 옷을 살 여유가 없는 사람들에게 혜택인 것처럼 보일지도 모르지만, 많은 사람들은 패스트 패션이 유지 비용을 고려하면 덜 부유한 사람들에게 좋지 않다고 생각한다. 그 상품들의 더 낮은 품질은 <u>처음에 돈이 덜 드는 것이 항상 절약을 의미하는 것은 아니라는 것</u>을 보여 주는데, 이는 그것들이 대개 꽤 빨리 낡아서 교체되거나 버려져야 하기 때문이다.

① 디자인의 천재성은 표절될 수 없다
② 디자이너들은 자신들의 옷에 너무 많은 값을 매기고 있다
③ 패스트 패션은 의류 산업에 해를 입히고 있다
④ 처음에 돈이 덜 드는 것이 항상 절약을 의미하는 것은 아니다

해설

빈칸 앞 문장에 많은 사람들은 유지 비용을 고려하면 패스트 패션이 덜 부유한 사람들에게 좋지 않다고 생각한다는 내용이 있고, 빈칸 뒷부분에 패스트 패션 상품들은 꽤 빨리 낡아서 교체되거나 버려져야 한다는 내용이 있으므로, 패스트 패션 상품의 낮은 질은 '처음에 돈이 덜 드는 것이 항상 절약을 의미하는 것은 아니'라는 것을 보여 준다고 한 ④번이 정답이다.

정답 ④

어휘

relatively 비교적 **retailer** 소매업체, 소매상 **high-end** 고급의
recreate 재현하다, 되살리다 **garment** 옷 **fabric** 직물
hardware 쇠붙이류, 금속 제품 **a fraction of** 몇 분의 일 **affluent** 부유한
maintenance 유지, 보수 관리 **inferior** 더 낮은, 열등한
wear out (낡아서) 떨어지다 **rather** 꽤, 오히려 **throw out** ~을 버리다
genius 천재(성) **charge** 값을 매기다, 충전하다

DAY 02 하프모의고사 02회

정답
p. 18

01	②	어휘	06	②	독해
02	④	문법	07	③	문법
03	②	생활영어	08	④	독해
04	②	독해	09	③	독해
05	②	독해	10	①	독해

취약영역 분석표

영역	맞힌 답의 개수
어휘	/1
생활영어	/1
문법	/2
독해	/6
TOTAL	/10

---

01 어휘 impractical 난이도 중 ●●○

밑줄 친 부분에 들어갈 말로 적절한 것은?

Implementing the changes he proposed right now is _____ as there hasn't been nearly enough time to fully test the updates.

① current
② impractical
③ progressive
④ possible

[해석]
그가 제안한 변화를 당장 실행하는 것은 비현실적인데, 이는 변경 사항들을 완전히 시험할 충분한 시간이 거의 없었기 때문이다.
① 현재의
② 비현실적인
③ 혁신적인
④ 가능한

정답 ②

[어휘]
implement 실행하다 propose 제안하다 current 현재의, 지금의
impractical 비현실적인, 터무니없는 progressive 혁신적인, 진보적인
possible 가능한

---

02 문법 조동사 난이도 중 ●●○

밑줄 친 부분에 들어갈 말로 적절한 것은?

The detective working on the recent murder case says he has determined that the suspect _____ present at the crime scene because surveillance footage confirmed she was across town at the exact time of the incident.

① cannot be
② will not be
③ should not have been
④ could not have been

[해석]
최근의 그 살인 사건에 대해 알아보던 형사는 용의자가 사건이 있었던 바로 그 시간에 마을 반대편에 있었음이 감시 영상에 의해 확인되었기 때문에 그녀가 범죄 현장에 있었을 리 없다고 판단했다고 말한다.

[해설]
④ 조동사 관련 표현 빈칸은 동사 has determined의 목적어로 온 that 절의 동사 자리이다. 문맥상 '그는 그녀가 범죄 현장에 있었을 리 없다고 판단했다'라는 의미가 되어야 자연스러운데, '~했을 리가 없다'는 조동사 관련 표현 couldn't have p.p.를 사용하여 나타낼 수 있으므로 ④ could not have been이 정답이다.

정답 ④

[어휘]
detective 형사 murder case 살인 사건 suspect 용의자; 의심하다
present 있는, 현재의; 주다 surveillance 감시 footage 영상, 장면

---

03 생활영어 I should help him adjust and learn quickly. 난이도 하 ●○○

밑줄 친 부분에 들어갈 말로 적절한 것은?

A: You look upset. What's wrong?
B: It's my new secretary. He keeps messing up my schedule.
A: Did you miss anything important?
B: No. It's just really frustrating, though.
A: Well, give him some time. He's still learning your style.
B: You're right. Instead of grumbling about it, _____
_____

① I'm trying my hardest to help him.
② I should help him adjust and learn quickly.
③ a severe warning will be the only good solution.
④ an experienced secretary has agreed to join us soon.

DAY 02 하프모의고사 02회

해석

A: 너 좀 화나 보이는데. 무슨 일이야?
B: 새로 온 비서 때문에 그래. 그가 내 일정을 계속 엉망으로 만들고 있어.
A: 뭐 중요한 일이라도 놓쳤어?
B: 아니. 그래도 그냥 너무 답답해서.
A: 음, 그에게 시간을 좀 줘. 그는 네 방식을 아직 배우는 중이잖아.
B: 네 말이 맞아. 그것에 대해 투덜거리기보다, <u>그가 빨리 적응하고 배우도록 도와야 하겠지.</u>

① 나는 그를 돕기 위해 최선을 다하고 있어.
② 그가 빨리 적응하고 배우도록 도와야 하겠지.
③ 엄격한 경고만이 좋은 해결책일 거야.
④ 숙련된 비서 한 명이 곧 합류하기로 했어.

해설

새로 온 비서는 B의 업무 방식을 아직 배우는 중이므로 시간이 필요하다는 A의 조언에 대해 B가 빈칸 앞에서 You're right(네 말이 맞아)이라고 동의하고 있으므로, '그가 빨리 적응하고 배우도록 도와야 하겠지'라는 의미의 ② 'I should help him adjust and learn quickly'가 정답이다.

정답 ②

어휘

secretary 비서 mess up ~을 엉망으로 만들다
frustrating 답답하게 하는, 불만스러운 grumble 투덜거리다, 넋두리하다
adjust 적응하다, 조정하다 severe 엄격한, 심각한 warning 경고
experienced 숙련된, 경험 많은

---

04 독해 목적 파악 난이도 하 ●○○

다음 글의 목적으로 적절한 것은?

To: customers@TravelGurus.com
From: alerts@TravelGurus.com
Date: October 14
Subject: Holiday travel

Dear Travel Lovers,

With the holiday travel season approaching, flight prices are rising. At Travel Gurus, we know you want to save money, so we've come up with a list of ways to get the best deals on flights. Use these tips and you can save on your holiday travel:

1. Book early to avoid last-minute price increases.
2. Be flexible and consider traveling on weekdays, when prices are lower.
3. Compare offers on different airlines and routes including those with longer layovers, which tend to be cheaper.
4. Fly into an airport near your destination if possible. Even with the required ground transportation, it can sometimes cost less overall.

These tips should help you save money, but our travel experts are here to help, too. Just call Travel Gurus, and one of our agents will be glad to help you find the best flights within your budget.

Happy Travels,
Travel Gurus

① to tell customers about an increase in airfare
② to explain methods for reducing flight expenses
③ to inform travelers about optimal booking times
④ to highlight the benefits of ground transportation

해석

수신: customers@TravelGurus.com
발신: alerts@TravelGurus.com
날짜: 10월 14일
제목: 휴가 여행철

여행 애호가 여러분께,

휴가 여행철이 다가옴에 따라, 항공권 가격이 오르고 있습니다. Travel Gurus에서는 여러분이 돈을 절약하길 원한다는 것을 알고 있기에, 항공권에 대한 최선의 구매에 성공할 수 있는 방법 목록을 제안드립니다. 이 조언들을 활용하시면 여러분은 휴가 여행에서 절약하실 수 있습니다.

1. 마지막 순간의 가격 인상을 피하기 위해 일찍 예약하세요.
2. 융통성 있게 대응하시고 가격이 더 낮은 때인 평일에 여행하는 것을 고려하세요.
3. 더 저렴한 경향의 경유 시간이 더 긴 것들을 포함하여, 다양한 항공사와 노선의 제안(항공권)들을 비교하세요.
4. 가능하시면 목적지 근처의 공항으로 비행하세요. 필요한 육로 교통수단까지 감안하면, 그것은 종종 전반적으로 비용이 덜 들 수 있습니다.

이 조언들은 귀하께서 돈을 절약하시도록 돕겠지만, 저희 여행 전문가들도 도움을 드리기 위해 여기 있습니다. Travel Gurus에 전화하시기만 하면 저희 상담원 중 한 명이 귀하의 예산 내에서 최고의 항공편을 찾는 데 기꺼이 도움드릴 것입니다.

즐거운 여행이 되시기를 바라며,
Travel Gurus

① 고객에게 항공료 인상에 대해 알리려고
② 항공권 지출을 줄일 방법을 설명하려고
③ 여행자들에게 최적의 예약 시간대를 알려 주려고
④ 육로 교통수단의 이점을 강조하려고

해설

지문 앞부분에서 항공료가 인상되는 휴가 여행철에 최선의 항공권 구매로 비용을 절약할 수 있는 방법들을 제안한다고 했으므로, ② '항공권 지출을 줄일 방법을 설명하려고'가 이 글의 목적이다.

정답 ②

어휘

come up with ~을 제안하다, 생각해내다 flexible 융통성 있는, 유연한
compare 비교하다 layover 경유 destination 목적지 expert 전문가
budget 예산 airfare 항공료 optimal 최적의, 최선의 highlight 강조하다

05~06 다음 글을 읽고 물음에 답하시오.

Dance-A-Thon
http://ChildhoodCancer.org/Dance-a-thon

HOME ABOUT DANCE-A-THON FAQ   🔍 SEARCH

HOME > DANCE-A-THON

[A]

July is Childhood Cancer Awareness Month. Each year, university students hold 48-hour dance marathons during which they dance continuously without sitting or sleeping. These events not only bring attention to those who suffer from the disease but also raise funds for their treatment. By soliciting donations from sponsors, participants raise millions of dollars each year.

The student dance-a-thons began at Pennsylvania State University in 1973 but have since spread to universities across the country. Shorter versions are now also held for high school and elementary school students who wish to help out as well.

This devastating disease affects more than 15,000 young people each year. But thanks to research funded in part by the dance-a-thons, survival rates are steadily increasing.

Do your part to help childhood cancer sufferers.

How will you help?
☐ Take part in a dance-a-thon
☐ Volunteer to organize an event
☐ Sponsor a dancer for $5 per hour
☐ Direct cash donation

Dancer Sponsorship:
☐ I would like to sponsor _____ (dancer name) for _____ hours of dancing.

Direct Cash Donations:
☐ $25   ☐ $50   ☐ $75   ☐ Other: _____

해석

(A) 소아암에 맞서는 데 함께하세요

7월은 소아암 인식의 달입니다. 매년 대학생들은 앉거나 잠을 안 자고 계속해서 춤을 추는 48시간의 댄스 마라톤을 개최합니다. 이러한 행사들은 질병으로 고통받는 사람들에게 관심을 가져올 뿐만 아니라 그들의 치료를 위한 기금을 모읍니다. 참가자들은 후원자들로부터 기부금을 간청하여, 매년 수백만 달러를 마련합니다.

학생 댄스 마라톤은 1973년에 펜실베이니아 주립 대학에서 시작되었지만, 이후 전국의 대학으로 확산되어 왔습니다. 이제는 도움을 주고자 하는 고등학생과 초등학생들을 위한 짧은 버전도 개최됩니다.

이 치명적인 질병은 매년 15,000명 이상의 젊은이들에게 영향을 미칩니다. 그러나 댄스 마라톤을 통해 일부 자금을 지원받는 연구 덕분에, 생존율이 꾸준히 상승하고 있습니다.

소아암 환자들을 돕기 위해 여러분의 역할을 해 주세요.

어떻게 도움을 주시겠습니까?
☐ 댄스 마라톤에 참여하기
☐ 행사 준비를 위한 자원봉사하기
☐ 시간당 5달러로 댄서를 후원하기
☐ 직접 현금 기부하기

댄서 후원:
☐ 저는 _____ (댄서 이름)을(를) 춤추는 _____ 시간에 대해 후원하고 싶습니다.

직접 현금 기부하기:
☐ 25달러   ☐ 50달러   ☐ 75달러   ☐ 다른 금액: _____

어휘

solicit 간청하다, 요청하다   **devastating** 치명적인, 파괴적인

---

05 독해 제목 파악   난이도 중 ●●○

(A)에 들어갈 윗글의 제목으로 적절한 것은?

① Development of Childhood Cancer Treatment
② Join the Fight against Childhood Cancer
③ Learn about Ways to Prevent Diseases in Children
④ Signs of Cancer in Young People

해석

① 소아암 치료법의 개발
② 소아암에 맞서는 데 함께하세요
③ 어린이의 질병 예방 방법에 대해 알아보세요
④ 젊은이들에게서 암이 발생하는 징후

해설

지문 앞부분에서 소아암 치료 기금 마련을 위한 대학생 댄스 마라톤이 개최된다고 하고, 지문 중간에서 소아암 환자들을 돕기 위해 자신의 역할을 해 달라고 권하고 있으므로, ② '소아암에 맞서는 데 함께하세요'가 이 글의 제목이다.

정답 ②

---

06 독해 내용 불일치 파악   난이도 중 ●●○

윗글에서 캠페인에 관한 내용과 일치하지 않는 것은?

① 이틀 내내 계속된다.
② 펜실베이니아 대학이 매년 수백만 달러를 후원한다.
③ 청소년들을 위한 별도의 행사가 준비되어 있다.
④ 기부는 두 가지 방법으로 할 수 있다.

해설

②번의 키워드인 '수백만 달러'가 그대로 언급된 지문의 millions of dollars 주변의 내용에서 참가자들은 후원자들로부터 기부금을 간청하여 매년 수백만 달러를 마련한다고 했으므로, ② '펜실베이니아 대학이 매년 수백만 달러

를 후원한다'는 지문의 내용과 다르다.

정답 ②

07 문법 병치 구문 | 수동태 | 명사절 | 분사 난이도 중 ●●○

밑줄 친 부분 중 어법상 옳은 것은?

> Education experts are ① interesting in the effects of e-book reading on comprehension. Despite the improved quality of digital books and their low cost, many wonder ② that reading from paper might be more beneficial than reading an electronic file. One reason for this is that reading text on screens irritates the eyes and ③ makes reading uncomfortable. Another reason is that many find e-book reading ④ highly distracted due to pop-up notifications.

해석

교육 전문가들은 전자책 읽기가 이해력에 미치는 영향에 대해 흥미로워한다. 디지털 책의 향상된 질과 낮은 비용에도 불구하고, 다수는 종이로 읽는 것이 전자 파일을 읽는 것보다 더 유익할 수 있을지 궁금해한다. 이것의 한 가지 이유는 화면의 텍스트를 읽는 것이 눈을 자극하고 읽기를 불편하게 만들 수 있다는 것이다. 또 다른 이유는 많은 이들이 전자책 읽기가 팝업 알림으로 인해 매우 주의를 산만하게 함을 알게 된다는 것이다.

해설

③ 병치 구문 접속사(and)로 연결된 병치 구문에서는 같은 구조끼리 연결되어야 하는데, and 앞에 단수 동사 irritates가 왔으므로 and 뒤에도 단수 동사 makes가 올바르게 쓰였다.

[오답 분석]
① 3형식 동사의 수동태 감정을 나타내는 동사(interest)는 주어가 감정의 원인이면 능동태를, 감정을 느끼는 주체이면 수동태를 쓰는데, 문맥상 '교육 전문가들은 흥미로워한다'라는 의미로 주어 Education experts가 감정을 느끼는 주체이므로, 현재분사 interesting을 be 동사(are)와 함께 수동태를 완성하는 과거분사 interested로 고쳐야 한다.
② 명사절 접속사 문맥상 '다수가 불확실한 사실(종이로 읽는 것이 전자 파일을 읽는 것보다 더 유익할 수 있을지)에 대해 궁금해한다'는 의미가 되어야 자연스러운데, 명사절 접속사 that은 확실한 사실을 나타내므로 의미상 적절하지 않다. 따라서 명사절 접속사 that을 불확실한 사실을 나타내는 명사절 접속사 if / whether(~인지 아닌지)로 고쳐야 한다.
④ 현재분사 vs. 과거분사 분사가 목적격 보어일 경우 목적어와 보어가 능동 관계면 현재분사, 수동 관계면 과거분사를 쓰는데, 목적어 e-book reading과 보어가 '전자책 읽기가 주의를 산만하게 하다'라는 의미의 능동 관계이므로 과거분사 distracted를 현재분사 distracting으로 고쳐야 한다. 참고로, 부사(highly)는 형용사를 앞에서 수식하므로 분사 앞에 쓰였다.

정답 ③

어휘

irritate 자극하다, 짜증나게 하다 distract 주의를 산만하게 하다

08 독해 무관한 문장 삭제 난이도 중 ●●○

다음 글의 흐름상 어색한 문장은?

> Representative money includes checks, debit cards, and credit cards, which are a type of money that represents actual currency. It has no value as a physical object but is useful when carrying large sums of money is inconvenient and enables more secure digital transactions. ① The value of representative money is that it can be used to pay for something even when one does not have cash on their person. ② Unlike cash that can be stolen or lost, these payment methods offer security features like PIN protection and fraud monitoring. ③ Digital transactions also create traceable records, providing protection against unauthorized use and enabling dispute resolution. ④ Furthermore, the advantage of paying with cash is that the transaction can proceed more quickly. As technology advances, these digital payment methods continue to evolve with additional security features like biometric authentication and instant fraud alerts, making them increasingly preferred over actual currency.

해석

대표 화폐는 수표, 직불 카드 및 신용 카드를 포함하는데, 이것들은 실제 화폐를 대신하는 돈의 형태이다. 그것은 물리적인 물체만으로는 가치가 없지만 많은 양의 돈을 들고 다니는 것이 불편할 때 유용하고 더 많은 안전한 디지털 거래를 가능하게 한다. ① 대표 화폐의 가치는 현금을 몸에 지니고 있지 않을 때조차도 무언가의 값을 지불하기 위해 사용될 수 있다는 점이다. ② 도난이나 분실될 수 있는 현금과 달리, 이러한 결제 수단은 PIN 보호 및 사기 감시와 같은 보안 기능을 제공한다. ③ 디지털 거래는 또한 추적 가능한 기록을 생성하는데, 이는 무단 사용에 대한 보호를 제공하고 분쟁 해결을 가능하게 한다. ④ 더 나아가, 현금으로 지불하는 것의 이점은 거래가 더욱 빠르게 진행될 수 있다는 것이다. 기술이 발전함에 따라, 이러한 디지털 결제 방식들은 생체 인증과 즉각적인 사기 경보와 같은 추가적인 보안 기능과 함께 계속해서 진화하고 있는데, 이는 그것들이 실제 화폐보다 점점 더 선호되도록 만든다.

해설

지문 앞부분에서 실제 화폐를 대신하는 돈의 형태인 대표 화폐는 현금이 불편할 때 유용하고 더 안전한 디지털 거래를 가능하게 한다고 언급한 뒤, ①, ②, ③번에서 '현금에 비해 대표 화폐가 가진 구체적인 장점들'에 대해 설명하고 있다. 그러나 ④번은 '현금 거래의 이점'에 대한 내용으로, 지문 앞부분의 내용과 관련이 없다.

정답 ④

어휘

debit card 직불 카드, 현금 카드 credit card 신용 카드
currency 화폐, 통화 transaction 거래 fraud 사기
traceable 추적 가능한 unauthorized 무단의, 승인되지 않은
dispute 분쟁; 반박하다 resolution 해결, 결심 biometric 생체 (측정)의
authentication 인증, 증명 instant 즉각적인 alert 경보; 기민한

09 독해 문장 삽입   난이도 중 ●●○

주어진 문장이 들어갈 위치로 적절한 것은?

Unfortunately, the sink was made of plastic and the tin set it on fire.

In a science laboratory in the 1970s, a teacher was demonstrating to his students what happens in a thermite reaction. (①) By accident, a single spark from a burner landed in a tin can of magnesium, which should have been closed but had been left open. (②) The teacher grabbed the tin and threw it in the sink, thinking to put the fire out with water. (③) The teacher then picked up a fire blanket to cover it but that too caught fire, effectively blocking the only exit in the room. (④) Everyone did manage to get out; needless to say, the rules for laboratory use were revised and flammable items were summarily replaced.

해석

유감스럽게도, 그 싱크대는 플라스틱으로 만들어져 있어서 그 통은 싱크대에 불을 붙였다.

1970년대의 한 과학 실험실에서, 한 교사가 학생들에게 테르밋 반응에서 어떤 일이 일어나는지 보여 주고 있었다. ① 우연히 화로에서 나온 불꽃 하나가 마그네슘 통에 떨어졌는데, 이 통은 닫혀 있었어야 했지만 열려 있던 것이었다. ② 교사는 물로 불을 끌 생각으로 통을 잡아서 싱크대에 던졌다. ③ 그러고 나서 교사는 그것을 덮기 위해 방화용 모포를 집어 들었지만, 그것 역시 불이 붙어서, 교실에 있는 유일한 출구를 사실상 막았다. ④ 모두가 가까스로 빠져나갔고, 말할 필요도 없이, 실험실 사용 규칙이 개정되고 인화성 물품은 즉시 교체되었다.

해설

③번 앞 문장에 교사는 물로 불을 끌 생각으로 불이 붙은 통을 싱크대에 던졌다는 내용이 있고, 뒤 문장에 그러고 나서(then) 교사는 그것(it)을 덮기 위해 방화용 모포를 집어 들었지만 그것 역시 불이 붙어 출구를 막았다는 내용이 있으므로, ③번 자리에 유감스럽게도 그 싱크대(the sink)는 플라스틱으로 만들어져 있어서 불이 옮겨 붙었다는 내용, 즉 마그네슘 통에 붙은 불이 출구를 막을 정도로 커지게 된 과정을 설명하는 주어진 문장이 나와야 지문이 자연스럽게 연결된다.

정답 ③

어휘

tin 통 set on fire 불을 붙이다 laboratory 실험실
demonstrate 보여 주다, 입증하다 by accident 우연히 grab 잡다
put out fire 불을 끄다, (화재를) 진화하다 effectively 사실상, 효과적으로
flammable 인화성의, 불에 잘 타는 summarily 즉시, 즉석에서

10 독해 빈칸 완성 – 구   난이도 중 ●●○

밑줄 친 부분에 들어갈 말로 적절한 것은?

When I think back to the teachers I had in my school days, the one who stands out for me the most is my first-grade teacher. She was a kind, soft-voiced, and perceptive woman who always did her best for everyone in her class. And of all the likeable qualities she displayed, the one that was most extraordinary for me was her _____. This became especially clear when foreign students who spoke little English joined her class, of which I was one. She was extremely patient with us when we had difficulty reading, making sure we all had the chance to practice. She treated all the students in the same way and never favored some above the others. I felt comfortable around her because she had no biases. She will always be a great role model for me.

① sense of fairness
② style of communication
③ creative instructional technique
④ empathetic listening skills

해석

내가 학창 시절 있었던 선생님들에 대해 돌이켜 볼 때, 나에게 가장 돋보이는 사람은 내 1학년 선생님이다. 그녀는 항상 반의 모든 사람을 위해 최선을 다하는, 친절하고 부드러운 목소리를 가진 통찰력 있는 여성이었다. 그리고 그녀가 보여 준 모든 호감 가는 자질들 중에서, 나에게 가장 특별했던 것은 그녀의 공정한 감각이었다. 이것은 특히 영어를 거의 하지 못하는 외국인 학생들이 그녀의 수업에 참여했을 때 분명해졌는데, 나는 그중 하나였다. 그녀는 우리가 읽는 데 어려움을 겪었을 때, 우리 모두가 연습할 기회를 반드시 가지게 하면서 매우 인내심을 보였다. 그녀는 그 모든 학생들을 같은 방식으로 대했고 결코 어떤 학생들을 다른 학생들보다 편애한 적이 없었다. 그녀가 편견이 없었기 때문에 나는 그녀 가까이에서 편안함을 느꼈다. 그녀는 항상 나에게 훌륭한 역할 모델일 것이다.

① 공정한 감각
② 의사소통 방식
③ 창의적인 교육 방법
④ 공감하는 경청 기술

해설

빈칸 뒷부분에서 필자의 1학년 선생님은 영어를 거의 하지 못하는 외국인 학생들을 수업에서 같은 방식으로 대했고 결코 특정 학생을 편애한 적이 없었다고 했으므로, 그녀의 자질들 중에서 필자에게 가장 특별했던 것은 그녀의 '공정한 감각'이라고 한 ①번이 정답이다.

정답 ①

어휘

stand out 돋보이다, 뛰어나다 perceptive 통찰력 있는; 시각, 전망
likeable 호감이 가는, 마음에 드는 extraordinary 특별한, 비범한 bias 편견
instructional 교육의 empathetic 공감하는

DAY 03 하프모의고사 03회

정답
p. 22

01	②	어휘	06	④	독해
02	②	문법	07	③	독해
03	④	문법	08	④	독해
04	③	생활영어	09	③	독해
05	②	독해	10	③	독해

취약영역 분석표

영역	맞힌 답의 개수
어휘	/1
생활영어	/1
문법	/2
독해	/6
TOTAL	/10

---

01 어휘 address   난이도 중 ●●○

밑줄 친 부분에 들어갈 말로 적절한 것은?

Many civil rights activists believe that the government should ＿＿＿＿＿ problems caused by social injustice to create a more equal society.

① overlook   ② address
③ deny   ④ build

[해석]
많은 시민권 운동가들은 정부가 더 평등한 사회를 만들기 위해 사회적 불평등에 의해 야기된 문제들을 해결해야 한다고 생각한다.

① 간과하다   ② 해결하다
③ 부인하다   ④ 만들어내다

정답 ②

[어휘]
activist 운동가, 활동가 injustice 불평등, 부당함
overlook 간과하다, 못 본 체하다 address 해결하다, 연설하다; 주소
deny 부인하다 build 만들어내다, 짓다

---

02 문법 to 부정사   난이도 중 ●●○

밑줄 친 부분에 들어갈 말로 적절한 것은?

The controversial theory about climate change proved to ＿＿＿＿＿ related policies positively despite initial skepticism.

① influence   ② have influenced
③ be influenced   ④ have been influenced

[해석]
기후 변화에 대한, 논란의 여지가 있는 그 이론은 초기의 회의론에도 불구하고 관련 정책들에 긍정적으로 영향을 미친 것으로 입증되었다.

[해설]
② to 부정사의 형태 to 부정사가 가리키는 명사(The controversial theory)와 to 부정사가 '논란의 여지가 있는 그 이론이 영향을 미치다'라는 의미의 능동 관계이므로 to 부정사의 능동태를 완성하는 ① influence, ② have influenced가 정답 후보이다. 이때 '영향을 미친' 시점이 '(영향을 미친) 것으로 입증된' 시점보다 이전이므로, to 부정사의 능동태 완료형을 완성하는 ② have influenced가 정답이다.

정답 ②

[어휘]
controversial 논란의 여지가 있는 theory 이론 initial 초기의, 처음의
skepticism 회의론

---

03 문법 비교 구문|보어|전치사|주어   난이도 중 ●●○

밑줄 친 부분 중 어법상 옳지 않은 것은?

Parents in Scandinavia consider friluftsliv, the Nordic concept of being outdoors, ① fundamental to human beings. Therefore, they will give their children, even babies, ample time outdoors ② regardless of rain, snow, and freezing temperatures. ③ It is believed that exposure to inclement weather creates resilience and immunity in young children. Also, the more children are taught to enjoy the outdoors and live spontaneously, the ④ easiest they are to manage.

[해석]
스칸디나비아의 부모들은 야외에 있는 것에 대한 북유럽의 개념인 '프리루프트슬리프'가 인간에게 필수적이라고 믿는다. 그래서, 비, 눈 그리고 영하의 기온에도 불구하고 그들은 자신의 자녀들, 심지어 아기들에게도 충분한 야외 시간을 줄 것이다. 궂은 날씨에의 노출은 어린아이들에게 있어서 회복력과 면역력을 이끌어내는 것으로 보인다. 또한, 아이들이 야외 활동을 즐기면서 자발적으로 사는 것을 더 많이 배울수록, 그들은 관리하기 더 쉽다.

---

12 공무원시험전문 해커스공무원 gosi.Hackers.com

해설

④ **비교급** 문맥상 '아이들이 ~ 더 많이 배울수록, 그들은 관리하기 더 쉽다'라는 의미가 되어야 자연스러운데, '더 ~할수록, 더 -하다'는 비교급 표현 'the + 비교급(more) + 주어(children) + 동사(are taught) ~, the + 비교급 + 주어(they) + 동사(are) -'의 형태로 나타낼 수 있다. 따라서 최상급 easiest를 비교급 easier로 고쳐야 한다.

[오답 분석]

① **보어 자리** 5형식 동사 consider는 'consider + 목적어(*friluftsliv* ~ outdoors) + 목적격 보어'의 형태로 쓰이는데, 보어 자리에는 명사나 형용사 역할을 하는 것이 와야 하므로 형용사 fundamental이 올바르게 쓰였다.

② **전치사** 문맥상 '비, 눈 그리고 영하의 기온에도 불구하고'라는 의미가 되어야 자연스러우므로, 명사구(rain ~ temperatures) 앞에서 '~에도 불구하고'라는 의미를 나타낼 수 있는 전치사 regardless of 가 올바르게 쓰였다.

③ **가짜 주어 구문** that절(that exposure ~ young children)과 같이 긴 주어가 오면 진주어인 that절을 맨 뒤로 보내고 가주어 it이 주어 자리에 대신해서 쓰이므로, 가주어 It이 올바르게 쓰였다.

정답 ④

어휘

Nordic 북유럽의 fundamental 필수적인, 근본적인 ample 충분한, 풍부한
freezing 영하의, 너무나 추운 exposure 노출 inclement (날씨가) 궂은
resilience 회복력 immunity 면역력 spontaneously 자발적으로

---

04 생활영어 Do you have any particular menu in mind?
난이도 중 ●●○

밑줄 친 부분에 들어갈 말로 적절한 것은?

 Henry Cooper
Hi! I want to know about your catering services.
10:10

Emma Williams
Of course. How many people are you expecting?
10:11

 Henry Cooper
We're planning for about 150 attendees in our company conference center on June 15.
10:12

Emma Williams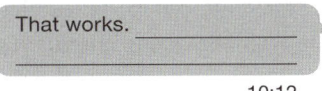
That works. _____
10:12

Henry Cooper
I saw your three-course formal dinner in the online reviews.
10:13

Emma Williams
In that case, we offer four different meal options. I can email you the options and pricing.
10:13

 Henry Cooper
It would be great if you could send it by today.
10:14

① What is your budget range for this service?
② Did you enjoy the meal options we provided?
③ Do you have any particular menu in mind?
④ Would you like to schedule this for lunchtime?

해석

Henry Cooper: 안녕하세요! 귀사의 케이터링 서비스에 대해 알고 싶어요.
Emma Williams: 물론입니다. 인원을 몇 명으로 예상하고 계세요?
Henry Cooper: 저희는 6월 15일에 회사 회의장에서 약 150명의 참석자를 계획하고 있습니다.
Emma Williams: 가능합니다. 특별히 염두에 둔 메뉴가 있으신가요?
Henry Cooper: 저는 인터넷 후기에서 세 가지 코스로 된 귀사의 저녁 정찬을 봤어요.
Emma Williams: 그 경우에, 저희는 네 가지의 서로 다른 식사 선택지를 제공합니다. 제가 그 선택지와 가격을 메일로 보내 드릴 수 있어요.
Henry Cooper: 그것을 오늘까지 보내 주신다면 정말 좋을 것 같습니다.

① 이 서비스를 위한 예산 범위가 어떻게 되나요?
② 저희가 제공했던 식사 선택지가 마음에 드셨나요?
③ 특별히 염두에 둔 메뉴가 있으신가요?
④ 점심 시간으로 일정을 잡으려 하시나요?

해설

6월 15일 회의장에서 약 150명이 참석하는 행사를 계획하고 있다는 Henry에게 Emma가 케이터링 서비스가 가능하다고 대답하고, 빈칸 뒤에서 다시 Henry가 I saw your three-course formal dinner in the online reviews(저는 인터넷 후기에서 세 가지 코스로 된 귀사의 저녁 정찬을 봤어요)라고 설명하고 있으므로, '특별히 염두에 둔 메뉴가 있으신가요?'라는 의미의 ③ 'Do you have any particular menu in mind?'가 정답이다.

정답 ③

어휘

attendee 참석자 budget 예산 range 범위

05~06 다음 글을 읽고 물음에 답하시오.

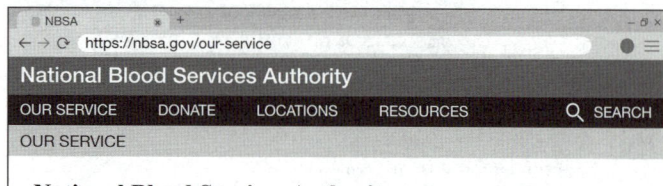

National Blood Services Authority

What We Do
We operate the largest network of blood banks in the country, collecting and testing blood before distributing it to hospitals and clinics for medical needs. We also organize nationwide blood donation drives and maintain a reserve supply of blood that medical facilities can access in the event of domestic emergencies such as natural disasters or major accidents.

Our Goals
We endeavor to eliminate blood shortages by promoting voluntary blood donation and building a reliable base of regular donors, and to continue research into blood storage technologies in order to enhance the safety and longevity of blood products.

Our Values
We uphold rigorous ethical and medical standards, ensuring every donation is handled with care and precision. We are committed to transparency, accountability, and making sure our practices adhere to global safety protocols.

05 독해 내용 일치 파악

윗글에서 National Blood Services Authority에 관한 내용과 일치하는 것은?

① It maintains a reserve supply of blood for export to other countries.
② It wants people to give blood voluntarily so there is always enough of it.
③ It has increased the budget for research into blood storage technologies.
④ It sets international safety standards for blood banks.

06 독해 유의어 파악　　　난이도 중 ●●○

밑줄 친 regular의 의미와 가장 가까운 것은?

① generous
② random
③ potential
④ consistent

해석
① 관대한
② 무작위의
③ 잠재적인
④ 일관된

해설
밑줄 친 부분이 포함된 문장에서 regular는 문맥상 '정기(적인)' 헌혈 기증자라는 의미로 쓰였으므로, '일관된'이라는 의미의 ④ consistent가 정답이다.

정답 ④

어휘
generous 관대한, 넉넉한　random 무작위의　potential 잠재적인
consistent 일관된, 한결 같은

07 독해 제목 파악　　　난이도 중 ●●○

(A)에 들어갈 글의 제목으로 적절한 것은?

[A]

A day pass for Namid National Park can be purchased for $10, but those intending to spend more time at the park are encouraged to purchase the Explorer Pass for $75, which provides 12 months of access not just to Namid National Park but to more than 100 protected sites across the country. Passes can be obtained at park entrances or online and must be displayed on your vehicle dashboard.

Namid National Park is open throughout the year, but visitors wishing to use campgrounds in the winter are advised to come prepared. Please note that winter temperatures average -5°C during the day and can occasionally drop as low as -30°C at night.

Fishing is allowed in designated areas with a valid fishing license. Hunting, however, is strictly prohibited and punishable by law.

For more information, please call 1 (888) 343-9536.

① Explorer Pass Benefits across Protected Sites
② Seasonal Camping Restrictions in National Parks
③ Comprehensive Visitor Guidelines for Namid National Park
④ Temperature Fluctuations in Mountain National Parks

해석

> **(A) Namid 국립 공원의 포괄적인 방문자 지침**
>
> Namid 국립 공원의 일일 패스는 10달러에 구매될 수 있지만, 공원에서 더 많은 시간을 보내고자 하는 분들은 75달러짜리 Explorer 패스를 구매하실 것이 권장되는데, 이 패스는 Namid 국립 공원뿐만 아니라 전국의 100개 이상의 보호 구역들에 12개월의 접근 권한을 제공합니다. 패스는 공원 입구나 온라인에서 구하실 수 있으며 여러분의 차량 대시보드 위에서 보여야 합니다.
>
> Namid 국립 공원은 일 년 내내 개방되지만, 겨울에 캠핑장을 이용하고자 하는 방문객분들은 준비하고 오시기를 권고드립니다. 겨울 기온은 낮 동안 평균 영하 5도이며, 밤에는 이따금씩 영하 30도까지 내려갈 수 있음을 참고하시기 바랍니다.
>
> 낚시는 유효한 낚시 면허를 소지하신 경우 지정된 구역에서 허용됩니다. 하지만, 사냥은 엄격히 금지되어 있으며 법적으로 처벌받을 수 있습니다.
>
> 더 자세한 정보는 1 (888) 343-9536으로 연락 주시기 바랍니다.

① 보호 구역 전역에 걸친 Explorer 패스의 혜택
② 국립 공원 내 계절별 캠핑 제한 사항
③ Namid 국립 공원의 포괄적인 방문자 지침
④ 산악 국립 공원에서의 기온 변화

해설
지문 전반에 걸쳐 Namid 국립 공원의 입장 패스 종류, 개방 시기, 캠핑장 이용 시 주의 사항, 낚시 및 사냥의 허용 여부를 알려 주고 있으므로, ③ 'Namid 국립 공원의 포괄적인 방문자 지침'이 이 글의 제목이다.

정답 ③

어휘
encourage 권장하다, 장려하다　obtain 구하다, 얻다　enterance 입구
display 보이다, 전시하다　dashboard 대시보드(계기판)
average 평균 ~이다; 평균　occasionally 이따금씩, 때때로
designate 지정하다　valid 유효한　strictly 엄격히　prohibit 금지하다
punishable 처벌받을 수 있는　restriction 제한 사항
comprehensive 포괄적인, 종합적인　guideline 지침
fluctuation 변화, 변동

08 독해 무관한 문장 삭제　　　난이도 중 ●●○

다음 글의 흐름상 어색한 문장은?

Color is easily the most obvious physical property of a mineral, but it is not useful in identifying it. This is because the real color in some minerals is hidden. ① The bare eye may see a strong blue or green, but it cannot perceive traces of other colors that affect the true color, causing it to appear different in hue. ② Mineral color can also change because of the presence of other minerals. ③ For example, quartz, a glossy mineral that is crystal in form, is colorless, but small amounts of titanium or iron can make it appear pink. ④ Quartz rocks, especially those that are dark, can be damaged by constant exposure to direct heat and sunlight.

DAY 03 하프모의고사 03회

해석

색은 아마도 광물의 가장 확실한 물리적 성질이지만, 그것(광물)을 식별하는 데 있어 유용하지는 않다. 이는 일부 광물의 실제 색이 숨겨져 있기 때문이다. ① 맨눈은 강렬한 파란색이나 녹색을 볼 수도 있지만, 진짜 색에 영향을 주는 다른 색의 흔적들은 인지할 수 없는데, 이는 그것이 다른 색조로 보이게 한다. ② 광물의 색은 또한 다른 광물의 존재로 인해 바뀔 수 있다. ③ 예를 들어, 수정 형태인 윤이 나는 광물인 석영은 색이 없지만, 적은 양의 티타늄이나 철이 그것을 분홍색인 것처럼 보이게 할 수 있다. ④ 석영암, 특히 어두운 것들은 직접적인 열이나 햇빛에의 지속적인 노출에 의해 손상될 수 있다.

해설

첫 문장에서 '광물을 식별하는 데 있어 유용하지 않은 성질인 색'에 대해 언급하고, ①번은 '맨눈으로는 인지할 수 없는 광물의 진짜 색', ②번은 '다른 광물의 존재로 인해 변하는 광물의 색', ③번은 '원래는 색이 없지만 티타늄이나 철이 섞여 분홍색으로 보일 수 있는 석영의 사례'에 대해 설명하고 있다. 그러나 ④번은 '열 또는 햇빛에의 지속적인 노출에 의해 손상될 수 있는 석영암'에 대한 내용으로, 첫 문장의 내용과 관련이 없다.

정답 ④

어휘

obvious 확실한, 분명한　property 성질, 재산　mineral 광물; 광물의
identify 식별하다, 확인하다　bare 맨, 벌거벗은　perceive 인지하다
trace 흔적; 추적하다　hue 색조, 색깔　presence 존재　glossy 윤이 나는
iron 철　constant 지속적인　exposure 노출

---

09 독해 문장 삽입　난이도 중 ●●○

주어진 문장이 들어갈 위치로 적절한 것은?

In early 19th century Germany, though, directors began to appear, and actors were no longer tasked with making these choices.

Works by Shakespeare have been staged continually since he wrote them in the 16th and 17th centuries, but how they are performed has changed immensely. (①) This is largely due to the change in direction in theaters. (②) In Shakespeare's time, theaters lacked the position of a dedicated director, relying instead on actors to direct themselves in how they delivered lines on stage. (③) This change was prompted by the increased complexity of stage productions of the time; someone was needed to oversee the larger casts of extras and more advanced stagecraft. (④) Interestingly, over the next century, directing evolved into an artistic position of its own, with people considering the director's vision to be as important as actors' performances.

해석

그러나, 19세기 초 독일에서 감독들이 등장하기 시작했고, 배우들은 더 이상 이러한 선택을 하는 과업을 맡지 않아도 되었다.

Shakespeare의 작품들은 그가 그것들을 16세기와 17세기에 집필한 이후 계속해서 무대에 올려졌지만, 그것들이 공연되는 방식은 엄청나게 변해왔다. ① 이는 대체로 극장 연출의 변화로 인한 것이다. ② Shakespeare 시대에, 극장에는 전담 감독의 지위가 없었고, 대신 무대 위에서 대사를 전달하는 방식에 있어서 직접 감독하는 배우들에 의존했다. ③ 이러한 변화는 당시 무대 제작의 복잡성이 증가함에 따라 유발되었는데, 더 많은 엑스트라 출연진과 더 선진적인 연출 기법을 감독하기 위해 누군가가 필요했다. ④ 흥미롭게도, 그 다음 세기에 걸쳐 감독은 그것만의 예술적인 지위로 진화했으며, 사람들은 감독의 통찰력이 배우들의 연기만큼이나 중요하다고 여겼다.

해설

③번 앞 문장에 Shakespeare 시대에는 감독의 지위가 없어 무대 위에서 대사를 전달하는 방식을 배우들이 직접 감독했다는 내용이 있고, 뒤 문장에 이러한 변화(This change)는 당시 무대 연출의 복잡성이 증가함에 따라 유발되었으며 더 많은 엑스트라 출연진과 더 선진적인 연출 기법을 감독하는 인력이 필요했다는 내용이 있으므로, ③번 자리에 그러나(though) 19세기 초 독일에서 감독들이 등장하기 시작했다는 내용, 즉 무대 제작이 복잡해짐에 따라 공연 감독이라는 지위가 생겨난 시점에 대해 언급하는 주어진 문장이 나와야 지문이 자연스럽게 연결된다.

정답 ③

어휘

director 감독　task 과업을 맡기다　immensely 엄청나게
direction 연출, 감독, 방향　dedicated 전담하는, 전념하는
rely on ~에 의존하다　prompt 유발하다; 즉각적인　complexity 복잡성
oversee 감독하다　cast 출연진; 던지다　stagecraft 연출 기법
evolve 진화하다, 발달하다

---

10 독해 빈칸 완성 - 구　난이도 중 ●●○

밑줄 친 부분에 들어갈 말로 적절한 것은?

Air traffic controllers are not workers that many people think about often. However, their work is vitally important in the modern world due to the global reliance on aircraft for transporting cargo and personnel by companies and economies worldwide. These highly trained professionals monitor all of the aircraft in the sky and coordinate their movement to ensure that they remain at a safe distance from one another. Performing this task requires immense planning, as it relies on ensuring that all planes have clear flight paths in order to maintain air traffic separation rules. So essential is their work that if they were to decide to stop performing it, they could _____. This was exactly what happened when American air traffic controllers went on strike in 1981. Without their assistance, more than 7,000 passenger and cargo flights had to be canceled, sending shockwaves through numerous sectors.

① cause the government to increase safety rules
② direct flights to less convenient locations
③ disrupt the aviation and logistics industries

④ increase the fares that passengers pay for flights

[해석]

항공 교통 관제사는 많은 사람들이 흔히 생각하는 근로자는 아니다. 하지만, 현대 세계에서 그들의 업무는 전 세계의 기업과 국가들이 화물과 사람들을 수송하는 것에 있어 항공기에 전 세계적으로 의존하고 있기 때문에 실로 중요하다. 이 고도로 훈련된 전문가들은 하늘에 있는 모든 항공기를 감시하고 그것들이 반드시 서로로부터 안전한 거리를 유지하게 하기 위해 그것들의 움직임을 조정한다. 이와 같은 업무를 수행하는 것은 그것이 항공 교통 분리 규칙을 유지하기 위해 모든 비행기가 반드시 명확한 항공로를 가지고 있게 하는 데 달려 있어서, 엄청난 계획을 필요로 한다. 그들의 일은 매우 중요하기 때문에 만약 그들이 그것을 수행하는 것을 그만두기로 결정한다면, 그들은 항공과 물류 산업을 중단시킬 수 있다. 이것이 바로 1981년에 미국 항공 교통 관제사들이 파업에 들어갔을 때 일어난 일이었다. 그들의 도움이 없어서, 7,000편이 넘는 여객기와 화물기가 취소되어야만 했고, 이것은 수많은 분야들에 충격을 주었다.

① 정부가 안전 수칙을 늘리게 하다
② 항공기를 덜 편리한 장소로 향하게 하다
③ 항공과 물류 산업을 중단시키다
④ 승객들이 항공편에 지불하는 요금을 인상하다

[해설]

지문 앞부분에서 화물과 사람들을 수송하는 것에 있어 항공기에 대한 세계적인 의존도로 인해 항공 교통 관제사의 업무가 중요하다고 하고, 빈칸 뒷부분에서 미국 항공 교통 관제사들의 파업으로 인해 7,000편이 넘는 여객기와 화물기가 취소되었던 1981년 미국의 사례를 들고 있으므로, 만약 항공 교통 관제사들이 일을 수행하는 것을 그만두기로 결정한다면 그들은 '항공과 물류 산업을 중단시킬' 수 있다고 한 ③번이 정답이다.

정답 ③

[어휘]

vitally 실로, 매우 reliance 의존(도), 의지 aircraft 항공기
transport 수송하다 cargo 화물 personnel 사람들, 인사과
economy 국가, 경제 coordinate 조정하다 immense 엄청난, 거대한
separation 분리, 구분 exactly 바로, 정확하게
go on strike 파업에 들어가다 shockwave 충격(파)
direct 향하게 하다, 지도하다 convenient 편리한
disrupt 중단시키다, 방해하다 aviation 항공 logistics 물류 fare 요금

DAY 04 하프모의고사 04회

▶ 정답 p. 26

01	④	어휘	06	②	독해
02	④	문법	07	④	독해
03	④	문법	08	③	독해
04	③	생활영어	09	②	독해
05	②	독해	10	③	독해

▶ 취약영역 분석표

영역	맞힌 답의 개수
어휘	/1
생활영어	/1
문법	/2
독해	/6
TOTAL	/10

---

01 어휘 essential 난이도 중 ●●○

밑줄 친 부분에 들어갈 말로 적절한 것은?

Social media was once considered nothing more than a means of communication, but it is now understood to play a(n) _____ role in everyday life.

① secondary ② conventional
③ reasonable ④ essential

[해석]
소셜 미디어는 한때 의사소통 수단에 불과한 것으로 여겨졌지만, 이제 그것은 일상생활에 필수적인 역할을 하는 것으로 파악된다.
① 이차적인 ② 관습적인
③ 합리적인 ④ 필수적인

정답 ④

[어휘]
means 수단, 방법 secondary 이차적인, 부차적인
conventional 관습적인, 형식적인 reasonable 합리적인, 이성적인
essential 필수적인

---

02 문법 시제 난이도 하 ●○○

밑줄 친 부분에 들어갈 말로 적절한 것은?

Until the government _____ stricter environmental regulations, some companies will continue to prioritize profits over sustainability.

① will have implemented ② have implemented
③ will implement ④ implements

[해석]
정부가 더 엄격한 환경 규제를 시행할 때까지, 일부 기업들은 지속 가능성보다 이익을 계속해서 우선시할 것이다.

[해설]
④ 현재 시제 빈칸은 부사절의 동사 자리이다. 시간을 나타내는 부사절(Until ~ regulations)에서는 미래를 나타내기 위해 현재 시제를 사용하므로, 현재 시제가 쓰인 ④ implements가 정답이다.

정답 ④

[어휘]
prioritize 우선시하다 sustainability 지속 가능성 implement 시행하다

---

03 문법 수동태 | 어순 | 조동사 | 관계절 난이도 중 ●●○

밑줄 친 부분 중 어법상 옳지 않은 것은?

Gardens have ① a timeless beauty, so growing flowers and vegetation naturally appeals to many homeowners. However, it is imperative that a gardener ② utilize the right mix of plants to promote healthy growth. Some plants have substances that repel certain bugs, and these are helpful to plants ③ that attract those insects. Additionally, some flowers and shrubs should never ④ place near each other as they compete for soil and water.

[해석]
텃밭은 세월이 흘러도 변치 않는 아름다움을 지니고 있어서, 꽃과 초목을 재배하는 것은 많은 집주인들의 관심을 끈다. 하지만, 정원을 가꾸는 사람이라면 건강한 성장을 촉진하는, 올바른 식물 조합을 활용하는 것이 필수적이다. 어떤 식물들은 특정한 곤충들을 쫓아버리는 물질을 가지고 있고, 이것들은 그 곤충들을 끌어들이는 식물들에게 도움이 된다. 게다가, 어떤 꽃과 관목들은 흙과 물을 두고 경쟁하기 때문에 서로 가까이 놓여서는 안 된다.

[해설]
④ 능동태 · 수동태 구별 문맥상 주어 some flowers and shrubs와 동사가 '어떤 꽃과 관목들이 놓이다'라는 의미의 수동 관계이므로 능동태 place를 수동태 be placed로 고쳐야 한다. 참고로, 조동사(should) 다음에는 동사원형이 와야 한다.

[오답 분석]
① 명사를 수식하는 여러 요소들의 어순 여러 품사가 함께 명사를 수식하는 경우 '(관사 +) 형용사 + 명사'의 어순이 되어야 하므로, 명사 beauty 앞에 a timeless beauty가 올바르게 쓰였다.
② 조동사 should의 생략 주절에 의무를 나타내는 형용사 imperative가 나오면 종속절에는 '(should +) 동사원형'이 와야 하므로, (should) utilize가 올바르게 쓰였다.
③ 관계대명사 선행사(plants)가 사물이고, 관계절 내에서 동사 attract의 주어 역할을 하므로 사물을 나타내는 주격 관계대명사 that이 올바르게 쓰였다.

정답 ④

어휘
vegetation 초목 appeal 관심을 끌다 imperative 필수적인
utilize 활용하다 promote 촉진하다, 홍보하다 repel 쫓아버리다, 격퇴하다
attract 끌어들이다 shrub 관목 compete 경쟁하다

04 생활영어 Download the latest operating system.
난이도 하 ●○○

밑줄 친 부분에 들어갈 말로 적절한 것은?

A: Are there any electronics service centers around here? My phone isn't working properly.
B: I might be able to help. What's the problem?
A: It keeps showing an error message, and I can't send texts.
B: Oh, that's a well-known software issue.
A: So what do I need to do?
B: _____
A: That's simpler than I thought. Thanks for letting me know!

① How about getting a new phone this time?
② Maybe you should back up your data first.
③ Download the latest operating system.
④ There's nothing you can do.

해석
A: 이 근처에 전자 제품 서비스 센터가 있나? 내 휴대폰이 제대로 작동하지 않아.
B: 내가 도와줄 수 있을지도 몰라. 뭐가 문제인데?
A: 오류 메시지가 계속 떠 있어서, 내가 문자를 보낼 수가 없어.
B: 아, 그건 잘 알려진 소프트웨어 문제야.
A: 그래서 내가 무엇을 해야 하는데?
B: 최신 운영 체제를 다운로드해.
A: 생각보다 간단하네. 알려 줘서 고마워!

① 이번 기회에 새 휴대폰을 사는 건 어때?
② 아마도 너는 데이터를 먼저 백업해야 할 거야.
③ 최신 운영 체제를 다운로드해.
④ 네가 할 수 있는 건 없어.

해설
오류 메시지가 계속 떠 있는 현상이 잘 알려진 소프트웨어 문제라는 B의 설명에 대해 A가 해결 방법을 묻고, 빈칸 뒤에서 다시 A가 That's simpler than I thought. Thanks for letting me know!(생각보다 간단하네. 알려 줘서 고마워!)라고 대답하고 있으므로, '최신 운영 체제를 다운로드해'라는 의미의 ③ 'Download the latest operating system'이 정답이다.

정답 ③

어휘
electronic 전자 제품의, 전자 공학의 properly 제대로, 적절히 latest 최신의
operate 운영하다, 작동하다, 수술하다

05~06 다음 글을 읽고 물음에 답하시오.

(A) _____

The Cleveport Community Center is happy to announce that it will be offering computer literacy classes for seniors, a perfect way for older residents to improve their abilities and confidence in using technology. Don't miss this opportunity to learn and grow!

Class Schedule
- **Dates**: Monday, May 5 - Friday, May 30
- **Times**: 10 a.m. - 12 p.m.
  (Monday, Wednesday, and Friday)
- **Location**: Cleveport Community Center,
  1624 Adams Boulevard

What You'll Learn
- **Tech Basics**
Discover how to operate a computer, connect to the internet, and send email.

- **_____ Digital Skills**
Go on step further, and master the skills needed for shopping online, using online banking, and making video calls with friends and family.

- **Internet Security**
Get tips for staying safe while enjoying the services of the internet.

Classes are offered at no cost for those 60 years old and over. To sign up, call (985) 555-8472.

해석

(A) 기술 교육을 통해 어르신분들께 힘을 실어 드립니다

저희 Cleveport 시민 문화 회관은 어르신분들을 위해, 나이 든 주민 여러분께서 기술을 사용하는 능력과 자신감을 향상시키는 완벽한 방법인, 컴퓨터 사용 능력 수업을 제공할 것임을 알릴 수 있어 기쁩니다. 배우고 성장할 수 있는 이 기회를 놓치지 마세요!

수업 일정
- **날짜**: 5월 5일 월요일 – 5월 30일 금요일

DAY 04 하프모의고사 04회

- **시간**: 오전 10시 – 오후 12시
  (월요일, 수요일, 금요일)
- **장소**: Cleveport 시민 문화 회관, Adams로 1624

배우시게 될 것들
- **기술 기초**
컴퓨터를 작동시키는 방법, 인터넷에 연결하는 방법, 이메일을 보내는 방법을 알아보세요.
- **심화된 디지털 기술들**
한 걸음 더 나아가서 온라인으로 쇼핑하고, 온라인 뱅킹을 사용하고, 친구 및 가족들과 화상 통화를 하는 데 필요한 기술들을 숙달하세요.
- **인터넷 보안**
인터넷 서비스를 즐기는 동시에 안전하게 이용하기 위한 조언을 얻으세요.

60세 이상이신 분들께는 비용 없이 수업이 제공됩니다. 신청하시려면, (985) 555-8472로 전화 주세요.

어휘

computer literacy 컴퓨터 사용 능력 senior 어르신, 고령자
confidence 자신감 operate 작동시키다 security 보안
sign up 신청하다

05 독해 제목 파악 난이도 하 ●○○

(A)에 들어갈 윗글의 제목으로 적절한 것은?

① Stay Safe While Online Shopping
② Empower Seniors through Technology Education
③ Connect with Family through Video Calls
④ Fundamental Computer Skills for Modern Living

해석
① 온라인 쇼핑 시 안전하게 이용하세요
② 기술 교육을 통해 어르신분들께 힘을 실어 드립니다
③ 가족분들과 화상 통화로 연락하세요
④ 문화생활을 위해 필수적인 컴퓨터 기술

해설
지문 처음에서 나이 든 주민들을 위해 컴퓨터 사용 능력 수업을 제공할 것이라고 했으므로, ② '기술 교육을 통해 어르신분들께 힘을 실어 드립니다'가 이 글의 제목이다.

정답 ②

어휘
empower 힘을 실어 주다, 자율권을 주다 fundamental 필수적인, 근본적인
modern living 문화생활

06 독해 빈칸 완성 – 단어 난이도 중 ●●○

윗글의 밑줄 친 부분에 들어갈 말로 적절한 것은?

① Formal ② Advanced
③ Communal ④ Unexpected

해석
① 형식적인 ② 심화된
③ 공동의 ④ 예기치 않은

해설
빈칸 뒷부분에서 한 걸음 더 나아가 온라인 쇼핑, 온라인 뱅킹, 화상 통화 등을 숙달할 것을 제안하고 있으므로, '심화된' 디지털 기술들이라고 한 ②번이 정답이다.

정답 ②

어휘
formal 형식적인, 공식적인 advanced 심화된 communal 공동의, 공용의
unexpected 예기치 않은

07 독해 내용 불일치 파악 난이도 중 ●●○

FactsOnly에 관한 다음 글의 내용과 일치하지 않는 것은?

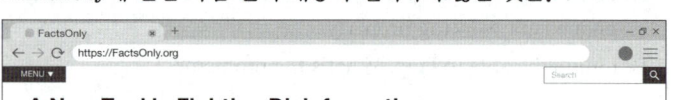

A New Tool in Fighting Disinformation

FactsOnly is the government's latest tool in the battle against online misinformation. The site features a list of the top false stories currently circulating on the Internet, along with detailed fact-checks, allowing users to quickly learn the truth. There is also a search feature to look for specific stories or topics. In addition to an explanation of the issue, all articles are accompanied by a list of sources for firsthand research. The FactsOnly website is offered free of charge and contains no advertising or user data collection. Users can also download a browser extension that uses AI to scan webpages and suggest articles on FactsOnly.org related to the content.

① It is part of an effort to fight against false information on the Internet.
② Users can look for articles about particular subjects.
③ No personal information about users is collected by the site.
④ It creates new articles using artificial intelligence.

해석

허위 정보와 싸우는 새로운 도구
FactsOnly는 온라인 허위 정보에 맞선 싸움에 사용되는 정부의 가장 최신 도구입니다. 사이트는 현재 인터넷에서 유통되는 주요한 가짜 뉴스 목록을 특징으로 하는데, 이는 상세한 사실 확인과 함께 사용자들로 하여금 진실을 빠르게 알아보게 합니다. 특정 이야기나 주제를 찾아볼 수 있는 검색 기능 또한 있습니다. 문제에 대한 설명 외에

도, 모든 기사들에는 직접 연구할 목적으로 출처 목록이 수반됩니다. FactsOnly 웹사이트는 무료로 제공되며 광고나 사용자 데이터 수집을 포함하지 않습니다. 사용자 여러분은 인공 지능을 활용하여 웹페이지를 스캔하고 해당 콘텐츠와 관련된 FactsOnly.org의 기사를 제시하는 브라우저 확장 프로그램도 다운로드하실 수 있습니다.

① 그것은 인터넷상의 허위 정보에 맞서 싸우기 위한 노력의 일환이다.
② 사용자들은 특정 주제에 대한 기사들을 찾아볼 수 있다.
③ 사용자에 대한 개인 정보가 사이트에 의해 수집되지 않는다.
④ 그것은 인공 지능을 활용하여 새로운 기사를 만들어낸다.

해설

④번의 키워드인 artificial intelligence(인공 지능)가 그대로 언급된 지문의 AI 주변의 내용에서 FactsOnly는 사용자들이 인공 지능을 활용하여 웹페이지를 스캔하고 관련 기사를 제시하는 브라우저 확장 프로그램을 다운로드할 수 있게 한다고는 했지만, ④ '그것은 인공 지능을 활용하여 새로운 기사를 만들어낸다'는지는 알 수 없다.

정답 ④

어휘

disinformation 허위 정보 misinformation 허위 정보
feature 특징으로 하다; 기능 circulate 유통시키다, 순환시키다
article 기사 accompany 수반하다, 동행하다 firsthand 직접
free of charge 무료로 advertising 광고 extension 확장

08 독해 주제 파악 난이도 중 ●●○

다음 글의 주제로 적절한 것은?

Humility may be regarded as the very root of all other virtues that lead to personal growth. Without this quality, which is an acceptance of one's shortcomings with the ultimate goal of making oneself a better person, no other virtues can develop. A humble person makes other people comfortable, whereas someone who is arrogant is unpleasant to be around because he only thinks of himself. Humility can therefore be a profitable trait to have no matter what environment a person is in. Among family and friends, it can keep relationships running smoothly, as a humble person is capable of setting their pride aside to resolve conflicts. In the workplace, it confers advantages as well, making employees receptive to change and willing to work with others. On the whole, developing the trait of humility can improve one's life and make it more peaceful.

① weaknesses that are hard to manage
② the problems associated with humility
③ advantages of being a humble person
④ ways to develop a humble character

해석

겸손은 개인적인 성장으로 이어지는 다른 모든 미덕의 근원으로 간주될지도 모른다. 자신을 더 나은 사람으로 만들겠다는 궁극적인 목표를 가지고 자신의 단점들을 수용하는 이 자질(겸손)이 없다면, 다른 어떤 미덕도 발전할 수 없다. 겸손한 사람은 다른 사람들을 편안하게 해 주는 반면, 거만한 사람은 자신만을 생각하기 때문에 주위에 있는 것이 불쾌하다. 그러므로 겸손은 한 사람이 어떤 환경에 있더라도 갖추어야 할 유익한 특성이 될 수 있다. 가족과 친구들 사이에서, 그것은 관계가 계속 순탄하게 진행되도록 할 수 있는데, 이는 겸손한 사람은 갈등을 해결하기 위해 자신의 자존심을 제쳐 놓을 수 있기 때문이다. 직장에서도 그것은 역시 이점을 주는데, 이는 직원들을 변화에 수용적이고 다른 사람들과 함께 기꺼이 일하도록 만든다. 전반적으로, 겸손의 특성을 발전시키는 것은 삶을 개선하고 그것을 더 평화롭게 만들 수 있다.

① 감당하기 어려운 약점
② 겸손과 관련된 문제점들
③ 겸손한 사람이 되는 것의 이점들
④ 겸손한 성격을 함양하는 방법

해설

지문 처음에서 겸손은 개인적인 성장으로 이어지는 다른 모든 미덕의 근원으로 간주될지도 모른다고 하고, 지문 뒷부분에서 겸손은 한 사람이 어떤 환경에 있더라도 유익한 특성이 될 수 있음을 가족·친구 관계와 직장 상황을 예로 들어 설명하고 있다. 따라서 ③ '겸손한 사람이 되는 것의 이점들' 이 이 글의 주제이다.

정답 ③

어휘

humility 겸손 virtue 미덕 shortcoming 단점 ultimate 궁극적인
humble 겸손한, 소박한 arrogant 거만한 trait 특성, 특징
set aside ~을 제쳐 놓다 resolve 해결하다, 다짐하다 conflict 갈등
confer 주다, 수여하다 receptive 수용적인 advantage 이점

09 독해 문장 삽입 난이도 중 ●●○

주어진 문장이 들어갈 위치로 적절한 것은?

This book, like others before it, was based on the notion that there was a perfect society that once existed or had yet to be discovered.

Utopian novels can be traced back to the writings of Plato, where he described the lost continent of Atlantis. Novels and stories featuring utopias, perfect societies, have appeared occasionally throughout history ever since. (①) However, they were truly popularized by Thomas More's work Utopia, which introduced the word into the English language. (②) Then, Edward Bellamy's 1888 novel Looking Backward elaborated on the idea and speculated about a utopia in the distant future. (③) This piece of fiction was immensely popular, leading to a wealth of utopian novels describing the perfection that would be reached in the future. (④) Eventually, the genre grew outdated and was replaced by the more critical and satirical, yet equally speculative, dystopian novel.

DAY 04 하프모의고사 04회

해석

> 그것 이전의 다른 것들과 마찬가지로, 이 책은 한때 존재했거나 아직 발견되지 않은 완벽한 사회가 있다는 관념에 기초했다.

'유토피아' 소설들은 그 기원이 Plato의 저서들까지 거슬러 올라갈 수 있는데, 이것들에서 그는 잃어버린 대륙 Atlantis를 묘사했다. 완벽한 사회인 유토피아를 특징으로 하는 소설과 이야기들은 그때 이후로 역사를 통틀어 가끔 등장해왔다. ① 하지만, 그것들은 Thomas More의 작품 『유토피아』에 의해 진정으로 대중화되었는데, 이것은 그 단어(utopia)를 영어에 도입했다. ② 그러고 나서, Edward Bellamy의 1888년 소설 『뒤를 돌아보며』는 그 개념에 대해 자세히 말했고 먼 미래의 유토피아에 대해 사색적으로 서술했다. ③ 이 소설 작품은 엄청나게 인기 있었고, 미래에 도달하게 될 이상을 묘사하는 많은 유토피아 소설들로 이어졌다. ④ 결국, 그 장르는 구식이 되었고, 더 비판적이고 풍자적이면서도 똑같이 사색적인 반이상향적인 소설에 의해 대체되었다.

해설

②번 앞 문장에 유토피아를 특징으로 한 소설들은 Thomas More의 『유토피아』로 인해 대중화되었다는 내용이 있고, 뒤 문장에 Edward Bellamy의 소설 『뒤를 돌아보며』가 그 개념(the idea)에 대해 자세히 말했다는 내용이 있으므로, ②번 자리에 이 책(This book)이 한때 존재했거나 아직 발견되지 않은 완벽한 사회가 있다는 관념(the notion)에 기초했다고 설명하는 내용, 즉 Thomas More의 『유토피아』에 의해 대중화되어 Edward Bellamy에 의해 구체화된 유토피아의 개념에 대해 설명하는 주어진 문장이 나와야 지문이 자연스럽게 연결된다.

정답 ②

어휘

notion 관념, 생각 trace back to 기원이 ~까지 거슬러 올라가다
feature ~을 특징으로 하다; 특징 occasionally 가끔
popularize 대중화하다 elaborate 자세히 말하다
speculate 사색적으로 서술하다, 깊이 생각하다 immensely 엄청나게
perfection 이상, 완벽 outdated 구식인 satirical 풍자적인
dystopian 반이상향적인

---

10 독해 빈칸 완성 - 구   난이도 중 ●●○

밑줄 친 부분에 들어갈 말로 적절한 것은?

> Adolescents undergo social and emotional changes beginning at puberty, and this can have an impact on their education in middle and high school. Even from early adolescence, their thinking is on a higher level than in childhood, which causes them to _____.
> Psychologists say that with this new mindset, teenagers are more likely to challenge classroom norms and educational goals. Hence, teens are less receptive to attempts to control and mold them into high-achieving adults. Education can become less effective when teachers are unsympathetic to the social and emotional upheavals that adolescent students are undergoing. In addition, that students are more technologically advanced than their teachers can cause them to be less respectful toward them. Therefore, education for adolescents should take into consideration the challenges posed by students during a time when they are learning to find their way and become independent.

① prefer emotional experiences over learning
② demand more technological approaches
③ explore and search for their identity
④ resist social and emotional upheavals

해석

청소년들은 사춘기에 시작되는 사회적, 그리고 정서적 변화를 겪으며, 이것은 그들의 중·고등학교 교육에도 영향을 미칠 수 있다. 청소년기 초반부터, 그들의 사고는 아동기보다 더 높은 수준인데, 이는 그들이 자신의 정체성을 탐구하고 모색하게 한다. 심리학자들은 이 새로운 사고방식으로 인해, 십 대들이 교실 규범과 교육적인 목표에 이의를 제기할 가능성이 더 크다고 말한다. 따라서, 십 대들은 그들을 통제하고 성취도가 높은 성인으로 만들려는 시도에 덜 수용적이다. 청소년기 학생들이 겪고 있는 사회적, 그리고 정서적 격변에 교사들이 공감하지 않을 때 교육이 덜 효과적이게 될 수 있다. 게다가, 학생들이 선생님들보다 기술적으로 더 앞서 있다는 것은 그들이 선생님들에게 덜 존경심을 보이게 할 수 있다. 그러므로, 청소년들을 위한 교육은 학생들이 자신들의 길을 찾고 독립적이게 되는 것을 배울 시기 동안에 그들에 의해 제기되는 이의들을 고려해야 한다.

① 학습보다 정서적 경험을 선호하다
② 더 많은 기술적 접근법을 요구하다
③ 자신의 정체성을 탐구하고 모색하다
④ 사회적 및 정서적 격변에 저항하다

해설

빈칸 뒤 문장에 이 새로운 사고방식으로 인해 십 대들은 교실 규범과 교육 목표에 이의를 제기할 가능성이 더 크다는 내용이 있고, 지문 마지막에 청소년을 위한 교육은 학생들이 자신들의 길을 찾는 것을 배울 시기 동안에 그들이 제기하는 이의들을 고려해야 한다고 했으므로, 청소년들의 사고는 그들이 '자신의 정체성을 탐구하고 모색'하게 한다고 한 ③번이 정답이다.

정답 ③

어휘

adolescent 청소년, 청소년기 undergo 겪다 puberty 사춘기
mindset 사고방식 norm 규범 receptive 수용적인
mold (틀에 넣어) 만들다 unsympathetic 공감하지 않는 upheaval 격변
take into consideration ~을 고려하다 pose 제기하다, 주장하다
independent 독립적인 explore 탐구하다 identity 정체성
resist 저항하다

DAY 05 하프모의고사 05회

정답   p. 30

01	②	어휘	06	①	독해
02	②	문법	07	②	독해
03	④	문법	08	②	독해
04	①	생활영어	09	③	독해
05	②	독해	10	②	독해

취약영역 분석표

영역	맞힌 답의 개수
어휘	/1
생활영어	/1
문법	/2
독해	/6
TOTAL	/10

---

01 어휘 undertake   난이도 중 ●●○

밑줄 친 부분에 들어갈 말로 적절한 것은?

The sustainable waste management bill passed this month indicates that the legislature will _____ drastic reforms to environmental conditions in the country.

① separate
② undertake
③ abandon
④ interpret

해석
이번 달 통과된 지속 가능한 폐기물 관리 법안은 입법부가 국가의 환경 상태에 대해 과감한 개혁에 착수할 것임을 시사한다.

① 분리하다
② 착수하다
③ 그만두다
④ 해석하다

정답 ②

어휘
sustainable 지속 가능한 bill 법안, 고지서 legislature 입법부
drastic 과감한 reform 개혁; 개혁하다 separate 분리하다
undertake 착수하다 abandon 그만두다, 버리다
interpret 해석하다, 설명하다

---

02 문법 부사절   난이도 하 ●○○

밑줄 친 부분에 들어갈 말로 적절한 것은?

We packed extra supplies _____ the camping trip lasted longer than expected.

① even though
② in case
③ whereas
④ unless

해석
우리는 캠핑 여행이 예정보다 더 오래 지속될 경우에 대비하여 여분의 물품을 챙겼다.

해설
② 부사절 접속사 빈칸은 절(the camping ~ expected)을 이끄는 접속사 자리이다. 문맥상 '캠핑 여행이 예정보다 더 오래 지속될 경우에 대비하여'라는 의미가 되어야 자연스러우므로, ① even though(비록 ~이지만), ③ whereas(반면에), ④ unless(만약 ~이 아니라면)가 아닌, '~(의 경우)에 대비하여'라는 의미의 부사절 접속사 ② in case가 정답이다.

정답 ②

---

03 문법 분사 | 수 일치 | 수동태 | 명사절   난이도 중 ●●○

밑줄 친 부분 중 어법상 옳지 않은 것은?

A recent study conducted by a research team in Japan ① suggests that a specific protein amino acid, called LP7, can slow down the development of dementia. Although this study has not yet reached clinical trials, it is expected ② to provide help for those at risk of the condition. Researchers will conduct further experiments to see ③ if their findings prove valid. If so, then a simple LP7 supplement ④ taking daily may be sufficient to inhibit brain cells from dying.

해석
일본의 한 연구 팀에 의해 수행된 최근의 한 연구는 LP7으로 불리는 특정 단백질 아미노산이 치매의 발생을 늦출 수 있다는 것을 시사한다. 비록 이 연구가 아직 임상 시험에 도달하지는 못했지만, 그것은 그 질환의 위험이 있는 사람들에게 도움을 줄 것으로 기대된다. 연구진은 그들의 연구 결과가 유효한지 알아보기 위해 추가 실험을 수행할 것이다. 만약 연구 결과가 유효하다면, 그 후에는 매일 섭취되는 간단한 LP7 보충제가 뇌세포가 죽는 것을 막기에 충분할지도 모른다.

해설
④ 현재분사 vs. 과거분사 수식받는 명사 a simple LP7 supplement와 분사가 '간단한 LP7 보충제가 섭취되다'라는 의미의 수동 관계이므로 현재분사 taking을 과거분사 taken으로 고쳐야 한다.

[오답 분석]
① **주어와 동사의 수 일치** 주어 자리에 단수 명사 A recent study가 왔으므로 단수 동사 suggests가 올바르게 쓰였다. 참고로, 주어와 동사 사이의 수식어 거품(conducted by ~ Japan)은 동사의 수 결정에 영향을 주지 않는다.
② **5형식 동사의 수동태** to 부정사를 목적격 보어로 취하는 5형식 동사(expect)가 수동태가 되면 to 부정사는 수동태 동사(is expected) 뒤에 그대로 남아야 하므로 is expected 뒤에 to 부정사 to provide가 올바르게 쓰였다.
③ **명사절 접속사** 문맥상 '그들의 연구 결과가 유효한지 (아닌지)'라는 의미가 되어야 자연스러우므로, '~인지 아닌지'라는 의미의 불확실한 사실을 나타내는 명사절 접속사 if가 올바르게 쓰였다.

정답 ④

어휘
conduct 수행하다 protein 단백질 dementia 치매
clinical trial 임상 시험 valid 유효한, 타당한 supplement 보충(제); 보충하다
sufficient 충분한 inhibit 막다, 방지하다

해석

> Liam Anderson: 널 위해 오늘 밤에 있는 코미디 쇼 티켓을 샀어.
> Camila Nelson: 고마워, 하지만 난 코미디에는 별로 관심이 없는걸.
> Liam Anderson: 너도 가고 싶을 거야, 날 믿어. Ryan이 공연을 할 거야.
> Camila Nelson: 와! 그 경우라면, 나도 보고 싶어. <u>공연이 언제 어디에서 있니?</u>
> Liam Anderson: 내가 네게 온라인 티켓을 보낼게. 거기에 공연에 대한 정보들이 모두 나와 있거든.
> Camila Nelson: 확인해 볼게. 표를 구해 줘서 고마워.

① 공연이 언제 어디에서 있니?
② Ryan이 대학에서 공연 예술을 전공했어?
③ 공연 후에 Ryan을 만날 기회가 있을까?
④ 너는 그가 오늘 밤 공연할 거라는 걸 알았어?

해설
Ryan이 공연을 할 것이라는 Liam의 말에 대해 Camila가 그 경우라면 코미디 쇼를 보고 싶다고 말하고, 빈칸 뒤에서 다시 Liam이 I'll send you the online ticket. It has all the information about the performance (내가 네게 온라인 티켓을 보낼게. 거기에 공연에 대한 정보들이 모두 나와 있거든)라고 대답하고 있으므로, '공연이 언제 어디에서 있니?'라는 의미의 ① 'When and where is the performance?'가 정답이다.

정답 ①

04 생활영어 When and where is the performance?

난이도 하 ●○○

밑줄 친 부분에 들어갈 말로 적절한 것은?

Liam Anderson
I bought you a ticket for the comedy show tonight.
11:05

Camila Nelson
Thanks, but I'm not really interested in comedy.
11:06

Liam Anderson
You'll want to go, trust me. Ryan is going to be performing.
11:06

Camila Nelson
Wow! In that case, I'd love to see it too.
11:07

Liam Anderson
I'll send you the online ticket. It has all the information about the performance.
11:08

Camila Nelson
I'll check it out. Thanks for getting me the ticket.
11:09

① When and where is the performance?
② Did Ryan study performing arts in university?
③ Is there a chance to meet Ryan after the performance?
④ Did you know that he's performing tonight?

05~06 다음 글을 읽고 물음에 답하시오.

A Growing Threat to Public Health
A growing concern for the National Disease Prevention Agency (NDPA) is the global public health threat posed by antibiotic resistance. Not only is antibiotic resistance responsible for at least a million deaths each year, but it also complicates what should be routine medical procedures, leading to prolonged hospital stays and increased medical costs.

Antibiotic Resistance
Antibiotic resistance occurs when disease-causing bacteria adapt to the antibiotic medications that previously killed them. Those who use antibiotics incorrectly, whether by taking them unnecessarily or failing to complete treatments as prescribed, facilitate the development of resistant strains that can spread to others.

The NDPA educates healthcare providers and the public about the proper use of antibiotics and funds research to develop new treatments. When a resistant infection is identified, the NDPA works with hospitals to <u>contain</u> its spread and provide guidance on treatment options.

해석

공중 보건에 대한 증가하는 위협

국립질병예방센터(NDPA)에 있어 점점 커지는 우려는 항생제 내성으로 인해 제기되는, 전 세계적인 공중 보건 위협입니다. 항생제 내성은 매년 최소 백만 명의 사망에 대한 책임이 있을 뿐만 아니라, 그것은 일상적인 의료 절차여야 하는 것을 복잡하게 만드는데, 이는 장기간의 병원 입원 기간과 증가된 의료 비용을 초래합니다.

항생제 내성

항생제 내성은 질병을 유발하는 박테리아가 이전에는 그것들을 죽였던 항생제 약물에 적응할 때 발생합니다. 불필요하게 항생제를 복용하거나 처방된 대로 치료를 완료하지 않는 등, 항생제를 잘못 사용하는 사람들은 다른 사람들에게 퍼질 수 있는, 내성이 있는 변종의 발생을 촉진합니다.

국립질병예방센터는 의료 서비스 제공자와 대중에게 항생제의 올바른 사용법을 교육하고, 새로운 치료법을 개발하기 위한 연구에 자금을 지원합니다. 내성 감염이 확인되면, 국립질병예방센터는 병원과 협력하여 그것의 확산을 방지하고 치료 선택지들에 관한 지침을 제공합니다.

어휘

pose 제기하다 antibiotic 항생제 resistance 내성, 저항(력)
complicate 복잡하게 만들다 procedure 절차 prolonged 장기간의
adapt 적응하다 treatment 치료(법) prescribe 처방하다
facilitate 촉진하다, 가능케 하다 strain 변종, 부담, 압력 infection 감염
contain 방지하다, 억누르다, 포함하다

---

05 독해 요지 파악 난이도 중 ●●○

윗글의 요지로 적절한 것은?

① The NDPA ensures that people use antibiotic medications as prescribed.
② The NDPA aims to combat bacteria's growing ability to withstand treatments.
③ The NDPA tracks deaths resulting from global public health threats.
④ The NDPA tests new treatments designed to replace antibiotics.

해석
① 국립질병예방센터는 사람들이 항생제 약물을 처방받은 대로 사용하게 한다.
② 국립질병예방센터는 치료에 저항하는 박테리아의 능력 증대와 싸우는 것을 목표로 한다.
③ 국립질병예방센터는 전 세계적인 공중 보건 위협으로 인한 사망자를 추적한다.
④ 국립질병예방센터는 항생제를 대체하기 위해 고안된 새로운 치료법을 시험한다.

해설
지문 처음에서 국립질병예방센터의 커지는 우려는 항생제 내성으로 인한 공중 보건 위협이라고 하고, 지문 뒷부분에서 항생제 내성에 대비하여 의료 서비스 제공자와 대중에게 항생제의 올바른 사용법을 교육하고 새로운 치료법을 개발하기 위한 연구에 자금을 지원한다고 했으므로, ② '국립질병예방센터는 치료에 저항하는 박테리아의 능력 증대와 싸우는 것을 목표로 한다'가 이 글의 요지이다.

정답 ②

어휘
combat 싸우다 withstand 저항하다, 견디다 replace 대체하다

---

06 독해 유의어 파악 난이도 중 ●●○

밑줄 친 contain의 의미와 가장 가까운 것은?

① prevent
② estimate
③ perform
④ document

해석
① 방지하다
② 추정하다
③ 수행하다
④ 기록하다

해설
밑줄 친 부분이 포함된 문장에서 contain은 문맥상 내성 감염의 확산을 '방지한다'는 의미로 쓰였으므로, '방지하다'라는 의미의 ① prevent가 정답이다.

정답 ①

어휘
prevent 방지하다, 예방하다 estimate 추정하다, 예상하다
perform 수행하다 document 기록하다; 기록

---

07 독해 내용 일치 파악 난이도 하 ●○○

National Technology in Education Conference에 관한 다음 글의 내용과 일치하는 것은?

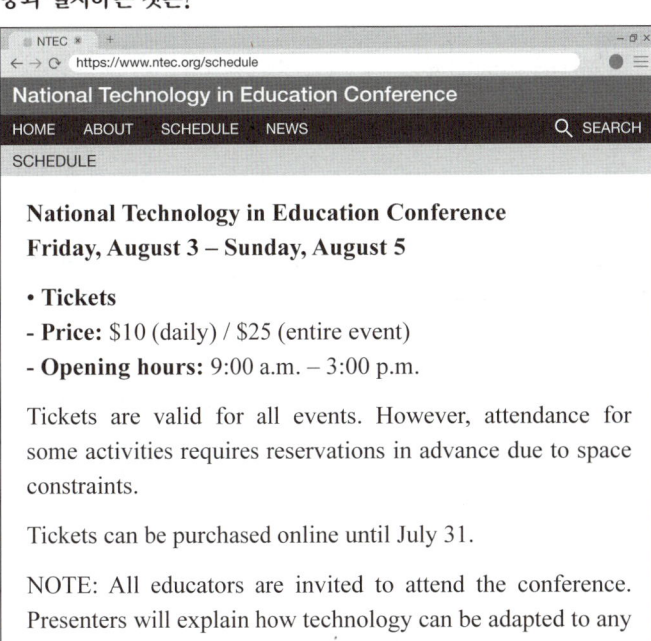

National Technology in Education Conference
Friday, August 3 – Sunday, August 5

- **Tickets**
- **Price:** $10 (daily) / $25 (entire event)
- **Opening hours:** 9:00 a.m. – 3:00 p.m.

Tickets are valid for all events. However, attendance for some activities requires reservations in advance due to space constraints.

Tickets can be purchased online until July 31.

NOTE: All educators are invited to attend the conference. Presenters will explain how technology can be adapted to any subject to improve educational outcomes for students.

DAY 05 하프모의고사 05회

① 일일권은 할인이 적용된다.
② 일부 행사는 사전 예약이 필요하다.
③ 티켓은 7월 31일까지 현장에서 구매할 수 있다.
④ 기술 분야에 종사하는 교육자들만 초대받았다.

해석

국립 교육 기술 컨퍼런스
8월 3일 금요일 – 8월 5일 일요일
• 티켓 정보
– 가격: 10달러 (일일권) / 25달러 (행사 전체)
– 운영 시간: 오전 9시 – 오후 3시
티켓은 모든 행사에 대해 유효합니다. 하지만, 공간 제약으로 인해 일부 활동의 참석은 사전 예약을 필요로 합니다.
티켓은 7월 31일까지 온라인으로 구매하실 수 있습니다.
참고 바랍니다: 모든 교육자분들께서는 이번 컨퍼런스에 참석하도록 초대받으셨습니다. 발표자분들께서 학생들의 교육 성과를 향상시키기 위해 기술이 어떻게 모든 과목에 적용될 수 있는지를 설명해 주실 예정입니다.

해설

②번의 키워드인 '사전 예약'이 그대로 언급된 지문의 reservations in advance 주변의 내용에서 공간 제약으로 인해 일부 활동의 참석은 사전 예약을 필요로 한다고 했으므로, ② '일부 행사는 사전 예약이 필요하다'가 지문의 내용과 일치한다.

[오답 분석]
① 일일권이 10달러라고는 했지만, 일일권은 할인이 적용되는지는 알 수 없다.
③ 티켓은 7월 31일까지 온라인으로 구매할 수 있다고 했으므로, 티켓이 7월 31일까지 현장에서 구매할 수 있다는 것은 지문의 내용과 다르다.
④ 모든 교육자들이 컨퍼런스에 초대받았다고 했으므로, 기술 분야에 종사하는 교육자들만 초대받았다는 것은 지문의 내용과 다르다.

정답 ②

어휘

attendance 참석 in advance 사전에 constraint 제약, 제한
adapt 적용하다, 적응하다 outcome 성과, 결과

08 독해 주제 파악   난이도 중 ●●○

다음 글의 주제로 적절한 것은?

The longest-living land animal is a giant tortoise named Jonathan, who is approximately 192 years old. Similarly, other species of turtles such as sea turtles and the smaller box turtles can also live up to a century. The evolutionary reason for turtles' long lifespans is relatively simple. Their eggs and hatchlings frequently become the prey of snakes, birds, and raccoons. Therefore, turtles need to breed often and lay eggs throughout their long lives so that they have more chances of producing offspring that survive into adulthood. On the other hand, the biological explanation for turtles' longevity is still not fully understood. What experts are beginning to suspect is that certain turtle species are able to initiate a controlled process in the body that quickly destroys damaged cells. This mechanism prolongs life because it blocks the replication of compromised cells that could otherwise develop into tumors and later into cancer.

① reasons turtle eggs are targeted by predators
② the rationale for turtles' extended lifespans
③ advantages of a prolonged breeding period
④ the anatomy of duplicated cancer cells

해석

가장 오래 산 육상 동물은 대략 192살이 된 Jonathan이라는 이름의 코끼리거북이다. 마찬가지로, 바다거북과 작은상자거북 같은 다른 종의 거북들도 한 세기까지 살 수 있다. 거북의 긴 수명에 대한 진화적인 이유는 비교적 간단하다. 그것들의 알과 부화한 새끼들은 뱀, 새, 그리고 너구리의 먹이가 되는 일이 흔하다. 그래서, 거북들은 성체까지 생존하는 새끼를 낳는 것에 있어 더 많은 가능성을 갖기 위해 그것들의 긴 일생 동안 자주 번식하고 알을 낳을 필요가 있다. 반면에, 거북의 장수에 대한 생물학적인 이유는 아직 완전히 이해되지 않았다. 전문가들이 추측하기 시작하고 있는 것은 특정 거북 종들이 신체 내에서 손상된 세포를 빠르게 파괴하는 통제 과정을 일으킬 수 있다는 것이다. 이러한 기제는 만약 그렇지 않았다면 종양으로, 후에는 암으로 발전할 수 있는 손상된 세포의 복제를 차단하기 때문에 생명을 연장시킨다.

① 거북의 알이 포식자의 표적이 되는 이유
② 거북의 수명이 늘어난 이유
③ 연장된 번식 기간의 이점
④ 복제된 암세포의 구조

해설

지문 전반에 걸쳐 거북의 긴 수명에 대해서는 성체까지 생존하는 새끼를 낳을 더 많은 가능성을 위한 것이라는 진화적인 이유가 있고, 전문가들이 추측하는 생물학적인 이유로 특정 거북 종들이 신체 내 손상 세포를 빠르게 파괴할 수 있는 점을 설명하고 있다. 따라서 ② '거북의 수명이 늘어난 이유'가 이 글의 주제이다.

정답 ②

어휘

evolutionary 진화적인 lifespan 수명 relatively 비교적
hatchling 부화한 새끼 breed 번식하다, 새끼를 낳다 offspring 새끼
explanation 이유, 해명 longevity 장수, 오래 지속됨
suspect 추측하다, 의심하다 initiate 일으키다, 시작하다
prolong 연장시키다 replication 복제
compromise 손상시키다, 타협시키다 tumor 종양 predator 포식자
rationale 이유 extend 늘리다, 연장시키다 anatomy (해부학적) 구조, 해부

09 독해 무관한 문장 삭제   난이도 중 ●●○

다음 글의 흐름상 어색한 문장은?

Positive economics studies the economy by relying on objective analysis, completely free of endorsements and disapprovals. ① John Keynes was the first economist credited with developing positive economic theories based solely on fact-supported logic. ② He posited that better financial decisions can be made when the facts of the economy are prioritized over value judgements and unsubstantiated predictions. ③ Financial decisions based solely on positive economics often lead to economically inefficient outcomes. ④ Critics, however, point out that there are many factors to consider when making an economic decision apart from objective truths. They insist that a mix of positive and normative economics, the latter of which incorporates subjectivity, is needed for sound economic decision-making.

해석

실증 경제학은 지지와 반대에서 완전히 벗어나서, 객관적인 분석에 의존함으로써 경제를 연구한다. ① John Keynes는 오직 사실에 의해 뒷받침되는 논리만을 바탕으로 한 실증 경제 이론을 발전시킨 것으로 인정받은 최초의 경제학자였다. ② 그는 가치 판단과 검증되지 않은 예측보다 경제에 대한 사실이 우선시될 때 더 나은 재정적인 결정을 내릴 수 있다고 가정했다. ③ 실증 경제학에만 기반한 재정적인 결정은 종종 경제적으로 비효율적인 결과로 이어진다. ④ 하지만, 비판하는 사람들은 객관적인 진실 외에도 경제적 결정을 내릴 때 고려해야 할 요소가 많음을 지적한다. 그들은 건전한 경제적 의사 결정을 위해서는 실증 경제학과 규범 경제학의 혼합이 필요하다고 주장하는데, 이 중 후자는 주관성을 포함한다.

해설

첫 문장에서 실증 경제학은 객관적인 분석에 의존하여 경제를 연구한다고 언급한 뒤, ①, ②번은 '가치 판단과 검증되지 않은 예측보다 경제에 대한 사실이 우선시될 때 더 나은 재정적인 결정을 내릴 수 있음을 전제로 한 John Keynes의 실증 경제학', ④번은 '경제적 결정을 내릴 때 객관적인 진실 외에도 고려해야 할 요소가 많다는 비판론자들의 주장'에 대해 설명하고 있다. 그러나 ③번은 '실증 경제학의 경제적 비효율성'에 대한 내용으로, 지문 전반의 내용과 관련이 없다.

정답 ③

어휘

positive economics 실증 경제학 objective 객관적인; 목적
analysis 분석 endorsement 지지, 승인 disapproval 반대
credit 인정하다, 믿다; 신용 posit 가정하다, 단정하다 prioritize 우선시하다
unsubstantiated 검증되지 않은 critic 비판하는 사람, 비평가
point out ~을 지적하다 apart from ~외에도
normative economics 규범 경제학 incorporate 포함하다, 설립하다
subjectivity 주관성 sound 건전한; 소리

---

10 독해 빈칸 완성 – 구 난이도 중 ●●○

밑줄 친 부분에 들어갈 말로 적절한 것은?

Mindfulness practices such as meditation and breathing exercises are portrayed in popular media as ways to become aware of the emotions that cause stress in everyday life. Many people believe that by recognizing feelings instead of running away from them, an individual should be able to relieve themselves from the anxiety related to their emotions. However, actual research from cognitive psychologists suggests that a person who is merely cognizant of their emotions may suppress uncomfortable feelings, which in turn exacerbates stress levels. Therefore, experts insist that participants can derive more value from a mindfulness approach that _____ rather than just awareness of them. Doing this effectively involves identifying and acknowledging feelings without ascribing any judgment to them. With enough practice, individuals who embrace their emotions while refraining from mentally and physically reacting to them should gradually experience lower levels of anxiety.

① promotes various meditation exercises
② incorporates acceptance of emotions
③ reflects academic experiment results
④ describes the consequences of stress

해석

명상과 호흡 운동과 같은 마음 챙김 연습은 일상생활에서 스트레스를 유발하는 감정들을 알게 되는 방법으로 대중 매체에서 묘사된다. 많은 사람들은 그것들(감정)에서 도망가는 대신에 감정을 인식함으로써, 개인이 자신의 감정과 관련된 불안으로부터 스스로를 해방시킬 수 있어야 한다고 생각한다. 하지만, 인지심리학자들의 실제 연구는 그저 자신의 감정을 인지하고 있기만 하는 사람이 불편한 감정을 억누를 수도 있다는 것을 시사하는데, 이것은 결국 스트레스 수준을 악화시킬 수 있다. 따라서, 전문가들은 참가자들이 감정에 대한 단순한 인식보다 감정에 대한 수용을 포함하는 마음 챙김 접근법으로부터 더 많은 가치를 얻을 수 있다고 주장한다. 이것을 효과적으로 하는 것은 어떤 판단도 그것들(감정)의 탓으로 돌리지 않으면서 감정을 식별하고 인정하는 것을 포함한다. 충분한 연습으로, 그것들(감정)에 대해 정신적·육체적으로 반응하는 것을 자제하면서 감정을 수용하는 개인들은 점차 낮은 수준의 불안감을 경험할 것이다.

① 다양한 명상 연습을 장려하다
② 감정에 대한 수용을 포함하다
③ 학문적 실험 결과를 반영하다
④ 스트레스의 결과를 묘사하다

해설

빈칸 뒤 문장에 이것을 효과적으로 하는 것은 어떤 판단이라도 감정의 탓으로 돌리지 않으면서 감정을 식별하고 인정하는 것을 포함한다는 내용이 있으므로, '감정에 대한 수용을 포함하는' 마음 챙김 접근법이라고 한 ②번이 정답이다.

정답 ②

어휘

mindfulness 마음 챙김 relieve 해방시키다, 완화하다 cognitive 인지의
suppress 억누르다, 진압하다 exacerbate 악화시키다
derive (이익·즐거움 등을) 얻다, 끌어내다 acknowledge 인정하다
ascribe A to B A를 B의 탓으로 돌리다 embrace 수용하다, 받아들이다
refrain from ~을 자제하다 incorporate 포함하다, 설립하다

DAY 06 하프모의고사 06회

정답   p. 34

01	③	어휘	06	③	독해
02	①	문법	07	①	독해
03	①	문법	08	④	독해
04	①	생활영어	09	④	독해
05	③	독해	10	④	독해

취약영역 분석표

영역	맞힌 답의 개수
어휘	/1
생활영어	/1
문법	/2
독해	/6
TOTAL	/10

---

01 어휘 blame   난이도 중 ●●○

밑줄 친 부분에 들어갈 말로 적절한 것은?

Those who forget their past accomplishments and focus on their failures tend to ＿＿＿＿ themselves for not succeeding.

① welcome
② copy
③ blame
④ analyze

[해석]
과거의 자신들의 성취를 잊고 실패에만 집중하는 사람들은 성공하지 못한 것에 대해 스스로를 탓하는 경향이 있다.

① 환영하다
② 따라 하다
③ 탓하다
④ 분석하다

정답 ③

[어휘]
accomplishment 성취, 업적   copy 따라 하다, 복사하다; 복사, 한 부
blame ~을 탓하다; 책임   analyze 분석하다

---

02 문법 수동태|부사|비교 구문|대명사   난이도 중 ●●○

밑줄 친 부분 중 어법상 옳지 않은 것은?

Being the youngest in a family of four children, I would not ① be surprising if my siblings were to treat me indifferently. However, instead of dominating all conversations, my brothers and sisters have ② always considered my opinion to be as ③ important as ④ theirs.

[해석]
네 아이가 있는 가정에서 막내이기 때문에, 나는 만약 형제자매들이 나를 무관심하게 대한다고 해도 놀라지 않을 것이다. 하지만, 모든 대화를 주도하는 것 대신에, 형과 누나들은 내 의견을 그들의 의견만큼 항상 중요하게 여겨 왔다.

[해설]
① 3형식 동사의 수동태   감정을 나타내는 동사(surprise)는 주어가 감정의 원인이면 능동태를, 감정을 느끼는 주체이면 수동태를 써야 하는데, '내가 놀라다'라는 의미로 주어(I)가 감정을 느끼는 주체이므로, 능동태 be surprising을 수동태 be surprised로 고쳐야 한다.

[오답 분석]
② 부사 자리   완료형 동사(have considered)를 수식할 때 부사(always)는 '조동사 + p.p.' 사이나 그 뒤에 와야 하므로 have와 considered 사이에 부사 always가 올바르게 쓰였다.
③ 원급   문맥상 '그들의 의견만큼 중요한'이라는 의미가 되어야 자연스러운데, '~만큼 -한'은 원급 표현 'as + 형용사의 원급(important) + as'의 형태로 나타낼 수 있으므로 as, as 사이에 형용사 important가 올바르게 쓰였다
④ 인칭대명사   문맥상 '내 의견을 그들의 의견만큼 중요하게 여겨 왔다'라는 의미가 되어야 자연스러우므로 대명사가 지시하는 것은 '그들의 의견'이다. 이때 '소유격(their) + 명사(opinion)'는 소유대명사로 나타낼 수 있으므로 소유대명사 theirs가 올바르게 쓰였다.

정답 ①

[어휘]
sibling 형제자매   indifferently 무관심하게   dominate 주도하다, 지배하다

---

03 문법 동사의 종류|전치사|조동사|수동태|시제|부사절   난이도 중 ●●○

밑줄 친 부분이 어법상 옳지 않은 것은?

① Her resolve to avoid relationship problems stopped her from get to know people.
② First-time skiers cannot be too careful about choosing appropriate slopes.
③ My visa had been denied by the consulate and I had to wait six months to reapply.
④ She will take the train to visit her parents however crowded it may be.

해석

① 관계 문제를 피하겠다는 그녀의 결심은 그녀가 사람들과 사귀지 못하게 했다.
② 스키를 처음 타는 사람들은 적절한 슬로프를 고르는 것에 대해 아무리 주의해도 지나치지 않다.
③ 내 비자가 영사관에 의해 발급 거부당했었고 나는 재신청하기 위해 6개월을 기다려야 했다.
④ 기차가 아무리 붐비더라도 그녀는 부모님을 방문하기 위해 그것을 탈 것이다.

해설

① 타동사 | 전치사 자리 동사 stop은 '~이 -하지 못하게 하다'라는 의미로 쓰일 때 'stop + 목적어 + from'의 형태를 취하는데, 전치사(from) 뒤에는 명사 역할을 하는 것이 와야 하므로 동사원형이 쓰인 from get을 동명사가 쓰인 from getting으로 고쳐야 한다.

[오답 분석]

② 조동사 관련 표현 문맥상 '적절한 슬로프를 고르는 것에 대해 아무리 주의해도 지나치지 않다'라는 의미가 되어야 자연스러우므로 조동사 관련 표현 cannot ~ too(아무리 ~해도 지나치지 않다)가 올 수 있다. 이때 조동사(cannot) 뒤에는 동사원형이 와야 하므로 cannot be too careful이 올바르게 쓰였다.
③ 능동태·수동태 구별 | 과거완료 시제 주어 My visa와 동사가 '내 비자가 (발급) 거부당했었다'라는 의미의 수동 관계이므로 수동태가 와야 한다. 이때 문맥상 '내 비자가 발급 거부당한' 시점이 '내가 6개월을 기다려야 했던' 특정 시점보다 더 이전에 일어난 일이므로 수동태 과거완료 had been denied가 올바르게 쓰였다.
④ 복합관계부사 '기차가 아무리 붐비더라도'는 복합관계부사 however (아무리 ~하더라도)로 나타낼 수 있는데, 복합관계부사 however가 이끄는 절은 'however + 형용사 + 주어 + 동사'의 형태가 되어야 하므로 however 뒤에 crowded it may be가 올바르게 쓰였다.

정답 ①

어휘

resolve 결심; 결심하다, 해결하다 deny 거부하다, 부인하다
consulate 영사관 reapply 재신청하다, 다시 지원하다 crowded 붐비는

---

04 생활영어 What am I supposed to do with it?
난이도 하 ●○○

밑줄 친 부분에 들어갈 말로 적절한 것은?

A: How's it going with the move into your new place?
B: Well, it's going OK, but also not OK. I'm having a bit of a problem.
A: What sort of problem?
B: The former tenant left a lot of stuff. _____?
A: You're within your rights to throw it out if it says so in the lease. Check the terms.
B: Oh, I didn't know that. I'd better look at what it says.

① What am I supposed to do with it
② Do you know if I can buy his stuff
③ Have you had a chance to take a look
④ How long am I allowed to keep it

해석

A: 새집으로 이사하는 건 어떻게 되어 가?
B: 글쎄, 잘 되고 있지만, 잘 안되고 있기도 해. 약간의 문제가 있어.
A: 어떤 문제인데?
B: 이전 세입자가 많은 물건을 두고 갔어. <u>내가 그것을 어떻게 해야 할까</u>?
A: 임대차 계약서에 그렇게 적혀 있다면 너는 그것을 버릴 권리가 있어. 계약 조건을 확인해 봐.
B: 아, 그건 몰랐네. 뭐라고 쓰여 있는지 봐야겠다.

① 내가 그것을 어떻게 해야 할까
② 내가 그의 물건을 살 수 있는지 아니
③ 너는 한번 볼 기회가 있었니
④ 내가 얼마 동안 그것을 보관해도 될까

해설

새집에 어떤 문제가 있는지 묻는 A의 질문에 대해 B가 이전 세입자가 많은 물건을 두고 갔다고 대답하고, 빈칸 뒤에서 다시 A가 You're within your rights to throw it out if it says so in the lease(임대차 계약서에 그렇게 적혀 있다면 너는 그것을 버릴 권리가 있어)라고 알려 주고 있으므로, '내가 그것을 어떻게 해야 할까'라는 의미의 ① 'What am I supposed to do with it'이 정답이다.

정답 ①

어휘

former 이전의 tenant 세입자 stuff 물건 throw out ~을 버리다
lease 임대차 계약(서); 임대하다 terms (합의·계약 등의) 조건

05~06 다음 글을 읽고 물음에 답하시오.

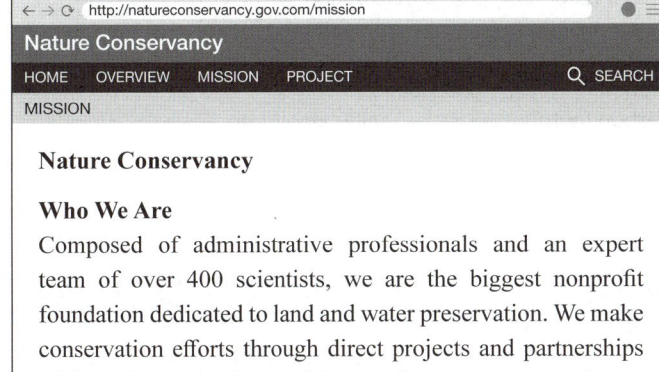

Nature Conservancy

Who We Are

Composed of administrative professionals and an expert team of over 400 scientists, we are the biggest nonprofit foundation dedicated to land and water preservation. We make conservation efforts through direct projects and partnerships with local organizations in 81 countries.

What We Do

Through funding from private donations, we fight climate change by giving a voice to local leaders and lobbying for

DAY 06 하프모의고사 06회

environment-first policies on both the domestic and international levels. Our main goal for the next decade is to protect 10 percent of the world's oceans through conservation programs and sustainable fishing initiatives.

How To Help
- Volunteer: Plant trees or restore a green space in your area.
- Donate: All monetary contributions directly support our mission.
- Lower your carbon footprint: Use our carbon footprint calculator to determine your footprint and _____ to reduce it.

해석

자연보호관리단

우리는 누구일까요
행정 전문가들과 400명 이상의 과학자가 있는 전문가 팀으로 구성된 우리는 토지와 수자원 보존에 전념하는, 가장 큰 규모의 비영리 재단입니다. 우리는 81개국에서 직접 진행하는 프로젝트와 지역 단체와의 동반자 관계를 통해 보전에 노력을 기울이고 있습니다.

우리는 무슨 일을 할까요
민간 기부금으로 모은 자금을 통해, 우리는 지역 지도자들에게 발언권을 부여하고 국내외 모두의 수준에서 환경 우선 정책을 위해 로비 활동을 함으로써 기후 변화에 맞섭니다. 우리의 다음 10년간의 주요 목표는 보전 프로그램과 지속 가능한 어업 계획을 통해 전 세계 바다의 10퍼센트를 보호하는 것입니다.

어떻게 도울 수 있을까요
- 자발적으로 참여하세요: 나무를 심거나 여러분의 지역 내 녹지 공간을 복원하세요.
- 기부하세요: 모든 금전적인 기부는 우리의 사명을 직접 지원합니다.
- 여러분의 탄소 발자국을 줄이세요: 저희의 탄소 발자국 계산기를 사용해서 여러분의 (탄소) 발자국을 확인하고 줄이기 위한 <u>조치를 취하세요</u>.

어휘

compose 구성하다   administrative 행정의   professional 전문가
expert 전문가의; 전문가   foundation 재단   dedicate 전념하다, 헌신하다
preservation 보존, 보호   conservation 보전, 보호
direct 직접 진행하는, 직접적인   domestic 국내의, 가정의
sustainable 지속 가능한   initiative 계획   restore 복원하다
monetary 금전적인   contribution 기여, 공헌
carbon footprint 탄소 발자국   calculator 계산기

05 독해 내용 일치 파악   난이도 중 ●●○

윗글에서 Nature Conservancy에 관한 내용과 일치하는 것은?

① It exclusively works through collaboration with local groups.
② It receives funding from government subsidies.
③ It advocates for domestic and international environmentally friendly policies.
④ It aims to protect 10 percent of all land areas in the next 10 years.

해석

① 그것은 오직 지역 단체와의 협업을 통해서 활동한다.
② 그것은 정부 보조금으로 자금 지원을 받는다.
③ 그것은 국내외 환경친화적인 정책들을 옹호한다.
④ 그것은 향후 10년 안에 모든 내륙 지역의 10퍼센트를 보호하는 것을 목표로 한다.

해설

③번의 키워드인 environmentally friendly policies(환경친화적인 정책들)를 바꾸어 표현한 지문의 environment-first policies(환경 우선 정책) 주변의 내용에서 자연보호관리단은 국내외 수준에서 환경 우선 정책을 위해 로비 활동을 한다고 했으므로, ③ '그것은 국내외 환경친화적인 정책들을 옹호한다'가 지문의 내용과 일치한다.

[오답 분석]
① 자연보호관리단은 직접 진행하는 프로젝트와 지역 단체와의 동반자 관계를 통해 보존에 노력을 기울인다고 했으므로, 그것이 오직 지역 단체와의 협업을 통해서 활동한다는 것은 지문의 내용과 다르다.
② 자연보호관리단은 민간 기부금으로 모은 자금을 통해 기후 변화에 맞선다고 했으므로, 그것이 정부 보조금으로 자금 지원을 받는다는 것은 지문의 내용과 다르다.
④ 자연보호관리단의 다음 10년간의 주요 목표로 전 세계 바다의 10퍼센트를 보호하는 것이 있다고 했지만, 그것이 향후 10년 안에 모든 내륙 지역의 10퍼센트를 보호하는 것을 목표로 하는지는 알 수 없다.

정답 ③

어휘

exclusively 오직, 배타적으로   subsidy 보조금   advocate 옹호하다, 지지하다

06 독해 빈칸 완성 - 구   난이도 중 ●●○

윗글의 밑줄 친 부분에 들어갈 말로 적절한 것은?

① keep in touch   ② hit the road
③ take action   ④ run away

해석

① 연락하다   ② 먼 길을 나서다
③ 조치를 취하다   ④ 달아나다

해설

빈칸이 있는 문장에서 탄소 발자국을 줄이기 위해 탄소 발자국 계산기를 사용하여 자신의 탄소 발자국을 확인하라고 했으므로, 탄소 발자국을 줄이기 위한 '조치를 취하'라고 한 ③번이 정답이다.

정답 ③

어휘

keep in touch 연락하다   hit the road 먼 길을 나서다
take action 조치를 취하다   run away 달아나다

07 독해 목적 파악   난이도 중 ●●○

다음 글의 목적으로 적절한 것은?

To	clients@signalinvestments.com
From	no-reply@signalinvestments.com
Date	June 10
Subject	Meeting investment goals

Dear Valued Customers,

Signal Investments knows that planning for your future is about more than simply setting financial goals. You need to make smart, intentional choices to secure your life after retirement. Here are five ways that you can do that:

1. Consistently contribute to your investment account to maximize growth.
2. As your income grows, consider increasing your contributions to retirement or investment accounts to boost your long-term financial benefits.
3. Build wealth strategically through age-appropriate investments: consider aggressive portfolios in your early career, then gradually shift toward more conservative investments.
4. Diversify your investments to protect yourself from sudden changes in the market and optimize long-term returns.
5. Periodically review your investment plan to track your savings and make changes as your needs and goals shift.

For more strategies to maximize your retirement investing, please visit the Signal Retirement Planning Center on our website.

Sincerely,

Signal Investments

① to notify customers of ways to optimize their finances for retirement
② to notify customers of a new strategy to diversify investments
③ to notify customers of the importance of retirement plans
④ to notify customers of the need to review their investment plans

해석

수신: clients@signalinvestments.com
발신: no-reply@signalinvestments.com
날짜: 6월 10일
제목: 투자 목표 충족시키기

소중하신 고객 여러분께,

Signal 투자 회사는 여러분의 미래를 계획하는 것이 단순히 재정 목표를 설정하는 것 이상이라는 점을 알고 있습니다. 여러분은 퇴직 이후의 삶을 보장하기 위해 현명하고, 의도적인 선택을 하셔야 합니다. 여기 여러분이 그것을 실천할 수 있는 다섯 가지 방법이 있습니다.

1. 성장을 극대화하기 위해 투자 계좌에 지속적으로 기여하세요.
2. 여러분의 수입이 증가함에 따라, 장기적인 재정 이익을 늘리기 위해 퇴직 연금 계좌나 투자 계좌에 대한 기여금을 늘리는 것을 고려하세요.
3. 연령대에 적합한 투자를 통해 전략적으로 부를 축적하세요: 직장 생활 초기에는 공격적인 포트폴리오를 고려하고, 그 후에 점차 더 보수적인 투자로 전환해 가세요.
4. 시장의 급격한 변화로부터 스스로를 보호하기 위해 투자를 다각화하고 장기적인 수익을 최적화하세요.
5. 정기적으로 투자 계획을 검토하여 저축 상황을 확인하고 필요와 목표 전환에 따라 변화를 주세요.

퇴직 연금 투자를 극대화하기 위한 더 많은 전략이 궁금하시다면, 당사 웹사이트의 Signal 퇴직 연금 설계 센터를 방문해 주세요.

진심을 담아,

Signal 투자 회사

① 고객에게 은퇴를 위한 재정을 최적화하는 방법에 대해 알리려고
② 고객에게 투자를 다각화하는 새로운 전략에 대해 알리려고
③ 고객에게 퇴직 연금 제도의 중요성에 대해 알리려고
④ 고객에게 투자 계획을 검토해야 할 필요성에 대해 알리려고

해설

지문 처음에서 퇴직 이후의 삶을 보장하기 위한 다섯 가지 방법이 있다고 하고, 지문 중간에서 퇴직 연금 투자를 극대화하는 전략들을 소개하고 있으므로, ① '고객에게 은퇴를 위한 재정을 최적화하는 방법에 대해 알리려고'가 이 글의 목적이다.

정답 ①

어휘

financial 재정적인   intentional 의도적인   retirement 퇴직 (연금), 은퇴
contribute 기여하다   account 계좌, 계정   maximize 극대화하다
strategically 전략적으로   appropriate 적합한   aggressive 공격적인
gradually 점차   conservative 보수적인   diversify 다각화하다, 다양화하다
optimize 최적화하다   long-term 장기적인   return 수익, 반환; 돌아오다
periodically 정기적으로   track 확인하다, 추적하다; 길   saving 저축

08 독해 제목 파악   난이도 중 ●●○

다음 글의 제목으로 적절한 것은?

The upper levels of Earth's atmosphere contain narrow bands of strong winds known as jet streams. These streams form when warm air masses converge with cold air masses. They play a strong role in influencing the weather, and are thus of great interest to meteorologists. As a general rule, greater differences in temperature cause the jet stream to flow faster, with mixtures of winter polar and subtropical air sometimes generating winds exceeding 200 miles per hour. When this occurs, these powerful jet streams dip southward, bringing sudden cold waves and triggering heavy snowfall in regions that normally experience milder conditions. As demonstrated by such effects, the jet stream's power gives it the capacity to generate powerful storms and to shape weather systems on a large scale.

① How Jet Streams Regulate Temperature
② Cold Wave Warning: Increasing Weather Volatility
③ Tracking the Formation of Tropical Storms
④ The Influence of the Jet Stream on Weather

해석
지구 대기의 상층부는 제트 기류라고 알려진 좁은 강풍 대역을 포함하고 있다. 이 기류는 따뜻한 기단이 차가운 기단과 만날 때 형성된다. 그것들은 날씨에 영향을 주는 데 있어 강력한 역할을 하고, 그래서 기상학자들의 큰 관심사이다. 일반적으로, 더 큰 기온 차이는 제트 기류가 더 빨리 흐르게 하며, 겨울인 극지방의 공기와 아열대 공기의 혼합은 때때로 시속 200마일이 넘는 바람을 일으킨다. 이 현상이 일어나면, 이 강력한 제트 기류는 남쪽으로 내려가고, 평소에는 더 온화한 기후를 경험하는 지역들에 갑작스러운 한파를 가져오고 폭설을 유발한다. 이와 같은 결과들에 의해 증명된 것처럼, 제트 기류의 힘은 그것에 강한 폭풍을 일으키고 대규모로 날씨 체계를 형성하는 능력을 부여한다.

① 제트 기류가 기온을 조절하는 방법
② 한파 경보: 증가하는 날씨 변동성
③ 열대 폭풍의 형성 추적하기
④ 제트 기류가 날씨에 미치는 영향

해설
지문 전반에 걸쳐 지구 대기의 상층부에서 기단의 온도 차이로 인해 생성되는 제트 기류는 날씨에 강력한 영향을 주는데, 이것에는 강한 폭풍을 일으키고 대규모로 날씨 체계를 형성하는 능력이 있다고 설명하고 있다. 따라서 ④ '제트 기류가 날씨에 미치는 영향'이 이 글의 제목이다.

정답 ④

어휘
atmosphere 대기, 분위기 stream 기류, 흐름, 추세 air mass 기단
converge 만나다, 모이다 meteorologist 기상학자
polar 극지방의, 양극의 subtropical 아열대의
generate 일으키다, 발생시키다 exceed 넘다, 초과하다
dip 내려가다, 살짝 담그다 sudden 갑작스러운 cold wave 한파
trigger 유발하다 demonstrate 증명하다 capacity 능력, 수용력
on a large scale 대규모로 regulate 조절하다 volatility 변동성, 휘발성

---

09 독해 문단 순서 배열   난이도 중 ●●○

주어진 글 다음에 이어질 글의 순서로 적절한 것은?

Archaeologists had long assumed that all inhabitants of Herculaneum, an ancient city located at the western base of Mount Vesuvius, consumed the same type of food. But an analysis of the remains revealed some interesting details about them.

(A) Archaeologists now know that, based on these gender differences, the men had a higher proportion of seafood in their diet compared to the women, whose main source of protein came from animal products rather than fish.

(B) However, the researchers found a significant difference between what the men ate and what the women ate upon further examination of this dietary pattern. Ratios of carbon and nitrogen isotopes of amino acids collected from the skeletons showed that women mostly took in a different source of protein.

(C) The amino acids from 17 adult skeletons indicated that the people ingested plenty of seafood. It appears that, overall, they ingested three times more fish than their modern counterparts.

*isotope: (화학) 동위 원소

① (A) – (C) – (B)   ② (B) – (A) – (C)
③ (C) – (A) – (B)   ④ (C) – (B) – (A)

해석
고고학자들은 오랫동안 베수비오 산의 서쪽 기슭에 위치한 고대 도시 Herculaneum의 모든 주민들이 같은 종류의 음식을 먹었다고 추측해 왔다. 그러나 유골에 대한 분석 연구는 그들에 대한 몇 가지 흥미로운 세부 사항을 밝혀냈다.

(A) 고고학자들은 이 성별 차이에 기반하여, 단백질의 주요 공급원이 생선보다는 동물성 식품이었던 여성들에 비해, 남성들이 그들의 식사에서 해산물의 비율이 더 높았음을 이제 알고 있다.

(B) 하지만, 연구원들은 이 식이 패턴에 대한 추가적인 조사에서 남성들이 먹은 것과 여성들이 먹은 것 사이의 상당한 차이를 발견했다. 해골에서 채취된 아미노산의 탄소와 질소 동위원소의 비율은 여성들이 주로 다른 단백질원을 섭취했다는 것을 보여 주었다.

(C) 17개의 성인 해골에서 나온 아미노산은 그 사람들이 많은 해산물을 섭취했다는 것을 나타냈다. 전반적으로, 그들은 현대의 사람들보다 세 배 더 많은 생선을 섭취한 것으로 보인다.

해설
주어진 문장에서 고대 도시 Herculaneum의 주민들의 유골 분석 연구 결과 몇 가지 흥미로운 세부 사항이 밝혀졌다고 언급한 후, (C)에서 전반적으로(overall) 그들은 현대인들보다 세 배 더 많은 생선을 섭취한 것으로 보인다고 알려 주고 있다. 이어서 (B)에서 하지만(However) 이 식이 패턴(this dietary pattern)에 대한 추가 조사에서 연구원들은 남성과 여성이 섭취한 단백질원이 서로 다름을 발견했다고 하고, (A)에서 이 성별 차이(these gender differences)에 기반하여 남성은 주로 해산물을, 여성은 동물성 식품을 먹었다고 설명하고 있다. 따라서 ④ (C) – (B) – (A)가 정답이다.

정답 ④

어휘
archaeologist 고고학자 inhabitant 주민 consume 먹다, 섭취하다
remains 유골, 나머지 gender 성(별) proportion 비율 protein 단백질
examination 조사, 검사 dietary 식이 (요법)의 ratio 비율 skeleton 해골
take in ~을 섭취하다, 흡수하다 ingest 섭취하다
counterpart (대응 관계에 있는) 사람

10 독해 문장 삽입 난이도 중 ●●○

주어진 문장이 들어갈 위치로 적절한 것은?

> They obtain our profiles and follow what we click on online, and then provide tailored product choices based on our surfing habits.

> Matthew Tobin Anderson's 2002 novel *Feed* introduced us to a culture that was strongly influenced by advertising and the use of Internet-capable brain implants called "feed." (①) Feed is designed not only to give people constant access to databases of music, movies, and other entertainment products but also to detect an individual's personal preferences and to communicate with the user through the implant. (②) This idea of directly connecting to the brains of people is comparable to the marketing landscape today. (③) Like a prediction of what we're experiencing now, Anderson's feed is a portrayal of how companies control our shopping behavior. (④) Indeed, present-day consumerism shares similarities with the strategy in *Feed*.

해석

그것들은 우리의 프로필을 입수하고 우리가 온라인에서 클릭하는 것을 따라간 다음, 우리의 인터넷 검색 습관에 기반하여 맞춤형 제품 선택지들을 제공한다.

Matthew Tobin Anderson의 2002년 소설 『피드』는 우리에게 광고와 '피드'로 불리는, 인터넷에 접속 가능한 뇌 임플란트에 강하게 영향받은 문화를 소개했다. ① 피드는 사람들에게 음악, 영화, 그리고 다른 엔터테인먼트 제품들의 데이터베이스로의 지속적인 접근권을 부여하기 위해서뿐만 아니라 개인적인 선호를 감지하고 (뇌) 임플란트를 통해 사용자와 소통할 수 있도록 고안된다. ② 사람들의 뇌에 직접 연결한다는 이 발상은 오늘날의 마케팅 분야와 유사하다. ③ 현재 우리가 경험하고 있는 것에 대한 예측처럼, Anderson의 피드는 기업들이 어떻게 우리의 구매 행동을 통제하는지에 대한 묘사이다. ④ 실제로, 오늘날의 소비지상주의는 『피드』 속 전략과 유사점을 공유한다.

해설

④번 앞 문장에 사람들의 뇌에 직접 연결한다는 발상의 Anderson의 피드는 기업들이 어떻게 우리의 구매 행동을 통제하는지에 대한 묘사라는 내용이 있고, 뒤 문장에 실제로 오늘날의 소비지상주의는 『피드』 속 전략과 유사점을 공유한다는 내용이 있으므로, ④번 자리에 그것들은(They)은 대중의 인터넷 검색 습관에 기반하여 맞춤형 제품 선택지들을 제공한다는 내용, 즉 『피드』 속 전략과 유사점을 갖는, 오늘날의 기업들이 우리의 구매 행동을 통제하는 방법에 대해 설명하는 주어진 문장이 나와야 지문이 자연스럽게 연결된다.

정답 ④

어휘

obtain 입수하다, 존재하다 tailored 맞춤의 detect 감지하다
preference 선호(도) comparable 유사한, 동등한 landscape 분야, 풍경
prediction 예측 portrayal 묘사 consumerism 소비지상주의

DAY 07 하프모의고사 07회

정답   p. 38

01	④	어휘	06	③	독해
02	②	문법	07	①	독해
03	②	문법	08	④	독해
04	②	생활영어	09	②	독해
05	④	독해	10	②	독해

취약영역 분석표

영역	맞힌 답의 개수
어휘	/1
생활영어	/1
문법	/2
독해	/6
TOTAL	/10

---

01 어휘 face   난이도 중 ●●○

밑줄 친 부분에 들어갈 말로 적절한 것은?

After the weather report warned of an approaching hurricane, citizens rushed to gather supplies necessary to _____ the disaster.

① reveal   ② ignore
③ accept   ④ face

[해석]
일기 예보가 다가오는 허리케인에 대해 경고하자, 시민들은 재난에 직면하는 데 필수적인 물자들을 서둘러 모았다.
① 폭로하다   ② 무시하다
③ 받아들이다   ④ 직면하다

정답 ④

[어휘]
rush 서두르다; 혼잡 supply 물자, 공급; 공급하다 reveal 폭로하다, 밝히다
ignore 무시하다 accept 받아들이다 face 직면하다, 맞서다

---

02 문법 병치 구문 | to 부정사   난이도 중 ●●○

밑줄 친 부분에 들어갈 말로 적절한 것은?

Maslow's hierarchy of needs enables us to understand basic human needs and _____ the insights in practical settings, categorizing human motivations into different levels.

① applying   ② apply
③ applied   ④ is applied

[해석]
Maslow의 욕구 단계는 우리로 하여금 인간의 기본적인 욕구를 이해하고 그 통찰을 실제 환경에 적용할 수 있게 하는데, 이것은 인간의 동기를 다양한 수준으로 분류한다.

[해설]
② 병치 구문 | to 부정사를 취하는 동사 빈칸은 등위접속사(and) 뒤에 오는 것의 자리이다. 등위접속사(and)로 연결된 병치 구문에서는 같은 구조끼리 연결되어야 하는데, and 앞에 동사 enable의 목적격 보어로 to 부정사 to understand가 왔으므로 and 뒤에도 to 부정사가 와야 한다. 이때 병치 구문에서 두 번째 나온 to는 생략될 수 있으므로 ② (to) apply가 정답이다.

정답 ②

[어휘]
hierarchy 단계, 계급 insight 통찰(력) practical 실제적인, 현실적인
categorize 분류하다 motivation 동기

---

03 문법 to 부정사 | 전치사 | 동사의 종류 | 목적어 | 어순   난이도 중 ●●○

밑줄 친 부분 중 어법상 옳지 않은 것은?

Thank you all for ① attending today's Get Out and Conquer webinar. This is your first step to freeing yourself from your office and becoming a digital nomad, allowing you ② working from anywhere in the world. Telecommunications advances have made ③ it possible to do a great number of jobs without being physically present in the office. Get Out and Conquer will teach you how ④ you can work outside the office so that you can offer your abilities to companies all over the world.

[해석]
오늘 인터넷 세미나 'Get Out and Conquer'에 참석해 주신 모든 분들께 감사드립니다. 이것은 여러분 자신을 사무실에서 해방시켜 디지털 유목민이 되기 위한 첫걸음이며, 이는 여러분이 세계 어디에서든 일할 수 있게 합니다. 통신의 발달은 사무실에 실제로 있지 않고도 많은 일들을 하는 것을 가능하게 만들었습니다. 'Get Out and Conquer'는 여러분이 전 세계 기업들에 능력을 제공하실 수 있도록 여러분께 사무실 밖에서 일할 수 있는 방법을 알려 드릴 것입니다.

해설

② **to 부정사를 취하는 동사**   동사 allow는 to 부정사를 목적격 보어로 취하므로 목적격 보어 자리의 working을 to 부정사 to work로 고쳐야 한다.

[오답 분석]

① **전치사 자리 | 타동사**   전치사(for) 뒤에는 명사 역할을 하는 것이 와야 한다. 이때 동사 attend는 전치사 없이 목적어를 바로 취하는 타동사이므로 목적어(today's Get Out and Conquer webinar) 앞에 동명사 attending이 올바르게 쓰였다.

③ **목적어 자리**   to 부정사구 목적어(to do ~ office)가 목적격 보어(possible)와 함께 오면 '가짜 목적어 it + 목적격 보어 + 진짜 목적어'의 형태가 되어야 하므로 가짜 목적어 it이 올바르게 쓰였다.

④ **어순**   간접 의문문은 '의문사 + 주어 + 동사'의 어순이 되어야 하므로 의문사 how 뒤에 you can이 올바르게 쓰였다.

정답 ②

어휘

webinar 인터넷 세미나   **nomad** 유목민   **physically** 실제로, 육체적으로

---

04 생활영어 I'll call and see if they can push back our reservation.   난이도 하 ●○○

밑줄 친 부분에 들어갈 말로 적절한 것은?

Luna Martinez
Did you book hotel rooms for our E Corp trip?
15:03

Joseph Hughes
Yes, I reserved rooms at the Lux Hotel for the 14th to 17th.
15:04

Luna Martinez
Hmm… We may need to change the reservation.
15:04

Joseph Hughes
Why? Is there a problem with that hotel?
15:05

Luna Martinez
No, the hotel's fine. But the E Corp meeting will be postponed until the 21st.
15:06

Joseph Hughes
I see.
15:07

① Let's stay at the Lux Hotel in that case.
② I'll call and see if they can push back our reservation.
③ We should prepare our presentation for the client.
④ I'll check the availability of closer accommodations.

해석

Luna Martinez: E 회사 출장을 위해 호텔 객실을 예약했나요?
Joseph Hughes: 네, Lux 호텔의 객실을 14일부터 17일까지 예약해 두었습니다.
Luna Martinez: 음… 우리는 예약을 변경할 필요가 있어요.
Joseph Hughes: 왜죠? 그 호텔에 무슨 문제라도 있나요?
Luna Martinez: 아뇨, 호텔은 괜찮아요. 그런데 E 회사와의 회의가 21일까지 연기될 거예요.
Joseph Hughes: 그렇군요. 제가 전화해서 예약을 미룰 수 있는지 알아보겠습니다.

① 그런 경우라면 Lux 호텔에서 머뭅시다.
② 제가 전화해서 예약을 미룰 수 있는지 알아보겠습니다.
③ 우리는 고객을 위해 발표를 준비해야 합니다.
④ 더 가까운 숙박 시설의 이용 가능 여부를 확인해 보겠습니다.

해설

E 회사 출장을 위해 14일부터 17일까지 Lux 호텔을 예약해 두었다는 Joseph에게 빈칸 앞에서 Luna가 But the E Corp meeting will be postponed until the 21st(그런데 E 회사와의 회의가 21일까지 연기될 거예요)라고 말하고 있으므로, '제가 전화해서 예약을 미룰 수 있는지 알아보겠습니다'라는 의미의 ② 'I'll call and see if they can push back our reservation'이 정답이다.

정답 ②

어휘

push back (시간·날짜를) 미루다   **accommodation** 숙박 시설

05~06 다음 글을 읽고 물음에 답하시오.

To	City Planning and Development Office
From	Arthur Mahoney
Date	September 19
Subject	Concerns Regarding an Abandoned Building

Dear Director of City Planning and Development,

This letter concerns the abandoned warehouse located off Highway 17, near the Cantu Street exit. Despite the city's assurances that this structure would be demolished, it has remained standing, which is a matter of concern for many residents.

In addition to being an eyesore, the structure appears to be unstable, with shattered windows and a partially collapsed roof. The presence of graffiti on its exterior walls suggests that people are illegally accessing the property. Given the _____ state of the structure, I feel like it is only a matter of time until someone gets hurt.

DAY 07 하프모의고사 07회

I kindly request that, for the good of the community, you honor the city's original commitment to tear down this hazardous building as soon as possible. Thank you for your attention to this pressing matter.

Respectfully yours,

Arthur Mahoney

해석

수신: 도시기획개발공단
발신: Arthur Mahoney
날짜: 9월 19일
제목: 버려진 건물들에 대한 우려 사항

도시기획개발공단의 책임자분께,

이 편지는 17번 고속도로에서 떨어진 곳에 위치한, Cantu로 출구 근처의 버려진 창고와 관련한 것입니다. 이 건물을 철거할 것이라는 시의 확언에도 불구하고, 그것은 여전히 남아 있어서 많은 주민들에게 우려의 대상이 되고 있습니다.

보기 흉할 뿐만 아니라, 그 건물은 산산이 부서진 창문들과 부분적으로 무너진 지붕 때문에 불안정해 보입니다. 외벽에 있는 낙서의 존재는 사람들이 불법적으로 그 건물에 접근하고 있음을 암시합니다. 건물의 열악한 상태를 고려할 때, 저는 누군가가 다치게 되는 것이 시간 문제일 뿐이라고 생각합니다.

지역 사회를 위하여, 이 위험한 건물을 가능한 한 빨리 해체하겠다는 시의 원래 약속을 지켜 주시길 정중히 요청드립니다. 이 시급한 문제에 관심을 가져 주신 데 감사드립니다.

당신을 존경하는,
Arthur Mahoney

어휘

abandoned 버려진, 유기된 warehouse 창고 assurance 확언, 보증
demolish 철거하다 eyesore 보기 흉한 것 unstable 불안정한
shatter 산산이 부수다 collapse 무너지다, 붕괴되다 graffiti 낙서
exterior 외부의 property 건물, 부동산, 재산
honor (약속을) 지키다, 존경하다, 명예를 주다 commitment 약속, 헌신
tear down ~을 해체하다, 파괴하다 hazardous 위험한 pressing 시급한

---

05 독해 목적 파악   난이도 중 ●●○

윗글의 목적으로 적절한 것은?

① 근처 고속도로가 훼손된 상황을 알리려고
② 건물 외벽의 불법 낙서에 대해 신고하려고
③ 불법 건축물로 인해 부상을 입은 사실을 공유하려고
④ 시에서 약속한 폐건물의 철거에 대해 상기시키려고

해설

지문 전반에 걸쳐 17번 고속도로 출구 근처에 버려진 창고는 철거할 것이라는 시의 확언에도 불구하고 아직 남아 있는데, 건물이 보기 흉할 뿐 아니라 불안정한 상태이므로 이 위험한 건물을 빨리 해체하겠다는 시의 원래

약속을 지켜 달라고 요청하고 있다. 따라서 ④ '시에서 약속한 폐건물의 철거에 대해 상기시키려고'가 이 글의 목적이다.

정답 ④

---

06 독해 빈칸 완성 - 단어   난이도 하 ●○○

윗글의 밑줄 친 부분에 들어갈 말로 적절한 것은?

① uneven   ② firm
③ poor   ④ light

해석

① 평평하지 않은   ② 견고한
③ 열악한   ④ 가벼운

해설

빈칸 앞부분에서 그 건물은 산산이 부서진 창문들과 부분적으로 무너진 지붕 때문에 불안정해 보인다고 하고, 빈칸이 있는 문장에서 누군가가 다치게 되는 것이 시간 문제라고 생각한다고 했으므로, 건물의 '열악한' 상태라고 한 ③번이 정답이다.

정답 ③

어휘

uneven 평평하지 않은, 고르지 않은 firm 견고한, 딱딱한 poor 열악한, 가난한
light 가벼운, 밝은

---

07 독해 요지 파악   난이도 상 ●●●

다음 글의 요지로 적절한 것은?

Companies and public figures in the US frequently file lawsuits that they don't intend to win, solely to damage the defendant by costing them money. These suits are known as "strategic lawsuits against public participation," or SLAPP suits. Such suits are generally punitive in nature, being filed in response to some form of perceived defamation, and are aimed at discouraging others from speaking out about an issue. SLAPP suits are problematic, yet effective in leaving media outlets and individuals fearful of criticizing many public figures. While some states have legislation limiting such practices, far too many plaintiffs simply file their suits in another state.

① SLAPP suits are designed to punish defendants through excessive legal costs.
② Public figures should be careful not to insult others in their public statements.
③ Media outlets have a responsibility to defend honest news coverage.
④ Legislation preventing SLAPP suits needs to be revised.

07회 정답·해석·해설

해커스공무원 비비안 영어 매일 하프모의고사

해석

미국에서 기업들과 유명 인사들은 그들이 승소할 의도가 없고, 오로지 비용을 지불하게 함으로써 피고에게 해를 입히기 위한 의도의 소송을 빈번히 제기한다. 이러한 소송은 '전략적 봉쇄 소송', 즉 SLAPP 소송으로 알려져 있다. 그러한 소송들은 일반적으로 사실상 처벌을 위한 것인데, 일종의 인지된 명예 훼손에 대한 대응으로 제기되며, 다른 사람들이 어떤 쟁점에 대해 공개적으로 말하지 못하게 막으려는 것을 목표로 삼는다. 전략적 봉쇄 소송은 문제가 있지만, 매스컴과 개인들이 많은 유명 인사들을 비판하는 것에 두려움을 느끼게 하는 데 효과적이다. 일부 주들은 그러한 관행을 제한하는 법안을 가지고 있지만, 너무 많은 고소인들이 단순히 또 다른 주에서 소송을 제기한다.

① 전략적 봉쇄 소송은 과도한 법적 비용을 통해 피고들을 처벌하기 위해 고안된다.
② 유명 인사들은 공개적 발언에서 타인을 모독하지 않도록 주의해야 한다.
③ 매스컴은 정직한 뉴스 보도를 옹호할 책임이 있다.
④ 전략적 봉쇄 소송을 막는 법안이 개정될 필요가 있다.

해설

지문 처음에서 기업들과 유명 인사들은 승소할 의도 없이 오로지 비용 지불로써 피고에게 해를 입히기 위한 전략적 봉쇄 소송을 빈번히 제기한다고 하고, 지문 중간에서 전략적 봉쇄 소송이 명예 훼손에 대한 대응으로 제기되는 처벌성 소송임을 알려 주고 있다. 따라서 ① '전략적 봉쇄 소송은 과도한 법적 비용을 통해 피고들을 처벌하기 위해 고안된다'가 이 글의 요지이다.

정답 ①

어휘

figure 인물, 숫자 file 제기하다, 제출하다, 보관하다 lawsuit 소송
solely 오로지 defendant 피고 suit 소송 strategic 전략적인
punitive 처벌을 위한, 가혹한 in nature 사실상 perceive 인지하다
defamation 명예 훼손 discourage 막다, 단념시키다
media outlet 매스컴 legislation 법안 plaintiff 고소인, 원고
excessive 과도한 insult 모독하다 statement 발언, 진술
defend 옹호하다 coverage 보도 revise 개정하다, 수정하다

---

08 독해 내용 일치 파악   난이도 중 ●●○

Glacier Conservation Agency에 관한 다음 글의 내용과 일치하는 것은?

About the Glacier Conservation Agency (GCA)

The Glacier Conservation Agency (GCA) is a government agency dedicated to the preservation of the nation's glaciers. Guided by a strong commitment to science and innovation, the GCA employs advanced satellite imaging, as well as ground-based surveys, to monitor glacier size, movement, and melt rates. It shares the information it obtains with international research institutions, which it collaborates with to develop new strategies to save these vital ecosystems. In addition to research, the GCA works with other government agencies to implement legislation limiting land use in sensitive glacier areas. It has the authority to enforce this legislation through the imposition of fines, the suspension of permits, and, when necessary, legal action.

① It develops strategies to address glacier melting.
② It provides funding to international research institutions.
③ It is the only government body authorized to determine land-use policies.
④ It can impose fines to enforce related legislation.

해석

빙하보존연구원(GCA)에 대해

빙하보존연구원은 국가의 빙하 보존에 전념하는 정부 기관입니다. 과학과 혁신에 대한 강한 헌신을 지침 삼아, 빙하보존연구원은 빙하의 크기, 이동, 그리고 해빙 속도를 관찰하기 위해 지상 기반의 조사뿐만 아니라 첨단 위성 영상을 활용합니다. 기관은 획득한 정보를 국제 연구 기관들과 공유하는데, 이 국제 연구 기관들은 이러한 필수 생태계를 살리는 새로운 전략을 개발하기 위해 빙하보존연구원과 협력하는 것입니다. 연구 외에도, 빙하보존연구원은 민감한 빙하 지역에서의 토지 이용을 제한하는 법안을 시행하기 위해 다른 정부 기관들과 함께 일합니다. 기관은 벌금 부과, 허가 중지, 그리고 필요한 경우, 법적 조치를 통해 이러한 법안을 집행할 권한을 가지고 있습니다.

① 그것은 해빙을 해결하기 위해 전략을 개발한다.
② 그것은 국제 연구 기관들에 자금을 제공한다.
③ 그것은 토지 이용 정책을 결정할 권한이 부여된 유일한 정부 기관이다.
④ 그것은 관련 법률을 집행하기 위해 벌금을 부과할 수 있다.

해설

④번의 키워드인 impose fines(벌금을 부과하다)를 바꾸어 표현한 지문의 imposition of fines(벌금 부과) 주변의 내용에서 빙하보존연구원은 벌금 부과 등의 조치를 통해 민감한 빙하 지역에서의 토지 이용을 제한하는 법안을 집행할 권한을 가지고 있다고 했으므로, ④ '그것은 관련 법률을 집행하기 위해 벌금을 부과할 수 있다'가 지문의 내용과 일치한다.

[오답 분석]
① 빙하보존연구원이 빙하의 해빙 속도를 관찰하기 위해 조사하고 위성 영상을 활용한다고는 했지만, 그것이 해빙을 해결하기 위해 전략을 개발하는지는 알 수 없다.
② 빙하보존연구원이 획득한 정보를 국제 연구 기관들과 공유한다고는 했지만, 그것이 국제 연구 기관들에 자금을 제공하는지는 알 수 없다.
③ 빙하보존연구원은 토지 이용 제한 법안 시행을 위해 다른 정부 기관들과 함께 일한다고 했으므로, 그것이 토지 이용 정책을 결정할 권한이 부여된 유일한 정부 기관이라는 것은 지문의 내용과 다르다.

정답 ④

어휘

glacier 빙하 conservation 보존, 보호 dedicate 전념하다
preservation 보존, 보호 commitment 헌신, 약속 innovation 혁신
employ 활용하다, 고용하다 advanced 첨단의, 선진의 satellite 위성
survey 조사; 조사하다 obtain 획득하다 institution 기관
collaborate 협력하다 strategy 전략 vital 필수적인 ecosystem 생태계

DAY 07 하프모의고사 07회

implement 시행하다 legislation 법안 sensitive 민감한 authority 권한
enforce 집행하다 imposition 부과 suspension 중지
authorized 권한이 부여된

09 독해 무관한 문장 삭제 난이도 중 ●●○

다음 글의 흐름상 어색한 문장은?

A 2009 study showed guppies can evolve in under 30 generations, making it observable to humans. A number of guppies from the Yarra River were divided into two groups. ① One of these groups was introduced to an area that had been cleared of predators, while the other was put in a section of the river that had extra predators added. ② The evolutionary changes observed in guppies were primarily caused by temperature fluctuations rather than predation levels. ③ Eight years later, within 30 generations, those in the low-predation area had evolved to have fewer babies, and become larger. ④ This evolution helped them survive the increased competition that comes from higher survival rates. Those in the high-predation area, on the other hand, had evolved to have much faster reproductive cycles with more offspring, which were generally smaller.

해석

2009년 연구는 구피가 30세대도 안 되어서 진화할 수 있음을 보여 주었는데, 이는 인간에게 관찰할 만한 것이었다. Yarra 강에 사는 많은 구피들이 두 집단으로 나뉘었다. ① 이 집단들 중 하나는 포식자가 전혀 없는 지역에 들여와진 반면, 또 다른 무리는 추가적인 포식자들이 더해진 강의 한 구역에 풀어졌다. ② 구피에게서 관찰된 진화적 변화는 주로 포식 수준보다는 온도 변동에 의해 일어났다. ③ 8년 후, 30세대 내에서 포식 수준이 낮은 지역에 있던 구피들은 더 적은 새끼를 가지도록 진화했고 더 커졌다. ④ 이 진화는 그것들이 더 높은 생존율에서 기인한 치열해진 경쟁에서 살아남도록 도왔다. 반면에, 포식 수준이 높은 지역에 있는 구피들은 더 많은 새끼들을 갖는, 훨씬 더 빠른 번식 주기를 가지도록 진화했는데, 이것들은 일반적으로 더 작았다.

해설

지문 앞부분에서 30세대 내에서 진화할 수 있는 구피 연구를 위해 Yarra 강에 사는 구피들을 두 집단으로 나누었다고 언급한 뒤, ①번은 '서식 환경의 포식자의 유무에 따른 구피 집단 구분', ③, ④번은 '8년 후 각 집단에 나타난 진화 결과'에 대해 설명하고 있다. 그러나 ②번은 '포식 수준보다 온도 변동에 의해 일어난 구피의 진화'에 대한 내용으로, 지문 전반의 내용과 관련이 없다.

정답 ②

어휘

evolve 진화하다 generation 세대 observable 관찰할 수 있는
divide 나누다 predator 포식자, 약탈자 section 구역, 부분
primarily 주로 fluctuation 변동 competition 경쟁
reproductive 번식의, 생식의 offspring 새끼

10 독해 문장 삽입 난이도 중 ●●○

주어진 문장이 들어갈 위치로 적절한 것은?

As a result, most advertisements try to communicate how a person might feel with the marketed product in their lives.

Many advertising agencies employ psychologists in an attempt to maximize the effectiveness of their ads. The crossover between these disciplines is particularly pronounced in emotional advertisements. (①) Numerous studies have shown that customers react more strongly to emotions than reason. (②) Rather than listing a product's features, letting you imagine its application, advertising will often show the users' emotional responses, such as a sense of relief or satisfaction. (③) This invariable tactic has been used since the 1700s, when a brewery's contents were being auctioned off. (④) Advertisers said, "We are not here to sell boilers and vats, but the potential for extraordinary wealth and success."

해석

그 결과, 대부분의 광고는 한 사람이 인생에서 그 홍보되는 상품으로 인해 어떤 기분이 들지를 전달하려고 한다.

많은 광고 대행사들은 그들 광고의 유효성을 극대화하기 위해 심리학자들을 고용한다. 이 분야들(광고와 심리학) 사이의 교차는 특히 감정을 자극하는 광고들에서 확연하다. ① 수많은 연구들이 소비자들이 이성보다는 감정에 더 강하게 반응한다는 것을 보여 주었다. ② 어떤 상품의 특징들을 열거하기보다는, 당신이 그것을 이용하는 것을 상상하게 하면서, 광고는 종종 안도감이나 만족감과 같이 사용자들의 감정적 반응들을 보여 줄 것이다. ③ 이 변치 않는 전략은 어느 양조장의 내용물이 경매로 처분되고 있던 1700년대 이래로 사용되어 왔다. ④ 광고주들은 "우리는 보일러나 대형 통이 아니라, 대단히 부유해지고 성공할 잠재성을 팔기 위해 여기에 있습니다"라고 말했다.

해설

②번 앞 문장에 많은 연구들이 소비자들이 이성보다는 감정에 더 강하게 반응한다는 것을 보여 주었다는 내용이 있고, 뒤 문장에 광고는 어떤 상품의 특징들을 열거하기보다는 안도감이나 만족감과 같이 사용자들이 그 상품으로 인해 어떤 기분이 드는지를 보여 줄 것이라고 했으므로, ②번 자리에 그 결과(As a result) 대부분의 광고는 한 사람이 그 홍보되는 상품으로 인해 어떤 기분이 들지를 전달하려고 한다는 내용, 즉 연구 결과에 따른 광고 전략을 설명하는 주어진 문장이 나와야 지문이 자연스럽게 연결된다.

정답 ②

어휘

agency 대행사 employ 고용하다 psychologist 심리학자
maximize 극대화하다 crossover 교차, 교차로 discipline 분야, 규율
pronounced 확연한, 단호한 feature 특징, 특집 기사
application 이용, 적용 relief 안도, 안심 invariable 변치 않는
tactic 전략 brewery 양조장 auction off ~을 경매로 처분하다 vat 대형 통
extraordinary 대단한, 비범한 wealth 부유함, 재산

DAY 08 하프모의고사 08회

정답

p. 42

01	②	어휘	06	②	독해
02	②	문법	07	②	독해
03	①	문법	08	②	독해
04	④	생활영어	09	③	독해
05	④	독해	10	②	독해

취약영역 분석표

영역	맞힌 답의 개수
어휘	/1
생활영어	/1
문법	/2
독해	/6
TOTAL	/10

---

01 어휘 prioritize   난이도 중 ●●○

밑줄 친 부분에 들어갈 말로 적절한 것은?

The couple _____ saving money rather than living luxuriously, with the goal of building up a sizable sum of money for their retirement.

① stopped
② prioritized
③ postponed
④ minded

해석

그 두 사람은 자신들의 은퇴를 위해 많은 액수의 돈을 마련하겠다는 목표를 갖고, 호화스럽게 사는 것보다 절약하는 것을 <u>우선시했다</u>.

① 멈추었다
② 우선시했다
③ 미뤘다
④ 꺼렸다

정답 ②

어휘

sizable 많은, 상당한   retirement 은퇴   prioritize 우선시하다
postpone 미루다   mind 꺼리다

---

02 문법 수동태|수 일치   난이도 중 ●●○

밑줄 친 부분에 들어갈 말로 적절한 것은?

Furniture created by expert designers for small apartments _____ at the exhibition.

① showcased
② is showcased
③ are showcased
④ have been showcased

해석

작은 아파트 전용으로 전문 디자이너들에 의해 만들어진 가구들이 전시회에서 선보여졌다.

해설

② 능동태·수동태 구별 | 주어와 동사의 수 일치   빈칸은 문장의 동사 자리이다. 주어 Furniture와 동사가 '가구가 선보여졌다'라는 의미의 수동 관계이므로 수동태 형태로 쓰인 ② is showcased, ③ are showcased, ④ have been showcased가 정답 후보이다. 이때 주어 자리에 단수 취급하는 불가산 명사 Furniture가 왔으므로 단수 수동태로 쓰인 ② is showcased가 정답이다.

정답 ②

어휘

furniture 가구   exhibition 전시(회)

---

03 문법 대명사|명사절|부사|동사의 종류|수 일치   난이도 중 ●●○

밑줄 친 부분 중 어법상 옳지 않은 것은?

The platypus has a broad, flat bill that resembles ① <u>those</u> of ducks and a furry body like a beaver, which surprised European biologists. ② <u>What</u> was later learned about the platypus made it seem like an ③ <u>even</u> stranger creature. It was discovered that the platypus does not give birth to live young like nearly every other mammal, but instead ④ <u>lays</u> eggs like a bird.

해석

오리너구리는 오리의 것과 닮은 넓고 평평한 부리와, 비버처럼 털로 덮인 몸을 가지고 있는데, 이는 유럽의 생물학자들을 놀라게 했다. 오리너구리에 대해 더 나중에 알려진 것은 그것이 훨씬 더 이상한 생물인 것처럼 보이게 만들었다. 오리너구리가 다른 거의 모든 포유류와 같이 살아 있는 새끼를 낳지 않고, 그 대신 새처럼 알을 낳는다는 사실이 밝혀진 것이었다.

해설

① 지시대명사   대명사가 지시하는 명사가 단수 명사(bill)이므로 복수 지시대명사 those를 단수 지시대명사 that으로 고쳐야 한다.

DAY 08 하프모의고사 08회

[오답 분석]

② **명사절 접속사** 주어가 없는 불완전한 절(was later ~ platypus)을 이끌면서 문장의 주어 자리에 올 수 있는 명사절 접속사 What이 올바르게 쓰였다.

③ **강조 부사** 비교급(stranger) 앞에 비교급을 강조할 수 있는 강조 부사 even이 올바르게 쓰였다.

④ **혼동하기 쉬운 자동사와 타동사 | 주어와 동사의 수 일치** 문맥상 '알을 낳다'라는 의미가 되어야 자연스러우므로 타동사 lay((알을) 낳다)가 올 수 있고, that절의 주어 자리에 단수 명사 the platypus가 왔으므로 단수 동사 lays가 올바르게 쓰였다.

정답 ①

어휘

broad 넓은 flat 평평한 bill 부리, 계산서 resemble 닮다 furry 털로 덮인 give birth to ~을 낳다 lay (알을) 낳다

---

04 생활영어 I'll bring you the bill.   난이도 하 ●○○

두 사람의 대화 중 가장 어색한 것은?

① A: Where can I find the closest convenience store?
   B: It's just two blocks ahead on your right.

② A: What do you do to relax after work?
   B: I pour myself a glass of wine.

③ A: Do you think you can come and lend me a hand?
   B: Hold on, I'll be there in a minute.

④ A: Can you recommend a dish on the menu?
   B: Yes, of course. I'll bring you the bill.

해석

① A: 가장 가까운 편의점을 어디서 찾을 수 있나요?
   B: 두 블록만 가시면 오른쪽에 있어요.

② A: 퇴근 후에 휴식을 취하기 위해 무엇을 하시나요?
   B: 저는 와인 한 잔을 따라 마셔요.

③ A: 와서 저를 좀 도와주실 수 있나요?
   B: 잠시 기다려요, 금방 갈게요.

④ A: 메뉴에 있는 요리 좀 추천해 주시겠어요?
   B: 네, 물론이죠. 계산서를 가져다드릴게요.

해설

④번에서 A는 메뉴에 있는 요리를 추천해 달라고 요청하고 있으므로, 계산서를 가져다주겠다는 B의 대답 ④ 'I'll bring you the bill'(계산서를 가져다드릴게요)은 어울리지 않는다.

정답 ④

어휘

lend a hand 도움을 주다 hold on (잠시) 기다리다 recommend 추천하다 bill 계산서

05~06   다음 글을 읽고 물음에 답하시오.

_____(A)_____

If you have a sweet tooth and a big heart, come support the bake sale for the Art for Everyone Association.

This charity organization provides children in need with opportunities to experience and participate in art. Your support helps kids discover their artistic passion!

A wide variety of baked goods will be provided by local bakeries and home cooks. All proceeds from the bake sale will be used to purchase art supplies and fund field trips to museums and other cultural centers.

Give the gift of art!

Organized by Art for Everyone

- **Location**: Sheraton Farmer's Market, Booth 121
- **Date**: Saturday, February 20
- **Time**: 8:00 a.m. to 2:00 p.m.

If you are unable to attend but would like to donate, monetary contributions can be given at www.artforeveryoneassoc.org/donationpage.

해석

(A) 아이들의 예술적 기회를 위한 모금 행사

달콤한 것을 좋아하고 따뜻한 마음씨를 가지셨다면, 예술온누리협회를 위한 빵 판매에 오셔서 후원해 주세요.

이 자선 단체는 도움이 필요한 아이들에게 예술을 경험하고 예술에 참여할 수 있는 기회를 제공합니다. 여러분의 후원은 아이들이 스스로의 예술적인 열정을 발견하도록 돕습니다!

현지 베이커리와 가정 요리사들에 의해 매우 다양한 종류의 빵 품목들이 제공될 것입니다. 빵 판매의 모든 수익금은 예술 용품을 구입하고 박물관 및 기타 문화 센터로의 현장 학습에 자금을 대는 데 사용될 것입니다.

예술이라는 선물을 나누어 주세요!

예술온누리협회 주최

- **장소**: Sheraton 농산물 직판장, 121번 부스
- **날짜**: 2월 20일 토요일
- **시간**: 오전 8시부터 오후 2시까지

참석하실 수 없지만 기부를 원하시는 경우, www.artforeveryoneassoc.org/donationpage에서 금전적인 기부를 하실 수 있습니다.

어휘

sweet tooth 단것을 좋아함 association 협회, 연관 charity 자선 단체 passion 열정 proceeds 수익금 field trip 현장 학습 organize 기획하다, 조직하다 donate 기부하다 monetary 금전적인 contribution 기부(금), 기여

05 독해 제목 파악　　　　난이도 중 ●●○

(A)에 들어갈 윗글의 제목으로 적절한 것은?

① Appreciation for Our Local Artists
② Fun at the Farmer's Market Art Booth
③ Homemade Desserts by Art Teachers
④ Fundraiser for Children's Art Opportunities

해석

① 우리 지역 예술가들에 대한 감사
② 농산물 직판장 예술 부스에서의 즐거움
③ 미술 교사들이 만든 수제 디저트
④ 아이들의 예술적 기회를 위한 모금 행사

해설

지문 앞부분에서 도움이 필요한 아이들에게 예술을 경험하고 예술에 참여할 수 있는 기회를 제공하는 자선 단체에서 주관하는 빵 판매의 모든 수익금은 어린이들의 예술 용품과 문화 시설 현장 학습 비용을 충당하는 데 사용될 것이라고 했으므로, ④ '아이들의 예술적 기회를 위한 모금 행사'가 이 글의 제목이다.

정답 ④

어휘

appreciation 감사, 감상　fundraiser 모금 행사

06 독해 내용 불일치 파악　　　　난이도 하 ●○○

위 안내문의 내용과 일치하지 않는 것은?

① 전문 베이커리에서 만든 빵을 구매할 수 있다.
② 지역 미술관에서 행사를 주최한다.
③ 행사는 농산물 직판장에서 단 하루 동안 열린다.
④ 웹페이지를 통해 기부금을 전달할 수 있다.

해설

②번의 키워드인 '주최한다'가 그대로 언급된 지문의 Organized 주변의 내용에서 예술온누리협회가 주최한다고 했으므로, ② '지역 미술관에서 행사를 주최한다'는 지문의 내용과 다르다.

정답 ②

07 독해 요지 파악　　　　난이도 중 ●●○

다음 글의 요지로 적절한 것은?

If you were to estimate the length of a line in a photograph, how would you do it? Some people simply look intently at the line and provide a rough estimate. But others examine the line in relation to another object in the picture to gauge its length. Either group may think that the method used by the other seems illogical; in truth, it really depends on how you were raised. People who were raised to be more independent try to solve problems directly; hence, they focus on the line itself to measure it. Individuals who were encouraged to have a group mentality, on the other hand, consider the context, which is why they look at things other than the line. A similar difference occurs when taking a picture. The more independent person will aim at something in the frame, while the other will look at the picture in its entirety. It's like using a zoom lens versus taking a panoramic shot.

① Personal attitudes can have an impact on how one poses for a photograph.
② The perspective of an individual can depend on the way the person was reared.
③ Thinking of the group and not just the individual is more caring.
④ The choices one makes are largely determined by how one views culture.

해석

만약 당신이 사진 속 선의 길이를 추정한다면, 어떻게 하겠는가? 일부 사람들은 그저 그 선을 집중하여 바라보고 대강의 추정치를 제시한다. 그러나 다른 사람들은 그것의 길이를 가늠하기 위해 사진 속의 또 다른 물체와 비교하여 그 선을 살펴본다. 어느 집단이든 다른 한쪽에 의해 사용되는 방법이 비논리적으로 보인다고 생각할 수도 있는데, 사실 그것은 당신이 어떻게 자랐는지에 달려 있다. 보다 독립적으로 길러진 사람들은 문제를 곧바로 해결하려고 하고, 그리하여 그들은 그것을 측정하기 위해 그 선 자체에 집중한다. 반면에 집단적 사고방식을 갖도록 독려된 사람들은 맥락을 고려하는데, 이것이 그들이 그 선 이외의 다른 것들을 보는 이유이다. 비슷한 차이점이 사진을 찍을 때 발생한다. 보다 독립적인 사람은 프레임 속의 무언가를 겨냥하는 데 반해, 다른 사람은 그 사진을 전체적으로 볼 것이다. 그것은 줌 렌즈를 사용하느냐 파노라마 촬영을 하느냐와 같은 문제이다.

① 개인의 태도는 사람이 사진을 찍기 위해 포즈를 취하는 방식에 영향을 미칠 수 있다.
② 한 개인의 관점은 그 사람이 길러진 방식에 달려 있다.
③ 개인뿐만 아니라 집단을 생각하는 것이 더 배려하는 것이다.
④ 한 사람이 내리는 선택들은 대체로 사람이 문화를 바라보는 방식에 의해 결정된다.

해설

지문 중간에서 사진 속 선의 길이를 추정하는 방식은 사람이 자란 방식에 달려 있다고 한 후, 독립적으로 양육된 사람들은 문제를 곧바로 해결하기 위해 선 자체에 집중하는 반면, 집단적 사고방식을 갖도록 양육된 사람들은 맥락을 고려하기 때문에 선 이외의 다른 것들을 본다고 설명하고 있다. 따라서 ② '한 개인의 관점은 그 사람이 길러진 방식에 달려 있다'가 이 글의 요지이다.

정답 ②

어휘

estimate 추정하다; 추정(치), 견적　intently 집중하여　rough 대강의, 거친
in relation to ~과 비교하여, 관련하여　gauge 가늠하다, 측정하다
illogical 비논리적인　independent 독립적인　mentality 사고방식, 심리, 성향
context 맥락　in its entirety 전체적으로, 전부　perspective 관점
rear (아이를) 기르다　caring 배려하는, 보살피는

DAY 08 하프모의고사 08회

08 독해 내용 일치 파악   난이도 하 ●○○

다음 이메일의 내용과 일치하는 것은?

To	inquiries@vera_print.com
From	helen_strickland@FowlerRoth.com
Date	May 2
Subject	Custom T-Shirt Order Inquiry
Attachment	company_logo.pdf

Good afternoon,

Our company is planning an upcoming volunteer day and is interested in placing an order for custom T-shirts.

We need 150 navy blue cotton shirts with our company logo printed on the front left chest area and "Fowler-Roth Volunteer Day" printed on the back in white. The order should include 40 small, 50 medium, 45 large, and 15 extra-large shirts, all of which should be unisex with a standard fit. We have a strict budget of no more than $2,200 for this order.

We need the shirts delivered to us by May 25. I realize this is a tight timeline, so I would appreciate it if you could let me know if you are able to fulfill this request as soon as possible.

I hope to hear from you soon.

Best regards,

Helen Strickland, Event Organizer

① 흰색 면 셔츠 150장이 필요하다.
② 네 가지의 서로 다른 사이즈를 주문할 예정이다.
③ 각 사이즈마다 2,200달러의 예산을 편성했다.
④ 답변 기한은 5월 25일까지이다.

해석

수신: inquiries@vera_print.com
발신: helen_strickland@FowlerRoth.com
날짜: 5월 2일
제목: 맞춤 제작 티셔츠 주문 관련 문의
첨부파일: company_logo.pdf

좋은 오후입니다,

저희 회사는 다가오는 자원봉사의 날을 계획하고 있어서, 맞춤 제작 티셔츠를 주문하는 것에 관심이 있습니다.

저희는 앞면 왼쪽 가슴 부분에 회사 로고가 인쇄되고, 등 쪽에 'Fowler-Roth 자원봉사의 날'이 흰색으로 인쇄된 짙은 남색 면 셔츠 150장이 필요합니다. 주문은 스몰 사이즈 40장, 미디엄 50장, 라지 45장, 엑스트라 라지 15장을 포함해야 하는데, 이것들 모두는 표준 크기로 남녀 공용이어야 합니다. 저희는 이 주문 건에 대해 2,200달러 이내의 엄격한 예산을 가지고 있습니다.

저희는 5월 25일까지 셔츠를 배송받아야 합니다. 이것이 촉박한 일정임을 알고 있어서, 가능한 한 빨리 이 요청을 이행하실 수 있을지 알려 주시면 감사하겠습니다.

곧 답변 받기를 바랍니다.

안부를 전합니다,

행사 기획자 Helen Strickland

해설

지문 중간에서 주문은 스몰 40장, 미디엄 50장, 라지 45장, 엑스트라 라지 15장을 포함해야 한다고 했으므로, ② '네 가지의 서로 다른 사이즈를 주문할 예정이다'가 지문의 내용과 일치한다.

[오답 분석]
① 짙은 남색 면 셔츠 150장이 필요하다고 했으므로, 흰색 면 셔츠 150장이 필요하다는 것은 지문의 내용과 다르다.
③ 전체 주문 건에 대해 2,200달러 이내의 예산이 있다고 했으므로, 각 사이즈마다 2,200달러의 예산을 편성했다는 것은 지문의 내용과 다르다.
④ 5월 25일까지 셔츠를 배송받아야 한다고 했으므로, 답변 기한이 5월 25일까지라는 것은 지문의 내용과 다르다.

정답 ②

어휘

upcoming 다가오는   chest 가슴   unisex 남녀 공용의
standard 표준의; 기준   strict 엄격한   budget 예산   tight 촉박한, 꽉 조이는
fulfill 이행하다

09 독해 무관한 문장 삭제   난이도 중 ●●○

다음 글의 흐름상 어색한 문장은?

The brain is at its peak in one's early to mid-twenties and then begins to weaken, but this does not worsen thinking ability. ① Despite the physical decline, the older brain can accomplish some things better than the younger brain can. ② For example, it can process information in a superior way when it comes to making moral decisions, controlling emotions, and assessing social situations. ③ To reduce the consequences of negative changes to the brain, older people should engage in activities that keep the brain active. This is partly because older people have learned to focus better, control anxiety, and avoid distractions. ④ As a result, in tasks involving problem-solving and abstract reasoning, older adults often do better than younger people.

해석

뇌는 사람의 20대 초중반에 절정에 달해 있다가 약해지기 시작하지만, 이것이 사고력을 악화시키지는 않는다. ① 신체적 쇠퇴에도 불구하고, 나이 든 뇌는 젊은 뇌가 하는 것보다 몇몇 일들을 더 잘 해낼 수 있다. ② 예를 들어, 그것(나이 든 뇌)은 도덕적 결정을 내리고, 감정을 통제하고, 그리고 사회적 상황을 판단하는 것에 관해서라면 정보를 더 뛰어난 방식으로 처리할 수 있다. ③ 뇌의 부정적인 변화로 인한 영향들을 줄이기 위해, 나이 든 사람들은 뇌를 활발하게 유지하는 활동들에 참여해야 한다. 이것은 일정 부분은 나이 든 사람들이 더 잘 집중하고, 불안을 통제하고, 산만함을 피하는 법을 배워 왔기 때문이다. ④ 결과적으로, 문제 해결과 추상

적 추론을 수반하는 일들에 있어서는, 나이 든 사람들이 종종 젊은 사람들보다 더 잘 수행한다.

해설

첫 문장에서 뇌가 사람의 20대 초중반에 절정에 달한 후 약해지기 시작하지만 이로 인해 사고력이 악화되는 것은 아니라고 한 후, ①, ②, ④번에서 나이 든 뇌가 젊은 뇌보다 더 잘 해낼 수 있는 일들을 설명하고 있다. 그러나 ③번은 '나이 든 사람들이 뇌의 부정적인 변화를 줄이기 위한 활동들에 참여할 필요성'에 대한 내용으로, 첫 문장의 내용과 관련이 없다.

정답 ③

어휘

peak 절정 **weaken** 약해지다 **worsen** 악화시키다 **decline** 쇠퇴, 감소
accomplish 해내다, 성취하다 **superior** 뛰어난, 상급의
when it comes to ~에 관해서라면 **moral** 도덕적인
assess 판단하다, 평가하다 **engage in** ~에 참여하다, 종사하다
distraction 산만함 **abstract** 추상적인 **reasoning** 추론

10 독해 문단 순서 배열   난이도 중 ●●○

주어진 글 다음에 이어질 글의 순서로 적절한 것은?

Utilitarianism is a form of decision-making that emphasizes outcomes that produce the greatest good for the greatest number of people. Many everyday decisions are easy to rationalize through a utilitarian lens.

(A) In hypothetical scenarios, though, this reasoning becomes more difficult when the outcomes are unclear. Suppose a group of 100 and a group of five are both in imminent danger. The utilitarian would say that saving the group of 100 is clearly better.

(B) For example, a parent may buy their children ice cream to make them happy rather than save a little money and deny them a slightly unhealthy snack.

(C) However, the group of 100 is made up of adventure enthusiasts who knowingly took risks, while the five are a group of scientists about to complete a vaccine for a deadly epidemic. The utilitarian must weigh 100 immediate lives against the potential to save hundreds of thousands in the future, which is not an easy task.

① (A) – (C) – (B)
② (B) – (A) – (C)
③ (B) – (C) – (A)
④ (C) – (A) – (B)

해석

공리주의는 최대 다수의 사람들을 위한 최대한의 행복을 도출하는 결과를 강조하는 의사 결정 방식이다. 많은 일상적인 결정들은 공리주의 관점을 통해 합리화하기 쉽다.

(A) 그러나 가상의 시나리오에서, 결과가 불명확할 때 이러한 추론은 훨씬 더 어려워진다. 100명인 한 집단과 5명인 한 집단 모두가 임박한 위험에 처해 있다고 가정해 보라. 공리주의자는 100명의 목숨을 구하는 것이 명백히 더 낫다고 말할 것이다.

(B) 예를 들어, 어떤 부모는 약간의 돈을 아끼고 아이들에게 조금 건강에 해로운 간식을 허락하지 않기보다는, 그들을 행복하게 만들기 위해 아이스크림을 사 줄 것이다.

(C) 하지만, 100명인 집단은 알면서도 위험을 받아들였던 모험 애호가들로 구성되어 있는 반면, 5명은 치명적인 전염병에 대한 백신을 완성하기 직전에 있는 과학자 집단이다. 공리주의자는 눈앞에 있는 100명의 생명과 미래에 수십만 명을 구할 가능성 사이에서 저울질해야 하는데, 이는 결코 쉬운 과제가 아니다.

해설

주어진 글에서 최대 다수의 사람들을 위한 최대의 행복을 도출하는 결과를 강조하는 공리주의는 일상적인 결정을 합리화하기 쉽다고 한 뒤, (B)에서 일상적인 결정의 예로 부모가 돈을 아끼는 대신 아이들을 행복하게 하기 위해 아이스크림을 사 주는 상황을 제시하고 있다. 이어서 (A)에서 그러나(though) 결과가 불명확할 때 이러한 추론(this reasoning)은 훨씬 더 어려워지는데, 위기에 처한 100명의 집단과 5명의 집단을 가정할 때 공리주의자는 100명의 목숨을 살리는 것을 선택할 것이라고 하고, (C)에서 하지만(However) 각 집단의 세부적인 상황이 다르므로 공리주의자가 어느 쪽의 목숨을 살릴지 결정하는 것은 쉽지 않다고 설명하고 있다. 따라서 ② (B) – (A) – (C)가 정답이다.

정답 ②

어휘

utilitarianism 공리주의 **emphasize** 강조하다 **outcome** 결과
rationalize 합리화하다 **hypothetical** 가상의, 가설적인
reasoning 추론, 추리 **imminent** 임박한 **enthusiast** 애호가
epidemic 전염병 **weigh** 저울질하다, 무게가 ~이다
immediate 눈앞의, 즉각적인 **potential** 가능성, 잠재력; 가능성 있는

DAY 09 하프모의고사 09회

정답   p. 46

01	③	어휘	06	①	독해
02	④	문법	07	①	독해
03	②	문법	08	④	독해
04	②	생활영어	09	④	독해
05	②	독해	10	①	독해

취약영역 분석표

영역	맞힌 답의 개수
어휘	/1
생활영어	/1
문법	/2
독해	/6
TOTAL	/10

---

01 어휘 unclear 난이도 하 ●○○

밑줄 친 부분에 들어갈 말로 적절한 것은?

> To others, the young child's attempts at speech were _____, but his parents were able to interpret what he was trying to say.

① extra
② junior
③ unclear
④ pure

[해석]
다른 사람들에게는 그 어린아이의 말하려는 시도가 불분명했지만, 그의 부모는 그가 무슨 말을 하려고 하는지 이해할 수 있었다.

① 추가적인 ② 청소년의
③ 불분명한 ④ 순수한

정답 ③

[어휘]
interpret 이해하다, 해석하다   extra 추가적인, 여분의
junior 청소년의; 아랫사람   unclear 불분명한, 불확실한   pure 순수한

---

02 문법 수동태 | 시제 난이도 상 ●●●

밑줄 친 부분에 들어갈 말로 적절한 것은?

> The ancient city _____ the birthplace of democracy by historians since the 5th century BCE.

① refers to as
② has been referred
③ was referred to as
④ has been referred to as

[해석]
그 고대 도시는 기원전 5세기 이후로 역사가들에 의해 민주주의의 발상지로 불려 왔다.

[해설]
④ 동사구의 수동태 | 시제 일치   빈칸은 문장의 동사 자리이다. 문맥상 주어 The ancient city와 동사가 '그 고대 도시가 ~로 불려 왔다'라는 의미의 수동 관계이므로 능동태 ① refers to as는 정답이 될 수 없다. 동사 refer는 '~을 -이라고 부르다'라는 의미로 쓰일 때 'refer to + 목적어 + as + 명사'의 형태를 취하는데, 목적어(the ancient city)가 주어 자리에 가서 수동태가 되면 수동태 동사 뒤에 'as + 명사'는 그대로 남으므로 ③ was referred to as, ④ has been referred to as가 정답 후보이다. 이때 문장에 현재완료 시제와 자주 함께 쓰이는 시간 표현 'since + 과거 시간 표현'(since the 5th century BCE)이 왔으므로, 현재완료 수동태 ④ has been referred to as가 정답이다.

정답 ④

[어휘]
birthplace 발상지   democracy 민주주의

---

03 문법 동명사 | 관계절 | 분사 | 비교 구문 난이도 중 ●●○

밑줄 친 부분 중 어법상 옳지 않은 것은?

> Ramadan is a holy time ① when Muslims around the world reflect on their spiritual lives and focus on their faith by avoiding ② consume food and drink from sunup to sundown. The purpose of this practice is to allow those ③ fasting to escape the distractions of the material world. By concentrating solely on the spiritual world, they can dedicate themselves to ④ the healthiest practices for their moral well-being.

[해석]
라마단은 전 세계 이슬람교도들이 먼동이 틀 때부터 해가 질 때까지 음식과 음료를 섭취하는 것을 피함으로써 그들의 영적인 삶을 되돌아보고 그들의 신앙에 집중하는 경건한 시간이다. 이 관습의 목적은 금식하는 사람들로 하여금 집중을 방해하는 물질 세계의 것들에서 벗어나게 하기 위함이다. 오로지 영적인 세계에 집중함으로써, 그들은 도덕적인 행복을 위해 가장 건전한 실천에 스스로 전념할 수 있다.

해설

② **동명사를 목적어로 취하는 동사** 동사 avoid는 동명사를 목적어로 취하므로 동사원형 consume을 동명사 consuming으로 고쳐야 한다.

[오답 분석]
① **관계부사** 선행사(a holy time)가 시간을 나타내고, 관계사 뒤에 완전한 절(Muslims ~ sundown)이 왔으므로 시간을 나타내면서 완전한 절을 이끄는 관계부사 when이 올바르게 쓰였다.
③ **현재분사 vs. 과거분사** 수식받는 명사(those)와 분사가 '사람들이 금식하다'라는 의미의 능동 관계이므로 현재분사 fasting이 올바르게 쓰였다.
④ **최상급** '최상급 + 명사' 앞에는 정관사 the가 와야 하므로 최상급 healthiest 앞에 정관사 the가 올바르게 쓰였다.

정답 ②

어휘

holy 경건한, 신성한 reflect on ~을 되돌아보다, 반성하다
spiritual 영적인, 정신적인 faith 신앙 consume 섭취하다, 소비하다
from sunup to sundown 먼동이 틀 때부터 해가 질 때까지
fast 금식하다, 단식시키다; 빠른 distraction 집중을 방해하는 것
concentrate on ~에 집중하다 solely 오로지 dedicate 전념하다
moral 도덕적인

---

04 생활영어 Just let Sarah know you're interested.
난이도 하 ●○○

밑줄 친 부분에 들어갈 말로 적절한 것은?

Mia Anderson
Are you planning to attend the marketing seminar next month?
14:15

Owen Bailey
I attended a similar seminar last year, so I might skip this one.
14:16

Mia Anderson
This year's seminar is actually quite different from last year's.
14:16

Owen Bailey
Really? What are the differences?
14:17

Mia Anderson
It highlights AI marketing tools and how to implement them in our campaigns.
14:17

Owen Bailey
That sounds interesting! How can I register?
14:18

Mia Anderson
_____
14:18

Owen Bailey
Great, I'll do that today. Thanks for letting me know!
14:19

① The registration deadline is next Friday.
② Just let Sarah know you're interested.
③ We need your employee ID.
④ It's the pre-registration period now.

해석

Mia Anderson: 다음 달에 있을 마케팅 세미나에 참석할 계획이신가요?
Owen Bailey: 제가 작년에 비슷한 세미나에 참석했거든요, 그래서 이번 세미나는 건너뛸 것 같아요.
Mia Anderson: 올해 세미나는 사실 작년 것과 상당히 달라요.
Owen Bailey: 정말요? 차이점이 뭐데요?
Mia Anderson: 그것은 AI 마케팅 도구들과 그것들을 우리의 광고 캠페인에 구현하는 방법을 강조해요.
Owen Bailey: 흥미롭네요! 어떻게 등록할 수 있나요?
Mia Anderson: Sarah가 당신이 관심 있다는 것을 알게 하기만 하면 돼요.
Owen Bailey: 좋아요, 오늘 그렇게 할게요. 알려 주셔서 감사합니다!

① 등록 마감일은 다음 주 금요일입니다.
② Sarah가 당신이 관심 있다는 걸 알게 하기만 하면 돼요.
③ 저희는 당신의 직원 ID가 필요합니다.
④ 지금은 사전 등록 기간입니다.

해설

다음 달 마케팅 세미나에 등록하는 방법을 묻는 Owen에게 Mia가 대답하고, 빈칸 뒤에서 다시 Owen이 Great, I'll do that today. Thanks for letting me know!(좋아요, 오늘 그렇게 할게요. 알려 주셔서 감사합니다!)라고 말하고 있으므로, 'Sarah가 당신이 관심 있다는 걸 알게 하기만 하면 돼요'라는 의미의 ② 'Just let Sarah know you're interested'가 정답이다.

정답 ②

어휘

highlight 강조하다 implement 구현하다, 실행하다 register 등록하다

05~06 다음 글을 읽고 물음에 답하시오.

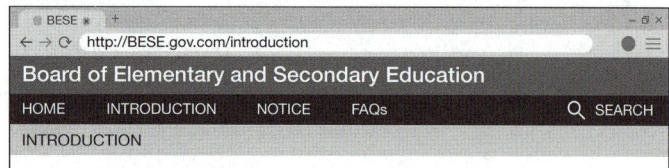

Board of Elementary and Secondary Education

Goals

We are dedicated to providing students a high-quality education that prepares them for future career success by fostering academic excellence and supporting educators. We also strive to create a more just education system and close achievement gaps.

Actions

We create educational policies and allocate resources to strengthen schools and give educators the tools they need to deliver effective instruction. This includes establishing curriculum guidelines, administering standardized testing, and providing on-going training. In addition, we collaborate with local school districts to implement programs that enhance learning and school performance.

Organizational Values

- Equity: Fairness in education is a top priority and we work to provide a high-quality education to all, regardless of background.
- Innovation: We develop new approaches to teaching and continuously seek policies and practices to improve education.

05 독해 내용 일치 파악

윗글에서 Board of Elementary and Secondary Education에 관한 내용과 일치하는 것은?

① It focuses on ensuring educators have successful careers.
② It creates rules and regulations related to education.
③ It works with local businesses to provide resources to schools.
④ It tailors education to students' individual backgrounds.

| 06 | 독해 유의어 파악 | 난이도 하 ●○○ |

밑줄 친 just의 의미와 가장 가까운 것은?

① fair
② global
③ famous
④ affordable

[해석]

① 공정한
② 세계적인
③ 유명한
④ 가격이 알맞은

[해설]

밑줄 친 부분이 포함된 문장에서 just는 문맥상 보다 '공평한' 교육 시스템을 만들고 학업 성취 격차를 좁히기 위해 노력한다는 의미로 쓰였으므로, '공정한'이라는 의미의 ① fair가 정답이다.

정답 ①

[어휘]

fair 공정한   affordable 가격이 알맞은, 감당할 수 있는

| 07 | 독해 제목 파악 | 난이도 중 ●●○ |

다음 글의 제목으로 가장 적절한 것은?

When Europeans colonized North America, they found a massive passenger pigeon population. The birds were so numerous that it was said that large flocks could darken the sky for days. However, within a short time, the species disappeared altogether. The reason for the quick demise of a population of animals estimated at between three and five billion amazed scientists. While it seemed to be influenced by the new settlers, this didn't fully explain the extinction. Surprisingly, modern genetic research suggests that the species was in decline before the arrival of the Europeans. In fact, researchers believe that the pigeon population would have fallen to only a few hundred thousand had Europeans not arrived in North America. However, this doesn't completely free settlers from responsibility. It is likely that overhunting by the Europeans pushed the struggling species to its ultimate extinction.

① The Reality of the Passenger Pigeon's Disappearance
② The Reason North America's Pigeon Population Increased
③ Pigeon Hunting: A Source of Nourishment for European Settlers
④ Ecological Damage Caused by Colonization

[해석]

유럽인들이 북아메리카를 식민지로 만들었을 때, 그들은 대규모의 나그네비둘기 개체군을 발견했다. 그 새들은 너무 많아서 큰 무리가 며칠간 하늘을 어둡게 할 수 있었다고 전해진다. 하지만, 단시간 내에 그 종은 완전히 사라졌다. 30억에서 50억 마리 사이로 추정되는 그 동물 개체군의 빠른 종말에 대한 이유는 과학자들을 놀라게 했다. 그것이 새로운 정착민들에 의해 영향을 받은 것처럼 보이기는 했지만, 이것이 그 멸종을 충분히 설명하지는 못했다. 놀랍게도, 현대의 유전학 연구는 그 종이 유럽인들의 출현 이전에 감소세에 있었음을 시사한다. 실제로, 연구원들은 유럽인들이 북아메리카에 도착하지 않았더라도, 그 비둘기 개체군은 겨우 몇십 만 정도로 감소했을 것이라고 생각한다. 하지만, 이것이 정착민들을 책임으로부터 완전히 자유롭게 하지는 않는다. 유럽인들에 의한 과도한 사냥은 그 분투하는 종을 궁극적인 멸종으로 내몰았을 가능성이 크다.

① 나그네비둘기 소멸의 진실
② 북아메리카의 비둘기 개체군이 늘어난 이유
③ 비둘기 사냥: 유럽 정착민들의 영양분의 원천
④ 식민지화에 의해 야기된 생태계의 피해

[해설]

지문 전반에 걸쳐 유럽인들이 북아메리카를 식민지로 만든 뒤 단시간 내에 멸종한 나그네비둘기 개체군은 유럽인들이 정착하기 전부터 이미 감소세에 있었지만, 유럽인들의 과도한 사냥 역시 결정적인 영향을 주었을 것이라고 설명하고 있으므로, ① '나그네비둘기 소멸의 진실'이 이 글의 제목이다.

정답 ①

[어휘]

colonize 식민지로 만들다, 대량 서식하다   massive 대규모의, 거대한
flock 무리, 떼   altogether 완전히, 전적으로   demise 종말, 죽음
estimate 추정하다   amaze 놀라게 하다   extinction 멸종, 소멸
genetic 유전학의   decline 감소, 쇠퇴   settler 정착민
responsibility 책임   overhunt 과도하게 사냥하다
struggle 분투하다, 애쓰다   ultimate 궁극적인, 최후의
nourishment 영양분, 음식물   ecological 생태계의

| 08 | 독해 요지 파악 | 난이도 중 ●●○ |

다음 글의 요지로 가장 적절한 것은?

Safe Travels
Protecting travelers on the nation's transportation systems is the main function of the Passenger Safety Administration (PSA). Effective safety measures protect passengers, crew, and cargo across the country's vast road-, rail-, and air-travel systems.

Weapons, Explosives, and Incendiaries
Weapons, explosives, and incendiaries (WEIs) are prohibited items on passenger travel, especially air travel. These include firearms, knives, and flammable materials that pose security threats.

The PSA employs teams of inspectors working around the clock using scanners and police dogs at departure points to detect WEIs on passengers and in their luggage. When a WEI is detected, PSA staff order additional screening to positively identify the item and determine whether it is a safety threat, often ordering its confiscation and detaining the traveler if he or she is suspected of having a dangerous intent.

*incendiary: 발연성 물질

DAY 09 하프모의고사 09회

① PSA supervises the functioning of the nation's transportation systems.
② PSA aims to create detection systems that accurately identify items in luggage.
③ PSA creates lists of WEIs that are prohibited for air travelers to carry.
④ PSA's main focus is protecting travelers from transportation security threats.

해석

안전한 여행

국가 교통 시스템에서 여행자를 보호하는 것이 승객안전관리청(PSA)의 주요 기능입니다. 효과적인 안전 조치는 전국의 광범위한 도로, 철도 및 항공 여행 시스템 전반에서 승객, 승무원 및 화물을 보호합니다.

무기, 폭발물 및 발연성 물질

무기류, 폭발물 및 발연성 물질(WEIs)은 승객분들의 여행에 있어서 금지된 품목들인데, 특히 항공 여행에서 그렇습니다. 여기에는 보안에 위협을 가하는 화기, 도검류 및 인화성 물질이 포함됩니다.

승객안전관리청은 스캐너와 경찰견을 이용하여 출발 지점에서 승객과 그들의 수하물에서 무기, 폭발물 및 발연성 물질을 탐지하기 위해 24시간 근무하는 조사단을 고용합니다. 무기, 폭발물 및 발연성 물질이 탐지되면, 승객안전관리청 직원은 해당 물품을 분명히 식별하고 그것이 안전 관련 위협인지 판단하기 위해 추가 검사를 명령하는데, 여행자가 위험한 의도를 가진 것으로 의심되는 경우 종종 그것(물품)의 압수와 여행자의 구금을 명령합니다.

① 승객안전관리청은 국가 교통 시스템의 기능을 감독한다.
② 승객안전관리청은 수하물에 든 물품을 정확하게 식별하는 탐지 시스템을 만드는 것을 목표로 한다.
③ 승객안전관리청은 항공 여행자들이 소지하는 것이 금지된 무기, 폭발물 및 발연성 물질의 목록을 만든다.
④ 승객안전관리청의 주된 초점은 여행자를 교통 보안 위협으로부터 보호하는 것이다.

해설

지문 처음에서 승객안전관리청의 주요 기능은 국가 교통 시스템에서 여행자를 보호하는 것이라고 하고, 지문 뒷부분에서 보안에 위협을 제기하는 무기, 폭발물 및 발연성 물질을 탐지하기 위해 취하고 있는 조치들을 설명하고 있으므로, ④ '승객안전관리청의 주된 초점은 여행자를 교통 보안 위협으로부터 보호하는 것이다'가 이 글의 요지이다.

정답 ④

어휘

transportation 교통 effective 효과적인 measure 조치, 측정; 측정하다
crew 승무원 cargo 화물 weapon 무기 explosive 폭발물; 폭발성의
prohibit 금지하다 firearm 화기 flammable 인화성의
pose 가하다, 제기하다 inspector 조사관, 검사관
around the clock 24시간 내내 detect 탐지하다 confiscation 압수
detain 구금하다 suspect 의심하다; 용의자 intent 의도
supervise 감독하다

09 독해 문장 삽입   난이도 중 ●●○

주어진 문장이 들어갈 위치로 적절한 것은?

In fact, it sparked the enactment of the Meat Inspection Act and the Pure Food and Drug Act.

In his novel *The Jungle*, journalist Upton Sinclair portrayed the terrible working conditions immigrant workers experienced in the early 1900s. Sinclair documented the truth through the life of a young Lithuanian, Jurgis Rudkus, who had recently immigrated. (①) In the novel, young immigrant men faced an environment that destroyed whatever optimism they had at the start. (②) For instance, they stood for ten hours a day in dirty, poorly-ventilated meatpacking factories for five dollars a day. (③) Sinclair hoped the book would help these men; instead, the public expressed strong concerns about food hygiene. (④) Encouragingly, over a century after the book's publication, significant progress has been made in the meatpacking industry through strengthened labor regulations, technological automation, and worker rights advocacy.

해석

실제로, 그것은 육류검사법과 순수식품의약품법의 제정을 촉발했다.

자신의 소설 『정글』에서, 기자인 Upton Sinclair는 1900년대 초반에 이주 노동자들이 겪은 끔찍한 노동 환경을 묘사했다. Sinclair는 최근에 이주해 온 젊은 리투아니아인 Jurgis Rudkus의 삶을 통해 진실을 기록했다. ① 그 소설에서, 젊은 이민자들은 그들이 애초에 가졌던 어떠한 낙관도 무너뜨리는 환경에 직면했다. ② 예를 들어, 그들은 하루 5달러를 벌기 위해 더럽고 환기가 잘 되지 않는 육류 가공 공장에서 하루에 10시간씩 서 있었다. ③ Sinclair는 그 책이 이 사람들을 돕길 바랐는데, 그 대신 대중들은 식품 위생에 대해 강한 우려를 표현했다. ④ 고무적이게도, 이 책의 출간 후 한 세기가 넘는 시간 동안, 강화된 노동 규정, 기술 자동화 그리고 노동자 권익 옹호를 통해 육류 가공 산업에서 상당한 진전이 이루어져 왔다.

해설

④번 앞 문장에 이 책을 읽은 대중들이 식품 위생에 강한 우려를 표현했다는 내용이 있고, 뒤 문장에 출간 후 한 세기가 지나는 동안 강화된 노동 규제, 기술적 자동화, 노동자 권익 옹호를 통해 육류 가공 산업에서의 진전이 있었다는 내용이 있으므로, ④번 자리에 실제로(In fact) 그것(it)이 식품 위생과 관련한 여러 법의 제정을 촉발했다는 내용, 즉 대중들이 우려를 표현한 결과로 발생한, 오늘날의 육류 가공 산업에서의 진전의 시발점에 대해 언급하는 주어진 문장이 나와야 지문이 자연스럽게 연결된다.

정답 ④

어휘

spark 촉발하다, 유발하다; 불꽃 enactment (법률) 제정 inspection 검사
portray 묘사하다 immigrant 이주민, 이민자 document 기록하다; 기록
optimism 낙관 ventilate 환기하다 meatpacking 육류 가공
hygiene 위생 publication 출간 strengthen 강화하다
regulation 규정, 규제 automation 자동화 advocacy 옹호, 지지

10 독해 빈칸 완성 – 구 난이도 중 ●●○

밑줄 친 부분에 들어갈 말로 적절한 것은?

Today, robots complete 50 percent of all tasks in numerous fields including agriculture, the automotive industry, and supply chain management. As robots become even more prevalent, they will need to improve their ability to _____, which will increase their efficiency and productivity. That's why a team of researchers from MIT has devised a framework that allows robots to develop human-like social skills through an interactive model. These robots were each given a goal and programmed to recognize the aims of others. An algorithm collected data from the social interactions between them and then decided if the other machines needed help achieving their goals or not. While still early, this type of social recognition would be beneficial at an assisted living center, for example, where robots could assess how much aid an elderly person requires.

① understand and respond to social cues
② update their algorithms
③ establish task objectives independently
④ identify mechanical failures

어휘
agriculture 농업 automotive 자동차의 prevalent 널리 쓰이는, 일반적인
efficiency 효율성, 능률 productivity 생산성 devise 고안하다
framework 구조, 틀 interactive 상호 작용을 하는 recognize 인지하다
aim 목표 beneficial 유익한, 이로운 assess 가늠하다 objective 목표
identify 식별하다, 확인하다

해석
오늘날, 로봇은 농업, 자동차 산업 그리고 공급망 관리를 포함하는 수많은 분야의 모든 업무 중 50퍼센트를 완수한다. 로봇이 훨씬 더 널리 쓰이게 됨에 따라, 그것들은 사회적 신호를 이해하고 그에 반응하는 능력을 향상시킬 필요가 있을 것인데, 이는 그것들의 효율성과 생산성을 증가시킬 것이다. 그것이 MIT의 한 연구팀이 상호 작용을 하는 모델을 통해 로봇들이 인간과 같은 사회적 기술을 발달시키게 하는 구조를 고안한 이유이다. 이 로봇들은 각자 하나의 목표를 받고 다른 것들의 목표를 인지하도록 설정되어 있었다. 알고리즘은 그것들 간의 사회적 상호 작용으로부터 자료를 수집한 다음, 다른 기계들이 그것들의 목표를 완수하는 데 도움이 필요한지 아닌지를 결정했다. 아직 이르기는 하지만, 이러한 종류의 사회 인지는 예를 들어 생활 지원 시설에서 유익할 것인데, 이곳에서 로봇들은 노인 한 명이 얼마나 많은 도움을 필요로 하는지를 가늠할 수 있을 것이다.

① 사회적 신호를 이해하고 그에 반응하다
② 그것들의 알고리즘을 업데이트하다
③ 독자적으로 작업 목표를 설정하다
④ 기계적 고장을 식별하다

해설
빈칸 뒤 문장에 한 연구팀이 상호 작용을 하는 모델을 통해 로봇들이 인간과 같은 사회적 기술을 발달시키게 하는 구조를 고안했다는 내용이 있고, 지문 마지막에서 사회 인지 로봇들은 노인 한 명이 얼마나 많은 도움을 필요로 하는지 가늠할 수 있다고 했으므로, 로봇들이 '사회적 신호를 이해하고 그에 반응하는' 능력을 향상시킬 필요가 있다고 한 ①번이 정답이다.

정답 ①

DAY 10 하프모의고사 10회

정답   p. 50

01	②	어휘	06	②	독해
02	④	문법	07	②	독해
03	④	문법	08	②	독해
04	④	생활영어	09	①	독해
05	②	독해	10	②	독해

취약영역 분석표

영역	맞힌 답의 개수
어휘	/1
생활영어	/1
문법	/2
독해	/6
TOTAL	/10

---

01 어휘 bias   난이도 중 ●●○

밑줄 친 부분에 들어갈 말로 적절한 것은?

> Freedom from _____ is essential for Consumer Protection Committee members when evaluating the circumstances of consumers with dissatisfaction.

① alarm   ② bias
③ honesty   ④ cooperation

해석

편견으로부터의 자유로움은 불만을 가진 소비자들의 상황을 파악할 때 소비자 보호 위원회 구성원들에게 필수적이다.
① 불안   ② 편견
③ 정직함   ④ 협력

정답 ②

어휘

evaluate 파악하다, 평가하다   circumstance 상황
alarm 불안, 경보   bias 편견   honesty 정직함   cooperation 협력

---

02 문법 조동사   난이도 하 ●○○

밑줄 친 부분에 들어갈 말로 적절한 것은?

> The citizens asked that the government _____ taxes on basic necessities.

① reduced   ② reduces
③ to reduce   ④ reduce

해석

시민들은 정부가 기초 생필품에 대한 세금을 인하할 것을 요청했다.

해설

④ 조동사 should의 생략   빈칸은 종속절(that ~ necessities)의 동사 자리이다. 주절에 요구를 나타내는 동사(ask)가 나오면 종속절에는 '(should +) 동사원형'이 와야 하므로, ④ (should) reduce가 정답이다.

정답 ④

어휘

tax 세금   necessity 필수품, 필요(성)

---

03 문법 동사의 종류 | to 부정사 | 대명사   난이도 중 ●●○

밑줄 친 부분 중 어법상 옳지 않은 것은?

> In *Charlotte's Web*, Charlotte, a spider, weaves a message into her web ① in order to save Wilbur, a pig who faces death. Upon seeing the message, Wilbur's owner decides ② not to kill the animal. Two lessons emerge. One is that deep friendships can form even among very different creatures, and ③ the other is that sacrifice can have a lasting impact. Wilbur's decision to protect Charlotte's eggs after she dies lets readers ④ to see the enduring bond between the two characters.

해석

『샬럿의 거미줄』에서 거미 샬럿은 죽음에 직면한 돼지 윌버를 구하기 위해 거미줄을 엮어서 메시지를 남긴다. 메시지를 보고, 윌버의 주인은 그 동물을 죽이지 않기로 결정한다. 두 가지 교훈이 모습을 드러낸다. 하나는 아주 다른 생물들 사이에서조차 깊은 우정이 형성될 수 있다는 것이고, 다른 하나는 희생이 지속적인 영향을 미칠 수 있다는 것이다. 샬럿이 죽은 뒤 그녀의 알을 보호하겠다는 윌버의 결심은 독자들로 하여금 두 등장인물의 지속되는 유대감을 보게 한다.

해설

④ **원형 부정사를 목적격 보어로 취하는 동사** 사역동사 let은 원형 부정사를 목적격 보어로 취하므로 to 부정사 to see를 원형 부정사 see로 고쳐야 한다.

[오답 분석]
① **to 부정사의 역할** 문맥상 '구하기 위해'라는 의미가 되어야 자연스러우므로, to 부정사가 목적을 나타낼 때 to 대신 쓸 수 있는 in order to(~하기 위해서)가 올바르게 쓰였다.
② **to 부정사의 형태** to 부정사의 부정형을 만들 때는 to 앞에 not이 와야 하므로, not to kill이 올바르게 쓰였다.
③ **부정대명사** 문맥상 '(두 가지 교훈 중) 다른 하나'라는 의미가 되어야 자연스러우므로, '정해진 것 중 남은 것 전부'라는 의미의 부정대명사 the other가 올바르게 쓰였다.

정답 ④

어휘

weave 짜다, 엮어서 만들다 **emerge** 드러나다, 나타나다 **sacrifice** 희생
lasting 지속되는 **enduring** 지속되는 **bond** 유대(감); 결합시키다

---

04 생활영어 How about getting some feedback on it?

난이도 하 ●○○

밑줄 친 부분에 들어갈 말로 적절한 것은?

A: Can I get someone else to give the talk for me?
B: Why? Did something suddenly come up?
A: Not really. But I feel like I'm going to mess up the speech.
B: You will be fine. If you're too worried, _____
_____
A: That's a good idea. Can you help me?
B: Of course. Deliver the speech to me now, and I'll give you my thoughts.

① I'd be happy to give the speech for you.
② why don't you reschedule the speech for next week?
③ you can use note cards instead of the script.
④ how about getting some feedback on it?

해석

A: 내 강연을 대신할 다른 누군가를 구할 수 있을까?
B: 왜? 갑자기 무슨 일이라도 생겼니?
A: 그건 아니야. 하지만 나는 연설을 망칠 것 같은 기분이 들어.
B: 잘될 거야. 너무 걱정된다면, 그것에 대해 피드백을 좀 들어 보는 게 어때?
A: 좋은 생각이네. 네가 도와줄 수 있어?
B: 물론이지. 지금 연설을 나에게 들려줘, 그러면 내가 내 생각을 얘기해 줄게.

① 너를 위해 내가 연설을 해도 좋아.
② 연설 일정을 다음 주로 변경하면 어때?
③ 너는 원고 대신 메모 카드를 사용할 수 있어.
④ 그것에 대해 피드백을 좀 들어 보는 게 어때?

해설

A가 연설을 망칠 것 같다고 하자 B가 잘될 거라고 안심시키고, 빈칸 뒤에서 도와줄 수 있는지 묻는 A에게 B가 Deliver the speech to me now, and I'll give you my thoughts(지금 연설을 나에게 들려줘, 그러면 내가 내 생각을 얘기해 줄게)라고 대답하고 있으므로, '그것에 대해 피드백을 좀 들어 보는 게 어때?'라는 의미의 ④ 'how about getting some feedback on it?'이 정답이다.

정답 ④

어휘

mess up ~을 망치다 **script** 원고, 대본

05~06 다음 글을 읽고 물음에 답하시오.

To: Mapleton Municipal Council
From: Jean Richards
Date: November 5
Subject: Improvement to the Town's Online Complaint System

Dear Council Members,

I trust everyone on the council is well. I am sending this letter in regard to the town's online system for filing complaints, which I believe can be improved.

The current system requires the complainant to provide their name and phone number. While I understand there are situations when the complainant must be contacted for more information, I think some complaints, like those about road or park conditions, can be made anonymously.

As we live in a small community, it's easy for rumors to spread or for personal information to be shared. By allowing anonymous complaints for certain issues, more residents would feel comfortable voicing their concerns, which in turn would lead to greater _____ in improving our town. Thank you for considering this suggestion.

With sincere regards,

Jean Richards

해석

수신: Mapleton 시 의회
발신: Jean Richards
날짜: 11월 5일
제목: 마을의 온라인 민원 시스템 개선

의원분들께,

의회에 계신 모든 분이 건강하실 것을 믿습니다. 저는 마을의 온라인 민원 접수 시스템에 대해 말씀드리고자 이 편지를 보내는데, 저는 이 시스템이 개선될 수 있다고 믿습니다.

DAY 10 하프모의고사 10회

현재의 시스템은 민원인이 이름과 전화번호를 제공하도록 요구하고 있습니다. 추가 정보를 위해 민원인이 연락받아야 하는 상황이 있다는 것을 이해하지만, 도로나 공원 상태에 관한 것들과 같은 일부 민원들은 익명으로 작성될 수 있다고 생각합니다.

우리가 작은 공동체에 살고 있기 때문에, 소문이 퍼지거나 개인 정보가 공유되기 쉽습니다. 특정 문제들에 대해 익명 민원을 허용함으로써, 더 많은 주민들이 자신들의 우려 사항을 표현하는 데 편안함을 느낄 것이고, 이는 우리 마을을 개선하는 것에 있어서 더 많은 <u>참여</u>로 이어질 것입니다. 이 제안을 고려해 주셔서 감사합니다.

진심 어린 안부를 담아,
Jean Richards

어휘
municipal council 시 의회 **complaint** 민원, 불만
complainant 민원인, 고소인 **anonymously** 익명으로 **rumor** 소문
comfortable 편안한 **concern** 우려 (사항); 걱정시키다, 관련되다

---

05 독해 목적 파악 난이도 중 ●●○

윗글의 목적으로 적절한 것은?

① to ask for road repairs near the park
② to propose a change to the town's online complaint process
③ to complain about the unauthorized sharing of private data
④ to suggest ways to improve the security of the town's website

해석
① 공원 근처의 도로 수리를 요청하려고
② 마을의 온라인 민원 처리 절차에 변경을 제안하려고
③ 개인 정보의 무단 공유에 대해 항의하려고
④ 마을 웹사이트의 보안을 개선하는 방법을 제안하려고

해설
지문 처음에서 온라인 민원 접수 시스템이 개선될 수 있음을 믿는다고 하고, 지문 중간에서 민원인이 이름과 전화번호를 제공해야 하는 현재 시스템을 언급한 후, 지문 뒷부분에서 특정 문제들에 대해 익명 민원을 허용하는 제안을 고려해 달라고 요청하고 있으므로, ② '마을의 온라인 민원 처리 절차에 변경을 제안하려고'가 이 글의 목적이다.

정답 ②

어휘
unauthorized 무단의, 승인되지 않은

---

06 독해 빈칸 완성 - 단어 난이도 중 ●●○

윗글의 밑줄 친 부분에 들어갈 말로 적절한 것은?

① residence
② participation
③ generosity
④ indifference

해석
① 거주
② 참여
③ 너그러움
④ 무관심

해설
빈칸이 있는 문장에서 익명 민원의 허용으로 많은 주민들이 우려 사항을 표현하는 데 편안함을 느낄 것이라고 했으므로, 마을을 개선하는 것에 있어서 더 많은 '참여'로 이어질 것이라고 한 ②번이 정답이다.

정답 ②

어휘
residence 거주(지), 주택 **participation** 참여 **generosity** 너그러움
indifference 무관심

---

07 독해 내용 불일치 파악 난이도 중 ●●○

다음 글의 내용과 일치하지 않는 것은?

The historic Loma Manor is accessible by public transportation. Visitors can take the Green Line to Freeman Station and walk north for five minutes from Exit 6 or take the 115 bus to Wolfe Avenue and walk west for three blocks. Taxis and rideshare service vehicles can enter the parking lot for free to access the pick-up and drop-off area. For those driving, parking is available for a flat fee of $20 per vehicle. Cash is no longer accepted.

General admission tickets do not cover specially ticketed programs or events. The cost of a standard adult ticket is $40. When accompanied by a ticketed adult, children under three are admitted for free. A complimentary mobile audio guide app is included with general admission.

NOTE: Although Loma Manor is open for tours daily from 9:30 a.m. – 5:00 p.m., its gardens close at 4:00 p.m. on Mondays and Tuesdays.

① Loma Manor can be accessed by foot from Freeman Station.
② The cost of on-site parking depends on duration.
③ The $40 admission does not provide all-inclusive access.
④ Loma Manor's gardens close early twice a week.

해석
역사적인 Loma Manor는 대중교통으로 접근 가능합니다. 방문객 여러분은 Green 라인을 타고 Freeman 역까지 가신 후 6번 출구에서 북쪽으로 5분 걸어가시거나, 115번 버스를 타고 Wolfe로까지 가신 후 서쪽으로 세 블록 걸어가실 수 있습니다. 택시와 승차 공유 서비스 차량은 승하차 구역에 접근하기 위해 무료로 주차장에 진입하실 수 있습니다. 운전해서 오시는 분들은, 차량 한 대당 20달러의 고정 요금으로 주차가 가능합니다. 현금은 더 이상 받지 않습니다.

일반 입장 티켓은 별도로 티켓이 발권되는 프로그램이나 이벤트에 적용되지 않습니다. 일반 성인 티켓의 가격은 40달러입니다. 티켓을 구매한 성인과 동반하는 3세 미만 어린이들은 입장이 무료입니다. 무료

10회 정답·해석·해설 해커스공무원 비비안 영어 매일 하프모의고사

> 모바일 오디오 가이드 앱은 일반 입장에 포함되어 있습니다.
>
> **참고 부탁드립니다**: Loma Manor는 매일 오전 9시 30분부터 오후 5시까지 투어를 위해 개방되지만, 월요일과 화요일에는 정원이 오후 4시에 문을 닫습니다.

① Loma Manor는 Freeman 역에서 도보로 접근할 수 있다.
② 현장 주차 비용은 주차한 시간에 따라 다르다.
③ 40달러의 입장료가 모든 접근권을 제공하지는 않는다.
④ Loma Manor의 정원은 일주일에 두 번 일찍 문을 닫는다.

해설
②번의 키워드인 parking(주차)이 그대로 언급된 지문 주변의 내용에서 차량 한 대당 20달러의 고정 요금으로 주차가 가능하다고 했으므로, ② '현장 주차 비용은 주차한 시간에 따라 다르다'는 지문의 내용과 다르다.

정답 ②

어휘
public transportation 대중교통 rideshare 승차 공유 pick-up 승차
drop-off 하차 flat fee 고정 요금 accompany 동반하다
complimentary 무료의, 칭찬하는 on-site 현장의

---

08 독해 주제 파악   난이도 중 ●●○

다음 글의 주제로 적절한 것은?

> If you feel that you're stuck and can't get things moving forward, you may need to start saying "yes" more often, according to Shonda Rhimes. In her memoir, *Year of Yes*, the award-winning TV producer and show creator says that she was always an introvert who was scared to try many things. However, she decided to change when a relative told her that she never said yes to anything. Rhimes pledged to say yes to everything for one year. And the results were amazing. As Rhimes confronted new fears, she not only overcame them but also became more confident in facing other fears, so they lost their power. But it was not all about getting over things that made her uncomfortable; she also said yes to allowing herself more time for fun, which she says unlocked her creative potential. As a result, she was able to improve the level of her work and advance her career even further.

① strategies for managing reluctance effectively
② life transformation through positive responses
③ role of family support in career choices
④ TV industry challenges for female producers

해석
Shonda Rhimes에 따르면, 만약 당신이 꼼짝 못 하고 앞으로 나아갈 수 없다고 느낀다면, 당신은 더 자주 '좋다'라고 말하기 시작할 필요가 있을지도 모른다. 수상 경력이 있는 TV 프로듀서이자 쇼 제작자인 그녀는 회고록 『Year of Yes』에서 자신이 항상 많은 것을 시도하기를 두려워했던 내성적인 사람이었다고 말한다. 하지만, 그녀는 한 친척이 그녀에게 그녀가 어떤 것에도 결코 좋다고 말하지 않는다고 했을 때 변하기로 결심했다. Rhimes는 일 년 동안 모든 것에 좋다고 말하겠다고 맹세했다. 그리고 결과는 놀라웠다. Rhimes는 새로운 공포에 맞닥뜨릴 때 그것을 극복했을 뿐만 아니라, 다른 공포에 직면하는 것에 대해 더욱 자신만만해져서, 그것(공포)은 힘을 잃었다. 그러나 그녀를 불편하게 만든 것들을 극복하는 것이 전부는 아니었다. 그녀는 그녀 자신에게 즐거움을 위한 더 많은 시간을 주는 것에도 좋다고 말했는데, 이것은 그녀가 말하기로는 그녀의 창의적인 가능성을 열어 주었다. 그 결과, 그녀는 자신의 일의 수준을 향상시키고 경력을 훨씬 더 발전시킬 수 있었다.

① 주저함을 효과적으로 관리하는 전략들
② 긍정적 반응을 통한 삶의 변화
③ 직업 선택에 있어 가족의 지지가 하는 역할
④ 여성 프로듀서들에게 있어 TV 업계의 어려움

해설
지문 전반에 걸쳐 TV 프로듀서이자 쇼 제작자 Shonda Rhime는 원래 시도를 두려워하는 내성적인 사람이었지만, 일 년 동안 모든 것에 '좋다'고 말할 것을 맹세한 결과 스스로를 불편하게 만드는 것들을 극복하고 일의 수준을 향상시키며 경력을 발전시킬 수 있었다고 알려 주고 있다. 따라서 ② '긍정적 반응을 통한 삶의 변화'가 이 글의 주제이다.

정답 ②

어휘
memoir 회고록 introvert 내성적인 사람; 내성적인 relative 친척
pledge 맹세하다 confront 맞닥뜨리다, 직면하다 overcome 극복하다
get over ~을 극복하다 unlock 열다, 자물쇠를 열다 reluctance 주저함
transformation 변화

---

09 독해 문단 순서 배열   난이도 중 ●●○

주어진 글 다음에 이어질 글의 순서로 적절한 것은?

> Some fruits and vegetables are easy to classify because they are either sweet or not sweet. This method of categorization is subjective, and can lead to different groups of people categorizing the same plant differently.

(A) For example, confusion may occur because some consider a tomato a sweet fruit, while others insist it is a non-sweet vegetable. The criterion of sweetness will make yams, carrots, and beets fruits as they all have a degree of sweetness.

(B) Instead of using taste as a classifier, botanists concur that fruits and vegetables should be viewed botanically, that is, based on which part of the plant they come from.

(C) If it emerges from the plant's flower, then it is a fruit, and this would include apples, cucumbers, and eggplants. In contrast, if it comes from any other part of the plant, such as the roots, stems, or leaves, it is a vegetable.

① (A) – (B) – (C)
② (A) – (C) – (B)
③ (C) – (A) – (B)
④ (C) – (B) – (A)

DAY 10 하프모의고사 10회

해석

일부 과일과 채소는 달거나 달지 않거나 둘 중 하나이기 때문에 분류하기 쉽다. 이러한 범주화의 방법은 주관적이며, 서로 다른 집단의 사람들이 똑같은 식물을 다른 범주로 분류하는 것으로 이어질 수 있다.

(A) 예를 들어, 어떤 사람들은 토마토를 단 과일로 간주하는 반면 다른 사람들은 그것이 달지 않은 채소라고 주장하기 때문에 혼란이 발생할 수도 있다. 참마, 당근, 그리고 무는 모두 어느 정도의 단맛이 있기 때문에 단맛이라는 기준은 그것들을 과일로 만들 것이다.

(B) 분류하기로써 맛을 사용하는 대신에, 식물학자들은 과일과 채소는 식물학적으로, 즉 그것들이 식물의 어느 부분에서 나오는지에 근거하여 판단되어야 한다는 것에 동의한다.

(C) 만약 그것이 식물의 꽃에서 나온다면 그것은 과일이고, 여기에는 사과, 오이, 그리고 가지가 포함될 것이다. 대조적으로, 그것이 뿌리, 줄기, 또는 잎과 같은 식물의 그 밖의 다른 부분에서 나온다면, 그것은 채소이다.

해설

주어진 글에서 과일과 채소를 단맛을 기준으로 분류하는 것은 서로 다른 사람들이 똑같은 식물을 다르게 분류하게 할 수 있다고 한 후, (A)에서 예를 들어(For example) 토마토, 참마, 당근, 무는 단맛이라는 기준에서 보면 과일로 주장될 수 있다고 설명하고 있다. 이어서 (B)에서 대신에(Instead) 식물학자들에 따르면 과일과 채소는 식물의 어느 부분에서 나오는지에 근거하여 판단되어야 한다고 하고, (C)에서 식물의 꽃에서 나오는 것은 과일인 반면 식물의 그 밖의 부분에서 나오는 것은 채소라고 구체적으로 알려 주고 있다. 따라서 ① (A) – (B) – (C)가 정답이다.

정답 ①

어휘

classify 분류하다 categorization 범주화 subjective 주관적인
confusion 혼란 criterion 기준 botanist 식물학자 concur 동의하다
botanically 식물학적으로 emerge 나오다 stem 줄기

---

10 독해 빈칸 완성 – 절   난이도 상 ●●●

밑줄 친 부분에 들어갈 말로 적절한 것은?

A comprehensive outline of civil, political, economic, social, and cultural rights is the basis for the Universal Declaration of Human Rights adopted by the United Nations in 1948. The Declaration has its origins in the abuses of World War II, when governments used police and armed forces to infringe people's human rights, and was written by representatives from various cultural backgrounds. Explicit in the document is the intent to accord all human beings the right to dignity, governance participation, and remedy for rights violations given its legitimacy in all countries. Although it is considered the most significant development in the history of human rights, many see it as imperfect because _____. Should rights violations occur in any country, such as the state's use of military might against the citizenry or the denial of human rights by society, the UN does not have the legal power to act.

① the limits do not go far enough
② its principles are not binding
③ concepts of human rights change over time
④ few countries have signed on

해석

시민, 정치, 경제, 사회, 그리고 문화권의 포괄적인 개요는 1948년에 유엔에 의해 채택된 세계 인권 선언의 근간이다. 그 선언은 정부가 사람들의 인권을 침해하기 위해 경찰과 군대를 이용했던 제2차 세계대전의 폐해에 그것의 기원을 두고 있으며, 다양한 문화적 배경 출신의 대표들에 의해 작성되었다. 그 문서에서 명시적인 것은 모든 국가에서 그것의 합법성을 고려하여 모든 인간에게 존엄성, 통치 참여, 그리고 권리 침해의 해결책에 대한 권리를 부여하려는 의도이다. 그것이 인권의 역사에 있어 가장 중요한 발전이라고 여겨지기는 하지만, 많은 사람들은 그것을 불완전한 것으로 여기는데, 이는 그것의 원칙들이 법적 구속력이 없기 때문이다. 만약 시민들에게 불리한 국가의 군사력 사용이나 누군가의 권리에 대한 사회의 부정과 같은 인권 침해가 어떤 나라에서라도 일어나더라도, 유엔은 행동을 취할 합법적인 권력을 갖고 있지 않다.

① 제한이 충분하지 않기
② 그것의 원칙들이 법적 구속력이 없기
③ 인권의 개념이 시간이 지나면서 변하기
④ 서명했던 국가가 거의 없기

해설

빈칸이 있는 문장에서 많은 사람들이 유엔이 선포한 세계 인권 선언을 불완전한 것으로 여긴다고 하고, 빈칸 뒤 문장에서 시민들에게 불리한 국가 군사력 사용이나 누군가의 권리에 대한 사회의 부정과 같은 권리 침해가 일어나더라도 유엔이 행동을 취할 합법적인 권력을 갖고 있지 않다고 했으므로, 이는 '그것의 원칙들이 법적 구속력이 없기' 때문이라고 한 ②번이 정답이다.

정답 ②

어휘

comprehensive 포괄적인, 종합적인 outline 개요, 일반 원칙
declaration 선언 adopt 채택하다 abuse 폐해, 남용, 오용
infringe 침해하다 representative 대표; 대표하는
explicit 명시적인, 명백한 accord 부여하다, 조화시키다 dignity 존엄성, 위엄
remedy 해결책, 치료 legitimacy 합법성 imperfect 불완전한
citizenry 시민들 denial 부정, 부인 binding 법적 구속력이 있는
sign on ~에 서명하다

DAY 11 하프모의고사 11회

정답   p. 54

01	①	어휘	06	④	독해
02	③	문법	07	③	독해
03	③	문법	08	②	독해
04	③	생활영어	09	④	독해
05	③	독해	10	①	독해

취약영역 분석표

영역	맞힌 답의 개수
어휘	/1
생활영어	/1
문법	/2
독해	/6
TOTAL	/10

---

01 어휘 attack = criticize   난이도 중 ●●○

밑줄 친 부분의 의미와 가장 가까운 것은?

The ambassador was recently <u>attacked</u> by the international community for his ignorant remarks about the ongoing refugee crisis.

① criticized   ② evaluated
③ avoided   ④ suspended

[해석]
그 대사는 진행 중인 난민 위기에 대한 그의 무지한 발언으로 국제 사회에 의해 최근 공격받았다.
① 비난받은   ② 평가받은
③ 외면당한   ④ 중단된

정답 ①

[어휘]
ambassador (외교) 대사 attack 공격하다, 습격하다 ignorant 무지한
remark 발언; 언급하다 ongoing 진행 중인 refugee 난민 crisis 위기
criticize 비난하다 evaluate 평가하다 avoid 외면하다, 피하다
suspend 중단하다, 보류하다

---

02 문법 분사   난이도 하 ●○○

밑줄 친 부분에 들어갈 말로 적절한 것은?

Three-fourths of books _____ online are typically delivered within two business days.

① is purchased   ② purchasing
③ purchased   ④ are purchased

[해석]
온라인으로 구매된 도서의 4분의 3은 일반적으로 영업일 기준 2일 이내에 배송됩니다.

[해설]
③ 현재분사 vs. 과거분사 주어(Three-fourths of books)와 동사(are ~ delivered)를 모두 갖춘 절에 또 다른 동사는 올 수 없으므로, 빈칸은 명사 books를 수식하는 수식어 거품 자리이다. 따라서 동사 형태의 ① is purchased와 ④ are purchased는 정답이 될 수 없다. 이때 수식받는 명사(books)와 분사가 '도서가 구매되다'라는 의미의 수동 관계이므로, 현재분사 ② purchasing이 아닌 과거분사 ③ purchased가 정답이다.

정답 ③

---

03 문법 to 부정사 | 전치사 | 도치 구문 | 부사   난이도 중 ●●○

밑줄 친 부분 중 어법상 옳지 않은 것은?

In Western countries, social workers tend to keep parents and children together ① <u>despite</u> any issues that may be present in the home. Only when the risk is deemed too high ② <u>does the social worker make</u> a recommendation for intervention to a family court. Before that, however, social workers are willing to ③ <u>doing</u> everything to improve the situation of a family. If a family ④ <u>successfully</u> applies the advice, then there will be no need to take the step of separating children from their parents.

[해석]
서구 국가들에서, 사회 복지사들은 가정에 있을지도 모르는 어떠한 문제들에도 불구하고 부모와 자녀를 같이 두려는 경향이 있다. 오직 그 위험이 너무 크다고 간주될 때에 한해 사회 복지사는 가정 법원에 개입을 건의한다. 하지만, 그전에 사회 복지사들은 가족의 상황을 개선하기 위해 기꺼이 모든 일을 할 것이다. 만약 가족이 성공적으로 조언을 적용한다면, 그 후 아이들을 부모로부터 분리하는 조치를 취할 필요가 없을 것이다.

[해설]
③ to 부정사 관련 표현 문맥상 '기꺼이 모든 일을 할 것이다'라는 의미가 되어야 자연스러운데, '기꺼이 ~하다'는 to 부정사 관련 표현 be willing to로 나타낼 수 있다. 따라서 doing을 to 뒤에서 to 부정사를 완성하는

DAY 11 하프모의고사 11회

동사원형 do로 고쳐야 한다.

[오답 분석]
① **전치사 자리** 명사구(any issues ~ home) 앞에는 전치사가 와야 하고, 문맥상 '가정에 있을지도 모르는 어떠한 문제들에도 불구하고'라는 의미가 되어야 자연스러우므로 전치사 despite(~에도 불구하고)가 올바르게 쓰였다.
② **도치 구문** 제한을 나타내는 부사절(Only when ~ too high)이 강조되어 문장의 맨 앞에 나오면 주절의 주어와 조동사가 도치되어 '조동사(does) + 주어(the social worker) + 동사(make)'의 어순이 되어야 하므로 does the social worker make가 올바르게 쓰였다.
④ **부사 자리** 부사(successfully)는 '동사(applies) + 목적어(the advice)'의 앞이나 뒤에 오므로 applies the advice 앞에 부사 successfully가 올바르게 쓰였다.

정답 ③

어휘

social worker 사회 복지사 deem 간주하다, 여기다
make a recommendation 건의하다 intervention 개입, 간섭
court 법원 separate 분리하다; 별개의

04 생활영어 Have you thought about what you're going to do then?
난이도 하 ●○○

밑줄 친 부분에 들어갈 말로 적절한 것은?

 Grace Moore
How's it going?
16:00

Chris Morgan
Great! I just got some really good news.
16:01

 Grace Moore
Oh, really? What is that?
16:02

Chris Morgan
We're all getting an extra week off at Christmas this year.
16:02

 Grace Moore
I know. My colleague on the HR team told me about it a week ago.
16:03

Chris Morgan
_____
16:03

 Grace Moore
I'm actually planning to visit my parents for a week.
16:04

① Why didn't you mention this to me earlier?
② When do you prefer to take your vacation?
③ Have you thought about what you're going to do then?
④ How many vacation days do you have left this year?

해석

Grace Moore: 요즘 좀 어때?
Chris Morgan: 잘 지내! 방금 정말 좋은 소식을 들었어.
Grace Moore: 아, 정말? 그게 뭔데?
Chris Morgan: 우리가 모두 올해 크리스마스에 한 주 더 쉬게 될 거래.
Grace Moore: 알고 있어. 일주일 전에 인사팀에 있는 동료가 그것에 대해 말해 줬거든.
Chris Morgan: 그때 뭘 할지 생각해 봤니?
Grace Moore: 사실 나는 일주일 동안 부모님을 방문할 계획이야.

① 왜 이걸 내게 더 일찍 말해 주지 않았니?
② 언제 휴가 가는 것을 선호하니?
③ 그때 뭘 할지 생각해 봤니?
④ 올해 남은 휴가일이 며칠이나 되니?

해설

올해 크리스마스에 한 주 더 쉬게 될 것이라는 Chris의 말에 대해 Grace가 인사팀 동료에게 들어 이미 알고 있던 사실이라고 반응하고, 빈칸 뒤에서 다시 Grace가 I'm actually planning to visit my parents for a week (사실 나는 일주일 동안 부모님을 방문할 계획이야)라고 대답하고 있으므로, '그때 뭘 할지 생각해 봤니?'라는 의미의 ③ 'Have you thought about what you're going to do then?'이 정답이다.

정답 ③

05~06 다음 글을 읽고 물음에 답하시오.

_____(A)

Pottersville invites everyone to its New Year's Eve Ball, an annual celebration of the coming of the new year that has been held for 75 years. You don't want to miss out on this fun event.

Details
• **Date**: Thursday, December 31
• **Time**: Events start at 6 p.m.
• **Location**: Doré Arena at the Pottersville Convention Center
• **Dress Code**: Formal attire required
• **Ticket Cost**: $25 per person

Highlights

- **Entertainment**
  Enjoy the talents of an assortment of musicians, dancers, and other entertainers as they put on shows throughout the evening.
- **Countdown and Fireworks**
  Count down the last moments of this year and take pleasure in the city's fireworks show at midnight in comfort from the arena's rooftop.

To request tickets, please call the city events manager at 555-2821.

해석

(A) Pottersville에서 황홀한 밤을 경험하세요

Pottersville에서 75년간 개최되어 온, 새해 맞이 연례 축하 행사인 새해 전야 무도제에 여러분 모두를 초대합니다. 이 즐거운 행사를 놓치지 마세요.

상세 정보
- **날짜**: 12월 31일, 목요일
- **시간**: 행사는 오후 6시에 시작합니다.
- **장소**: Pottersville 컨벤션 센터 내 Doré 공연장
- **복장 규정**: 격식을 차린 복장이 요구됩니다
- **입장료**: 1인당 25달러

주요 행사
- 오락 활동
  다양한 음악가, 댄서 및 기타 연예인들이 저녁 내내 공연하는 동안 그들의 재능을 즐기세요.
- 카운트다운과 불꽃놀이
  올해의 마지막 순간을 카운트다운하고 자정에는 공연장 옥상에서 도시의 불꽃놀이 쇼를 편안하게 즐기세요.

티켓을 요청하시려면, 시 행사 관리자에게 555-2821번으로 전화 주시기 바랍니다.

어휘

ball 무도제, 무도회 arena 공연장, 경기장 formal 격식을 차린, 정중한
attire 복장 an assortment of 다양한 put on 공연을 하다, 상연하다
entertainer 연예인 in comfort 편안하게

---

05 독해 제목 파악 난이도 중 ●●○

(A)에 들어갈 윗글의 제목으로 적절한 것은?

① Visit Pottersville in the Coming Year
② See How Pottersville Changed over the Years
③ Experience a Magical Night in Pottersville
④ Be Inspired by Pottersville Creative Passion

해석

① 내년에 Pottersville을 방문하세요
② Pottersville이 수년간 어떻게 변화했는지 확인하세요
③ Pottersville에서 황홀한 밤을 경험하세요
④ Pottersville의 창의적인 열정에서 영감을 얻으세요

해설

지문 처음에서 새해 맞이 행사인 Pottersville의 새해 전야 무도제에 초대한다고 하고, 지문 뒷부분에서 주요 행사로 새해 전날 밤 카운트다운과 불꽃놀이를 소개하고 있다. 따라서 ③ 'Pottersville에서 황홀한 밤을 경험하세요'가 이 글의 제목이다.

정답 ③

어휘

magical 황홀한, 마법 같은 inspire 영감을 주다, 고무하다

---

06 독해 내용 불일치 파악 난이도 하 ●○○

New Year's Eve Ball에 관한 윗글의 내용과 일치하지 않는 것은?

① 75년 동안 진행되어 왔다.
② 별도의 복장 규정이 있다.
③ 연예인들의 무대를 볼 수 있다.
④ 티켓은 현장에서 구매 가능하다.

해설

④번의 키워드인 '티켓'이 그대로 언급된 지문의 tickets 주변의 내용에서 티켓을 요청하려면 시 행사 관리자에게 전화해 달라고 했으므로, ④ '티켓은 현장에서 구매 가능하다'는 지문의 내용과 다르다.

정답 ④

---

07 독해 요지 파악 난이도 중 ●●○

다음 글의 요지로 적절한 것은?

One of the principal theories for the interactions of people and societies is that of structural functionalism. This idea looks to explain how societies and personal relationships develop over time. The theory posits that societies evolve much in the same way that biological organisms do, with different components each serving a specific purpose, much in the same way that organs do with organisms. Sectors of a society could include education, religion, philosophy, economics, and countless other arenas. Each sector has the goal of reaching its own equilibrium, or state of stability. This, in turn, brings stability to the entirety of the organism. This theory has come under tremendous scrutiny for flaws such as taking too much of a macroscopic view of society and ignoring human nature and genetics, yet it remains influential even today.

① Social sectors operate independently for overall stability.
② Evolutionary biology determines societal structural development exclusively.

③ Structural functionalism compares society to biological organisms.
④ Human nature primarily contradicts structural functionalism principles.

해석

사람과 사회의 상호작용에 대한 주요 이론들 중 하나는 '구조기능주의' 이론이다. 이 개념은 사회와 개인의 관계가 시간이 지나면서 어떻게 발전하는지 설명하려고 한다. 그 이론은 사회가 생물학적인 유기체가 진화하는 것과 동일한 방식으로 진화하며, (신체) 장기들이 유기체에서 하는 것과 동일한 방식으로 서로 다른 요소들이 각각 특정한 목적을 수행한다고 상정한다. 사회의 분야들은 교육, 종교, 철학, 경제 그리고 수많은 다른 계통들을 포함할 수 있다. 각 분야는 그것만의 균형 또는 안정 상태에 이른다는 목표를 갖고 있다. 이것은 결국 유기체 전체에 안정을 가져온다. 이 이론은 사회에 대해 지나치게 거시적인 관점을 취하는 것과 인간의 본성과 유전적 특징을 무시하는 것과 같은 결점들 때문에 엄청나게 철저한 검토를 받게 되었지만, 그것은 오늘날에도 여전히 영향력이 있다.
① 사회의 분야들은 전체 안정성을 위해 독립적으로 작동한다.
② 진화 생물학은 전적으로 사회의 구조적 발전을 결정한다.
③ 구조기능주의는 사회를 생물학적 유기체와 비교한다.
④ 인간 본성은 주로 구조기능주의 원칙과 모순된다.

해설

지문 전반에 걸쳐 구조기능주의는 사회가 생물학적인 유기체처럼 진화한다는 견해인데, 이 이론에 따르면 사회의 각 분야는 유기체의 장기들이 그러하듯 저마다의 균형 상태에 이름으로써 결과적으로 사회 전체의 안정성을 가져올 수 있다고 설명하고 있으므로, ③ '구조기능주의는 사회를 생물학적 유기체와 비교한다'가 이 글의 요지이다.

정답 ③

어휘

principal 주요한 **structural** 구조(상)의 **functionalism** 기능주의
posit (사실로) 상정하다 **evolve** 진화하다 **biological** 생물학적인
organism 유기체, 생물 **component** 요소, 부품 **organ** (신체) 장기
sector 분야 **countless** 수많은 **arena** 계, 영역, 경기장
equilibrium 균형 (상태), 평정 **stability** 안정(성) **in turn** 결국, 차례차례
entirety 전체, 전부 **come under** (비난을) 받게 되다, ~의 통제를 받다
scrutiny 철저한 검토, 정밀 조사 **macroscopic** 거시적인
genetics 유전적 특징, 유전학 **independently** 독립적으로
exclusively 전적으로, 배타적으로 **compare** 비교하다 **primarily** 주로
contradict 모순되다, 부인하다 **principle** 원칙

08 독해 무관한 문장 삭제   난이도 중 ●●○

다음 글의 흐름상 어색한 문장은?

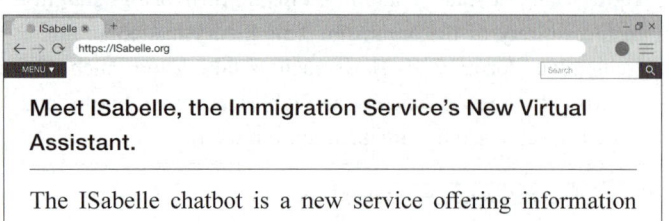

Meet ISabelle, the Immigration Service's New Virtual Assistant.

The ISabelle chatbot is a new service offering information from the Immigration Service. ISabelle can assist users with commonly asked questions about the immigration process, including explaining visa categories, giving directions for filling out applications, and checking one's case status, all using the latest information to provide accurate and timely help. ① As part of the Immigration Service's efforts to improve customer service, the chatbot will be available around the clock. ② The Immigration Service warns users that ISabelle frequently provides outdated visa information from 2010. ③ For questions that cannot be answered, ISabelle offers users access to live operators who can provide more in-depth assistance. ④ Currently available in English, Spanish, and Chinese, the service will add additional languages in future updates, including Korean, Portuguese, and Arabic.

해석

출입국관리사무소의 새로운 가상 도우미 ISabelle을 만나 보세요.

ISabelle 챗봇은 출입국관리사무소의 정보를 제공하는 새로운 서비스입니다. ISabelle은 사용자분들이 자주 묻는 이민 절차에 관한 질문들에 대해 도움을 드릴 수 있는데, 여기에는 비자 종류 설명, 신청서 작성 방법 안내 그리고 신청 건 진행 상황 확인 등이 포함되며, 이것들은 모두 정확하고 시기 적절한 도움을 드리기 위해 가장 최신의 정보를 이용합니다. ① 출입국관리사무소의 고객 서비스를 향상시키기 위한 노력의 일환으로, 그 챗봇을 24시간 내내 이용하실 수 있을 것입니다. ② 출입국관리사무소는 ISabelle이 2010년의 오래된 비자 정보를 자주 제공한다는 점을 사용자분들에게 경고합니다. ③ 답변할 수 없는 질문에 대해서는, ISabelle이 사용자분들을 더 심층적인 도움을 제공할 수 있는 실시간 상담원에게 연결해 줍니다. ④ 현재 영어, 스페인어, 중국어로 이용 가능하며, 이 서비스는 향후 업데이트에서 한국어, 포르투갈어, 아랍어를 포함한 추가 언어들을 더할 것입니다.

해설

지문 앞부분에서 출입국관리사무소의 정보를 제공하는 ISabelle 챗봇은 사용자들이 자주 묻는 이민 절차 관련 질문들에 최신 정보를 이용하여 답변하는 서비스라고 언급한 후, ①번은 'ISabelle 이용 가능 시간', ③번은 'ISabelle의 상담원 연결 기능', ④번은 '추후 추가 예정인 ISabelle의 이용 가능 언어 선택지들'에 대해 설명하고 있다. 그러나 ②번은 'ISabelle이 오래된 비자 정보를 제공하는 점에 대한 경고'에 대한 내용으로, 지문 앞부분의 내용과 관련이 없다.

정답 ②

어휘

immigration 출입국관리사무소, 이민 **virtual** 가상의 **direction** 방법, 방향
fill out ~을 작성하다 **application** 신청(서) **status** (진행) 상태
accurate 정확한 **timely** 시기적절한 **around the clock** 24시간 내내
warn 경고하다 **frequently** 자주 **outdated** 오래된, 구식의
operator 상담원, (기계) 조작자

09 독해 문장 삽입   난이도 중 ●●○

주어진 문장이 들어갈 위치로 적절한 것은?

> But the truth is that discipline—forcing oneself to sit at the desk to write first without motivation— leads to inspiration.

> Many wannabe fiction authors with dreams of producing best-selling novels struggle to write. (①) This doesn't mean that they don't have the talent to produce coherent or even artful prose. (②) Rather, their writing difficulties emerge from their inability to make themselves physically sit with an open notebook or a word processor and get to work. (③) For many aspiring authors, this problem seems to stem from the misconception that they must wait for inspiration to strike before they can start writing. (④) Famed writer William Somerset Maugham, among other established authors, seemed to agree with this regimen when he said, "I write only when inspiration strikes, which fortunately strikes every morning at nine o'clock sharp."

해석

그러나 사실은 동기 부여 없이 먼저 글을 쓰기 위해 스스로를 책상에 앉게 만드는 수련법이 영감을 이끌어낸다는 것이다.

베스트셀러 소설을 만들겠다는 꿈을 가진 많은 소설 작가 지망생들은 힘겹게 글을 쓴다. ① 이는 그들이 논리 정연하거나 심지어 예술적인 산문을 창작할 재능이 없다는 것을 의미하지 않는다. ② 그보다는, 빈 노트나 문서 작성기를 가지고 스스로를 물리적으로 앉혀 놓고 일을 시작하게 하지 못하는 데서 그들의 글쓰기 어려움이 생긴다. ③ 많은 작가 지망생들에게, 이 문제는 그들이 글을 쓰기 시작하기 전에 영감이 떠오르기를 기다려야 한다는 잘못된 생각에서 기인하는 것으로 보인다. ④ 다른 저명한 작가들 중에서도 유명한 작가인 William Somerset Maugham이 "나는 영감이 떠오를 때만 글을 쓰는데, 이것은 다행히 매일 아침 9시 정각에 떠오른다"라고 말했을 때, 그는 이 방식에 동의하는 것처럼 보였다.

해설

④번 앞 문장에 많은 작가 지망생들이 글쓰기를 어려워하는 것은 글을 쓰기 시작하기 전에 영감이 떠오르기를 기다려야 한다는 잘못된 생각에서 기인한 것으로 보인다는 내용이 있고, 뒤 문장에서 매일 아침 9시 정각에 글을 쓴 유명 작가 William Somerset Maugham도 이 방식(this regimen)에 동의하는 것처럼 보인다고 했으므로, ④번 자리에 그러나(But) 사실은 동기 부여 없이도 스스로를 책상에 앉게 만드는 수련법이 영감을 이끌어낸다는 내용, 즉 영감이 떠오르기를 기다리지 않고 책상에 앉아 글부터 쓰는 수련법을 제안하는 주어진 문장이 나와야 지문이 자연스럽게 연결된다.

정답 ④

어휘

discipline 수련법, 훈육 motivation 동기 부여 inspiration 영감
struggle 힘겹게 하다, 애쓰다 coherent 논리 정연한, 일관성 있는
prose 산문 inability 할 수 없음, 무능 aspiring 장차 ~이 되려는, 포부가 있는
stem from ~에서 기인하다 misconception 잘못된 생각, 오해
established 저명한, 인정받는 regimen 방식, 식이 요법
sharp 정각에; 날카로운

10 독해 빈칸 완성 – 구   난이도 중 ●●○

밑줄 친 부분에 들어갈 말로 적절한 것은?

> With the enormous geographical and meteorological changes occurring on Earth, it has become more important than ever to collect information related to natural disasters. The use of modern monitoring and imaging technology has allowed scientists to understand, forecast, and respond to volcanic eruptions, earthquakes, and landslides. In addition, being able to observe and predict glacier and ice-sheet melt and the resulting sea-level change can provide governments with data for disaster response support and mitigation. In short, _____ is critical for protecting life on the planet.

① the precise monitoring of changes on and inside Earth
② international collaboration among governments
③ studies on natural disasters that occurred previously
④ sustainable infrastructure in vulnerable regions

해석

지구상에서 지리학적·기상학적인 거대한 변화들이 발생하면서, 자연재해와 관련된 정보를 수집하는 것은 그 어느 때보다도 더욱 중요해졌다. 현대식의 관측과 영상 기술의 사용은 과학자들이 화산 폭발, 지진 그리고 산사태를 이해하고 예측하며 대응할 수 있게 해 주었다. 게다가, 빙하와 빙판 용해 그리고 그 결과로 초래된 해수면 변화를 관찰하고 예상할 수 있는 능력은 정부에게 재해 대책 지원과 (재해) 완화를 위한 데이터를 제공할 수 있다. 요약하자면, 지구 표면과 내부의 변화에 대한 정밀한 관찰은 지구의 생명체를 보호하는 데 중요하다.

① 지구 표면과 내부의 변화에 대한 정밀한 관찰
② 정부들 간의 국제적인 협력
③ 이전에 발생했던 자연재해들에 대한 연구
④ 취약한 지역들에 있는 지속 가능한 기반 시설

해설

지문 전반에 걸쳐 지구상에 일어나는 다양한 지리학적·기상학적 변화들로 인해 재해 관련 정보 수집이 그 어느 때보다도 더욱 중요해졌다고 하고, 현대식의 관측을 통해 화산 폭발, 지진, 산사태, 해수면 변화 등에 대해 이해하고 예상함으로써 재해 대책 지원과 재해 완화를 위한 데이터를 제공할 수 있다고 했으므로, '지구 표면과 내부의 변화에 대한 정밀한 관찰'이 지구의 생명체를 보호하는 데 중요하다고 한 ①번이 정답이다.

정답 ①

어휘

geographical 지리학적 meteorological 기상학적
forecast 예측하다, 예보하다 volcanic 화산의 eruption 폭발, 분출
landslide 산사태 observe 관찰하다 predict 예상하다 glacier 빙하
mitigation 완화, 경감 critical 중요한, 결정적인 precise 정밀한
collaboration 협력 sustainable 지속 가능한 vulnerable 취약한

DAY 12 하프모의고사 12회

정답 p. 58

01	④	어휘	06	②	독해
02	①	문법	07	②	독해
03	③	문법	08	④	독해
04	②	생활영어	09	③	독해
05	③	독해	10	②	독해

취약영역 분석표

영역	맞힌 답의 개수
어휘	/1
생활영어	/1
문법	/2
독해	/6
TOTAL	/10

---

01 어휘 distracted 난이도 중 ●●○

밑줄 친 부분에 들어갈 말로 적절한 것은?

It is usually harder for _____ people to remember information presented at meetings than it is for those who are attentive.

① friendly
② dedicated
③ independent
④ distracted

해석

산만한 사람들이 회의에서 제시된 정보를 기억해 두는 것은 주의 깊은 사람들에게 그것이 그러한 것보다 보통 더 어렵다.

① 친절한
② 헌신적인
③ 독립적인
④ 산만한

정답 ④

어휘

present 제시하다, 나타내다 attentive 주의 깊은, 배려하는 friendly 친절한 dedicated 헌신적인, 전념하는 independent 독립적인 distracted 산만한

---

02 문법 형용사 | 수 일치 난이도 중 ●●○

밑줄 친 부분에 들어갈 말로 적절한 것은?

_____ people attending the international food festival was remarkable, which reflected the event's popularity.

① The number of
② A number of
③ A variety of
④ A little of

해석

국제 음식 축제에 참석한 사람들의 수는 주목할 만했는데, 이는 그 행사의 인기를 반영하는 것이었다.

해설

① 수량 표현 | 수량 표현의 수 일치 빈칸은 문장의 주어 역할을 하는 명사 people 앞에 쓸 수 있는 수량 표현의 자리이다. 명사 people은 복수 가산 명사이므로 불가산 명사 앞에 오는 수량 표현 ④ A little of는 정답이 될 수 없다. 문맥상 '국제 음식 축제에 참석한 사람들의 수는 주목할 만했다'라는 의미가 되어야 자연스럽고, 문장의 동사 자리에 단수 동사 was가 왔으므로, 주어 자리에서 단수 취급하는 수량 표현 'the number of + 명사'의 형태를 완성하는 ① The number of가 정답이다. ② A number of(많은)와 ③ A variety of(다양한)가 주어 자리에 오면 동사는 복수 동사를 써야 하므로 정답이 될 수 없다.

정답 ①

어휘

remarkable 주목할 만한 reflect 반영하다 popularity 인기

---

03 문법 동사의 종류 | 수 일치 | 대명사 | 어순 난이도 중 ●●○

밑줄 친 부분 중 어법상 옳지 않은 것은?

The first "challenge" activity on social media to catch on ① was the Ice Bucket Challenge in which people poured large buckets of icy water on ② themselves to ③ rise treatment research funds for Lou Gehrig's disease. Unfortunately, a lot of challenges are now simply meant to create funny viral videos, lacking ④ such a worthwhile goal.

해석

소셜 미디어에서 인기를 얻은 첫 번째 '챌린지' 활동은 루게릭 병을 위한 치료 연구 기금을 모으기 위해 사람들이 찬물이 든 큰 버킷을 스스로에게 들이붓는 아이스 버킷 챌린지였다. 안타깝게도, 많은 챌린지들이 지금은 그러한 가치 있는 목표 없이, 단순히 우스꽝스러운 유명 영상을 만들어내려는 의도를 갖는다.

해설

③ 혼동하기 쉬운 자동사와 타동사 문맥상 '치료 연구 기금을 모으다'라는 의미가 되어야 자연스럽고, 전치사 없이 목적어(treatment research funds)를 바로 취하는 동사는 타동사이므로 '떠오르다'라는 의미의 자동사 rise를 '~을 모으다'라는 의미의 타동사 raise로 고쳐야 한다.

[오답 분석]
① 주어와 동사의 수 일치 주어 자리에 단수 명사 The first "challenge" activity가 왔으므로 단수 동사 was가 올바르게 쓰였다. 참고로, 주어와 동사 사이의 수식어 거품(on ~ catch on)은 동사의 수 결정에 영향을 주지 않는다.
② 재귀대명사 전치사 on의 목적어가 지칭하는 대상이 관계절의 주어(people)와 동일하므로 재귀대명사 themselves가 올바르게 쓰였다.
④ 혼동하기 쉬운 어순 such는 'such + a/an + 형용사 + 명사'의 어순이 되어야 하므로, 명사 goal 앞에 such a worthwhile이 올바르게 쓰였다.

정답 ③

어휘
catch on 인기를 얻다, 유행하다 viral video 유명 영상
worthwhile 가치 있는

---

04 생활영어 That's actually a good suggestion.
난이도 하 ●○○

밑줄 친 부분에 들어갈 말로 적절한 것은?

A: Have you planned anything for next week's mini-vacation?
B: The usual, I guess. I'll get some rest and watch TV.
A: Don't you usually go somewhere?
B: No, I hardly ever do anything special.
A: You should think about using this time to treat yourself. How about finding a nice restaurant to enjoy a meal?
B: _____ I'd like to do that.

① I'm trying to save money on food.
② That's actually a good suggestion.
③ I'd rather not waste my time.
④ Restaurants will be crowded.

해석
A: 다음 주 단기 휴가에 뭐 할지 계획했어?
B: 늘 하던 걸 할 것 같아. 좀 쉬고 TV 보려고.
A: 너 보통 어디 가지 않아?
B: 아니, 나는 거의 특별한 무언가를 하진 않아.
A: 너는 스스로를 대접하는 데 이 시간을 사용하는 걸 생각해 봐야 해. 식사를 즐길 근사한 식당을 찾아 보는 건 어때?
B: 그거 정말 좋은 제안이다. 그렇게 하고 싶어.

① 먹는 데 돈을 아끼려 하고 있어.
② 그거 정말 좋은 제안이다.
③ 내 시간을 낭비하고 싶지는 않아.
④ 식당들이 붐빌 거야.

해설
휴가에 특별한 일을 하진 않는다는 B에게 A가 근사한 식당에서 식사를 즐기는 등 스스로를 대접하는 데 휴가 시간을 사용하는 걸 생각해 보라고 제안하고, 빈칸 뒤에서 다시 B가 I'd like to do that(그렇게 하고 싶어)이라고 말하고 있으므로, '그거 정말 좋은 제안이다'라는 의미의 ② 'That's actually a good suggestion'이 정답이다.

정답 ②

05~06 다음 글을 읽고 물음에 답하시오.

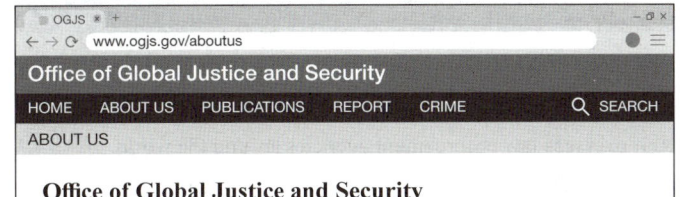

Office of Global Justice and Security

About
We are committed to creating a safer world through coordination with law enforcement authorities in over 180 countries. Together, we collect and share evidence to assist investigators and facilitate the secure transfer of prisoners across international borders for prosecution within the proper geographic jurisdictions.

CLOUD Act
In response to the new era of digitization, the Clarifying Lawful Overseas Use of Data (CLOUD) Act was passed in 2018 to accelerate the process of approving and sharing digital and electronic evidence among the department's network of international partners.

Points of Emphasis
- Balancing the protection of public safety with the individual's right to privacy
- Fighting corruption at the global level by identifying high-ranking officials guilty of bribery and similar crimes

해석

국제사법보안처

소개
저희는 180개국 이상의 법 집행 당국들과의 조율을 통해 더 안전한 세계를 만드는 데 전념합니다. 수사관들을 지원하기 위해 저희는 함께 증거를 수집하고 공유하며, 적절한 지리적 관할권 내에서의 기소를 위해 국경 너머로 수감자들의 안전한 이송을 용이하게 합니다.

데이터의 합법적 해외 사용 명확화(CLOUD) 법안
디지털화의 새로운 시대에 대응하여, 부처의 국제 파트너 조직망에서 디지털 및 전자 증거를 승인하고 공유하는 과정을 가속화하기 위해, 데이터의 합법적 해외 사용 명확화 법안이 2018년에 제정되었습니다.

DAY 12 하프모의고사 12회

강조점
- 공공 안전의 보호와 개인의 사생활 권리의 균형 맞추기
- 뇌물 수수 및 유사 범죄를 저지른 고위 공직자들을 식별함으로써 세계적인 차원에서 부패와 맞서기

어휘

coordination 조율, 조정 enforcement 집행 authorities 당국
investigator 수사관 facilitate 용이하게 하다, 촉진하다 prisoner 수감자
border 국경 prosecution 기소 geographic 지리적인
jurisdiction 관할권 clarify 명확히 하다 emphasis 강조
corruption 부패 guilty 죄가 있는, 죄책감이 드는 bribery 뇌물 수수

---

05 독해 내용 일치 파악 난이도 중 ●●○

윗글에서 Office of Global Justice and Security에 관한 내용과 일치하는 것은?

① It oversees law enforcement agencies around the world.
② It dispatches investigators to prosecute prisoners.
③ It applies a law to enable the quick sharing of digital evidence.
④ It prioritizes public safety over individuals' right to privacy.

해석
① 그것은 전 세계 법 집행 기관들을 감독한다.
② 그것은 수감자들을 기소하기 위해 조사관을 파견한다.
③ 그것은 디지털 증거의 신속한 공유를 가능케 하기 위해 법률을 적용한다.
④ 그것은 개인의 사생활 권리보다 공공 안전을 우선시한다.

해설
③번의 키워드인 digital evidence(디지털 증거)를 바꾸어 표현한 지문의 digital and electronic evidence(디지털 및 전자 증거) 주변의 내용에서 디지털 및 전자 증거를 공유하는 과정을 가속화하기 위해 데이터의 합법적 해외 사용 명확화 법안이 제정되었다고 했으므로, ③ '그것은 디지털 증거의 신속한 공유를 가능케 하기 위해 법률을 적용한다'가 지문의 내용과 일치한다.

[오답 분석]
① 국제사법보안처가 180개국 이상의 법 집행 당국들과 업무를 조율한다고는 했지만, 그것이 전 세계 법 집행 기관들을 감독하는지 알 수 없다.
② 국제사법보안처는 적절한 지리적 관할권 내에서의 기소를 위해 국경 너머 수감자들의 이송을 용이하게 한다고는 했지만, 그것이 수감자들을 기소하기 위해 조사관을 파견하는지는 알 수 없다.
④ 국제사법보안처는 공공 안전의 보호와 개인의 사생활 권리의 균형 맞추기를 강조한다고 했으므로, 그것이 개인의 사생활 권리보다 공공 안전을 우선시한다는 것은 지문의 내용과 다르다.

정답 ③

어휘
oversee 감독하다 dispatch 파견하다 prioritize 우선시하다

---

06 독해 유의어 파악 난이도 중 ●●○

밑줄 친 network의 의미와 가장 가까운 것은?

① authority
② community
③ access
④ agreement

해석
① 권한
② 공동체
③ 접근권
④ 합의

해설
밑줄 친 부분이 포함된 문장에서 network는 문맥상 부처의 국제 파트너 '조직망'에서 디지털 및 전자 증거를 승인하고 공유하는 과정을 가속화하기 위해 법안이 제정되었다는 의미로 쓰였으므로, '공동체'라는 의미의 ② community가 정답이다.

정답 ②

어휘
authority 권한, 당국 community 공동체, 지역 사회 access 접근(권)
agreement 합의, 동의

---

07 독해 주제 파악 난이도 중 ●●○

다음 글의 주제로 적절한 것은?

> Culture shock is a well-known phenomenon; still, returning home after years of living abroad can subject one to an even bigger episode—that of reverse culture shock. People have good memories of their homeland, but once the initial euphoria of being back home wears off, they may start feeling like a foreigner in their own country, especially if the withdrawal from their previous life was too swift. Having adjusted to the culture of a Western nation in surroundings very different from their motherland, native traditions can seem unfamiliar, and before long, they begin to feel foreign. The language, the sights, smells and sounds, and even the conversation can become overwhelming. Moreover, the feeling of being socially distant from people one is close to can be distressing. Like culture shock, it takes time and the empathy of loved ones to help persons readjust when they return home.

① a comparison of culture shock and reverse culture shock
② a surprising reaction to returning to one's homeland
③ the difficulties of learning new customs and traditions
④ the benefits of living in a foreign land

해석
문화 충격은 잘 알려진 현상이지만, 그럼에도 불구하고 해외에서 수년간 산 후에 귀국하는 것은 훨씬 큰 사건, 즉 역문화 충격의 사건을 겪게 만들 수 있다. 사람들은 고국에 대해 좋은 기억을 가지고 있지만, 귀국한 것에 대한 처음의 행복감이 사라지면, 특히 그들의 이전 생활로부터의 철수가 너무 급작스러웠다면, 그들은 모국에서 이방인처럼 느끼기 시작할 수도

있다. 그들의 모국과 매우 다른 환경의 서구 국가의 문화에 적응했기 때문에, 모국의 전통들은 낯설어 보일 수 있고, 머지않아 그들은 이질감을 느끼기 시작한다. 언어, 풍경, 냄새와 소리, 그리고 심지어 대화조차도 대응하기 힘들어질 수 있다. 게다가, 가까운 사람들로부터 사회적으로 동떨어져 있는 느낌은 비참할 수 있다. 문화 충격처럼, 사람들이 귀국했을 때 다시 적응하는 것을 돕는 데에는 시간과 사랑하는 사람들의 공감이 필요하다.

① 문화 충격과 역문화 충격의 비교
② 고국으로 돌아가는 것에 대한 의외의 반작용
③ 새로운 관습과 전통을 배우는 것의 어려움
④ 외국에서 사는 것의 이점

해설

지문 전반에 걸쳐 해외에서 수년간 살다가 고국으로 돌아가면 처음에는 행복감을 느끼지만 곧 고국의 많은 것들이 생경해 보이고, 사회적으로 동떨어져 있는 느낌을 받는 현상인 역문화 충격에 대해 설명하고 있다. 따라서 ② '고국으로 돌아가는 것에 대한 의외의 반작용'이 이 글의 주제이다.

정답 ②

어휘

phenomenon 현상 subject A to B A로 하여금 B를 겪게 만들다
reverse 역의, 정반대의; 역 euphoria 행복감, 희열
wear off 사라지다, 점점 줄어들다 withdrawal 철수, 퇴거, 취소
swift 급작스러운, 빠른, 신속한 adjust 적응하다, 조정하다
surroundings 환경 overwhelming 대응하기 힘든, 압도적인
distressing 비참한, 괴로움을 주는 empathy 공감, 감정이입
comparison 비교, 비유 reaction 반작용, 반응

---

08 독해 내용 불일치 파악 난이도 하 ●○○

National Transportation Safety Convention에 관한 다음 글의 내용과 일치하지 않는 것은?

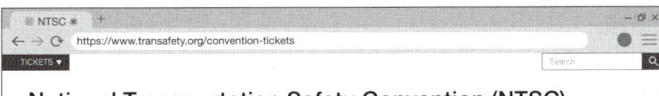

National Transportation Safety Convention (NTSC)

Tuesday, January 12 – Friday, January 15
Tickets:
- Price: $25.00
- Hours: Tuesday: Noon – 5:00 p.m.
         Wednesday-Friday: 10:00 a.m. – 5:00 p.m.

Tickets will be available online or at the convention center box office beginning December 1.

Sponsors and exhibitors can receive free tickets for their employees. Ticket allocation will be determined by sponsorship level or display booth size.

Tickets ensure entrance to the exhibit hall, all lectures, and most additional events. Special passes are required for VIP activities.

① 화요일 회의는 오후 12시에 열린다.
② 입장권은 12월 1일부터 판매된다.
③ 무료 입장권 제공 수량은 업체마다 다를 수 있다.
④ 입장권 소지자는 VIP 행사에 참여할 수 있다.

해석

국가교통안전회의(NTSC)
1월 12일 화요일 – 1월 15일 금요일
입장권:
- 가격: 25달러
- 시간: 화요일: 오후 12시 – 오후 5시
        수요일-금요일: 오전 10시 – 오후 5시

입장권은 12월 1일부터 온라인 또는 회의장 매표소에서 구매하실 수 있습니다.

후원 업체와 전시 업체 분들께서는 직원들을 위한 무료 입장권을 받으실 수 있습니다. 입장권 할당량은 후원 수준 또는 전시 부스 크기에 따라 결정될 것입니다.

입장권은 전시장, 모든 강연, 그리고 대부분의 추가 행사에 대한 입장을 보장합니다. VIP 활동에는 특별 출입증이 필요합니다.

해설

④번의 키워드인 'VIP'가 그대로 언급된 지문 주변의 내용에서 VIP 활동에는 특별 출입증이 필요하다고 했으므로, ④ '입장권 소지자는 VIP 행사에 참여할 수 있다'는 지문의 내용과 다르다.

정답 ④

---

09 독해 문단 순서 배열 난이도 중 ●●○

주어진 글 다음에 이어질 글의 순서로 적절한 것은?

Door-to-door selling in the US began in the mid-1800s when David McConnell went house to house to sell books. But he struggled to find buyers, and women only opened their doors because they liked his free samples of perfume.

(A) On top of that, he wasn't the best salesperson when it came to talking to women about perfumes. So, he hired a sales force of women who loved talking about perfumes, and that is how his perfume company became successful.
(B) Looking reality in the face, McConnell realized that he should focus on selling the more popular product. He began selling fragrances with hopes they would appeal to the women who made up the majority of his customers. He experienced a degree of success, but there were still barriers.
(C) The largest obstacle was that there was only one of him. Walking for the whole day was tiring, and the profits he earned alone were less than he had anticipated.

① (A) – (C) – (B) ② (B) – (A) – (C)
③ (B) – (C) – (A) ④ (C) – (A) – (B)

DAY 12 하프모의고사 12회

해석

미국의 방문 판매는 1800년대 중반에 David McConnell이 책을 팔기 위해 집집마다 다녔을 때 시작되었다. 그러나 그는 구매자들을 찾는 데 어려움을 겪었는데, 여성들은 단지 그의 무료 향수 샘플을 좋아했기 때문에 문을 열어 주었다.

(A) 그뿐 아니라, 여성들에게 향수에 대해 말하는 것에 관한 한 그는 최고의 판매원이 아니었다. 그래서, 그는 향수에 대해 이야기하기를 좋아하는 여성 판매 인력을 고용했고, 그렇게 해서 그의 향수 회사는 성공했다.

(B) 직면한 현실을 보면서, McConnell은 그가 더 인기 있는 상품을 파는 것에 집중해야 한다는 것을 깨달았다. 그는 향수들이 그의 고객 중 대다수를 이룬 여성들의 관심을 끌기를 바라면서 그것들을 팔기 시작했다. 그는 어느 정도의 성공을 경험했지만, 여전히 장벽들이 있었다.

(C) 가장 큰 장애물은 오로지 그밖에 없었다는 것이었다. 하루 종일 걸어 다니는 것은 고되었고, 그가 홀로 번 수익은 기대했던 것보다 적었다.

해설

주어진 글에서 David McConnell이 책을 팔기 위해 방문 판매를 시작했지만 여성 고객들은 단지 그의 무료 향수 샘플을 좋아했기 때문에 문을 열어 주었다고 한 뒤, (B)에서 그가 책 대신 더 인기 있는 상품(the more popular product)인 향수를 팔기 시작했지만 장벽들이 있었다고 설명하고 있다. 뒤이어 (C)에서 가장 큰 장애물(The largest obstacle)은 판매원이 오로지 그밖에 없어서 고되고 수익이 적은 것이었다고 한 뒤, (A)에서 그뿐 아니라(On top of that) 그가 여성들에게 향수에 대해 말하는 것에 있어서는 최고의 판매원이 아니었다는 추가적인 장애물을 설명하고 있다. 따라서 ③ (B) – (C) – (A)가 정답이다.

정답 ③

어휘

door-to-door selling 방문 판매 on top of ~뿐 아니라
when it comes to ~에 관한 한 fragrance 향수, 향기
appeal 관심을 끌다, 호소하다 make up ~을 이루다 barrier 장벽, 장애물
obstacle 장애물 tiring 고된, 피로하게 하는 anticipate 기대하다, 예상하다

---

10 독해 빈칸 완성 – 단어   난이도 중 ●●○

밑줄 친 부분에 들어갈 말로 적절한 것은?

Called the big cities of the sea, coral reefs have plenty of natural competition, from organisms that feed on them to jellyfish that invade their territory. But nothing has been more destructive to reefs than ocean acidification due to rising carbon dioxide levels, and by 2011, only half of the reefs that previously existed remained. A year later, scientists thought of transplanting healthy coral that could withstand warming water onto damaged reefs. Subsequently, the method was challenged because it was slow and expensive. _____, sturdier, slow-growing coral species began being used to bolster weak ones by embedding baby coral onto damaged reefs, which is less costly and shows greater promise. In addition, by designating areas where coral reefs grow as "protected," fish that consume organisms that prey on coral can thrive, thus reducing the pest population and giving corals added protection.

① Theoretically   ② Ultimately
③ Obviously   ④ Honestly

해석

바다의 대도시라고 불리는 산호초에게는 그것들을 먹고 사는 생물들부터 그것들의 영역에 침입하는 해파리까지 많은 자연의 경쟁 상대가 있다. 그러나 다른 어떤 것도 증가하고 있는 이산화탄소 수치로 인한 해양 산성화보다 산호초에 더 해를 끼치지는 않았고, 2011년에는 이전에 존재했던 산호초 중 절반만이 살아남았다. 1년 후, 과학자들은 따뜻한 물을 견뎌낼 수 있는 건강한 산호를 손상된 산호초에 옮겨 심는 것을 생각해냈다. 나중에, 그 방법은 시간이 걸리고 비용이 많이 든다는 이유로 이의를 제기받았다. 결국, 어린 산호를 손상된 산호초에 끼워 넣음으로써 허약한 것(산호 종)들을 강화하기 위해 보다 튼튼하고 천천히 자라는 산호 종이 사용되기 시작했는데, 이것은 비용이 덜 들고 더 유망하다. 뿐만 아니라, 산호초가 '보호되어' 자라는 지역을 지정함으로써, 산호를 먹이로 하는 생물들을 섭취하는 물고기가 잘 자랄 수 있고, 따라서 유해 동물 개체 수를 줄이고 산호에 추가적인 보호를 제공할 수 있다.

① 이론적으로   ② 결국
③ 분명히   ④ 솔직히

해설

빈칸 앞부분에 2012년에 과학자들은 따뜻한 물을 견딜 수 있는 건강한 산호를 손상된 산호초에 옮겨 심는 방법을 생각했지만 시간과 비용이 많이 든다는 이유로 이의를 제기받았다는 내용이 있고, 빈칸 뒤 문장에 비용이 덜 들고 더 유망한 방법이 사용되기 시작했다는 내용이 있으므로, '결국' 다른 방법으로 보다 튼튼하고 천천히 자라는 어린 산호를 손상된 산호초에 끼워 넣는 것이 사용되기 시작했다고 한 ② Ultimately가 정답이다.

정답 ②

어휘

coral reef 산호초 feed on ~을 먹고 살다 jellyfish 해파리
invade 침입하다 destructive 해를 끼치는, 파괴적인 acidification 산성화
carbon dioxide 이산화탄소 transplant 옮겨 심다, 이식하다
withstand 견뎌내다 sturdy 튼튼한 bolster 강화하다
embed 끼워 넣다, 박다 show promise 유망하다
designate 지정하다, 지명하다 prey on ~을 먹이로 하다
thrive 잘 자라다, 번영하다 pest 유해 동물, 해충 theoretically 이론적으로
obviously 분명히

DAY 13 하프모의고사 13회

정답 (p. 62)

01	②	어휘	06	②	독해
02	②	문법	07	④	독해
03	④	문법	08	④	독해
04	④	생활영어	09	③	독해
05	③	독해	10	③	독해

취약영역 분석표

영역	맞힌 답의 개수
어휘	/1
생활영어	/1
문법	/2
독해	/6
TOTAL	/10

---

01 어휘 withdraw — 난이도 중 ●●○

밑줄 친 부분에 들어갈 말로 적절한 것은?

Conservationists refused to _____ their opposition to cutting the budget allocated for protecting endangered animals.

① admit
② withdraw
③ complete
④ pursue

[해석]
환경 보호 활동가들은 멸종 위기에 처한 동물들을 보호하는 데 할당된 예산을 삭감하는 것에 대한 그들의 반대를 철회하기를 거절했다.

① 인정하다
② 철회하다
③ 완료하다
④ 추구하다

정답 ②

[어휘]
conservationist 환경 보호 활동가 opposition 반대 budget 예산
allocate 할당하다 endangered 멸종 위기에 처한 admit 인정하다
withdraw 철회하다, 중단하다, 취소하다 complete 완료하다
pursue 추구하다

---

02 문법 동사의 종류 — 난이도 중 ●●○

밑줄 친 부분에 들어갈 말로 적절한 것은?

During our home renovation project, I decided to have all the windows _____, which dramatically improved the insulation in our century-old house.

① replace
② replaced
③ replacing
④ to be replaced

[해석]
우리 집 개조 작업 동안, 나는 모든 창문을 교체되게 하기로 결정했는데, 이는 100년이 된 우리 집의 단열을 극적으로 개선했다.

[해설]
② 5형식 동사 빈칸은 사역동사 have의 목적격 보어 자리이다. 사역동사 have는 목적어와 목적격 보어가 능동 관계이면 목적격 보어로 원형 부정사를, 목적어와 목적격 보어가 수동 관계이면 목적격 보어로 과거분사를 취하는데, 문맥상 목적어(all the windows)와 목적격 보어가 '모든 창문이 교체되다'라는 의미의 수동 관계이므로 과거분사 ② replaced가 정답이다.

정답 ②

[어휘]
insulation 단열

---

03 문법 수동태|to 부정사|보어|대명사 — 난이도 중 ●●○

밑줄 친 부분 중 어법상 옳지 않은 것은?

As the fictional character Sherlock Holmes grew ever more beloved, his creator Arthur Conan Doyle began ① to resent him. The success of the Holmes detective series left Doyle's other literary works ② overshadowed. The author's seven historical novels were his real passion, but ③ they attracted little attention among his readers because they ④ were obsessing with the enigmatic Holmes.

[해석]
소설 속 등장인물인 Sherlock Holmes가 점점 더 사랑을 받게 되면서, 그의 창작자 Arthur Conan Doyle은 그를 원망하기 시작했다. Holmes의 탐정 수사 시리즈의 성공은 Doyle의 다른 문학 작품들을 빛을 잃은 상태가 되게 했다. 그 작가의 일곱 편의 역사 소설은 그의 진정한 열정의 대상이었지만, 그의 독자들이 수수께끼 같은 Holmes에게 사로잡혔기 때문에 그들 사이에서 그것들(일곱 편의 역사 소설)은 거의 관심을 받지 못했다.

DAY 13 하프모의고사 13회

해설

④ **3형식 동사의 수동태** 감정을 나타내는 동사(obsess)는 주어가 감정의 원인이면 능동태를, 감정을 느끼는 주체이면 수동태를 써야 하는데, '그들(독자들)이 사로잡히다'라는 의미로 주어(they)가 감정을 느끼는 주체이므로 능동태 were obsessing을 수동태 were obsessed로 고쳐야 한다.

[오답 분석]
① **동명사와 to 부정사 둘 다 목적어로 취하는 동사** 동사 begin은 동명사가 목적어일 때와 to 부정사가 목적어일 때 의미가 동일하므로 began의 목적어 자리에 to 부정사 to resent가 올바르게 쓰였다.
② **보어 자리** 동사 leave는 '~을 -한 상태가 되게 하다'의 뜻으로 쓰일 때 목적격 보어를 취하는데, 보어 자리에는 형용사 역할을 하는 것이 와야 하므로 분사 overshadowed가 올바르게 쓰였다. 참고로, 문맥상 목적어 Doyle's other literary works와 목적격 보어가 'Doyle의 다른 문학 작품들이 빛을 잃게 되다'라는 의미의 수동 관계이므로 과거분사가 쓰였다.
③ **인칭대명사** 대명사가 지시하는 명사(The author's seven historical novels)가 복수이므로, 복수 대명사 they가 올바르게 쓰였다.

정답 ④

어휘

resent 원망하다, 분하게 여기다 literary 문학의, 문학적인
overshadow 빛을 잃게 만들다, 무색하게 만들다 passion 열정
obsess (마음을) 사로잡다 enigmatic 수수께끼 같은

---

04 생활영어 Wasn't it a fixed rate regardless of changes in volume?

난이도 중 ●●○

밑줄 친 부분에 들어갈 말로 적절한 것은?

 Emily Lewis
How may I help you today?
11:00

 Ryan Murphy
I'd like to renew our current delivery service contract.
11:01

 Emily Lewis
We appreciate your continued business. How long would you like to extend the contract?
11:02

 Ryan Murphy
One year. The services we need would be the same as before. What about the cost?
11:03

 Emily Lewis
The cost might change depending on the delivery volume.
11:03

 Ryan Murphy
_____
11:04

 Emily Lewis
Our pricing policy has changed. A fixed rate applies up to a certain number of deliveries, with extra charges for more.
11:05

① Do you offer any discounts for regular customers?
② We typically use delivery services twice a week.
③ I'm not certain about our exact delivery needs for next year.
④ Wasn't it a fixed rate regardless of changes in volume?

해석

> Emily Lewis: 오늘 무엇을 도와드릴까요?
> Ryan Murphy: 저의 현재 배송 서비스 계약을 갱신하고 싶습니다.
> Emily Lewis: 계속 이용해 주셔서 감사합니다. 계약을 얼마나 연장하고 싶으신가요?
> Ryan Murphy: 1년이요. 저희가 필요로 하는 서비스는 이전과 동일할 것입니다. 비용은 어떻게 되나요?
> Emily Lewis: 비용은 배송량에 따라 변동될 수 있습니다.
> Ryan Murphy: 물량 변동에 상관없이 고정 요금이 아니었나요?
> Emily Lewis: 가격 정책이 변경되어서요. 일정 수량까지의 배송에는 고정 요금이 적용되며, 초과 시에는 추가 요금이 부과됩니다.

① 정기 고객을 위한 할인을 제공하시나요?
② 저희는 보통 일주일에 두 번 배송 서비스를 이용합니다.
③ 내년의 정확한 배송 필요량에 대해서는 확신할 수 없어요.
④ 물량 변동에 상관없이 고정 요금이 아니었나요?

해설

이전과 동일한 서비스의 계약을 연장할 경우의 비용을 묻는 Ryan에게 Emily가 배송량에 따라 비용이 변동될 수 있다고 알려 주고, 빈칸 뒤에서 다시 Emily가 Our pricing policy has changed. A fixed rate applies up to a certain number of deliveries, with extra charges for more(가격 정책이 변경되어서요. 일정 수량까지의 배송에는 고정 요금이 적용되며, 초과 시에는 추가 요금이 부과됩니다)라고 설명하고 있으므로, '물량 변동에 상관없이 고정 요금이 아니었나요?'라는 의미의 ④ 'Wasn't it a fixed rate regardless of changes in volume?'이 정답이다.

정답 ④

어휘

renew 갱신하다 contract 계약; 계약하다 appreciate 감사하다, 감상하다
extend 연장하다, 확대하다 volume 양, 음량, (출판물) 권 fixed 고정된
rate 요금, 속도, 비율 charge 요금, 청구; 청구하다
regardless of ~에 상관없이

05~06 다음 글을 읽고 물음에 답하시오.

Appeal Review

Appeals Courts (AC) look at legal decisions to make sure they follow the law correctly. These courts are an important part of our justice system. They fix mistakes that could lead to people being treated unfairly under the law.

Legal Precedent

Legal precedent (LP) means decisions made by courts in the past that set rules for future cases. When courts follow LP, similar cases get similar outcomes. This makes our legal system fairer and more consistent. If judges don't follow these precedents, people might be confused about what the law really means.

AC judges check cases where legal precedent may have been used incorrectly. They study past court decisions carefully. Then they write opinions that explain legal standards clearly. This helps make sure the law works the same way for everyone across the whole court system. By doing this important work, AC judges protect everyone's right _____.

05 독해 요지 파악

윗글의 요지로 적절한 것은?

① AC's top concern is looking for problems in the judicial system.
② AC is charged with establishing precedent in legal cases.
③ AC aims to be sure that laws are clear and fairly applied.
④ AC trains judges to look for inconsistencies in LP.

정답 ③

06 독해 빈칸 완성 - 구

윗글의 빈칸에 들어갈 말로 적절한 것은?

① to supervise lower court decisions
② to receive fair treatment under the law
③ to evaluate court procedure compliance
④ to reinforce existing legal standards

정답 ②

evaluate 평가하다   procedure 절차   compliance 준수
reinforce 강화하다

07 독해 목적 파악   난이도 하 ●○○

다음 글의 목적으로 적절한 것은?

To: Residents@LesterCity.com
From: Info@LesterCity.com
Date: April 11
Subject: Household waste

Dear Residents,

The City of Lester is committed to reducing pollution caused by household waste. But we can't do it alone. Here are five ways residents can minimize waste:

1. Reduce the number of single-use items used by opting for reusable bags, bottles, and containers.
2. Compost food scraps and yard waste instead of throwing them out.
3. Follow recycling guidelines and sort all recyclables rather than putting them in household trash.
4. Donate or repurpose unwanted clothing, furniture, or other household items that are still in good condition to help others.
5. When shopping, be mindful to avoid purchasing products with unnecessary packaging.

Following these steps can help keep our community clean and sustainable. For more tips and resources, visit the Sanitation Department's website. Remember, small changes can have a big impact!

Sincerely,

City of Lester

① to tell residents how to separate trash properly
② to tell residents how to use food scraps to produce compost
③ to tell residents how to save money while shopping
④ to tell residents how to reduce the amount of waste they produce

해석

수신: Residents@LesterCity.com
발신: Info@LesterCity.com
날짜: 4월 11일
제목: 가정용 쓰레기 관련

주민 여러분께,

Lester 시는 가정용 쓰레기로 인한 오염을 줄이는 데 전념하고 있습니다. 그러나 저희 혼자서는 그것을 해낼 수 없습니다. 다음은 주민 여러분이 쓰레기를 최소화할 수 있는 다섯 가지 방법들입니다.

1. 재사용 가능한 봉투, 병 및 용기를 선택함으로써 사용되는 일회용품의 수를 줄이세요.
2. 음식물 찌꺼기와 정원 쓰레기를 버리는 대신 퇴비로 만드세요.
3. 재활용 지침을 따르고, 모든 재활용품들을 가정용 쓰레기에 넣지 말고 분류하세요.
4. 다른 이들을 돕기 위해 여전히 상태가 좋은 원치 않는 의류, 가구 또는 기타 가정용품을 기부하거나 다른 용도로 사용하세요.
5. 쇼핑할 때, 불필요한 포장이 있는 제품 구매를 피하도록 유의하세요.

이러한 단계들을 따르는 것은 우리 마을을 깨끗하고 지속 가능하게 유지하도록 도울 수 있습니다. 더 많은 조언과 자료를 위해, 공중 위생과 웹사이트를 방문하세요. 작은 변화가 큰 영향을 미칠 수 있음을 기억하세요!

진심을 담아,
Lester 시

① 주민들에게 제대로 분리수거하는 방법을 알려 주려고
② 주민들에게 음식물 찌꺼기를 활용하여 퇴비를 생산하는 방법을 알려 주려고
③ 주민들에게 쇼핑할 때 돈을 절약할 방법을 알려 주려고
④ 주민들에게 그들이 배출하는 쓰레기의 양을 줄일 방법을 알려 주려고

해설

지문 앞부분에서 주민들이 가정용 쓰레기를 최소화할 수 있는 다섯 가지 방법들이 있다고 한 뒤, 그 방법들을 알려 주고 있으므로, ④ '주민들에게 그들이 배출하는 쓰레기의 양을 줄일 방법을 알려 주려고'가 이 글의 목적이다.

정답 ④

어휘

commit 전념하다   pollution 오염   household 가정(용)의
minimize 최소화하다   opt 선택하다   reusable 재사용 가능한
compost 퇴비로 만들다; 퇴비   scrap 찌꺼기, 한 조각, 오려낸 것
yard 정원, 마당   throw out ~을 버리다   sort 분류하다   donate 기부하다
repurpose 다른 용도로 사용하다   mindful 유의하는
sustainable 지속 가능한   sanitation (공중) 위생

08 독해 제목 파악   난이도 중 ●●○

다음 글의 제목으로 적절한 것은?

Asperger syndrome is a relatively common condition, affecting roughly 37 million people worldwide. It is classified as a form of autism, but sufferers do not exhibit the same symptoms shown by those with other forms of autism. Most notably, people with Asperger syndrome do not seem to have any form of cognitive impairment. Instead, they tend to have a decreased level of displayed emotional responses, and they may not be as perceptive as those without the condition in noticing the emotional responses of others. Additionally, they display odd peculiarities in their speech, often engaging in wordy monologues about topics they are knowledgeable about. The condition was misunderstood for a long period of time, and the public carried tremendous negative perceptions about those who had it. But as public awareness has increased, these stigmas have begun to change.

① Recent Increases in the Number of Asperger Patients
② Asperger Syndrome: The Most Common Form of Autism
③ Treatment Strategies for Asperger Syndrome
④ Common Symptoms of Those with Asperger Syndrome

해석

'아스퍼거 증후군'은 비교적 흔한 질환이며, 전 세계적으로 대략 3,700만 명에게서 발생한다. 그것은 자폐증의 한 종류로 분류되지만, 환자들은 다른 종류의 자폐증이 있는 사람들에게서 보이는 것과 같은 증상을 보이지는 않는다. 가장 눈에 띄는 것은, 아스퍼거 증후군이 있는 사람들은 어떤 종류의 인지 장애도 가지고 있지 않은 것처럼 보인다는 것이다. 그 대신, 그들은 낮은 수준의 정서 반응을 보이는 경향이 있으며, 그들은 다른 사람들의 정서 반응을 알아채는 데 있어 그 질환이 없는 사람들만큼 민감하지 않을 수도 있다. 게다가, 그들은 말투에 있어서 이상한 특이점을 보이는데, 종종 그들이 많이 아는 주제들에 대한 장황한 독백에 몰두한다. 그 질환은 오랜 기간 동안 제대로 이해되지 못했고, 대중들은 그 병이 있는 사람들에 대해 엄청나게 부정적인 인식을 가지고 있었다. 그러나 대중의 인식이 높아지면서, 이러한 낙인은 바뀌기 시작했다.

① 최근 아스퍼거 환자 수의 증가
② 아스퍼거 증후군: 자폐증의 가장 흔한 종류
③ 아스퍼거 증후군 치료 전략
④ 아스퍼거 증후군이 있는 사람들에게 흔한 증상들

해설

지문 전반에 걸쳐 자폐증의 일종인 아스퍼거 증후군이 있는 환자들이 다른 종류의 자폐증이 있는 사람들과는 다른 증상들을 보인다고 하며, 아스퍼거 증후군 환자들이 보이는 대표적인 증상들을 설명하고 있다. 따라서 ④ '아스퍼거 증후군이 있는 사람들에게 흔한 증상들'이 이 글의 제목이다.

정답 ④

어휘

relatively 비교적 affect (사람이나 신체 부위에) 발생하다, 병이 나게 하다
roughly 대략, 거의 classify 분류하다 autism 자폐증 symptom 증상
cognitive 인지적인 impairment 장애, 손상
perceptive 민감한, 지각력이 있는 odd 이상한 peculiarity 특이점, 특성
engage in ~에 몰두하다, 참여하다 wordy 장황한 monologue 독백
knowledgeable 많이 아는 tremendous 엄청난 awareness 인식
stigma 낙인, 오명

09 독해 문장 삽입 난이도 상 ●●●

주어진 문장이 들어갈 위치로 적절한 것은?

However, these claims expose a fundamental misunderstanding of this constitutional provision.

Over the last decade, the spread of information has become increasingly democratized as more and more people have turned to social media platforms or user-created content. (①) This has in turn led to negative reactions when one of these sites requires fact-checking, or blocks inaccurate or harmful information. (②) Certain users declare that such actions infringe upon their right to free speech guaranteed by the First Amendment of the United States Constitution. (③) The first right protected by the First Amendment is free speech, but this only limits the interference of the government. (④) Companies and other private entities are free to place whatever restrictions they want on the actions or speech of their users and members. Moreover, laws may require that these organizations limit or edit content if there is a risk associated with not doing so.

*First Amendment: (미국 헌법) 수정 제1조

해석

하지만, 이러한 주장들은 이 헌법 조항에 대한 근본적인 오해를 드러낸다.

지난 10년에 걸쳐, 점점 더 많은 사람들이 소셜 미디어 플랫폼이나 사용자 제작 콘텐츠에 의지하면서 정보의 확산이 점차 더 민주화되어 왔다. ① 이것은 이 사이트들 중 하나가 사실 확인을 요구하거나, 부정확하거나 해로운 정보를 차단할 때 결국 부정적인 반응들로 이어져 왔다. ② 어떤 사용자들은 그러한 행위가 미국의 헌법 수정 제1조에 의해 보장되는 그들의 권리인 언론의 자유를 침해한다고 단언한다. ③ 헌법 수정 제1조에 의해 보호되는 첫 번째 권리가 언론의 자유이지만, 이것은 오직 정부의 간섭만을 제한한다. ④ 회사들과 다른 민간 단체들은 그들의 사용자와 구성원들의 행위나 말에 그들이 원하는 어떤 제약이든 자유롭게 둘 수 있다. 게다가, 만약 그렇게 하지 않는 것과 관련된 위험이 있다면, 법은 이러한 조직들이 콘텐츠를 제한하거나 편집하도록 요구할 수도 있다.

해설

③번 앞 문장에 일부 사용자는 대중 미디어 사이트가 사실 확인을 요구하거나 해로운 정보를 차단하는 것이 미국의 헌법 수정 제1조의 언론의 자유를 침해한다고 단언한다는 내용이 있고, 뒤 문장에 헌법 수정 제1조에 의해 보호되는 언론의 자유는 오직 정부의 간섭만을 제한한다는 내용이 있으므로, ③번 자리에 하지만(However) 이러한 주장들(these claims)은 미국 헌법 수정 제1조에 대한 근본적인 오해를 드러낸다는 내용, 즉 대중 미디어 사이트에 대한 부정적인 반응 이면의 이유에 대해 설명하는 주어진 문장이 나와야 지문이 자연스럽게 연결된다.

정답 ③

어휘

fundamental 근본적인, 필수적인 constitutional 헌법의
provision 조항, 규정 democratize 민주화하다 turn to ~에 의지하다
in turn 결국 inaccurate 부정확한 declare 단언하다, 분명히 말하다
infringe upon ~을 침해하다, 제한하다 free speech 언론의 자유
guarantee 보장하다 interference 간섭, 개입 entity 단체, 기업
associate 관련짓다

DAY 13 하프모의고사 13회

10 독해 무관한 문장 삭제 　　　난이도 중 ●●○

다음 글의 흐름상 어색한 문장은?

The disposition effect refers to a change in humans' outlook due to the perceived potential for loss or gain. This was first identified in a 1985 paper written by Hersh Shefrin and Meir Statman. In the paper, they discuss investing, where they found that people are far more likely to sell stocks that increase in value, and to hold on to stocks that have lost value over time. ① Based on this research, the two researchers concluded that humans have a stronger emotional connection to negative outcomes than they do to perceived gains. ② By holding on to falling stocks, people retain hope that their fortunes may turn around. ③ The main purpose of implementing stock market regulations was to protect investors from the risks of the disposition effect. ④ Along with this, more importantly, they avoid acknowledging or finalizing a situation that would cause regret. As a result, they often end up losing additional money.

해석

'처분 효과'는 손실 또는 이득에 대해 인지된 가능성으로 인한 사람들의 관점의 변화를 의미한다. 이것은 Hersh Shefrin과 Meir Statman에 의해 1985년에 집필된 한 논문에서 처음 확인되었다. 그 논문에서, 그들은 투자에 대해 논하는데, 이것에서 그들은 사람들이 가치가 오르는 주식은 팔고, 시간이 지나면서 가치를 잃은 주식은 계속 보유할 가능성이 훨씬 더 크다는 것을 발견했다. ① 이 연구에 근거하여, 그 두 연구자들은 인간이 인지된 이득보다는 부정적인 결과에 더 강한 정서적 연결 고리를 갖는다는 결론을 내렸다. ② 하락하는 주식을 계속 보유함으로써, 사람들은 그들의 자산이 회복될 수 있다는 희망을 마음에 간직한다. ③ 처분 효과의 위험으로부터 투자자를 보호하는 것이 주식 시장 규제를 도입하는 것의 주된 목적이었다. ④ 이것과 함께, 더욱 중요한 것은 그들이 후회를 유발할 상황을 인정하거나 마무리 짓지 않으려고 한다는 점이다. 그 결과, 그들은 종종 결국 추가적인 돈을 잃게 된다.

해설

지문 앞부분에서 사람들이 가치가 오르는 주식을 파는 반면 가치를 잃은 주식을 보유하는 처분 효과를 언급한 후, ①, ②, ④번에서 인간은 인지된 이득보다 부정적인 결과에 더 강한 정서적 연결 고리를 갖기 때문에 하락하는 주식을 계속 보유하면서 후회를 유발할 상황을 인정하거나 마무리 짓지 않는 경향이 있다고 설명하고 있다. 그러나 ③번은 '주식 시장 규제 도입의 취지'에 대한 내용으로, 지문 앞부분의 내용과 관련이 없다.

정답 ③

어휘

disposition 처분, 매각　outlook 관점, 전망　potential 가능성; 잠재적인
investing 투자　stock 주식　hold on to ~을 계속 보유하다
outcome 결과　retain 마음에 간직하다, 보유하다　fortune 자산, 행운
turn around 회복되다, 호전되다　implement 도입하다, 시행하다
acknowledge 인정하다　regret 후회; 후회하다

DAY 14 하프모의고사 14회

정답   p. 66

01	④	어휘	06	①	독해
02	③	문법	07	②	독해
03	③	문법	08	③	독해
04	③	생활영어	09	②	독해
05	③	독해	10	③	독해

취약영역 분석표

영역	맞힌 답의 개수
어휘	/1
생활영어	/1
문법	/2
독해	/6
TOTAL	/10

---

01 어휘 reform   난이도 중 ●●○

밑줄 친 부분에 들어갈 말로 적절한 것은?

> It is unnecessary to _____ the existing system, seeing that it works well as it is and the people are accustomed to the system.

① comprehend ② establish
③ conceal ④ reform

해석
기존의 체계가 그대로도 잘 작동하고 사람들이 그 체계에 익숙한 것으로 보아, 그것을 개편하는 것은 불필요하다.
① 이해하다 ② 확립하다
③ 숨기다 ④ 개편하다

정답 ④

어휘
accustomed 익숙한   comprehend 이해하다   establish 확립하다
conceal 숨기다   reform 개편하다, 개혁하다; 개혁

---

02 문법 가정법   난이도 중 ●●○

밑줄 친 부분에 들어갈 말로 적절한 것은?

> Were the policy implemented without proper consideration of economic factors, it _____ numerous problems.

① created ② will create
③ would create ④ would have created

해석
그 정책이 경제 요소들에 대한 적절한 고려 없이 시행된다면, 그것은 수많은 문제들을 불러일으킬 것이다.

해설
③ 가정법 과거 | 가정법 도치   문맥상 '그 정책이 경제 요소들에 대한 적절한 고려 없이 시행된다면, 그것은 수많은 문제들을 불러일으킬 것이다'라는 의미로 현재의 반대 상황을 가정하고 있고, if절에 가정법 과거 'if + 주어 + 과거 동사(be 동사는 were)'에서 if가 생략되어 주어(the policy)와 동사(were)가 도치된 형태가 왔으므로, 주절에도 가정법 과거 '주어 + would + 동사원형' 형태가 와야 한다. 따라서 ③ would create가 정답이다.

정답 ③

어휘
implement 시행하다   consideration 고려 (사항)

---

03 문법 수동태 | 분사 | 관계절 | 대명사   난이도 중 ●●○

밑줄 친 부분 중 어법상 옳지 않은 것은?

> Competitive skating today is marked by a higher level of physical ability, ① <u>compared</u> to the figure skating of the twentieth century. While the jumps have become complex, the circular patterns, ② <u>which</u> gave "figure skating" its name, are seen less frequently. This means that skaters who performed with grace in the past can no longer compete in events where athletic jumps ③ <u>performed</u> by young and powerful skaters. Points for elegance are lower than ④ <u>those</u> for fantastic jumps.

해석
오늘날 스케이팅 경기는 20세기의 피겨 스케이팅과 비교했을 때 더 높은 수준의 신체 능력으로 특징지어진다. 점프는 복잡해져 온 반면, '피겨 스케이팅'에 그 이름을 부여했던 빙빙 도는 패턴들이 덜 빈번하게 보인다. 이는 과거에 우아하게 연기했던 스케이트 선수들이 젊고 힘이 넘치는 스케이트 선수들에 의해 힘찬 점프가 연출되는 대회들에서 더 이상 경쟁할 수 없다는 것을 의미한다. 고상함에 대한 점수는 환상적인 점프에 대한 점수보다 낮다.

DAY 14 하프모의고사 14회

해설

③ **능동태·수동태 구별** 주어 athletic jumps와 동사가 '힘찬 점프가 연출되다'라는 의미의 수동 관계이므로 능동태 performed를 수동태 are performed로 고쳐야 한다.

[오답 분석]
① **분사구문의 형태** 주절의 주어(Competitive skating)와 분사구문이 '스케이팅 경기가 비교되다'라는 의미의 수동 관계이므로 과거분사 compared가 올바르게 쓰였다.
② **관계대명사** 선행사(the circular patterns)가 사물이고, 관계절(which ~ name) 내에서 동사 gave의 주어 역할을 하므로 사물을 가리키는 주격 관계대명사 which가 올바르게 쓰였다.
④ **지시대명사** 대명사가 지시하는 명사 Points가 복수이므로 복수 지시대명사 those가 올바르게 쓰였다.

정답 ③

어휘

mark 특징짓다, 표시하다; 자국 compare 비교하다 circular 빙빙 도는, 원형의 frequently 빈번하게, 자주 grace 우아함; 품위 elegance 고상함

---

04 생활영어 You should have planned time for questions. 난이도 하 ●○○

밑줄 친 부분에 들어갈 말로 적절한 것은?

A: We had to stop the presentation midway today.
B: Your team spent weeks preparing everything. Why weren't you able to finish?
A: Because we kept getting interrupted by the audience asking for more details.
B: _____
A: You're right. I think we scheduled the presentation too tightly.
B: And it would be better to have the Q&A session after finishing the presentation.

① Setting priorities can save us time.
② Add more visuals to your presentation.
③ You should have planned time for questions.
④ We typically get fewer attendees than we hope for.

해석

A: 우리는 오늘 발표를 도중에 멈춰야 했어.
B: 너희 팀은 모든 걸 준비하는 데 몇 주를 보냈잖아. 왜 끝낼 수 없었던 거야?
A: 추가적인 세부 사항에 대해 물어보는 청중들이 계속 끼어들었거든.
B: 너희는 질문을 위한 시간을 계획했어야 했어.
A: 네 말이 맞아. 우리가 발표 일정을 너무 빠듯하게 짠 것 같아.
B: 그리고 질의응답 시간은 발표를 마친 뒤에 갖는 게 더 나을 거야.

① 우선 순위를 정하면 시간을 절약할 수 있어.
② 발표에 더 많은 시각 자료를 더해 봐.
③ 너희는 질문을 위한 시간을 계획했어야 했어.
④ 우리가 바라는 것보다 일반적으로 참석자 수가 더 적어.

해설

몇 주간 준비한 발표를 왜 끝내지 못했는지 묻는 B에게 A가 추가 세부 사항에 대해 물어보는 청중들이 계속 끼어들었다고 대답하고, 빈칸 뒤에서 다시 A가 You're right. I think we scheduled the presentation too tightly(네 말이 맞아. 우리가 발표 일정을 너무 빠듯하게 짠 것 같아)라고 동의하고 있으므로, '너희는 질문을 위한 시간을 계획했어야 했어'라는 의미의 ③ 'You should have planned time for questions'가 정답이다.

정답 ③

어휘

midway 도중에 interrupt 끼어들다, 방해하다, 중단시키다
tightly 빠듯하게, 빽빽히 priority 우선 (순위)
typically 일반적으로, 전형적으로

05~06 다음 글을 읽고 물음에 답하시오.

To	Consumer Protection Office
From	Ron Banks
Date	April 24
Subject	Hidden Online Fees

To whom it may concern,

I hope that you are well. I'm writing today about a problem I have encountered when shopping online, specifically hidden fees that are being charged when making purchases.

Like most people, I enjoy the convenience and selection of shopping online. However, many online retailers are now tacking on hidden fees for making purchases. Prices of items initially seem low, but at payment, the price is inflated by processing fees, unincluded basic options, or high shipping costs. So, I don't know the true cost until the last minute. This feels like false advertising.

I would like your agency to investigate this problematic practice and determine what can be done. I hope you can make advertised online prices clearer.

Respectfully,

Ron Banks

해석

수신: 소비자 보호 진흥원
발신: Ron Banks
날짜: 4월 24일
제목: 숨겨진 온라인 수수료

관계자분께,

잘 지내고 계신지요. 저는 오늘 온라인 쇼핑을 하면서 접한 문제, 특히 구매할 때 부과되고 있는 숨겨진 수수료에 대해 말씀드리고자 합니다.

대부분의 사람들처럼, 저도 온라인 쇼핑의 편리함과 다양한 선택지를 즐깁니다. 하지만, 요즘 많은 온라인 소매 업체들이 구매 시 숨겨진 수수료를 덧붙이고 있습니다. 처음에는 상품 가격이 낮아 보이지만, 결제 시점에서 처리 수수료, 포함되지 않은 기본 옵션, 또는 높은 배송비에 의해 가격이 올라갑니다. 그래서, 저는 마지막 순간까지 실제 비용을 알 수가 없습니다. 이것은 허위 광고처럼 느껴집니다.

여러분의 기관에서 이러한 문제가 되는 관행을 조사하고 무엇이 행해질 수 있을지 판단해 주시기를 바랍니다. 저는 온라인에서 광고되는 가격이 더 명확해지기를 희망합니다.

경의를 표하며,
Ron Banks

어휘

fee 수수료 encounter 접하다, 마주치다 charge 부과하다, 청구하다; 요금
convenience 편리함 retailer 소매 업체 tack on ~을 덧붙이다
initially 처음에 payment 결제 inflate 올리다, 부풀리다 advertising 광고
investigate 조사하다 problematic 문제가 되는
practice 관행, 연습, 실습; 연습하다

05 독해 목적 파악 | 난이도 중 ●●○

윗글의 목적으로 적절한 것은?

① To request help finding a product in an online store
② To complain about the selection of items offered online
③ To ask that a common tactic of online stores be stopped
④ To inquire about the fees charged by online retailers

해석
① 온라인 상점에서 제품을 찾는 것에 도움을 요청하려고
② 온라인에서 제공되는 물품 선택지에 대해 항의하려고
③ 온라인 상점의 일반적인 전략을 중단해 달라고 요청하려고
④ 온라인 소매 업체에 의해 부과되는 수수료에 대해 문의하려고

해설
지문 중간에서 많은 온라인 소매 업체들이 덧붙이는 숨은 수수료 항목들 때문에 결제 마지막 순간까지 실제 비용을 알 수가 없다는 문제를 언급한 후, 지문 마지막에서 소비자 보호 진흥원에서 이러한 관행을 조사하고 이에 대해 무엇이 행해질 수 있을지 결정해 달라고 요청하고 있으므로, ③ '온라인 상점의 일반적인 전략을 중단해 달라고 요청하려고'가 이 글의 목적이다.

정답 ③

어휘
complain 항의하다, 불평하다 tactic 전략, 전술 inquire 문의하다

06 독해 유의어 파악 | 난이도 하 ●○○

밑줄 친 problematic의 의미와 가장 가까운 것은?

① troublesome   ② difficult
③ messy   ④ famous

해석
① 골칫거리인   ② 어려운
③ 어질러진   ④ 유명한

해설
밑줄 친 부분이 포함된 문장에서 problematic은 문맥상 '문제가 되는' 관행을 조사한다는 의미로 쓰였으므로, '골칫거리인'이라는 의미의 ① troublesome이 정답이다.

정답 ①

어휘
troublesome 골칫거리인, 성가신 difficult 어려운 messy 어질러진
famous 유명한

07 독해 내용 일치 파악 | 난이도 중 ●●○

Ministry of Digital Advancement에 관한 다음 글의 내용과 일치하는 것은?

Introduction of the Ministry of Digital Advancement (MDA)

The MDA is at the forefront of the country's push to modernize public services. The MDA focuses on developing and implementing digital versions of many government services, including permit applications, identification cards and passports, and tax payments. The MDA also offers online literacy programs to help citizens uncomfortable with technology adapt to the use of the new system. We see the MDA's actions as a step toward both improving government engagement with citizens and a mechanism for increased transparency. The MDA envisions a future in which nearly all government services will be available to citizens using their computer or other Internet-connected device.

① It does not provide passport-related services.
② It supports programs to teach people to use its new system.
③ It wants people to engage with each other online more.
④ Its plan is to distribute Internet-connected devices to all citizens.

해석

디지털혁신연구소(MDA) 소개

디지털혁신연구소는 공공 서비스를 현대화하는 국가 노력의 최전선에 있습니다. 디지털혁신연구소는 허가 신청, 신분증 및 여권, 그리고 세금 납부를 포함하여, 다양한 정부 서비스의 디지털 버전을 개발하고

DAY 14 하프모의고사 14회

구현하는 데 중점을 돕니다. 디지털혁신연구소는 기술에 익숙하지 않은 시민분들이 새로운 시스템 사용에 적응하시는 것을 돕기 위해 온라인 사용 능력 프로그램 또한 제공합니다. 저희는 디지털혁신연구소의 활동을 시민분들과 함께하는 정부 참여를 개선하는 것과 증대된 투명성의 기제 둘 다로 향하는 하나의 단계로 봅니다. 디지털혁신연구소는 거의 모든 정부 서비스가 컴퓨터나 기타 인터넷 연결 기기를 사용하여 시민분들에게 이용 가능해질 미래를 구상합니다.

① 그것은 여권 관련 서비스는 제공하지 않는다.
② 그것은 사람들에게 새로운 시스템을 사용하는 것을 가르치기 위한 프로그램을 지원한다.
③ 그것은 사람들이 온라인에서 서로 더 많이 소통하기를 원한다.
④ 그것의 계획은 인터넷 연결 기기를 모든 시민에게 보급하는 것이다.

[해설]
②번의 키워드인 supports programs(프로그램을 지원한다)를 바꾸어 표현한 지문의 offers online literacy programs(온라인 사용 능력 프로그램을 제공한다) 주변의 내용에서 디지털혁신연구소는 기술에 익숙하지 않은 시민들의 새로운 시스템 사용을 돕기 위해 온라인 사용 능력 프로그램을 제공한다고 했으므로, ② '그것은 사람들에게 새로운 시스템을 사용하는 것을 가르치기 위한 프로그램을 지원한다'가 지문의 내용과 일치한다.

[오답 분석]
① 디지털혁신연구소는 신분증 및 여권을 포함하여 정부 서비스의 디지털 버전을 개발하고 구현하는 데 중점을 둔다고 했으므로, 그것이 여권 관련 서비스는 제공하지 않는다는 것은 지문의 내용과 다르다.
③ 디지털혁신연구소는 그것의 활동을 시민들과 함께하는 정부 참여를 개선하는 단계로 보고 있다고는 했지만, 그것이 사람들이 온라인에서 서로 더 많이 소통하기를 원하는지는 알 수 없다.
④ 디지털혁신연구소는 거의 모든 정부 서비스가 컴퓨터나 기타 인터넷 연결 기기를 통해 이용 가능해질 미래를 구상한다고는 했지만, 그것의 계획이 인터넷 연결 기기를 모든 시민에게 보급하는 것인지는 알 수 없다.

정답 ②

[어휘]
forefront 최전선 modernize 현대화하다 implement 구현하다, 실행하다
permit 허가(증); 허가하다 application 신청 identification 신분증
literacy (특정 분야의)사용, 능력, 문해력 adapt 적응하다
engagement 참여, 관여 transparency 투명성 envision 구상하다

08 독해 제목 파악 난이도 중 ●●○

다음 글의 제목으로 적절한 것은?

It's quite common for moms and dads to look over and correct their kids' homework during the early years of their education. Sometimes, this continues on into high school and even to college. If this is your habit, you as a parent are not contributing to your child's education and self-esteem. The message conveyed through such behavior is doubt regarding your child's abilities. While answering a few questions children may have is perfectly fine, going through their reports and papers meticulously is unnecessary. Reviewing and then fixing errors only reinforces the notion that you believe they are not skilled enough to do the work on their own. Instead, they should be left to find their own way with gentle guidance, not with excessive interference. The mistakes they are allowed to make will ultimately benefit them.

① The Benefits of Parental Oversight
② Ways to Motivate Lazy Students
③ Proper Role for Parents in Children's Schoolwork
④ The Connection between Education and Self-Esteem

[해석]
엄마와 아빠가 아이들의 초기 교육 기간 동안에 그들의 숙제를 검토하고 고치는 것은 꽤 흔하다. 때때로, 이것은 고등학교 그리고 심지어는 대학교까지도 이어진다. 만약 이것이 당신의 습관이라면, 당신은 부모로서 아이의 교육과 자존감에 기여하고 있지 않다. 그러한 행동을 통해 전달되는 메시지는 당신 아이의 능력에 대한 불신이다. 아이들이 가질 수도 있는 몇몇 질문에 답하는 것은 더할 나위 없이 좋지만, 그들의 리포트와 과제물을 꼼꼼하게 검토하는 것은 불필요하다. 검토하고 나서 오류를 바로잡는 것은 단지 당신이 그들 스스로 과제를 하기에 충분히 능숙하지 않다고 생각한다는 인상을 강화할 뿐이다. 대신에, 그들이 지나친 간섭이 아닌 적당한 지도하에 그들만의 방법을 찾도록 내버려 두어야 한다. 그들이 저지르도록 허락된 실수는 궁극적으로 그들에게 이로울 것이다.

① 부모가 감독하는 것의 이점
② 게으른 학생들에게 동기 부여하는 방법
③ 아이들의 학업에 있어 부모의 올바른 역할
④ 교육과 자존감 사이의 연관성

[해설]
지문 전반에 걸쳐 부모가 아이의 숙제를 검토하고 고치는 행동은 아이의 교육이나 자존감에 기여하지 않는데, 그러한 행동을 통해 전달되는 메시지는 아이의 능력에 대한 불신이므로, 지나친 간섭이 아닌 적당한 지도 하에 아이들이 그들만의 방법을 찾도록 내버려 두어야 한다고 주장하고 있다. 따라서 ③ '아이들의 학업에 있어 부모의 올바른 역할'이 이 글의 제목이다.

정답 ③

[어휘]
correct 고치다, 수정하다 contribute 기여하다
self-esteem 자존감, 자긍심 convey 전달하다 doubt 불신, 의심; 의심하다
go through ~을 검토하다, 겪다 meticulously 꼼꼼하게
reinforce 강화하다 notion 인상, 개념 interference 간섭
oversight 감독, 감시 motivate 동기 부여하다

09 독해 주제 파악 난이도 중 ●●○

다음 글의 주제로 적절한 것은?

With its brutal winters and short summers, Siberia has long been known as one of the coldest places on Earth. However, it began to experience unusually high temperatures in the first half of 2020, even reaching an unprecedented 38 degrees

Celsius in June, which led to wildfires and the appearance of insects and animals that never existed in the area previously. Today, climate change continues, and the rise in Siberia's temperature remains a persistent issue. Though scientists have identified large-scale wind patterns as the primary cause for the fastest warming recorded anywhere in the world, another factor was decreased snow cover. This lack of cover reduced ground moisture and exposed the ground to solar radiation, triggering the melting of the area's permafrost.

* permafrost: 영구 동토층 (지층의 온도가 연중 0°C 이하인 땅)

① increased wildfire rates in the northern hemisphere
② extreme changes to the climate of Siberia
③ ways that animal species are affected by global warming
④ benefits of snow cover on temperature regulation

해석

혹독한 겨울과 짧은 여름으로 인해, 시베리아는 오랫동안 지구에서 가장 추운 곳들 중 하나로 알려져 왔다. 하지만, 그것은 2020년 상반기에 평소와 달리 높은 온도를 경험하기 시작했고, 심지어 6월에는 전례 없는 섭씨 38도에 달했는데, 이것은 들불과 이전에 그 지역에 한 번도 존재하지 않던 곤충과 동물들의 출현으로 이어졌다. 오늘날, 기후 변화가 계속되고 있으며, 시베리아의 기온 상승은 여전히 지속적인 문제로 남아 있다. 과학자들은 대규모의 바람 패턴이 전 세계 어디에서나 기록된 것 중 가장 빠른 온난화에 대한 주된 원인이라고 밝히기는 했지만, 또 다른 요인은 줄어든 적설량이었다. 이러한 눈 부족은 땅의 수분을 줄이고 지면을 태양 복사열에 노출시켜서, 그 지역(시베리아)의 영구 동토층이 녹는 것을 촉발했다.

① 북반구에서의 증가된 들불 발생률
② 시베리아 기후의 극심한 변화
③ 동물 종들이 지구 온난화에 의해 영향을 받는 방식들
④ 기온 조절에 있어 적설의 이점들

해설

지문 전반에 걸쳐 추운 날씨로 잘 알려진 시베리아가 2020년 초에 이례적으로 높은 기온을 겪었고 심지어 6월에 38도까지 상승했는데, 이런 이상 고온 현상이 오늘날 계속되고 있으며, 이것의 주된 원인은 대규모의 바람 패턴과 줄어든 적설량이라고 설명하고 있다. 따라서 ② '시베리아 기후의 극심한 변화'가 이 글의 주제이다.

정답 ②

어휘

brutal 혹독한, 잔인한 unprecedented 전례 없는 wildfire 들불
persistent 지속적인 primary 주된, 주요한 snow cover 적설(량)
expose 노출시키다 solar radiation 태양 복사열 trigger 촉발하다; 방아쇠
hemisphere 반구 extreme 극심한 regulation 조절, 규제

10 독해 빈칸 완성 - 구   난이도 중 ●●○

밑줄 친 부분에 들어갈 말로 적절한 것은?

Long recognized for their curiosity and superior intelligence, dolphins also seem to have other important abilities that make them special. One of these is the capability _____, which they use for determining where they are and where they are going. Surprisingly, unlike in other animals that are thought to have this capacity, it has been proven in dolphins. In studies, researchers presented the marine mammals with two identical objects, one with a magnetic charge and the other without. In almost all cases, the dolphins approached the magnetized object more quickly, proving that they could detect its charge and were attracted to it. From this, researchers concluded that dolphins could most likely sense Earth's magnetism and use it in their navigation.

① to remember previous journeys
② to recognize identical items
③ to sense magnetic fields
④ to use objects around them as tools

해석

호기심과 우수한 지능으로 오랫동안 인정받아 온 돌고래는 또한 그것(돌고래)들을 특별하게 만드는 다른 중요한 능력들을 가지고 있는 것처럼 보인다. 이것들 중 하나는 자기장을 감지하는 능력인데, 그것들은 이것을 자신들이 어디에 있고 어디로 가고 있는지를 알아내기 위해 사용한다. 놀랍게도, 이 능력을 갖고 있다고 여겨지는 다른 동물들과는 다르게, 그것은 돌고래에게서는 입증되었다. 연구들에서, 연구원들은 그 해양 포유동물들에게 두 개의 동일한 물체를 주었는데, 하나는 자기량이 있는 것이었고 다른 하나는 없는 것이었다. 거의 모든 경우에, 돌고래는 자력을 띤 물체에 더 빠르게 다가갔고, 이는 그것들이 그것의 전하를 감지할 수 있어서 그것에 유인된 것임을 입증했다. 이로부터, 연구원들은 돌고래가 지구의 자성을 감지하여 그것을 그것들의 항해에 이용할 가능성이 크다고 결론지었다.

① 이전의 여정을 기억하는
② 동일한 물체를 알아보는
③ 자기장을 감지하는
④ 그것들 주변의 물체를 도구로 사용하는

해설

지문 뒷부분에 연구에서 돌고래는 자력을 띤 물체에 더 빠르게 다가갔는데, 이로부터 연구원들은 돌고래가 지구의 자성을 감지하여 그것을 항해에 이용할 가능성이 크다고 결론지었다는 내용이 있으므로, 돌고래를 특별하게 만드는 능력들 중 하나가 '자기장을 감지하는' 능력이라고 한 ③번이 정답이다.

정답 ③

어휘

recognized 인정받은, 알려진 curiosity 호기심 superior 우수한
intelligence 지능 capability 능력 determine 알아내다, 결정하다
capacity 능력, 용량 identical 동일한 magnetic charge 자기량
detect 감지하다 attract 유인하다, 끌어당기다 navigation 항해, 항법

DAY 15 하프모의고사 15회

정답   p. 70

01	③	어휘	06	②	독해
02	①	문법	07	④	독해
03	③	문법	08	①	독해
04	③	생활영어	09	③	독해
05	③	독해	10	①	독해

취약영역 분석표

영역	맞힌 답의 개수
어휘	/1
생활영어	/1
문법	/2
독해	/6
TOTAL	/10

---

01 어휘 vulnerable = helpless   난이도 중 ●●○

밑줄 친 부분의 의미와 가장 가까운 것은?

Agricultural workers are hesitant to abandon pesticides because doing so would leave their crops <u>vulnerable</u> to insect attacks.

① superior
② similar
③ helpless
④ immune

해석

농업 종사자들은 살충제를 포기하는 것을 주저하는데, 그렇게 하는 것이 그들의 작물을 곤충의 공격에 <u>취약한</u> 상태가 되게 할 것이기 때문이다.

① 우월한
② 비슷한
③ 무력한
④ 면역력 있는

정답 ③

어휘

agricultural 농업의 hesitant 주저하는, 망설이는
abandon 포기하다, 버리다 pesticide 살충제, 농약
vulnerable 취약한, 연약한 insect 곤충 superior 우월한 similar 비슷한
helpless 무력한, 취약한 immune 면역력 있는

---

02 문법 to 부정사   난이도 중 ●●○

밑줄 친 부분에 들어갈 말로 적절한 것은?

The pilot program, advertised as a breakthrough in online education, turned out to _____ for teachers with limited classroom experience, raising questions about its true intent.

① have been designed
② have designed
③ being designed
④ be designed

해석

온라인 교육의 큰 발전이라고 광고되던 그 시범 프로그램은 교실 수업 경험이 부족한 교사들을 위해 고안된 것으로 밝혀졌는데, 이는 그것의 진정한 의도에 대한 의문을 불러일으켰다.

해설

① to 부정사의 형태 to 부정사가 가리키는 명사(The pilot program)와 to 부정사가 '그 시범 프로그램이 고안된 것으로 밝혀지다'라는 의미의 수동 관계이므로 to 부정사의 수동태를 완성하는 ① have been designed와 ④ be designed가 정답 후보이다. 이때 '프로그램이 고안된' 시점이 '(고안된 것으로) 밝혀진'(turned out) 시점보다 이전이므로, to 부정사의 수동태 완료형을 완성하는 ① have been designed가 정답이다.

정답 ①

어휘

pilot 시범용(의); 조종사 advertise 광고하다 breakthrough 큰 발전, 돌파구

---

03 문법 명사절 | 시제 | 동명사   난이도 중 ●●○

밑줄 친 부분 중 어법상 옳지 않은 것은?

In 2021, Sotheby's hosted its first "Natively Digital" event, and ① <u>has continued</u> to showcase digital arts in the form of non-fungible tokens (NFTs) since that time. NFTs are digital files based on the same blockchain technology as Bitcoin and Ethereum. ② <u>Being published</u> as an NFT allows these digital art pieces to be owned and traded in a secure, verifiable manner. ③ <u>What</u> Sotheby's would keep ④ <u>boosting</u> the new form of art remains to be seen because blockchain asset could fluctuate anytime.

해석

2021년, 소더비는 제1회 '선천적으로 디지털' 행사를 주최했고, 그때 이후로 대체 불가능한 토큰(NFTs) 형태인 디지털 예술품들을 계속해서 선

보여 왔다. 대체 불가능한 토큰은 비트코인 및 이더리움과 같이 동일한 블록체인 기술에 기반을 둔 디지털 파일들이다. 대체 불가능한 토큰으로 발행되는 것은 이 디지털 예술품들이 안전하고 검증 가능한 방식으로 소유되고 거래되게 한다. 소더비가 그 새로운 형태의 예술을 계속해서 신장시킬 것인지는 지켜봐야 하는데, 블록체인 자산은 언제라도 등락을 거듭할 수 있기 때문이다.

해설

③ **명사절 접속사** 완전한 절(Sotheby's ~ art)을 이끌며 '소더비가 그 새로운 형태의 예술을 계속해서 신장시킬 것인지 (아닌지)'라는 의미를 나타낼 수 있는 것은 명사절 접속사 whether(~인지 아닌지)이므로, 불완전한 절을 이끄는 명사절 접속사 What을 Whether로 고쳐야 한다.

[오답 분석]
① **시제 일치** 현재완료 시제와 자주 함께 쓰이는 시간 표현 'since + 과거 시간 표현'(since that time)이 왔고, 문맥상 '선보여 왔다'라는 의미로 과거에 시작된 일이 현재까지 계속되고 있음을 표현하고 있으므로 현재완료 시제 has continued가 올바르게 쓰였다.
② **동명사의 형태** 동명사(Being published) 뒤에 목적어가 없고 문맥상 '대체 불가능한 토큰으로 발행되다'라는 의미의 수동 관계가 되어야 자연스러우므로 동명사의 수동형 Being published가 올바르게 쓰였다.
④ **동명사를 목적어로 취하는 동사** 동사 keep은 동명사를 목적어로 취하므로 동명사 boosting이 올바르게 쓰였다.

정답 ③

어휘

host 주최하다; 주인 showcase 선보이다, 전시하다; 공개 행사
non-fungible token 대체 불가능한 토큰(NFT)
publish 발행하다, 출판하다, 발표하다 trade 거래하다; 무역
verifiable 검증 가능한 boost 신장시키다, 북돋우다 asset 자산, 재산
fluctuate 등락을 거듭하다

---

04 생활영어 How long is the task force expected to operate?
난이도 하 ●○○

밑줄 친 부분에 들어갈 말로 적절한 것은?

 Mason Parker
Are you going to apply for the new customer service task force?
14:40

Chloe Wright
I'm not sure.
14:41

 Mason Parker
Why not? It's a great opportunity to learn how to deal with customer complaints and common issues effectively.
14:42

Chloe Wright
That's true. I've been wanting to develop those kinds of practical skills.
14:42

 Mason Parker
Then why are you hesitating?
14:43

Chloe Wright
I'm worried that I might be away from my current job for too long. _____
14:44

 Mason Parker
I think it will last at least a quarter.
14:44

① How many people are allowed to join the task force?
② Where will the task force be working primarily?
③ How long is the task force expected to operate?
④ Are you interested in other training seminars?

해석

Mason Parker: 새로운 고객 서비스 전담반에 지원하실 건가요?
Chloe Wright: 잘 모르겠어요.
Mason Parker: 왜요? 그건 고객 불만과 일반적인 문제들을 효과적으로 다루는 방법을 배울 좋은 기회예요.
Chloe Wright: 맞아요. 저는 그런 종류의 실용적인 기술들을 개발하기를 원해 왔어요.
Mason Parker: 그럼 왜 주저하시나요?
Chloe Wright: 제가 현재 업무를 너무 오래 떠나게 될까 봐 걱정이에요. 전담반은 얼마나 오래 운영될 것으로 예상되나요?
Mason Parker: 제 생각에 최소 1분기는 지속될 거예요.

① 전담반에 몇 명이 참여할 수 있나요?
② 전담반은 주로 어디서 일하게 되나요?
③ 전담반은 얼마나 오래 운영될 것으로 예상되나요?
④ 다른 교육 세미나에 관심 있으신가요?

해설

고객 서비스 전담반 지원을 왜 주저하는지 묻는 Mason에게 Chloe가 현재 하고 있는 업무를 너무 오래 떠나게 될까 봐 걱정이라고 대답하고, 빈칸 뒤에서 다시 Mason이 I think it will last at least a quarter(제 생각에 최소 1분기는 지속될 거예요)라고 말하고 있으므로, '전담반은 얼마나 오래 운영될 것으로 예상되나요?'라는 의미의 ③ 'How long is the task force expected to operate?'가 정답이다.

정답 ③

어휘

apply for ~에 지원하다 task force 전담반, 대책 위원회
deal with ~을 다루다 complaint 불만 practical 실용적인
hesitate 주저하다, 망설이다 quarter 1분기(3개월), 4분의 1
primarily 주로 operate 운영되다, 작동되다, 수술하다

05~06 다음 글을 읽고 물음에 답하시오.

___(A)___

As a Hawaiian resident, you need to know what you can do to save the state bird.

Although their numbers have slightly improved, the nene is still not safe from extinction. So, let's all do what we can to protect the native goose that serves as Hawaii's state bird.

The Nene Conservation Team is working on a plan to help the bird's population grow. They will hold an information session for the public next week. Attend and you can learn more about their efforts and what you can do too.

Can you imagine the state without its most iconic native bird?

- **Location**: Diamondhead Outdoor Pavilion
  (event will be held in the Assembly Hall in case of bad weather.)
- **Date**: Wednesday, April 10
- **Time**: 6:30 p.m.

To donate to the group, please visit www.savethenene.com or call (808) 555-6363.

05 독해 제목 파악

(A)에 들어갈 윗글의 제목으로 적절한 것은?

① Join the Hawaiian Bird Watching Network
② Hawaii's Ecosystem Needs Your Attention
③ Hawaii's State Bird is in Danger
④ Volunteer to Save Hawaiian Traditions

정답 ③

06 독해 내용 불일치 파악

위 안내문의 내용과 일치하지 않는 것은?

① 하와이의 상징적인 새를 보존하려는 단체가 있다.
② 하와이 주조의 개체 수는 현재 감소하고 있다.
③ 행사는 야외 공간에서 개최될 예정이다.
④ 기부는 웹사이트를 통해 할 수 있다.

정답 ②

07 독해 무관한 문장 삭제

다음 글의 흐름상 어색한 문장은?

Timing plays an important role in how events are presented to the world, and poor timing can cause important events to be overlooked. One example of this occurred with the early aviation pioneer Harriet Quimby. On April 16, 1912, the American pilot set off from Dover, England, and landed on a beach near Calais, France. ① The 40-kilometer flight may not seem particularly impressive today, but it marked a great feat in aviation at the time since Quimby had become the first female pilot to fly across the English Channel. ② Unfortunately, her accomplishment went largely unnoticed. ③ That's because most of the world was focused on the sinking of the *Titanic*, which had happened the previous day. ④ The *Titanic*'s tragic sinking is still a source of fascination to many people today. In fact, in *The New York Times*, the only mention of Quimby's accomplishment came in a short article on page 15.

해석

타이밍은 사건이 세상에 어떻게 보여지는지에 있어서 중요한 역할을 하며, 좋지 않은 타이밍은 중요한 사건이 간과되게 할 수 있다. 이것의 한 예는 초기 항공 선구자 Harriet Quimby에게 일어났다. 1912년 4월 16일에, 그 미국인 조종사는 영국 Dover에서 출발하여 프랑스 Calais 근처의 해변에 착륙했다. ① 40킬로미터의 비행은 오늘날 특별히 인상적으로 보이지 않을 수도 있지만, 그것은 Quimby가 영국 해협을 횡단한 최초의 여성 조종사가 되었다는 이유로 그 당시 항공 분야에서 대단한 위업을 남겼다. ② 안타깝게도, 그녀의 업적은 크게 눈에 띄지 않았다. ③ 그것은 전 세계 대부분이 전날 발생했던 Titanic호 침몰에 집중하고 있었기 때문이다. ④ Titanic호의 비극적인 침몰은 오늘날에도 여전히 많은 사람들에게 매력적인 소재이다. 실제로, 『뉴욕 타임스』에서 Quimby의 업적에 대한 언급은 15페이지에 짧은 기사로만 실렸을 뿐이었다.

해설

첫 문장에서 좋지 않은 타이밍에 발생한 사건은 간과될 수 있다고 하면서, 항공 선구자 Harriet Quimby의 사례를 언급한 후, ①번은 Quimby의 40킬로미터 비행이 그 당시 항공 분야에서 대단한 위업이었다는 것, ②, ③번은 안타깝게도 그녀의 업적이 비행 전날 발생한 Titanic호 침몰 때문에 크게 눈에 띄지 않았음을 설명하고 있다. 그러나 ④번은 '여전히 매력적인 소재인 Titanic호 침몰'이라는 내용으로, 첫 문장의 내용과 관련이 없다.

정답 ④

어휘

present 보여 주다, 나타내다 overlook 간과하다 aviation 항공, 비행
pioneer 선구자 set off 출발하다 feat 위업 channel 해협, 수로
accomplishment 업적, 성취 unnoticed 눈에 띄지 않는 sinking 침몰
tragic 비극적인 fascination 매력, 흥미 article 기사, 논문

---

08 독해 요지 파악   난이도 중 ●●○

다음 글의 요지로 적절한 것은?

After working for years in a children's psychiatric clinic, British psychiatrist John Bowlby formulated his theory of attachment in 1958. His attachment theory considered the significance of the relationship between mothers and babies in regard to their cognitive, social, and emotional development. Without this link, Bowlby argued, young children would not receive sufficient care and support and thus would be more likely to develop attachment issues and disorders. Subsequent studies in the 1960s were conducted to understand how healthy attachments form. Interestingly, researchers found that babies established stronger relationships not with those who satisfied their physical needs—those who fed them or spent the most time with them—but with those who were attuned to their emotional state. This sensitive responsiveness is the key to forming deep attachments, and it can be fostered through play and appropriate and timely communication.

① Attachment theory explains the importance and formation of relationships.
② Children will be poorly adjusted without sufficient care.
③ Emotional states are more important to well-being than physical states.
④ Fundamental attachment is determined in childhood and does not change.

해석

아동 정신 병원에서 수년간 근무한 후, 영국의 정신과 의사 John Bowlby는 1958년에 그의 애착 이론을 공식화했다. 그의 애착 이론은 아기들의 인지적, 사회적, 그리고 정서적 발달에 관해 엄마와 아기 간의 관계의 중요성을 고려했다. Bowlby는 이 관계가 없다면, 어린아이들이 충분한 보살핌과 지지를 받지 못할 것이고 그리하여 애착 문제와 이상이 생길 가능성이 더 크다고 주장했다. 1960년대의 뒤이은 연구들은 어떻게 건전한 애착이 형성되는지를 알기 위해 수행되었다. 흥미롭게도, 연구원들은 아기들이 그들의 신체적 욕구를 충족시켜 준 사람들, 즉 그들에게 먹을 것을 주었거나 그들과 가장 많은 시간을 보냈던 사람들이 아니라, 그들의 정서적 상태에 적절히 대응했던 사람들과 더 강한 관계를 맺는다는 것을 발견했다. 이 세심한 반응성은 깊은 애착을 형성하는 비결이며, 그것은 놀이와 적절하고 시기에 맞는 의사소통을 통해 발달될 수 있다.

① 애착 이론은 관계의 중요성과 형성 과정을 설명한다.
② 아이들은 충분한 돌봄이 없다면 불완전하게 적응할 것이다.
③ 정서적 상태는 행복에 있어 신체적 상태보다 더 중요하다.
④ 근본적인 애착은 유년기에 결정되어 변하지 않는다.

해설

지문 전반에 걸쳐 John Bowlby의 애착 이론은 아기들의 인지·사회·정서적 발달에 있어 엄마와의 관계가 중요함을 보여 주었고, 뒤이은 연구들은 아기들의 건전한 애착이 형성되는 방식에 대해 밝혔다고 설명하고 있으므로, ① '애착 이론은 관계의 중요성과 형성 과정을 설명한다'가 이 글의 요지이다.

정답 ①

어휘

psychiatric 정신과의 formulate 공식화하다, 만들어내다
attachment 애착 significance 중요성 cognitive 인지의
sufficient 충분한 disorder 이상, 무질서 subsequent 뒤이은, 그다음의
conduct 수행하다 feed 먹을 것을 주다, 양육하다
be attuned to ~에 적절히 대응하다 emotional 정서적인, 감정적인
sensitive 세심한, 민감한 responsiveness 반응성, 응답
foster 발달시키다, 조성하다 appropriate 적절한 timely 시기에 맞는
formation 형성 (과정) poorly 불완전하게, 형편없이
adjust 적응하다, 조정하다 fundamental 근본적인

09 독해 문단 순서 배열

주어진 글 다음에 이어질 글의 순서로 적절한 것은?

Can people who are blind be trained to use bat-like echolocation to move through their environment? According to neurobiologist Lutz Wiegrebe, it is possible.

(A) Depending on the sound that is returned, they can perceive how objects are arranged and even detect their composition. Knowing what is near them and exactly where it is located allows them to move around unaided much more easily.

(B) Wiegrebe has found a small number of blind people who have developed a rudimentary form of echolocation that helps them navigate their surroundings with ease. By making clicking sounds with their mouths and then listening for the echo, they form a mental image of the objects around them.

(C) In fact, some blind people have become so adept at this skill that they can even ride a bicycle. Such impressive mastery of echolocation is perhaps the most compelling evidence that Wiegrebe's research will continue to open new possibilities for the visually impaired.

*echolocation: 음파 탐지, 반향 위치 결정법

① (A) – (B) – (C)
② (A) – (C) – (B)
③ (B) – (A) – (C)
④ (B) – (C) – (A)

해석

맹인들은 그들의 주변 환경을 옮겨 다니기 위해 박쥐와 같은 음파 탐지를 사용하도록 훈련될 수 있을까? 신경생리학자 Lutz Wiegrebe에 따르면 그것은 가능하다.

(A) 되돌아오는 소리에 따라, 그들은 물체들이 어떻게 배열되어 있는지를 인식하고 그것들의 구도까지도 감지할 수 있다. 그들 주변에 무엇이 있는지, 그리고 그것이 정확히 어디에 위치해 있는지를 아는 것은 그들이 도움을 받지 않고 훨씬 더 쉽게 돌아다니게 해 준다.

(B) Wiegrebe는 주변 환경을 쉽게 탐색하는 데 도움이 되는, 기본적인 형태의 음파 탐지를 발달시킨 얼마 안 되는 맹인들을 발견했다. 입으로 딸깍거리는 소리를 낸 후 그 울림을 들음으로써, 그들은 주변의 물체에 대한 심상을 만들어낸다.

(C) 실제로, 일부 맹인들은 이 기술에 매우 능숙해져서 자전거를 탈 수도 있다. 음파 탐지에 대한 이러한 인상적인 숙달은 아마도 Wiegrebe의 연구가 시각이 손상된 사람에게 새로운 가능성을 계속해서 열어 줄 것이라는 가장 설득력 있는 증거이다.

해설

주어진 문장에서 신경생리학자 Lutz Wiegrebe에 따르면 맹인들이 주변을 옮겨 다니기 위해 음파 탐지를 사용할 수 있다고 한 뒤, (B)에서 Wiegrebe가 발견한 소수의 맹인들은 소리 울림을 통해 주변 물체에 대한 심상을 만들어낸다고 설명하고 있다. 이어서 (A)에서 그들(they)은 되돌아오는 소리에 따라 주변 물체들의 배열과 구도를 감지함으로써 도움 없이 쉽게 돌아다닐 수 있다고 하고, (C)에서 실제로(In fact) 일부 맹인들은 이 기술(this skill)에 능숙해져서 자전거 타기까지 가능한데, 이는 시각이 손상된 사람에게 새로운 가능성을 열어 줄 것이라고 주장하고 있다. 따라서 ③ (B) – (A) – (C)가 정답이다.

정답 ③

어휘

blind 맹인인 neurobiologist 신경생리학자 perceive 인식하다, 감지하다
arrange 배열하다, (일을) 처리하다 detect 감지하다
composition 구도, 작곡 unaided 도움을 받지 않는
rudimentary 기본적인 navigate 탐색하다, 길을 찾다
surroundings (주변) 환경 with ease 쉽게 click 딸깍거리는 소리를 내다
adept 능숙한 compelling 설득력 있는 impair 손상시키다

10 독해 빈칸 완성 – 절

밑줄 친 부분에 들어갈 말로 적절한 것은?

In Thailand, people are often called by a nickname rather than their legal name. In fact, the practice is so prevalent that people can be friends for years without knowing each other's official names. While many outsiders believe that these terms of endearment are simply easier versions of the person's longer name, there is actually another reason for them. According to a traditional Thai belief, evil spirits lurk around children and try to interfere with their lives. However, it is thought that their malicious attempts can be prevented _____ _____. Therefore, Thai parents assign their children nicknames at birth and use these to refer to them instead of their actual names. Interestingly, these often take the form of names that may seem insulting, like "fatty" or "frog," as these are thought to be less likely to cause jealousy in the spirits than nicer nicknames.

① if they do not know the child's actual name
② if special charms are worn to repel evil spirits
③ if spiritual protection ceremonies are regularly performed
④ if parents maintain secrecy about their child's existence

해석

태국에서, 사람들은 그들의 법적인 이름보다는 별명으로 자주 불린다. 실제로, 그 관행은 너무 만연해서 사람들은 서로의 공식적인 이름을 알지 못한 채 수년간 친구가 될 수 있다. 많은 외부인들은 이러한 애칭이 단지 그 사람의 긴 이름의 더 쉬운 형태라고 여기지만, 그것들에는 사실 또 다른 이유가 있다. 전통적인 태국 믿음에 따르면, 악령들은 아이들 주변에 숨어서 그들의 삶에 훼방을 놓으려고 한다. 하지만, 만약 그들이 아이의 실제 이름을 알지 못한다면 그들의 악의적인 시도는 막을 수 있다고 생각된다. 그러므로, 태국 부모들은 그들의 아이들에게 태어날 때 별명을 지어 주고 그들을 부르기 위해 실제 이름 대신 그것들을 사용한다. 흥미롭게도, 이것들은 종종 '뚱뚱보'나 '개구리'와 같이 모욕적으로 보일지도 모르는 이름의 형태를 띠는데, 이것들이 더 멋진 별명보다 그 영혼들의 질투를 유발할 가능성이 더 적다고 생각되기 때문이다.

① 만약 그들이 아이의 실제 이름을 알지 못한다면
② 만약 악령을 물리치기 위한 특별한 부적이 착용된다면
③ 만약 영적 보호 의식이 정기적으로 행해진다면
④ 만약 부모들이 자녀의 존재에 대해 비밀을 유지한다면

해설

빈칸 앞 문장에 태국의 전통 믿음에 따르면 악령들은 아이들 주변에 숨어서 그들의 삶에 훼방을 놓으려 한다는 내용이 있고, 빈칸 뒤 문장에 태국 부모들은 아이들이 태어날 때 별명을 지어 주고 그 별명을 실제 이름 대신 사용한다는 내용이 있으므로, '만약 그들이 아이의 실제 이름을 알지 못한다면' 악령들의 악의적인 시도는 막을 수 있다고 생각된다고 한 ①번이 정답이다.

정답 ①

어휘

nickname 별명 legal 법적인 prevalent 만연한, 일반적인
a term of endearment 애칭 evil spirit 악령 lurk 숨어 있다, 도사리다
interfere 훼방을 놓다, 간섭하다 malicious 악의적인
attempt 시도; 시도하다 prevent 막다, 예방하다 refer to ~를 부르다
insulting 모욕적인, 무례한 jealousy 질투 charm 부적, 매력; 매혹하다
repel 물리치다 secrecy 비밀 유지 existence 존재

DAY 16 하프모의고사 16회

▶ 정답 p. 74

01	③	어휘	06	②	독해
02	①	문법	07	③	독해
03	③	문법	08	③	독해
04	②	생활영어	09	②	독해
05	③	독해	10	④	독해

▶ 취약영역 분석표

영역	맞힌 답의 개수
어휘	/1
생활영어	/1
문법	/2
독해	/6
TOTAL	/10

---

01 어휘 break 난이도 하 ●○○

밑줄 친 부분에 들어갈 말로 적절한 것은?

At the start of the year, people plan to _____ self-limiting habits in order to remove barriers to their progress.

① adopt
② strengthen
③ break
④ revive

[해석]
연초에, 사람들은 그들의 발전에 대한 장애물을 제거하기 위해 자기 제한적인 습관들을 중단할 계획을 세운다.

① 채택하다
② 강화하다
③ 중단하다
④ 되살리다

정답 ③

[어휘]
self-limiting 자기 제한적인 habit 습관 barrier 장애물, 장벽
progress 발전; 진행하다 adopt 채택하다 strengthen 강화하다
break 중단하다, 깨뜨리다 revive 되살리다, 부활시키다

---

02 문법 시제 난이도 하 ●○○

밑줄 친 부분에 들어갈 말로 적절한 것은?

As long as students _____ their assignments on time, they will receive full credit, which will be reflected in their final grades.

① submit
② will submit
③ were submitting
④ will have submitted

[해석]
학생들은 제시간에 그들의 과제를 제출하기만 하면 만점을 받을 것인데, 이것은 그들의 최종 성적에 반영될 것이다.

[해설]
① 현재 시제 빈칸은 부사절의 동사 자리이다. 조건을 나타내는 부사절(As long as ~)에서는 미래를 나타내기 위해 현재 시제를 사용하므로, 현재 시제가 쓰인 ① submit가 정답이다.

정답 ①

[어휘]
assignment 과제 on time 제시간에 credit 학점, 신용
final grade 최종 성적

---

03 문법 수식어|분사|수 일치|대명사|어순 난이도 중 ●●○

밑줄 친 부분 중 어법상 옳지 않은 것은?

The mechanical double clocks in competitive chess ① keep track of time as one player or ② the other makes a move. In international tournaments, a player is permitted forty moves in two hours. If the player does not make the number of moves ③ require during the game, he loses the game—except when the opponent lacks ④ enough pieces to win the match.

[해석]
겨루기 체스에서 기계로 작동되는 두 시계는 한 선수나 다른 한 선수가 수를 둘 때 시간을 기록한다. 국제 경기에서, 선수는 두 시간에 40번의 수가 허용된다. 만약 그 선수가 게임 동안 요구되는 수(數)의 수를 두지 못하면, 그는 상대가 시합에 이길 만큼 충분한 말이 없는 경우 외에는 그 시합에서 진다.

[해설]
③ 수식어 거품 자리 | 현재분사 vs. 과거분사 주어(the player)와 동사(has not made)를 모두 갖춘 완전한 절에 또 다른 동사(require)는 올 수 없으므로, 명사(the number of moves)를 수식하는 분사가 와야 한다. 이때 수식받는 명사 the number of moves와 분사가 '수(數)의 수가 요구되다'라는 의미의 수동 관계이므로 동사 require를 과거분사 required로 고쳐야 한다.

[오답 분석]
① **주어와 동사의 수 일치** 주어 자리에 복수 명사 The mechanical double clocks가 왔으므로 복수 명사 keep이 올바르게 쓰였다. 참고로, 주어와 동사 사이의 수식어 거품(in competitive chess)은 동사의 수 결정에 영향을 주지 않는다.
② **부정대명사** 문맥상 '(두 선수 중 나머지) 다른 선수'라는 의미가 되어야 자연스러우므로 '정해진 것 중 남은 사람[것] 전부'라는 의미의 부정대명사 the other가 올바르게 쓰였다.
④ **혼동하기 쉬운 어순** enough는 명사(pieces)를 앞에서 수식하므로 enough pieces가 올바르게 쓰였다.

정답 ③

어휘
mechanical 기계로 작동되는, 기계적인 keep track of ~을 기록하다, 파악하다
tournament 경기, 시합 opponent 상대; 반대의 piece (게임) 말, 조각

04 생활영어 You can never be too careful.
난이도 하 ●○○

밑줄 친 부분에 들어갈 말로 적절한 것은?

A: Don't forget to bring an umbrella for our trip today.
B: The forecast said the sky would be clear.
A: I know, but it's the rainy season and the weather on the island is unpredictable.
B: Well, in that case, should I bring a waterproof jacket too?
A: That's not a bad idea. _____
B: You're right. I wouldn't want to get soaked.

① Let's go indoors if it starts raining.
② You can never be too careful.
③ The rainy season is almost over anyway.
④ I've checked multiple weather sources.

해석

A: 오늘 우리 여행에 우산 가져오는 거 잊지 마.
B: 일기 예보에서는 하늘이 맑을 거라고 하던데.
A: 알아, 그렇지만 지금은 장마철이고 섬 날씨는 예측할 수 없어.
B: 음, 그렇다면, 방수 재킷도 가져가야 할까?
A: 괜찮은 생각이네. 아무리 조심해도 지나치지 않지.
B: 네 말이 맞아. 나는 젖고 싶지 않아.

① 비가 오기 시작하면 실내로 가자.
② 아무리 조심해도 지나치지 않지.
③ 장마철이 거의 끝났어.
④ 다양한 날씨 자료들을 찾아 봤어.

해설
장마철이고 섬 날씨는 예측할 수 없다는 A의 말에 대해 B가 방수 재킷도 가져가야 할지 묻자, 빈칸 뒤에서 다시 B가 You're right. I wouldn't want to get soaked(네 말이 맞아. 나는 젖고 싶지 않아)라고 말하고 있으므로, '아무리 조심해도 지나치지 않지'라는 의미의 ② 'You can never be too careful'이 정답이다.

정답 ②

어휘
forecast 일기 예보; 예보하다 unpredictable 예측할 수 없는
waterproof 방수의 get soaked 젖다

05~06 다음 글을 읽고 물음에 답하시오.

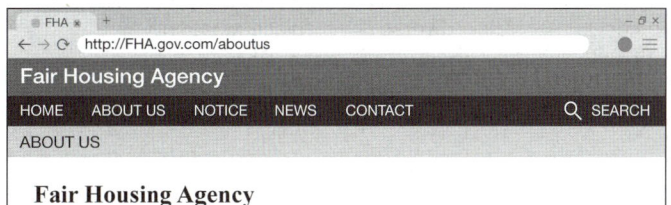

Fair Housing Agency

Purpose
Our agency was founded to advance equal access to housing regardless of race, social class, and other demographic characteristics. Our programs are meant to make sure that safe, affordable housing is available to everyone in the country and free from unlawful barriers.

Activities
We investigate complaints received from the public to ensure fair housing practices are upheld and hold violators accountable for their actions. In addition, we provide resources and training to help individuals understand their rights and give housing providers the tools necessary to foster diverse communities. We also partner with outside organizations to help those facing housing discrimination.

Guiding Principles
• Equity & Accessibility: We promote equal opportunity and the removal of systemic barriers to housing.
• Accountability & Transparency: We champion ethical standards and maintain openness in all our actions.

해석

공정주거지원청
목적
저희 기관은 인종, 사회 계층 및 기타 인구통계학적 특성에 관계없이 주택에 대한 동등한 접근권을 증진시키기 위해 설립되었습니다. 저희 프로그램들은 안전하고 저렴한 주택이 국내 모든 사람에게 이용 가능하고 불법적인 장벽으로부터 자유롭도록 보장하기 위해 의도되었습니다.

활동
저희는 공정한 주택 관행이 확실하게 유지되고 위반한 사람들에게 그들의 행동에 대한 책임을 묻기 위해 대중들로부터 받은 불만 사항들을 조사합니다. 게다가, 저희는 개인들이 자신의 권리를 이해하도록 돕고 주택 제공자들이 다양한 지역 사회를 조성하는 데 필요한 도구들을

주기 위해 자원과 교육 훈련을 제공합니다. 저희는 또한 주거 차별에 직면한 사람들을 돕기 위해 외부 기관들과 협력합니다.

지도 원칙
- 형평성 및 접근성: 저희는 동등한 기회와 주거에 대한 구조적인 장벽의 제거를 촉진합니다.
- 책임성 및 투명성: 저희는 윤리적 기준을 옹호하고 저희의 모든 행동에 개방성을 유지합니다.

어휘

demographic 인구통계학적인　affordable 저렴한, 가격이 알맞은
unlawful 불법적인　investigate 조사하다　complaint 불만 사항, 항의
uphold 유지시키다　hold A accountable for B A에게 B의 책임을 묻다
foster 조성하다, 기르다　diverse 다양한　discrimination 차별
principle 원칙, 주의　equity 형평성　accessibility 접근성
accountability 책임성　transparency 투명성　champion 옹호하다
ethical 윤리적인

05 독해 내용 일치 파악　난이도 중 ●●○

윗글에서 Fair Housing Agency에 관한 내용과 일치하는 것은?

① It was founded to build more affordable housing units.
② It has no power to punish violators of housing laws.
③ It offers educational tools to people supplying housing.
④ It pays outside organizations to provide housing for individuals.

해석
① 그것은 더 많은 저렴한 주택들을 건설하기 위해 설립되었다.
② 그것은 주택 법을 위반한 사람들을 처벌할 권한이 없다.
③ 그것은 주택을 공급하는 사람들에게 교육적 도구를 제공한다.
④ 그것은 개인들에게 주택을 제공하기 위해 외부 조직에 비용을 지불한다.

해설
③번의 키워드인 educational tools(교육적 도구)를 바꾸어 표현한 지문의 training(교육 훈련) 주변의 내용에서 공정주거지원청은 주택 제공자들이 다양한 지역 사회를 조성하는 데 필요한 도구들을 주기 위해 교육 훈련을 제공한다고 했으므로, ③ '그것은 주택을 공급하는 사람들에게 교육적 도구를 제공한다'가 지문의 내용과 일치한다.

[오답 분석]
① 공정주거지원청은 누구나 주택에 동등한 접근권을 갖게 하기 위해 설립되었다고 했으므로, 그것이 더 많은 저렴한 주택들을 건설하기 위해 설립되었다는 것은 지문의 내용과 다르다.
② 공정주거지원청은 공정한 주택 관행을 위반한 사람들에게 행동에 대한 책임을 묻는다고 했으므로, 그것이 주택 법을 위반한 사람들을 처벌할 권한이 없다는 것은 지문의 내용과 다르다.
④ 공정주거지원청이 주거 차별에 직면한 사람들을 돕기 위해 외부 기관들과 협력한다고는 했지만, 그것이 개인들에게 주택을 제공하기 위해 외부 조직에 비용을 지불하는지는 알 수 없다.

정답 ③

06 독해 유의어 파악　난이도 하 ●○○

밑줄 친 diverse의 의미와 가장 가까운 것은?

① busy　　　　　　② varied
③ local　　　　　　④ strong

해석
① 붐비는　　　　　② 다양한
③ 현지의　　　　　④ 튼튼한

해설
밑줄 친 부분이 포함된 문장에서 diverse는 문맥상 주택 제공자들에게 '다양한' 지역 사회를 조성하는 데 필수적인 도구들을 제공한다는 의미로 쓰였으므로, '다양한'이라는 의미의 ② varied가 정답이다.

정답 ②

07 독해 무관한 문장 삭제　난이도 중 ●●○

다음 글의 흐름상 어색한 문장은?

Some personality traits may predict the likelihood of success in life. Studies led by psychologists point to diligence as one such trait. It reflects a tendency to work hard, set goals, take responsibility, obey rules, and be organized. People who have this trait regulate themselves and control their impulses. ① For instance, while most people choose enjoyment at the moment, industrious individuals will go home and study for a big exam or make sure they're in bed early so they can be at work on time. ② They are also the ones who avoid driving over the speed limit even when there are no other cars around. ③ Studies show that diligence is directly linked to decreased creativity since rule-following limits innovative thinking. ④ The trait is especially significant in critical areas such as relationships, financial security, and health. They are aware of the consequences of certain actions and are thus apt to be more careful than others.

해석
어떤 성격 특성들은 인생에서 성공의 가능성을 예견할지도 모른다. 심리학자들에 의해 주도된 연구들은 그러한 특성의 하나로 성실함을 지목한다. 그것은 열심히 일하고, 목표를 세우고, 책임감을 가지고, 규칙을 준수하며 체계적인 성향을 나타낸다. 이러한 특성을 가진 사람들은 그들 자신을 통제하며 충동을 자제한다. ① 예를 들어, 많은 사람들이 그 순간의 즐거움을 선택하는 반면, 근면한 사람들은 중요한 시험을 위해 집에 가서 공부를 하거나 그들이 제시간에 출근할 수 있도록 반드시 일찍 잠들 것이다. ② 그들은 또한 다른 차들이 주변에 없더라도 제한 속도 이상으로 운전하는 것을 피하는 사람들이다. ③ 연구들은 규칙 준수가 혁신적인 사고를 제한하기 때문에 성실함이 창의성 감소와 직접적으로 연관된다는 것을 보여준다. ④ 그 특성은 관계, 경제적 안정 그리고 건강과 같이 중요한 영역들에서 특히 의미가 있다. 그들은 특정 행동의 결과에 대해 알고 있으므로 다른 사람들에 비해 더욱 주의 깊은 경향이 있다.

해설

지문 앞부분에서 인생에서 성공의 가능성을 예견하는 성격 특성들 중 하나인 성실함을 가진 사람들은 스스로를 통제하고 충동을 자제한다고 언급한 뒤, ①, ②번에서 '실생활 속 성실함의 사례들', ④번에서 '삶의 중요한 영역들에 영향을 미치는 성실함'에 대해 설명하고 있다. 그러나 ③번은 '성실함과 창의성 감소의 연관성'에 대한 내용으로, 지문 앞부분의 내용과 관련이 없다.

정답 ③

어휘

personality 성격 trait 특성 likelihood 가능성 diligence 성실, 근면
tendency 성향, 경향 organized 체계적인, 정리된 regulate 통제하다
impulse 충동 industrious 근면한 significant 의미가 있는, 중요한
consequence 결과 be apt to ~하는 경향이 있다

---

08 독해 내용 불일치 파악 난이도 중 ●●○

다음 글의 내용과 일치하지 않는 것은?

> To: Reservations@TimesSquareHosp.com
> From: VicHadid@SimpsportCity.com
> Date: July 5
> Subject: Banquet Facilities
>
> Dear Sir or Madam,
>
> I would like to get more information about possibly reserving the facilities at your hotel.
>
> We will be hosting an event for a delegation visiting from China on September 10. We need to book a facility that can provide a space where we can have a show by a local theater troupe. Before the performance, we need to have a catered cocktail party. After, we will have a sit-down dinner. We expect approximately 100 guests at the event, but would like preparations for at least 20 additional people to be safe.
>
> Could you please let me know if your hotel can accommodate our needs? If so, please send me a sample menu and the price for such an event.
>
> I hope to hear from you soon.
>
> Kind regards,
> Vic Hadid
> Simpsport City Event Planner

① Visitors from another country will attend the event.
② An area for a performance is necessary.
③ Food needs to be prepared for 100 people.
④ A menu and cost estimate should be provided.

해석

수신: Reservations@TimesSquareHosp.com
발신: VicHadid@SimpsportCity.com
날짜: 7월 5일
제목: 연회 시설 관련

담당자님께,

귀하의 호텔 시설 예약 가능성에 관해 더 많은 정보를 얻고자 합니다.

저희는 9월 10일에 중국에서 방문하는 대표단을 위한 행사를 개최할 예정입니다. 저희는 현지 극단의 공연을 진행할 수 있는 공간이 제공 가능한 시설을 예약해야 합니다. 공연 전에는, 케이터링 서비스가 있는 칵테일 파티를 진행해야 합니다. 공연 후에는, 앉아서 하는 저녁 식사를 진행할 예정입니다. 행사에는 약 100명의 손님들을 예상하지만, 안전하게 최소 20명의 추가 인원을 위한 준비를 하고 싶습니다.

귀하의 호텔이 저희의 요구를 수용할 수 있는지 알려 주시겠습니까? 가능하다면, 견본 메뉴와 이러한 행사에 대한 가격을 보내 주시기 바랍니다.

곧 소식을 듣기를 바라겠습니다.

안부를 전하며,
Vic Hadid
Simpsport 도시 행사 책임자

① 다른 나라에서 온 방문객들이 행사에 참석할 것이다.
② 공연을 위한 공간이 필요하다.
③ 100명을 위한 음식이 준비되어야 한다.
④ 메뉴와 비용의 견적이 제공되어야 한다.

해설

③번의 키워드인 100 people(100명)을 바꾸어 표현한 지문의 100 guests(100명의 손님들) 주변의 내용에서 행사에 약 100명의 손님들을 예상하지만 최소 20명의 추가 인원을 위한 준비를 하고 싶다고 했으므로, ③ '100명을 위한 음식이 준비되어야 한다'는 지문의 내용과 다르다.

정답 ③

어휘

banquet 연회 reserve 예약하다 host 주최하다 delegation 대표단
theater troupe 극단 accommodate 수용하다
estimate 견적, 예상치; 예상하다

---

09 독해 주제 파악 난이도 중 ●●○

다음 글의 주제로 적절한 것은?

> In the early 1990s, zero-tolerance policies were enacted in schools throughout the US in an effort to keep students safe by strictly enforcing rules against minor offenses that administrators believed could lead to more serious crimes. Under zero tolerance, those in violation of school rules were automatically punished, no matter the circumstances or rationale behind the violation. In theory, the threat of a strict penalty for even minor offenses would deter students

DAY 16 하프모의고사 16회

from misbehaving. In practice, however, the results were less successful. Increased suspension rates didn't improve school discipline but rather caused students to fall behind in their studies, which led to discouragement and eventually more poor conduct. To make matters worse, there were even cases where victims and attackers were punished equally. For example, a student defending him- or herself against a bully would receive the same penalty as the initiator because they were both technically involved in a fight.

① Origins of zero-tolerance policies in American education
② Negative impacts of strict disciplinary approaches in education
③ The historical development of school punishment systems
④ Educational reforms aimed at reducing student misconduct

해석
1990년대 초반에, 무관용 정책은 행정관들이 생각하기에 더 중대한 범죄로 이어질 수 있는 가벼운 위반 사항에 대해 규칙을 엄격하게 집행함으로써 학생들을 계속 안전하게 하기 위한 노력의 일환으로 미국 전역의 학교에서 규정되었다. 무관용 정책에 따르면, 교칙을 위반한 학생들은 그 위반 이면의 상황이나 이유에 관계없이 자동적으로 처벌을 받았다. 이론상으로, 심지어 가벼운 위반 사항에도 적용되는 엄격한 처벌의 위협은 학생들이 비행을 저지르는 것을 단념시킬 것이었다. 하지만, 실제 결과는 덜 성공적이었다. 증가한 정학률은 학교의 규율을 개선시키지 못했고 오히려 학생들이 학업에서 뒤처지게 했는데, 이것은 낙담과 결국에는 더 불량한 행실로 이어졌다. 설상가상으로, 심지어 피해자들과 가해자들이 똑같이 처벌을 받는 경우도 있었다. 예를 들어, 괴롭히는 학생으로부터 자신을 방어한 학생은 (싸움을) 시작한 사람과 같은 처벌을 받았는데, 이는 그들 둘 다 엄밀히 따지면 싸움에 연루되었기 때문이다.

① 미국 교육에서 무관용 정책의 기원
② 교육에서 엄격한 징계 방식의 부정적인 영향
③ 학교 처벌 제도의 역사적인 발전
④ 학생의 비행을 줄이는 것을 목표로 하는 교육 개혁

해설
지문 전반에 걸쳐 무관용 정책의 의도는 가벼운 위반 사항에조차 엄격한 벌칙을 적용하여 학생들의 비행을 단념시키는 것이었지만, 그로 인해 증가한 정학률은 학교의 규율을 개선시키지 못하고 오히려 학생들이 학업에서 뒤처지게 하여 더욱 불량한 행실로 이어졌다고 설명하고 있다. 따라서 ② '교육에서 엄격한 징계 방식의 부정적인 영향'이 이 글의 주제이다.

정답 ②

어휘
tolerance 관용 enact 규정하다, 제정하다 strictly 엄격하게
enforce 집행하다, 강요하다 offense 위반 (사항)
administrator 행정관, 관리자 violation 위반, 방해 punish 처벌하다
rationale 이유 deter A from B A가 B하는 것을 단념시키다
misbehave 비행을 저지르다 suspension 정학, 보류
discipline 규율, 징계 fall behind 뒤처지다, 늦어지다
to make matters worse 설상가상으로 victim 피해자
attacker 가해자, 공격자 bully 괴롭히는 사람; 괴롭히다
initiator 시작하는 사람 technically 엄밀히 따지면, 기술적으로
misconduct 비행

---

10 독해 문단 순서 배열 난이도 중●●○

주어진 글 다음에 이어질 글의 순서로 적절한 것은?

The political decision to commit injustice for the sake of the citizenry is a philosophical dilemma. In Ursula Le Guin's short story which takes place in the fictional city of Omelas, this choice is aptly described.

(A) Every day in the real world, immigrants and refugees often appear at the borders of countries and are subjected to detention, deprivation, and trauma. Everyone in the country sees it but, just like in Le Guin's tale, they accept the norms they find immoral.

(B) One resident after another visits the child and feels sickened by the conditions he lives in, but no one ever tries to free him. They know that the happiness of Omelas will vanish if anyone dares to bring the child out.

(C) It is the name of a peaceful place that radiates happiness, but the contentment is dependent upon the suffering of one child. Everyone knows that he is kept in a filthy basement.

① (A) – (C) – (B)
② (B) – (A) – (C)
③ (C) – (A) – (B)
④ (C) – (B) – (A)

해석
시민들을 위해 부정을 저지르겠다는 정치적 결정은 철학적 딜레마이다. 허구의 도시 Omelas에서 일어나는 일에 대한 Ursula Le Guin의 단편 소설에는, 이 선택이 적절히 묘사되어 있다.

(A) 매일 현실 세계에서는, 이민자들과 난민들이 종종 국경에 나타나며 그들은 구금, 빈곤 그리고 정신적 외상의 대상이 된다. 그 나라의 모든 사람이 그것을 목격하지만, Le Guin의 이야기에서처럼, 그들은 자신들이 비윤리적이라고 여기는 규범들을 용인한다.

(B) 주민들은 차례로 그 아이를 방문하고는 그가 살고 있는 환경에 역겨워하지만, 아무도 결코 그를 구해 주려 하지 않는다. 그들은 누구라도 감히 그 아이를 데리고 나가면 Omelas의 행복이 사라질 것임을 안다.

(C) 그것은 행복을 발산하는 평화로운 장소의 이름이지만, 그 만족은 한 아이의 고통에 의존하고 있다. 모든 사람은 그가 더러운 지하실에 갇혀 있다는 것을 안다.

해설
주어진 글에서 시민들을 위해 부정을 저지르는 딜레마가 Omelas라는 허구의 도시에 대한 소설에 적절히 묘사되어 있다고 한 후, (C)에서 그것(It)은 평화로운 장소의 이름이지만 이곳의 만족은 지하실에 갇혀 있는 한 아이의 고통에 의존한다고 언급하고 있다. 이어서 (B)에서 주민들은 그 아이(the child)를 도와주면 Omelas의 행복이 사라질 것임을 알기에 아무도 그 아이를 구해 주지 않는다고 하고, (A)에서 Le Guin의 이야기처럼 현실 세계에서도 사람들은 이민자와 난민들이 고통에 시달리는 것을 알면서도 그들을 돕지 않는다고 설명하고 있다. 따라서 ④ (C) – (B) – (A)가 정답이다.

정답 ④

어휘
injustice 부정(의) aptly 적절히 refugee 난민 detention 구금
vanish 사라지다 dare to 감히 ~하다 radiate 발산하다, 내뿜다
contentment 만족(감) filthy 더러운 basement 지하실, 지하층

DAY 17 하프모의고사 17회

정답   p. 78

01	④	어휘	06	④	독해
02	③	문법	07	③	독해
03	③	문법	08	④	독해
04	④	생활영어	09	②	독해
05	②	독해	10	③	독해

취약영역 분석표

영역	맞힌 답의 개수
어휘	/1
생활영어	/1
문법	/2
독해	/6
TOTAL	/10

---

01 어휘 utilize   난이도 중 ●●○

밑줄 친 부분에 들어갈 말로 적절한 것은?

The man decided to pursue a career as a lawyer, hoping to effectively _____ his combative nature by arguing court cases.

① forgive ② doubt
③ overcome ④ utilize

[해석]
그 남자는 변호사로서의 경력을 추구하기로 결심했는데, 그는 법정 소송 사건을 입증함으로써 자신의 논쟁하기 좋아하는 성격을 효과적으로 활용할 수 있기를 바랐다.

① 용서하다 ② 의심하다
③ 극복하다 ④ 활용하다

정답 ④

[어휘]
effectively 효과적으로, 효율적으로 combative 논쟁하기 좋아하는, 전투적인
nature 성격, 본성 argue 입증하다, 주장하다 forgive 용서하다
doubt 의심하다 overcome 극복하다 utilize 활용하다

---

02 문법 동사의 종류 | 비교 구문 | 동명사 | to 부정사   난이도 중 ●●○

밑줄 친 부분 중 어법상 옳지 않은 것은?

Nothing made me ① more uneasy than the sense that I had no control over my life. Over the years, I found my family and supervisors taking over every significant decision in my life. I realized it was time to stop ② feeling so helpless. I told ③ to them that I wanted my choices to be respected, and after they started to allow me ④ to make my own decisions, I began feeling that I was capable of taking responsibility for myself.

[해석]
다른 어떤 것도 내가 내 삶을 통제할 수 없다는 느낌보다 나를 더 불안하게 만들지는 않았다. 수년 동안, 나는 가족과 관리자들이 내 인생에서 모든 중요한 결정을 넘겨받았음을 알게 되었다. 나는 이토록 무력하게 느끼는 것을 멈춰야 할 때라고 깨달았다. 나는 그들에게 내 선택이 존중받기를 원한다고 말했고, 그들이 나로 하여금 스스로 결정을 내리도록 해 주기 시작한 뒤로 나는 내 자신을 책임질 수 있다고 느끼기 시작했다.

[해설]
③ 4형식 동사 동사 tell은 'tell + 간접 목적어 + 직접 목적어(that절)'의 형태를 취하는 4형식 동사이므로 to them that을 them that으로 고쳐야 한다.

[오답 분석]
① 비교급 형태로 최상급 의미를 만드는 표현 문맥상 '다른 어떤 것도 ~ 느낌보다 나를 더 불안하게 만들지는 않았다'라는 의미가 되어야 자연스러운데, '다른 어떤 것도 -보다 더 ~하지 않다'는 비교급 형태로 최상급 의미를 만드는 표현 'nothing ~ 비교급 + than'의 형태를 사용하여 나타낼 수 있으므로, 비교급 more uneasy가 올바르게 쓰였다.
② 동명사와 to 부정사 둘 다 목적어로 취하는 동사 문맥상 '이토록 무력하게 느끼는 것을 멈추다'라는 의미가 되어야 자연스러운데, 동사 stop은 '~하는 것을 멈추다'라는 의미일 때 동명사를 목적어로 취하므로 동명사 feeling이 올바르게 쓰였다.
④ to 부정사를 취하는 동사 동사 allow는 to 부정사를 목적격 보어로 취하므로 to 부정사 to make가 올바르게 쓰였다.

정답 ③

[어휘]
uneasy 불안한, 불편한 supervisor 관리자, 감독관
take over ~을 넘겨받다, 인계받다 significant 중요한, 상당한
helpless 무력한 take responsibility for ~을 책임지다

DAY 17 하프모의고사 17회

03 문법 비교 구문 | 부사절 | 동사의 종류 | 수 일치
난이도 중 ●●○

밑줄 친 부분이 어법상 옳은 것은?

① I have to leave for work an hour early lest I <u>ran</u> into rush-hour traffic.
② She turned down her music because she heard someone <u>knocked</u> on the door.
③ <u>By far</u> the most influential scientist of all time was Sir Isaac Newton.
④ One fifth of our clients <u>has</u> been using our services for at least 10 years.

해석
① 나는 러시아워의 교통 혼잡을 겪지 않도록 한 시간 일찍 출근해야 한다.
② 그녀는 누군가가 문을 두드리는 것을 들어서 음악 소리를 낮췄다.
③ 역사상 단연코 가장 영향력 있는 과학자는 Isaac Newton 경이었다.
④ 우리 고객들 중 5분의 1이 적어도 10년 동안 우리의 서비스를 이용해 오고 있다.

해설
③ **최상급 강조 표현** 최상급을 강조하기 위해 최상급 표현 앞에 강조 표현(by far)이 올 수 있으므로 최상급 the most influential 앞에 By far가 올바르게 쓰였다.

[오답 분석]
① **부사절 접속사** 문맥상 '러시아워의 교통 혼잡을 겪지 않도록'이라는 의미가 되어야 자연스러우므로 부사절 접속사 lest(~하지 않도록)가 쓰였는데, 접속사 lest가 이끄는 절의 동사는 '(should +) 동사원형'의 형태를 취하므로 과거동사 ran을 (should) run으로 고쳐야 한다.
② **5형식 동사** 지각동사 hear는 목적어와 목적격 보어가 능동 관계일 때 목적격 보어로 원형 부정사나 현재분사를, 목적어와 목적격 보어가 수동 관계일 때 목적격 보어로 과거분사를 취하는데, 문맥상 목적어(someone)와 목적격 보어가 '누군가가 두드리다'라는 의미의 능동 관계이므로 과거분사 knocked를 원형 부정사 knock 또는 현재분사 knocking으로 고쳐야 한다. 참고로, 현재분사가 올 경우 동작의 진행을 강조한다.
④ **부분 표현의 수 일치** 부분을 나타내는 분수 표현(One fifth of)을 포함한 주어는 of 뒤 명사(our clients)에 동사를 수 일치시켜야 하므로, 단수 동사 has를 복수 동사 have로 고쳐야 한다.

정답 ③

어휘
run into ~을 겪다, ~와 우연히 만나다 rush-hour 러시아워(출퇴근 시간)

04 생활영어 Well, I'm more of a night person.
난이도 중 ●●○

밑줄 친 부분에 들어갈 말로 적절한 것은?

 Elizabeth Clark
You must be enjoying working the day shift now.
11:15

Logan Phillips
Not really. I'm thinking of switching back to the late shift.
11:16

 **Elizabeth Clark**
I didn't expect that. What seems to be the problem?
11:16

Logan Phillips
_____
11:17

 Elizabeth Clark
Oh, I see. It must be difficult for you to get up so early.
11:18

Logan Phillips
Yes. And I still go to sleep late, so I'm running late every morning.
11:18

① I try to sleep eight hours every night.
② There isn't a lot to do in the morning.
③ The night shift pays better than the day shift.
④ Well, I'm more of a night person.

해석
Elizabeth Clark: 너 이제 주간 근무조로 일하니 좋겠다.
Logan Phillips: 그다지. 난 다시 야간 근무조로 바꿀까 생각 중인걸.
Elizabeth Clark: 그건 예상하지 못했는데. 무슨 문제가 있는 거야?
Logan Phillips: 음, 나는 저녁형 인간에 더 가깝거든.
Elizabeth Clark: 아, 그렇구나. 네가 그렇게 일찍 일어나는 건 분명 어렵겠네.
Logan Phillips: 맞아. 그리고 난 아직도 늦게 잠이 들어서, 매일 아침 지각하고 있어.

① 나는 매일 밤 여덟 시간을 자려고 해.
② 아침에 할 일이 많지 않아.
③ 야간 근무조 수당이 주간 근무조보다 더 낫거든.
④ 음, 나는 저녁형 인간에 더 가깝거든.

해설
다시 야간 근무조로 바꾸려는 이유를 묻는 Elizabeth에게 Logan이 대답하고, 빈칸 뒤에서 다시 Elizabeth가 It must be difficult for you to get up so early(네가 그렇게 일찍 일어나는 건 분명 어렵겠네)라고 말하고 있으므로, '음, 나는 저녁형 인간에 더 가깝거든'이라는 의미의 ④ 'Well, I'm more of a night person'이 정답이다.

정답 ④

어휘

day shift 주간 근무조 switch 바꾸다, 전환하다 late shift 야간 근무조

05~06 다음 글을 읽고 물음에 답하시오.

To	Subscribers@OrangeSecurity.com
From	Support@OrangeSecurity.com
Date	January 18
Subject	Security Notice

Dear Orange Security Subscribers,

The security of your data is now more important than ever. With a major computer virus spreading, Orange Computer Security wants to help. Here are four steps you can take to stay protected:

1. Ensure your operating system, antivirus software, and applications are up-to-date.
2. Do not open suspicious emails, attachments, or links from unknown sources.
3. Use firewalls, strong antivirus software, and two-factor authentication on your accounts to add an extra layer of security to your devices and information. Please note that these advanced security services may require additional fees.
4. Back up your important files in the cloud or on a separate external drive to prevent data loss in case you are affected by a virus.

Remaining proactive is the key to keeping your devices and information safe. To learn more about security threats and ways to protect yourself, visit the Safety & Security tab on our website.

Respectfully,

Orange Computer Security

해석

수신: Subscribers@OrangeSecurity.com
발신: Support@OrangeSecurity.com
날짜: 1월 18일
제목: 보안 관련 알림

Orange 보안 서비스 구독자분들께,

여러분의 데이터 보안이 현재 그 어느 때보다 중요해졌습니다. 주요 컴퓨터 바이러스가 확산됨에 따라, Orange 컴퓨터 보안팀에서 도움을 드리고자 합니다. 보호 상태를 유지하기 위해 취할 수 있는 네 가지 단계는 다음과 같습니다.

1. 운영 체제, 바이러스 백신 소프트웨어 및 응용 프로그램이 최신 상태인지 확인하세요.
2. 불분명한 출처의 의심스러운 이메일, 첨부 파일 또는 링크를 열지 마세요.
3. 방화벽, 강력한 바이러스 백신 소프트웨어 및 계정에 이중 인증을 사용하여 기기와 정보에 추가적인 보안 단계를 더해 보세요. 이 고급 보안 서비스는 추가 비용을 필요로 한다는 점에 유의하세요.
4. 바이러스에 감염되는 경우의 데이터 손실을 막기 위해 중요한 파일을 클라우드나 별도의 외장 드라이브에 백업해 두세요.

사전 대책을 강구하는 것이 여러분의 기기와 정보를 안전하게 지키는 핵심입니다. 보안 위협과 자신을 보호하는 방법에 대해 더 알아보시려면, 저희 웹사이트의 안전 및 보안 탭을 방문해 주세요.

존경을 담아,
Orange 컴퓨터 보안팀

어휘

security 보안 subscriber 구독자 operate 운영하다, 작동하다, 수술하다
antivirus 바이러스 백신 up-to-date 최신의 suspicious 의심스러운
attachment 첨부 파일, 애착 firewall 방화벽 authentication 인증
account 계정, 계좌 external 외장의, 외부의
proactive 사전 대책을 강구하는 threat 위협, 협박

---

05 독해 목적 파악 난이도 중 ●●○

윗글의 목적으로 적절한 것은?

① to alert subscribers about the threat of a computer virus
② to notify subscribers about what they can do to protect their data
③ to advise subscribers on how to update their computer's software
④ to instruct subscribers to use a cloud-based service for backing up information

해석

① 구독자들에게 컴퓨터 바이러스의 위협에 대해 경고하려고
② 구독자들에게 자신들의 데이터를 보호하기 위해 할 수 있는 일에 대해 알리려고
③ 구독자들에게 컴퓨터 소프트웨어를 업데이트하는 방법에 대해 조언하려고
④ 구독자들에게 정보를 백업하기 위한 클라우드 기반 서비스를 사용하도록 지시하려고

해설

지문 앞부분에서 개인 컴퓨터 보호 상태를 유지하기 위한 네 가지 단계가 있다고 했으므로, ② '구독자들에게 자신들의 데이터를 보호하기 위해 할 수 있는 일에 대해 알리려고'가 이 글의 목적이다.

정답 ②

어휘

alert 경고하다; 경고, 알림 notify 알리다 instruct 가르치다, 지시하다

DAY 17 하프모의고사 17회

06 독해 내용 불일치 파악   난이도 중 ●●○

위 이메일의 내용과 일치하지 않는 것은?

① 주요 컴퓨터 바이러스가 확산 중이다.
② 운영 체제를 최신 상태로 유지할 것을 권장한다.
③ 이중 인증 기능은 유료로 제공된다.
④ 데이터를 외장 드라이브로 유출해서는 안 된다.

해설

④번의 키워드인 '외장 드라이브'가 그대로 언급된 지문의 external drive 주변의 내용에서 바이러스에 감염되는 경우의 데이터 손실을 막기 위해 중요한 파일을 클라우드나 별도의 외장 드라이브에 백업해 두라고 했으므로, ④ '데이터를 외장 드라이브로 유출해서는 안 된다'가 지문의 내용과 다르다.

정답 ④

07 독해 주제 파악   난이도 중 ●●○

다음 글의 주제로 적절한 것은?

Since it was published in the early 17th century, the inns that the main character in Miguel de Cervantes's *Don Quixote* stops at along his journey have been analyzed in great detail. On the surface, these can be seen for what they are literally, places of rest and refuge for tired travelers. However, if viewed more metaphorically, they can be seen in an entirely different way. The guest houses that Don Quixote and his travel partner Sancho Panza stop in are filled with a variety of characters from different social classes, from servants to nobles. In these, Panza finds comfort and a connection to others. However, Quixote is uncomfortable and would prefer to spend his nights in the wilderness under the stars. And even when he is convinced to lodge at an inn, Quixote remains disconnected from the events that occur there, much as he is with reality and society.

① Don Quixote's friendship with Sancho Panza
② The importance of buildings in Cervantes's works
③ Cervantes's use of symbolism to represent society
④ A comparison of nature and civilization in *Don Quixote*

해석

17세기 초에 출간된 이래로, Miguel de Cervantes의 『돈키호테』의 주인공이 그의 여정 도중에 머무는 여관들은 아주 자세히 분석되어 왔다. 겉보기에, 이것들은 문자 그대로 지친 여행객들을 위한 휴식과 보호의 장소로 보일 수 있다. 하지만, 더 비유적으로 바라본다면, 그것들은 완전히 다른 방식으로 보일 수 있다. 돈키호테와 그의 여행 동반자인 산초 판자가 머무는 손님용 숙소는 하인부터 귀족까지 서로 다른 사회 계층 출신의 다양한 등장인물들로 가득 차 있다. 여기서, 판자는 안락함과 다른 사람들과의 유대감을 찾는다. 하지만, 돈키호테는 불편해하고 별 아래 황야에서 그의 밤을 보내는 것을 선호한다. 그리고 돈키호테가 여관에서 묵는 것을 납득했을 때조차도, 그는 그가 현실과 사회에서 그러한 것처럼 그곳에서 일어나는 사건들로부터 여전히 동떨어져 있다.

① 돈키호테와 산초 판자의 우정
② Cervantes의 작품들에서 건물의 중요성
③ 사회를 묘사하는 Cervantes의 상징적 표현 사용
④ 『돈키호테』에서 자연과 문명의 비교

해설

지문 전반에 걸쳐 돈키호테와 그의 여행 동반자 산초 판자가 머무는 여관을 비유적으로 바라보면 여관은 단순히 휴식을 위한 장소가 아니라 서로 다른 사회 계층 출신의 사람들로 가득 찬 장소인데, 돈키호테가 그곳에서 불편함을 느끼고 그곳에서 일어나는 사건들로부터 동떨어져 있는 것은 그가 현실과 사회에서 그러한 것과 같다고 설명하고 있다. 따라서 ③ '사회를 묘사하는 Cervantes의 상징적 표현 사용'이 이 글의 주제이다.

정답 ③

어휘

inn 여관 analyze 분석하다 on the surface 겉보기에
literally 문자 그대로 refuge 보호, 피신 metaphorically 비유적으로
servant 하인 noble 귀족, 상류층; 고결한 wilderness 황야, 황무지
convince 납득시키다 lodge 묵다, 숙박하다 disconnected 동떨어진
symbolism 상징적 표현, 상징주의 represent 묘사하다, 나타내다
civilization 문명

08 독해 요지 파악   난이도 중 ●●○

다음 글의 요지로 적절한 것은?

Federal Marshal Service

As the country's oldest law enforcement department, the Federal Marshal Service (FMS) is committed to protecting its citizens. In addition to enforcing federal law, the FMS oversees special initiatives aimed at improving the well-being of those impacted by crime.

Security and Benefit Programs

The FMS manages the Witness Security Program, which provides 24-hour protection for individuals and their families who testify against dangerous criminals. Since its foundation in 1971, over 19,000 witnesses have entered the program's guardianship, and no participant has been harmed.

The FMS also has the authority to seize illegally obtained assets. Once a suspect is found guilty, these assets, including real estate, vehicles, art, and jewelry, are sold at auction, with a portion—about $500 million per year—of the total proceeds used to compensate victims of crimes.

① FMS maintains financial stability through the seizure and sale of assets.
② FMS is specially qualified to recommend changes to federal law.
③ FMS ensures that suspects appear for federal court trials.
④ FMS operates programs to aid crime victims and witnesses.

17회 정답·해석·해설

해커스공무원 비비안 영어 매일 하프모의고사

해석

연방 보안관 서비스

국가의 가장 오래된 법 집행 부서로서, 연방 보안관 서비스(FMS)는 시민분들을 보호하는 것에 헌신하고 있습니다. 연방법을 집행하는 것 외에도, 연방 보안관 서비스는 범죄로 인해 영향받은 사람들의 복지를 향상시키는 것을 목표로 하는 특별 계획들을 감독합니다.

보안 및 혜택 프로그램

연방 보안관 서비스는 증인 보안 프로그램을 관리하는데, 이것은 위험한 범죄자들에 대해 증언을 하는 개인과 그 가족분들에게 24시간 보호를 제공해 드립니다. 1971년 설립 이후, 19,000명 이상의 증인이 프로그램의 보호를 받았으며, 어떤 참가자도 해를 입지 않았습니다.

또한 연방 보안관 서비스는 불법적으로 획득한 자산을 압수할 권한이 있습니다. 용의자가 유죄로 판명되면, 부동산, 차량, 예술품 및 보석을 포함한 이러한 자산들은 경매로 판매되며, 총 수익금의 일부—연간 약 5억 달러—가 범죄 피해자들에게 보상하는 것에 사용됩니다.

① 연방 보안관 서비스는 자산의 압수 및 매각을 통해 재정적 안정성을 유지한다.
② 연방 보안관 서비스는 연방법 개정을 권고하는 것에 특별한 자격을 갖추고 있다.
③ 연방 보안관 서비스는 용의자들이 연방 법원 재판에 출석하도록 보장한다.
④ 연방 보안관 서비스는 범죄 피해자와 증인들을 돕기 위한 프로그램을 운영한다.

해설

지문 전반에 걸쳐 연방 보안관 서비스는 범죄로 인해 영향받은 사람들의 복지를 향상시키는 계획들을 감독하기 위해, 증인 보안 프로그램을 관리하고, 용의자가 유죄로 판명되면 불법적으로 획득된 용의자의 자산을 처분하여 수익금 일부를 범죄 피해자들에게 보상하는 데 사용한다고 했으므로, ④ '연방 보안관 서비스는 범죄 피해자와 증인들을 돕기 위한 프로그램을 운영한다'가 이 글의 요지이다.

정답 ④

어휘

federal 연방의 marshal 보안관, 집행관 enforcement 집행
commit 헌신하다 oversee 감독하다 initiative 계획
well-being 복지, 안녕 crime 범죄 witness 증인, 목격자; 목격하다
testify 증언하다 foundation 설립, 기초 guardianship 보호, 후견
authority 권한 seize 압수하다 illegally 불법적으로 obtain 획득하다
asset 자산 suspect 용의자 guilty 유죄의 real estate 부동산, 건물
auction 경매 proceeds 수익금 compensate 보상하다 victim 피해자
stability 안정성 seizure 압수 qualify 자격을 주다 court 법원
trial 재판, 시험

---

09 독해 문장 삽입 난이도 중 ●●○

주어진 문장이 들어갈 위치로 적절한 것은?

Over the three-month experiment, the mice in the former group were revealed to have much better long-term memories.

Though intermittent fasting (IF) is being advocated as a means of losing weight and increasing longevity, it may have another, less publicized benefit—improving memory retention. Researchers from King's College London conducted an experiment on three groups of lab mice. (①) While one group was subjected to IF, the two others had normal and calorie restricted (CR) diets. (②) The mice on the CR diet exhibited an improvement too, but the results were not as impressive. (③) Scans of the brains of the IF mice also showed that they had undergone greater neurogenesis—the creation of new neurons, the process of which supports the speed and recovery of cognitive abilities. (④) Based on their results, the researchers hypothesized that IF could be an effective means of improving long-term memory and brain function in humans.

해석

그 3개월간의 실험을 통해, 전자 집단의 쥐들은 훨씬 더 좋은 장기 기억력을 가진 것으로 밝혀졌다.

간헐적 단식이 체중을 감량하고 수명을 늘리는 방법으로써 지지받고 있긴 하지만, 그것에는 또 다른 덜 알려진 이점이 있는데, 바로 기억 유지력을 향상시키는 것이다. 킹스 칼리지 런던의 연구원들은 세 집단의 실험실 쥐에 관한 실험을 했다. ① 한 집단은 간헐적 단식을 받은 반면, 다른 두 집단은 일반 식단 및 칼로리 제한 식단을 받았다. ② 칼로리 제한 식단을 받은 쥐들도 향상을 보였지만, 결과가 그만큼 인상적이지는 않았다. ③ 간헐적 단식을 한 쥐들의 뇌 정밀 검사 사진은 그것들이 더 큰 신경 조직 발생, 즉 새로운 신경 세포의 생성을 경험했다는 것을 보여 주었는데, 이 과정은 인지 능력의 속도와 회복을 지원한다. ④ 그들의 결과에 근거하여, 연구원들은 간헐적 단식이 인간의 장기 기억력과 뇌 기능을 향상시키는 효과적인 방법이 될 수 있다는 가설을 세웠다.

해설

②번 앞부분에서 간헐적 단식이 기억 유지력을 향상시키는지를 확인하는 실험에서 한 집단의 쥐는 간헐적 단식을 받은 반면 다른 두 집단은 일반 식단 및 칼로리 제한 식단을 받았다고 하고, 뒤 문장에서 칼로리 제한 식단을 받은 쥐들도 향상을 보였지만 결과가 그만큼 인상적이지는 않았다(not as impressive)는 내용이 있으므로, ②번 자리에 그 3개월간의 실험을 통해 전자 집단(the former group)의 쥐들이 훨씬 더 좋은 장기 기억력을 가진 것으로 밝혀졌다는 내용, 즉 세 집단의 실험 대상 중 간헐적 단식을 한 집단이 보인 차별적인 실험 결과를 언급하는 주어진 문장이 나와야 지문이 자연스럽게 연결된다.

정답 ②

DAY 17 하프모의고사 17회

어휘
reveal 밝히다   long-term 장기적인   intermittent fasting 간헐적 단식
advocate 지지하다, 옹호하다   longevity 수명, 장수
publicize 알리다, 홍보하다   retention 유지, 보유
be subjected to ~을 받다, 당하다   undergo 경험하다   neuron 신경 세포
cognitive 인지의   hypothesize 가설을 세우다, 제기하다

어휘
cognitive 인지의   bias 편향   name after ~의 이름을 따서 짓다
assembly 조립   fold 접다   expert 전문가   excessive 과도한
phenomenon 현상   fall apart 망가지다, 부서지다
boost 힘, 상승; 밀어올리다   skilled 숙련된   distinct 분명한, 별개의
valuable 귀중한   functional 실용적인, 기능적인

10 독해 빈칸 완성 – 단어   난이도 하 ●○○

밑줄 친 부분에 들어갈 말로 적절한 것은?

In 2011, a study introduced a cognitive bias called the "IKEA effect," named after the Swedish company that produces and sells furniture that sometimes requires assembly by the purchaser. In the study, participants who had folded their own origami figures considered their amateur work to be of equal quality and more _____ than origami made by experts. Researchers concluded that individuals would place excessive worth on a product that they helped to create through their own labor. But this phenomenon only occurred when the labor resulted in success. In other words, origami structures that fell apart did not receive the same perceived boost in worth.

*origami: 종이접기

① skilled   ② distinct
③ valuable   ④ functional

해석
2011년에, 한 연구는 '이케아 효과'로 불리는 인지 편향을 소개했는데, 이것은 때때로 구매자에 의한 조립을 요하는 가구를 생산하고 판매하는 스웨덴 회사의 이름을 따서 지어진 것이었다. 그 연구에서, 자신만의 종이접기 모형을 접었던 참가자들은 그들의 미숙한 작품이 전문가들에 의해 만들어진 종이접기와 품질이 동일하며, 더 귀중하다고 여겼다. 연구원들은 사람들이 자신의 노동을 통해 만드는 데 도움을 준 물건에 과도한 가치를 둔다는 결론을 내렸다. 그러나 이 현상은 그 노동이 성공이라는 결과를 낳을 때만 일어났다. 다시 말해서, 망가진 종이접기 조립품은 가치에 있어서 동일한 인지적 힘을 얻지 못했다.

① 숙련된   ② 분명한
③ 귀중한   ④ 실용적인

해설
빈칸 뒤 문장에 사람들은 자신의 노동을 통해 직접 만든 물건에 과도한 가치를 둔다는 내용이 있으므로, 자신만의 종이접기 모형을 접었던 참가자들이 그들의 미숙한 작품이 전문가들의 작품보다 더 '귀중하'다고 여겼다고 한 ③번이 정답이다.

정답 ③

DAY 18 하프모의고사 18회

정답 p. 82

01	④	어휘	06	④	독해
02	④	문법	07	③	독해
03	③	문법	08	③	독해
04	④	생활영어	09	④	독해
05	③	독해	10	②	독해

취약영역 분석표

영역	맞힌 답의 개수
어휘	/1
생활영어	/1
문법	/2
독해	/6
TOTAL	/10

---

01 어휘 bored 난이도 중 ●●○

밑줄 친 부분에 들어갈 말로 적절한 것은?

Tasks are repeated hour after hour for days, with little variation or rest, leaving assembly line workers at the factory feeling _____.

① patient ② jealous
③ ashamed ④ bored

해석
작업들은 변화나 휴식이 거의 없이 수일 동안 매시간 반복되는데, 이는 그 공장에서 일하는 조립 라인 근로자들이 지루함을 느끼게 한다.
① 인내심 있는 ② 질투하는
③ 부끄러운 ④ 지루한

정답 ④

어휘
repetitively 반복적으로 variation 변화 assembly 조립
patient 인내심 있는 jealous 질투하는 ashamed 부끄러운
bored 지루한, 따분한

해석
최근 설문조사는 대부분의 소비자들이 환경 비용이 더 높은 저렴한 대안제를 선택하기보다 환경 친화적인 제품을 사용하기를 선호한다는 것을 밝혔다.

해설
(A) what vs. that 완전한 절(most consumers ~ costs)을 이끌면서 동사 revealed의 목적어 자리에 올 수 있는 것은 명사절 접속사 that이므로, 불완전한 절을 이끄는 명사절 접속사 what이 아닌 that이 들어가야 적절하다.
(B) 병치 구문 than 대신 to를 쓰는 비교 표현 prefer A to B(B보다 A를 선호하다)에서 비교 대상은 같은 구조끼리 연결되어야 하는데, to 앞에 동명사 using이 왔으므로 to 뒤에 동사원형 choose가 아니라 동명사 choosing이 들어가야 적절하다. 참고로, 'prefer + 동명사 + to + 동명사'는 'prefer + to 부정사 + rather than + to 부정사'의 형태로 바꾸어 표현할 수도 있다.
따라서 ④ (A) that - (B) choosing이 정답이다.

정답 ④

어휘
reveal 밝히다, 폭로하다 alternative 대안; 대체의

---

02 문법 명사절|병치 구문 난이도 중 ●●○

다음 (A), (B) 중, 어법상 옳은 것끼리 고른 것은?

A recent survey revealed (A) (what / that) most consumers prefer using environmentally friendly products to (B) (choose / choosing) cheaper alternatives with higher environmental costs.

　(A)　　(B)　　　　(A)　　(B)
① what　choose　② what　choosing
③ that　choose　④ that　choosing

---

03 문법 동사의 종류|시제|전치사|to 부정사 난이도 중 ●●○

밑줄 친 부분 중 어법상 옳지 않은 것은?

The Isle of Man ① is enjoying the benefits of Internet connectedness as it continues to see infrastructure development advance year by year. ② For several years, the number of people using the Internet to obtain official documents has been ③ raising. Government officials are now looking for ways ④ to offer more services online.

DAY 18 / 하프모의고사 18회　93

DAY 18 하프모의고사 18회

해석
Man섬은 기반 시설 개발이 해마다 진척되는 것을 계속해서 지켜보면서 인터넷 연결의 혜택을 누리고 있다. 수년 동안, 공식 문서를 받기 위해 인터넷을 사용하는 사람들의 수가 증가해 오고 있는 것이다. 정부 관료들은 이제 온라인으로 더 많은 서비스를 제공할 방법들을 찾고 있다.

해설
③ **혼동하기 쉬운 자동사와 타동사** 문맥상 '인터넷을 사용하는 사람들의 수가 증가해 오고 있다'라는 의미가 되어야 자연스러우므로 타동사 raise(증가시키다)의 분사형 raising을 자동사 rise(증가하다)의 분사형 rising으로 고쳐야 한다.

[오답 분석]
① **현재진행 시제** 문맥상 '혜택을 누리고 있다'라는 의미가 되어야 자연스러우므로 현재진행 시제 is enjoying이 올바르게 쓰였다.
② **전치사** 문맥상 '수년 동안'이라는 의미가 되어야 자연스러우므로, '얼마나 오래 지속되는가'를 나타내는 전치사 for(~동안)가 올바르게 쓰였다.
④ **to 부정사를 취하는 명사** 명사 way는 to 부정사를 취하므로 ways 뒤에 to 부정사 to offer가 올바르게 쓰였다.

정답 ③

어휘
connectedness 연결(성) infrastructure 기반 시설
document 문서, 기록; 기록하다

---

04 생활영어 In what way is their exchange policy strict?
난이도 중 ●●○

밑줄 친 부분에 들어갈 말로 적절한 것은?

A: It looks like there's a tear in the suit you just bought.
B: Then I'll have to take it back and exchange it for one in good condition.
A: The store has a really rigid exchange policy.
B: _____
A: They don't allow exchanges for simply changing your mind, and the packaging can't be damaged.
B: I see. I'd better check their policy before going.

① Do I need to present my receipt for the exchange?
② Have you ever exchanged anything at that store?
③ What if the suit was damaged before I purchased it?
④ In what way is their exchange policy strict?

해석
A: 네가 방금 산 정장에 찢어진 부분이 있는 것 같아.
B: 그럼 그걸 다시 가져가서 상태가 좋은 것으로 교환해야겠어.
A: 그 가게는 아주 엄격한 교환 방침을 가지고 있어.
B: 어떤 점에서 그들의 교환 방침이 엄격한데?
A: 그들은 단순한 변심으로 인한 교환을 허용하지 않고, 포장도 훼손되면 안 돼.
B: 그렇구나. 가기 전에 그들의 방침을 확인하는 게 좋겠어.

① 교환을 위해 영수증을 제시해야 하니?
② 그 가게에서 뭐라도 교환해 본 적 있어?
③ 내가 구매하기 전에 그 정장이 훼손되어 있었던 거면 어쩌지?
④ 어떤 점에서 그들의 교환 방침이 엄격한데?

해설
B가 찢어져 있는 새 옷을 가져가서 교환하겠다고 하자 A가 그 가게에는 엄격한 교환 방침이 있다고 하고, 빈칸 뒤에서 다시 A가 They don't allow exchanges for simply changing your mind, and the packaging can't be damaged(그들은 단순한 변심으로 인한 교환을 허용하지 않고, 포장도 훼손되면 안 돼)라고 말하고 있으므로, '어떤 점에서 그들의 교환 방침이 엄격한데?'라는 의미의 ④ 'In what way is their exchange policy strict?'가 정답이다.

정답 ④

어휘
tear 찢어진 부분; 찢다 exchange 교환하다; 교환 rigid 엄격한
strict 엄격한

05~06 다음 글을 읽고 물음에 답하시오.

National Security Service
The National Security Service (NSS) is dedicated to ensuring secure and effective foreign diplomacy by protecting the nation's assets worldwide. To fulfill this mission, the NSS is one of the largest security agencies in the government, with over 100 locations across the country.

Protecting People and Property
NSS agents provide 24/7 protection for the minister during their travels and official visits. They also collaborate with personal protection teams to safeguard visiting important foreign officials, including heads of state, members of royal families, and foreign ministers.

Present at over 100 government buildings throughout the country, NSS personnel are responsible for maintaining security. Selected locations feature trained police dogs that patrol government buildings and other sites of national importance. On the digital front, NSS engineers design and manage advanced security systems that protect these facilities from unauthorized access and cyberattacks.

해석

국가외교보안국
국가외교보안국(NSS)은 전 세계적으로 국가의 자산을 보호함으로써 안전하고 효과적인 해외 외교 활동을 보장하기 위해 헌신합니다. 이러한 임무를 수행하기 위해, 국가외교보안국은 전국 각지에 100개

이상의 현장을 갖춘, 정부 내 가장 큰 보안 기관 중 하나입니다.

인력 및 재산 보호

국가외교보안국 요원들은 장관의 출장과 공식 방문 동안 24시간 보호를 제공합니다. 그들은 또한 국가 원수, 왕족 구성원, 외무장관을 포함하여, 방문하는 중요 외국 관리들을 보호하기 위해 개인 보호팀과 협력합니다.

전국 100개 이상의 정부 건물에 주재하면서, 국가외교보안국의 직원들은 보안 유지를 담당하고 있습니다. 선별된 장소들은 정부 건물과 국가적으로 중요한 다른 시설들을 순찰하는 훈련된 경찰견들을 포함합니다. 디지털 측면에서는, 국가외교보안국 엔지니어들이 이러한 시설들을 무단 접근과 사이버 공격으로부터 보호하는 첨단 보안 시스템을 설계하고 관리합니다.

[어휘]

dedicate 헌신하다 effective 효과적인 diplomacy 외교 asset 자산
fulfill 수행하다, 이행하다 property 재산 minister 장관
collaborate 협력하다 safeguard 보호하다 personnel 직원, 인력
feature (특별히) 포함하다, 특징으로 하다; 특징 patrol 순찰하다
unauthorized 무단의, 허가되지 않은 cyberattack 사이버 공격

05 독해 요지 파악 난이도 중 ●●○

윗글의 요지로 적절한 것은?

① NSS emphasizes a technology-based approach to security.
② NSS is committed to deploying police dogs.
③ NSS promotes diplomacy by providing comprehensive security.
④ NSS strives to become the most widespread security organization in the government sector.

[해석]
① 국가외교보안국은 보안에 대해 기술 기반 접근법을 강조한다.
② 국가외교보안국은 경찰견들을 배치하는 데 전념한다.
③ 국가외교보안국은 포괄적인 보안을 제공함으로써 외교를 촉진한다.
④ 국가외교보안국은 정부 부문에서 가장 광범위한 보안 기관이 되기 위해 노력한다.

[해설]
지문 전반에 걸쳐 국가외교보안국은 국가의 자산을 보호함으로써 안전하고 효과적인 외교 활동을 보장한다고 하고, 해외 활동을 하는 장관과 국가를 방문하는 고위 인사들을 보호할 뿐만 아니라, 물리적·디지털적 측면에서 정부 건물의 보안을 유지한다고 했으므로, ③ '국가외교보안국은 포괄적인 보안을 제공함으로써 외교를 촉진한다'가 이 글의 요지이다.

정답 ③

[어휘]
emphasize 강조하다 deploy 배치하다 promote 촉진하다, 홍보하다
comprehensive 포괄적인 strive 노력하다 widespread 광범위한

06 독해 유의어 파악 난이도 중 ●●○

밑줄 친 feature의 의미와 가장 가까운 것은?

① exclude ② leave
③ pick ④ contain

[해석]
① 제외시키다 ② 남겨 두다
③ 고르다 ④ 포함하다

[해설]
밑줄 친 부분이 포함된 문장에서 feature는 문맥상 선별된 장소들은 훈련된 경찰견들을 '포함한다'는 의미로 쓰였으므로, '포함하다'라는 의미의 ④ contain이 정답이다.

정답 ④

[어휘]
exclude 제외시키다 leave 남겨 두다, 떠나다 pick 고르다, 선택하다
contain 포함하다

07 독해 내용 불일치 파악 난이도 중 ●●○

National Institute of Origin에 관한 다음 글의 내용과 일치하지 않는 것은?

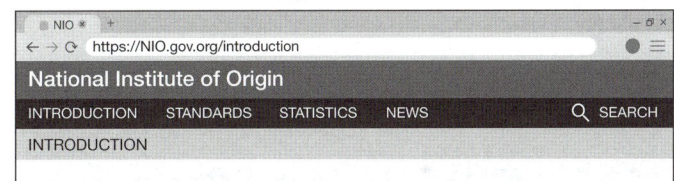

National Institute of Origin (NIO) Responsibilities

The NIO is a French regulatory body charged with ensuring wine, dairy products, and other agricultural goods are produced in specific regions using traditional methods. Only products that receive NIO approval can use regional names and designations of authenticity. This protects local farmers and artisans, as well as product reputations, from imitations produced elsewhere. It also protects consumers, as soil in other regions or different production methods can negatively affect the flavors of the finished products they buy. The institute files notices with appropriate authorities and may offer support for legal enforcement of regulations when products are marketed using region-specific names without certification.

① 전통적인 생산 방법이 사용될 것을 보장한다.
② 제품에 지역 이름이 쓰일 수 있는지를 결정한다.
③ 소비자들로부터 지역 농부와 장인들을 보호한다.
④ 관련 규정의 집행에 관여할 수 있다.

DAY 18 하프모의고사 18회

해석

국립원산지연구소(NIO)의 책무

국립원산지연구소는 와인, 유제품 및 기타 농산물이 전통적인 방법을 사용하여 특정 지역에서 생산되는 것을 보장하는 책임을 맡은 프랑스의 규제 기관입니다. 국립원산지연구소의 승인을 받은 제품들만이 지역 이름과 진품이라는 명칭을 사용할 수 있습니다. 이는 지역 농부들과 장인들, 뿐만 아니라 다른 곳에서 생산된 모조품들로부터 제품의 명성을 보호합니다. 그것은 또한 소비자들도 보호하는데, 다른 지역의 토양이나 다른 생산 방법이 소비자들이 구매하는 완제품의 풍미에 부정적으로 영향을 미칠 수 있기 때문입니다. 연구소가 적절한 당국에 통지서를 제출하며 인증 없이 해당 지역의 특정 이름을 사용하여 제품이 거래될 때 규정의 법적 집행을 위한 지원을 제공할 수 있습니다.

해설

③번의 키워드인 '소비자들'이 그대로 언급된 지문의 consumers 주변의 내용에서 국립원산지연구소는 소비자들에게 부정적인 영향을 미칠 수 있는 완제품으로부터 소비자들을 보호한다고 했으므로, ③ '소비자들로부터 지역 농부와 장인들을 보호한다'는 것은 지문의 내용과 다르다.

정답 ③

어휘

origin 원산지 **responsibility** 책무, 책임 **regulatory** 규제의
be charged with ~할 책임을 맡다 **dairy** 유제품 **agricultural** 농업의
approval 승인 **designation** 명칭, 지명 **authenticity** 진품, 진실성
artisan 장인 **reputation** 명성 **imitation** 모조품, 모방 **flavor** 풍미
institute 연구소, 협회 **file** 제출하다, 제기하다, 보관하다 **appropriate** 적절한
authorities 당국 **enforcement** 집행 **market** 거래하다; 시장
certification 인증

해석

유럽의 추상 미술의 정확한 시작을 찾아내는 것은 어렵다. 그 미술 자체는 자유로운 표현을 장려하는 예술적 환경에서 발전해 온 것으로 보인다. 이렇게 하여, 관람객들은 익숙하고 잘 배열된 그림으로 나타낸 주제보다는 역동적이고 힘 있는 방식으로 그려진 선, 색 그리고 형태를 보기 시작했는데, 이것들은 추상 미술의 잘 알려진 특성들이다. 그것은 또한 활용된 양식들의 큰 다양성으로 인정받는데, 이것이 어떤 한 가지 양식도 그 예술 운동과 연관지을 수 없는 이유이다. 주목할 만한 점은, 양식에 상관없이 초기의 미술품들이 현재 우리가 추상 표현주의라고 부르는 것, 즉 실재하는 것은 그 무엇도 표현하지 않는 미술의 특징들을 지녔다는 것이다.

① 유럽 풍경화에서 선과 색을 통한 역동적 표현
② 유럽 박물관에서의 추상 미술 전시에 대한 대중의 반응
③ 추상 미술의 역사적 배경과 특징
④ 유럽 갤러리의 추상 미술 전시 전략

해설

지문 앞부분에서 유럽 추상 미술은 자유로운 표현을 강조하는 환경에서 발전해 온 것으로 보이며, 역동적인 선, 색, 형태와 함께 활용된 양식의 큰 다양성으로 인정받는다고 설명하고 있다. 따라서 ③ '추상 미술의 역사적 배경과 특징'이 이 글의 주제이다.

정답 ③

어휘

pinpoint 정확히 찾아내다 **abstract art** 추상 미술 **evolve** 발전하다, 진화하다
landscape 환경, 풍경(화) **spectator** 관객, 관중 **dynamic** 역동적인
pictorial 그림으로 나타낸, 회화의 **attribute** 특성; (결과를) ~에 돌리다
associate 연관짓다 **reception** 반응, 접수 **exhibition** 전시(회)

---

08 독해 주제 파악 난이도 중

다음 글의 주제로 적절한 것은?

It is difficult to pinpoint the exact beginnings of abstract art in Europe. The art itself seems to have evolved from an artistic landscape that encouraged free expression. Thus, spectators began seeing lines, colors, and shapes painted in a dynamic and forceful manner rather than the familiar well-arranged pictorial subject, attributes that abstract art became well known for. It is also recognized for the great variety of styles utilized, which is the reason no single style can be associated with the movement. Notably, regardless of style, the early artworks had the characteristics of what we now call abstract expressionism—art that does not represent anything that is real.

① Dynamic expression through lines and colors in European landscapes
② Public reception of abstract art exhibitions across European museums
③ The historical context and features of abstract art
④ Exhibition strategies for abstract art in European galleries

---

09 독해 문단 순서 배열 난이도 하

주어진 글 다음에 이어질 글의 순서로 적절한 것은?

There was once a busy couple who worked hard so that they could prepare for their son's future. Their only child was a curious boy who kept asking his parents about everything in life.

(A) He hardly talked to them, however, and it was then that the parents regretted not giving their son time when he wanted to talk.
(B) He grew indifferent to his parents, preferring to study or relax alone, or spend time with his friends. But his parents were aging, and they longed to know more about what their son was doing and what his thoughts were.
(C) Despite his flourishing curiosity, his mother and father were so tired in the evenings and weekends that they just wanted to rest or do some activity with minimal conversation. As he got older, he began seeking his own identity.

① (B) – (A) – (C) ② (B) – (C) – (A)
③ (C) – (A) – (B) ④ (C) – (B) – (A)

18회 정답·해석·해설 해커스공무원 비비안 영어 매일 하프모의고사

해석

> 옛날에 아들의 미래를 대비할 수 있도록 열심히 일하는 바쁜 부부가 있었다. 그들의 외동아들은 부모에게 인생의 모든 것에 대해 계속 질문하던 호기심 많은 소년이었다.

(A) 하지만, 그는 부모와 거의 이야기하지 않았고, 부모가 아들이 이야기하기를 원할 때 그에게 시간을 내주지 않았던 것을 후회한 것은 바로 그때였다.

(B) 그는 부모에게 무관심해져서, 혼자 공부하거나 휴식을 취하거나 또는 친구들과 시간을 보내는 것을 선호하게 되었다. 그러나 그의 부모는 나이가 들어 갔고, 그들은 아들이 무엇을 하고 있는지 그리고 그의 생각이 무엇인지에 대해 더 알기를 간절히 바랐다.

(C) 그의 자라나는 호기심에도 불구하고, 그의 엄마와 아빠는 저녁과 주말에 너무 지쳐서 그저 쉬거나 최소한의 대화를 하는 약간의 활동만 하기를 원했다. 나이가 들어가면서, 그는 자신만의 정체성을 찾기 시작했다.

해설

주어진 문장에서 한 바쁜 부부의 외동아들은 호기심 많은 소년이었다고 소개한 뒤, (C)에서 그의 자라나는 호기심(his flourishing curiosity)에도 불구하고 부모는 일상에 지쳐 아들과 약간의 활동만 하기를 원했는데, 나이가 듦에 따라 소년은 차츰 자신만의 정체성을 찾기 시작했다고 설명하고 있다. 이어서 (B)에서 그가 부모에게 무관심해진 반면 부모는 아들에 대해 더 알기를 바랐다고 하고, (A)에서 하지만(however) 아들은 부모와 거의 이야기하지 않았고 그제서야 부모는 그에게 대화 시간을 내주지 않은 것을 후회했다고 이야기하고 있다. 따라서 ④ (C) – (B) – (A)가 정답이다.

정답 ④

어휘

curious 호기심 많은, 궁금한 indifferent 무관심한
long to ~하기를 간절히 바라다 flourish 자라다, 번창하다
minimal 최소한의 identity 정체성, 신원

---

10 독해 빈칸 완성 – 구   난이도 중 ●●○

밑줄 친 부분에 들어갈 말로 적절한 것은?

> Studies show that people's cognitive decline after turning 20 is greater than the growth that occurs prior to that point. Intellectual growth during a person's developmental years is often swifter, more positive, and more dramatic than growth that takes place during adulthood. Other studies confirm that tasks that require the recall of information become more complex in adulthood, particularly when people's names and contextual details are involved. In addition, the slowing down of information processing due to deteriorating vision and hearing is evident in later adulthood. While such intense handicaps may seem overwhelming, people develop other methods of approaching problems and numerous coping mechanisms throughout adulthood to _____.

① accelerate cognitive development
② make up for these deficits
③ restore previous physical capacities
④ complicate memory recall processing

해석

연구들은 20살이 된 후 사람들의 인지 저하가 그 시점에 앞서 일어난 발달보다 더 크다는 것을 보여 준다. 사람의 성장기 동안의 지능 발달은 종종 성인기 동안에 일어나는 성장보다 더 빠르고, 더 긍정적이며, 더 극적이다. 다른 연구들은 정보의 회상을 필요로 하는 일이 성인기에 더 복잡해진다는 것을 확인하는데, 이는 특히 사람들의 이름과 문맥상의 세부 사항들이 포함될 때 그렇다. 게다가, 성인기 후반에 악화되는 시력과 청력으로 인해 정보 처리가 느려지는 것이 명백하다. 이러한 극심하게 불리한 조건들이 저항할 수 없는 것처럼 보일지도 모르지만, 사람들은 성인기 내내 이러한 결함들을 보완하기 위해 문제에 접근할 다른 방법들과 다양한 대처 기제들을 발달시킨다.

① 인지 발달을 가속화하다
② 이러한 결함들을 보완하다
③ 이전의 신체적 능력들을 회복하다
④ 기억 회상 처리 과정을 복잡하게 하다

해설

빈칸 앞부분에 성인기가 되면 정보의 회상을 필요로 하는 일이 더 복잡해지는 동시에 감퇴하는 시력과 청력으로 인해 정보 처리가 느려진다는 내용이 있고, 빈칸이 있는 문장에 사람들은 성인기 내내 문제에 접근할 다른 방법들과 다양한 대체 기제들을 발달시킨다는 내용이 있으므로, '이러한 결함들을 보완하기' 위해서라고 한 ②번이 정답이다.

정답 ②

어휘

cognitive 인지의 intellectual 지능의, 지적인
developmental year 성장기 adulthood 성인기, 성년
confirm 확인하다, 사실임을 보여 주다 recall 회상, 기억력; 기억해내다
contextual 문맥상의 deteriorate 악화되다 evident 명백한
intense 극심한 overwhelming 저항할 수 없는, 압도적인 cope 대처하다
make up for ~을 보완하다, 만회하다 deficit 결함, 적자
restore 회복하다, 복원하다

DAY 19 하프모의고사 19회

정답   p. 86

01	④	어휘	06	①	독해
02	③	문법	07	③	독해
03	④	문법	08	③	독해
04	②	생활영어	09	③	독해
05	③	독해	10	③	독해

취약영역 분석표

영역	맞힌 답의 개수
어휘	/1
생활영어	/1
문법	/2
독해	/6
TOTAL	/10

01 어휘 exaggerate   난이도 중 ●●○

밑줄 친 부분에 들어갈 말로 적절한 것은?

If someone _____ an action or event, it could be impressive in style, often to the point of seeming pretentious.

① observes
② approves
③ resolves
④ exaggerates

해석

누군가가 어떤 행동이나 사건을 과장한다면, 그것은 종종 허세 부리는 것처럼 보인다고 할 정도로 표현의 측면에서 인상적일 수 있다.

① 관찰한다
② 승인한다
③ 해결한다
④ 과장한다

정답 ④

어휘

impressive 인상적인   to the point of ~라고 할 정도로
pretentious 허세 부리는, 건방진, 가식적인   observe 관찰하다
approve 승인하다, 찬성하다   resolve 해결하다   exaggerate 과장하다

02 문법 분사   난이도 중 ●●○

밑줄 친 부분에 들어갈 말로 적절한 것은?

The students took detailed notes _____ to the professor's lecture on ancient history.

① listen
② listened
③ while listening
④ with listened

해석

학생들은 고대사에 대한 교수의 강의를 듣는 동안에 자세한 필기를 했다.

해설

③ 분사구문의 형태 빈칸은 주어(The students)와 동사(took)를 모두 갖춘 완전한 절 다음에 와서 부사절 역할을 하는 것의 자리이므로, 동사 형태의 ① listen은 정답이 될 수 없다. 또한 전치사 뒤에는 명사 역할을 하는 것이 와야 하므로 ④ with listened도 정답이 될 수 없고, 분사구문 형태의 ② listened와 ③ while listening이 정답 후보이다. 이때 주절의 주어 The students와 분사구문이 '학생들이 듣다'라는 의미의 능동 관계이므로 현재분사가 쓰인 ③ while listening이 정답이다. 참고로, 분사구문의 의미를 분명하게 하기 위해 부사절 접속사 while이 분사구문 앞에 쓰였다.

정답 ③

03 문법 수동태 | 상관접속사 | to 부정사 | 관계절   난이도 중 ●●○

밑줄 친 부분 중 어법상 옳지 않은 것은?

Responsibility for a crime usually requires not only a guilty mind, ① but also a guilty act. ② To be considered a guilty act, the act needs to take place voluntarily. Unintentional actions would not qualify as guilty acts. Situations ③ in which the actor is unaware of his behavior are also deemed involuntary. On the other hand, the voluntary aspect of a guilty act includes deliberate inaction. Crimes or injuries that ④ are resulted from intentional inaction can constitute guilty conduct.

해석

범죄의 책임은 보통 유죄 의식뿐만 아니라, 유죄인 행위도 필요로 한다. 유죄인 행위로 간주되기 위해, 그 행위는 자발적으로 일어나야 한다. 의도하지 않은 행동은 유죄 행위의 자격을 얻지 못할 것이다. 행위자가 자신의 행동을 의식하지 못하는 상황 또한 비자발적인 것으로 간주된다. 한편, 유죄인 행위의 자발적인 측면은 의도적으로 행동하지 않음을 포함한다. 의도적으로 행동하지 않은 결과로 발생하는 범죄나 부상은 유죄 행동이 되는 것으로 여겨질 수 있다.

19회 정답·해석·해설
해커스공무원 비비안 영어 매일 하프모의고사

해설

④ **수동태로 쓸 수 없는 동사** 동사 result(결과로 발생하다)는 목적어를 취하지 않는 자동사이기 때문에 수동태로 쓸 수 없으므로, are resulted를 능동태 result로 고쳐야 한다.

[오답 분석]
① **상관접속사** 문맥상 '유죄 의식뿐만 아니라 유죄인 행위도'라는 의미가 되어야 자연스러운데, 'A뿐만 아니라 B도'는 상관접속사 not only A but also B를 사용하여 나타낼 수 있다. 따라서 not only와 짝을 이루는 but also가 올바르게 쓰였다.
② **to 부정사의 역할 | to 부정사의 형태** 문맥상 '유죄인 행위로 간주되기 위해'라는 의미가 되어야 자연스러우므로, 부사 역할을 하는 to 부정사가 와야 한다. 이때 to 부정사가 가리키는 명사(the act)와 to 부정사가 '행위가 간주되다'라는 의미의 수동 관계이므로, to 부정사의 수동형 To be considered가 올바르게 쓰였다.
③ **전치사 + 관계대명사** 관계사 뒤에 완전한 절(the actor ~ behavior)이 왔으므로 '전치사 + 관계대명사'가 올 수 있다. 이때 '전치사 + 관계대명사'에서 전치사는 선행사(Situations) 또는 관계절의 동사에 따라 결정되는데, 문맥상 '상황에서'라는 의미가 되어야 자연스러우므로 전치사 in(~에서)이 관계대명사 which 앞에 온 in which가 올바르게 쓰였다.

정답 ④

어휘
guilty 유죄의, 죄책감이 드는 voluntarily 자발적으로
unintentional 의도하지 않은 deliberate 의도적인
constitute ~이 되는 것으로 여겨지다, 구성하다 conduct 행동, 지도, 경영

---

04 생활영어 Do we need to order any additional supplies?
난이도 하 ●○○

밑줄 친 부분에 들어갈 말로 적절한 것은?

Harper White
I think it's time to buy printer paper and toner.
10:18

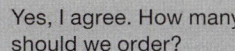
Morgan Russell
Yes, I agree. How many should we order?
10:19

Harper White
2 toners and 5 packs of printer paper would be fine. We have to order them this week.
10:19

Morgan Russell
I see. I will place an order this afternoon. _____
10:20

Harper White
I noticed that we're running out of paper cups. Maybe we should order those too.
10:21

Morgan Russell
We won't be buying paper cups anymore because they create a lot of waste.
10:22

① Could you check when our last order was placed?
② Do we need to order any additional supplies?
③ Should we order from the supplier we used before?
④ Do you know how much of our budget is left?

해석

Harper White: 프린터 용지와 토너를 살 때가 된 것 같아요.
Morgan Russell: 네, 동의합니다. 몇 개를 주문해야 할까요?
Harper White: 토너 2개와 프린터 용지 5팩이면 되겠어요. 우리는 그것들을 이번 주에 주문해야 합니다.
Morgan Russell: 알겠습니다. 제가 오늘 오후에 주문할게요. 추가로 주문해야 하는 비품이 있을까요?
Harper White: 종이컵을 다 써 가는 걸 알아요. 아마 그것들도 주문해야 할 겁니다.
Morgan Russell: 저희는 종이컵이 많은 쓰레기를 배출하기 때문에 더 이상 구매하지 않으려고 해요.

① 마지막 주문이 언제 들어갔는지 확인해 주실 수 있나요?
② 추가로 주문해야 하는 비품이 있을까요?
③ 우리가 이전에 이용했던 공급 업체에 주문해야 하나요?
④ 우리 예산 중에 얼마가 남아 있는지 아시나요?

해설
Morgan이 토너와 프린터 용지를 오후에 주문하겠다고 하고, 빈칸 뒤에서 Harper가 I noticed that we're running out of paper cups. Maybe we should order those too(종이컵을 다 써 가는 걸 알아요. 아마 그것들도 주문해야 할 겁니다)라고 말하고 있으므로, '추가로 주문해야 하는 비품이 있을까요?'라는 의미의 ② 'Do we need to order any additional supplies?'가 정답이다.

정답 ②

어휘
place an order 주문하다 run out of ~을 다 써버리다
supply 비품, 공급 업체 budget 예산

05~06 다음 글을 읽고 물음에 답하시오.

To	Highway Safety Bureau
From	Sadie Bates
Date	November 12
Subject	Road conditions

Dear Sir or Madam,

Today, I am writing to you about a growing problem that

I have noticed on public highways over the last year. I am referring to the increase in the number and size of potholes, which have become a driving hazard.

Since I work in sales, I must often commute to meet clients in other cities using the highway system. Recently, these trips have been affected by the condition of the roadways. As drivers have to slow down to avoid the potholes, traffic jams form. In addition, I have seen many cars sustain damage or get into accidents after hitting a broken part of the road.

The conditions of the roadways are dangerous and _____. I implore you to repair the roadways so that everyone can travel safely once again.

Respectfully,

Sadie Bates

05 윗글의 목적으로 적절한 것은?

① 도로 위 움푹 패인 곳의 잦은 발생 원인을 문의하려고
② 출퇴근 시간에 혼잡한 고속도로 상황을 공유하려고
③ 안전하지 않은 공공 시설물에 대한 복구를 요청하려고
④ 고속도로에 교통량이 증가한 이유를 설명하려고

06 윗글의 밑줄 친 부분에 들어갈 말로 적절한 것은?

① unacceptable
② narrow
③ sensitive
④ empty

07 Future City Engineering Competition에 관한 다음 글의 내용과 일치하는 것은?

Team Registration Deadline: August 30

- **Registration Fee**: $25.00 (per team)
- **Competition Date**: 11:00 a.m., November 15

Teams must consist of at least three students of middle school age. There is no maximum limit on team size.

Final projects, which include an essay, a model of the future city, and a presentation, will be judged by a panel of engineers.

Please note: Registration must be completed by a team coach on the competition portal. Spots are limited, so we recommend registering as soon as possible.

① Each student must pay $25 to register.
② Teams can have no more than three members.
③ The competition will be evaluated by engineering experts.
④ A representative student must complete the registration online.

[해석]

미래 도시 설계 경진 대회 (FCEC)

팀 등록 마감 기한: 8월 30일

-등록비: 25달러 (팀당)
-경진 대회 날짜: 11월 15일, 오전 11시

팀은 중학생 연령의 학생 최소 3명으로 구성되어야 합니다. 팀 규모의 최대 (인원) 제한은 없습니다.

에세이, 미래 도시 모형 그리고 발표를 포함하는 최종 프로젝트가 공학자 심사원단에 의해 심사될 것입니다.

주의사항: 등록은 경진 대회 포털 사이트에서 팀 코치에 의해 완료되어야 합니다. 자리가 제한되어 있으므로, 가능한 한 빨리 등록하시기를 권장드립니다.

① 학생당 등록을 위해 25달러를 지불해야 한다.
② 팀은 3명을 초과할 수 없다.
③ 경진 대회는 공학 전문가들에 의해 평가될 것이다.
④ 대표 학생이 온라인 등록을 완료해야 한다.

[해설]

③번의 키워드인 engineering experts(공학 전문가들)를 바꾸어 표현한 지문의 a panel of engineers(공학자 심사원단) 주변의 내용에서 경진 대회의 최종 프로젝트는 공학자 심사원단에 의해 심사될 것이라고 했으므로, ③ '경진 대회는 공학 전문가들에 의해 평가될 것이다'는 지문의 내용과 일치한다.

[오답 분석]
① 경진 대회 등록비는 팀당 25달러라고 했으므로, 학생당 등록을 위해 25달러를 지불해야 한다는 것은 지문의 내용과 다르다.
② 팀은 최소 3명으로 구성되어야 하며 최대 인원 제한은 없다고 했으므로, 팀이 3명을 초과할 수 없다는 것은 지문의 내용과 다르다.
④ 등록은 관련 사이트에서 팀 코치에 의해 완료되어야 한다고 했으므로, 대표 학생이 온라인 등록을 완료해야 한다는 것은 지문의 내용과 다르다.

정답 ③

[어휘]

competition 경진 대회, 경쟁 registration 등록 presentation 발표, 제출 judge 심사하다 evaluate 평가하다 representative 대표; 대표하는

08 독해 문단 순서 배열   난이도 하 ●○○

주어진 글 다음에 이어질 글의 순서로 적절한 것은?

Although the Vietnamese soup pho is a laborious dish to prepare, it is so pleasing that you may not mind the burden of making it.

(A) Once all the items are prepared, put the soup together. The meat should be thinly sliced and arranged in bowls with the vegetables and noodles. Pour the hot stock over it, and garnish the dish with bean sprouts, lime wedges, and cilantro.

(B) The secret to a great pho is the stock. Start with high-quality beef bones and rinse them repeatedly to reduce the oil. The bones must then be cooked slowly for at least three hours.

(C) When the stock is cooked, it should be strained to remove fat and bits of bone, after which it can be flavored with fish sauce, salt, and sugar. Next, prepare the other ingredients. This includes boiling and cooling the noodles and slightly burning the onions and ginger.

① (A) – (C) – (B) ② (B) – (A) – (C)
③ (B) – (C) – (A) ④ (C) – (A) – (B)

[해석]

비록 베트남 수프인 쌀국수(포)는 준비하기 힘든 음식이지만, 그것은 매우 만족스러워서 당신은 그것을 만드는 부담을 마다하지 않을지도 모른다.

(A) 일단 모든 재료가 준비되면, 국물을 함께 넣어라. 고기는 얇게 썰려서 그릇에 채소와 국수와 함께 갖춰져야 한다. 그것 위에 뜨거운 국물을 붓고 숙주 나물, 라임 조각과 고수 잎으로 고명을 얹어라.

(B) 맛있는 쌀국수의 비결은 국물이다. 좋은 품질의 소 뼈와 함께 시작하고 기름을 제거하기 위해 그것들을 반복해서 씻어내라. 그 다음에 뼈는 적어도 세 시간 동안 천천히 요리되어야 한다.

(C) 그 국물이 조리될 때, 지방과 뼈 조각들을 제거하기 위해 그것은 체에 걸러져야 하고, 그 이후에 액젓, 소금 그리고 설탕으로 맛을 낼 수 있다. 다음으로, 다른 재료들을 준비하라. 이것은 국수를 끓여서 식히는 것과 양파와 생강을 불에 살짝 굽는 것을 포함한다.

[해설]

주어진 문장에서 베트남 쌀국수는 준비하기 힘든 음식이지만 매우 만족스러워서 만드는 부담을 마다하지 않을 음식이라고 한 후, (B)에서 맛있는 쌀국수를 위한 시작으로 좋은 소 뼈로 국물을 내는 법에 대해 알려 주고 있다. (C)에서 그 국물(the stock)을 체에 걸러 간을 맞춘 다음 다른 재료들을 준비하라고 말하고, (A)에서 모든 재료(all the items)가 준비되면

국물을 함께 넣고 고명을 곁들이는 마무리 단계를 설명하고 있다. 따라서 ③ (B) - (C) - (A)가 정답이다.

정답 ③

어휘

laborious 힘든, 인내를 요하는 pleasing 만족스러운 burden 부담, 짐
arrange 갖추다, 정돈하다 stock 국물, 재고품 garnish 고명을 얹다
rinse 씻어내다 strain (체에) 거르다, 잡아당기다; 긴장 flavor 맛을 내다
ingredient 재료 boil 끓이다

09 독해 문장 삽입   난이도 중 ●●○

주어진 문장이 들어갈 위치로 적절한 것은?

In pursuit of these goals, minimalists dispose of items or habits that do not provide value.

Voluntary simplicity, otherwise more commonly known as minimalism, has been linked to higher rates of happiness. (①) One reason for this is that partakers in a minimalist lifestyle, which is centered on limiting consumption and ownership, tend to take better care of their psychological needs. (②) Instead of focusing on acquiring material objects, they pay more attention to maintaining individual autonomy, overall awareness, and positive emotions. (③) As a result, they also get rid of many sources of stress in their lives, leaving them with excess energy to support their psychological well-being. (④) The immense mental and emotional benefits that come from removing unnecessary items and simplifying one's lifestyle make voluntary simplicity a powerful tool in the search for happiness.

해석

이러한 목표들을 추구하며, 미니멀리스트들은 가치를 제공하지 않는 물건이나 습관들을 버린다.

미니멀리즘으로 더 흔히 알려져 있는 자발적 단순함은 더 높은 수준의 행복감과 연관되어 왔다. ① 이것의 한 가지 이유는 소비와 소유를 제한하는 것에 집중하는 미니멀리스트 생활 양식의 참여자들이 그들의 심리적 욕구를 더 잘 돌보는 경향이 있기 때문이다. ② 물질적인 것들을 얻는 데 치중하는 대신, 그들은 개인의 자율성, 전반적인 의식 그리고 긍정적인 감정을 유지하는 데 더 많은 주의를 기울인다. ③ 결과적으로, 그들은 자신들의 삶에서 스트레스의 많은 원인을 제거하기도 하는데, 이는 그들에게 심리적 행복을 지속시킬 여분의 에너지를 남긴다. ④ 불필요한 물건들을 없애고 한 사람의 생활 양식을 간소화하는 것에서 오는 정신적이고 정서적으로 엄청난 이점들은 자발적 단순함을 행복을 찾는 강력한 수단으로 만든다.

해설

③번 앞 문장에 미니멀리스트들은 물질적인 것들 대신 개인의 자율성, 전반적 의식, 긍정적인 감정을 유지하는 데 많은 주의를 기울인다는 내용이 있고, 뒤 문장에 결과적으로(As a result) 그들은 삶에서 스트레스의 원인을 제거함으로써 심리적 행복을 지속시킬 에너지를 남긴다는 내용이 있으므로, ③번 자리에 이러한 목표들(these goals)을 추구하며 미니멀리스트들이 가치를 제공하지 않는 물건이나 습관들을 버린다는 내용, 즉 심리적 행복에 초점을 맞추는 미니멀리스트들이 스트레스의 원인을 제거하는 방법에 대해 설명하는 주어진 문장이 나와야 지문이 자연스럽게 연결된다.

정답 ③

어휘

in pursuit of ~을 추구하여 dispose of ~을 버리다, 처분하다
voluntary 자발적인 partaker 참여자, 관계자 consumption 소비
ownership 소유 psychological 심리적인 acquire 얻다
maintain 유지하다 autonomy 자율성 awareness 의식, 인식
get rid of ~을 제거하다 support 지속시키다, 돕다 immense 엄청난

10 독해 빈칸 완성 - 연결어   난이도 중 ●●○

밑줄 친 (A), (B)에 들어갈 말로 적절한 것은?

Even if humans were to stop using fossil fuels this very moment, the carbon dioxide already in the atmosphere would remain. This lingering carbon dioxide would cause temperatures to rise for centuries. _____(A)_____, scientists are looking for solutions to remove this gas from the atmosphere. Of course, plants and trees do this naturally. Unfortunately, while trees reliably absorb carbon dioxide and convert it to oxygen, they do so too slowly. As a result, a large number of trees would be needed to influence climate change in a meaningful way. Planting more trees requires lots of land, which may be unavailable or better used for growing crop-producing plants. A unique solution already being implemented is the planting of hyper-efficient fake trees. _____(B)_____, the leaves of these artificial trees can soak up one thousand times more carbon dioxide compared to real leaves that use photosynthesis. This increased efficiency would help rid the Earth of carbon dioxide emissions and keep more land available for other purposes.

	(A)	(B)
①	Thus	In contrast
②	For example	Recently
③	Consequently	In fact
④	In the same way	However

해석

인간이 화석 연료 사용을 당장 멈춘다고 할지라도, 이미 대기 중에 있는 이산화탄소는 남아 있을 것이다. 좀처럼 사라지지 않는 이 이산화탄소는 수 세기 동안 기온이 오르게 할 것이다. (A) 결과적으로, 과학자들은 이 가스를 대기에서 없애기 위한 해결책들을 찾고 있다. 물론, 식물과 나무는 자연히 이것을 한다. 안타깝게도, 나무는 이산화탄소를 확실하게 흡수하여 그것을 산소로 전환시키지만, 그것들은 너무 느리게 그렇게 한다. 그 결과, 의미 있는 방식으로 기후 변화에 영향을 주기 위해서는 많은 수의 나무들이 필요할 것이다. 더 많은 나무를 심는 것은 넓은 땅을 필요로 하는데, 이 땅은 이용할 수 없거나, 작물을 생산하는 식물 재배를 위해 더 잘 사용될지도 모른다. 이미 시행되고 있는 독특한 해결책은 고효율의 인공 나무를 심는 것이다. (B) 실제로, 이 인공 나무의 잎은 광합성을 이용하는 진짜 잎에 비해 이산화탄소를 1,000배 더 많이 빨아들일 수 있다. 이 높아진 효

율은 이산화탄소 배출물을 없애는 데 도움을 주고 더 많은 땅을 다른 목적을 위해 이용 가능하도록 유지할 것이다.

	(A)	(B)
①	그러므로	대조적으로
②	예를 들어	최근에
③	결과적으로	실제로
④	같은 방법으로	하지만

해설

(A) 빈칸 앞 문장은 대기 중에 있는 이산화탄소가 사라지지 않고 수세기 동안 기온이 오르게 할 것이라는 내용이고, 빈칸 뒤 문장은 과학자들은 이 가스를 대기에서 없애기 위한 해결책들을 찾고 있다는 결론적인 내용이다. 따라서 빈칸에는 결론을 나타내는 연결어인 Thus(그러므로) 또는 Consequently(결과적으로)가 들어가야 한다.

(B) 빈칸 앞 문장은 일부 도시에서 시행되고 있는 고효율의 인공 나무를 심는 방안에 대한 내용이고, 빈칸 뒤 문장은 이 인공 나무의 잎이 광합성을 이용하는 진짜 잎에 비해 이산화탄소를 1,000배 더 많이 빨아들일 수 있다고 강조하는 내용이다. 따라서 빈칸에는 강조를 나타내는 연결어인 In fact(실제로)가 들어가야 한다.

정답 ③

어휘

fossil fuel 화석 연료 **carbon dioxide** 이산화탄소 **atmosphere** 대기
linger 좀처럼 사라지지 않는, 남아 있는 **naturally** 자연히, 저절로
reliably 확실하게, 신뢰할 수 있게 **absorb** 흡수하다 **convert** 전환시키다
unavailable 이용할 수 없는, 손에 넣을 수 없는 **implement** 시행하다
fake 인공의, 가짜의 **artificial** 인공의 **soak up** ~을 빨아들이다, 흡수하다
photosynthesis 광합성 **efficiency** 효율 **rid of** ~을 없애다
emission 배출(물)

DAY 20 하프모의고사 20회

정답   p. 90

01	②	어휘	06	④	독해
02	②	문법	07	④	독해
03	①	문법	08	④	독해
04	③	생활영어	09	②	독해
05	③	독해	10	②	독해

취약영역 분석표

영역	맞힌 답의 개수
어휘	/1
생활영어	/1
문법	/2
독해	/6
TOTAL	/10

---

01 어휘 vital | accumulate   난이도 중 ●●○

밑줄 친 (A), (B)에 들어갈 말로 적절한 것은?

Journalists with know-how and experience are ___(A)___ to newspapers because practical skills ___(B)___ in the field enable them to quickly produce compelling stories under tight deadlines.

	(A)	(B)
①	challenging	admired
②	vital	accumulated
③	challenging	combined
④	vital	distorted

해석
노하우와 경험이 있는 기자들은 현장에서 (B) 축적된 실용적인 능력이 그들로 하여금 빠듯한 마감일 속에서도 설득력 있는 이야기들을 빠르게 제작할 수 있게 하기 때문에 신문사에 (A) 매우 중요하다.

	(A)	(B)
①	도전적인	존경받는
②	매우 중요한	축적된
③	도전적인	합쳐진
④	매우 중요한	왜곡된

정답 ②

어휘
practical 실용적인, 현실적인   field 현장, 들판
compelling 설득력 있는, 강제적인   challenging 도전적인, 힘든
admire 존경하다   vital 매우 중요한   accumulate 축적하다, 모으다
combine 합치다   distort 왜곡하다

---

02 문법 수동태 | to 부정사   난이도 중 ●●○

밑줄 친 부분에 들어갈 말로 적절한 것은?

The damaged vehicles are required _____ before insurance claims can proceed.

① to inspect
② to be inspected
③ inspecting
④ being inspected

해석
손상된 차량들은 보험 청구가 진행될 수 있기 전에 검사를 받도록 요구된다.

해설
② 5형식 동사의 수동태 | to 부정사의 형태 to 부정사를 목적격 보어로 취하는 5형식 동사(require)가 수동태가 되면 to 부정사는 수동태 동사(are required) 뒤에 그대로 남아야 하므로, to 부정사 형태의 ① to inspect와 ② to be inspected가 정답 후보이다. 이때 to 부정사가 가리키는 명사(The damaged vehicles)와 to 부정사가 '손상된 차량들이 검사받다'라는 의미의 수동 관계이므로 to 부정사의 수동형 ② to be inspected가 정답이다.

정답 ②

어휘
insurance 보험   claim 청구: 주장하다   inspect 검사하다

---

03 문법 도치 구문 | 수 일치 | to 부정사 | 명사절 | 부사절   난이도 중 ●●○

밑줄 친 부분 중 어법상 옳지 않은 것은?

From unexpected places ① comes the best ideas. That's why the city government is accepting proposals ② to improve the quality of urban life from all citizens. ③ Whoever submits a proposal will present their ideas before a committee that will review them in order to select the best ones, lest too many projects ④ overwhelm the limited funding.

해석
예기치 못한 곳에서 최선의 생각들이 나온다. 그것이 시 정부가 모든 시민들로부터 도시 생활의 질을 향상시킬 안을 받고 있는 이유이다. 안을 제출하는 누구든 최선의 것들을 선택하기 위해 그들의 제안을 검토할 위원회 앞에서 그것들을 발표할 것인데, 이는 너무 많은 프로젝트가 제한된 자금을 압도하지 않도록 한다.

해설
① 도치 구문 | 주어와 동사의 수 일치   장소를 나타내는 부사구(From unexpected places)가 강조되어 문장의 맨 앞에 오면 주어와 동사가 도치되어 '동사 + 주어'의 어순이 된다. 이때 주어 자리에 복수 명사 the best ideas가 왔으므로 단수 동사 comes를 복수 동사 come으로 고쳐야 한다.

[오답 분석]
② to 부정사의 역할   문맥상 '도시 생활의 질을 향상시킬 안'이라는 의미가 되어야 자연스러우므로, 명사(proposals) 뒤에서 명사를 수식하는 형용사 역할을 하는 to 부정사 to improve가 올바르게 쓰였다.
③ 복합관계대명사   문맥상 '안을 제출하는 누구든'이라는 의미가 되어야 하므로 '누구든'이라는 의미의 복합관계대명사 Whoever가 올바르게 쓰였다.
④ 부사절 접속사   문맥상 '제한된 자금을 압도하지 않도록'이라는 의미가 되어야 자연스러운데, '~하지 않도록'은 부사절 접속사 lest를 사용하여 나타낼 수 있다. 이때 접속사 lest가 이끄는 절의 동사는 '(should) + 동사원형'의 형태를 취하므로 (should) overwhelm이 올바르게 쓰였다.

정답 ①

어휘
proposal 안, 청혼   urban 도시의   committee 위원회
overwhelm 압도하다

---

04   생활영어   Doesn't it go straight to the area?
난이도 하 ●○○

밑줄 친 부분에 들어갈 말로 적절한 것은?

A: What is the quickest way to get to the shopping district from here?
B: That would definitely be the subway.
A: Thanks. Isn't there a bus that goes there?
B: Sure. But it will take more than an hour.
A: It takes longer than expected. _____
B: It makes many stops along the way.

① Is this area always so congested with traffic?
② How long would it take by subway?
③ Doesn't it go straight to the area?
④ Has the road construction been completed?

해석
A: 여기에서 상점가로 가는 가장 빠른 방법이 뭔가요?
B: 그건 분명 지하철일 거예요.
A: 감사해요. 거기로 가는 버스는 없나요?
B: 물론 있지요. 그런데 한 시간 이상이 걸릴 겁니다.
A: 예상한 것보다 오래 걸리네요. <u>그곳으로 곧장 가지 않나 봐요?</u>
B: 가는 도중에 정차를 많이 하거든요.

① 이 지역은 원래 교통이 혼잡한가요?
② 지하철로는 얼마나 걸릴까요?
③ 그곳으로 곧장 가지 않나 봐요?
④ 도로 공사가 끝났나요?

해설
상점가로 버스를 타고 가면 한 시간 이상이 걸린다는 B의 말에 대해 A가 예상한 것보다 오래 걸린다고 대답하고, 빈칸 뒤에서 다시 B가 It makes many stops along the way(가는 도중에 정차를 많이 하거든요)라고 덧붙이고 있으므로, '그곳으로 곧장 가지 않나 봐요?'라는 의미의 ③ 'Doesn't it go straight to the area?'가 정답이다.

정답 ③

어휘
definitely 분명, 절대   congested 혼잡한, 붐비는   straight 곧장, 똑바로
construction 공사, 건설

05~06   다음 글을 읽고 물음에 답하시오.

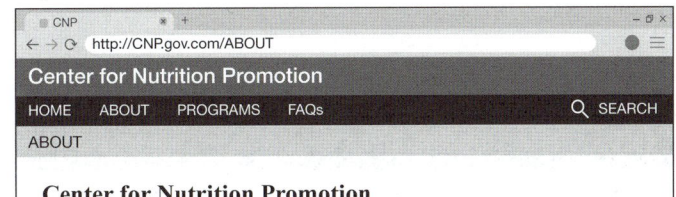

Center for Nutrition Promotion

Our Purpose
We provide science-based guidance and resources to help people make informed nutrition choices. By creating and implementing policies, we promote healthier eating and natural well-being to prevent diseases and conditions often related to diet, such as obesity, hypertension, and diabetes.

What We Do
We create nutrition guidelines that highlight eating a balanced diet rich in natural foods, fruits, and vegetables. This enables people to understand the importance of their dietary choices. In addition, we support policymakers, educators, and health professionals in providing the public with practical, accurate nutrition information.

Our Commitment
- Scientific Integrity: We conduct research experiments and studies to base recommendations on fact-based research.

DAY 20 하프모의고사 20회

- Impactful Cooperation: We partner with public health experts and organizations to encourage healthy eating habits.

[해석]

영양진흥원

우리의 목적
우리는 사람들이 정보에 기반한 영양 선택을 하도록 돕기 위해 과학에 기반한 지침과 자원을 제공합니다. 정책을 수립하고 시행함으로써 우리는 비만, 고혈압, 당뇨병과 같이 흔히 식단과 관련된 질병과 질환들을 예방하기 위해 더 건강한 식습관과 자연스러운 행복을 증진시킵니다.

우리가 하는 일
우리는 자연 식품, 과일 및 채소가 풍부한, 균형 잡힌 식단을 강조하는 영양 지침을 만듭니다. 이것은 사람들이 그들의 식단 선택의 중요성을 이해할 수 있게 합니다. 뿐만 아니라, 우리는 대중에게 실용적이고 정확한 영양 정보를 제공하는 것에 있어 정책 입안자, 교육자 그리고 보건 관련 전문가들을 지원합니다.

우리의 약속
- 과학적 진실성: 우리는 추천의 근거를 사실에 기반한 연구에 두고자 실험과 연구를 수행합니다.
- 영향력을 미치는 협력: 우리는 건강한 식습관을 장려하기 위해 공중 보건 전문가 및 기관들과 함께 일합니다.

[어휘]
nutrition 영양 (섭취) implement 시행하다 promote 증진시키다, 홍보하다
well-being 행복 obesity 비만 hypertension 고혈압 diabetes 당뇨병
policymaker 정책 입안자 practical 실용적인 accurate 정확한
commitment 약속, 헌신 integrity 진실성, 정직 conduct 수행하다
cooperation 협력 partner 함께 일하다, 제휴하다

05 독해 내용 일치 파악   난이도 중 ●●○

윗글에서 Center for Nutrition Promotion에 관한 내용과 일치하는 것은?

① It provides resources to help people lose weight.
② It offers medical treatment to people with hypertension and diabetes.
③ It encourages people to eat more natural foods.
④ It gives classes to the public about practical nutrition.

[해석]
① 그것은 사람들이 체중을 감량하는 데 도움이 되는 자원을 제공한다.
② 그것은 고혈압과 당뇨병이 있는 사람들에게 의학적 치료를 제공한다.
③ 그것은 사람들이 더 많은 자연 식품을 섭취하도록 권장한다.
④ 그것은 실용적인 영양 섭취에 대한 수업을 대중에게 제공한다.

[해설]
③번의 키워드인 natural foods(자연 식품)가 그대로 언급된 지문 주변의 내용에서 영양진흥원은 자연 식품이 풍부한 식단의 중요성을 강조하는 영양 지침을 만든다고 했으므로, ③ '그것은 사람들이 더 많은 자연 식품을 섭취하도록 권장한다'가 지문의 내용과 일치한다.

[오답 분석]
① 영향진흥원은 사람들이 정보에 기반한 영양 선택을 하도록 돕기 위해 과학에 기반한 지침과 자원을 제공한다고 했으므로, 그것이 사람들이 체중을 감량하는 데 도움이 되는 자원을 제공한다는 것은 지문의 내용과 다르다.
② 영양진흥원이 비만, 고혈압 및 당뇨병과 같은 식단 관련 질병들을 예방하기 위해 더 건강한 식습관을 증진시킨다고는 했지만, 그것이 고혈압과 당뇨병 환자들에게 의학적 치료를 제공하는지는 알 수 없다.
④ 영양진흥원은 대중에게 실용적인 영양 정보를 제공하는 것에 있어 교육자들을 지원한다고는 했지만, 그것이 실용적인 영양 섭취에 대한 수업을 대중에게 제공하는지는 알 수 없다.

정답 ③

06 독해 유의어 파악   난이도 중 ●●○

밑줄 친 partner의 의미와 가장 가까운 것은?

① pair   ② assist
③ interact   ④ collaborate

[해석]
① 짝을 짓다   ② 돕다
③ 소통하다   ④ 협력하다

[해설]
밑줄 친 부분이 포함된 문장에서 partner는 문맥상 공중 보건 전문가 및 기관들과 '함께 일한다'라는 의미로 쓰였으므로, '협력하다'라는 의미의 ④ collaborate가 정답이다.

정답 ④

[어휘]
pair 짝을 짓다; 짝 assist 돕다 interact 소통하다 collaborate 협력하다

07 독해 주제 파악   난이도 중 ●●○

다음 글의 주제로 적절한 것은?

Readers around the world have read the popular decades-old mystery books by an author named Carolyn Keene. As it turns out, this was a pen name for all the writers who penned the actual Nancy Drew stories, which were produced by the Stratemeyer Syndicate. These writers, whose names never appeared on the book covers, did ghostwriting, a job that involves writing something and then never claiming authorship of the material. Ghostwriting has had a long history, with the practice being used in earlier times by prominent and high-ranking persons who needed others to write for them. In later times, it was kept a secret by publishers, but perceptive readers recognized that many famous individuals did not have the time to write their memoirs. Today, however, ghostwriting is considered a profession, with as much as 25 percent of bestselling books having been written by surrogate writers in the US and Europe.

① history of pen names in literary publishing
② significance of authorship in mystery book series
③ famous celebrities hiring writers for memoirs
④ modern acceptance of ghostwriting as a profession

해석

전 세계의 독자들은 Carolyn Keene이라는 이름의 작가가 집필한 수십 년 된 인기 있는 추리 소설들을 읽어 왔다. 알고 보니, 이것은 Stratemeyer 배급사에 의해 제작되었던 실제 Nancy Drew 이야기를 썼던 모든 작가들의 필명이었다. 자신들의 이름이 결코 책 표지에 나오지 않는 이 작가들은 대필, 즉 글을 쓰고 그 내용의 원작자임을 절대 주장하지 않는 것을 수반하는 일을 했다. 대필은 긴 역사를 가지고 있는데, 그 관행은 이전 시대에는 그들을 위해 글을 써 줄 다른 사람이 필요했던, 유명한 상류 계층 사람들에 의해 사용되었다. 후에, 그것은 출판사들에 의해 비밀로 부쳐졌지만, 분별력 있는 독자들은 많은 유명한 사람들이 그들의 회고록을 쓸 시간이 없다는 것을 알았다. 하지만, 오늘날 대필은 하나의 직업으로 여겨지며, 미국과 유럽에서는 베스트셀러 책들의 무려 25퍼센트나 대리 작가들에 의해 쓰여지고 있다.

① 문학 작품 출판에 있어서 필명의 역사
② 미스터리 책 시리즈에서 원작자의 중요성
③ 회고록을 위해 작가를 고용하는 유명 인사들
④ 직업으로서의 대필의 현대적 수용

해설

지문 중간에서 대필은 긴 역사를 가지고 있는데, 이전에는 출판사들에 의해 비밀에 부쳐졌던 반면 오늘날에는, 하나의 직업으로 여겨지며 미국과 유럽에서 활발하게 활동하고 있다고 설명하고 있다. 따라서 ④ '직업으로서의 대필의 현대적 수용'이 이 글의 주제이다.

정답 ④

어휘

pen name 필명 pen 쓰다 syndicate 배급사, 연합체 ghostwriting 대필
involve 수반하다 claim 주장하다, 요구하다 authorship 원작자, 저술 작업
prominent 유명한, 중요한 perceptive 분별력 있는, 인지의 memoir 회고록
profession 직업 surrogate 대리의, 대용의 acceptance 수용

---

08 독해 요지 파악   난이도 중 ●●○

다음 글의 요지로 적절한 것은?

Volcanic eruptions can range from relatively harmless to extremely calamitous. Whether the explosion is a harmless slow flow or a devastating outpouring depends on the makeup of the molten rock, known as magma, which resides beneath the earth's surface. Magma contains dissolved gases that expand in response to shifts in pressure in the surrounding rock. Those gases then seek to escape their confinement and pull the magma up to the surface with them, causing an eruption. The severity of this eruption depends on how sticky, or resistant to flow, the magma is. The stickier the magma is, the more difficulty the gases have escaping and the more intense the eruption is. When the magma is more fluid, the gases meet less resistance and create a gentler flow. Of course, the amount of gas suspended in the magma is another factor. High concentrations of gas bubbles provoke violent eruptions; lower concentrations have less disastrous outcomes.

① Magma collides with volcanic gases to produce eruptions.
② Sticky magma is present in all types of volcanic eruptions.
③ Different kinds of magma have various concentrations of gas.
④ Magma composition determines the intensity of a volcanic eruption.

해석

화산 분출은 그 범위가 비교적 해를 끼치지 않는 것에서부터 극단적으로 재앙을 초래하는 것까지 이를 수 있다. 그 폭발이 피해를 주지 않는 느린 흐름일지 아니면 대단히 파괴적인 분출일지는 지표면 아래에 있는 마그마라고 알려진 녹은 암석의 성질에 달려 있다. 마그마는 주변 암석들 사이 압력의 변화에 대한 반응으로 팽창하는, 용해된 가스를 함유하고 있다. 그 후에 그 가스는 속박에서 벗어나려고 하면서 마그마를 그것(유용성 가스)들과 함께 지표면까지 끌어당겨, 분출을 야기한다. 이 분출의 격렬함은 마그마가 얼마나 끈적거리는지, 또는 얼마나 흐름에 저항력이 있는지에 달려 있다. 마그마가 더 끈적거릴수록, 가스가 새어 나오는 것이 더 어렵고 분출은 더 격렬해진다. 마그마가 더 유동성이 있을 때, 가스는 저항을 덜 받으면서 더 부드러운 흐름을 만든다. 물론, 마그마 속에 떠도는 가스의 양은 또 다른 요소이다. 고농도의 가스 기포는 격렬한 분출을 유발하고, 더 낮은 농도의 것들은 덜 처참한 결과를 낳는다.

① 마그마는 화산 가스와 충돌하여 분출을 일으킨다.
② 끈적거리는 마그마는 모든 종류의 화산 분출에 존재한다.
③ 서로 다른 종류의 마그마는 각양각색의 가스 농도를 갖는다.
④ 마그마의 성질이 화산 분출의 강도를 결정한다.

해설

지문 앞부분에서 범위가 비교적 위험하지 않은 것에서부터 재앙을 초래하는 것까지 이르는 다양한 화산 분출의 형태는 지표면 아래에 있는 마그마의 성질에 달려 있다고 하고, 지문 뒷부분에서 마그마의 점성과 유동성과 포함하는 가스 농도에 따라 화산 분출의 강도가 달라진다고 설명하고 있다. 따라서 ④ '마그마의 성질이 화산 분출의 강도를 결정한다'가 이 글의 요지이다.

정답 ④

어휘

eruption 분출, 폭발 calamitous 재앙을 초래하는 explosion 폭발
devastating 대단히 파괴적인 outpouring 분출 makeup 성질, 구성
molten 녹은 dissolve 용해되다, 녹다 escape 벗어나다, 새어 나오다
confinement 속박, 감금 severity 격렬함 sticky 끈적거리는
resistant 저항력이 있는 intense 격렬한 fluid 유동성 있는; 액체
suspend 떠돌게 하다, 띄우다 concentration 농도, 집중
provoke 유발하다 collide 충돌하다 composition 성질, 구성

DAY 20 하프모의고사 20회

09 독해 문단 순서 배열   난이도 상 ●●●

주어진 글 다음에 이어질 글의 순서로 적절한 것은?

In the town of Baarle, your location can be in Belgium or the Netherlands depending on which side of the border you're standing on. Due to centuries of treaties, land exchanges, and purchases, the town consists of enclaves, pieces of territory completely surrounded by the other country.

(A) All the sections of Belgian land in Baarle are enclosed by their Dutch neighbors, while these Belgian exclaves also contain areas of land belonging to the Netherlands.

(B) As a more interesting example, in the past, the Dutch food establishments in this particular town shut down earlier than their Belgian counterparts, so patrons would simply move to the Belgian side of the restaurant at closing time to continue eating.

(C) In other words, there are Dutch exclaves inside these Belgian ones. In fact, citizens of Baarle can enjoy a meal in their Belgian dining room, play in their backyard situated in the Netherlands, and then travel back to Belgium when it's time to sleep in the bedroom.

① (A) – (B) – (C)
② (A) – (C) – (B)
③ (B) – (A) – (C)
④ (B) – (C) – (A)

[해석]

Baarle 마을에서는, 당신이 어느 쪽의 국경에 서 있는지에 따라 위치가 벨기에가 될 수도 있고 네덜란드가 될 수도 있다. 수세기 동안의 조약, 땅 교환과 매각으로 인해, 그 마을은 다른 나라에 의해 완전히 둘러싸인 영토의 일부, 고립 영토들로 이루어져 있다.

(A) Baarle에 있는 벨기에 땅의 모든 구역들은 이웃하는 네덜란드 구역으로 에워싸여 있으며, 동시에 이 벨기에의 고립 영토들은 네덜란드에 속하는 땅의 지역을 포함하기도 한다.

(B) 더 재미있는 일례로, 과거에 이 특별한 마을 안에 있는 네덜란드의 음식점들이 벨기에의 것들보다 더 일찍 문을 닫아서, 단골들은 계속 식사를 하기 위해 폐점 시간에 식당의 벨기에 쪽으로 자리를 그냥 옮기고는 했다.

(C) 다시 말해서, 이 벨기에의 고립 영토 안에 네덜란드의 고립 영토가 있는 것이다. 실제로, Baarle의 시민들은 벨기에 식당에서 식사를 즐기고, 네덜란드에 위치한 그들의 뒷마당에서 놀다가, 잘 시간이 되면 침실에 있는 벨기에로 돌아갈 수 있다.

[해설]

주어진 문장에서 Baarle 마을은 조약, 땅 교환 및 매각으로 인해 고립 영토들로 이루어져 있다고 한 뒤, (A)에서 Baarle에 있는 모든 벨기에 땅들은 네덜란드 구역에 의해 에워싸인 동시에 그 안에 고립된 네덜란드 영토를 포함한다고 설명하고 있다. 이어서 (C)에서 다시 말해서(In other words) 이 벨기에의 고립 영토(these Belgian ones) 안에 네덜란드의 고립 영토가 있는데, 이로 인해 Baarle의 시민들은 국경을 수시로 넘나든다고 하고, (B)에서 더 재미있는 일례(a more interesting example)로 음식점의 네덜란드 구역이 문을 닫으면 단골들은 더 늦게 문을 닫는 벨기에 쪽으로 자리를 옮겼다고 설명하고 있다. 따라서 ② (A) – (C) – (B)가 정답이다.

정답 ②

[어휘]

border 국경   treaty 조약   exclave 고립 영토 (타국 내 자국 영토)
territory 영토   surround 둘러싸다   enclose 에워싸다, 두르다
Dutch 네덜란드의   establishment 점포, 시설   shut down 문을 닫다
counterpart 대응 관계에 있는 것(사람), 상대   patron 단골, 고객
situate 위치시키다

---

10 독해 빈칸 완성 – 구   난이도 중 ●●○

밑줄 친 부분에 들어갈 말로 적절한 것은?

To: patients@VirtuHealthNet.org
From: patientcare@VirtuHealthNet.org
Date: August 7
Subject: Virtual Visits

Dear Valued Patients,

Virtual doctor visits are a convenient way to access quality healthcare from the comfort of your home. If you've booked an online checkup, here are five simple steps to help you get ready for it:

1. Ensure your device is fully charged and has a working camera, microphone, and internet connection. Test these features in advance.
2. Find a quiet space where you won't be interrupted and you are comfortable talking about your medical concerns.
3. Have a list of your current medications, allergies, and any recent symptoms.
4. Write down questions you wish to address with the physician so you don't forget anything important.
5. Log in to the VirtuHealthNet platform five to ten minutes before your scheduled appointment time using the link sent to your email.

By following these steps, you'll be well-prepared for _____. If you need technical assistance or wish to cancel or modify an appointment time, support is available 24/7 at www.VirtuHealthNet.org/support.

Best regards,

VirtuHealthNet Patient Care Team

① finding a quiet space for telehealth interactions
② having a productive consultation with your doctor
③ keeping your digital privacy safe
④ navigating the telehealth platform

해석

수신: patients@VirtuHealthNet.org
발신: patientcare@VirtuHealthNet.org
날짜: 8월 7일
제목: 가상 현실의 방문

친애하는 환자 여러분께,

가상 현실 의사의 방문은 안락한 댁에서 양질의 의료 서비스에 접근하는 편리한 방법입니다. 만약 온라인 검진을 예약하셨다면, 여기 여러분의 준비를 도울 다섯 가지 간단한 단계가 있습니다.

1. 기기가 완전히 충전되어 있고 작동하는 카메라, 마이크 및 인터넷 연결을 갖추었는지 확인하세요. 이러한 기능들을 미리 테스트해 두세요.
2. 방해받지 않고 여러분의 의료 관련 우려 사항에 대해 편안하게 이야기할 수 있는, 조용한 공간을 찾으세요.
3. 현재 복용 중인 약물, 알레르기 및 최근 증상에 대한 목록을 준비하세요.
4. 의사와 해결하고 싶은 질문들을 적어 두세요. 그러면 중요한 내용을 잊지 않으실 겁니다.
5. 이메일로 전송된 링크를 사용하여 예정된 약속 시간 5~10분 전에 VirtuHealthNet 플랫폼에 로그인하세요.

이러한 단계들을 따름으로써, 여러분은 <u>의사와의 생산적인 상담을 하는 것</u>에 알맞게 준비하실 수 있습니다. 기술적 지원이 필요하시거나, 약속 시간을 취소 또는 변경하기 원하시는 경우, www.VirtuHealthNet.org/support에서 24시간 지원을 받으실 수 있습니다.

안부를 전하며,
VirtuHealthNet 환자 관리 팀

① 원격 의료 의사소통을 위한 조용한 공간을 찾는 것
② 의사와의 생산적인 상담을 하는 것
③ 디지털 개인 정보를 안전하게 유지하는 것
④ 원격 의료 플랫폼을 탐색하는 것

해설

지문 전반에 걸쳐 가상 현실 의사와의 온라인 상담을 위한 다섯 가지의 준비 단계를 설명하고 있으므로, 이러한 단계들을 따름으로써 '의사와의 생산적인 상담을 하는 것'에 알맞게 준비할 수 있다고 한 ②번이 정답이다.

정답 ②

어휘

virtual 가상 (현실)의 patient 환자 convenient 편리한 comfort 안락함
checkup 검진, 점검 charge 충전하다, 청구하다 feature 기능; 특징으로 삼다
interrupt 방해하다 medication 약물 symptom 증상
address 해결하다, 주소를 적다 physician 의사 appointment 약속
modify 변경하다, 수정하다 telehealth 원격 의료
interaction 의사 소통, 교류 productive 생산적인 consultation 상담
navigate 탐색하다, 길을 찾다

DAY 21 하프모의고사 21회

◉ 정답
p. 94

01	②	어휘	06	④	독해
02	②	문법	07	④	독해
03	③	문법	08	④	독해
04	④	생활영어	09	②	독해
05	③	독해	10	④	독해

◉ 취약영역 분석표

영역	맞힌 답의 개수
어휘	/1
생활영어	/1
문법	/2
독해	/6
TOTAL	/10

---

01 어휘 discipline — 난이도 중 ●●○

밑줄 친 부분에 들어갈 말로 적절한 것은?

> Because the student consistently misbehaved, the principal decided to _____ her according to school regulations.

① motivate
② discipline
③ dislike
④ praise

[해석]
그 학생이 지속적으로 나쁜 행동을 했기 때문에, 그 교장 선생님은 그녀를 학교 규정에 따라 징계하기로 했다.

① 동기를 부여하다 ② 징계하다
③ 싫어하다 ④ 칭찬하다

정답 ②

[어휘]
consistently 지속적으로, 항상 misbehave 나쁜 행동을 하다
motivate 동기를 부여하다 discipline 징계하다, 훈육하다 dislike 싫어하다
praise 칭찬하다; 칭찬

---

02 문법 동사의 종류 — 난이도 중 ●●○

밑줄 친 부분에 들어갈 말로 적절한 것은?

> The judge let the defendant _____ by a public defender because he could not afford a private attorney.

① represented
② be represented
③ to represent
④ to be represented

[해석]
판사는 피고인이 개인 변호사를 선임할 여유가 없었기 때문에 그가 국선 변호인에 의해 변호받도록 했다.

[해설]
② 5형식 동사   빈칸은 사역동사 let의 목적격 보어 자리이다. 사역동사 let은 목적어와 목적격 보어가 수동 관계일 때 목적격 보어로 'be + p.p.' 형태를 취하는데, 목적어 the defendant와 목적격 보어가 '피고인이 변호받다'라는 의미의 수동 관계이므로 'be + p.p.' 형태인 ② be represented가 정답이다.

정답 ②

[어휘]
judge 판사; 판단하다 defendant 피고 public defender 국선 변호인
afford ~할 여유가 되다 attorney 변호사 represent 변호하다, 대표하다

---

03 문법 동사의 종류 | 수 일치 | 대명사 | 분사 — 난이도 중 ●●○

밑줄 친 부분 중 어법상 옳지 않은 것은?

> It is reported that a substantial portion of all bankruptcies in America ① are due to medical bills. The medical costs are clearly burdensome even for ② those with insurance, and such costs can keep people without coverage ③ seeking necessary treatment. The government is working to expand coverage, including programs like Medicaid, which is a health insurance program for low-income individuals and people with disabilities, ④ operated by both the federal and state governments.

[해석]
미국의 모든 파산 중에서 상당 부분은 의료비로 인한 것으로 보고된다. 그 의료 비용은 보험이 있는 사람들에게마저도 분명히 부담이 되며, 그러한 비용은 보상 범위가 없는 사람들을 필수적인 치료를 받지 못하게 할 수 있다. 정부는 Medicaid와 같은 프로그램을 포함해 보상 범위를 확대하기 위해 노력하고 있는데, 이것(Medicaid)은 연방 정부와 주 정부 모두에 의해 운용되는, 저소득층과 장애인들을 위한 건강 보험 프로그램이다.

해설

③ **타동사** 문맥상 '보상 범위가 없는 사람들을 필수적인 치료를 받지 못하게 하다'라는 의미가 되어야 자연스러운데, 동사 keep이 '~을 -하지 못하게 하다'의 의미로 쓰일 때는 'keep + 목적어(people without coverage) + from'의 형태를 취하므로, seeking을 from seeking으로 고쳐야 한다. 참고로, 전치사(from) 뒤에는 명사 역할을 하는 것이 와야 한다.

[오답 분석]
① **부분 표현의 수 일치** 부분을 나타내는 표현(a substantial portion of)을 포함한 주어는 of 뒤 명사(all bankruptcies)에 동사를 수 일치시켜야 하므로 복수 동사 are가 올바르게 쓰였다.
② **지시대명사** 문맥상 '보험이 있는 사람들'이라는 의미가 되어야 자연스러우므로, 수식어구(with insurance)의 꾸밈을 받아 '~한 사람들'이라는 의미를 나타내는 지시대명사 those가 올바르게 쓰였다.
④ **현재분사 vs. 과거분사** 수식받는 명사(Medicaid)와 분사가 'Medicaid가 운용되다'라는 의미의 수동 관계이므로 과거분사 operated가 올바르게 쓰였다.

정답 ③

어휘

substantial 상당한 bankruptcy 파산 burdensome 부담스러운
insurance 보험 coverage 보상 범위, 보도 treatment 치료, 대우
disability 장애 operate 운용하다, 작동되다, 수술하다 federal 연방의

---

04 생활영어 The host organization is probably inexperienced.
난이도 하 ●○○

밑줄 친 부분에 들어갈 말로 적절한 것은?

 Nora Hill
Welcome back to the office!
15:40

How was the conference?
15:40

Caleb Russell
Well, there were pros and cons.
The presentations were good.
15:41

 Nora Hill
Then what were the problems?
15:42

Caleb Russell
There was a lot of downtime between speeches and confusion about where to go.
15:43

 Nora Hill
_____
15:44

Caleb Russell
Definitely. It'll probably improve next time.
15:44

① I'm glad it was a productive experience.
② At least you were constantly stimulated.
③ You probably didn't stay for the whole event.
④ The host organization is probably inexperienced.

해석

> Nora Hill: 사무실에 돌아온 걸 환영해요!
> 학회는 어땠어요?
> Caleb Russell: 글쎄요, 장단점이 있었어요. 발표는 좋았죠.
> Nora Hill: 그럼 뭐가 문제였나요?
> Caleb Russell: 연설 사이에 중단 시간이 많았고 어디로 가야 하는 지에 대한 혼란이 있었어요.
> Nora Hill: 주최 기관이 아마 미숙했나 보네요.
> Caleb Russell: 정말로요. 다음번에는 나아지겠죠.

① 생산적인 경험이었다니 기쁘네요.
② 적어도 끊임없이 흥미가 생기긴 했겠네요.
③ 당신은 아마 행사 내내 머물지는 않았겠네요.
④ 주최 기관이 아마 미숙했나 보네요.

해설

학회에서 무엇이 문제였는지 묻는 Nora의 질문에 대해 Caleb이 연설 사이에 중단 시간이 많았고 어디로 가야 하는지에 대한 혼란이 있었다고 대답하고, 빈칸 뒤에서 다시 Caleb이 Definitely. It'll probably improve next time(정말로요. 다음번에는 나아지겠죠)이라고 말하고 있으므로, '주최 기관이 아마 미숙했나 보네요'라는 의미의 ④ 'The host organization is probably inexperienced'가 정답이다.

정답 ④

어휘

pros and cons 장단점, 찬반 양론 organize 준비하다
downtime 중단 시간, 한가한 시간 confusion 혼란 productive 생산적인
constantly 끊임없이, 항상 stimulate 흥미를 불러일으키다, 자극하다
inexperienced 미숙한, 경험이 부족한

05~06 다음 글을 읽고 물음에 답하시오.

_____(A)_____

Everyone has the power to make a difference in the lives of animals in need.

DAY 21 하프모의고사 21회

At the shelter, we try our best to make the animals comfortable, but there are many that require more individualized care and special attention. By fostering, you can provide a safe and caring space for these animals before they are adopted.

We invite you to attend an information seminar to learn more about the fostering process. You will also get a chance to meet some of the furry friends you might be able to help.

Come see if fostering is right for you.

- **Location**: Coopersville Animal Shelter
- **Date**: Saturday, April 12
- **Time**: 10:00 a.m. (Animal meet-and-greet starts at 10:30 a.m.)

For more information or to browse photos of animals available for fostering, please visit our website at www.coopersvilleanimalshelter.com/fosterprogram.

해석

(A) 반려동물에게 여러분의 집을 개방하세요

모든 사람은 도움이 필요한 동물들의 삶에 변화를 줄 수 있는 힘을 가지고 있습니다.

보호소에서, 저희는 동물들이 편안하게 지낼 수 있도록 최선을 다하지만, 더 개별적인 돌봄과 특별한 관심을 필요로 하는 많은 동물들이 있습니다. 위탁 양육함으로써, 여러분은 그들(동물들)이 입양되기 전에 안전한 돌봄의 공간을 제공할 수 있습니다.

위탁 양육 과정에 대해 더 자세히 알아보기 위한 정보 세미나에 여러분들을 초대합니다. 여러분은 도울 수 있을지 모를 많은 친구들을 만날 기회도 얻게 될 것입니다.

위탁 양육이 여러분에게 적합한지 오셔서 확인해 보세요.

- 장소: Coopersville 동물 보호소
- 날짜: 4월 12일, 토요일
- 시간: 오전 10시 (동물 만남 및 인사는 오전 10시 30분에 시작합니다)

더 많은 정보를 원하시거나 위탁 양육이 가능한 동물들의 사진을 둘러보시려면, 저희 웹사이트 www.coopersvilleanimalshelter.com/fosterprogram을 방문해 주세요.

어휘

shelter 보호소　**comfortable** 편안한　**individualize** 개별화하다
foster 위탁 양육하다, 기르다　**caring** 돌보는, 배려하는
adopt 입양하다, 채택하다　**furry** 털이 많은　**browse** 둘러보다

05 독해 제목 파악　난이도 중 ●●○

(A)에 들어갈 윗글의 제목으로 적절한 것은?

① Meet Other Pet Owners
② Respect for Shelter Volunteers
③ Open Your Homes to Pets
④ Gratitude for Animal Adoption

해석

① 다른 반려동물 주인들을 만나 보세요
② 보호소 봉사자분들에 대한 존경
③ 반려동물에게 여러분의 집을 개방하세요
④ 동물 입양에 대한 감사

해설

지문 중간에서 동물들에게 안전한 돌봄의 공간을 제공하는 위탁 양육에 대한 정보를 제공하는 세미나에 참석할 것을 권장하고 있으므로, ③ '반려동물에게 여러분의 집을 개방하세요'가 이 글의 제목이다.

정답 ③

어휘

respect 존경; 존경하다　**gratitude** 감사

06 독해 내용 불일치 파악　난이도 중 ●●○

위 안내문의 내용과 일치하지 않는 것은?

① 일부 동물들은 위탁 양육 가정에서 특별한 돌봄이 필요하다.
② 세미나에서 참석자들은 일부 보호소 동물들을 볼 수 있다.
③ 세미나는 토요일 아침에 열릴 것이다.
④ 웹사이트에 위탁 양육 중인 동물들의 사진이 있다.

해설

④번의 키워드인 '웹사이트'가 그대로 언급된 지문의 website 주변의 내용에서 위탁 양육이 가능한 동물들의 사진을 둘러보려면 웹사이트를 방문하라고는 했지만, ④ '웹사이트에 위탁 양육 중인 동물들의 사진이 있'는지는 알 수 없다.

정답 ④

07 독해 주제 파악　난이도 중 ●●○

다음 글의 주제로 적절한 것은?

Asthma is a chronic condition resulting in more than 400,000 deaths yearly, and there has been a marked increase in diagnoses since the 1960s. The disease has been recognized since the empires of ancient Egypt. Life for sufferers involves constant management of the condition, as there is no cure. Asthma is characterized by inflammation of the airways in the lungs, causing attacks of shortness of breath, wheezing, coughing, and general difficulty breathing. Those afflicted with the condition may be more susceptible to or suffer more severe reactions to infections of the lungs, like pneumonia. The condition ordinarily begins in childhood, and while symptoms may become less severe, with asthma attacks occurring less frequently, they persist for life. Given the increasing prevalence of the condition, it is well worth investing in its research.

*asthma: 천식
*pneumonia: 폐렴

① Ancient treatments for chronic conditions
② Various symptoms of lung diseases today
③ Lung infections complicating existing health problems
④ The need for more asthma research due to rising case numbers

[해석]

천식은 매년 40만 명 이상의 사망자를 낳는 만성 질환으로, 1960년대 이후 진단에서 뚜렷한 증가가 있어 왔다. 그 질병은 고대 이집트 제국 이래로 인식되어 왔다. 치료할 방법이 없기 때문에 환자들의 생활에는 그 질환의 지속적인 관리가 수반된다. 천식은 폐에 있는 기도의 염증으로 특징지어지는데, 이것은 숨 가쁨, 쌕쌕거림, 기침 그리고 전반적인 호흡 곤란의 발병을 야기한다. 그 질환에 시달리는 사람들은 폐렴과 같은 폐의 감염에 더 걸리기 쉽거나 더 심각한 반응을 겪을 수도 있다. 그 질환은 대개 어린 시절에 시작되며, 비록 천식 발작이 덜 자주 일어나면서 증상이 덜 심해질 수도 있기는 하지만, 그것들(증상들)은 평생 지속된다. 그 질환의 증가하는 발병률을 고려했을 때, 그것의 연구에 투자할 가치가 충분히 있다.

① 만성 질환들에 대한 고대 치료법
② 오늘날 폐 질병들의 다양한 증상들
③ 기존의 건강 문제들을 복잡하게 만드는 폐 감염
④ 증가하는 환자 수로 인한 더 많은 천식 연구의 필요성

[해설]

지문 전반에 걸쳐 1960년대 이후 진단 사례가 증가해 온 천식은 호흡을 방해하는 증상들을 야기하고 폐를 감염되기 쉬운 상태로 만들며 발병률이 증가하고 있으므로 관련 연구에 투자할 가치가 있다고 주장하고 있다. 따라서 ④ '증가하는 환자 수로 인한 더 많은 천식 연구의 필요성'이 이 글의 주제이다.

정답 ④

[어휘]

chronic 만성의 marked 뚜렷한 diagnosis 진단; 진단하다 empire 제국
sufferer 환자 characterize 특징짓다 inflammation 염증 airway 기도
attack 발병, 발작; 공격하다 wheezing 쌕쌕거림 coughing 기침
afflict 시달리게 하다, 괴롭히다 susceptible 걸리기 쉬운, 민감한
infection 감염 symptom 증상 severe 심한 persist 지속되다
prevalence 발병률, 널리 퍼짐 complicate 복잡하게 만들다
existing 기존의

08 독해 무관한 문장 삭제   난이도 하 ●○○

다음 글의 흐름상 어색한 문장은?

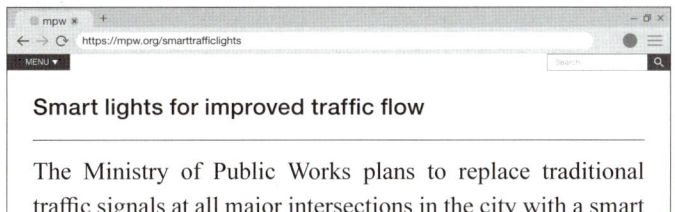

Smart lights for improved traffic flow

The Ministry of Public Works plans to replace traditional traffic signals at all major intersections in the city with a smart traffic light control system. ① Unlike standard signals, smart traffic lights use sensors to detect real-time traffic conditions, automatically adjusting traffic light timing based on the volume of traffic they detect. ② The implementation of the new system is expected to reduce unnecessary wait times during off-peak hours by as much as 25 percent. ③ It is also expected to improve response times for emergency vehicles, as the system can identify them and activate green lights to prioritize their movement through intersections. ④ Unfortunately, citizens' concerns about surveillance technology have resulted in the indefinite postponement of the smart traffic light system. The installation will begin in March and conclude in September.

[해석]

교통 흐름 개선을 위한 스마트 신호등

공공 사업 관리부는 도시 내 모든 주요 교차로에 있는 기존의 교통 신호들을 스마트 교통 신호등 제어 시스템으로 교체할 계획이다. ① 일반 신호와 달리, 스마트 교통 신호등은 센서를 사용하여 실시간 교통 상황을 감지하는데, 그것들이 감지한 교통량을 바탕으로 신호등의 타이밍을 자동으로 조정한다. ② 그 새로운 시스템의 실행은 한산한 시간대 동안의 불필요한 대기 시간을 최대 25퍼센트까지 줄일 것으로 예상된다. ③ 시스템이 구급 차량을 식별하고 교차로를 통과하는 그것들의 이동을 우선시하기 위해 녹색 신호를 활성화할 수 있기 때문에, 그것(스마트 교통 신호등)은 구급 차량의 대응 시간 또한 개선할 것으로 예상된다. ④ 안타깝게도, 감시 기술에 대한 시민들의 우려는 스마트 교통 신호등 시스템의 무기한 연기를 초래했다. 그것의 설치는 3월에 시작되어 9월에 끝날 것이다.

[해설]

첫 문장에서 공공 사업 관리부가 기존 교통 신호들을 스마트 교통 신호등 시스템으로 교체할 계획임을 언급한 뒤, ①번은 '일반 신호와 다른 스마트 교통 신호등의 작동 원리', ②, ③번은 '스마트 교통 신호등 실행으로 예상되는 교통 흐름 개선 효과'를 설명하고 있다. 그러나 ④번은 '감시 기술에 대한 시민들의 우려로 인해 무기한 연기된 스마트 신호등 도입'에 대한 내용으로, 첫 문장의 내용과 관련이 없다.

정답 ④

[어휘]

traffic 교통(량) ministry (정부의) 부 replace 교체하다
intersection 교차로 detect 감지하다 automatically 자동으로
adjust 조정하다 implementation 실행, 시행 off-peak 한산한, 비수기의
emergency 구급, 비상 사태 identify 식별하다, 확인하다
activate 활성화하다 prioritize 우선시하다 surveillance 감시
indefinite 무기한의 postponement 연기, 지연

09 독해 문단 순서 배열   난이도 상 ●●●

주어진 글 다음에 이어질 글의 순서로 적절한 것은?

Prisons in America are often said to have a "revolving door," as exiting the system often leads to re-entry for ex-prisoners.

DAY 21 하프모의고사 21회

New research indicates that this may be directly related to punishments imposed during release.

(A) It was found that, on average, people who were sent to prison had a 20 percent higher chance of returning later than those who had only been sentenced to probation. These findings reinforce countless other studies in the field.

(B) In a 2017 study from the University of Michigan, the post-release progress of individuals in the Michigan state corrections system was tracked.

(C) These studies seem to point to the conditional release system as the main cause of these alarming statistics. Former prisoners were much more likely to be sent back to prison for violating one of the many restrictions placed on conditionally released individuals, despite the fact that such violations were not actually crimes.

*probation: 집행 유예

① (A) – (B) – (C)
② (B) – (A) – (C)
③ (B) – (C) – (A)
④ (C) – (A) – (B)

해석

미국의 교도소들은 종종 '회전문'을 가지고 있다고 일컬어지는데, 이는 그 체계에서 나가는 것이 종종 전 수감자들이 다시 (교도소에) 들어가는 것으로 이어지기 때문이다. 새로운 연구는 이것이 석방 기간 동안에 부과된 처벌과 직접적으로 관련 있을 수 있음을 보여 준다.

(A) 평균적으로, 교도소로 보내졌던 사람들은 집행 유예만 선고받았던 사람들보다 이후에 (교도소로) 다시 돌아갈 확률이 20퍼센트 더 높은 것으로 밝혀졌다. 이 연구 결과는 그 분야의 수많은 다른 연구들을 보강한다.

(B) 2017년 미시간 대학의 한 연구에서, 미시간 주 교정 체계에 있는 사람들의 석방 후 추이가 추적되었다.

(C) 이 연구들은 이 걱정스러운 통계치의 주원인으로 가석방 제도를 지목하는 것처럼 보인다. 이전 수감자들은 가석방으로 풀려난 개인들에게 부과된 많은 제약들 중 한 가지를 위반한 것 때문에, 그러한 위반들이 실제로 범죄는 아니었다는 사실에도 불구하고 다시 교도소로 보내질 가능성이 훨씬 더 컸다.

해설

주어진 문장에서 미국 교도소에서 수감자들이 다시 교도소에 들어가는 현상이 석방 기간 동안의 처벌과 관련 있음을 보여 준 연구를 언급한 후, (B)에서 미시간 대학에서 죄수들의 석방 후 추적 연구를 진행했다고 알려 주고 있다. 이어서 (A)에서 연구 결과 수감자들은 집행 유예만 선고받은 사람들보다 교도소로 돌아갈 확률이 더 높았는데, 이는 다른 연구들을 뒷받침했다고 하고, (C)에서 이 연구들(These studies)은 이 걱정스러운 통계치(these alarming statistics)의 주원인으로 풀려난 수감자들에게 많은 제약들을 부과하는 가석방 제도를 지목한다고 설명하고 있다. 따라서 ② (B) – (A) – (C)가 정답이다.

정답 ②

어휘

prison 교도소 revolve 회전하다 punishment 처벌 impose 부과하다 release 석방, 공개, 발표; 풀어 주다 on average 평균적으로 sentence 선고하다; 선고, 문장 reinforce 보강하다, 강화하다 correction 교정, 정정 conditional release 가석방 alarming 걱정스러운 statistics 통계 violate 위반하다 restriction 제약, 제한 crime 범죄

---

10 독해 빈칸 완성 – 단어   난이도 중 ●●○

밑줄 친 부분에 들어갈 말로 적절한 것은?

The normalcy bias is an inescapable aspect of human nature, greatly affecting the public's reaction to everything from natural disasters to financial market collapses. This cognitive bias causes people to disregard warnings of impending threats. As a result, they often fail to act, believing the disaster won't happen or won't result in negative consequences for them. Studies have indicated that 70 percent of people display this characteristic when faced with serious threats. Some researchers believe that our inaction is a result of our being inherently _____ and considering any vagueness we detect in the warnings or threats as a sign that they won't be as serious as thought.

① realistic
② romantic
③ energetic
④ optimistic

해석

'정상화 편향'은 인간 본성의 피할 수 없는 측면인데, 이는 자연재해부터 금융 시장 붕괴에까지 이르는 모든 것에 대한 대중의 반응에 크게 영향을 끼친다. 이 인지적 편향은 사람들이 임박한 위험에 대한 경고를 무시하게 만든다. 그 결과, 그들은 그 재앙이 일어나지 않거나 그들에게 부정적인 결과를 초래하지 않을 것이라고 믿기 때문에 종종 행동하지 않는다. 연구들은 70퍼센트의 사람들이 심각한 위험에 직면했을 때 이러한 특성을 보인다는 것을 시사해 왔다. 일부 연구자들은 우리의 행동하지 않음이 우리가 선천적으로 낙관적인 것, 그리고 우리가 경고나 위협에서 감지하는 어떤 모호함을 그것들(경고나 위협들)이 생각만큼 심각하지는 않을 것이라는 신호로 간주하는 것의 결과라고 믿는다.

① 현실적인
② 낭만적인
③ 활기찬
④ 낙관적인

해설

지문 중간에서 정상화 편향 때문에 사람들은 재앙이 일어나지 않거나 그들에게 부정적인 결과를 초래하지 않을 것이라 믿고 행동하지 않는다고 했고, 빈칸이 있는 문장 뒷부분에서 우리가 경고나 위협에서 감지하는 어떤 모호함을 그것들이 생각만큼 심각하지는 않을 것이라는 신호로 간주한다고 했으므로, 우리의 행동하지 않음이 선천적으로 '낙관적인' 것의 결과라고 한 ④번이 정답이다.

정답 ④

어휘

normalcy 정상(화) bias 편향 inescapable 피할 수 없는 reaction 반응 collapse 붕괴 cognitive 인지적인 disregard 무시하다; 무시, 묵살 impending 임박한 consequence 결과 characteristic 특성, 성격 inaction 행동하지 않음, 활동 부족 inherently 선천적으로, 본질적으로 vagueness 모호함, 분명하지 않음 detect 감지하다 optimistic 낙관적인

DAY 22 하프모의고사 22회

정답 p. 98

01	③	어휘	06	②	독해
02	④	문법	07	②	독해
03	④	문법	08	③	독해
04	④	생활영어	09	③	독해
05	②	독해	10	②	독해

취약영역 분석표

영역	맞힌 답의 개수
어휘	/1
생활영어	/1
문법	/2
독해	/6
TOTAL	/10

---

01 어휘 severe 난이도 중 ●●○

밑줄 친 부분에 들어갈 말로 적절한 것은?

Some victims had such _____ injuries that they required more urgent transport to the hospital than others.

① accidental ② intentional
③ severe ④ external

[해석]
일부 피해자들이 부상이 너무 심각해서 그들은 다른 이들보다 병원으로의 더 신속한 이송을 필요로 했다.
① 우연한 ② 고의적인
③ 심각한 ④ 외부적인

정답 ③

[어휘]
victim 피해자, 희생자 injury 부상 urgent 신속한 accidental 우연한
intentional 고의적인 severe 심각한 external 외부적인

---

02 문법 어순|동명사 난이도 중 ●●○

밑줄 친 부분에 들어갈 말로 적절한 것은?

Isabella's friend asked _____ a mistake during the team project.

① when would I admit to make ② when would I admit making
③ when I would admit to make ④ when I would admit making

[해석]
Isabella의 친구는 내가 팀 프로젝트 중 실수를 한 것을 언제 받아들일 것인지 물었다.

[해설]
④ 어순 | 동명사를 목적어로 취하는 동사 빈칸은 동사 asked의 목적어 역할을 하는 간접 의문문 자리이다. 간접 의문문은 '의문사(when) + 주어(I) + 동사(would admit)'의 어순이 되어야 하므로 ③, ④번이 정답 후보이다. 이때 동사 admit은 동명사를 목적어로 취하므로, 동명사 making이 쓰인 ④ when I would admit making이 정답이다.

정답 ④

[어휘]
admit 받아들이다, 인정하다

---

03 문법 전치사|형용사|수 일치 난이도 하 ●○○

밑줄 친 부분 중 어법상 옳지 않은 것은?

Solar geoengineering is ① different from other methods of lowering atmospheric temperatures in ② a number of ways. It may have negative repercussions caused by the use of technologies that ③ are untested. Reducing temperatures can be done by ④ emit sulfur into the upper atmosphere or altering cloud cover over the ocean, both of which carry risks.

[해석]
태양지구공학은 대기 온도를 낮추는 다른 방법들과 많은 면에서 다르다. 그것은 검증되지 않은 기술의 사용에 의해 야기되는 부정적인 영향들을 미칠지도 모른다. 온도를 낮추는 것은 황을 더 높은 대기권으로 방출하거나 바다 위의 구름양을 변화시킴으로써 이루어질 수 있는데, 이것들 모두 위험을 수반한다.

[해설]
④ 전치사 자리 전치사(by) 뒤에는 명사 역할을 하는 것이 와야 하므로 동사원형 emit을 동명사 emitting으로 고쳐야 한다.

[오답 분석]
① 기타 전치사 형용사 different는 전치사 from과 함께 different from(~과 다르다)의 형태로 자주 쓰이므로 different from이 올바

② **수량 표현** 문맥상 '많은 면에서'라는 의미가 되어야 자연스럽고, 수량 표현 a number of(많은)는 복수 명사(ways)와 함께 쓰이므로 a number of ways가 올바르게 쓰였다.

③ **주격 관계절의 수 일치** 주격 관계절(that ~ untested) 내의 동사는 선행사(technologies)에 수 일치시켜야 하므로 복수 동사 are가 올바르게 쓰였다.

정답 ④

어휘

geoengineering 지구공학 lower 낮추다 atmospheric 대기의
temperature 온도 repercussion 영향 untested 검증되지 않은
emit 방출하다, 내뿜다 sulfur 황 alter 변화시키다
cloud cover 구름양, 운량

해설

다른 연사가 Mr. Bell의 강연 시간을 대신하게 되면 Mr. Bell의 강연은 어떻게 할지 묻는 B의 질문에 대해 A가 그는 다른 연사가 비운 시간대를 대신해야 할 것이라고 대답하고, 빈칸 앞에서 다시 B가 that's a relief(다행이네요)라고 덧붙이고 있으므로, '늦게 참석하는 것이 안 하는 것보다 낫지요'라는 의미의 ④ 'Late participation is better than no participation'이 정답이다.

정답 ④

어휘

make it 시간 맞춰 가다, 성공하다 slot 자리, 시간, 틈 vacate 비우다, 떠나다
complain 불평하다, 항의하다 participation 참석, 참여

04 생활영어 Late participation is better than no participation. 난이도 하 ●○○

밑줄 친 부분에 들어갈 말로 적절한 것은?

A: I just got word from Mr. Bell that he's not going to make it on time.
B: Oh, no! Everyone's expecting him to give the first talk.
A: I know, so I asked the other speaker to take his slot.
B: That's probably the best option under the circumstances. But what about Mr. Bell?
A: He'll have to take the time slot vacated by the other speaker.
B: Well, that's a relief. _____

① Mr. Bell has never been late before.
② We should push back the first talk time.
③ The audience will complain about the change.
④ Late participation is better than no participation.

해석

A: 방금 Mr. Bell로부터 그가 제시간에 못 올 거라는 말을 들었어요.
B: 오, 안 돼요! 모두들 그가 첫 번째 강연을 하기를 기대하고 있다고요.
A: 알아요, 그래서 다른 연사에게 그의 자리를 대신해 달라고 요청해 뒀어요.
B: 그 상황에선 아마 그게 최선의 선택일 거예요. 그럼 Mr. Bell은 어쩌죠?
A: 그는 그냥 그 다른 연사가 비운 시간대를 대신해야 할 거예요.
B: 음, 다행이네요. 늦게 참석하는 것이 안 하는 것보다 낫지요.

① Mr. Bell은 결코 지각한 적이 없어요.
② 우리는 첫 번째 강연 시간을 늦춰야 해요.
③ 청중은 그 변경 사항에 대해 불평할 거예요.
④ 늦게 참석하는 것이 안 하는 것보다 낫지요.

05~06 다음 글을 읽고 물음에 답하시오.

To	Federal Communications Board
From	Richard Collins
Date	April 10
Subject	Television Content

Dear FCB Representatives,

As a concerned viewer and media consumer, I feel compelled to address the increasing amount of inappropriate content in television shows and movies, specifically how much violence is being shown.

I appreciate the variety of programs aired by the networks. However, the rising levels of graphic violence being depicted are troubling, especially given their impact on young people. Repeated exposure to violent and distressing scenes can desensitize and negatively influence young minds.

I ask that the FCB review the content and issue stronger guidelines to take care of the problem and ensure content aligns with the audience's expectations and family values.

I thank you for your time and hope steps are taken to promote responsible media content.

Respectfully,
Richard Collins

해석

수신: 연방 방송 통신 감독 위원회
발신: Richard Collins
날짜: 4월 10일
제목: TV 콘텐츠

연방 방송 통신 감독 위원회(FCB) 담당자분들께,

관심 있는 시청자이자 미디어 소비자로서, 저는 TV 프로그램과 영화에서 특히 얼마나 많은 폭력이 보여지고 있는지와 같이, 부적절한 콘텐츠가 증가하는 상황에 대해 꼭 말해야겠다는 생각이 듭니다.

저는 방송망에서 제공되는 다양한 프로그램들에 대해 감사드립니다. 하지만, 묘사되는 폭력의 생생함의 정도가 높아지는 것은 걱정스러운 일인데, 특히 젊은 사람들에게 미치는 그것들의 영향을 고려할 때 그렇습니다. 폭력적이고 비참한 장면들에의 반복적인 노출은 어린 마음들을 무감각하게 만들고 부정적으로 영향을 줄 수 있습니다.

저는 연방 방송 통신 감독 위원회가 콘텐츠를 검토하고, 문제 상황을 다루고 콘텐츠가 시청자들의 기대와 가족적 가치에 맞추도록 보장하기 위해 더 강력한 지침을 발행할 것을 요청드립니다.

귀하의 시간을 내어 주신 데 감사드리며 책임감 있는 미디어 콘텐츠를 촉진하기 위해 조치가 취해지기를 바랍니다.

존경을 담아,
Richard Collins

어휘

representative 담당자, 대표; 대표하는   compel ~하게 만들다, 강요하다
inappropriate 부적절한   violence 폭력   appreciate 감사하다, 감상하다
graphic 생생한, 그래픽의   depict 묘사하다   troubling 걱정스러운
exposure 노출   distressing 비참한, 고통스러운
desensitize 무감각하게 만들다   align with ~에 맞추다, 맞추어 조정하다
promote 촉진하다, 홍보하다

05　독해　목적 파악　난이도 중 ●●○

윗글의 목적으로 적절한 것은?

① 다양한 프로그램을 방송하는 방송사에 감사를 표하려고
② 개별 콘텐츠에 대한 심의를 강화할 것을 부탁하려고
③ 최근 방영된 TV 프로그램의 아쉬운 점을 전달하려고
④ 가족적 가치를 반영하는 새로운 콘텐츠를 제안하려고

해설

지문 중간에서 TV 프로그램과 영화에서 묘사되는 폭력의 생생함의 정도가 높아지는 것이 걱정스러운 일이라고 하고, 지문 마지막에서 연방 방송 통신 감독 위원회가 문제 상황을 다루기 위해 더 강력한 지침을 발행할 것을 요청한다고 했으므로, ② '개별 콘텐츠에 대한 심의를 강화할 것을 부탁하려고'가 이 글의 목적이다.

정답 ②

06　독해　유의어 파악　난이도 중 ●●○

밑줄 친 aligns with의 의미와 가장 가까운 것은?

① adapts to　　　　　② conforms to
③ interferes with　　④ copes with

해석

① ~에 적응한다　　② ~을 따른다
③ ~를 방해한다　　④ ~에 대처한다

해설

밑줄 친 부분이 포함된 문장에서 aligns with는 문맥상 시청자들의 기대와 가족적 가치'에 맞추다'라는 의미로 쓰였으므로, '~을 따른다'라는 의미의 ② conforms to가 정답이다.

정답 ②

어휘

adapt to ~에 적응하다   conform to ~을 따르다, 순응하다
interfere with ~를 방해하다   cope with ~에 대처하다

07　독해　내용 불일치 파악　난이도 중 ●●○

다음 글의 내용과 일치하지 않는 것은?

Tickets for the Yung Tower Observation Deck can be purchased in the first-floor lobby of the visitor center located at the base of Mount Slev. Admission is $15 for adults and $10 for senior citizens and children 13 years old and younger. Please note that tickets are valid only on the day of purchase from the time of purchase until the observation deck closes for the day.

Visitors must take the Mount Slev Cable Car from the visitor center up to the Yung Tower entrance, where there are elevators to the Observation Deck. During peak hours, visitors can expect to wait in line for the cable car, which has a capacity of approximately 40 people.

- If you have a reservation for Flame, the fine-dining restaurant at the highest point of the tower, please confirm your reservation at the visitor center before taking the cable car.

Please call 1 (800) 926-6543 for more information.

① The cost of admission is lower for senior citizens and children.
② Tickets for the observation deck can be purchased days in advance.
③ About 40 people can be transported from the visitor center to the tower at a time.
④ Visitors must take a cable car to get to Flame.

해석

Yung 타워 전망대 티켓은 Slev 산기슭에 위치한 방문자 센터 1층 로비에서 구매하실 수 있습니다. 입장료는 성인 15달러, 노인과 13세 이하 어린이는 10달러입니다. 티켓은 구매 당일에 구매 시점부터 그날 전망대가 문을 닫을 때까지만 유효하다는 점을 유의하세요.

방문객분들은 방문자 센터에서 Yung 타워 입구까지 Slev 산 케이블카를 타고 올라가셔야 하며, 이곳에 전망대로 가는 엘리베이터가 있습니다. 혼잡 시간대에, 방문객분들은 수용 인원이 약 40명인 케이블카를 타기 위해 줄 서서 기다리는 것을 예상하실 수 있습니다.

- 타워의 가장 꼭대기에 위치한 고급 레스토랑 Flame에 예약이 있으시다면, 케이블카를 타기 전에 방문자 센터에서 예약을 확인해 주세요.

DAY 22 하프모의고사 22회

더 많은 정보를 원하시면 1 (800) 926-6543으로 전화 주세요.

① 입장 요금은 노인과 어린이의 것이 더 낮다.
② 전망대 티켓은 며칠 앞서 구매될 수 있다.
③ 약 40명의 사람들이 방문자 센터부터 타워까지 한 번에 이동될 수 있다.
④ 방문객들은 Flame에 가기 위해 케이블카를 타야 한다.

해설
②번의 키워드인 be purchased(구매되다)를 바꾸어 표현한 지문의 purchase(구매) 주변의 내용에서 티켓은 구매 당일에 구매 시점부터 그날 전망대가 문을 닫을 때까지 유효하다고 했으므로, ② '전망대 티켓은 며칠 앞서 구매될 수 있다'는 지문의 내용과 다르다.

정답 ②

어휘
observation deck 전망대   admission 입장(료)   valid 유효한
capacity 수용 인원, 능력   approximately 약, 대략   confirm 확인하다
at a time 한 번에

08 독해 문단 순서 배열   난이도 중 ●●○

주어진 글 다음에 이어질 글의 순서로 적절한 것은?

Deep-sea mining is the extraction of valuable metals and minerals by cutting away wide areas of ocean floor with robotic equipment. While it provides a source of metals used in electronics, it is now at issue because of its projected environmental impacts.

(A) Once the foundations needed for survival are damaged, deep-sea organisms will die off. The same can be said of ocean floor corals, where many creatures live.

(B) One is the destruction of landforms through the use of techniques similar to surface mining for coal. The process involves the pressing of the sea floor, which releases masses of sediment that make the water dirty and toxic. Another disruption is the hindering of natural water flows.

(C) These two ways will alter the basic geological elements necessary for life in the deepest parts of the ocean. Resources that support biodiversity will be destroyed, and the natural transport of nutrients will be halted.

① (A) – (B) – (C) ② (B) – (A) – (C)
③ (B) – (C) – (A) ④ (C) – (A) – (B)

해석
심해 채굴은 로봇 장비로 해저의 넓은 구획을 잘라냄으로써 귀중한 금속과 광물을 추출하는 것이다. 그것은 전자 장치에 사용되는 금속의 원천을 제공하지만, 예상되는 환경에 미치는 영향들 때문에 현재 문제가 되고 있다.

(A) 일단 생존에 필요한 그 기반들이 손상되면, 심해 생물들은 죽게 될 것이다. 많은 생명체들이 살고 있는 해저 산호들에 대해서도 같은 말을 할 수 있다.

(B) 하나는 석탄의 노천 채굴과 유사한 기술의 사용을 통한 지형 파괴이다. 그 과정은 해저에 압력 가하기를 수반하는데, 이것은 물을 더럽히고 유독성으로 만드는 퇴적물 덩어리를 배출한다. 또 다른 환경 파괴는 자연스러운 물의 흐름을 방해하는 것이다.

(C) 이 두 가지 방식들은 바다 가장 깊은 부분에 있는 생명체에게 필요한 기본적인 지질학적 요소들을 변화시킬 것이다. 생물 다양성을 유지하는 자원들이 파괴될 것이고 영양소의 자연스러운 이동이 중단될 것이다.

해설
주어진 문장에서 심해 채굴은 환경에 미치는 영향들 때문에 문제가 되고 있다고 한 후, (B)에서 그 환경 영향 중 하나(One)는 지형 파괴이고, 또 다른(Another) 것은 자연스러운 물의 흐름 방해라고 설명하고 있다. 이어서 (C)에서 이 두 가지 방식들(These two ways)은 바다의 생명체에게 필요한 기본적인 지질학적 요소들을 변화시킬 것이라고 하고, (A)에서 생존에 필요한 그 기반들(the foundations needed for survival)이 손상되면 많은 심해 생물들이 죽게 될 것이라고 예측하고 있다. 따라서 ③ (B) – (C) – (A)가 정답이다.

정답 ③

어휘
mining 채굴, 광업   extraction 추출   projected 예상되는
foundation 기반   organism 생물   coral 산호   destruction 파괴
coal 석탄   sediment 퇴적물   toxic 유독성의
disruption (환경) 파괴, 붕괴, 혼란   hinder 방해하다   alter 변화시키다
geological 지질학적   element 요소   biodiversity 생물 다양성
nutrient 영양소   halt 중단시키다

09 독해 문장 삽입   난이도 중 ●●○

주어진 문장이 들어갈 위치로 적절한 것은?

The idea that general people could belong to a superior social class stimulated luxury goods consumption.

People are natural consumers, but before the 1900s, they mostly bought the necessities of life, such as food, clothing, and shelter. (①) Overconsumption became a lifestyle when industrialization made it possible for everyday people to purchase goods freely. (②) It was especially evident after the end of World War II, a period when marketers promoted greater spending by making it seem necessary for ordinary people to climb socially. (③) Families thought they could attain this status if they owned items that were considered luxurious back then—cars, cigarettes, and electric iceboxes. (④) It became crucial to have these possessions in order to meet the standard.

해석
일반인들이 상위의 사회 계층에 속할 수 있다는 생각은 사치품 소비를 활발하게 했다.

사람들은 타고난 소비자이지만, 1900년대 이전에는 주로 음식, 옷, 그리고 주거지와 같은 생활 필수품을 구입했다. ① 산업화가 평범한 사람들이 자유롭게 물건을 구매하는 것을 가능하게 만들면서 과소비가 하나의 생활 방식이 되었다. ② 그것은 특히 판매자들이 보통의 사람들이 사회적으로 상승하기 위해 더 큰 소비가 필요한 것처럼 보이게 함으로써 그것을 촉진했던 시기인 제2차 세계 대전 종전 후 특히 눈에 띄게 되었다. ③ 가정들은 자동차, 담배 그리고 냉장고 등 당시 사치스러운 것으로 여겨졌던 물건들을 소유하면 이 지위를 얻을 수 있을 것이라고 생각했다. ④ 그 기준을 충족시키기 위해서는 이러한 소유물들을 갖는 것이 아주 중요해졌다.

[해설]

③번 앞 문장에서 판매자들은 보통 사람들이 사회적으로 상승하기 위해 더 큰 소비가 필요한 것처럼 보이게 했다고 하고, 뒤 문장에서 가정들이 당시 사치스러운 것으로 여겨졌던 물건들을 소유하면 이 지위(this status)를 얻을 수 있을 것이라고 생각했다고 했으므로, ③번 자리에 일반인들이 상위 계층에 속할 수 있다는 생각이 사치품 소비를 활발하게 했다는 내용, 즉 가정들이 사치품 소비를 통해 얻고자 했던 지위가 무엇이었는지 언급하는 주어진 문장이 나와야 지문이 자연스럽게 연결된다.

정답 ③

[어휘]

superior 상위의, 우월한 stimulate 활발하게 하다, 자극하다
consumption 소비 shelter 주거지, 대피처 industrialization 산업화
evident 눈에 띄는, 분명한 promote 촉진하다, 홍보하다
attain 얻다, 도달하다 status 지위, 신분 crucial 아주 중요한, 결정적인
possession 소유(물)

10 독해 빈칸 완성 - 구   난이도 중 ●●○

밑줄 친 부분에 들어갈 말로 적절한 것은?

> Just decades ago, people who got tattoos were part of a cultural subgroup and had to make a special effort to find a tattoo shop. Today, pigmenting the skin is so popular that parlors can be easily found in downtown areas. About 30 percent of people in the US and in Britain have had markings etched onto their skin. Now that it is more widely accepted, more careful thought and planning is put into getting a tattoo. People who got one while in their early 20s now realize they were too young and the motif on their skin no longer suits them. This has increased the demand for skin clinics that offer laser tattoo removal. Since it can be costly and painful, professional tattoo artists encourage clients to _____ just in case they may come to dislike their body art in the future.

① consider tattoo design trends that are currently popular
② mull over the desired design before getting tattooed
③ be aware of the physical side effects of tattoos
④ choose tattoo artists with proper medical certification

[해석]

수십 년 전만 해도, 문신을 한 사람들은 문화적 하위 집단의 일부였고 문신 가게를 찾기 위해 특별한 노력을 해야 했다. 오늘날에는 피부에 그림을 입히는 것이 매우 인기가 많아서 시술실들을 도심 지역들에서 쉽게 찾아볼 수 있다. 미국과 영국 사람들의 약 30퍼센트가 그들의 피부에 무늬를 새겼다. 그것이 더 널리 받아들여지고 있기 때문에, 문신을 하는 데에는 보다 신중한 생각과 계획이 적용된다. 20대 초반에 문신을 한 사람들은 자신이 너무 어렸고 피부의 무늬가 그들에게 더 이상 어울리지 않는다는 것을 이제 깨닫는다. 이것은 레이저 문신 제거를 제공하는 피부 클리닉에 대한 수요를 증가시켜 왔다. 그것은 비용이 많이 들고 고통스러울 수 있기 때문에, 전문 문신사들은 고객들이 미래에 그들이 자신들의 신체에 한 예술을 싫어하게 될지도 모를 경우에 대비해 문신을 받기 전에 원하는 디자인을 숙고할 것을 권한다.

① 현재 인기 있는 문신 디자인 경향을 고려하다
② 문신을 받기 전에 원하는 디자인을 숙고하다
③ 문신의 신체적 부작용들을 인식하다
④ 적절한 의료 자격증이 있는 문신사를 선택하다

[해설]

빈칸 앞부분에 20대 초반에 문신을 한 사람들은 피부의 무늬가 그들에게 더 이상 어울리지 않는다는 것을 이제 깨닫는다는 내용이 있고, 빈칸이 있는 문장에 문신 제거는 비용이 많이 들고 고통스러울 수 있다는 내용이 있으므로, 문신사들이 '문신을 받기 전에 원하는 디자인을 숙고할' 것을 권한다고 한 ②번이 정답이다.

정답 ②

[어휘]

tattoo 문신 subgroup 하위 집단 make an effort 노력하다
pigment 그림을 입히다, 채색하다 parlor 시술실, 가게 marking 무늬
etch 새기다, 선명하게 그리다 motif 무늬, 주제 mull over ~을 숙고하다
side effect 부작용 certification 자격증

DAY 23 하프모의고사 23회

정답
p. 102

01	②	어휘	06	①	독해
02	③	문법	07	③	독해
03	③	문법	08	③	독해
04	②	생활영어	09	③	독해
05	③	독해	10	②	독해

취약영역 분석표

영역	맞힌 답의 개수
어휘	/1
생활영어	/1
문법	/2
독해	/6
TOTAL	/10

---

01 어휘 complain   난이도 하 ●○○

밑줄 친 부분에 들어갈 말로 적절한 것은?

The newly opened restaurant is receiving negative reviews from customers, as many _____ that the staff are unprofessional and make frequent mistakes during service.

① question   ② complain
③ promise   ④ reject

해석
새로 문을 연 식당은 고객들로부터 부정적인 평가를 받고 있는데, 고객 다수가 직원들이 전문가답지 못하고 서비스 도중 잦은 실수를 한다고 불평하기 때문이다.

① 질문하다   ② 불평하다
③ 약속하다   ④ 거절하다

정답 ②

어휘
unprofessional 전문가답지 못한 frequent 잦은 question 질문하다
complain 불평하다, 항의하다 promise 약속하다 reject 거절하다

---

02 문법 병치 구문   난이도 중 ●●○

밑줄 친 부분에 들어갈 말로 적절한 것은?

Standing at the edge of the flooded road as rain continued to pour heavily, the driver knew it was no use attempting to cross the dangerous waters or _____ for the storm to subside.

① wait   ② waited
③ waiting   ④ had waited

해석
비가 계속해서 거세게 쏟아질 때 침수된 도로 가장자리에 서 있으면서, 그 운전자는 위험한 물을 건너려 하거나 폭풍이 가라앉기를 기다리는 것이 소용없다는 것을 알았다.

해설
③ 병치 구문 빈칸은 등위접속사(or) 뒤에 오는 것의 자리이다. 등위접속사(or)로 연결된 병치 구문에서는 같은 구조끼리 연결되어야 하는데, 문맥상 '위험한 물을 건너려 하거나 폭풍이 가라앉기를 기다리는 것이 소용없다'라는 의미가 되어야 자연스럽고, or 앞에 동명사 관련 표현 it's no use -ing(-해도 소용없다)를 완성하는 동명사 attempting이 왔으므로, or 뒤에도 동명사가 와야 한다. 따라서 동명사 ③ waiting이 정답이다.

정답 ③

어휘
flood 침수시키다, 물에 잠기다; 홍수 pour 쏟아지다, 따르다 heavily 거세게
attempt 시도하다; 시도 subside 가라앉다

---

03 문법 동사의 종류 | to 부정사 | 부사절   난이도 중 ●●○

밑줄 친 부분 중 어법상 옳지 않은 것은?

When applying for jobs, there are several things that can be done ① to enable one to stand out. First, tailor your résumé to the industry. For instance, in creative fields, it is advisable ② for applicants to take a more artistic approach, such as formatting their résumés in a more flexible manner. In addition, include key words from the job listings so that it can help the hiring manager ③ finding your résumé ④ when they search through job sites.

해석
입사 지원을 할 때, 쉽게 눈에 띄게 하기 위해 행해질 수 있는 몇 가지 것들이 있다. 우선, 이력서를 업계에 맞추어라. 예를 들어, 창작 분야의 경우, 지원자들이 보다 유연한 방식으로 자신들의 이력서를 구성하는 것과 같이 더 예술적인 접근법을 취하는 것이 바람직하다. 뿐만 아니라, 구인 목록에

있는 핵심어들을 포함해서 그것이 인사 담당자가 구인 사이트를 통해 검색할 때 당신의 이력서를 발견하는 것을 돕도록 하라.

해설

③ 원형 부정사를 목적격 보어로 취하는 동사 준 사역동사 help는 to 부정사 또는 원형 부정사를 목적격 보어로 취하므로, 목적격 보어 자리의 finding을 (to) find로 고쳐야 한다.

[오답 분석]

① to 부정사의 역할 문맥상 '쉽게 눈에 띄게 하기 위해'라는 의미가 되어야 자연스러우므로 부사 역할을 할 때 목적을 나타내는 to 부정사 to enable이 올바르게 쓰였다.

② to 부정사의 의미상 주어 문장의 주어(it)와 to 부정사의 행위 주체(applicants)가 달라 to 부정사의 의미상 주어가 필요한 경우 'for + 명사'를 to 부정사 앞에 써야 하므로, 'for + 명사' 형태의 for applicants가 to 부정사 to take 앞에 올바르게 쓰였다.

④ 부사절 접속사 문맥상 '인사 담당자가 구인 사이트를 통해 검색할 때'라는 의미가 되어야 자연스러운데, '~할 때'라는 의미는 부사절 접속사 when을 사용하여 나타낼 수 있다. 이때 when이 이끄는 부사절은 '부사절 접속사 + 주어 + 동사'의 형태가 되어야 하므로 when they search가 올바르게 쓰였다.

정답 ③

어휘

stand out 쉽게 눈에 띄다, 두드러지다 tailor 맞추다, 조정하다
résumé 이력서 advisable 바람직한 applicant 지원자

---

04 생활영어 Can I do a practice run for the meeting that morning?
난이도 하 ●○○

밑줄 친 부분에 들어갈 말로 적절한 것은?

 Riley Scott
How's the preparation for the annual performance review coming along?
11:25

Ethan Davis
All the data and reports are ready. I'm planning to ask you to review them this afternoon.
11:26

 Riley Scott
Then I'll give you feedback tomorrow morning.
11:27

Ethan Davis
Also, I've reserved meeting room A for the annual performance review on Friday.
11:28

 Riley Scott
Good. What time is the meeting?
11:28

Ethan Davis
It's 2 p.m. _____
_____
11:29

 Riley Scott
Of course. It's a very important meeting, so make sure to take enough time to prepare.
11:30

① What is the time limit for the presentation?
② Can I do a practice run for the meeting that morning?
③ How long does the meeting usually last?
④ Should I book an earlier reservation time?

해석

Riley Scott: 연례 성과 검토 준비는 어떻게 진행되고 있나요?
Ethan Davis: 모든 데이터와 보고서가 준비되었어요. 오늘 오후에 검토를 요청드릴 계획입니다.
Riley Scott: 그럼 제가 내일 아침에 의견을 드릴게요.
Ethan Davis: 그리고, 연례 성과 검토를 위해 금요일에 A 회의실을 예약해 두었습니다.
Riley Scott: 좋아요. 회의는 몇 시인가요?
Ethan Davis: 오후 2시입니다. <u>그날 오전에 제가 회의를 위한 예행연습을 해도 될까요?</u>
Riley Scott: 물론이죠. 매우 중요한 회의인 만큼 충분한 시간을 내어 준비하세요.

① 발표 제한 시간은 얼마인가요?
② 그날 오전에 제가 회의를 위한 예행연습을 해도 될까요?
③ 회의는 보통 얼마나 오래 진행되나요?
④ 제가 더 빠른 시간을 예약해야 할까요?

해설

연례 성과 검토를 위한 회의가 금요일 몇 시인지 묻는 Riley에게 Ethan이 오후 2시라고 대답하고, 빈칸 뒤에서 다시 Riley가 Of course. It's a very important meeting, so make sure to take enough time to prepare(물론이죠. 매우 중요한 회의인 만큼 충분한 시간을 내어 준비하세요)라고 대답하고 있으므로, '그날 오전에 제가 회의를 위한 예행연습을 해도 될까요?'라는 의미의 ② 'Can I do a practice run for the meeting that morning?'이 정답이다.

정답 ②

어휘

preparation 준비 annual 연례의, 한 해의 practice run 예행연습

05~06 다음 글을 읽고 물음에 답하시오.

Bank Failures

Guaranteeing the deposits of accountholders during bank failures is the main function of the Federal Banking Insurance Agency (FBIA). Ensuring the safety of money held by the country's banks gives consumers more confidence in their financial institutions and protects their assets.

Deposit Insurance

Deposit insurance is a _____ with the backing of the federal government that ensures the money accountholders deposit is safe, up to a predetermined limit, even in cases in which a bank goes out of business.

In the event of a bank failure and closure, the FBIA acts as a receiver for the business. It dispatches teams of professionals to take over the bank, sell off its assets, and attempt to find other banks to purchase the business. This allows it to reimburse depositors in a timely fashion, usually within the course of one business day, and minimizes disruptions for consumers.

해석

은행 파산
계좌 소유자들의 예금을 은행 파산 시에 보장하는 것이 연방 은행 보장 기관(FBIA)의 주요 기능입니다. 국가의 은행들에 의해 보유된 자금의 안전을 지키는 일은 소비자들에게 그들의 금융 기관에 대한 더 큰 신뢰를 주고 그들의 자산을 보호합니다.

예금 보험
예금 보험은 계좌 소유자들이 예금한 돈이 은행이 도산하는 경우라 할지라도 미리 정해진 한도까지 안전할 것을 보장하는, 연방 정부의 지원에 따른 보호 장치입니다.

은행 파산 및 폐쇄의 경우, 연방 은행 보장 기관은 해당 사업체의 파산 관리인으로서 역할을 합니다. 기관은 그 은행을 인수하고, 그것의 자산을 매각하며, 해당 사업체를 사들일 다른 은행들을 찾으려고 시도하기 위해 전문가 팀을 파견합니다. 이는 그것으로 하여금 제때에, 일반적으로 영업일 하루 이내에 예금자들에게 상환하게 하고, 소비자들의 혼란을 최소화 합니다.

어휘
deposit 예금, 보증금; 예금하다 accountholder 계좌 소유자
confidence 신뢰, 자신(감) institution 기관 asset 자산
predetermined 미리 정해진 go out of business 도산하다, 폐업하다
receiver 파산 관리인, 수취인 dispatch 파견하다, 보내다
take over ~을 인수하다 reimburse 상환하다, 환급하다 depositor 예금자
in a timely fashion 제때에 minimize 최소화하다 disruption 혼란, 중단

---

05 독해 요지 파악 난이도 중 ●●○

윗글의 요지로 적절한 것은?

① FBIA aims to assist consumers in increasing their assets.
② FBIA focuses on ensuring banks do not fail.
③ FBIA's main purpose is to protect funds held by banks.
④ FBIA tries to sell banks that are in financial trouble before they fail.

해석
① 연방 은행 보장 기관은 소비자들이 그들의 자산을 증가시키는 데 있어 돕는 것을 목표로 한다.
② 연방 은행 보장 기관은 은행들이 파산하지 않게 하는 데 중점을 둔다.
③ 연방 은행 보장 기관의 주요 목적은 은행에 보유된 자금을 보호하는 것이다.
④ 연방 은행 보장 기관은 재정적 어려움에 처한 은행들이 파산하기 전 그것들을 매각하려고 노력한다.

해설
지문 처음에서 계좌 소유자들의 예금을 은행 파산 시에 보장하는 것이 연방 은행 보장 기관의 주요 기능이라고 하고, 지문 뒷부분에서 은행 파산 및 폐쇄의 경우 파산 관리인 역할을 하며 예금자들에게 예금이 상환되게 함으로써 소비자들의 혼란을 최소화한다고 했으므로, ③ '연방 은행 보장 기관의 주요 목적은 은행에 보유된 자금을 보호하는 것이다'가 이 글의 요지이다.

정답 ③

---

06 독해 빈칸 완성 – 단어 난이도 중 ●●○

윗글의 밑줄 친 부분에 들어갈 말로 적절한 것은?

① safeguard   ② barrier
③ hardship   ④ permit

해석
① 보호 장치   ② 장애물
③ 고난   ④ 허가

해설
빈칸이 있는 문장에서 예금 보험으로 계좌 소유자들의 예금은 은행이 도산하는 경우라 할지라도 미리 정해진 한도까지 안전하다고 했으므로, 연방 정부의 지원에 따른 '보호 장치'라고 한 ①번이 정답이다.

정답 ①

어휘
safeguard 보호 장치; 보호하다 barrier 장애물 hardship 고난, 어려움
permit 허가

---

07 독해 내용 일치 파악 난이도 하 ●○○

The National Archive에 관한 다음 글의 내용과 일치하는 것은?

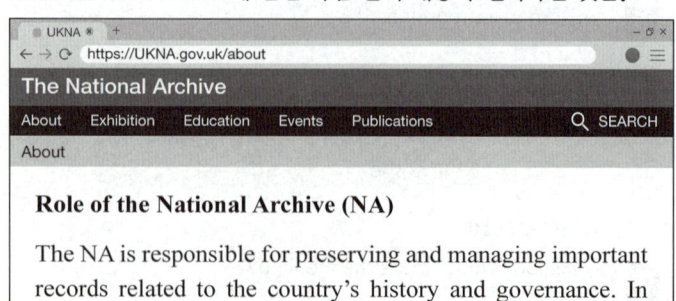

Role of the National Archive (NA)

The NA is responsible for preserving and managing important records related to the country's history and governance. In keeping with this mission, it advises government agencies on how to properly manage records to follow all legal requirements. It also facilitates online public access to these documents in order to ensure transparency. Because of the digitization efforts of the NA, ordinary citizens and researchers can easily access records dating back hundreds of years at no cost. Materials in the archive can even be printed or bound for a modest fee.

① It allows citizens to store important documents and items.
② It encourages people to visit the archive and access documents.
③ It makes centuries-old documents available to the public.
④ It will print out any record at no cost to users.

해석

국가 기록원(NA)의 역할

국가 기록원은 국가의 역사 및 통치와 관련된 중요한 기록들을 보존하고 관리하는 일을 담당합니다. 이러한 사명에 따라, 국가 기록원은 정부 기관들에게 모든 법적 요건을 준수하여 기록을 적절히 관리하는 방법에 대해 조언합니다. 국가 기록원은 또한 투명성을 보장하기 위해 이러한 문서들에 대해 온라인을 통한 일반인 접근을 가능하게 합니다. 국가 기록원의 디지털화 노력 덕분에, 일반 시민들과 연구자들은 수백 년 전으로 거슬러 올라가는 기록들에 무료로 쉽게 접근할 수 있습니다. 기록 보관소의 자료들은 소정의 수수료를 지불하면 인쇄하거나 제본할 수도 있습니다.

① 그것은 시민들이 중요한 기록과 물품을 보관하게 한다.
② 그것은 사람들이 기록원을 방문하여 기록에 접근하도록 장려한다.
③ 그것은 수백 년 된 문서들을 일반 대중이 이용할 수 있도록 한다.
④ 그것은 사용자들에게 어떤 기록이든 무료로 인쇄해 준다.

해설

③번의 키워드인 centuries-old documents(수백 년 된 문서들)를 바꾸어 표현한 지문의 records dating back hundreds of years(수백 년 전으로 거슬러 올라가는 기록들) 주변의 내용에서 국가 기록원은 일반 시민들과 연구자들이 수백 년 전으로 거슬러 올라가는 기록들에 쉽게 접근할 수 있게 한다고 했으므로, ③ '그것은 수백 년 된 문서들을 일반 대중이 이용할 수 있도록 한다'가 지문의 내용과 일치한다.

[오답 분석]
① 국가 기록원은 국가의 역사 및 통치와 관련된 기록들을 보존 및 관리한다고 했으므로, 그것이 시민들이 중요한 기록과 물품을 보관하게 한다는 것은 지문의 내용과 다르다.
② 국가 기록원은 온라인으로 일반인이 자료에 접근하는 것을 가능하게 한다고 했으므로, 그것이 사람들이 기록원을 방문하여 기록에 접근하도록 장려한다는 것은 지문의 내용과 다르다.
④ 국가 기록원의 자료들은 소정의 수수료를 지불하면 인쇄할 수 있다고 했으므로, 그것이 사용자들에게 어떤 기록이든 무료로 인쇄해 준다는 것은 지문의 내용과 다르다.

정답 ③

어휘

archive 기록 보관소; 보관하다 preserve 보존하다, 관리하다
governance 통치 legal 법적인 requirement 요건
facilitate 가능하게 하다 transparency 투명성 digitization 디지털화
bind 제본하다, 묶다 modest 적당한, 별로 많지 않은, 겸손한

---

08 독해 주제 파악 난이도 중 ●●○

다음 글의 주제로 적절한 것은?

Narcolepsy is a sleep disorder that results in not being able to stay awake for long periods of time. People who suffer from this condition often have extreme daytime drowsiness and find themselves falling asleep at random times. In fact, they may suddenly be overcome by their sleepiness while in the middle of performing a task, or even in the middle of a conversation. Sometimes, this causes them to slur their words or even collapse. Unfortunately, there is no cure for narcolepsy at this time. Instead, sleep specialists offer medications that can help reduce the disorder's impact on sufferers' lives and guide them in changing their behavior to manage their symptoms. Most often, this encompasses devising sleep schedules that prevent drowsiness at inopportune times. These not only have strict nighttime sleep rules, but can also include scheduled naps so the patient can stay awake at other times.

① causes of extreme daytime sleepiness disorders
② the impact of sleep disorders on social life
③ managing narcolepsy through medication and schedules
④ novel surgical procedures for narcolepsy patients

해석

기면증은 오랜 시간 동안 깨어 있지 못하게 하는 수면 장애이다. 이 질환으로 고통받는 사람들은 종종 낮 시간의 극심한 졸음을 겪으며, 닥치는 대로 잠이 드는 스스로를 발견한다. 실제로, 그들은 작업을 하는 도중이나 심지어 대화 도중에도 갑자기 졸음에 꼼짝 못하게 될 수 있다. 때때로, 이 질환은 그들이 불분명하게 말을 하거나 심지어 쓰러지게 한다. 안타깝게도, 현재 기면증에 대한 치료법은 없다. 대신, 수면 전문가들은 환자들의 생활에 미치는 그 장애의 영향을 줄이는 데 도움이 될 수 있는 약을 제공하고 증상을 관리하기 위해 그들이 행동을 변화시키도록 인도한다. 대부분의 경우, 이것은 부적절한 때의 졸음을 예방하는 수면 일정을 계획하는 것을 포함한다. 이것들은 엄격한 야간 수면 규칙을 가질 뿐만 아니라, 환자가 다른 시간에 깨어 있을 수 있도록 예정된 낮잠도 포함할 수 있다.

① 낮 시간의 극심한 졸림 장애의 원인들
② 수면 장애가 사회 생활에 미치는 영향
③ 약물과 일정을 통해 기면증 관리하기
④ 기면증 환자를 위한 새로운 수술 절차

해설

지문 전반에 걸쳐 기면증은 오랜 시간 깨어 있지 못하는 수면 장애인데, 현재 기면증에 대한 치료법은 없지만 그 장애의 영향을 줄이는 약을 제공하고 증상을 관리하기 위해 특정한 수면 일정을 계획하게 하는 수면 전문가들의 도움을 받을 수 있다고 알려 주고 있다. 따라서 ③ '약물과 일정을 통해 기면증 관리하기'가 이 글의 주제이다.

정답 ③

어휘

disorder 장애, 병, 엉망 stay awake 깨어 있다 extreme 극심한
drowsiness 졸음 random 닥치는 대로의, 임의의
overcome 꼼짝 못하게 하다, 극복하다 slur 불분명하게 말하다
collapse 쓰러지다 medication 약 encompass 포함하다

DAY 23 하프모의고사 23회

devise 계획하다, 고안하다 inopportune 부적절한, 시기가 나쁜
strict 엄격한 nap 낮잠 novel 새로운; 소설 surgical 수술의

09 독해 무관한 문장 삭제   난이도 중 ●●○

다음 글의 흐름상 어색한 문장은?

After a series of studies, researchers have determined that the traditional practice of preventing foreign-language learners from using bilingual dictionaries while reading may not be wise. ① To test the effect of using a dictionary while reading, the researchers split students into two groups—one with access to electronic dictionaries and one without them—and had them read a passage in the second language. ② They then gave the students a vocabulary test to see how well they understood the new words that they had encountered. ③ It was found that the average modern English dictionary includes more than 175,000 distinct words. ④ When the results were analyzed, they showed that the students who were able to look up words understood and retained them much better than those who guessed their meaning from the context.

해석

일련의 연구 끝에, 연구원들은 외국어 학습자들이 책을 읽는 동안 두 가지 언어로 된 사전을 사용하지 못하게 하는 종래의 관행이 현명하지 않을 수도 있다는 것을 밝혔다. ① 책을 읽는 동안 사전을 사용하는 것의 효과를 시험하기 위해, 연구원들은 학생들을 전자사전을 사용할 수 있는 집단과 사용할 수 없는 집단 두 개로 나누었고, 그들에게 제2외국어로 쓰인 한 구절을 읽게 했다. ② 그리고 나서 그들은 학생들이 접했던 새로운 단어를 얼마나 잘 이해했는지 알아보기 위해 단어 시험을 실시했다. ③ 일반적인 현대 영어 사전은 17만 5천 개 이상의 다른 단어들을 포함하는 것으로 밝혀졌다. ④ 결과가 분석되었을 때, 그것들은 (전자사전에서) 단어들을 찾아볼 수 있었던 학생들이 문맥에서 의미를 추측한 학생들보다 그것들(단어들)을 훨씬 더 잘 이해하고 기억한다는 것을 보여 주었다.

해설

첫 문장에서 외국어 학습자들에게 두 가지 언어로 된 사전을 사용하지 못하게 하는 관행은 바람직하지 않을 수도 있다고 언급한 뒤, ①, ②, ④번에서 전자사전 사용 여부에 따라 나눈 두 집단에게 제 2외국어 구절을 읽히고 단어 시험을 치른 결과, 전자사전을 사용한 학생들이 단어들을 훨씬 더 잘 이해하고 기억했다고 설명하고 있다. 그러나 ③번은 '현대 영어 사전이 포함하고 있는 단어 수'에 대한 내용으로, 첫 문장의 내용과 관련이 없다.

정답 ③

어휘

bilingual 두 언어로 쓰인, 이중 언어 사용자의 split 나누다
encounter 접하다, 마주치다 distinct 다른, 구분되는 analyze 분석하다
look up ~을 찾아보다 retain 기억하다, 유지하다 context 문맥, 전후 사정

10 독해 문장 삽입   난이도 중 ●●○

주어진 문장이 들어갈 위치로 적절한 것은?

In addition to inferior care, they argue it results in a great cost for the government.

Critics of nationalized health care contend that it has many disadvantages over a system in which care is provided on a for-profit basis. (①) They claim that a government-run system is inefficient and reduces the quality and the range of treatment options available. (②) In the United States, for example, estimates indicate that implementing a universal health care program would require an outlay of more than 15 trillion dollars over the first ten years. (③) Opponents also point to relatively longer wait times for diagnostic tests like MRIs in countries with publicly-run systems. (④) They commonly cite the Canadian system as the perfect example of this, as being sent to a specialist there can take nearly six months in some provinces.

해석

질 낮은 의료에 더해, 그들은 그것이 정부에 큰 비용을 초래한다고 주장한다.

국유화된 의료에 대한 비판론자들은 영리를 목적으로 의료가 제공되는 체제에 비해 많은 단점이 있다고 주장한다. ① 그들은 정부가 운영하는 체제가 비효율적이고, 이용 가능한 치료 선택지의 질과 범위를 감소시킨다고 주장한다. ② 예를 들어, 미국에서는 보편적 의료 보장 프로그램을 실시하려면 처음 10년 동안 15조 달러 이상의 지출이 필요하다는 것을 시사하는 추정치가 있다. ③ 반대론자들은 또한 공적으로 운영되는 체제를 갖춘 국가들에서 MRI와 같은 진단 검사를 위한 대기 시간이 상대적으로 더 길다는 점을 지적한다. ④ 그들은 흔히 이것의 완벽한 예시로 캐나다의 체제를 언급하는데, 일부 지방에서는 전문의에게로 보내지는 데 거의 6개월이 걸릴 수 있기 때문이다.

해설

②번 앞 문장에서 국유화된 의료가 이용 가능한 치료 선택지의 질을 감소시킨다고 하고, 뒤 문장에서 미국에서 보편적 의료 보장 프로그램 실시하려면 처음 10년 동안 15조 달러 이상의 지출이 필요하다는 추정치를 예시로 언급했으므로, ②번 자리에 비판론자들은 질 낮은 의료에 더해 국유화된 의료 시스템이 정부에 큰 비용을 초래한다고 주장한다는 내용, 즉 국유화된 의료의 질적 저하에서 더 나아가 재정적 측면의 단점을 추가로 언급하는 주어진 문장이 나와야 지문이 자연스럽게 연결된다.

정답 ②

어휘

inferior 질 낮은, 열등한 nationalize 국유화하다 contend 주장하다
disadvantage 단점 for-profit 영리 목적의 inefficient 비효율적인
estimate 추정치; 추정하다 universal 보편적인, 전 세계적인
outlay 지출, 소비 trillion 1조 opponent 반대론자, 상대
diagnostic 진단의 cite 언급하다, 인용하다 province 지방, 주

DAY 24 하프모의고사 24회

정답 (p. 106)

01	②	어휘	06	④	독해
02	①	문법	07	②	독해
03	②	문법	08	③	독해
04	②	생활영어	09	④	독해
05	②	독해	10	①	독해

취약영역 분석표

영역	맞힌 답의 개수
어휘	/1
생활영어	/1
문법	/2
독해	/6
TOTAL	/10

---

01 어휘 figure out 난이도 상 ●●●

밑줄 친 부분에 들어갈 말로 적절한 것은?

Readers can often _____ the meaning of unknown words thanks to context clues.

① set about
② figure out
③ carry on
④ hold onto

해석

독자들은 종종 문맥상의 단서들 덕분에 알 수 없는 단어들의 의미를 이해할 수 있다.

① ~을 시작하다
② ~을 이해하다
③ ~을 계속하다
④ ~을 고수하다

정답 ②

어휘

unknown 알 수 없는, 알려지지 않은 context 문맥상의; 문맥 clue 단서
set about ~을 시작하다, 착수하다 figure out ~을 이해하다
carry on ~을 계속하다 hold onto ~을 고수하다, 꼭 잡다

---

02 문법 비교 구문 난이도 중 ●●○

밑줄 친 부분에 들어갈 말로 적절한 것은?

The new stadium is _____ the previous one, accommodating many more spectators.

① three times as large as
② three times as largely as
③ three times as larger than
④ three times as large than

해석

새 경기장은 이전 경기장의 세 배만큼 커서, 더 많은 관중을 수용할 수 있다.

해설

① 원급 문맥상 '이전 경기장의 세 배만큼 크다'라는 의미가 되어야 자연스러운데, '~배만큼 –하다'는 원급 표현 '배수사 + as + 원급 + as'의 형태로 나타낼 수 있으므로 ①, ②번이 정답 후보이다. 이때 as ~ as 사이가 형용사 자리인지 부사 자리인지는 as, as를 지우고 구별하는데, be동사(is)의 보어 자리에는 형용사 역할을 하는 것이 와야 하므로 형용사 large가 쓰인 ① three times as large as가 정답이다.

정답 ①

어휘

stadium 경기장 previous 이전의 accommodate 수용하다, 숙박시키다
spectator 관중, 구경꾼

---

03 문법 수 일치|비교 구문|관계절|분사 난이도 중 ●●○

밑줄 친 부분 중 어법상 옳지 않은 것은?

One of the ① oldest forms of the English novel ② are the Robinsonade. It takes its name from modern English novels, *Robinson Crusoe*. The original novel is about a man ③ who was shipwrecked on an island and had to survive before escaping. Books in this genre share themes with the genre's origin, ④ centering around stories of isolation, survival, and rebuilding both the self and society.

해석

영어 소설의 가장 오래된 형태들 중 하나는 '로빈슨 크루소 부류의 문학'이다. 그것은 그 이름을 현대 영어 소설 『로빈슨 크루소』에서 따왔다. 그 원작 소설은 섬에 난파되어 탈출하기까지 살아남아야 했던 한 남자에 관한 것이다. 이 장르의 책들은 그 장르의 기원(로빈슨 크루소)과 주제를 공유하는데, 이것들은 고립, 생존 그리고 자아와 사회 모두를 재건하는 이야기에 중점을 둔다.

DAY 24 하프모의고사 24회

해설

② **수량 표현의 수 일치** 주어 자리에 단수 취급하는 수량 표현 'one of + 복수 명사'(One of the oldest forms)가 왔으므로 복수 동사 are를 단수 동사 is로 고쳐야 한다.

[오답 분석]
① **최상급 관련 표현** 문맥상 '가장 오래된 형태들 중 하나'라는 의미가 되어야 자연스러운데, '가장 ~한 -중 하나'는 최상급 관련 표현 'one of the + 최상급'의 형태로 나타낼 수 있으므로 최상급 oldest가 올바르게 쓰였다.
③ **관계대명사** 선행사(a man)가 사람이고 관계절 내에서 동사 was shipwrecked의 주어 역할을 하므로, 사람을 나타내는 주격 관계대명사 who가 올바르게 쓰였다.
④ **분사구문의 형태** 주절의 주어(Books)와 분사구문이 '책들이 ~에 중점을 두다'라는 의미의 능동 관계이므로 현재분사 centering이 올바르게 쓰였다.

정답 ②

어휘

shipwreck 난파시키다 escape 탈출하다; 탈출
center around ~에 중점을 두다 isolation 고립 rebuild 재건하다

---

04 생활영어 Is there any way we can reschedule?
난이도 하 ●○○

밑줄 친 부분에 들어갈 말로 적절한 것은?

A: Any interest in visiting my hometown with me?
B: I'd love to. When are you going?
A: I'm going this weekend.
B: I'll be in the office all weekend. _____?
A: Unfortunately, I need to go soon, and this is my only free weekend for a while.
B: I see. That's too bad. I want to join you next time, though.

① Are we still able to get tickets
② Is there any way we can reschedule
③ What time does the flight leave
④ How long will you be out of town

해석

A: 나랑 같이 내 고향에 가 볼 생각 있어?
B: 나야 좋지. 언제 갈 건데?
A: 이번 주말에 가려고.
B: 나는 주말 내내 사무실에 있을 거야. 우리가 일정을 변경할 수 있는 방법은 없을까?
A: 안타깝지만 나는 빨리 가 봐야 하고, 당분간은 이번 주말이 유일하게 한가로워.
B: 알겠어. 아쉽다. 그래도 다음번에는 함께하길 바라.

① 우리가 아직 표를 구할 수 있을까
② 우리가 일정을 변경할 수 있는 방법은 없을까
③ 비행기가 몇 시에 출발해
④ 얼마나 오랫동안 시내를 떠나 있을 거야

해설

이번 주말에 같이 고향에 가자는 A의 제안에 대해 B가 주말 내내 사무실에 있을 예정이라고 대답하고, 빈칸 뒤에서 다시 A가 Unfortunately, I need to go soon, and this is my only free weekend for a while(안타깝지만 나는 빨리 가 봐야 하고, 당분간은 이번 주말이 유일하게 한가로워)이라고 말하고 있으므로, '우리가 일정을 변경할 수 있는 방법은 없을까'라는 의미의 ② 'Is there any way we can reschedule'이 정답이다.

정답 ②

05~06 다음 글을 읽고 물음에 답하시오.

_____(A)_____

Don't be a couch potato—join us for the Ridgemont Potato Festival, the province's longest-running festival. Bring the entire family for a weekend of fun that celebrates our city's most important crop!

Details
- **Date and Time:** Saturday, April 8 – Sunday, April 9; 11:00 a.m. – 7:00 p.m.
- **Admission:** Entry is free; food vendors and certain activities require cash.
- **Location:** Ridgemont Fairgrounds

Attractions
- **Global Potato Feast**
  Enjoy potato-based dishes from around the world, including potato pancakes, soups, and salads. For a classic treat, don't miss out on complimentary French fries!
- **Potato Contests**
  Take part in the fun with potato peeling races and "hot" potato toss competitions, open to both children and adults.

For the safety of all guests, pets are not allowed on the fairgrounds. Additional information about the festival's schedule can be found at ridgemontpotatofestival.com.

해석

(A) 훌륭한 작물과 함께 즐겨 보세요

소파에만 누워 계시지 말고, 가장 오래 지속되고 있는 도 축제인 Ridgemont 감자 축제에 참여하세요. 우리 시의 가장 중요한 작물을 기념하는 즐거운 주말에 온 가족을 데려오세요!

상세 정보
- **날짜 및 시간:** 4월 8일 토요일 – 4월 9일 일요일, 오전 11시 – 오후 7시

- **입장료**: 입장은 무료입니다. 음식 노점상들과 일부 활동들이 현금을 필요로 합니다.
- **장소**: Ridgemont 박람회장

즐길 거리
- **세계 감자 축제**
  감자로 만든 팬케이크, 수프, 샐러드 등 감자를 기반으로 한 전 세계 요리들을 즐겨 보세요. 고전적인 간식으로는, 무료 감자 튀김을 놓치시면 안 됩니다!
- **감자 경연 대회**
  어린이와 성인 모두에게 열려 있는 감자 껍질 벗기기 경주와 '뜨거운' 감자 던지기 대회의 즐거움에 참여하세요.

모든 방문객분들의 안전을 위해, 반려동물은 박람회장에 출입이 허용되지 않습니다. 축제 일정에 관한 추가 정보는 ridgemontpotatofestival.com에서 확인하실 수 있습니다.

어휘

couch potato 소파에만 누워 있는 사람 province 도, 행정 구역
vendor 노점상 fairground 박람회장 attraction 즐길 거리, 매력
feast 축제 treat 간식, 대접; 대하다 complimentary 무료의
peel 껍질을 벗기다; 껍질

05 독해 제목 파악 난이도 중 ●●○

(A)에 들어갈 윗글의 제목으로 적절한 것은?

① Learn Delicious Potato Recipes
② Have Fun with a Cool Crop
③ Teach Children How to Use Potatoes
④ Expand Tourism in Our Province

해석

① 맛있는 감자 요리법들을 배워 보세요
② 훌륭한 작물과 함께 즐겨 보세요
③ 아이들에게 감자를 활용하는 법을 가르치세요
④ 우리 도의 관광업을 확장해 봅시다

해설

지문 앞부분에서 시의 가장 중요한 작물인 감자를 기념하는 축제에 가족과 함께 참여하라고 하고, 지문 중간에서 감자를 활용한 축제 행사들을 소개하고 있으므로, ② '훌륭한 작물과 함께 즐겨 보세요'가 이 글의 제목이다.

정답 ②

어휘

expand 확장하다, 확대하다 tourism 관광 (사업)

06 독해 내용 불일치 파악 난이도 하 ●○○

Ridgemont Potato Festival에 관한 윗글의 내용과 일치하지 않는 것은?

① 이틀 모두 같은 시간에 끝난다.
② 축제 입장료가 없다.
③ 모든 연령대의 사람들이 대회에 참가할 수 있다.
④ 축제는 반려동물 친화적인 행사이다.

해설

④번의 키워드인 '반려동물'이 그대로 언급된 지문의 pets 주변 내용에서 방문객들의 안전을 위해 반려동물은 박람회장에 출입이 허용되지 않는다고 했으므로, ④ '축제는 반려동물 친화적인 행사이다'는 지문의 내용과 다르다.

정답 ④

07 독해 빈칸 완성 - 구 난이도 중 ●●○

밑줄 친 부분에 들어갈 말로 적절한 것은?

To	equipment@UrbanEvents.com
From	CarlaLandis@Tidewater.gov
Date	August 26
Subject	Equipment Rental

Dear Rental Manager,

I am writing to inquire about renting some audio equipment for the city's annual employee appreciation picnic.

We will be holding the picnic at Triton Park Pavilion the first Sunday of November. For the four-hour picnic, we will need to rent microphones and speakers to be used during speeches and various events. We will also need a projector so that we can present a slide show of the city's achievements over the last year. Keep in mind that everything will be done in the park, so all of the equipment needs to be able to be used outdoors.

Please send me a list of equipment options that _____ _____. In addition, please note that someone will need to drop off and pick up the equipment on the day of the event.

I thank you for your time.

Respectfully,

Carla Landis, City Clerk

① would include weatherproof items
② would meet our needs for the event
③ would fall within our city's budget range
④ would support presentations throughout the entire day

DAY 24 하프모의고사 24회

해석

수신: equipment@UrbanEvents.com
발신: CarlaLandis@Tidewater.gov
날짜: 8월 26일
제목: 장비 대여 관련

대여 관리자님께,

저는 시의 연례 직원 감사 야유회를 위한 오디오 장비 대여에 관해 문의드리고자 글을 씁니다.

저희는 11월 첫째 주 일요일에 Triton 공원 파빌리온에서 야유회를 열 예정입니다. 4시간 동안 진행되는 이 야유회에서, 저희는 연설과 다양한 행사 중에 사용될 마이크와 스피커를 대여해야 할 것입니다. 저희는 지난해 시의 성과에 대한 슬라이드 쇼를 상영할 수 있도록 프로젝터 또한 필요합니다. 모든 행사가 공원에서 진행될 것임에 유념해 주세요, 그러므로 모든 장비는 야외에서 사용될 수 있어야 합니다.

행사에 대한 저희의 요구 사항에 부합할 장비 선택지 목록을 제게 보내 주시기 바랍니다. 뿐만 아니라, 행사 당일에 누군가가 장비를 배송하고 찾아가셔야 한다는 점을 명심해 주세요.

시간 내 주셔서 감사합니다.

존경을 담아,
시청 직원 Carla Landis

① 비바람을 잘 견디는 물품들을 포함할 것이다
② 행사에 대한 저희의 요구 사항에 부합할 것이다
③ 시의 예산 범위 내에 들 것이다
④ 하루 종일 발표를 지원할 것이다

해설

빈칸 앞부분에서 시의 연례 감사 야유회를 위해 대여할 장비의 조건들을 나열하고 있으므로, '행사에 대한 저희의 요구 사항에 부합할' 장비 선택지 목록을 보내 달라고 한 ②번이 정답이다.

정답 ②

어휘

inquire 문의하다, 묻다 annual 연례의, 해마다의 appreciation 감사, 인정
present 상영하다, 발표하다 drop off ~을 배송하다, (차로) 내려 주다
clerk 직원, 사무원 weatherproof 비바람을 잘 견디는

---

08 독해 요지 파악   난이도 상 ●●●

다음 글의 요지로 적절한 것은?

Of the more than 3,000 spoken languages that exist worldwide, indigenous peoples speak about 90 percent of them. This is why indigenous communities are considered the main source of language diversity in the world. Yet, it is these languages that are the most likely to disappear. As indigenous languages vanish when young people stop speaking them and elders pass away, communities lose their political standing as recognized tribes. This loss of recognition frequently leads to governments denying these peoples their fundamental right to self-governance and tribal autonomy. This makes it crucial to preserve these languages. There are many ways to save a language, some of which are encouraging its use in the home and offering language classes to the young. In addition, social media sites may be used to communicate in the language.

① All tribal languages hold sufficient educational value.
② Tribal communities should avoid political recognition systems.
③ Language preservation ensures tribal political rights.
④ Social media threatens indigenous language prevalence.

해석

전 세계에 존재하는 3,000개 이상의 구어 중에서, 토착민들은 그것들의 약 90퍼센트를 사용한다. 이것은 토착 공동체들이 전 세계 언어 다양성의 주요한 원천으로 여겨지는 이유이다. 그렇지만, 가장 소멸될 가능성이 높은 것들이 바로 이 언어들이다. 젊은이들이 토착 언어를 사용하지 않고 나이 든 사람들이 세상을 떠나면서 그것들이 사라질 때, 공동체들은 공식적으로 인정받은 부족으로서의 정치적 지위를 잃게 된다. 이러한 인정의 상실은 흔히 이 사람들에게 자치와 부족 자율성에 대한 기본적인 권리를 부정하는 정부로 이어진다. 이것은 그 언어들을 보존하는 것을 중요하게 만든다. 언어를 지켜내는 많은 방법이 있는데, 이것들 중 일부는 가정에서 그것의 사용을 장려하는 것, 그리고 젊은 사람들에게 언어 수업을 제공하는 것이다. 게다가, 소셜 미디어 사이트가 그 언어로 의사소통하기 위해 사용될 수도 있다.

① 모든 부족 언어는 충분한 교육적 가치를 가진다.
② 부족 공동체는 정치적 인정 시스템을 피해야 한다.
③ 언어 보존은 부족의 정치적 권리를 보장한다.
④ 소셜 미디어는 토착 언어의 보급을 위협한다.

해설

지문 전반에 걸쳐 토착민들에 의해 사용되는 언어들은 소멸 가능성이 높은데, 만약 이 언어들이 사라지면 토착 공동체는 공식적으로 인정받은 부족으로서의 정치적 지위를 잃게 되고 기본적인 권리들을 부정당할 수 있으므로 토착 언어의 보존이 중요하다고 주장하고 있다. 따라서 ③ '언어 보존은 부족의 정치적 권리를 보장한다'가 이 글의 요지이다.

정답 ③

어휘

indigenous 토착의, 원산의 diversity 다양성 vanish 사라지다, 소멸되다
pass away 세상을 떠나다 standing 지위, 위치
recognized (공식적으로) 인정받은 tribe 부족, 종족 frequently 흔히, 자주
fundamental 기본적인, 근본적인 governance 통치, 관리
autonomy 자율성, 자치권 crucial 중요한, 결정적인
preserve 보존하다, 지키다 prevalence 보급, 유행

09 독해 문단 순서 배열　　난이도 중 ●●○

주어진 글 다음에 이어질 글의 순서로 적절한 것은?

> Detecting when someone is lying is easier when the person is speaking a foreign language, according to the existing theory. This hypothesis states that lying and speaking a foreign language, respectively, are cognitively more demanding than telling the truth and using a native language.

(A) A new theory based on this knowledge asserts that it is actually simpler to discern when native speakers lie because the differences in response time between telling the truth and a falsehood are much more pronounced.
(B) However, recent findings show non-native speakers take a while to respond regardless of whether they are telling the truth or lying.
(C) Owing to this increased cognitive burden, telling a lie in a foreign language would have a suspiciously long and easily detectable response time.

① (A) – (C) – (B)　　② (B) – (A) – (C)
③ (C) – (A) – (B)　　④ (C) – (B) – (A)

해석

기존의 이론에 따르면, 누군가가 거짓말을 하고 있을 때를 감지하는 것은 그 사람이 외국어로 말하고 있을 때 더 쉽다. 이 가설은 거짓말을 하는 것과 외국어로 말하는 것이 각각 진실을 말하는 것과 모국어를 사용하는 것보다 인지적으로 더 큰 노력을 요한다고 진술한다.

(A) 이 정보에 기반한 새로운 이론은 모국어 사용자들이 거짓말할 때를 알아보는 것이 사실 더 간단한데, 이는 진실과 거짓을 말하는 것 간의 응답 시간 차이가 훨씬 더 뚜렷하기 때문이라고 주장한다.
(B) 하지만, 최근의 연구 결과들은 모국어 사용자가 아닌 사람들은 그들이 진실을 말하고 있든 거짓말을 하고 있든 간에 대답하는 데 시간이 좀 걸린다는 것을 보여 준다.
(C) 이 늘어난 인지적 부담 때문에, 외국어로 거짓말하는 것은 의심스럽게 길고 쉽게 감지할 수 있는 응답 시간을 보일 것이다.

해설

주어진 문장에서 거짓말을 하는 것과 외국어로 말하는 것은 진실을 말하는 것과 모국어로 말하는 것보다 더 큰 인지적 노력을 요하므로 외국어로 거짓말을 하고 있을 때 감지하는 것이 쉽다는 가설을 소개한 뒤, (C)에서 이 늘어난 인지적 부담(this increased cognitive burden) 때문에 외국어로 거짓말을 하는 것이 긴 응답 시간을 보일 것이라고 예측하고 있다. 이어서 (B)에서 하지만(However) 최근의 연구 결과는 외국어로 말하는 것이 진실이든 거짓말이든 대답하는 데 시간이 걸린다는 것을 보여 준다고 하고, (A)에서 이 정보(this knowledge)에 기반한 새로운 이론에 따르면 모국어 사용자들의 거짓말을 알아보는 것이 더 간단하다고 주장하고 있다. 따라서 ④ (C) – (B) – (A)가 정답이다.

정답 ④

어휘

detect 감지하다　hypothesis 가설　state 진술하다, 명시하다
respectively 각각　cognitively 인지적으로
demanding 큰 노력을 요하는, 힘든　assert 주장하다, 확실히 하다
discern 알아보다　falsehood 거짓　pronounced 뚜렷한
owing to ~때문에　burden 부담　suspiciously 의심스럽게, 수상하게도

10 독해 빈칸 완성 – 연결어　　난이도 중 ●●○

밑줄 친 (A), (B)에 들어갈 말로 적절한 것은?

> Scientists have long assumed that Jupiter's Great Red Spot has endured for centuries because of its very depth. Researchers from the National Aeronautics and Space Administration initially presumed that it was a shallow storm because of its flat appearance. ____(A)____, it turned out that the storm was much deeper than they believed. Scientists used Juno, a space probe with cutting-edge technology, to analyze the storm's top cloud layers. Microwaves measured the clouds down to 200 kilometers but could go no farther. A Juno scientist subsequently used deviations in Juno's flight path to examine more deeply and was able to report that the Great Red Spot is about 500 kilometers deep. ____(B)____, the storm's extent cannot compare with the brown and white stripes that go around the planet, which are about three thousand kilometers in depth.

*Great Red Spot: (목성) 대적점

	(A)	(B)
①	However	Nonetheless
②	Therefore	In addition
③	For instance	Consequently
④	Moreover	Hence

해석

오랫동안 과학자들은 목성의 대적점이 바로 그것의 깊이 때문에 수세기 동안 지속되어 왔다고 추정해 왔다. 미국 항공 우주국의 연구원들은 그것의 납작한 모습 때문에 처음에는 그것이 얕은 폭풍우라고 생각했다. (A) 하지만, 그 폭풍우는 그들이 생각한 것보다 훨씬 더 깊다는 것이 밝혀졌다. 과학자들은 그 폭풍우 꼭대기의 구름층을 분석하기 위해, 최첨단 기술을 갖춘 우주 탐사선인 Juno를 사용했다. 마이크로파는 그 구름을 2백 킬로미터 아래까지 측정했지만 그 이상은 갈 수 없었다. 한 Juno 과학자는 더욱 깊숙이 조사하기 위해 나중에 Juno의 비행 경로에서 항로를 변경했고, 그 대적점이 약 5백 킬로미터의 깊이라는 것을 발표할 수 있었다. (B) 그럼에도 불구하고, 그 폭풍우의 크기는 그 행성 주변을 도는 갈색과 흰색의 띠들과는 비교도 안 되는데, 이것들은 깊이가 약 3천 킬로미터이다.

	(A)	(B)
①	하지만	그럼에도 불구하고
②	그러므로	게다가
③	예를 들어	결과적으로
④	더욱이	이런 이유로

해설

(A) 빈칸 앞 문장은 목성 대적점의 납작한 모습 때문에 연구원들이 처음에는 그것을 얕은 폭풍우로 생각했다는 내용이고, 빈칸 뒤 문장은 그 폭풍우

DAY 24 하프모의고사 24회

가 생각보다 훨씬 더 깊은 것으로 밝혀졌다는 대조적인 내용이다. 따라서 빈칸에는 대조를 나타내는 연결어인 However(하지만)가 들어가야 한다.
(B) 빈칸 앞 문장은 한 Juno 과학자가 그 대적점이 약 5백 킬로미터의 깊이라는 것을 발표했다는 내용이고, 빈칸 뒤 문장은 그 폭풍우의 깊이는 행성 주변을 도는 약 3천 킬로미터 깊이의 갈색과 흰색 띠들과는 비교도 안 된다는 양보적인 내용이다. 따라서 빈칸에는 양보를 나타내는 연결어인 Nonetheless(그럼에도 불구하고)가 들어가야 한다.

정답 ①

어휘

assume 추정하다, 가정하다 endure 지속하다, 인내하다 depth 깊이
presume 생각하다, 추정하다 shallow 얕은 flat 납작한, 평평한
turn out ~으로 밝혀지다 probe 탐사선 cutting-edge 최첨단의
analyze 분석하다 subsequently 나중에 deviation 항로 변경, 일탈
path 경로, 길 examine 조사하다 extent 크기, 정도 compare 비교하다
stripe 띠, 줄무늬 go around ~을 돌다

DAY 25 하프모의고사 25회

정답
p. 110

01	②	어휘	06	②	독해
02	②	문법	07	④	문법
03	②	생활영어	08	④	독해
04	③	독해	09	②	독해
05	②	독해	10	②	독해

취약영역 분석표

영역	맞힌 답의 개수
어휘	/1
생활영어	/1
문법	/2
독해	/6
TOTAL	/10

---

01 어휘 compromise 난이도 중 ●●○

밑줄 친 부분에 들어갈 말로 적절한 것은?

> It's important to stand your ground and refuse to _____ on issues that matter to you. Otherwise, you may lose credibility with both yourself and others.

① concentrate ② compromise
③ continue ④ decide

[해석]
당신에게 중요한 문제에 대해서는 당신의 입장을 고수하고 타협하려고 하지 않는 것이 중요하다. 그렇지 않으면, 당신은 스스로와 다른 사람들 모두에게 신뢰를 잃을지도 모른다.
① 집중하다 ② 타협하다
③ 계속하다 ④ 결정하다

정답 ②

[어휘]
stand one's ground ~의 입장을 고수하다 credibility 신뢰
concentrate 집중하다 compromise 타협하다 continue 계속하다
decide 결정하다

---

02 문법 동사의 종류 | 명사절 난이도 상 ●●●

밑줄 친 부분에 들어갈 말로 적절한 것은?

> The doctor _____ regular exercise could significantly improve his condition.

① explained that the patient
② explained to the patient that
③ explained to the patient what
④ explained the patient that

[해석]
의사는 환자에게 규칙적인 운동이 그의 상태를 크게 개선할 수 있다고 설명했다.

[해설]
② 3형식 동사 | 명사절 접속사 that절 또는 의문사절을 목적어로 갖는 3형식 동사 explain 뒤에 '사람(the patient)'은 혼자 올 수 없고 'to + 사람'(to the patient)의 형태로 와야 하므로, ② explained to the patient that과 ③ explained to the patient what이 정답 후보이다. 이때 빈칸 뒤에 완전한 절(regular exercise ~ condition)이 왔으므로, 불완전한 절을 이끄는 의문사 what이 아닌, 완전한 절을 이끄는 명사절 접속사 that이 쓰인 ② explained to the patient that이 정답이다.

정답 ②

[어휘]
significantly 크게, 상당히 improve 개선하다, 향상시키다

---

03 생활영어 Do you have a preference for a particular position? 난이도 하 ●○○

밑줄 친 부분에 들어갈 말로 적절한 것은?

Samuel
Hello. I'm interested in volunteer opportunities at municipal animal shelters.
15:30

Municipal Shelter
Thank you! Volunteer positions are always open. _____
15:30

Samuel
Nothing specific, but I'm a dog groomer, so I could help with grooming work.
15:31

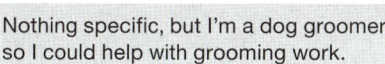

DAY 25 하프모의고사 25회

Municipal Shelter: The Best Friends shelter needs groomers. Would you be interested in volunteering there? 15:32

Samuel: Yes, that sounds perfect! How do I apply? 15:32

Municipal Shelter: You can apply online through the Best Friends shelter website. 15:33

Samuel: I'll do that today. 15:34

Municipal Shelter: Excellent! The shelter animals will benefit from your grooming service. 15:34

① Which days work best for you?
② Do you have a preference for a particular position?
③ Are you comfortable cleaning cages and walking dogs?
④ Do you know about the age requirements for volunteering?

해석

Samuel: 안녕하세요. 저는 시립 동물 보호소에서의 자원봉사 기회에 관심이 있습니다.
시립 보호소: 감사합니다! 자원봉사 자리는 항상 열려 있답니다. 특별히 선호하는 직무가 있으신가요?
Samuel: 구체적인 것은 없긴 하지만, 제가 반려견 미용사라서요, 그래서 미용 작업을 도울 수 있습니다.
시립 보호소: Best Friends 보호소에서 미용사를 필요로 합니다. 그곳에서 자원봉사하는 데 관심 있으신가요?
Samuel: 네, 완벽하네요! 어떻게 신청하면 되나요?
시립 보호소: Best Friends 보호소 웹사이트를 통해 온라인으로 신청하실 수 있습니다.
Samuel: 오늘 신청할게요.
시립 보호소: 좋아요! 보호소 동물들이 귀하의 미용 서비스로 도움을 받을 것입니다.

① 어느 날이 가장 괜찮으세요?
② 특별히 선호하는 직무가 있으신가요?
③ 반려견 집을 청소하고 산책시키는 것도 편하신가요?
④ 자원봉사의 나이 요건에 대해 아시나요?

해설

시립 동물 보호소의 자원봉사 기회에 관심이 있다는 Samuel의 말에 대해 시립 보호소 직원이 자원봉사 자리는 항상 열려 있다고 말하고, 빈칸 뒤에서 다시 Samuel이 Nothing specific, but I'm a dog groomer, so I could help with grooming work(구체적인 것은 없긴 하지만, 제가 반려견 미용사라서요, 그래서 미용 작업을 도울 수 있습니다)라고 대답하고 있으므로, '특별히 선호하는 직무가 있으신가요?'라는 의미의 ② 'Do you have a preference for a particular position?'이 정답이다.

정답 ②

어휘

municipal 시(립)의 **shelter** 보호소 **specific** 구체적인, 특정한
dog groomer 반려견 미용사 **preference** 선호 **cage** 개집, 우리

04~05 다음 글을 읽고 물음에 답하시오.

Citizen Services

A lost or stolen passport is a serious matter as it could lead to identity theft or illegal use. It must therefore be reported immediately to Citizen Services through our website or 24-hour helpline so that it can be canceled.

If you wish to apply for a replacement passport, you must visit a passport office or consulate in person with valid government-issued identification, two recent passport-sized photographs, a completed replacement form, and the replacement fee. If you have to travel urgently and would like an emergency passport, you will be required to submit proof of an upcoming flight.

In the event that you are abroad when your passport is lost or stolen, visit your nearest embassy for assistance obtaining an emergency travel document. Your identity will have to be <u>verified</u> through additional documentation, such as an image of your lost passport.

해석

시민 서비스

분실 또는 도난된 여권은 신원 도용이나 불법적 사용으로 이어질 수 있으므로 심각한 문제입니다. 따라서 여권이 취소될 수 있도록 즉시 웹사이트나 24시간 전화 상담 서비스를 통해 시민 서비스에 신고하셔야 합니다.

대체 여권을 신청하시려면, 유효한 정부 발행 신분증, 최근 여권용 사진 두 장, 작성된 대체 신청서, 그리고 대체 수수료를 지참하여 여권과나 영사관을 직접 방문하셔야 합니다. 급히 여행해야 해서 긴급 여권을 원하시는 경우, 예정된 항공편에 대한 증빙 자료를 제출하셔야 할 것입니다.

해외에 있을 때 여권을 분실하거나 도난당하신 경우, 긴급 여행 서류를 받을 도움을 요청하기 위해 가까운 대사관을 방문하세요. 분실된 여권의 이미지와 같이, 추가 서류를 통해 신원이 확인되어야 할 것입니다.

어휘

passport 여권 **identity theft** 신원 도용 **immediately** 즉시
helpline 전화 상담 서비스, 직통 전화 **replacement** 대체
consulate 영사관 **in person** 직접 **valid** 유효한 **identification** 신분증
complete 작성하다, 완성하다 **fee** 수수료 **urgently** 급히
upcoming 예정된, 다가오는 **embassy** 대사관 **verify** 확인하다, 검증하다

04 독해 유의어 파악 난이도 중 ●●○

밑줄 친 verified의 의미와 가장 가까운 것은?

① recorded   ② protected
③ confirmed   ④ shared

[해석]

① 기록된   ② 보호된
③ 확인된   ④ 공유된

[해설]

밑줄 친 부분이 포함된 문장에서 verified는 문맥상 추가 서류를 통해 신원이 '확인되어'야 한다는 의미로 쓰였으므로, '확인된'이라는 의미의 ③ confirmed가 정답이다.

정답 ③

[어휘]

record 기록하다; 기록, 음반 protect 보호하다 confirm 확인하다
share 공유하다

05 독해 목적 파악 난이도 중 ●●○

윗글의 목적으로 적절한 것은?

① to provide information about passport processing times
② to explain what to do after losing a passport
③ to announce new passport security features
④ to offer safety tips to international travelers

[해석]

① 여권 처리 소요 시간에 대한 정보를 제공하려고
② 여권 분실 후 무엇을 해야 하는지 설명하려고
③ 신규 여권 보안 기능을 알리려고
④ 해외 여행객들에게 안전 관련 조언을 제공하려고

[해설]

지문 전반에 걸쳐 여권을 분실하거나 도난당한 경우 즉시 여권을 취소해야 하며, 대체 여권을 신청하기 위해 여권과 또는 영사관을 방문하여 증빙 자료를 제출할 수 있는데, 해외에서는 대사관에 도움을 요청할 수 있다고 설명하고 있다. 따라서 ② '여권 분실 후 무엇을 해야 하는지 설명하려고'가 이 글의 목적이다.

정답 ②

[어휘]

announce 알리다, 발표하다 feature 기능, 특징

06 독해 내용 불일치 파악 난이도 중 ●●○

다음 글의 내용과 일치하지 않는 것은?

SUMMER SCIENCE SEMINARS

Explore, experiment, and learn at the Northshore Children's Museum during the Summer Science Seminars. Each seminar will feature hands-on exhibits, live demonstrations, and fun experiments to make science come alive.

ABOUT

Science educators and researchers from NCM and local universities will give weekly presentations examining a different scientific topic ranging from local ecosystems to space exploration. Participants will get first-hand experience with scientific topics and have their questions answered by experts.

RECOMMENDED AGES

Participants ages 6-18 are welcome.
All activities are split into three age groups, with materials and experiments tailored to the needs and knowledge of each.

SCIENCE FAIR

The summer series will end with a science fair in which participants can create a presentation about a topic they learned about during the seminars.

WHEN

Every Wednesday from June 1 to August 31
Seminars run from 10 a.m. to 3 p.m.

COST

$10 per seminar or $100 for the 13-week program when paid in advance

---

① A variety of scientific topics will be explored during the seminars.
② Students from local universities are invited to attend.
③ Participants will be grouped according to age for all exercises.
④ A discount is offered when paying for the full 13-week program.

[해석]

여름 과학 세미나

Northshore 어린이 박물관에서 열리는 여름 과학 세미나에서 탐구하고, 실험하고, 배워 보세요. 각 세미나는 과학을 재미있게 만드는 체험형 전시, 실시간 시연 및 흥미로운 실험들을 특징으로 합니다.

소개

Northshore 어린이 박물관과 지역 대학의 과학 교육자와 연구원들이 지역 생태계에서부터 우주 탐사에 이르기까지 다양한 과학 주제를 고찰하는 주간 발표를 진행할 것입니다. 참가자들은 과학 주제들을 직접 체험하고 전문가들에게 질문에 대한 답변을 받으실 수 있습니다.

권장 연령

6-18세 참가자분들을 환영합니다.
모든 활동은 세 개의 연령 그룹으로 나뉘며, 각 그룹의 필요와 지식에 맞춘 자료와 실험이 제공됩니다.

DAY 25 하프모의고사 25회

> **과학 박람회**
> 여름 시리즈는 참가자분들이 세미나 동안 배운 한 가지 주제에 대한 발표물을 만들 수 있는 과학 박람회로 마무리될 것입니다.
> **일시**
> 6월 1일부터 8월 31일까지 매주 수요일
> 세미나는 오전 10시부터 오후 3시까지 진행됩니다.
> **비용**
> 세미나당 10달러 또는 사전 결제 시 13주 프로그램 100달러

① 세미나 동안 다양한 과학 주제가 탐구될 것이다.
② 지역 대학의 학생들이 참석하도록 초대된다.
③ 참가자들은 모든 활동에 있어 연령에 따라 그룹 지어질 것이다.
④ 13주 프로그램 전체를 결제할 때 할인이 제공된다.

해설
②번의 키워드인 local universities(지역 대학)가 그대로 언급된 지문 주변의 내용에서 지역 대학의 과학 교육자와 연구원들이 세미나에서 주간 발표를 진행할 것이라고는 했지만, ② '지역 대학의 학생들이 참석하도록 초대되'는지는 알 수 없다.

정답 ②

어휘
explore 탐구하다, 탐험하다 experiment 실험하다; 실험
feature 특징으로 하다 hands-on 체험형의 exhibit 전시; 전시하다
demonstration 시연, 증명 come alive 재미있어지다, 활기를 띠다
ecosystem 생태계 first-hand 직접적인, 일차적인 split 나누다, 쪼개다
tailor (용도·목적에) 맞추다 fair 박람회 in advance 사전에, 미리
discount 할인

07 문법 전치사 | 부사절 | 보어 | 주어 | 관계절   난이도 중 ●●○

밑줄 친 부분 중 어법상 옳지 않은 것은?

> Smoking bans have become ① so commonplace that it's easy ② to forget that there was a time recently ③ in which cigarettes could be smoked in the majority of restaurants. In the United States, ④ although the initial worry that such a move would be incredibly detrimental to businesses that catered to smokers, bans followed California's successful prohibition of smoking in public restaurants in 1995.

해석
흡연 금지법은 매우 흔해져서 다수의 식당에서 담배를 피울 수 있었던 시절이 최근까지 있었다는 것을 잊기 쉽다. 미국에서는, 그러한 움직임이 흡연자들의 기호에 맞추던 가게들에 엄청나게 해로울 것이라는 초기의 우려에도 불구하고, 금지법은 1995년 공공 식당에서의 흡연에 대한 캘리포니아의 성공적인 금지 규정에 뒤이어 일어났다.

해설
④ 전치사 자리 명사구(the initial worry ~ smokers) 앞에는 전치사가 와야 하므로, 완전한 절을 이끄는 부사절 접속사 although(비록 ~이지만)를 양보를 나타내는 전치사 despite 또는 in spite of로 고쳐야 한다.

[오답 분석]
① 부사절 접속사 | 보어 자리 문맥상 '흡연 금지법은 매우 흔해져서 ~ 잊기 쉽다'라는 의미가 되어야 자연스러우므로 '매우 ~해서 −하다'라는 의미의 부사절 접속사 so ~ that이 올 수 있다. 이때 so ~ that 사이에 오는 것은 문장의 동사에 따라 결정되는데, 동사 become은 주격 보어를 취하고 보어 자리에는 명사나 형용사가 올 수 있으므로, so that 사이에 형용사가 온 so commonplace that이 올바르게 쓰였다.
② 가짜 주어 구문 to 부정사구(to forget ~ restaurants)와 같이 긴 주어가 오면 진주어인 to 부정사구를 문장 맨 뒤로 보내고 가주어 it이 주어 자리에 대신해서 쓰이므로, 진주어 자리에 to 부정사 to forget이 올바르게 쓰였다.
③ 전치사 + 관계대명사 완전한 절(cigarettes ~ restaurants) 앞에는 '전치사 + 관계대명사'가 올 수 있다. '전치사 + 관계대명사'에서 전치사는 선행사 또는 관계절의 동사에 따라 결정되는데, 선행사 a time이 사물이고 문맥상 '시절에'라는 의미가 되어야 자연스러우므로, 전치사 in(~에)이 사물을 나타내는 관계대명사 which 앞에 온 in which가 올바르게 쓰였다.

정답 ④

어휘
ban 금지(법) commonplace 흔한 cigarette 담배 majority of 다수의
initial 초기의, 처음의 cater to ~의 기호에 맞추다 incredibly 엄청나게
detrimental 해로운 prohibition 금지 (규정)

08 독해 주제 파악   난이도 중 ●●○

다음 글의 주제로 적절한 것은?

> While humans have no muscles that control the movement of the spine in the same way that hands and fingers can be manipulated with precision, it is arguably a far more important collection of bones than any other in the body. The spinal column is made up of a series of vertebrae separated by intervertebral discs, and it houses the nerves that connect the brain and heart to a person's four limbs. This structure is so integral to the functioning of the entire body. The slightest damage to any one of the spine's discs can cause severe pain and even impair movement in certain areas. Even though surgery and other forms of treatment can successfully alleviate these problems, the complexity of the spine is such that cures are often not so simple and take a long time to work.

*spinal column: 등골뼈
*vertebrae: 척추뼈
*intervertebral disc: 척추 사이 원반

① Precision control systems in human anatomy
② Similarities between hands and spine mobility
③ Medical treatments for spinal cord problems
④ Complex structure and vital role of the spine

25회 정답·해석·해설

해커스공무원 비비안 영어 매일 하프모의고사

해석

인간에게 손과 손가락이 정밀하게 움직여질 수 있는 것과 같은 방식으로 척추의 움직임을 제어하는 근육이 없기는 하지만, 그것(척추)은 거의 틀림없이 신체 내부의 다른 것보다 훨씬 더 중요한 뼈들의 집합체이다. 등골뼈는 척추 사이 원반들로 분리되는 일련의 척추뼈로 구성되고, 뇌와 심장을 사람의 네 팔다리로 연결하는 신경들을 안전한 장소에 넣어 둔다. 이 구조는 몸 전체가 기능하는 것에 매우 필수적이다. 척추 원반 중 어떤 하나의 가장 경미한 손상도 극심한 통증을 일으키고 심지어 특정 부위의 움직임을 약화시킬 수 있다. 비록 수술과 다른 형태의 치료법들이 이 문제들을 성공적으로 완화할 수는 있지만, 척추는 너무 복잡해서 대개 치유법들이 그다지 간단하지 않고 효능이 있기까지 오랜 시간이 걸린다.

① 인체 구조의 정밀한 제어 시스템
② 손과 척추 운동성의 유사점
③ 등골뼈 문제에 대한 의학적 치료
④ 척추의 복잡한 구조와 중요한 역할

해설

지문 처음에서 척추는 신체 내부의 다른 것보다 훨씬 더 중요한 뼈들의 집합체라고 하고, 지문 뒷부분에서 척추는 몸 전체가 기능하게 하는 데 필수적인데, 그 구조가 너무 복잡해서 대개 치료가 간단하지 않고 시간이 오래 걸린다고 설명하고 있다. 따라서 ④ '척추의 복잡한 구조와 중요한 역할'이 이 글의 주제이다.

정답 ④

어휘

spine 척추, 등뼈 manipulate 움직이다, 다루다
with precision 정밀하게, 정확하게 arguably 거의 틀림없이
house 안전한 장소에 넣어 두다, 수용하다 nerve 신경 limb 팔다리, 사지
integral 필수적인 impair 약화시키다, 손상시키다 surgery 수술
alleviate 완화하다 complexity 복잡성 cure 치료(법); 치료하다
anatomy 구조, 해부학 mobility 운동성 vital 중요한, 필수적인

해석

대부분의 사람들은 누군가가 우울하다는 것을 들을 때, 즉시 그 사람이 단순히 슬픈 것이라고 생각하지만, 임상 우울증은 우울한 감정뿐만 아니라, 많은 신체적 영향들도 야기하는 정신 질환이다.

(A) 실제로, 임상적으로 우울한 환자들은 종종 예상치 못한 급격한 체중 감소 또는 증가, 피로함 그리고 그들의 정신 운동 능력과 관련된 문제로 고통받는다.
(B) 다행히도, 대부분의 환자들에게 우울증과 그것의 영향은 정신 치료와 호르몬 수치를 조정하는 약물의 조합을 통해 제어될 수 있다.
(C) 이러한 증상들의 결과로, 환자들은 그들의 신체가 자신들의 기대에 어긋나는 것처럼 느껴져, 훨씬 더 극심한 절망감으로 고통받기 시작할 수 있다.

해설

주어진 문장에서 임상 우울증은 우울한 감정뿐만 아니라 신체적 영향들도 야기하는 정신 질환이라고 한 뒤, (A)에서 실제로(In fact) 임상적으로 우울한 환자들은 체중 변화, 피로함 등의 신체적 문제들을 겪는다고 설명하고 있다. 이어서 (C)에서 이러한 증상들의 결과로(As a result of these symptoms) 환자들은 훨씬 더 극심한 절망감으로 고통받을 수 있다고 하고, (B)에서 다행히도(Luckily), 대부분의 경우 우울증과 그것의 영향은 정신 치료와 약물의 조합을 통해 제어될 수 있다고 설명하고 있다. 따라서 ② (A) - (C) - (B)가 정답이다.

정답 ②

어휘

depressed 우울한 immediately 즉시 clinical 임상적인
suffer from ~으로 고통받다 rapid 급격한 exhaustion 피로, 소모
psychomotor 정신 운동(성)의 combination 조합, 결합
psychotherapy 정신 치료 medication 약물 symptom 증상
fail ~의 기대에 어긋나다, 실패하다

---

09 독해 문단 순서 배열   난이도 중 ●●○

주어진 문장 다음에 이어질 글의 순서로 적절한 것은?

When most people hear that someone is depressed, they immediately think that the person is simply sad, but clinical depression is a mental illness that causes not only depressed feelings, but also numerous physical effects.

(A) In fact, clinically depressed patients often suffer from rapid unexpected weight loss or gain, exhaustion, and trouble with their psychomotor abilities.
(B) Luckily, for most patients, depression and its effects can be controlled through a combination of psychotherapy and medications that balance hormone levels.
(C) As a result of these symptoms, the patients can begin to suffer even greater feelings of hopelessness, as their bodies seem to be failing them.

① (A) - (B) - (C)   ② (A) - (C) - (B)
③ (C) - (A) - (B)   ④ (C) - (B) - (A)

10 독해 빈칸 완성 - 절   난이도 중 ●●○

밑줄 친 부분에 들어갈 말로 적절한 것은?

One of the greatest challenges facing entrepreneurs today is effective marketing for their business. This is a critical aspect of developing new businesses of all sizes. Even after securing investors for their business, establishing the business and developing its operational and logistical capabilities can consume the majority of a new company's start-up capital, leaving little room in the budget to tell potential customers about their business. The most cost-effective way to do this is to focus initially on branding: reach out to those in your demographic and establish your business as a legitimate and trusted member of the community. This can mean participation in local events, doing charity work, and otherwise serving the interests of your future customers. This is often harder work than marketing a product directly. But, it ensures that customers trust you when you begin to market your products, guaranteeing that _____.

DAY 25 / 하프모의고사 25회 135

DAY 25 하프모의고사 25회

① you learn what products every age group would respond best to
② you get the most value possible for your marketing budget
③ you understand your customers' needs in future ad campaigns
④ you build efficient delivery processes for your upcoming products

해석

오늘날 기업가들이 직면한 가장 큰 도전 중 하나는 그들의 사업을 위한 효과적인 마케팅이다. 이것은 모든 규모의 새로운 사업을 성장시키는 데 있어 매우 중요한 측면이다. 심지어 사업을 위한 투자자들을 확보한 이후에도, 사업체를 설립하고 그것의 운영 및 물류 역량을 개발하는 것은 신규 회사의 창업 자본 대부분을 다 써버릴 수 있어서, 잠재 고객들에게 그들의 사업을 알릴 수 있는 예산에 여유를 거의 남기지 않는다. 이것(효과적인 마케팅)을 하기 위해 가장 비용 효율이 높은 방법은 초기에 브랜드화에 집중하는 것인데, 즉 당신의 인구 통계 집단에 있는 사람들에게 접근하여 당신의 사업을 지역 사회의 합법적이고 신뢰받는 일부분으로 지위를 확고히 하는 것이다. 이것은 지역 행사 참여, 자선 활동을 하는 것, 그 외에 당신의 미래 고객들의 이익을 위해 봉사하는 것을 의미할 수 있다. 이것은 종종 제품을 직접 마케팅하는 것보다 더 힘든 일이다. 그러나, 그것은 당신이 제품을 판매하기 시작할 때 고객들이 당신을 반드시 신뢰하게 하며, <u>당신이 마케팅 예산에서 가능한 최대의 가치를 얻는</u> 것을 보장한다.

① 당신이 각 연령 집단이 어떤 제품에 가장 잘 반응하는지 알게 된다
② 당신이 마케팅 예산에서 가능한 최대의 가치를 얻는다
③ 당신이 향후 광고 캠페인에서 고객들의 요구를 이해한다
④ 당신이 새로 나올 제품을 위한 효율적인 배송 절차를 구축한다

해설

빈칸 앞부분에서 효과적인 마케팅을 하는 가장 비용 효율이 높은 방법은 초기 브랜드화에 집중하는 것인데, 이것에는 지역 행사 참여, 자선 활동, 잠재 고객을 위한 봉사 등이 포함되어 제품을 직접 마케팅하는 것보다 더 힘들기는 하지만, 추후 제품 판매를 시작할 때 고객들의 신뢰를 얻게 한다고 설명하고 있다. 따라서 그것은 '당신이 마케팅 예산에서 가능한 최대의 가치를 얻는' 것을 보장한다고 한 ②번이 정답이다.

정답 ②

어휘

entrepreneur 기업가   critical 매우 중요한, 결정적인
secure 확보하다; 안전한   establish 설립하다, (지위를) 확고히 하다
operational 운영의, 작전의   logistical 물류의, 수송의   capability 역량
consume 다 써버리다, 섭취하다   start-up 창업의   capital 자본
budget 예산   potential 잠재적인; 가능성   initially 초기에, 처음에
branding 브랜드화   reach out to ~에게 접근하다
demographic 인구 통계 집단; 인구 통계학의   legitimate 합법적인, 정당한
charity 자선   serve 봉사하다   guarantee 보장하다
upcoming 새로 나올, 다가오는

DAY 26 하프모의고사 26회

정답
p. 114

01	①	어휘	06	②	독해
02	③	문법	07	③	독해
03	②	문법	08	③	독해
04	②	생활영어	09	④	독해
05	④	독해	10	③	독해

취약영역 분석표

영역	맞힌 답의 개수
어휘	/1
생활영어	/1
문법	/2
독해	/6
TOTAL	/10

---

01 어휘 execute 난이도 중 ●●○

밑줄 친 부분에 들어갈 말로 적절한 것은?

The leaders at the summit vowed to _____ the commitments they made to reduce global warming, which marked significant progress.

① execute ② mention
③ identify ④ relax

[해석]
정상 회담의 지도자들은 그들이 지구 온난화를 줄이기 위해 했던 약속들을 실행하기로 서약했는데, 이는 상당한 진전을 보여 주는 것이었다.

① 실행하다 ② 언급하다
③ 식별하다 ④ 완화하다

정답 ①

[어휘]
summit 정상 회담, 산꼭대기 vow 서약하다, 맹세하다
commitment 약속, 헌신 significant 상당한, 중요한 execute 실행하다
mention 언급하다 identify 식별하다 relax 완화하다, 편하게 하다

---

02 문법 어순 난이도 중 ●●○

밑줄 친 부분에 들어갈 말로 적절한 것은?

The instructions for assembling the bookshelf were _____ without any additional help, allowing even furniture assembly beginners to complete the task quickly.

① enough clear to follow ② enough clear to following
③ clear enough to follow ④ clear enough to following

[해석]
책장을 조립하기 위한 설명서는 추가적인 도움 없이도 따라 할 만큼 충분히 명료해서, 가구 조립 초보자들조차도 빠르게 작업을 완료하게 한다.

[해설]
③ 혼동하기 쉬운 어순 문맥상 '추가적인 도움 없이도 따라 할 만큼 충분히 명료하다'라는 의미가 되어야 자연스러운데, enough는 '형용사 + enough + to 부정사' 순으로 와서 '~하기에 충분히 -하다'라는 의미로 쓰이므로, ③ clear enough to follow가 정답이다.

정답 ③

[어휘]
instruction 설명(서), 지시 assemble 조립하다 bookshelf 책장, 책꽂이

---

03 문법 도치 구문 | 수 일치 | 조동사 | to 부정사 | 수동태 난이도 상 ●●●

밑줄 친 부분 중 어법상 옳지 않은 것은?

The school administration is requesting that parents ① pack an extra set of clothing for their children and make sure they wear rubber boots to school. On rain-soaked streets ② comes inconveniences like puddles, which can cause students' clothes and shoes wet, making them uncomfortable in class. In addition, a concerted effort ③ to protect against sickness during the wet months ④ is required to ensure the students' well-being.

[해석]
학교 당국은 학부모들에게 아이들을 위한 여분의 옷을 챙기고 그들(아이들)이 학교에 반드시 고무장화를 신고 오게 하도록 당부하고 있다. 비에 젖은 거리에는 물웅덩이와 같은 불편 사항들이 발생하는데, 이는 학생들의 옷과 신발을 젖게 해서, 그들로 하여금 교실에서 불쾌함을 느끼도록 만들 수 있다. 게다가, 학생들의 건강을 보장하기 위해서는 우기인 달 동안 질병을 막기 위한 협력이 요구된다.

DAY 26 하프모의고사 26회

해설

② **도치 구문 | 주어와 동사의 수 일치** 장소를 나타내는 부사구(On rain-soaked streets)가 강조되어 문장의 맨 앞에 나오면 주어와 동사가 도치되어 '동사 + 주어'의 어순이 되어야 하는데, 주어 자리에 복수 명사(inconveniences)가 왔으므로 단수 동사 comes를 복수 동사 come으로 고쳐야 한다.

[오답 분석]
① **조동사 should의 생략** 주절에 제안을 나타내는 동사 request가 오면 종속절에는 '(should +) 동사원형'이 와야 하므로 종속절에 (should) pack이 올바르게 쓰였다.
③ **to 부정사를 취하는 명사** 명사 effort는 to 부정사를 취하므로 to 부정사 to protect가 올바르게 쓰였다.
④ **능동태·수동태 구별 | 주어와 동사의 수 일치** 문맥상 주어 a concerted effort와 동사가 '협력이 요구된다'라는 의미의 수동 관계이므로 수동태가 와야 하는데, 주어 자리에 단수 명사 a concerted effort가 왔으므로 단수 수동태 is required가 올바르게 쓰였다. 참고로, 주어와 동사 사이의 수식어 거품(to protect ~ months)은 동사의 수 결정에 영향을 주지 않는다.

정답 ②

어휘

administration (행정) 당국, 관리, 집행 pack 챙기다, 싸다 rubber 고무
inconvenience 불편, 불편한 일 puddle 물웅덩이
concerted effort 협력 protect against ~을 막다

---

04 생활영어 It does seem like the best approach.
난이도 하 ●○○

밑줄 친 부분에 들어갈 말로 적절한 것은?

A: I won't be able to meet with the client next week.
B: Why not? What's going on?
A: He and I disagree rather strongly about the marketing plan. I'm not sure I'm the best fit for his vision, so I'd like you to take over the project.
B: That makes sense. _____
A: Thanks for being understanding.
B: No problem. We're all on the same team.

① How could you let this happen?
② It does seem like the best approach.
③ You need to adjust to the client's needs.
④ People should finish anything they start.

해석

A: 저는 다음 주에 그 고객과 만날 수 없을 것 같아요.
B: 왜 안 되죠? 무슨 일이 있나요?
A: 그와 제가 마케팅 계획에 대해 꽤 강경하게 의견이 달라서요. 제가 그의 미래상에 가장 적합한지 잘 모르겠어서, 당신이 그 프로젝트를 맡아 주시면 좋겠습니다.
B: 일리가 있네요. 그게 가장 좋은 방법인 것 같아요.
A: 이해해 주셔서 감사해요.
B: 괜찮아요. 우리는 모두 같은 팀이잖아요.

① 어떻게 이런 일이 일어나게 할 수 있죠?
② 그게 가장 좋은 방법인 것 같아요.
③ 당신은 그 고객의 요구에 맞추어야 해요.
④ 사람들은 자신이 시작한 것은 무엇이든 끝내야 해요.

해설

한 고객과 마케팅 계획에 대한 의견이 상당히 달라서 담당 프로젝트를 B가 맡아 주면 좋겠다는 A의 말에 대해 빈칸 앞에서 B가 That makes sense (일리가 있네요)라고 말하고 있으므로, '그게 가장 좋은 방법인 것 같아요'라는 의미의 ② 'It does seem like the best approach'가 정답이다.

정답 ②

어휘

client 고객, 의뢰인 disagree 의견이 다르다, 동의하지 않다
rather 꽤, 상당히 strongly 강경하게, 튼튼하게 fit 적합; 적당한; 꼭 맞다
take over ~을 맡다, 인수하다 adjust 맞추다, 적응하다

05~06 다음 글을 읽고 물음에 답하시오.

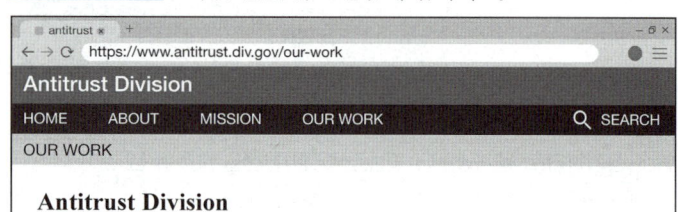

Antitrust Division

History
The Antitrust Division was established in 1919 to regulate competition among companies and protect consumers from unfair pricing. Since its foundation, it has passed three landmark laws that work to ensure competition in the marketplace so that consumers receive lower prices, more choices, and higher-quality goods.

Enforcing Regulations
When violations of antitrust laws occur, we pursue legal action against the offending company. If found guilty of monopolistic practices, companies may be issued significant fines, and key individuals involved may be sentenced to prison.

Competition Advocacy
We advocate for policies and laws that promote competition in nationally regulated industries like communications, transportation, and energy. We also review local legislation and provide legal recommendations to spur competition in areas such as real estate and professional licensing.

해석

독점 방지 정책실

역사

독점 방지 정책실은 기업들 간의 경쟁을 규제하고 소비자들을 불공정한 가격으로부터 보호하기 위해 1919년에 설립되었습니다. 설립 이후, 독점 방지 정책실은 시장에서의 경쟁을 보장하여 소비자들이 더 저렴한 가격, 더 많은 선택지 그리고 더 높은 품질의 상품을 받을 수 있도록 하는 세 가지 획기적인 법률을 통과시켰습니다.

규제를 집행하는 일

독점 방지법 위반이 발생할 때, 저희는 범죄를 저지른 기업에 대해 법적 조치를 취합니다. 독점적 관행으로 유죄 판결을 받게 되면, 기업들은 상당한 벌금을 부과받을 수도 있으며, 관련된 주요 인물들은 징역형을 선고받을 수도 있습니다.

경쟁 옹호

저희는 통신, 운수 및 에너지와 같이 국가적으로 규제되는 산업에서의 경쟁을 촉진하는 정책과 법률을 옹호합니다. 저희는 또한 부동산 및 전문 면허와 같은 분야에서 경쟁을 자극하기 위해 지역 법안을 검토하고 법적 권고를 제공합니다.

어휘

antitrust 독점 방지 regulate 규제하다 competition 경쟁
unfair 불공정한 foundation 설립, 토대, 재단
landmark 획기적인; 주요 지형지물 enforce 집행하다 violation 위반, 침해
pursue 실행하다, 추구하다 offend 범죄를 저지르다, 기분 상하게 하다
monopolistic 독점적인 practice 관행, 실행, 연습
issue 부과하다, 발표하다; 쟁점 significant 상당한 fine 벌금
sentence 선고하다; 문장 advocacy 옹호 promote 촉진하다, 홍보하다
transportation 운송 legislation 법안 recommendation 권고, 추천
spur 자극하다 real estate 부동산

---

05 독해 내용 일치 파악   난이도 상 ●●●

윗글에서 Antitrust Division에 관한 내용과 일치하는 것은?

① Protecting companies from unfair laws is its primary objective.
② Violations of laws will result in companies being issued warnings.
③ Energy sector regulations are beyond its advocacy scope.
④ It reviews local legislation to promote competition.

해석

① 불공정한 법으로부터 기업을 보호하는 것이 그것의 주요 목적이다.
② 독점 방지법 위반 시 기업에 경고가 내려지게 될 것이다.
③ 에너지 부문 규제는 그것의 옹호 범위를 넘어선다.
④ 그것은 경쟁을 촉진하기 위해 지역 법안을 검토한다.

해설

④번의 키워드인 reviews local legislation(지역 법안을 검토한다)이 그대로 언급된 지문 주변의 내용에서 독점 방지 정책실은 경쟁을 자극하기 위해 지역 법안을 검토한다고 했으므로, ④ '그것은 경쟁을 촉진하기 위해 지역 법안을 검토한다'가 지문의 내용과 일치한다.

[오답 분석]

① 독점 방지 정책실은 소비자들을 불공정한 가격으로부터 보호하기 위해 설립되었다고는 했지만, 불공정한 법으로부터 기업을 보호하는 것이 그것의 주요 목적인지는 알 수 없다.
② 독점 방지법 위반이 발생하면 독점 방지 정책실은 벌금 및 징역과 같은 법적 조치를 취한다고 했으므로, 독점 방지법 위반 시 기업에 경고가 내려지게 될 것이라는 것은 지문의 내용과 다르다.
③ 독점 방지 정책실은 에너지 등 국가적으로 규제되는 산업에서의 경쟁을 촉진하는 정책 및 법률을 옹호한다고 했으므로, 에너지 부문 규제가 그것의 옹호 범위를 넘어선다는 것은 지문의 내용과 다르다.

정답 ④

어휘

primary 주요한, 기본적인, 최초의 objective 목적; 객관적인
compliance 준수 scope 범위, 기회

---

06 독해 유의어 파악   난이도 중 ●●●

밑줄 친 landmark의 의미와 가장 가까운 것은?

① strict
② notable
③ costly
④ domestic

해석

① 엄격한
② 주목할 만한
③ 값비싼
④ 국내의

해설

밑줄 친 부분이 포함된 문장에서 landmark는 문맥상 시장에서의 경쟁을 보장하는 세 가지 '획기적인' 법률을 통과시켰다는 의미로 쓰였으므로, '주목할 만한'이라는 의미의 ② notable이 정답이다.

정답 ②

어휘

strict 엄격한 notable 주목할 만한 costly 값비싼 domestic 국내의, 가정의

---

07 독해 제목 파악   난이도 중 ●●●

다음 글의 제목으로 적절한 것은?

In cities where closed-circuit television (CCTV) cameras are a common sight, people generally believe them to be helpful in providing added security. The cameras give a heightened sense of protection from criminal activity and the benefit of records that can be checked to verify facts when an incident occurs. Some feel uncomfortable, however, and for good reason, for CCTV cameras can breach privacy in both public and nonpublic areas. That a person's every move can be monitored even when he or she is not carrying out lawless activity can be cause for discomfort and offense. In fact, some people have abused the technology to catch citizens engaged in immoral rather than illegal acts or to target certain persons for the purpose of threatening them, turning the system into a means by which crimes can be committed.

① Reasons Authorities Install CCTV Cameras in Public Areas
② Types of Illegal Activities Caught by Public Monitoring Devices
③ The Unethical Use of a Surveillance System
④ Why the Public Agrees to the Use of CCTV Cameras

해석

폐쇄 회로 텔레비전(CCTV) 카메라들이 흔한 광경인 도시에서, 사람들은 보통 그것들이 추가적인 보안을 제공하는 데 도움이 된다고 믿는다. 그 카메라들은 범죄 행위로부터 더 강화된 보호감과 사건이 발생할 때 사실을 입증하기 위해 확인될 수 있는 기록의 이점을 준다. 하지만, 일부 사람들은 CCTV 카메라가 공공 및 비공공 장소 모두에서 사생활을 침해할 수 있다는 정당한 이유로 불편함을 느낀다. 한 사람의 일거수일투족이 심지어 법에 어긋나는 행위를 수행하고 있지 않을 때에도 감시될 수 있다는 점은 불편함과 불쾌함의 원인일 수 있다. 실제로, 일부 사람들은 불법이라기보다는 부도덕한 행위에 관여된 시민들을 적발하거나 특정인들을 협박할 목적으로 그들을 겨냥하기 위해 그 기술을 악용하여, 그 시스템을 범죄가 저질러질 수 있는 수단이 되게 해 왔다.

① 정부가 공공 장소에 CCTV 카메라를 설치하는 이유
② 공공 감시 장치에 의해 적발되는 불법 행위의 종류
③ 감시 체계의 비윤리적 사용
④ 대중들이 CCTV 카메라의 사용에 동의하는 이유

해설

지문 전반에 걸쳐 폐쇄 회로 텔레비전(CCTV) 카메라의 이점에도 불구하고 일부 사람들은 그것이 사생활을 침해할 수 있다는 이유로 불편함을 느끼는데, 실제로 그 카메라는 불법이라기보다는 부도덕한 행위에 관여된 시민들을 적발하거나 협박하는 목적으로 종종 악용되어 왔다고 설명하고 있다. 따라서 ③ '감시 체계의 비윤리적 사용'이 이 글의 제목이다.

정답 ③

어휘

heighten 강화하다, 높이다 criminal 범죄의 verify 입증하다, 확인하다
incident 사건 for good reason 정당한 이유로 breach 침해하다, 위반하다
carry out ~을 수행하다 lawless 법에 어긋나는 discomfort 불편함
offense 불쾌함, 위반 abuse 악용하다, 남용하다 engage in ~에 관여하다
immoral 부도덕한 threaten 협박하다 commit 저지르다, 헌신하다
unethical 비윤리적인 surveillance 감시, 감독

---

08 독해 내용 불일치 파악   난이도 하 ●○○

National Wildlife Conservation Conference에 관한 다음 글의 내용과 일치하지 않는 것은?

National Wildlife Conservation Conference (NWCC)

Thursday, October 10
9 a.m. – 5 p.m.

Tickets
- Price: $50.00 (general); $75.00 (VIP)

All tickets are valid for admission to all events. VIP tickets include reserved seating in the designated VIP section.

Tickets are available online or through the venue box office. A $10 discount is offered for tickets purchased before September 1.

NOTE: NWCC invites attendees from government agencies, businesses, and members of the general public.

① 10월 중 단 하루 개최된다.
② VIP 티켓 구매자는 예약석을 이용할 수 있다.
③ 티켓 판매는 9월 1일까지 진행된다.
④ 일반인들도 회의에 참석할 수 있다.

해석

국립 야생 동물 보존 회의 (NWCC)

10월 10일 목요일
오전 9시 – 오후 5시

티켓
- 가격: 50달러 (일반), 75달러 (VIP)

모든 티켓은 모든 행사 입장에 유효합니다. VIP 티켓은 지정된 VIP 구역에서의 예약석을 포함합니다.

티켓은 온라인 또는 행사장 매표소를 통해 구매 가능합니다. 9월 1일 이전에 구매된 티켓에 대해서는 10달러 할인이 제공됩니다.

참고해 주세요: 국립 야생 동물 보존 회의는 정부 기관, 기업체 및 일반 대중 참석자분들을 초대합니다.

해설

③번의 키워드인 '9월 1일'이 그대로 언급된 지문의 September 1 주변의 내용에서 9월 1일 이전에 구매된 티켓에 대해 10달러 할인이 제공된다고 했으므로, ③ '티켓 판매는 9월 1일까지 진행된다'는 지문의 내용과 다르다.

정답 ③

어휘

conservation 보존, 보호 conference 회의, 학회 valid 유효한
designate 지정하다, 지명하다 venue 행사장 box office 매표소

---

09 독해 문단 순서 배열   난이도 중 ●●○

주어진 글 다음에 이어질 글의 순서로 적절한 것은?

It was in 1990 while on a train that J.K. Rowling conceived the idea for the first Harry Potter book that, over a span of ten years, would become a 7-book series selling more than 500 million copies.

(A) In time, the publishing house Bloomsbury would see some merit in her manuscript. They asked only that she change her name so that boys would be encouraged to read the book. Hence, the entire best-selling series was published under the name J.K. Rowling instead of Joanne Rowling.

(B) Rowling kept all these letters, most of which stated that her novel was too old-fashioned, too long, and too ordinary. She did not allow these refusals to make her despair but instead kept pushing forward with her book.

(C) Yet, the first book was rejected by twelve different publishers after it was completed in 1995. One publisher even sent her a rudely worded letter turning down her novel.

① (B) – (A) – (C)
② (B) – (C) – (A)
③ (C) – (A) – (B)
④ (C) – (B) – (A)

해석

J.K. Rowling이 10년의 기간에 걸쳐 5억 부 이상이 팔리는 일곱 권 짜리 시리즈가 될 첫 번째 해리 포터 책에 대한 구상을 생각해낸 것은 1990년에 한 기차에 타고 있을 때였다.

(A) 이윽고, Bloomsbury 출판사가 그녀의 원고에서 몇몇 훌륭한 점들을 보았다. 그들은 소년들이 그 책을 읽도록 장려하기 위해 그녀의 이름을 바꾸는 것만을 요구했다. 이런 이유로, 전 권의 베스트셀러 시리즈는 Joanne Rowling 대신 J.K. Rowling이라는 이름으로 출간되었다.

(B) Rowling은 이 모든 편지들을 간직하고 있었고, 이것들 중 대부분은 그녀의 소설이 너무 진부하고, 너무 길며, 너무 평범한 점을 언급했다. 그녀는 이 거절들이 그녀를 절망하게 두지 않았고 그 대신 그녀의 책을 계속해서 밀어붙였다.

(C) 그렇지만, 그 첫 번째 책은 1995년에 완성된 이후 열두 군데의 서로 다른 출판사들에 의해 거부되었다. 한 출판사는 그녀의 소설을 퇴짜 놓으며 무례하게 쓴 편지를 그녀에게 보내기까지 했다.

해설

주어진 문장에서 J.K. Rowling이 1990년에 한 기차에서 해리 포터 시리즈의 첫 번째 책에 대한 구상을 생각해냈다고 한 후, (C)에서 그렇지만(Yet) 그녀의 첫 번째 책은 여러 출판사들로부터 거부되었고, 그중 한 곳은 그녀에게 무례한 편지까지 보냈음을 알려 주고 있다. (B)에서 이 모든 편지들(all these letters)을 간직했던 그녀는 절망하지 않고 자신의 책을 계속해서 밀어붙였다고 하고, 뒤이어 (A)에서 이윽고(In time) Bloomsbury 출판사가 그녀의 원고에서 몇몇 훌륭한 점들을 보아 J.K. Rowling이라는 저자명으로 출간했다고 설명하고 있다. 따라서 ④ (C) – (B) – (A)가 정답이다.

정답 ④

어휘

conceive 생각해내다, 상상하다 span 기간 publishing house 출판사
merit 훌륭한 점, 장점 manuscript 원고 entire 전체의
old-fashioned 진부한, 구식의 ordinary 평범한 refusal 거절
despair 절망하다; 절망 push forward 밀어붙이다, 추진하다
rudely 무례하게 word 말을 쓰다; 단어, 말
turn down ~을 퇴짜 놓다, 거절하다

---

10 독해 빈칸 완성 – 단어 난이도 중 ●●○

밑줄 친 부분에 들어갈 말로 적절한 것은?

When teaching classrooms full of young learners, we have to be prepared to support the _____ of talent and abilities we are likely to encounter. Some students learn more efficiently through physical activity, while others thrive when allowed to express themselves artistically. Similarly, certain children thrive in groups, whereas other kids work best on their own. Before we can cater to each student's unique learning style and level, however, we have to recognize them. To do this, offer choices to the children. Allow them—within reason—to dictate how they learn most effectively, so they can showcase their talent. This requires that we offer a range of learning materials, such as books about various topics, and games and puzzles with tiered difficulty levels that can provide an appropriate challenge to students with different gifts.

① balance
② addition
③ variety
④ development

해석

어린 학습자들로 가득한 학급을 가르칠 때, 우리는 우리가 접할 가능성이 있는 재능과 능력의 다양성을 지지할 준비가 되어 있어야 한다. 어떤 학생들은 신체 활동을 통해 더 효율적으로 배우는 반면, 다른 학생들은 예술적으로 자신을 표현하는 것이 허용될 때 성공한다. 마찬가지로, 어떤 아이들은 집단 속에서 성공하는 반면, 다른 아이들은 혼자서 할 때 가장 잘한다. 하지만, 우리가 각 학생의 고유의 학습 방식과 수준을 충족시킬 수 있기 전에, 우리는 그것들을 알아야 한다. 이것을 하기 위해, 아이들에게 선택의 기회를 제공하라. 그들이 자신의 재능을 돋보이게 할 수 있도록, 이치에 맞는 선에서 그들이 가장 효과적으로 학습하는 방식을 결정하게 하라. 이것은 우리가 가지각색의 주제에 대한 책 그리고 서로 다른 재능을 가진 학생들에게 적절한 과제를 제공할 수 있는 단계별 난이도의 게임 및 퍼즐과 같은 다양한 학습 자료를 제공하는 것을 필요로 한다.

① 균형
② 추가
③ 다양성
④ 발달

해설

빈칸 뒷부분에 어떤 학생들은 신체 활동을 통해 더 효율적으로 배우는 반면 다른 학생들은 예술적인 표현이 허용될 때 성공하고, 어떤 아이들은 집단 속에서 성공하는 반면 다른 아이들은 혼자서 할 때 가장 잘한다는 내용이 있으므로, 어린 학습자들로 가득한 학급을 가르칠 때 우리는 재능과 능력의 '다양성'을 지지할 준비가 되어 있어야 한다고 한 ③번이 정답이다.

정답 ③

어휘

encounter 접하다, 직면하다 thrive 성공하다, 번창하다
on one's own 혼자서 cater to ~을 충족시키다 dictate 결정하다, 지시하다
showcase 돋보이게 하다, 전시하다 tiered 단계별의 appropriate 적절한
challenge 과제, 도전 gift 재능, 선물 variety 다양성

DAY 27 하프모의고사 27회

정답   p. 118

01	④	어휘	06	④	독해
02	③	문법	07	③	독해
03	③	문법	08	④	독해
04	②	생활영어	09	③	독해
05	①	독해	10	②	독해

취약영역 분석표

영역	맞힌 답의 개수
어휘	/1
생활영어	/1
문법	/2
독해	/6
TOTAL	/10

---

01 어휘 uncomfortable   난이도 중 ●●○

밑줄 친 부분에 들어갈 말로 적절한 것은?

> He finds it _____ to eat with his colleagues because they always bring up troublesome work-related issues during regular lunch times.

① ordinary
② inspiring
③ refreshing
④ uncomfortable

[해석]
그는 그의 동료들이 평상시의 점심시간 동안에 항상 일과 관련된 성가신 문제들을 꺼내기 때문에 그들과 식사하는 것을 불편하게 여긴다.

① 일상적인
② 고무적인
③ 신선한
④ 불편한

정답 ④

[어휘]
colleague 동료 troublesome 성가신, 귀찮은 regular 평상시의, 규칙적인
ordinary 일상적인, 평범한 inspiring 고무적인 refreshing 신선한
uncomfortable 불편한

---

02 문법 관계절   난이도 중 ●●○

밑줄 친 부분에 들어갈 말로 적절한 것은?

> The company implemented a six-month trial period _____ new policies were tested and refined.

① what
② where
③ during which
④ of which

[해석]
그 회사는 새로운 정책이 검사받고 개선되는 6개월간의 시험 기간을 시행했다.

[해설]
③ 전치사 + 관계대명사 빈칸은 완전한 절(new policies ~ refined)을 이끌면서 명사(a six-month trial period)를 수식하는 것의 자리이다. 따라서 불완전한 절을 이끄는 명사절 접속사 ① what은 정답이 될 수 없고, 관계절을 이끄는 ② where, ③ during which, ④ of which가 정답 후보이다. 이때 선행사 a six-month trial period가 시간을 나타내고, 문맥상 '6개월간'이라는 의미가 되어야 자연스러우므로, 전치사 during(~간)이 관계대명사 which 앞에 온 ③ during which가 정답이다.

정답 ③

[어휘]
implement 시행하다 trial 시험의 refine 개선하다, 정제하다

---

03 문법 동사의 종류 | 보어 | 명사 | 비교 구문   난이도 중 ●●○

밑줄 친 부분 중 어법상 옳지 않은 것은?

> Investors ① provide startup companies the initial financial backing in the hopes of reaping ② growth profit, but an excessive concentration on these types of investments can make the whole investment ③ riskily, so they typically take up ④ no more than 10 percent of an investor's portfolio.

[해석]
투자자들은 성장 수익을 거두겠다는 희망을 갖고 신생 기업들에 초기 재정적 지원을 제공하지만, 이 종류의 투자에 대한 과도한 집중은 전체 투자를 위태롭게 만들 수 있기 때문에, 그것들은 일반적으로 투자자의 포트폴리오의 단지 10퍼센트밖에 차지하지 않는다.

[해설]
③ 5형식 동사 | 보어 자리 동사 make는 '~을 -하게 만들다'의 뜻으로 쓰일 때 목적격 보어를 취하는데, 보어 자리에는 형용사 역할을 하는 것이 와야 하므로 부사 riskily를 형용사 risky로 고쳐야 한다.

[오답 분석]
① 4형식 동사 동사 provide는 두 개의 목적어를 '간접 목적어(startup companies) + 직접 목적어(the initial financial backing)'의 순서로 취하는 4형식 동사이므로 provide 뒤에 간접 목적어 startup companies가 올바르게 쓰였다.
② 복합명사 '명사 + 명사' 형태의 복합명사 growth profit이 올바르게 쓰였다.
④ 비교급 관련 표현 문맥상 '단지 10퍼센트밖에 차지하지 않는'이라는 의미가 되어야 자연스러우므로, '단지 ~밖에 안 되는'이라는 의미의 비교급 관련 표현 no more than이 올바르게 쓰였다.

정답 ③

어휘
investor 투자자 startup company 신생 기업 initial 초기의
financial 재정적인 backing 지원 reap 거두다, 획득하다 profit 수익, 이익
concentration 집중 typically 일반적으로 take up ~을 차지하다

04 생활영어 Where should we begin our corrections?
난이도 중 ●●○

밑줄 친 부분에 들어갈 말로 적절한 것은?

Jackson Evans
Have you read over the website copy?
11:32

Amelia Jones
Yes. The text requires lots of edits.
11:33

Jackson Evans
I thought so too. There are some unsupported claims in the promotional content.
11:34

Amelia Jones
Exactly. It puts us at risk of being penalized for false advertising.
11:34

Jackson Evans
The formatting and wording seem a little inconsistent too.
_____
11:35

Amelia Jones
Correcting the exaggerated parts is the most urgent.
11:36

Jackson Evans
I agree. Can you get started with it right away?
11:36

① When is the deadline for content revisions?
② Where should we begin our corrections?
③ Is there a problem with the content guidelines?
④ Didn't we proofread the entire copy?

해석
Jackson Evans: 웹사이트 광고문을 꼼꼼히 읽어 보셨나요?
Amelia Jones: 네. 본문에 수정을 필요로 하는 곳이 많던데요.
Jackson Evans: 저도 그렇게 생각했어요. 홍보 관련 내용에 몇몇 입증되지 않은 주장들이 있더라고요.
Amelia Jones: 맞아요. 그것은 우리를 허위 광고로 처벌받을 위험에 처하게 합니다.
Jackson Evans: 형식과 단어 사용도 좀 일관성이 없어 보여요. 우리가 어디서부터 수정을 시작해야 할까요?
Amelia Jones: 과장된 부분을 바로잡는 일이 가장 시급해요.
Jackson Evans: 저도 동의해요. 지금 바로 시작해 주실 수 있나요?

① 내용 수정 기한이 언제인가요?
② 우리가 어디서부터 수정을 시작해야 할까요?
③ 내용 지침에 어떤 문제가 있나요?
④ 우리가 전체 광고문을 교정 보지 않았나요?

해설
Amelia가 웹사이트 광고문에 입증되지 않은 주장들이 있어 허위 광고로 처벌받을 위험이 있다고 하자 Jackson이 형식과 단어 사용도 일관성이 없어 보인다고 하고, 빈칸 뒤에서 다시 Amelia가 Correcting the exaggerated parts is the most urgent(과장된 부분을 바로잡는 일이 가장 시급해요)라고 말하고 있으므로, '우리가 어디서부터 수정을 시작해야 할까요?'라는 의미의 ② 'Where should we begin our corrections?'가 정답이다.

정답 ②

어휘
copy 광고문, 원고, 사본 edit 수정; 수정하다 unsupported 입증되지 않은
claim 주장; 주장하다 promotional 홍보의 inconsistent 일관성이 없는
correct 수정하다; 올바른 exaggerated 과장된 urgent 시급한
revision 수정 proofread 교정하다

05~06 다음 글을 읽고 물음에 답하시오.

_____(A)_____

The Pritchard Municipal Transportation Department is excited to invite you to its upcoming Summer Bike Safety and Repair Clinics, a series of free events designed to promote safe and responsible cycling for everyone in the community.

DAY 27 하프모의고사 27회

Details
- **Dates:** Every Saturday, from the beginning of June through the end of August
- **Time:** 10:00 a.m. – 1:00 p.m.
- **Location:** Southside Mall Parking Lot, 300 Novak Avenue

What to Expect
- **Free Bike Tune-Ups**
  Experienced mechanics will be on site to offer free bike tune-ups.
- **Safety Lessons**
  Instructors will provide hands-on lessons on how to navigate city streets, signal turns, and wear appropriate safety gear.
- **Giveaways**
  To encourage safe riding, we will distribute free bike lights to children (while supplies last).

For more information, visit www.pritchardbikeclinics.org or contact the Municipal Transportation Department at (208) 987-6543.

해석

(A) 올여름 안전하게 자전거를 타세요

Pritchard 시 교통부는 지역 사회의 모든 분들을 위한 안전하고 책임감 있는 자전거 타기를 증진하기 위해 고안된 일련의 무료 행사인, 다가오는 자전거 안전 및 수리 여름 클리닉에 여러분을 초대하게 되어 기쁩니다.

세부 사항
- **날짜:** 6월 초부터 8월 말까지 매주 토요일
- **시간:** 오전 10시 – 오후 1시
- **장소:** Southside 쇼핑몰 주차장, Novak로 300

기대하실 수 있는 것
- **무료 자전거 점검**
  숙련된 정비사분들이 무료 자전거 점검 서비스를 제공하기 위해 현장에 계실 것입니다.
- **안전 교육**
  강사들이 도시의 거리들을 지나다니고, 방향 전환 신호를 보내고, 적절한 안전 장비를 착용하는 방법에 대한 실습수업을 제공할 것입니다.
- **증정품**
  안전한 주행을 장려하기 위해, 저희는 어린이들에게 무료 자전거 지시등을 나누어 줄 예정입니다(물품이 충분할 때까지).

더 자세한 정보를 위해서는 www.pritchardbikeclinics.org를 방문하시거나 (208) 987-6543번으로 시 교통부에 문의하십시오.

어휘
municipal 시의, 지방 자치제의 **promote** 증진하다, 홍보하다
tune-up 점검 **mechanic** 정비사 **on site** 현장에 **instructor** 강사
navigate 지나다니다, 길을 찾다 **appropriate** 적절한 **gear** 장비
giveaway 증정품 **distribute** 나누어 주다, 분배하다
supply 물품, 공급; 공급하다 **last** 충분하다, 지속되다; 마지막의, 가장 최근의

---

05 독해 제목 파악 난이도 중

(A)에 들어갈 윗글의 제목으로 적절한 것은?

① Ride Safely This Summer
② Upgrade Your Bike
③ Explore New Bike Paths
④ Get Fit Through Cycling

해석
① 올여름 안전하게 자전거를 타세요
② 여러분의 자전거를 업그레이드하세요
③ 새로운 자전거 경로를 탐험하세요
④ 자전거 타기를 통해 건강해지세요

해설
지문 앞부분에서 모든 시민들을 위한 안전하고 책임감 있는 자전거 타기를 증진하는 행사인 자전거 안전 및 수리 여름 클리닉에 초대한다고 했으므로, ① '올여름 안전하게 자전거를 타세요'가 이 글의 제목이다.

정답 ①

어휘
explore 탐험하다, 탐구하다 **path** 경로, 길 **get fit** 건강해지다

---

06 독해 내용 불일치 파악 난이도 하

Summer Bike Safety and Repair Clinics에 관한 윗글의 내용과 일치하지 않는 것은?

① 매주 개최될 것이다.
② 전문가들에게 자전거를 점검받을 기회가 있다.
③ 안전 장비에 대한 수업을 들을 수 있다.
④ 모든 참가자들은 자전거 지시등을 받을 수 있다.

해설
④번의 키워드인 '자전거 지시등'이 그대로 언급된 지문의 bike lights 주변의 내용에서 어린이들에게 무료 자전거 지시등을 나누어 줄 예정이라고 했으므로, ④ '모든 참가자들은 자전거 지시등을 받을 수 있다'는 지문의 내용과 다르다.

정답 ④

---

07 독해 문장 삽입 난이도 하

주어진 문장이 들어갈 위치로 적절한 것은?

This process is only required once at the very beginning, so you won't need to take photos multiple times.

IDforMe is a government-approved, digital identification app that can serve as a valid proof of ID. It can be used for various purposes, including picking up mail at the post office, accessing bank accounts online, buying age-restricted items, and signing up for government services. The app securely stores your personal information using advanced encryption, ensuring that your details are only accessible by you. (①) To get started, download the app for free and create an account. (②) You'll be prompted to take a selfie and scan a piece of government-issued ID, like a driver's license or passport to verify your identify. (③) With IDforMe, your proof of identity is always available as long as you have your phone. (④)

해석

이 과정은 맨 처음에 단 한 번만 요청될 것이므로, 여러분이 여러 번 사진을 찍으실 필요는 없습니다.

IDforMe는 유효한 신분 증명 역할을 할 수 있는, 정부 승인을 받은 디지털 신분증입니다. 그것은 우체국에서의 우편물 수령, 은행 계좌의 온라인 접속, 연령 제한이 있는 상품 구매 및 정부 서비스 가입 등 다양한 목적으로 사용될 수 있습니다. 앱은 고급 암호화를 사용하여 개인 정보를 안전하게 저장하는데, 이는 자신의 세부 사항에 오직 자신만이 접근할 수 있음을 보장합니다. ① 시작하시려면, 무료로 앱을 다운로드하고 계정을 만드세요. ② 여러분의 신원을 확인하기 위해 사진을 찍고 운전 면허증이나 여권과 같은 정부 발행 신분증을 스캔하도록 요청받을 것입니다. ③ IDforMe로, 여러분의 신분 증명은 휴대폰이 있는 한 언제든 이용 가능합니다. ④

해설

③번 앞 문장에 앱에서 신원을 확인하기 위해 사용자의 사진을 찍고 신분증을 스캔하라고 요청할 것이라는 내용이 있으므로, ③번 자리에 이 과정(This process)은 맨 처음에 한 번만 요청될 것이므로 여러 번 사진을 찍을 필요가 없다는 내용, 즉 사용자의 사진을 찍고 신분증을 스캔하도록 요청받는 단계에 대해 부연 설명하는 주어진 문장이 나와야 지문이 자연스럽게 연결된다.

정답 ③

어휘

identification 신분증 valid 유효한 proof 증명(서), 증거
account 계좌, 계정 age-restricted 연령 제한이 있는 securely 안전하게
store 저장하다, 보관하다; 가게 advanced 고급의, 선진의
encryption 암호화 accessible 접근 가능한 license 면허증
verify 확인하다 identity 신원, 신분 available 이용 가능한

08 독해 요지 파악 난이도 중 ●●○

다음 글의 요지로 적절한 것은?

Astronomers have gathered much information about the rings of Saturn in the 400 years since Galileo Galilei first spotted them. When viewed through telescopes on Earth, Saturn appears to have seven large rings that orbit it at different speeds depending on their distance from the planet. But through satellite imaging, these main rings have been determined to actually be a series of up to one thousand smaller ringlets that are grouped together. The rings consist of pieces of ice and shattered chunks of rock from comets, asteroids, and moons that were broken into pieces under the immense force of Saturn's gravity. Three other planets in the solar system have rings too, but they are darker, fainter, and do not fill the viewer with the same sense of awe as Saturn's. This is because of the ring system's sheer size, with a diameter of 270,000 kilometers, or more than half the distance between the Earth and the Moon.

① Astronomers disagree about Saturn's ring composition.
② Rings maintain consistent speeds around planets.
③ Moons remain intact despite Saturn's gravity.
④ Multiple tiny ringlets compose Saturn's rings.

해석

천문학자들은 Galileo Galilei가 토성의 고리를 처음 발견한 이후로 400년 동안 그것들에 대한 많은 정보를 수집해 왔다. 지구에서 망원경을 통해 관측될 때, 토성은 그 행성으로부터의 거리에 따라 다른 속도로 그것(토성)의 궤도를 도는 일곱 개의 큰 고리를 가지고 있는 것처럼 보인다. 그러나 위성 영상을 통해, 이 가장 큰 고리들이 실제로는 함께 모여 있는, 최대 1,000개의 일련의 더 작은 고리들인 것으로 밝혀졌다. 그 고리들은 얼음 조각들과 토성 중력의 어마어마한 힘에 의해 산산조각 난 혜성, 소행성 그리고 위성 조각으로 부서진 바윗 덩어리들로 이루어진다. 태양계의 다른 세 행성들도 고리들을 가지고 있지만, 그것들은 더 어둡고, 더 희미하며, 토성의 것처럼 관찰자들을 경외감에 사로잡히게 만들지 않는다. 이는 순전히 27만 킬로미터의 지름, 즉 지구와 달 사이의 거리의 절반이 넘는 그 고리 체계의 크기 때문이다.

① 천문학자들은 토성의 고리 구성에 대해 의견이 일치하지 않는다.
② 고리는 행성 주위에서 일정한 속도를 유지한다.
③ 위성은 토성의 중력에도 불구하고 온전하게 남아 있다.
④ 수많은 작은 고리들이 토성의 고리를 구성한다.

해설

지문 전반에 걸쳐 토성의 고리가 처음 발견된 이후 400년 동안 그것들에 대한 많은 정보가 수집되었는데, 일곱 개의 큰 고리로 보이는 것이 실제로는 약 1,000개의 작은 고리들이며, 토성 중력에 의해 산산조각 난 혜성·소행성·위성의 조각이 모여 27만 킬로미터의 지름을 이룬다고 알려 주고 있다. 따라서 ④ '수많은 작은 고리들이 토성의 고리를 구성한다'가 이 글의 요지이다.

정답 ④

어휘

astronomer 천문학자 Saturn 토성 spot 발견하다 telescope 망원경
orbit 궤도를 돌다; 궤도 satellite 위성 determine 밝히다, 결정하다
ringlet 작은 고리 shatter 산산이 부수다 chunk 덩어리 comet 혜성
asteroid 소행성 moon 위성, 달 immense 어마어마한, 엄청난
gravity 중력 faint 희미한 awe 경외감 sheer 순전한, 순수한
diameter 지름 composition 구성 intact 온전한 compose 구성하다

DAY 27 하프모의고사 27회

09 독해 무관한 문장 삭제   난이도 중 ●●○

다음 글의 흐름상 어색한 문장은?

A "cliff-hanger" is a storytelling tool that works to build suspense by placing the lead character in a dangerous situation or tricky dilemma at the end of a work of fiction. If executed correctly, a cliff-hanger will encourage the audience to tune back in for the next installment of the story. ① The technique itself has been in use for centuries in oral storytelling. ② However, the term only came into being in the 1930s, when British author Thomas Hardy published a serialized version of his novel *A Pair of Blue Eyes*. ③ Bookstores typically display cliff-hanger novels in prominent locations to maximize impulse purchases. ④ His work appeared in *Tinsley's Magazine* for more than six months, with each installment strategically ending in suspense. One memorable section ended with the main character literally left hanging on the edge of a cliff. Eager to learn the fate of this hero, readers purchased the following magazine issue enthusiastically.

[해석]

'클리프행어'는 소설 작품의 마지막에 주인공을 위험한 상황이나 곤란한 궁지에 빠트림으로써 긴장감을 자아내는 이야기 수단이다. 정확하게 행해진다면, 클리프행어는 독자들이 이야기의 다음 회에 귀를 기울이도록 부추길 것이다. ① 그 기법 자체는 구전 이야기에서 수세기 동안 사용되어 왔다. ② 하지만, 그 용어는 영국인 작가 Thomas Hardy가 그의 소설 『한 쌍의 푸른 눈』의 연재판을 출간한 1930년대에야 생겨났다. ③ 서점들은 충동 구매를 극대화하기 위해 클리프행어 소설들을 눈에 띄는 위치에 일반적으로 진열한다. ④ 그의 작품은 6개월 넘는 기간 동안 〈Tinsley's Magazine〉에 실렸는데, 각 회분이 전략적으로 긴장감 있게 끝났다. 기억할 만한 한 부분은 주인공이 말 그대로 절벽(cliff) 끝에 매달린(hanging) 채로 끝이 났다. 이 남자 주인공의 운명을 알기를 간절히 바라면서, 독자들은 열광적으로 다음 호 잡지를 구매했다.

[해설]

지문 앞부분에서 작품 마지막에 주인공을 위험한 상황에 빠트림으로써 긴장감을 만들어내는 '클리프행어' 기법에 대해 언급하고, ①번은 '구전 이야기에서 사용되어 온 클리프행어', ②번은 '용어의 유래로 여겨지는 Thomas Hardy의 소설 『한 쌍의 푸른 눈』', ④번은 '각 회분이 긴장감 있게 끝난 『한 쌍의 푸른 눈』'을 설명하고 있다. 그러나 ③번은 '클리프행어 소설들을 눈에 잘 띄는 위치에 진열하는 서점들'에 대한 내용으로, 지문 앞부분의 내용과 관련이 없다.

정답 ③

[어휘]

suspense 긴장감 lead character 주인공 tricky 곤란한, 까다로운
dilemma 궁지, 딜레마 execute 행하다, 처형하다
tune in 귀를 기울이다, (채널을) 맞추다 installment 1회분, 설치
oral 구전의, 구두의 term 용어, 기간 come into being 생겨나다, 태어나다
serialize 연재하다 prominent 눈에 띄는, 두드러진 impulse 충동
literally 말 그대로 edge 끝, 가장자리 eager 간절한, 열망하는 fate 운명
enthusiastically 열광적으로

10 독해 빈칸 완성 - 절   난이도 중 ●●○

밑줄 친 부분에 들어갈 말로 적절한 것은?

In 1952, the poet Dylan Thomas penned the now-famous refrain "Do not go gentle into that good night… Rage, … rage against the dying of the light." At the time, the lines expressed Thomas's grief for the impending death of his ailing father as well as his belief that a person should never simply be resigned to death. Since then, the poem has been used in popular culture to not only reflect on the end of life but also to evoke the notion that surrendering is unacceptable under any circumstances as long as there is still time and opportunity. In other words, the fundamental message of the poem is that, in the face of an inevitable and undesirable outcome, _____.

① life will go on no matter what
② one should fight until the end
③ acceptance will bring peace
④ nothing can be done about the past

[해석]

1952년에, 시인 Dylan Thomas는 이제는 유명한 후렴구인 "순순히 어두운 밤을 받아들이지 마세요… 빛이 꺼져감에 분노하고, 또 분노하세요"를 썼다. 그 당시에, 이 시구들은 한 사람이 결코 그저 죽음에 굴복해서는 안 된다는 그의 믿음뿐만 아니라 병든 아버지의 임박한 죽음에 대한 Thomas의 슬픔을 표현했다. 그 이후로, 그 시는 삶의 끝을 성찰하기 위해서뿐만 아니라 시간과 기회가 여전히 있는 한 어떠한 상황에서도 굴복하는 것은 용납되지 않는다는 생각을 일깨우기 위해 대중문화에서 사용되어 왔다. 즉, 그 시의 핵심적인 메시지는 불가피하고 원치 않는 결과에도 불구하고, 사람은 끝까지 맞서 싸워야 한다는 것이다.

① 어떤 일이 있더라도 삶은 계속될 것이다
② 사람은 끝까지 맞서 싸워야 한다
③ 받아들임이 평화를 가져올 것이다
④ 과거에 대해서는 아무것도 할 수 없다

[해설]

빈칸 앞 문장에 Dylan Thomas 시의 유명한 후렴구는 시간과 기회가 있는 한 어떠한 상황에서도 굴복하는 것은 용납되지 않는다는 생각을 일깨우기 위해 대중문화에서 사용되어 왔다는 내용이 있으므로, 그 시의 핵심적인 메시지는 불가피하고 원치 않는 결과에도 불구하고 '사람은 끝까지 맞서 싸워야 한다'는 것이라고 한 ②번이 정답이다.

정답 ②

[어휘]

pen (글을) 쓰다 refrain 후렴구, (상투적인) 문구; 삼가다
rage 분노하다, 몹시 화내다 grief 슬픔, 애도, 비탄
impending 임박한, 절박한, 곧 일어날 ailing 병든, 앓고 있는
be resigned to ~에 굴복하다, 따르다 reflect 성찰하다, 반성하다
evoke 일깨우다, 불러내다 surrender 굴복하다, 포기하다
circumstance 상황, 환경 fundamental 핵심적인, 기본적인
in the face of ~에도 불구하고, ~에 직면하여 inevitable 불가피한

DAY 28 하프모의고사 28회

정답   p. 122

01	②	어휘	06	①	독해
02	②	문법	07	③	독해
03	④	문법	08	①	독해
04	④	생활영어	09	③	독해
05	②	독해	10	③	독해

취약영역 분석표

영역	맞힌 답의 개수
어휘	/1
생활영어	/1
문법	/2
독해	/6
TOTAL	/10

---

01 어휘 concrete   난이도 중 ●●○

밑줄 친 부분에 들어갈 말로 적절한 것은?

After three days of trial, the plaintiff won the case as his opponent lacked _____ evidence.

① flexible   ② concrete
③ fake   ④ complex

[해석]
3일 동안의 재판 후에, 원고는 상대방에게 구체적인 증거가 없었기 때문에 승소했다.
① 융통성 있는   ② 구체적인
③ 가짜의   ④ 복잡한

정답 ②

[어휘]
trial 재판 plaintiff 원고, 고소인 win the case 승소하다
opponent 상대, 반대자 flexible 융통성 있는, 유연한 concrete 구체적인
fake 가짜의 complex 복잡한

---

02 문법 동사의 종류   난이도 중 ●●○

밑줄 친 부분에 들어갈 말로 적절한 것은?

The private investigator watched the subject who had been under surveillance _____ the abandoned building.

① to enter   ② enter
③ entered   ④ being entered

[해석]
그 사설 탐정은 감시를 받아 왔던 그 대상이 버려진 건물로 들어가는 것을 지켜보았다.

[해설]
② 원형 부정사를 목적격 보어로 취하는 동사   빈칸은 지각동사 watch의 목적격 보어 자리이다. 지각동사 watch는 목적어와 목적격 보어가 능동 관계일 때 목적격 보어로 원형 부정사나 현재분사를 취하는데, 목적어 the subject와 목적격 보어가 '그 대상이 들어가다'라는 의미의 능동 관계이므로 원형 부정사 ② enter가 정답이다.

정답 ②

[어휘]
private investigator 사설 탐정 subject 대상, 주제, 과목
surveillance 감시 abandon 버리다, 포기하다

---

03 문법 대명사|전치사|to 부정사|병치 구문   난이도 하 ●○○

밑줄 친 부분 중 어법상 옳지 않은 것은?

US schools are ① similar to European schools in a number of ways. Class size is limited, which allows a teacher ② to give each student adequate attention. Both systems are co-educational, offer the same basic subjects, and ③ require nine or ten years to complete. Yet, the rate of students who go on to university in the United States is about 10-20 percent higher than ④ those of Europe.

[해석]
미국의 학교들은 많은 방식에 있어 유럽의 학교들과 비슷하다. 학급 규모는 제한되는데, 이는 교사로 하여금 각각의 학생들에게 충분한 관심을 두게 한다. 두 나라의 체계 모두 남녀 공학이고, 동일한 기본 과목을 제공하며, 이수하는 데 9년에서 10년을 필요로 한다. 그렇지만, 미국에서 대학에 진행하는 학생의 비율은 유럽에서의 비율보다 약 10-20퍼센트 더 높다.

[해설]
④ 지시대명사   대명사가 지시하는 명사가 단수 명사(the rate)이므로 복수 지시대명사 those를 단수 지시대명사 that으로 고쳐야 한다.

DAY 28 하프모의고사 28회

[오답 분석]
① 기타 전치사 '유럽의 학교와 비슷한'을 나타내기 위해 전치사 숙어 표현 similar to(~와 비슷한)가 올바르게 쓰였다.
② to 부정사를 취하는 동사 동사 allow는 to 부정사를 목적격 보어로 취하므로 to 부정사 to give가 올바르게 쓰였다.
③ 병치 구문 세 개의 단어는 'A, B, + 등위접속사 + C'의 형태로 연결할 수 있는데, 등위접속사(and)로 연결된 병치 구문에서는 같은 품사끼리 연결되어야 하고, A와 B 자리에 복수 동사 are, offer가 왔으므로 C 자리에도 복수 동사 require가 올바르게 쓰였다.

정답 ④

어휘

adequate 충분한, 적절한 attention 관심, 주의
co-educational 남녀 공학의 subject 과목, 주제
complete 이수하다, 끝마치다, 완료하다 rate 비율, 속도, 요금

04 생활영어 I want to give them small bills as a gift.
난이도 하 ●○○

밑줄 친 부분에 들어갈 말로 적절한 것은?

A: Before we go to my sister's place, can we stop by the bank?
B: Can you do that tomorrow? We have a long drive ahead of us.
A: But I'm going to see my sister's kids for the first time.
B: I know, but why do you need to drop by the bank?
A: _____
B: Oh, I didn't think of that. Let's go to the bank, then.

① I need to deposit some money quickly.
② I'm going to open an account.
③ I have to check my balance.
④ I want to give them small bills as a gift.

해석

A: 우리 언니네 집에 가기 전에, 은행을 잠깐 들를 수 있을까?
B: 내일 가면 안 돼? 우리는 갈 길이 멀어.
A: 그렇지만 언니 아이들을 처음 보는 건데.
B: 나도 알지, 그런데 왜 은행에 들러야 해?
A: 그들에게 선물로 용돈을 조금 주고 싶어.
B: 아, 내가 그걸 생각 못했네. 그럼 은행에 가자.

① 돈을 빨리 입금해야 해.
② 계좌를 개설할 거야.
③ 내 잔고를 확인해야 해.
④ 그들에게 선물로 용돈을 조금 주고 싶어.

해설

언니 아이들을 처음 보러 가는 길에 은행에 들를 수 있는지 묻는 A의 말에 대해 B가 왜 들러야 하는지 묻고, 빈칸 뒤에서 다시 B가 I didn't think of that. Let's go to the bank, then(내가 그걸 생각 못했네. 그럼 은행에 가자)이라고 말하고 있으므로, '그들에게 선물로 용돈을 조금 주고 싶어'라는 의미의 ④ 'I want to give them small bills as a gift'가 정답이다.

정답 ④

어휘

stop by ~에 잠시 들르다 deposit 입금하다, 예금하다; 보증금
open an account 계좌를 개설하다 balance 잔고, 균형

05~06 다음 글을 읽고 물음에 답하시오.

Maritime Safety
Maintaining the safety and security of the nation's coastal waters is the core mission of the Coast Guard. The agency actively patrols to enforce law and provide protection in order to safeguard the country and its citizens and industries.

Search and Rescue Operations
Search and Rescue (SAR) operations, in which the Coast Guard looks for and assists people in distress at sea, such as lost boaters, those experiencing medical emergencies, and passengers on damaged or capsized vessels, are a critical aspect of the service's activities.

The Coast Guard's highly trained personnel are on duty 24 hours a day. They actively respond to distress signals and coordinate rapid responses to dangerous situations. When a distress call is received, SAR teams immediately mobilize and dispatch the necessary resources to conduct a timely rescue.

해석

해양 안전
국가 연안 수역의 안전과 보안을 유지하는 것은 해안 경비대의 핵심 임무입니다. 그 기관은 국가와 시민 및 산업을 보호하기 위해 법을 집행하고 보호를 제공하고자 적극적으로 순찰합니다.

수색 및 구조 작전
해안 경비대가 해상에서 조난당한 사람들, 예를 들어 길 잃은 보트 이용자, 응급 의료 상황을 겪고 있는 사람들, 그리고 손상되거나 전복된 선박의 승객들을 찾고 돕는 수색 및 구조 작전(SAR)은 해당 기관 활동들 중 중요한 한 측면입니다.

해안 경비대의 고도로 훈련된 직원들이 하루 24시간 근무합니다. 그들은 조난 신호에 적극적으로 대응하고 위험한 상황에 대해 신속한 대응을 조직화합니다. 조난 호출이 접수되면, 수색 및 구조대는 즉시 동원되어 시기적절한 구조를 수행하기 위해 필요한 자원을 배치합니다.

어휘

maritime 해양의, 바다의 coastal 연안의, 해안의 patrol 순찰하다
enforce 집행하다 safeguard 보호하다 rescue 구조; 구조하다
operation 작전, 활동, 수술 distress 조난, 곤경; 괴롭히다
capsize 전복시키다, 뒤집히다 vessel 선박 critical 중요한
personnel 직원, 인원 coordinate 조직화하다, 편성하다
mobilize 동원되다 dispatch 배치하다, 파견하다 conduct 수행하다
timely 시기적절한

05 독해 요지 파악　　　난이도 중 ●●○

윗글의 요지로 적절한 것은?

① The Coast Guard takes care of maintaining water quality.
② The Coast Guard is meant to protect people in the waters around the country.
③ The Coast Guard attempts to prevent boats from being damaged or capsizing.
④ The Coast Guard conducts SAR exercises to improve its operations.

해석
① 해안 경비대는 수질 유지에 대한 책임이 있다.
② 해안 경비대는 국가 주변 수역에서 사람들을 보호하도록 되어 있다.
③ 해안 경비대는 선박이 손상되거나 전복되는 것을 방지하려 한다.
④ 해안 경비대는 그것의 활동을 개선하기 위해 수색 및 구조 작전을 실시한다.

해설
지문 처음에서 국가 연안 수역의 안전 및 보안 유지가 해안 경비대의 핵심 임무라고 하고, 지문 중간에서 그 기관의 활동 중에서도 해상에서 조난당한 사람들을 찾고 돕는 작전은 중요한 한 측면이라고 설명하고 있으므로, ② '해안 경비대는 국가 주변 수역에서 사람들을 보호하도록 되어 있다'가 이 글의 요지이다.

정답 ②

06 독해 유의어 파악　　　난이도 중 ●●○

밑줄 친 dispatch의 의미와 가장 가까운 것은?

① deploy　　② secure
③ retrieve　　④ command

해석
① 배치하다　　② 확보하다
③ 회수하다　　④ 명령하다

해설
밑줄 친 부분이 포함된 문장에서 dispatch는 문맥상 수색 및 구조대가 시기적절한 구조를 수행하기 위해 필요한 자원을 '배치한다'는 의미로 쓰였으므로, '배치하다'라는 의미의 ① deploy가 정답이다.

정답 ①

어휘
deploy 배치하다　secure 확보하다; 안심하는, 안전한　retrieve 회수하다
command 명령하다; 명령

07 독해 내용 불일치 파악　　　난이도 중 ●●○

Hillary-Sanders 저택에 관한 다음 글의 내용과 일치하지 않는 것은?

> The Hillary-Sanders House is open to the public on weekdays from 11 a.m. to 7 p.m. and from 8 a.m. to 8 p.m. on Saturdays and national holidays. Tickets may be reserved up to one month in advance using the online ticket booking agency. Online purchasers will receive a QR code that can be scanned by the kiosks at the entrance of the museum.
>
> • **Online tickets**: Tickets.HSandersHouse.com
>
> The Hillary-Sanders House (part of the city's Historical District) charges $15 for full-priced adult admission. Children ages 6-18 and senior citizens can enter for $10. There is no charge for those under 5 years old. Guided tours can be arranged for an additional cost of $10 per ticket, regardless of age.
>
> • **CLOSED**: Sundays, New Year's Day, and Christmas week (December 25-31)
>
> There is no charge for school groups visiting the Hillary-Sanders House as part of an official field trip.
>
> For additional information, call 1 (800) 555-2814.

① 토요일에 더 늦게까지 개방한다.
② QR 스캔용 키오스크를 비치하고 있다.
③ 티켓 구매 시 무료 가이드 투어를 제공한다.
④ 현장 학습 학생들은 별도의 입장료가 없다.

해석

> Hillary-Sanders 저택은 평일에는 오전 11시부터 오후 7시까지, 토요일과 국경일에는 오전 8시부터 오후 8시까지 일반 대중분들께 개방됩니다. 티켓은 온라인 티켓 예매 대행 업체를 이용하시어 최대 한 달 전부터 예약하실 수 있습니다. 온라인으로 구매하신 분들은 박물관 입구에 있는 키오스크로 스캔될 수 있는 QR 코드를 받으실 겁니다.
>
> ■ 온라인 티켓: Tickets.HSandersHouse.com
>
> Hillary-Sanders 저택(도시 역사 지구의 일부)은 성인 입장료에 대해 정가 15달러를 청구합니다. 6-18세 아이들과 노인분들은 10달러에 입장하실 수 있습니다. 5세 미만인 아이들은 무료입니다. 연령에 관계 없이, 티켓당 추가 비용 10달러로 가이드 투어가 준비될 수 있습니다.
>
> ■ 휴관: 일요일, 새해 첫날, 크리스마스 주간(12월 25일-31일)
>
> 공식 현장 학습의 일환으로 Hillary-Sanders 저택을 방문하시는 학교 단체에는 입장료가 부과되지 않습니다.
>
> 더 알아보시려면, 1 (800) 555-2814로 전화해 주세요.

해설
③번의 키워드인 '가이드 투어'를 그대로 언급한 지문의 Guided tours 주변의 내용에서 티켓당 추가 비용 10달러로 가이드 투어가 준비될 수 있다고 했으므로, ③ '티켓 구매 시 무료 가이드 투어를 제공한다'는 지문의 내용과 다르다.

정답 ③

DAY 28 하프모의고사 28회

어휘
national holiday 국경일 district 지구, 구역 charge 청구하다; 요금
arrange 준비하다, 정리하다 field trip 현장 학습

08 독해 제목 파악 난이도 상

다음 글의 제목으로 적절한 것은?

In the days of old, sailors composed sayings about their situation when they were sailing the oceans. For example, "down in the doldrums" means that one is unable to make progress. For sailors, "the doldrums" meant that the ship could not move. Ships sailing between Europe and Africa relied on trade winds—steady breezes found north and south of the equator. These natural wind patterns essentially served as highways for ocean navigation. Specifically, Earth's rotation causes air to slope toward the equator in a counterclockwise direction in the southern hemisphere and in a clockwise direction in the northern hemisphere, known as the Coriolis effect. This effect, along with a high-pressure area, pushes the trade winds from east to west. However, the intense solar heat near the equator calms these winds, causing them to cease. This area is known as the doldrums, where ships stood still as there was no wind in their sails.

① The Science behind an Old Sailing Expression
② How Ships in the Past Navigated the Seas
③ Formation of Winds near Earth's Equator
④ The Effect of Wind on Trade in the Old Days

해석
옛날에, 선원들은 바다를 항해하고 있을 때 그들의 상황에 대한 격언들을 만들었다. 예를 들어, '적도 무풍대로 들어가다'는 나아가지 못하는 상태를 의미한다. 선원들에게 '적도 무풍대'는 배가 움직일 수 없다는 것을 의미했다. 유럽과 아프리카 사이를 항해하던 배들은 적도의 북쪽과 남쪽에서 발생하는 일정한 미풍인, 무역풍에 의존했다. 이러한 자연적인 바람 패턴은 본질적으로 바다 항해를 위한 고속도로 역할을 했다. 구체적으로 말하면, 지구의 자전은 공기가 남반구에서는 적도를 향해 시계 반대 방향으로, 북반구에서는 시계 방향으로 비스듬히 움직이게 하는데, 이것은 코리올리 효과로 알려져 있다. 고기압 지역을 따라, 이 효과는 무역풍을 동쪽에서 서쪽으로 밀어낸다. 하지만, 적도 근처에서는 강렬한 태양열이 이 바람들을 진정시켜서, 그것들이 그치게 한다. 이 지역이 바로 적도 무풍대로 알려져 있는데, 이곳에서 배들은 그것들의 돛에 바람이 불지 않아서 가만히 서 있었다.

① 옛 항해 표현 이면의 과학
② 과거의 배들이 바다를 항해했던 방법
③ 지구 적도 부근의 바람 형성
④ 옛날에 바람이 무역에 미친 영향

해설
지문 전반에 걸쳐 '적도 무풍대로 들어가다'라는 항해 관련 표현은 나아가지 못하는 상태를 의미하는 격언으로, 적도 근처에서 무역풍이 잦아들어 돛에 바람이 불지 않음에 따라 배들이 가만히 서 있었던 현상에서 유래되었음을 알려 주고 있다. 따라서 ① '옛 항해 표현 이면의 과학'이 이 글의 제목이다.

정답 ①

어휘
compose 만들다, 구성하다 saying 격언, 속담 sail 항해하다; 돛
progress 나아감, 진행; 나아가다 trade wind 무역풍
steady 일정한, 한결같은 breeze 미풍 equator 적도 highway 고속도로
navigation 항해 specifically 구체적으로 말하면
rotation (지구·천체의) 자전, 회전 slope 비스듬히 움직이다, 경사지다
counterclockwise 시계 반대 방향으로 hemisphere 반구
clockwise 시계 방향으로 high-pressure 고기압의, 강압적인
intense 강렬한 cease (바람이) 그치다, 그만두다

09 독해 문장 삽입 난이도 중

주어진 문장이 들어갈 위치로 적절한 곳은?

By that time, Benin had become a prosperous city, and it attracted the Europeans who were about to divide and conquer Africa.

In 800 AD, the people of Benin, a city located in what is now southern Nigeria, began building a defensive fortification. (①) Completed around 1460 AD, its earthen walls were 20 meters high in most parts and included defensive water channels. (②) When the Portuguese visited in 1472 AD, they described the earthwork as a structure so great that it was second only to China's Great Wall. (③) Because of its wealth, Benin was especially attractive to British traders who were attempting to convince the government to make the city a protected territory. (④) Aware of their motives, the rulers of Benin attacked first, causing the British army to invade the city in 1897 and completely destroy it.

해석
그때쯤, Benin은 번영하는 도시가 되었고, 그것은 아프리카를 분열시키고 정복하려는 유럽인들을 끌어들였다.

서기 800년, 오늘날 나이지리아 남부에 위치한 도시 Benin의 사람들은 방어용 요새를 건설하기 시작했다. ① 서기 1460년에 완성된 그것의 동쪽 벽은 거의 모든 곳이 20미터 높이였고 방어용 수로들을 포함하고 있었다. ② 포르투갈인들이 서기 1472년에 방문했을 때, 그들은 그 토공 작업을 중국의 만리장성에 버금가는 훌륭한 건축물이라고 묘사했다. ③ 그것의 부유함 때문에, Benin은 그 도시를 보호령으로 만들도록 정부를 설득하려 하고 있었던 영국 무역업자들에게 특히 매력적이었다. ④ 그들의 동기를 알게 되면서 Benin의 통치자들이 먼저 공격했는데, 이는 영국군이 1897년 그 도시를 침략해서 그것을 완전히 파괴하게 했다.

해설
③번 앞 문장에 포르투갈인들이 1472년에 Benin에 방문했을 때 Benin의 토공 작업을 훌륭하다고 묘사했다는 내용이 있고, 뒤 문장에 도시의 부유함 때문에 Benin은 그 도시를 보호령으로 만들도록 정부를 설득하던 영국 무

역업자들에게 특히 매력적이었다는 내용이 있으므로, ③번 자리에 그때쯤 (By that time) Benin은 번영했고 이것이 유럽인들을 끌어들였다는 내용, 즉 유럽의 영국 무역업자들이 Benin에 매력을 느낀 이유를 설명하는 주어진 문장이 나와야 지문이 자연스럽게 연결된다.

정답 ③

어휘

prosperous 번영한, 번창한　attract 끌어들이다, 불러일으키다
be about to 막 ~하려고 하다　conquer 정복하다　defensive 방어용의
fortification 요새, 방어 시설　complete 완성하다, 끝마치다
channel 수로, 운하, 경로　earthwork 토공 작업, 토목 공사　trader 무역업자
convince 설득하다　territory 영토　aware 알고 있는　invade 침략하다
destroy 파괴하다

10 독해 문단 순서 배열　난이도 중 ●●○

주어진 글 다음에 이어질 글의 순서로 적절한 것은?

Global agricultural systems strive to meet the dietary demands of growing populations, but this has impacted the environment negatively. The process begins with the planting of crops.

(A) Aside from this impact on water, nitrogen accumulation is a threat to land and air. It affects the health of native plant species, which reduces the biodiversity of the ecosystem. Fertilizers also contribute one-fifth of total greenhouse gas emissions in the atmosphere.

(B) To ensure food security, farmers use chemical fertilizers that double the rate of food produced but also increase nitrogen and phosphorus levels in the environment. These pollutants find their way into water bodies.

(C) One especially pronounced effect is the death of lakes. Washed-away fertilizers in these lakes result in algae blooms, which deplete oxygen in the waters and create dead zones where no living thing can thrive.

① (A) – (C) – (B)　　② (B) – (A) – (C)
③ (B) – (C) – (A)　　④ (C) – (B) – (A)

해석

전 세계 농업 시스템은 증가하는 인구의 음식 수요를 충족시키기 위해 애쓰지만, 이것은 환경에 부정적으로 영향을 주어 왔다. 그 과정은 농작물들을 심는 것으로 시작한다.

(A) 물에 대한 이러한 영향 외에도, 질소 축적은 토양과 공기에 위협적인 것이다. 그것은 토종 식물 종의 건강에 영향을 미치는데, 이것은 생태계의 생물 다양성을 감소시킨다. 또한 비료는 대기 중 온실가스 총 배출량의 5분의 1의 원인이 된다.

(B) 식량 안보를 보장하기 위해, 농부들은 생산되는 식량의 비율을 두 배로 만드는 화학 비료를 사용하지만, 환경에서의 질소와 인의 수치 또한 증가시킨다. 이 오염 물질들은 수역으로 흘러 들어간다.

(C) 한 가지 특히 두드러진 결과는 호수들의 죽음이다. 이 호수들로 씻겨 내려온 비료는 조류 대발생을 초래하는데, 이것은 물속 산소를 고갈시키고 어떤 생물도 잘 자랄 수 없는 죽음의 수역을 만들어낸다.

해설

주어진 문장에서 증가하는 인구의 음식 수요를 충족시키려는 농업 시스템이 환경에 부정적인 영향을 준다고 언급한 뒤, (B)에서 식량 안보를 위해 농부들이 화학 비료를 사용함으로써 증가한 수치의 질소와 인이 수역으로 흘러 들어간다고 설명하고 있다. 이어서 (C)에서 특히 두드러진 결과는 호수의 죽음이라고 하고, (A)에서 물에 대한 이러한 영향 외에(Aside from this impact on water) 질소 축적은 생물 다양성을 줄이고 온실가스의 원인이 되면서 토양과 공기도 위협한다고 설명하고 있다. 따라서 ③ (B) – (C) – (A)가 정답이다.

정답 ③

어휘

agricultural 농업의, 농사의　strive 애쓰다, 노력하다　dietary 음식의, 식사의
negatively 부정적으로, 소극적으로　crop 농작물
aside from ~ 외에, ~을 제외하고　accumulation 축적, 누적
native 토종의, 타고난　biodiversity 생물 다양성　ecosystem 생태계
fertilizer 비료　contribute ~의 원인이 되다, 기여하다
greenhouse gas 온실가스　emission 배출(량)　atmosphere 대기
food security 식량 안보　pollutant 오염 물질
pronounced 두드러진, 명백한　algae bloom 조류 대발생
deplete 고갈시키다, 대폭 감소시키다　thrive 잘 자라다, 번성하다

DAY 29 하프모의고사 29회

정답
p. 126

01	③	어휘	06	①	독해
02	②	문법	07	③	독해
03	③	문법	08	②	독해
04	③	생활영어	09	④	독해
05	③	독해	10	④	독해

취약영역 분석표

영역	맞힌 답의 개수
어휘	/1
생활영어	/1
문법	/2
독해	/6
TOTAL	/10

---

01 어휘 deceive · 난이도 중 ●●○

밑줄 친 부분에 들어갈 말로 적절한 것은?

She felt there was no reason to trust her former neighbor, who had _____ her so many times before.

① convinced
② respected
③ deceived
④ invited

[해석]
그녀는 이전에 자신을 아주 여러 번 속였던 옛 이웃을 믿을 이유가 없다고 느꼈다.

① 설득했던 ② 존경했던
③ 속였던 ④ 초대했던

정답 ③

[어휘]
convince 설득하다 respect 존경하다, 존중하다 deceive 속이다 invite 초대하다

---

02 문법 가정법 · 난이도 중 ●●○

밑줄 친 부분에 들어갈 말로 적절한 것은?

_____ the negotiation fail again, the government will have no choice but to implement stricter economic measures.

① If ② Should
③ That ④ Were

[해석]
혹시라도 협상이 다시 실패한다면, 정부는 더 엄격한 경제 조치를 시행할 수밖에 없을 것이다.

[해설]
② 가정법 미래 | 가정법 도치 문맥상 '혹시라도 협상이 다시 실패한다면'이라는 의미로 가능성이 희박한 미래를 가정하고 있고, 주절에 가정법 미래 '주어 + will + 동사원형' 형태가 왔으므로, if절에도 가정법 미래 'if + 주어 + should + 동사원형' 형태가 와야 한다. 이때 if절에 if가 생략되면 주어와 should가 도치되어 'Should + 주어(the negotiation) + 동사원형(fail)'의 형태가 되므로, ② Should가 정답이다. 참고로, 부사절 접속사 ① If도 주절 앞에서 부사절을 이끌 수 있지만, 이 경우 주어 자리에 쓰인 단수 명사 the negotiation에 수 일치시켜 동사도 단수 동사 fails가 쓰여야 한다.

정답 ②

[어휘]
negotiation 협상 implement 시행하다 measure 조치, 수단; 측정하다

---

03 문법 대명사 | to 부정사 | 조동사 | 수동태 | 어순 · 난이도 중 ●●○

밑줄 친 부분 중 어법상 옳지 않은 것은?

Humans are naturally inclined ① to seek patterns and habits. Breaking habits requires that the stimulus that results in the response ② be removed. We can also try an alternate strategy to replace the habit with another beneficial one. In this way, the catalyst that motivates detrimental behaviors instead inspires positive ③ one. ④ Such a systematic strategy can be an effective way to use our own tendencies toward patterned behavior to effect a change that we want to see in our lives.

[해석]
인간은 선천적으로 행동 양식과 습관을 추구하는 경향이 있다. 습관들을 그만두는 것은 그 반응을 불러일으키는 자극이 제거되는 것을 필요로 한다. 우리는 또한 그 습관을 또 다른 유익한 습관으로 바꾸는 대체 전략을 시도해 볼 수 있다. 이런 식으로, 해로운 행동들에 동기를 부여하는 촉매가 대신 긍정적인 행동들을 불러일으킨다. 이와 같은 체계적인 전략은

우리가 삶에서 보고 싶은 변화를 가져오기 위해 양식화된 행동을 향한 우리의 경향을 사용하는 효과적인 방법이 될 수 있다.

해설

③ 부정대명사 앞에서 언급된 명사(behaviors)와 같은 종류이지만 다른 대상을 가리킬 때 부정대명사 one을 쓸 수 있는데, 앞에 언급된 명사 behaviors가 복수 명사이므로 단수 부정대명사 one을 복수 부정대명사 ones로 고쳐야 한다.

[오답 분석]

① to 부정사 관련 표현 문맥상 '추구하는 경향이 있다'라는 의미가 되어야 자연스러운데, '~하는 경향이 있다'는 to 부정사 관련 표현 be inclined to로 나타낼 수 있으므로 are (naturally) inclined 뒤에 to 부정사 to seek가 올바르게 쓰였다.

② 조동사 should의 생략 | 능동태·수동태 구별 주절에 요청을 나타내는 동사(require)가 나오면 종속절에는 '(should +) 동사원형'이 와야 한다. 이때 문맥상 that절의 주어 the stimulus와 동사가 '자극이 제거되다'라는 의미의 수동 관계이므로 종속절에 (should) be removed가 올바르게 쓰였다.

④ 혼동하기 쉬운 어순 such는 'such + a/an + 형용사 + 명사'의 어순이 되어야 하므로 Such a systematic strategy가 올바르게 쓰였다.

정답 ③

어휘

seek 추구하다, 노력하다   stimuli 자극들(stimulus의 복수형)
alternate 대체의, 번갈아 하는   strategy 전략, 계획
replace 바꾸다, 대체하다   catalyst 촉매, 기폭제   motivate 동기를 부여하다
detrimental 해로운, 불리한   inspire 불러일으키다, 고무하다
tendency 성향, 경향, 추세

---

04 생활영어 After you reserve a time, we'll email you within three days.   난이도 하 ●○○

밑줄 친 부분에 들어갈 말로 적절한 것은?

 Isabella Wilson
I'm reaching out because we'd like to conduct a final interview with you.
11:20

Jack Foster
I appreciate the opportunity. When will the interview be scheduled?
11:20

 **Isabella Wilson**
It will be conducted online during the third week of this month.
11:21

Jack Foster
Could you let me know the exact date and time?
11:21

 Isabella Wilson
You can choose the time slot that works best for you through the 'Recruit' section of our website.
11:22

Jack Foster
I'll probably choose Wednesday or Thursday. How will I be notified of the confirmed interview schedule?
11:23

 Isabella Wilson
_____
11:24

① You can reschedule the interview if something urgent comes up.
② Time slots are available on a first-come, first-served basis.
③ After you reserve a time, we'll email you within three days.
④ The final candidates will be announced next Monday.

해석

| Isabella Wilson: 귀하와 최종 면접을 진행하고 싶어서 연락드렸습니다.
Jack Foster: 기회를 주셔서 감사합니다. 면접 일정은 언제인가요?
Isabella Wilson: 이번 달 셋째 주에 온라인으로 진행될 예정입니다.
Jack Foster: 정확한 날짜와 시간을 알려 주실 수 있나요?
Isabella Wilson: 저희 웹사이트의 '채용' 부분에서 귀하에게 가장 적합한 시간대를 선택하실 수 있습니다.
Jack Foster: 저는 아마 수요일이나 목요일로 선택할 것 같네요. 확정된 면접 일정은 어떻게 통보받게 되나요?
Isabella Wilson: 시간을 예약하시고 나면, 저희가 3일 안에 이메일을 보내드릴 것입니다. |

① 급한 일이 생기시면 면접 일정을 변경하실 수 있습니다.
② 시간대는 선착순으로 이용 가능합니다.
③ 시간을 예약하시고 나면, 저희가 3일 안에 이메일을 보내드릴 것입니다.
④ 최종 후보자는 다음 주 월요일에 발표될 것입니다.

해설

Isabella가 웹사이트에서 가장 적합한 면접 시간대를 선택할 수 있다고 하자 Jack이 셋째 주 수요일이나 목요일로 선택할 것 같다고 하며 빈칸 앞에서 How will I be notified of the confirmed interview schedule? (확정된 면접 일정은 어떻게 통보받게 되나요?)이라고 묻고 있으므로, '시간을 예약하시고 나면, 저희가 3일 안에 이메일을 보내드릴 것입니다'라는 의미의 ③ 'After you reserve a time, we'll email you within three days'가 정답이다.

정답 ③

어휘

reach out 연락하다   exact 정확한   time slot 시간대   recruit 채용하다
notify 통보하다, 알리다   confirm 확정하다, 확인하다
reschedule 일정을 변경하다   urgent 급한
first-come, first-served 선착순   candidate 후보자

05~06 다음 글을 읽고 물음에 답하시오.

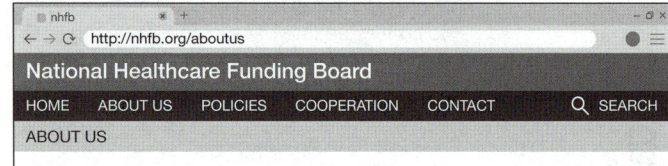

National Healthcare Funding Board

Our Primary Challenge

Life expectancy has risen thanks to advances in medicine, nutrition, and sanitation, but many individuals still spend their later years managing multiple health conditions, which not only reduces their quality of life but places a strain on the already overburdened healthcare system. The National Healthcare Funding Board was established to fund research into initiatives that predict, prevent, and reduce the impact of chronic diseases.

What We Fund

We invest in projects that promote early intervention. Through grants to academic institutions and medical research centers, we also help support studies that explore emerging diagnostic tools, technologies that monitor health conditions remotely, and interventions that delay cognitive decline in aging populations.

Our Core Values

- We consider it beneficial _____.
- All our funding decisions are based on rigorous, ethically sound research.

어휘

primary 주요한 life expectancy 기대 수명 strain 부담
overburdened 과부하가 걸린 initiative 계획 chronic 만성적인
intervention 개입 grant 보조금; 수여하다 emerging 최근 생겨난
diagnostic 진단의 remotely 원격으로 cognitive 인지의
decline 저하; 감소하다, 거절하다 beneficial 이로운, 유익한
rigorous 엄격한 ethically 윤리적으로 sound 건전한; 소리

05 독해 내용 일치 파악

윗글의 내용과 일치하는 것은?

① Life expectancy increases have contributed to the strain on healthcare systems.
② Chronic disease treatments can receive Board funding for clinical trials.
③ The Board supports research conducted at schools and research centers.
④ Remote technologies are only funded when focused on aging populations.

어휘

treatment 치료, 대우 clinical trial 임상 시험

정답 ③

06 독해 빈칸 완성 – 구   난이도 중 ●●○

윗글의 밑줄 친 부분에 들어갈 말로 적절한 것은?

① to shift the focus from treatment to prevention
② to expand medical insurance coverage
③ to unify the national healthcare system
④ to introduce market competition principles

[해석]

① 치료에서 예방으로 초점을 전환하는 것
② 의료 보험 보장 범위를 확대하는 것
③ 국가의 의료 시스템을 일원화하는 것
④ 시장 경쟁 원리를 도입하는 것

[해설]

지문 앞부분에 국가보건기금공단은 만성적인 질병을 예측 및 예방하는 연구에 자금을 댄다는 내용이 있고, 빈칸 앞부분에서 인지 기능 저하를 지연시키는 것을 포함하여 조기 개입을 촉진하는 프로젝트에 투자한다고 했으므로, '치료에서 예방으로 초점을 전환하는 것'이 이롭다고 생각한다고 한 ①번이 정답이다.

정답 ①

[어휘]

shift 전환하다, 이동시키다; 교대 근무 expand 확대하다, 확장하다
coverage 보장 범위 unify 일원화하다, 통일하다 competition 경쟁
principle 원리, 주의

07 독해 목적 파악   난이도 중 ●●○

다음 글의 목적으로 적절한 것은?

To: customers@globalsecuretravel.com
From: support@globalsecuretravel.com
Date: April 18
Subject: Travel Tips

Dear Customers,

Increased reliance on digital devices when in unfamiliar surroundings can make it easier for cybercriminals to steal your sensitive data. To help you stay safe while traveling, we've put together some essential tips to keep in mind:

1. Free Wi-Fi in public spaces can be a hotspot for cybercriminals. Use a VPN whenever possible.
2. Secure your accounts with unique passwords, and add an extra layer of protection by enabling two-factor authentication.
3. Make sure to turn off Bluetooth in public places when you don't need it. This protects your device from being detected by other nearby devices.
4. Use your own charger, and plug it into a power outlet instead of using public USB charging ports.
5. Check your bank and credit card statements frequently to catch any suspicious transactions early.

Travel with greater peace of mind by taking these precautions. For more travel and safety tips, visit our Traveler Safety Center.

Sincerely,

The Global Secure Travel Team

① to provide customers with instructions on how to find free Wi-Fi in public spaces
② to provide customers with information on how to set up a VPN before traveling
③ to provide customers with advice on how to protect their personal data during travel
④ to provide customers with details on how to turn on Bluetooth in public places

[해석]

수신: customers@globalsecuretravel.com
발신: support@globalsecuretravel.com
날짜: 4월 18일
제목: 여행 관련 조언

고객 여러분께,

익숙하지 않은 환경에서 디지털 기기에 대해 높아진 의존도는 사이버 범죄자들이 여러분의 민감한 데이터를 훔치기 더욱 쉽게 만들 수 있습니다. 여행하는 동안 여러분이 안전을 유지하시도록 돕기 위해, 유의하셔야 할 몇 가지 필수 조언들을 준비했습니다.

1. 공공장소의 무료 Wi-Fi는 사이버 범죄자들의 거점이 될 수 있습니다. 가능할 때마다 VPN을 사용하세요.
2. 고유한 비밀번호로 여러분의 계정을 보호하고, 이중 인증을 사용하셔서 추가적인 보호 단계를 더하세요.
3. 필요하지 않은 때에는 공공장소에서 블루투스를 반드시 끄세요. 이것은 주변의 다른 기기에 의해 여러분의 기기가 탐지되지 않게 보호합니다.
4. 자신만의 충전기를 사용하고, 공용 USB 충전 단자를 사용하는 것 대신 전원 콘센트에 연결하세요.
5. 의심스러운 거래를 조기에 발견하기 위해 은행 및 신용 카드 명세서를 자주 확인하세요.

이러한 예방책들을 취함으로써 더 큰 마음의 평화와 함께 여행하세요. 더 많은 여행 및 안전 관련 조언을 위해서는, 저희 여행자 안전 센터를 방문해 주세요.

진심을 담아,
세계안전여행단 드림

① 공공장소에서 무료 Wi-Fi를 찾는 방법에 대한 지침을 고객에게 제공하려고
② 여행 전에 VPN을 설정하는 방법에 대한 정보를 고객에게 제공하려고
③ 여행 동안 개인 데이터를 보호하는 방법에 대한 조언을 고객에게 제공하려고
④ 공공장소에서 블루투스를 켜는 방법에 대한 세부 정보를 고객에게 제공하려고

DAY 29 하프모의고사 29회

해설
지문 앞부분에서 여행하는 동안 개인 데이터를 훔치려는 사이버 범죄자들로부터 안전을 유지하도록 돕는 필수 조언들을 준비했다고 하고, 다섯 가지의 조언들을 알려 주고 있으므로, ③ '여행 동안 개인 데이터를 보호하는 방법에 대한 조언을 고객에게 제공하려고'가 이 글의 목적이다.

정답 ③

어휘
reliance 의존　surrounding (주변) 환경　cybercriminal 사이버 범죄자
put together (이것저것 모아) 준비하다　essential 필수적인
hotspot 거점, 활기 넘치는 곳　layer 단계, 층　authentication 인증
turn off ~을 끄다　detect 탐지하다, 감지하다
charger 충전기, 요금; 충전하다　outlet 콘센트　port 단자, 항구
statement 명세서, 진술(서)　suspicious 의심스러운　transaction 거래
precaution 예방책　instruction 지침, 설명　set up ~을 설치하다

08 독해 무관한 문장 삭제　난이도 중 ●●○

다음 글의 흐름상 어색한 문장은?

Some languages use a flexible order, with fluctuating word orders or meanings, depending on a variety of factors, while others employ a set order. ① Languages with fixed word orders require specific sequences for subjects, objects, and verbs, and deviating from these constructions will either change the meaning or be ungrammatical. ② Many languages have additional parts of speech that get inserted into a sentence, such as prepositions, articles, adjectives, and adverbs. ③ The most common word order to find is SOV, or subject-object-verb, accounting for around nearly 44 percent of languages. ④ Languages with a free order are substantially less common, only making up around 2 percent of languages. In these languages, words can be put in any order with little to no impact on the meaning.

해석
어떤 언어들은 다양한 요소들의 여부에 따라 어순이나 의미가 변동하는 유연한 어순을 쓰는 반면, 다른 언어들은 정해진 어순을 사용한다. ① 고정된 어순이 있는 언어들은 주어, 목적어 그리고 동사를 위한 특정한 순서를 필요로 하며, 이러한 구조에서 벗어나는 것은 의미를 바꾸거나 비문법적인 것일 것이다. ② 많은 언어들은 전치사, 관사, 형용사 그리고 부사 등과 같이 문장에 삽입되는 부가적인 품사들을 가지고 있다. ③ 발견할 수 있는 가장 일반적인 어순은 SOV, 즉 주어-목적어-동사인데, 이는 언어들의 거의 44퍼센트를 차지한다. ④ 순서가 자유로운 언어는 상당히 덜 일반적이며, 언어의 약 2퍼센트만을 구성한다. 이 언어들에서, 단어들은 의미에 거의 또는 전혀 영향을 주지 않으면서 어떤 순서로도 놓일 수 있다.

해설
첫 문장에서 유연한 어순을 사용하는 언어와 정해진 어순을 사용하는 언어에 대해 언급하고, ①번은 '고정된 어순이 있는 언어들의 특성', ③번은 '가장 일반적인 고정 어순인 주어-목적어-동사', ④번은 '상대적으로 적은 비중인 순서가 자유로운 언어'에 대해 설명하고 있다. 그러나 ②번은 '문장에 삽입되는 부가적인 품사들'에 대한 내용으로, 첫 문장의 내용과 관련이 없다.

정답 ②

어휘
flexible 유연한, 융통성 있는　fluctuate 변동하다, 오르내리다, 동요하다
a variety of 다양한, 여러 가지의　factor 요소, 요인
employ 사용하다, 고용하다　set 고정된　sequence 순서, 배열, 서열
subject 주어, 주제　deviate 벗어나다, 빗나가다　construction 구조, 공사
ungrammatical 비문법적인　insert 삽입하다　preposition 전치사
article 관사　adjective 형용사　adverb 부사
account for ~을 차지하다, 설명하다　substantially 상당히, 실질적으로
make up ~을 구성하다, 차지하다

09 독해 문장 삽입　난이도 중 ●●○

주어진 문장이 들어갈 위치로 적절한 곳은?

It also provides invaluable consumer data, allowing businesses to continuously refine their approaches.

Social media has fundamentally transformed how businesses interact with their audience through digital engagement strategies. Companies now require established digital presences across multiple platforms—from TikTok and Instagram to emerging metaverse spaces. (①) These digital platforms emphasize visual content and necessitate constant monitoring to maintain brand consistency. (②) Brand identities are increasingly shaped through personalized content and targeted demographic approaches. (③) Additionally, customer support has evolved to multi-channel solutions, with automated chatbots handling routine inquiries. (④) This automation resolves simple repetitive problems, conserving time and energy for human representatives who address complex issues publicly, creating transparent accountability.

해석
그것은 또한 귀중한 소비자 데이터를 제공해서, 기업들이 지속적으로 그들의 접근 방식을 개선하게 한다.

소셜 미디어는 디지털 참여 전략을 통해 기업이 고객과 상호 작용하는 방식을 근본적으로 변화시켜 왔다. 기업들은 이제 틱톡과 인스타그램에서부터 새롭게 등장하는 메타버스 공간에 이르기까지, 여러 플랫폼에 걸쳐 확립된 디지털 존재감을 요구한다. ① 이러한 디지털 플랫폼들은 시각적 콘텐츠를 강조하고 브랜드 일관성을 유지하기 위해 지속적인 모니터링을 필요로 한다. ② 브랜드 정체성이 개인화된 콘텐츠와 목표로 하는 인구 통계학적 접근법을 통해 점점 더 형성된다. ③ 게다가, 고객 지원은 자동화된 챗봇이 일상적인 문의를 처리하면서, 여러 경로의 해결책으로 발전해 왔다. ④ 이러한 자동화는 단순하고 반복적인 문제를 해결하여, 투명한 책임감을 만들어내면서 복잡한 문제를 공개적으로 다루는 인간 대리인을 위한 시간과 에너지를 절약한다.

해설
④번 앞 문장에 고객 지원은 자동화된 챗봇이 일상적인 문의를 처리하면서

여러 경로의 해결책으로 발전해 왔다는 내용이 있고, 뒤 문장에 이러한 자동화(This automation)는 인간 대리인을 위한 시간과 에너지를 절약한다는 내용이 있으므로, ④번 자리에 그것은 또한(also) 귀중한 소비자 데이터를 제공해서 기업들이 접근 방식을 개선하게 한다는 내용, 즉 고객 지원에 챗봇을 사용하는 것의 추가적인 이점에 대해 설명하는 주어진 문장이 들어가야 지문이 자연스럽게 연결된다.

정답 ④

어휘

fundamentally 근본적으로 transform 변화시키다 interact 상호 작용하다
audience 고객, 관객 engagement 참여 strategy 전략
establish 확립하다, 수립하다 presence 존재감 emerging 새롭게 등장하는
emphasize 강조하다 necessitate 필요로 하다 constant 지속적인
consistency 일관성 identity 정체성, 신분 personalize 개인화하다
demographic 인구 통계학적 evolve 발전하다 automate 자동화하다
routine 일상적인 resolve 해결하다 repetitive 반복적인
conserve 보존하다 representative 대리인, 대표; 대표하는
publicly 공개적으로 transparent 투명한 accountability 책임감

10 독해 빈칸 완성 – 단어   난이도 상 ●●●

밑줄 친 부분에 들어갈 말로 적절한 것은?

The rule of law is a principle of governance whereby government and all individuals and entities are accountable to the laws of the land. This presumes that the law is consistent with international human rights standards. People in positions of authority should treat law as something higher than politics and personal advantage. Similarly, citizens should obey the law even if aspects of it are inconvenient. If rule of law goes unrecognized, it becomes impossible to achieve peace and security and to attain economic, developmental, and social progress. Under the rule of law, the state acts within a legal framework that includes the obligation to protect human rights. In this context, when operating within legal systems aligned with international standards, states may take appropriate measures to protect their populations from serious human rights violations or crimes against humanity. This is the opposite of a government that controls its citizens in a random manner through laws that have no basis in _____.

① reality
② agreement
③ safety
④ universality

해석

법치주의는 정부와 모든 개인과 독립체들이 그 나라의 법률에 책임이 있는 통치 원칙이다. 이것은 법이 국제 인권 기준과 일치한다고 가정한다. 권력을 가진 자리에 있는 사람들은 법을 정치와 사적인 이익보다 더 중요한 것으로 여겨야 한다. 마찬가지로, 시민들은 법의 방향이 불편할지라도 법을 지켜야 한다. 만약 법치주의가 인정받지 못한다면, 평화와 안보를 달성하고 경제적, 발전적, 사회적 진보를 이루는 것이 불가능해진다. 법치주의 아래에서, 국가는 인권을 보호할 의무를 포함하는 법적 체제 내에서 행동한다. 이러한 맥락에서, 국제 기준에 맞는 법적 체계 내에서 운영될 때 국가는 심각한 인권 침해나 반인도적 범죄로부터 국민을 보호하기 위해 적절한 조치를 취할 수 있다. 이것은 보편성에 근거하지 않은 법들을 통해 임의 방식으로 시민들을 통제하는 정부와 반대되는 것이다.

① 진실성
② 동의
③ 안전
④ 보편성

해설

지문 앞부분에서 법치주의는 그 나라의 법률이 국제 인권 기준과 일치함을 가정한다고 하고, 빈칸 앞부분에서 국제 기준에 맞는 법적 체계 내에서 운영될 때 국가는 인권 침해나 반인도적 범죄로부터 국민을 보호할 수 있다고 했으므로, '보편성'에 근거하지 않은 법들을 통해 임의 방식으로 시민들을 통제하는 정부와 반대되는 것이라고 한 ④번이 정답이다.

정답 ④

어휘

rule of law 법치주의 principle 원칙, 원리, 주의 governance 통치, 관리
entity 독립체, 존재 accountable for ~에 책임이 있는
presume 가정하다, 추정하다 consistent with ~과 일치하는
authority 권력, 당국 obey 지키다, 따르다 aspect 방향, 측면
unrecognized 인정받지 못하는, 의식되지 못하는 attain 이루다, 획득하다
framework 체제, 틀 obligation 의무 align with ~에 맞추어 조정하다
appropriate 적절한 measure 조치, 측정; 측정하다 violation 침해, 위반
humanity 인도적임, 인간선 random 임의의, 무작위의
agreement 동의, 합의 universality 보편성, 일반성

DAY 30 하프모의고사 30회

▶ 정답　　　p. 130

01	①	어휘	06	③	독해
02	③	문법	07	③	독해
03	①	문법	08	③	독해
04	②	생활영어	09	④	독해
05	②	독해	10	③	독해

▶ 취약영역 분석표

영역	맞힌 답의 개수
어휘	/1
생활영어	/1
문법	/2
독해	/6
TOTAL	/10

01　어휘　desperate　난이도 중 ●●○

밑줄 친 부분에 들어갈 말로 적절한 것은?

> Finding no work in the city during the economic crisis put rural migrants in a(n) ＿＿＿＿ position. They even sold the land in the countryside that had been passed down through generations.

① desperate
② temporary
③ stable
④ individual

해석
경제 위기 동안 도시에서 일자리를 찾지 못한 것은 시골에서 이주해 온 사람들을 절박한 위치로 몰아넣었다. 그들은 심지어 여러 세대에 걸쳐 전해 내려 온, 시골 지역에 있는 땅을 팔기까지 했다.

① 절박한
② 일시적인
③ 안정적인
④ 개인적인

정답 ①

어휘
crisis 위기　rural 시골의　countryside 시골 지역, 전원 지대
pass down ~을 전해 주다, 물려주다　generation 세대　desperate 절박한
temporary 일시적인　stable 안정적인　individual 개인적인, 각각의

02　문법　도치 구문 | 시제　난이도 중 ●●○

밑줄 친 부분에 들어갈 말로 적절한 것은?

> No sooner ＿＿＿＿＿＿＿＿＿＿ than property development corporations sought exceptions to avoid the requirements.

① the new housing bill passed
② the new housing bill will pass
③ had the new housing bill passed
④ have the new housing bill passed

해석
새 주택 법안이 통과되자마자 부동산 개발 법인들은 요구 조건들을 피하기 위해 예외를 찾았다.

해설
③ 도치 구문 | 과거완료 시제　부정을 나타내는 부사구(No sooner)가 강조되어 절의 맨 앞에 나오면 주어와 조동사가 도치되므로 '조동사 + 주어 + 동사'의 어순으로 쓰인 ③, ④번이 정답 후보이다. 이때 문맥상 '새 주택 법안이 통과된' 시점이 '개발자들이 예외를 찾은' 특정 과거 시점보다 더 이전에 일어난 일이므로, 과거완료 시제가 쓰인 ③ had the new housing bill passed가 정답이다.

정답 ③

어휘
property 부동산, 재산　corporation 법인, 회사　exception 예외
requirement 요구 조건　bill 법안

03　문법　분사 | 상관접속사 | 명사　난이도 중 ●●○

밑줄 친 부분 중 어법상 옳지 않은 것은?

> With the world ① embraced digitalization, customers have come to rely on the convenient access to products that e-commerce provides. Nevertheless, they remain largely unaware of the enormous challenges ② involved in facilitating it. First, e-commerce businesses must ③ either hire a shipping company or have their own system of delivering goods. Furthermore, since ④ information that is sensitive is necessary in all online purchases, e-commerce firms are obligated to take special care when it comes to cyber security.

해석
세상이 디지털화를 수용하면서, 소비자들은 전자 상거래가 제공하는 상

품들에 대한 편리한 접근성에 의존해 오게 되었다. 그럼에도 불구하고, 그들은 그것을 가능하게 하는 데 수반되는 막대한 어려움들을 대부분 알지 못한 채로 남겨진다. 우선, 전자 상거래 기업들은 운송 회사를 고용하거나 제품들을 배송하는 자체 시스템을 갖춰야 한다. 더욱이, 민감한 정보는 모든 온라인 구매에서 필수이기 때문에, 전자 상거래 회사들은 사이버 보안에 관한 한 각별한 주의를 기울일 의무가 있다.

해설

① **분사구문의 역할** 동시에 일어나는 상황은 'with + 명사 + 분사'의 형태로 나타낼 수 있는데, 명사(the world)와 분사가 '세상이 수용하다'라는 의미의 능동 관계이므로 과거분사 embraced를 현재분사 embracing으로 고쳐야 한다.

[오답 분석]

② **현재분사 vs. 과거분사** 수식받는 명사(challenges)와 분사가 '어려움들이 수반되다'라는 의미의 수동 관계이므로 과거분사 involved가 올바르게 쓰였다.

③ **상관접속사** 문맥상 '운송 회사를 고용하거나 제품을 배송하는 자체 시스템을 갖추다'라는 의미가 되어야 자연스러운데, 'A 또는 B'는 상관접속사 either A or B를 사용하여 나타낼 수 있다. 따라서 or와 짝을 이루는 either가 올바르게 쓰였다.

④ **불가산명사** 불가산 명사(information)는 앞에 부정관사(an)를 쓰거나 복수형으로 쓸 수 없으므로, information이 올바르게 쓰였다.

정답 ①

어휘

embrace 수용하다 convenient 편리한 challenge 어려움, 도전; 도전하다
involve 수반하다, 포함하다 facilitate 가능하게 하다 hire 고용하다
sensitive 민감한 obligate 의무를 지우다

---

04 생활영어 Why don't you leave work early and get some rest? 난이도 하 ●○○

밑줄 친 부분에 들어갈 말로 적절한 것은?

A: What's wrong? You don't look well.
B: I know. I might have eaten something bad.
A: Do you want to see a doctor?
B: I don't think it's that serious.
A: _____
B: I can't. I have work that needs to be finished today.
A: We can probably adjust the schedule. Take care of yourself before your condition gets worse.

① How many days of sick leave can you take?
② Why don't you leave work early and get some rest?
③ Did you get the company's regular check-up?
④ Could you work from home until you're better?

해석

A: 무슨 일인가요? 안색이 안 좋아 보여요.
B: 저도 알아요. 아마 상한 음식을 먹었는지도 모르겠어요.
A: 병원에 가 볼래요?
B: 그렇게 심각하다고 생각하지 않아서요.
A: 조퇴하고 휴식을 좀 취하는 건 어때요?
B: 그럴 수는 없어요. 저는 오늘 끝내야 하는 일이 있는걸요.
A: 우리는 일정을 조정하는 게 가능할 거예요. 당신의 상태가 더 악화되기 전에 스스로를 돌봐야 해요.

① 병가를 며칠 사용할 수 있나요?
② 조퇴하고 휴식을 좀 취하는 건 어때요?
③ 회사의 정기 건강 검진을 받았나요?
④ 좀 괜찮아질 때까지 재택근무를 할 수 있나요?

해설

안색에 안 좋으니 병원에 갈 것을 권하는 A에게 B가 심각하게 생각하지 않는다고 대답하고, 빈칸 뒤에서 다시 B가 I can't. I have work that needs to be finished today(그럴 수는 없어요. 저는 오늘 끝내야 하는 일이 있는걸요)라고 말하고 있으므로, '조퇴하고 휴식을 좀 취하는 건 어때요?'라는 의미의 ② 'Why don't you leave work early and get some rest?'가 정답이다.

정답 ②

어휘

see a doctor 병원에 가다, 진찰을 받다 adjust 조정하다
check-up 건강검진 work from home 재택근무하다

05~06 다음 글을 읽고 물음에 답하시오.

To	Traffic Fines Processing Office
From	Aliyah Woods
Date	March 18
Subject	Issue with Online Traffic Fine Payment System

Dear Sir or Madam,

Please be advised of the challenges I've encountered when trying to pay a traffic fine through the official website.

Whenever I enter my citation number into the system, I receive an error message.

I have tried to submit my payment multiple times, using various devices and credit cards, and my repeated lack of success makes me feel that this problem is not unique to me but, rather, a problem with your website. My citation is due in a few days, and it would be very inconvenient for me to have to visit your office to pay it in person.

If this issue has not already been reported by other users, I ask that you address it promptly. In the meantime, is there an alternative remote payment option available?

Regards,
Aliyah Woods

DAY 30 하프모의고사 30회

해석

수신: 교통 범칙금 처리과
발신: Aliyah Woods
날짜: 3월 18일
제목: 교통 범칙금 온라인 납부 시스템 관련 문제

담당자분께,

공식 웹사이트를 통해 교통 범칙금을 납부하려고 할 때 제가 맞닥뜨린 어려움에 대한 조언을 요청드립니다.

제가 시스템에 위반 딱지 번호를 입력할 때마다, 저는 오류 메시지를 받습니다.

저는 다양한 기기와 신용 카드들을 사용하여 여러 번 납입금을 내려고 했지만, 반복되는 실패 상황은 저로 하여금 이 문제가 제게만 발생하는 것이 아니라, 오히려 귀하의 웹사이트 문제라고 생각하게 합니다. 제 위반 딱지가 지불 기일이 며칠 남지 않았고, 제가 귀하의 사무실을 직접 방문하여 납부해야 한다면 매우 불편할 것입니다.

만약 이 문제가 다른 사용자들에 의해 이미 보고된 것이 아니라면, 신속하게 해결해 주시기를 요청드립니다. 그동안에, 혹시 이용 가능한 대체 원격 납부 선택지가 있을까요?

안부를 전하며,
Aliyah Woods

어휘

payment 납부, 지불   encounter 맞닥뜨리다   citation 위반 딱지
due 지불 기일이 된   inconvenient 불편한   in person 직접, 몸소
report 보고하다; 보고(서)   promptly 신속하게
alternative 대체 가능한, 대안적인; 대안   remote 원격의

05 독해 목적 파악 | 난이도 중 ●●○

윗글의 목적으로 적절한 것은?

① 잘못 부과된 교통 범칙금에 대해 항의하려고
② 범칙금 납부와 관련된 기술적인 문제를 보고하려고
③ 웹사이트의 취약한 보안에 대한 조치를 요청하려고
④ 범칙금을 온라인으로 납부하는 방법을 제안하려고

해설

지문 중간에서 다양한 기기와 신용 카드들을 사용하여 교통 범칙금을 내려 했지만 반복해서 실패한 것으로 보아 웹사이트 문제로 생각된다고 하고, 지문 마지막에서 이 문제를 신속하게 해결해 달라고 요청하고 있으므로 ② '범칙금 납부와 관련된 기술적인 문제를 보고하려고'가 이 글의 목적이다.

정답 ②

06 독해 유의어 파악 | 난이도 하 ●○○

밑줄 친 reported의 의미와 가장 가까운 것은?

① weakened   ② corrected
③ raised   ④ achieved

해석

① 약화된   ② 수정된
③ 제기된   ④ 이뤄진

해설

밑줄 친 부분이 포함된 문장에서 reported는 문맥상 이 문제가 다른 사용자들에 의해 이미 '보고되지' 않았다는 의미로 쓰였으므로, '제기된'이라는 의미의 ③ raised가 정답이다.

정답 ③

어휘

weaken 약화시키다   correct 수정하다; 올바른   raise 제기하다, 들어올리다
achieve 이루다, 달성하다

07 독해 내용 불일치 파악 | 난이도 중 ●●○

ClearSky 앱에 관한 다음 글의 내용과 일치하지 않는 것은?

Check air quality with the ClearSky app.

The new ClearSky app helps residents stay informed about local air quality. ClearSky gives real-time readings of the air quality index, which provides information about various pollutants in the air. As part of the government's Environmental Health Awareness (EHA) initiative, the app allows users to make informed decisions about their outdoor activities. When pollution reaches dangerous levels, ClearSky provides an emergency alert warning. In the future, it will also offer seven-day forecasts for air quality. To use the app, simply download it from your mobile device's application store and turn on live location. ClearSky data can also be accessed via computer on the EHA website.

① It gives information about the quality of the air.
② Warnings are sent out when pollution becomes dangerously high.
③ Expected pollution levels are now available to users a week in advance.
④ Its information can be accessed using a computer.

해석

ClearSky 앱과 함께 공기 질을 확인하세요

새로운 ClearSky 앱은 주민분들이 지역 공기 질에 대해 계속해서 정보를 얻으실 수 있도록 돕습니다. ClearSky는 공기 중 다양한 오염 물

질에 관한 정보를 제공하는 공기 질 지수의 실시간 측정값을 제공합니다. 정부의 환경 건강 지킴이(EHA) 계획의 일환으로, 앱은 사용하시는 분들이 야외 활동에 대해 정보에 기반한 결정을 내리게 합니다. 오염이 위험한 수준에 도달하면, ClearSky는 비상 알림 경고를 제공합니다. 향후에는, 공기 질에 대한 7일 예보 또한 제공할 예정입니다. 앱을 사용하시려면, 모바일 기기의 앱 스토어에서 다운로드하시고 실시간 위치 기능을 켜기만 하면 됩니다. ClearSky 데이터는 환경 건강 지킴이 웹사이트를 통해 컴퓨터로도 접속하실 수 있습니다.

① 그것은 공기 질에 대한 정보를 제공한다.
② 오염이 위험할 정도로 높아지면 경고가 발송된다.
③ 예상 오염 수준은 사용자들이 현재 한 주 전에 이용 가능하다.
④ 그것의 정보는 컴퓨터를 사용하여 접근될 수 있다.

해설
③번의 키워드인 a week in advance(한 주 전에)를 바꾸어 표현한 지문의 seven-day forecasts(7일 예보) 주변의 내용에서 향후 공기 질에 대한 7일 예보가 제공될 예정이라고 했으므로, ③ '예상 오염 수준은 사용자들이 현재 한 주 전에 이용 가능하다'는 지문의 내용과 다르다.

정답 ③

어휘
real-time 실시간의 reading 측정값, 독서 index 지수, 색인
pollutant 오염 물질 initiative 계획, 주도권 outdoor 야외의
alert 알림; 경고하다 forecast 예보

08 독해 주제 파악   난이도 중 ●●○

다음 글의 주제로 적절한 것은?

Showing respect is customary in any society and is often displayed through gestures, but respectful body language differs according to culture. Western cultures demonstrate respect with the handshake, although there are variations when signifying deference, such as not putting the other hand in the pocket while shaking hands in Germany and not pumping the hand too hard in France. In other cultures, physical touch may even be considered disrespectful. For example, Eastern countries recognize someone's superiority by allowing them to remain higher in position and bestowing them more space, which is why those in a subordinate position bow about 15 degrees or bend their head and keep their limbs closer to their body. Other cultures have different ways to show respect without contact, such as the Zimbabwean clapping of the hands and the Tibetan extending of the tongue, and in certain Eastern cultures, individuals may fold their hands together or place their right hand above their heart.

① common expressions of respect across cultures
② physical space requirements for social interactions
③ global variations in respect through gestures
④ East-West perspectives on handshake practices

해석
존경심을 보이는 것은 어느 사회에서나 관습적이고 대개 몸짓들을 통해 나타나지만, 존경심을 보이는 신체 언어는 문화에 따라 다르다. 독일에서 악수를 하는 동안 다른 손을 주머니에 넣지 않는 것과 프랑스에서 손을 너무 세게 흔들지 않는 것과 같이, 경의를 나타낼 때 차이가 있기는 하지만 서구 문화권은 악수로 존경심을 보여 준다. 다른 문화권에서는, 신체적인 접촉이 심지어 무례하게 여겨질지 모른다. 예를 들어, 동양 국가들은 누군가의 우월성을 그 사람이 더 높은 위치에 머물게 하며 더 많은 공간을 줌으로써 인식하는데, 이는 지위가 아래인 사람들이 약 15도로 고개 숙여 인사하거나 그들의 머리를 숙이고 팔다리를 그들의 몸에 더 가까이 있게 하는 이유이다. 손뼉을 치는 짐바브웨인들과 혀를 내미는 티베트인들 그리고 손을 모으거나 오른손을 심장 위에 놓을지도 모르는 특정 동양 문화권에서처럼, 다른 문화들은 (신체) 접촉 없이 존경심을 보여 주는 별개의 방법들을 갖고 있다.

① 문화들에 걸쳐 나타나는 존경심의 공통적인 표현
② 사회적 상호 작용을 위한 물리적 공간의 요건
③ 몸짓들을 통한 존경심의 세계적인 차이
④ 악수 관행에 대한 동서양의 관점

해설
지문 처음에서 존경심을 보이는 신체 언어가 문화에 따라 다르다고 하고, 지문 중간에서 악수로 존경심을 보여 주는 서구 문화권과 더 높은 위치의 자리 또는 더 많은 공간을 줌으로써 우월성을 인식하는 동양 국가들의 사례를 구분 지어 제시하고 있으므로, ③ '몸짓들을 통한 존경심의 세계적인 차이'가 이 글의 주제이다.

정답 ③

어휘
respect 존경(심), 경의; 존경하다 customary 관습적인, 습관적인
display 나타내다, 전시하다 demonstrate 보여 주다, 입증하다
handshake 악수 variation 차이, 변화, 변형 signify 나타내다, 의미하다
deference 경의, 존중 pump 흔들다, 퍼 올리다
disrespectful 무례한, 경멸하는 superiority 우월성, 우세
bestow 주다, 부여하다 height 높이, 키
subordinate (지위가) 아래의, 열등한 bow 고개 숙여 인사하다, 머리를 숙이다
limb 팔다리 clap 손뼉을 치다 extend 내밀다, 뻗다
fold together ~을 맞잡다 perspective 관점

09 독해 제목 파악   난이도 하 ●○○

다음 글의 제목으로 적절한 것은?

Studies indicate that there are numerous health benefits that come with getting a pet, particularly if that pet is a dog. These benefits are especially notable for older individuals, as they face unique health challenges that pets can address. Pets can help combat feelings of loneliness and isolation, which is a significant factor in health decline for senior citizens. There are cognitive benefits as well, as studies show that cognitive deterioration in these individuals slows due to the presence of a pet in their lives. Furthermore, for those with dogs, the exercise boost from daily walks with the dog can translate into keeping people healthy and active as they age.

DAY 30 하프모의고사 30회

① Addressing Loneliness in Elderly Members of Society
② Ways to Keep Pets Healthy as a Person Ages
③ Effective Exercise Regimens for Senior Citizens
④ Seniors Remaining Healthier Longer by Keeping Pets

해석

연구들은 반려동물을 기르면서 얻는 수많은 건강상의 이점들이 있다는 것을 시사하는데, 그 반려동물이 개라면 특히 그렇다. 이러한 이점들은 나이 든 사람들에게 유난히 두드러지는데, 반려동물들이 해결할 수 있는 독특한 건강 문제에 그들이 직면하기 때문이다. 반려동물들은 외로움과 고립감과 싸우는 데 도움을 줄 수 있는데, 이것은 노인들의 건강 쇠약에 있어 중요한 요인이다. 연구들이 이 사람들의 인지 저하가 그들 삶에서 반려동물의 존재로 인해 둔화된다는 것을 보여 주듯이, 인지적인 이점들 또한 있다. 게다가, 개를 데리고 있는 사람들에게, 개와 매일 산책하는 것으로 인한 운동 증가는 나이가 들면서 그들을 건강하고 활동적으로 유지하는 것이 될 수 있다.

① 사회의 나이 든 구성원들의 외로움을 해결하기
② 사람이 나이 듦에 따라 반려동물들을 건강하게 기르는 방법
③ 노인들을 위한 효과적인 운동 관리
④ 반려동물들을 기름으로써 더 오래 건강을 유지하는 노인들

해설

지문 전반에 걸쳐 반려동물을 기를 때 얻는 건강상의 이점은 나이 든 사람들에게 두드러지는데, 반려동물이 노인들의 외로움과 고립감을 극복하는 데 도움을 주고, 그들의 인지 저하를 둔화시키며, 운동량을 증가시키기 때문이라고 설명하고 있으므로, ④ '반려동물들을 기름으로써 더 오래 건강을 유지하는 노인들'이 이 글의 제목이다.

정답 ④

어휘

indicate 시사하다, 보여 주다 notable 두드러진, 눈에 띄는
address 해결하다, 다루다, 연설하다; 주소 combat 싸우다, 분투하다; 전투
loneliness 외로움, 고독 isolation 고립감, 고독 factor 요인, 요소
senior citizen 노인 cognitive 인지의, 인지적인 deterioration 저하, 하락
presence 존재, 참석 boost 증가; 북돋우다
translate into (결과로서) ~이 되다 regimen 관리, 식이 요법

---

10 독해 문단 순서 배열 난이도 중 ●●○

주어진 글 다음에 이어질 글의 순서로 적절한 것은?

You make a to-do list. You're resolved to finish everything on your list. That's because it's your objective to be productive so that you can achieve your goals.

(A) In such cases, delaying is not an act of laziness. Laziness is an unwillingness to do anything, but delaying tasks is an active process of avoiding something important because it's difficult or unpleasant. Like any other bad habit, it takes hard work and discipline to overcome the habit of delaying tasks.

(B) Begin by recognizing the fact that you are delaying. Then, you need to adopt a strategy that is encouraging, such as changing your internal dialogue from "I have to do this," to "I choose to do this," after which you can reward yourself each time you complete a difficult task.

(C) Unfortunately, the same pattern has happened again: The most important task on your list was put off for another day not because you were busy but because you focused on the less essential things.

① (A) – (B) – (C)   ② (B) – (A) – (C)
③ (C) – (A) – (B)   ④ (C) – (B) – (A)

해석

당신은 할 일 목록을 만든다. 당신은 목록에 있는 모든 것을 끝내기 위해 굳게 결심한다. 그것은 당신이 목표를 달성할 수 있도록 생산적으로 되는 것이 당신의 목적이기 때문이다.

(A) 이러한 경우에, 미루는 것은 게으른 행동이 아니다. 게으름은 어떤 일을 하든 마음이 내키지 않는 것이지만, 과제를 미루는 것은 그것이 어렵거나 불쾌하기 때문에 중요한 무언가를 피하는 능동적인 과정이다. 다른 나쁜 버릇처럼, 과제를 미루는 버릇을 극복하기 위해서는 노력과 훈련이 필요하다.

(B) 당신이 미루고 있다는 사실을 인식하는 것으로부터 시작하라. 그런 다음, 당신은 내면의 대화를 '나는 이것을 해야 한다'에서 '나는 이것을 하기로 선택한다'로 바꾸는 것과 같이 격려하는 전략을 채택해야 하는데, 그 이후에 당신이 어려운 과제를 완수할 때마다 스스로에게 보상할 수 있다.

(C) 유감스럽게도, 똑같은 패턴이 다시 일어나게 되는데, 당신의 목록에서 가장 중요한 과제는 당신이 바빴기 때문이 아니라 덜 중요한 것들에 집중했기 때문에 하루 더 연기되었다.

해설

주어진 문장에서 목표 달성을 위해 할 일 목록에 있는 것을 끝내겠다고 굳게 결심하는 상황을 가정한 후, (C)에서 유감스럽게도(Unfortunately) 할 일 목록에서 가장 중요한 과제가 하루 더 연기됨에 따라 똑같은 패턴(the same pattern)이 다시 일어나게 된다고 설명하고 있다. 이어서 (A)에서 이러한 경우에(In such cases) 미루는 버릇을 극복하기 위해서는 노력과 훈련이 필요하다고 하고, (B)에서 스스로 미루고 있다는 사실을 인식하는 것을 시작으로 과제를 완수할 때마다 자기 보상하는 전략을 채택하라고 제안하고 있다. 따라서 ③ (C) – (A) – (B)가 정답이다.

정답 ③

어휘

resolved 굳게 결심한, 단호한 objective 목적; 객관적인
productive 생산적인, 풍부한 delay 미루다
unwillingness 마음이 내키지 않음 unpleasant 불쾌한
discipline 훈련, 연습; 징계하다 overcome 극복하다
adopt 채택하다, 입양하다 internal 내면의, 내부의 dialogue 대화
complete 완수하다, 완성하다 put off ~을 연기하다, 미루다
essential 중요한, 필수적인

MEMO

2025 최신판

해커스공무원

비비안 영어
매일 하프
모의고사

초판 1쇄 발행 2025년 5월 9일

지은이	해커스 공무원시험연구소
펴낸곳	해커스패스
펴낸이	해커스공무원 출판팀
주소	서울특별시 강남구 강남대로 428 해커스공무원
고객센터	1588-4055
교재 관련 문의	gosi@hackerspass.com
	해커스공무원 사이트(gosi.Hackers.com) 교재 Q&A 게시판
	카카오톡 플러스 친구 [해커스공무원 노량진캠퍼스]
학원 강의 및 동영상강의	gosi.Hackers.com
ISBN	979-11-7244-557-7 (13740)
Serial Number	01-01-01

저작권자 ⓒ 2025, 해커스공무원

이 책의 모든 내용, 이미지, 디자인, 편집 형태에 대한 저작권은 저자에게 있습니다.
서면에 의한 저자와 출판사의 허락 없이 내용의 일부 혹은 전부를 인용, 발췌하거나 복제, 배포할 수 없습니다.

공무원 교육 1위,
해커스공무원 gosi.Hackers.com

해커스공무원

- **해커스공무원 학원 및 인강**(교재 내 인강 할인쿠폰 수록)
- 해커스 스타강사의 **공무원 영어 무료 특강**
- **공무원 매일영어 학습, 출제예상 핵심 어휘리스트** 등 공무원 시험 합격을 위한 다양한 무료 학습 콘텐츠
- 정확한 성적 분석으로 약점 극복이 가능한 **합격예측 온라인 모의고사**(교재 내 응시권 및 해설강의 수강권 수록)
- 공무원 영어 기출 어휘를 언제 어디서나 외우는 **공무원 보카 어플**

한경비즈니스 2024 한국품질만족도 교육(온·오프라인 공무원학원) 1위